Civic Engagement in American Democracy

Civic Engagement in American Democracy

Theda Skocpol
Morris P. Fiorina
Editors

BROOKINGS INSTITUTION PRESS
Washington, D.C.

RUSSELL SAGE FOUNDATION
New York, N.Y.

Civic Engagement in American Democracy may be ordered from:

BROOKINGS INSTITUTION PRESS
1775 Massachusetts Avenue, N.W.
Washington, D.C. 20036
Tel: 1-800/275-1447 or 202/797-6258
Fax: 202/797-6004
www.brookings.edu

Library of Congress Cataloging-in-Publication data

Civic engagement in American democracy / Theda Skocpol and Morris
  P. Fiorina, editors.
    p.   cm.
Includes bibliographical references and index.
ISBN 0-8157-2810-7 (cloth : alk. paper)
ISBN 0-8157-2809-3 (pbk. : alk. paper)
1. Political participation—United States. 2. Civil society—
United States. 3. Democracy—United States. I. Skocpol,
Theda. II. Fiorina, Morris P.
JK1764 .C5266 1999   99-6407
323'.042'0973—dc21   CIP

9 8 7 6 5 4 3 2 1

The paper used in this publication meets minimum requirements of the American National Standard for Information Sciences—Permanence for Printed Library Materials, ANSI Z39.48-1984.

Typeset in Adobe Garamond

Composition by Northeastern Graphic Services
Hackensack, New Jersey

Printed by R. R. Donnelley and Sons
Harrisonburg, Virgina

Contents

Preface and Acknowledgments   vii

1 *Making Sense of the Civic Engagement Debate*   1
THEDA SKOCPOL AND MORRIS P. FIORINA

PART ONE
Between State and Society:
Roots of American Civic Engagement

2 *How Americans Became Civic*   27
THEDA SKOCPOL, WITH THE ASSISTANCE OF MARSHALL GANZ,
ZIAD MUNSON, BAYLISS CAMP, MICHELE SWERS, AND JENNIFER OSER

3 *Organizational Repertoires and Institutional Change:*
Women's Groups and the Transformation of American
Politics, 1890–1920   81
ELISABETH S. CLEMENS

4 *National Elections as Institutions for Generating*
Social Capital   111
WENDY M. RAHN, JOHN BREHM, AND NEIL CARLSON

PART TWO
Civic Life in a Changing Society

5 *Professions and Civic Engagement:
   Trends in Rhetoric and Practice, 1875–1995*   163
   STEVEN BRINT AND CHARLES S. LEVY

6 *Vital Signs: Organizational Population Trends
   and Civic Engagement in New Haven, Connecticut,
   1850–1998*   211
   PETER DOBKIN HALL

7 *Social Change and Civic Engagement:
   The Case of the PTA*   249
   SUSAN CRAWFORD AND PEGGY LEVITT

8 *Technological Change and Associational Life*   297
   MARCELLA RIDLEN RAY

9 *Mobilizing Civic Engagement: The Changing
   Impact of Religious Involvement*   331
   ROBERT WUTHNOW

PART THREE
The Ironies of Contemporary Activism

10 *The Rise of Citizen Groups*   367
    JEFFREY M. BERRY

11 *Extreme Voices: A Dark Side of Civic Engagement*   395
    MORRIS P. FIORINA

12 *Civic Participation and the Equality Problem*   427
    KAY LEHMAN SCHLOZMAN, SIDNEY VERBA, AND HENRY E. BRADY

13 *Advocates without Members:
    The Recent Transformation of American Civic Life*   461
    THEDA SKOCPOL

Contributors   511

Index   515

Preface and Acknowledgments

FOR THE TWO OF US, who have long studied American politics from somewhat different angles, the recent surge of interest in the health and prospects of our nation's democracy and civic life created a welcome opportunity for a collaborative project. What would be the result, we wondered, if we brought together political scientists, sociologists, and historians who were doing original empirical research using a variety of conceptual approaches? Each of us knew a different set of colleagues, and we suspected they might both enjoy and learn from discussions with one another. With support from a grant provided by the Russell Sage Foundation, we convened an intimate working conference on "Civic Engagement in American Democracy" in the pleasant surrounds of Portland, Maine, in September 1997. Conferences vary from excellent to dismal, but this one proved both delightful and unusually enlightening, as scholars with shared concerns met new colleagues and learned about work they did not already know. Organized around prepared drafts, conference discussions sharpened our questions about civic engagement in America, past and present, and probed the strengths, limits, and complementarities of the theoretical and research approaches surveyed in Chapter 1.

In addition to the authors represented in this volume, a number of other participants enriched the discussions of the Portland conference. We warmly acknowledge the contributions of Frank Baumgartner, Jocelyn Crowley, Gerald Gamm, H. W. Perry, Robert Putnam, Juliet Schor, and Steve Yonish. In addition we are deeply grateful for the financial support of the Russell Sage Foundation, and the efforts made by editors at both the Russell Sage Foundation and the Brookings Institution Press to obtain helpful critical reviews of the first draft of the manuscript. One anonymous reviewer, in particular, provided unusually sympathetic, detailed, and as-tute comments on each chapter. Janet Mowery edited the book, while Carlotta Ribar proofread and Julia Petrakis indexed the pages. During the production process, Janet Walker shepherded the contributors to this methodologically diverse collection. We appreciate her skill and patience. Finally, we thank Bill and Michael Skocpol and Mary and Joey Fiorina for their good-humored support.

THEDA SKOCPOL, Mount Desert, Maine

MORRIS FIORINA, Stanford, California

July 1999

Civic
Engagement
in American
Democracy

1 | *Making Sense of the Civic Engagement Debate*

THEDA SKOCPOL

MORRIS P. FIORINA

WHAT IS HAPPENING to American democracy? Scholars, public commentators, and thoughtful citizens alike are puzzling about the health of civic life in the United States. High-level commissions have issued reports with dire diagnoses and recommendations for amelioration, even as scholars publish articles and books by the dozens.[1] This ferment responds to a dizzying array of contradictory changes in recent decades, some of which have clearly enhanced democracy while others undercut our shared public life. For democracy in America, this may be, at once, the best and most worrisome of times.

The Civil Rights movement triumphed in the 1960s, ensuring that the promise of equality built into the Constitution was, by law, finally made good for everyone. African Americans struggled for and won basic rights, including the ability to register and vote in all parts of the country. In the wake of the momentous Civil Rights Movement, other formerly marginalized groups—feminists, the poor, homosexuals, the disabled—also raised their voices. More than ever before, the world's first mass democracy for white men became a nation where citizens of all colors and both genders could take part, where formerly excluded groups could speak up.

---

1. Scholarly works are cited throughout. For two recent commission reports, see Council on Civil Society (1998) and National Commission on Civic Renewal (1998).

1

The tenor of national politics has also changed. "Public interest" groups have proliferated, not only groups advocating the rights of the formerly marginalized, but also groups speaking for broad causes such as environmentalism and other understandings of what is good for society as a whole.[2] Many observers find such transformations heartening. In their view, the United States has moved away from a politics of narrow interest group maneuvers toward a more inclusive and pluralist debate about the public good. Civil society, the network of ties and groups through which people connect to one another and get drawn into community and political affairs, may simply be "reinventing" itself.[3]

But is this the whole story? Even as more voices speak up on behalf of social rights and broad conceptions of the public interest, millions of Americans seem to be drawing back from involvements with community affairs and politics. Most prominently, voting rates have dropped about 25 percent since the 1960s. Moreover, the proportion of Americans who tell pollsters that they "trust the federal government to do what is right" has plummeted from three-quarters in the early 1960s to less than a third at the turn of the twenty-first century. American civil society may also be weakening. Many commentators point to an erosion in "those forms of communal and associational life which are organized neither by the self-interest of the market nor by the coercive potential of the state."[4] Americans are participating less in many kinds of shared endeavors, from unions and political parties to religious groups and other sorts of voluntary membership organizations.[5]

Of course, some people are very active. But this may mean that small cadres push extreme or narrow causes, framing an overall public debate only tangentially relevant to the values and concerns of most citizens—who then pull further and further back from politics and community affairs.[6] Everyday Americans are increasingly mere spectators of public affairs. Much of the time they are benignly disinterested observers; at other moments angry or cynical. Either way, ordinary citizens have less and less involvement in shaping our common affairs—and, arguably, dwindling

---

2. Berry (1977); Berry (1997, pp. 29–34); Minkoff (1995); McFarland (1984); Dunlap and Mertig (1992); Pettinico (1996); and Walker (1991).

3. Able arguments along these lines can be found in Dionne (1998); Ladd (1999); Schudson (1996); Stengel (1996); and Wuthnow (1998); and in Jeffrey Berry's contribution to this volume.

4. Wolfe (1998, p. 17).

5. Galston and Levine (1998); Putnam (1995a).

6. For a variety of arguments indicating such possibilities, see Ganz (1994); King (1997); Judis (1992); Rauch (1998); and Skerry (1997).

leverage over powerful leaders and institutions. Who knows what might happen if times turn bad and America's leaders need active support for decisive steps to cope with social problems?

The Roots of an Intellectual Agenda

It is vital that we make sense of what is happening to American democracy and why—so say commentators across the partisan spectrum, ranging from William Bennett and George Will on the right to Michael Sandel and Robert Kuttner on the left. So say scholars of otherwise divergent theoretical and methodological persuasions. A surprisingly wide array of people agree that we need to dissect recent transformations in American democracy.

Many also want to find ways to *do* something about disturbing developments. Today's debate about civic engagement attracts both analysts and activists—in fact tends to blur the lines between them. For the first time since the 1960s, mainstream academics are talking openly about social reforms, not just analyzing trends from an olympian, detached standpoint. What Senator Bill Bradley calls the challenge of revitalizing our national community engages considerable scholarly energy these days.[7]

Americans of many persuasions agree that troubles for our democracy may lie in a loss of social ties or in the changing universe of voluntary associations. Observers suspect that solutions to current ills may involve rebuilding group life beyond as well as within formal politics. When people of different partisan or theoretical positions converge—not only on questions, but also on a sense of where the answers might lie—a new "agenda" is born. This has happened in today's debate about civic engagement in American democracy.

Several not mutually exclusive considerations help to explain why such a wide array of scholars and pundits have been drawn into the civic engagement debate—and also why so many Americans are paying attention. Several trends—disillusionment with U.S. government, innovations in the world of scholarship, and nostalgia for older folkways in an era of unsettling transformations—have led people to examine America's civic health more closely.

7. Bradley (1998).

Ironically, worries about the federal government explain the attraction for conservatives and liberals alike—although each group certainly has its own take on the civic debate and hopes to push the discussion in a congenial direction. In the 1960s, the federal government declared a "War on Poverty" and undertook to prod improvements in race relations. Correctly or not, many Americans believe problems in these areas have gotten worse, not better. Our national government appears to have bitten off much more than it could chew, and many conservatives and liberals are focusing instead on extragovernmental forms of activity.

Some ideologues on the right would prefer to have unfettered markets solve all social problems, but there are also "civic conservatives" who hope that families, churches, and voluntary groups at the local level can address social ills more effectively than "big government" or "the welfare state."[8] Many civic conservatives are interested in revitalizing local voluntary groups because they see them as an *alternative* to national government activities.[9]

Liberals, meanwhile, sense that increases in federal spending or regulation will be hard to legislate in an era of tax revolts, budget pressures, and festering distrust of government. Liberals are likely to think of civic group activities *in relation to government* and as the groundwork for widespread and meaningful participation in politics. They look for social welfare policies that work through partnerships between civil society and government. Many on the left also hope for a revival of populist organizations and social movements "from below," viewing the revitalization of civil society as a possible way to energize democratic politics and empower ordinary people.[10]

Happenings in academia have also fueled broad interest and lively debate about the health of American civil society and democracy. "Academic scribblers" are often dismissed as irrelevant, and certainly it is harder for intellectuals to have an impact on public policy in the United States than in many other industrial democracies. Nevertheless, writings by a major sociologist and a leading political scientist have combined to spark broad scholarly participation in the current civic engagement debate.

James Coleman was a sociologist who regularly addressed controversial public issues about schools and families. As a social theorist, Coleman built conceptual bridges between the individualistic, market-oriented thinking

---

8. Starobin (1997).

9. For an unadulterated statement from this perspective, see Joyce and Schambra (1996).

10. Weir and Ganz (1997).

of economists and sociologists' concern with social networks, norms, and values.[11] He deployed the concept of "social capital" to point to ways in which social ties and shared norms can enhance economic efficiency and help individuals to become better educated, find jobs, amass economic capital, raise well-socialized children, and make careers.[12] Coleman led the way in convincing economists—arguably the most powerful social scientists—that they should pay attention to social ties and culture.

Then political scientist Robert Putnam came along with a 1993 book, *Making Democracy Work*, that married aspects of Coleman's "social capital" theory to propositions about voluntary associations taken from Alexis de Tocqueville.[13] Putnam used his version of "social capital" to explain effective democratic governance in Italy. Tracing what happened after new forms of regional governance were legislated, Putnam found that institutions similar on paper worked very differently in different regions of Italy, depending on the degree to which each region had a rich array of voluntary social groups.[14] Regions with lots of associations had more effective governing arrangements, Putnam argued. Even groups apparently remote from politics, such as choral societies, enhanced effective governance.

Because his study of Italy portrayed social capital as deeply rooted in history—Putnam traced Italian regional differences all the way back to the thirteenth century—some were surprised when, a couple of years later, Putnam published "Bowling Alone," in which he argued that social capital has sharply eroded in the United States.[15] According to "Bowling Alone," the United States, long a democracy noted for high levels of civic engagement, has experienced a sharp downward spiral of social capital in the late twentieth century. Social capital might not necessarily be so persistent. Americans in the late twentieth century are increasingly going it alone, Putnam argued, rather than cohering in groups such as bowling leagues, or churches, or unions, or civic associations. Putnam has amassed a formidable array of social statistics to document declines in group involvements since the 1950s and 1960s.[16] In his view, the troubles of U.S. democracy

11. *Foundations of Social Theory* (Coleman 1990) is his major theoretical work.

12. Coleman (1988).

13. Tocqueville ([1835–40] 1969); Putnam (1993a).

14. For the cogent critical engagements with Putnam's (1993a) thesis, see Levi (1996) and Tarrow (1996).

15. Putnam (1995a).

16. In addition to Putnam (1995a) and (1995b), see Putnam (2000, forthcoming).

and governance are attributable to declining social trust and the unraveling of social connections.

"Bowling Alone" and subsequent writings by Robert Putnam have sparked much discussion within academia and beyond. Although many scholars differ with Putnam on empirical or theoretical grounds, legions of academics have nevertheless been happy to leap into the fray.[17] Scholars agree that Putnam has raised important questions about social and political change in America.

Beyond academia, not just "Bowling Alone" but other retrospections on declining community such as Alan Ehrenhalt's *The Lost City* have been widely featured in the mass media, indicating a cultural preoccupation with issues of civic health.[18] Indeed, popular yearnings may be even more decisive than intellectual conclusions, which will take a while to gel. Many Americans long for "the good old days"—even if renditions of the imagined past do not always line up with one another, let alone with the facts.

The 1980s was a time of economic anxiety, as giant corporations downsized and new technologies came on line, reducing people's certainty about lifetime careers. Everyone in the work force seems to be working harder, even as many strata of Americans feel they are falling behind in a roaring consumerist culture.[19] In the wake of the feminist movement and the entry of more and more wives and mothers into the paid labor force, men and women find themselves in new relationships, fraught with tensions. In the mass media age, children and parents often seem to be on different wavelengths. New waves of immigration and changing race relationships call old cultural and political certainties into question, while economic gaps have widened, even in periods of growth, between the most privileged Americans and all others.[20]

Amidst so many unsettling transformations, real or perceived, is it any wonder that social critics resonate when they contrast current social unravelings to an apparently simpler, more stable, and more sociable time in the past? Ehrenhalt, Putnam, Joyce and Schambra, and many other commentators who stress lost community bring to mind a half-remembered era in

17. For a range of views, see Dionne (1998); Galston and Levine (1998); Ladd (1999); and Nye, Zelikow, and King (1997).

18. Ehrenhalt (1996).

19. Schor (1992, 1998).

20. Danziger and Gottschalk (1995).

America—a time when bowling leagues met regularly and people sat on their porches or played bridge; a time when wives organized dinner parties and neighbors threw themselves into all kinds of community activities.[21] Who exactly did all of these things, how regularly, and at what cost is subject to investigation and debate. But the sense that the American past might have been better, more reassuring, is widespread—and understandable. More than mere "theory" or "data" is at stake in discussions of what is happening to civic engagement in America. Despite all of the progress in our economy and culture, there may be good things we Americans have lost. Even if we cannot turn back the tides of time, we can still remember and seek old advantages in new ways.

Lines of Scholarly Investigation

Public aspects of the civic engagement debate have rhythms of their own, driven by the rollercoaster logic of the mass media and the byzantine rhythms of partisan politics and issue advocacy. Meanwhile, though, dozens of scholars are analyzing data and probing the complex interrelationships of social and political change in the United States and beyond. Various methodologies are being deployed in challenging research projects inspired by overlapping yet partially divergent theoretical presumptions and hypotheses.

Much research on contemporary trends uses survey research methods to track changes in citizens' attitudes and self-reported behaviors. Surveys with national samples hold the promise of being comprehensive and representative. At their best, they yield data that can be probed with sophisticated statistical techniques.[22] Yet there are major limits to this approach. Surveys are powerful tools for getting at relationships among the attitudes, reported behaviors, and socioeconomic characteristics of individual respondents *at a given point in time*, but they can be used to measure change over time only when survey organizations have posed the same or very similar questions to national samples again and again. Scholars now studying civic patterns in the United States have had to rely on just a few surveys that happen to have done this in the past. At best, surveys such as

---

21. Ehrenhalt (1996); Putnam (1995a, 1995b); Joyce and Schambra (1996).
22. See studies such as Rosenstone and Hansen (1993); Verba, Schlozman, and Brady (1995); and Putnam (1995b).

the American National Election Studies and the General Social Survey have repeated questions only since the 1970s.

Even when certain questions have been repeated at regular intervals, they do not always turn out to be optimal from the point of view of latter-day researchers. Take the example of the question asked by the General Social Survey (GSS) from 1974 to 1994 about Americans' memberships in voluntary groups. People were asked to consider each of thirteen general *categories* of associations, such as fraternal groups, veterans' groups, school service groups, sports groups, professional groups, including a residual category for "other" groups. The respondent simply indicated if he or she was a member of one *or more* associations within that broad category. This approach probably seemed very detailed at the time the GSS first started asking this question. Today, however, researchers are concerned about exactly how many memberships Americans have in particular kinds of groups. The GSS categories do not say much about the types of groups involved in a category: membership groups are mixed together with mailing-list groups. And what if a person belongs to several groups within a single category: several professional associations, a number of sports groups, or (perhaps most likely of all) several "other" groups? He or she would, nevertheless, indicate the broad category only once, and evidence of multiple memberships concentrated within that category (rather than memberships spread across several categories) would be lost.[23] In "Bowling Alone," Robert Putnam used GSS data to argue that Americans in general were members of about 25 percent fewer groups in the 1990s than in the 1970s. But other scholars have challenged this finding.[24] They have objected to the fact that Putnam controlled for education levels; and they have argued that the General Social Survey data are not sufficiently fine-grained to support conclusions about declining memberships.

Currently, scholars are asking much more precise questions about the full range of individuals' involvements in groups, social activities, and political activities of all kinds.[25] Although we cannot redo past studies in order to create fresh standardized time series, today's investigations of American civic engagement are becoming ever more rich and varied. This is true within the world of survey research. It is even more true when we consider the full range

23. This point is developed in Baumgartner and Walker (1988).

24. Ladd (1996); Samuelson (1996).

25. For examples, see Guterbock and Fries (1997); Pew Research Center for the People and the Press (1997); and Verba, Schlozman, and Brady (1995).

of social science theories and methodologies currently being deployed to investigate the past and present of civic engagement in America.

The scholarly community especially benefits from research findings uncovered by a variety of methods. Consider Part III of this collection, about the nature and effects of contemporary American civic activism. Drawing on national survey data, Sidney Verba, Kay Schlozman, and Henry Brady give us an overall picture of which Americans are highly active in politics and civic life, and why. Morris Fiorina uses a community ethnography to probe the ironies of polarized advocacy in the local politics of Concord, Massachusetts. In their respective contributions, Jeff Berry and Theda Skocpol characterize the changing universe of civically active groups since the 1960s; each considers what changing types of groups may mean for national debates. The combination of these approaches affords a more nuanced picture than any one methodology deployed in isolation could generate.

Historical Approaches

Along with surveys and ethnographies, historical studies are a crucial part of the current repertoire of civic engagement research. How can we accurately describe, let alone causally diagnose, changes in American society and democracy over the past several generations unless we know more about trends during recent decades and about long-term patterns before the 1960s? A quest for deeper historical knowledge seems especially pertinent. Ever since the United States broke away from British colonial control, Americans have believed themselves to be an unusually free and equal people. When the French aristocrat Alexis de Tocqueville toured the fledgling republic in the 1830s, he celebrated the distinctive characteristics of "democracy in America." Tocqueville argued that egalitarian mores, a profusion of voluntary associations, vibrant religion, competitive elections, and decentralized governance all combined to make the United States an unusually civic democracy.[26] Subsequently, both foreign and native observers have commented upon Tocqueville's propositions, probing the changing characteristics of American democracy. Again and again from the nineteenth century to the early 1960s, the United States was found to be a "nation of joiners" and an unusually participatory democracy.[27]

26. Tocqueville ([1835–40] 1969).
27. Schlesinger (1944); Hausknecht (1962); and Almond and Verba (1963).

Characterizations of America's democratic past are invariably used as benchmarks for assessments of contemporary changes. In the current public debates, almost every contributor makes explicit or implicit claims about patterns in the past in the course of saying why things have become better or worse in recent times.[28] At times, however, commentators invoke a largely mythical past, rather than carefully measuring recent changes in society and politics against actual patterns in earlier phases of U.S. history. Richer and more accurate analyses of the dynamics of civic activity in America's past might well modify our assessments of what has gone wrong—and right—lately.

Alternative kinds of data and methods must be used to examine social and political developments before the 1970s, and especially before World War II. Representative statistical surveys based on national samples are not available; and we cannot do new ethnographies of past communities or associations. Scholars who want to hypothesize about changes in individuals' behaviors and attitudes have to find substitutes for survey data or direct interviews and observations. Many use historical voting data to get at participation in electoral politics and deduce broad conclusions about past social attitudes from partisan voting breakdowns.[29] Other scholars examine transformations in U.S. political parties, contrasting the highly participatory elections of nineteenth-century America with the low-key elections and smaller turnouts of much of the twentieth century.[30]

The challenge is greater when it comes to looking at past participation in voluntary associations. A few social historians have done detailed community studies, using actual membership lists enriched by individual documents such as diaries or letters. But there are no national data on Americans' membership (including multiple memberships) in voluntary groups in the nineteenth and early twentieth centuries. Too often we can only guess why people formed, led, joined, or abandoned groups or movements. Inferences must be made from very incomplete and fragmentary data—much as historians have always done.

Of course, students of the American past can look directly at the characteristics and trajectories of organized groups themselves. Historians

---

28. For example, claims about the past figure pivotally in the assessments of America's current civic health made in Council on Civil Society (1998); Joyce and Schambra (1996); and National Commission on Civic Renewal (1998).

29. Burnham (1970); Kleppner (1982).

30. Aldrich (1995); Burnham (1970); McGerr (1986).

have mapped the changing array of voluntary groups, political parties, churches, and social movements for each epoch of the U.S. past, mining a huge variety of primary documentary sources in the process (many examples and citations are given in Chapter 2 of this volume). Specific types of groups—ranging from temperance associations to women's groups and veterans' associations—have been studied over many decades in U.S. history. For some types of groups in the past, directories provided sketches of hundreds of groups.[31] Especially for the late nineteenth and early twentieth centuries, many cities and towns and some states had official "directories" that included year-by-year enumerations of associations. And for the period since 1955 the *Encyclopedia of Associations* gives data on both national and state-level U.S. associations. Triangulating from sources such as these, it is possible to gain an overview of the changing shape of the associational universe throughout American history.

For scholars who prefer to theorize about individuals' attitudes and choices, data about the incidence of groups function as an indirect substitute for survey data. But the substitution is imperfect, because even if group membership totals are known, one cannot deduce which people join or drop out. Memberships cannot even be added up and divided by the population, because many persons belonged to more than one group. The best that can be done is to divide total numbers of groups by the overall population of a known unit, such as a town or state, to arrive at "per capita" numbers of groups. This is the approach used by Gerald Gamm and Robert Putnam in their study of associational "density" in twenty-six American towns and cities between 1840 and 1940.[32] After counting numbers of groups in city directories decade by decade, Gamm and Putnam divide by city and town populations. Then they conclude that small towns and cities were more associationally inclined than big cities and begin to hypothesize about why individuals might have been more likely to join groups in smaller towns and cities than in larger cities.[33]

Other scholars regard groups and institutions as central in their own right and consequently are less dismayed by the absence of comprehensive

31. For an extraordinarily comprehensive example, see Stevens (1899).

32. Gamm and Putnam (1999).

33. A similar question was investigated by Hausknecht (1962), but he was able to analyze direct survey responses from individuals living in places of different sizes. Gamm and Putnam's indirect approach necessarily presumes that groups drew their memberships from inside town or city boundaries. However, in nineteenth- and early-twentieth-century America, very large proportions of group memberships could come from a surprisingly wide region around small cities or towns.

individual-level data from the past. Civil society and the democratic polity can be seen as populated by organized groups, political parties, government, and religious and economic institutions, all of which pattern social relationships in different ways at various times and places. The organizational characteristics of groups can be studied over time. Official documents from groups, including speeches by their leaders, can provide a sense of group goals and values.

A number of chapters in this collection rely on historical and macroscopic examinations of organizations, cultural themes, and institutional patterns. Contributors Elisabeth Clemens, Peter Dobkin Hall, and Jeffrey Berry explore the emergence and transformation of social movements and types of voluntary associations or interest groups, asking how groups have changed in relationship to governmental activities and changes in the broader American society, economy, and culture. For scholars exploring organizational characteristics and relationships, it may make good sense to trace the rise and fall of particular associations or sets of groups of a particular kind.[34] Rich data can be obtained from associational and public records on the origins of groups, their organizational structure, their activities, and their resources. In many cases, it is also possible to map group memberships over time and, if associations are large, the incidence of state, regional, and local units within a movement or national association. In this volume, for example, Chapter 2 by Theda Skocpol and her associates probes data about the nature, emergence, and development of dozens of large voluntary associations, using that information to explore relationships between U.S. government and civil society.

Social Capital, Rational Choice, and Historical-Institutionalism

Scholars involved in debates about civic engagement in American democracy are posing questions and seeking answers with the aid of somewhat different theoretical perspectives. People may generally agree that social dynamics are closely intertwined with the health of democracy. They may also agree that fundamental transformations are happening in American civic life—changes well worth exploring empirically and analyti-

34. See Clemens (1997).

cally. But different clusters of scholars emphasize disparate aspects of democratic governance; and they are certainly exploring different possible *causes* of contemporary transformations.

The "social capital" approach makes causal and normative assumptions along what may be called neo-Durkheimian lines, stressing the socialization of individuals into shared norms and cooperative societal action. Rational-choice scholars ask about the unintended effects for the American polity as a whole of transformed incentives for individual behavior. Meanwhile, historical-institutionalists probe changing organizational patterns, shifts in resources for collective social and political activity, and transformations in the relationships between elites and ordinary citizens in American society and politics. Varied theoretical frames of reference in civic engagement scholarship are not necessarily contradictory; scholars inspired by different concepts and frames of reference can arrive at complementary empirical findings and evaluative judgments. Nevertheless, at this early stage in the debate, it helps to delineate the basic assumptions and operating hypotheses used by scholars inspired by each of these major perspectives.

Social trust in general is at the heart of the matter for Robert Putnam and other adherents of the "social capital" perspective on democracy and its discontents. To the degree that the social capital approach is a causal theory rather than just a label for social networks and norms, it embodies a fundamentally social psychological proposition about the roots of efficient government and social institutions, focusing on the socialization of individuals into cooperative behavior.[35] According to Putnam, individuals who regularly interact with one another in face-to-face settings learn to work together to solve collective problems. They gain social trust, which spills over into trust in government. Wise public policies, robust economic development, and efficient public administration all flow from such social trust grounded in regular cooperative social interactions.[36]

Because he understands effective democracy as an outgrowth of dense small-group ties and the positive attitudes and actions these evoke from individuals, Putnam finds it alarming that Americans today are much less likely to interact with one another and trust government than survey research says they did three decades ago. He differs with analysts who discuss reform of U.S. democracy in terms of "such procedural issues as

35. Coleman (1988).
36. Putnam (1993a, 1993b).

term limits and campaign financing" because "the ills that afflict the American polity reflect deeper, largely unnoticed social changes."[37] The fundamental problem lies in sharply declining social trust and an overall fraying of the social fabric. In contrast to the "erosion of social capital" in the present, Putnam points to what he sees as a much healthier time in the American past. "Recent historical work on the Progressive Era," Putnam writes, "has uncovered evidence of the powerful role played by nominally non-political associations (such as women's literary societies) precisely because they provided a dense social network."[38]

Rational-choice scholars tend to be more skeptical than neo-Durkheimians about the automatic benefits of involvement in public affairs. What kind of civic engagement, by whom, to what ends? As Morris Fiorina's contribution to this volume shows, rational-choice scholars analyze the ways in which institutions and organizations create incentives for individuals to engage in various kind of behaviors. Then they ask whether the result, intended or unintended, adds up to a socially optimal outcome. Often it does not. Applied to the realm of civic engagement research, this approach can inject a healthy note of skepticism about any romanticization of sheer participation or group activism in community and government affairs.

From a different direction of evaluation and analysis, historical-institutionalists like Theda Skocpol also disagree with the neo-Durkheimian stress on social trust as the essence of democracy. Democracy, after all, grew up historically out of century-long struggles among social groups and between state authorities and their subjects.[39] In a very real sense, first liberal-parliamentary regimes and then democracies were a product of organized conflict and *distrust*. The energy to forge liberal and democratic regimes came when people crystallized their misgivings about concentrated or arbitrary political power. What is more, middling and subordinate groups in society had to organize, amass resources, and assert themselves. After much struggle, institutions were fashioned to guarantee civil rights, allowing people to organize and speak out. Then electoral arrangements emerged, allowing masses of citizens to participate in elections designed to choose among leaders and courses of public action.

---

37. Putnam (1993b, p. 41).
38. Ibid.
39. Bendix (1964); Moore (1966); Downing (1992); Ertman (1997); and Rueschemeyer, Stephens, and Stephens (1992).

As (many, not all) industrial-capitalist nations became democracies, most citizens won the right to vote. In addition, organized balances were institutionalized through which power-holders in the economy and government to some degree checked one another, leaving space for citizens to live their lives and, if necessary, exert leverage in public affairs. Democratic governments became strong enough to buffer market processes, but at the same time governments were limited and subject to popular influence. Incentives were created for leaders to attend to the wants and values of ordinary citizens—as expressed in elections and through mass-based political parties, social movements, and participation in popularly rooted voluntary associations. From an institutionalist perspective, voluntary associations matter as sources of popular leverage, not just as facilitators of individual participation and generalized social trust.

One example explains well how scholars of different theoretical persuasions regard the same sorts of voluntary groups. As we have seen, Robert Putnam understands U.S. women's groups during the Progressive Era as engaged in creating "dense" and relatively "nonpolitical" social ties. Social ties in general are what matter in Putnam's social capital perspective, and he sees American women as historically likely to have specialized in creating and sustaining rich social connections and generalized trust, particularly in local communities. But early-modern U.S. women's associations have a different place in the institutionalist approaches of Theda Skocpol and Elisabeth Clemens.[40] Each in her own way, Skocpol and Clemens note that the General Federation of Women's Clubs, the Woman's Christian Temperance Union, and the National Congress of Mothers (later the PTA) were doing a lot more than discussing literature, holding tea parties, and supporting local schools and projects for community betterment. These vast women's associations were also powerful shapers of local, state, and national legislation to aid families and communities. Both Clemens and Skocpol see historical U.S. women's associations as exercisers of popular leverage in democracy. American women's associations were active nationally and in states and regions as well as local communities. They were symbiotically tied to government—both influenced by government and aiming to influence it—and thus were not at all "nonpolitical." In the view of institutionalists like Skocpol and Clemens, women's associations were remarkable sources of popular power and public leverage in American democracy.

40. In addition to Chapters 2 and 3 in this volume, see Clemens (1997) and Skocpol (1992)

In short, both social capital theorists and historical-institutionalists may focus on voluntary associations in aspects of their empirical research, but they do so for different theoretical reasons. They ask different questions and probe different possible mechanisms and effects. From a historical-institutional perspective, the trouble with American democracy today does not lie in sheer social disconnection or simply in the generalized growth of social and political distrust. Institutionalists examine changing patterns of organization and resource balances. They ask who relates to whom, and who is organized for what purposes. They are especially interested in forms of participation and power that include—or exclude—average and less-privileged citizens.

Social and cultural changes may be probed by institutionalists to see what light they shed on issues of organization, resource distribution, and participation and leverage in the broader society and democracy. In this volume, for example, Robert Wuthnow suggests that emerging evangelical religious movements in contemporary America may channel believers' social commitments into intracongregational, rather than communitywide forms of group activity. This may differ from how Protestant evangelism worked in American society and democracy in the past. Peter Dobkin Hall charts the rise of religious social service organizations and their displacement of formerly more prevalent membership social groups in New Haven, Connecticut. And Susan Crawford and Peggy Levitt use a case study of the PTA over a century to explore the effects of racial and family changes on a broad civic association that has been centrally involved in American democracy.

Other institutionalist contributors focus more directly on the changing organizational infrastructure of public policy debates and political participation. Clemens argues that turn-of-the-twentieth-century women's movements and associations responded to political opportunities and exclusions in ways that ended up fashioning new associational approaches to popular lobbying that soon spread to other groups, restructuring the "rules of the game" for voluntary associations in relation to government. In her concluding contribution to the volume, Theda Skocpol argues that the universe of organized voluntary groups active in American public life has been sharply transformed since the 1950s. Broad-gauged, cross-class voluntary federations are in decline, while advocacy groups of all kinds have proliferated. New groups represent many new voices and causes in politics, but perhaps at the expense of encompassing citizen involvement and democratic leverage for average citizens.

Looking Ahead

In surveying contributions beyond as well as within this collection, we have used this introduction to offer a map not only of shared concerns but also of methodological and theoretical variations among researchers investigating changing patterns of civic engagement in American democracy. The distinctions we offer are intended to help readers sort out important theoretical and methodological variations, to think about the strengths and lacunae of each approach. But we do not mean to suggest that such differences should be causes for zero-sum conflict or obstacles to dialogue and shared efforts. In fact, we believe just the opposite. Pressing questions about changes in American society and democracy need to be tackled by scholars who, individually and together, use varied and complementary ideas and research approaches. Substantive questions and findings should be at the center of our concern.

The contributors to this volume have been inspired by concepts and hypotheses from all three major theoretical perspectives discussed above. Yet institutionalist and rational-choice arguments predominate in the pages that follow. Recently published scholarship on civic engagement in America has been preoccupied with sustaining or refuting social capital hypotheses, and this book aims to broaden the theoretical horizons of ongoing scholarly discussion. At the same time, the collection is proudly eclectic about empirical methodology. Major parts of the book are *not* sorted out by methodology; instead, each includes contributions by scholars who use an array of empirical approaches and kinds of evidence to address overlapping issues in complementary ways. Throughout this book, in fact, many individual chapters combine qualitative and quantitative sources of evidence to offer an especially rich picture of changes in American society and democracy.

Ranging from the beginning of American nationhood through recent times, the chapters of Part I offer an eagle-eye examination of the roots of civic engagement. In its own way each chapter challenges the too often taken-for-granted notion that civic engagement is something purely social and separate from the state and electoral politics. Democratic civil society is certainly a matter of individuals and social groups influencing government and public life, yet the opposite processes also occur—just as much in the United States as anywhere else. Chapter 2 by Theda Skocpol and her collaborators and Chapter 3 by Elisabeth Clemens both highlight ways in which the institutions and activities of American government have influ-

enced the identities, organizational forms, and strategies of voluntary associations at the center of "civil society," even as associations themselves have
helped to transform public policies and the very "rules of the game" in
politics and governance. Chapter 4 by Wendy Rahn, John Brehm, and Neil
Carlson uses survey analysis to probe ways in which national elections in the
United States influence the sense of civic involvement and political engagement of individuals. Just as the Skocpol chapter argues that national mobilizations for major wars have spurred Americans to launch and join an array
of voluntary associations, so do Rahn, Brehm, and Carlson show that participation in the shared ritual and organized contention of national elections
can strengthen Americans' sense of political efficacy and social solidarity.

Contributors to Part II explore long-term changes in American society
and culture, asking how they have influenced voluntary associations and
citizens' political involvements. In Chapter 5, Steven Brint and Charles
Levy analyze cultural and organizational changes among professionals,
who have always been leaders in modern American civic life. Showing that
contemporary leaders of professional associations do not address society-
wide civic values as much as their predecessors once did, Brint and Levy
dissect the strengths and weaknesses of today's more bureaucratized and
"compartmentalized" styles of professional engagement with public concerns. Examining voluntary, religious, and nonprofit "entities" in New
Haven over a similarly long stretch, Peter Dobkin Hall offers another
perspective on the professionalization of civic life, highlighting the rise of
tax-exempt nonprofit agencies devoted to delivering social services. Even
many churches may be experiencing the transformation of their "social
ministries" away from reliance on membership relationships and toward
the use of tax-exempt funds from foundations and public agencies to
deliver social services.

The other three chapters of Part II examine forces often thought to
have revolutionized American civic life. The National Congress of Parents
and Teachers (PTA) has been a major civic force throughout the twentieth
century. Because it has been so intimately involved with changing family
structures and with public schools that were once racially segregated and
then underwent legally enforced desegregation, the PTA makes an ideal
laboratory for exploring the impact of gender and racial transformations.
Using a remarkable combination of historical, ethnographic, and quantitative techniques, Crawford and Levitt reveal in Chapter 7 how racial and
family changes have influenced PTA membership and policies and suggest
how the PTA seeks to adapt to new social realities.

Technologies of communication have a profound impact on possibilities for group formation, Marcella Ray shows. But the nuanced and long-term perspective she offers in Chapter 8 suggests that each wave of technological innovation in some ways facilitates, and in other ways undercuts, the social ties that undergird civic engagement. In Chapter 9, Robert Wuthnow delivers a comparable message about the civic effects, direct and indirect, of ongoing religious transformations in American society. Historically, mainline Protestant denominations built bridges to engagement in the civic affairs of the larger society. Today, however, mainline Protestant denominations are losing ground, especially to evangelical denominations that tend to channel the energies of believers into intracongregational activities. Nevertheless, suggests Wuthnow, modes of reaching out by religious people may be changing, as formal partnerships are forged between religious and secular organizations to encourage volunteering, charity, and community development. Each of the chapters in Part II clarifies long-term transformations, while at the same time suggesting that current trends are anything but unidirectional.

Finally, the chapters of Part III probe the ironies of new forms of civic activism in late-twentieth-century America. Often those who discuss civic engagement speak as if all kinds of participation and activism were good (except perhaps totalitarian mobilization). Good for individuals: the good citizen is one who attends lots of meetings, always votes, reads the newspaper, and watches nothing more on television than "The NewsHour with Jim Lehrer." And good for the nation, too, because observers often presume that more voices and more groups are automatically better. However, contributors to Part III suggest that participation needs to be analyzed more critically.

In Chapter 10, Jeffrey Berry charts the rise of new "public interest" advocacy groups since the 1960s and 1970s, commenting on the ways in which such groups have enriched as well as placed limits on national democratic debates. Where Berry stresses the upside of recent participatory changes, Morris Fiorina by contrast probes their "dark side." In Chapter 11, Fiorina shows us the excesses of activism in the decision-making of one community, and uses his ethnographic snapshot to theorize about the conditions under which "extremists" may become too influential for the good of democracy. Fiorina's work leads toward the conclusion that the problem with American democracy today may be a combination of too-ready routes to participation by small groups of activists with intense commitments to (often) extreme causes, coupled with obstacles to routine participation by ambivalent citizens with everyday concerns.

Fiorina's concerns are further probed from additional methodological perspectives in the concluding two chapters. In Chapter 12, Schlozman, Verba, and Brady explore the inequalities that plague American democracy today, as money increasingly displaces time, and as chances to gain civic skills become concentrated in just a few institutional sectors, leaving ordinary Americans at a disadvantage in most spheres outside of religion. In Chapter 13, Skocpol surveys the changing universe of voluntary groups active in American national life since the 1950s. American democracy now has more organized activists than ever before—including activists representing formerly excluded groups and marginalized values. But are ordinary citizens being left by the wayside in a national polity organized by and for the most privileged? At one time, broad-gauged membership associations offered ladders into state and national affairs and facilitated exchanges among citizens and between leaders and the led. But nowadays the American civic universe is dominated by professionals.

Taken together and considered against the backdrop of the longer-term patterns and transformations analyzed in Parts I and II, the contributions to Part III underscore the paradoxes of civic engagement today: American civil society and democracy may have become more flexible and open than ever before. But the United States at the dawn of a new millennium may, nevertheless, be evolving into a system organized and directed by and for the most privileged of its citizens. The challenge of "revitalizing our national community" may require Americans to look long and hard at issues of power and inequality—matters that have always been at the heart of choice and contention in the world's first, most vibrant, and most enduring democracy.

References

Aldrich, John H. 1995. *Why Parties? The Origin and Transformation of Political Parties in America.* University of Chicago Press.

Almond, Gabriel A., and Sidney Verba. 1963. *The Civic Culture: Political Attitudes and Democracy in Five Nations.* Princeton University Press.

Baumgartner, Frank, and Jack L. Walker. 1988. "Survey Research and Membership in Voluntary Associations." *American Journal of Political Science* 32: 908–27.

Bendix, Reinhard. 1964. *Nation-Building and Citizenship.* New York: Wiley.

Berry, Jeffrey M. 1977. *Lobbying for the People: The Political Behavior of Public Interest Groups.* Princeton University Press.

———. 1997. *The Interest Group Society.* 3d ed. New York: Longman.

Bradley, Bill. 1998. "America's Challenge: Revitalizing Our National Community." In *Community Works*, edited by E. J. Dionne Jr. Brookings.

Burnham, Walter Dean. 1970. *Critical Elections and the Mainsprings of American Politics.* New York: Norton.

Clemens, Elisabeth S. 1997. *The People's Lobby: Organizational Innovation and the Rise of Interest Group Politics in the United States, 1890–1925.* University of Chicago Press.

Coleman, James. 1988. "Social Capital and the Creation of Human Capital." *American Journal of Sociology* 94 (Supplement): S95–S120.

———. 1990. *Foundations of Social Theory.* Harvard University Press.

Council on Civil Society. 1998. "A Call to Civil Society: Why Democracy Needs Moral Truths." New York: Institute for American Values.

Danziger, Sheldon, and Peter Gottschalk. 1995. *America Unequal.* New York: Russell Sage Foundation; Harvard University Press.

Dionne, E. J. Jr., ed. 1998. *Community Works: The Revival of Civil Society in America.* Brookings.

Downing, Brian. 1992. *The Military Revolution and Political Change: Origins of Democracy and Autocracy in Modern Europe.* Princeton University Press.

Dunlap, Riley E., and Angela G. Mertig. 1992. *American Environmentalism: The U.S. Environmental Movement, 1970–1990.* New York: Taylor and Francis.

Ehrenhalt, Alan. 1996. *The Lost City: Discovering the Forgotten Virtues of Community in the Chicago of the 1950s.* Basic Books.

Ertman, Thomas. 1997. *Birth of the Leviathan: Building States and Regimes in Medieval and Early Modern Europe.* Cambridge University Press.

Galston, William A., and Peter Levine. 1998. "America's Civic Condition: A Glance at the Evidence." In *Community Works*, edited by E. J. Dionne Jr. Brookings.

Gamm, Gerald, and Robert D. Putnam. 1999. "The Growth of Voluntary Associations in America, 1840–1940." *Journal of Interdisciplinary History* 29(3): 511–57.

Ganz, Marshall. 1994. "Voters in the Crosshairs: How Technology and the Market Are Destroying Politics." *American Prospect*, no. 16 (Winter): 100–109.

Guterbock, Thomas M., and John C. Fries. 1997. "Maintaining America's Social Fabric: The AARP Survey of Civic Involvement." Washington, D.C.: American Association of Retired Persons.

Hausknecht, Murray. 1962. *The Joiners: A Sociological Description of Voluntary Association Membership in the United States.* New York: Bedminster.

Joyce, Michael S., and William A. Schambra. 1996. "A New Civic Life." In *To Empower People: From State to Civil Society*, 2d ed., edited by Michael Novak. Washington, D.C.: AEI Press.

Judis, John B. 1992. "The Pressure Elite: Inside the Narrow World of Advocacy Group Politics." *American Prospect*, no. 9 (Spring): 15–29.

King, David C. 1997. "The Polarization of American Parties and Mistrust of Government." In *Why People Don't Trust Government*, edited by Joseph S. Nye Jr., Philip D. Zelikow, and David C. King. Harvard University Press.

Kleppner, Paul. 1982. *Who Voted? The Dynamics of Electoral Turnout, 1870–1980.* New York: Praeger.

Ladd, Everett C. 1996. "The Data Just Don't Show Erosion of America's 'Social Capital.'" *Public Perspective* 7(4): 1, 5–22.

———. 1999. *The Ladd Report.* New York: Free Press.

Levi, Margaret. 1996. "Social and Unsocial Capital." *Politics and Society* 24 (March): 45–55.

McFarland, Andrew S. 1984. *Common Cause: Lobbying in the Public Interest.* Chatham, N.J.: Chatham House Publishers.

McGerr, Michael. 1986. *The Decline of Popular Politics.* Oxford University Press.

Minkoff, Debra C. 1995. *Organizing for Equality: The Evolution of Women's and Racial-Ethnic Organizations in America, 1955–1985.* Temple University Press.

Mitchell, Robert Cameron, Angela C. Mertig, and Riley E. Dunlap. 1992. "Twenty Years of Environmental Mobilization: Trends among National Environmental Organizations." In *American Environmentalism: The U.S. Environmental Movement, 1970–1990*, edited by Riley E. Dunlap and Angela E. Mertig. New York: Taylor and Francis.

Moore, Barrington, Jr. 1966. *Social Origins of Dictatorship and Democracy: Lord and Peasant in the Making of the Modern World.* Boston: Beacon Press.

National Commission on Civic Renewal. 1998. "A Nation of Spectators: How Civic Disengagement Weakens America and What We Can Do about It." College Park, Md.: National Commission on Civic Renewal.

Nye, Joseph S., Jr., Philip D. Zelikow, and David C. King. 1997. *Why People Don't Trust Government.* Harvard University Press.

Pettinico, George. 1996. "Civic Participation Is Alive and Well in Today's Environmental Groups." *Public Perspective* 7(4): 27–30.

Pew Research Center for the People and the Press. 1997. "Trust and Citizen Engagement in Metropolitan Philadelphia: A Case Study." Washington, D.C.

Putnam, Robert D. 1993a. *Making Democracy Work: Civic Traditions in Modern Italy.* Princeton University Press.

———. 1993b. "The Prosperous Community: Social Capital and Public Life." *American Prospect*, no. 13 (Spring): 35–42.

———. 1995a. "Bowling Alone: America's Declining Social Capital." *Journal of Democracy* 6(1): 65–78.

———. 1995b. "Tuning In, Tuning Out: The Strange Disappearance of Social Capital in America." *PS: Political Science and Politics* (December 1995): 664–83.

———. 2000 (forthcoming). *Bowling Alone: Civic Disengagement in America.* Simon and Schuster.

Rauch, Jonathan. 1998. "Demosclerosis Returns." *Wall Street Journal*, April 14, A22.

Rosenstone, Steven J., and John Mark Hansen. 1993. *Mobilization, Participation, and Democracy in America.* New York: Macmillan.

Rueschemeyer, Dietrich, Evelyne Huber Stephens, and John D. Stephens. 1992. *Capitalist Development and Democracy.* University of Chicago Press.

Samuelson, Robert J. 1996. " 'Bowling Alone' Is Bunk." *Washington Post*, April 10, A19.

Schlesinger, Arthur M., Sr. 1944. "Biography of a Nation of Joiners." *American Historical Review* 50(1): 1–25.

Schlozman, Kay Lehman, and John T. Tierney. 1986. *Organized Interests and American Democracy.* Harper and Row.

Schor, Juliet B. 1992. *The Overworked American: The Unexpected Decline of Leisure.* Basic Books.

————. 1998. *The Overspent American: Upscaling, Downshifting and the New Consumer.* Basic Books.

Schudson, Michael. 1996. "What If Civic Life Didn't Die?" *American Prospect,* no. 25 (March–April): 17–20.

Skerry, Peter. 1997. "The Strange Politics of Affirmative Action." *Wilson Quarterly* (Winter): 39–46.

Skocpol, Theda. 1992. *Protecting Soldiers and Mothers: The Political Origins of Social Policy in the United States.* Belknap Press of Harvard University Press.

————. 1995. *Social Policy in the United States: Future Possibilities in Historical Perspective.* Princeton University Press.

————. 1996. "The Tocqueville Problem: Civic Engagement in American Democracy." *Social Science History* 21(4): 455–79.

Starobin, Paul. 1997. "Civilizing Capitalism." *National Journal* 29 (January): 106–9.

Stengel, Richard. 1996. "Bowling Together: Civic Engagement in America Isn't Disappearing but Reinventing Itself." *Time,* July 22, 35–36.

Stevens, Albert C. 1899. *The Cyclopedia of Fraternities.* New York: Hamilton.

Tarrow, Sidney. 1996. "Making Social Science Work across Space and Time: A Critical Reflection on Robert Putnam's *Making Democracy Work.*" *American Political Science Review* 90(2): 389–97.

Tocqueville, Alexis de. [1835–40] 1969. *Democracy in America.* Edited by J. P Mayer and translated by George Lawrence. Garden City, N.Y.: Doubleday, Anchor Books.

Turow, Joseph. 1997. *Breaking Up America: Advertising and the New Media World.* University of Chicago Press.

Verba, Sidney, Kay Lehman Schlozman, and Henry E. Brady. 1995. *Voice and Equality: Civic Voluntarism in American Politics.* Harvard University Press.

Walker, Jack L., Jr. 1991. *Mobilizing Interest Groups in America: Patrons, Professions, and Social Movements.* University of Michigan Press.

Weir, Margaret, and Marshall Ganz. 1997. "Reconnecting People and Politics." In *The New Majority: Toward a Popular Progressive Politics,* edited by Stanley B. Greenberg and Theda Skocpol. Yale University Press.

Wolfe, Alan. 1998. "Is Civil Society Obsolete?" In *Community Works,* edited by E. J. Dionne Jr. Brookings.

Wuthnow, Robert. 1994. *Sharing the Journey: Support Groups and America's New Quest for Community.* Free Press.

————. 1998. *Loose Connections: Joining Together in America's Fragmented Communities.* Harvard University Press.

PART ONE

Between State and Society:
Roots of American
Civic Engagement

2 | *How Americans Became Civic*

THEDA SKOCPOL
with the assistance of Marshall Ganz, Ziad Munson,
Bayliss Camp, Michele Swers, and Jennifer Oser

M ORE THAN A MILE down a narrow winding road, the earthly remains of William W. Durgin of North Lovell, Maine, lie in a small out-of-the-way cemetery peppered with tiny headstones nestled amidst trees along a brook. The unpretentiousness of Durgin's resting place is appropriate for a backwoods farmer, lumberman, and spool maker who lived most of his long life—just over ninety years stretching from December 18, 1839, through January 27, 1929—in this very rural region of woodlands, rocky fields, and small hamlets at the western

Many people and institutions contributed to the research reported in this chapter. Contributions came from dozens of researchers working with the Civic Engagement Project at Harvard University. In addition to those listed on the title page, I would especially like to thank David Siu, Andrew Karch, Julia Greene, Christine Woyshner, Jocelyn Crowley, Anne Marie Flores, Sandy Chung, Janna Hansen, Cameron Sheldon, Susan Crawford, Anita Renton, Ruth Aguilera, Robert Mickey, Christian Brunelli, Julianne Unsel, and Elizabeth Rybicki. Many archivists and representatives of the associations included in this study were very generous with information and assistance. Seed funding for the Civic Engagement Project came from the Bertelsmann Foundation and the Russell Sage Foundation. Further research funding has come from grants provided by the Pew Charitable Trusts, the John D. and Catherine T. MacArthur Foundation, and the Children's Studies at Harvard Program. In addition, the Ford Foundation supported research on the religious underpinnings of civic associations, especially women's associations, through a grant administered by Constance Buchanan in the Education, Media, Arts, and Culture Program. Many colleagues, too many to list, offered comments on earlier drafts. I am especially grateful for feedback received at meetings of the American Politics Workshop, Harvard University, and at the 1997 conference described in the preface to this volume. And thanks to Bill Skocpol for finding William Durgin's grave.

edge of Maine, bordering Kezar Lake and facing the foothills of the White Mountains in neighboring New Hampshire.[1]

But Durgin's headstone is a surprise. On a large granite slab towering above the others, an inscription tells of the life-defining moment when Durgin served as "One of Abraham Lincoln's bearers and escort to Springfield Ill. Helped to place Remains in tomb." After four years of service in the Union army during the Civil War, 1st Sergeant William W. Durgin was chosen to be one of eight pallbearers, including illustrious officers and four "first Sergeants . . . selected with reference to their Age, length of Service and good soldierly conduct for escort duty to the remains of President Lincoln to Springfield, Illinois."[2] He helped carry the presidential casket to the hearse, escorted it to the Capitol where Lincoln lay in state, and rode the famous funeral train as it made its lugubrious way from Washington, D.C., to Springfield, Illinois, passing through "Baltimore, Harrisburg, Philadelphia, New York, Albany, Buffalo, Cleveland, Columbus, Chicago, [and] Indianapolis," all of which Durgin still recalled many decades later just a year before his death, when he was interviewed by a newsman.[3]

As if serving as Lincoln's pallbearer were not enough, Durgin's gravestone tells us more about the man known in life by his middle name, Warren. Under the dates bracketing his birth and death, a boldly engraved line says that Durgin was a "G.A.R Commander"—that is, the elected head of his local post of the Grand Army of the Republic, the post–Civil War association of Union veterans. The next line of the stone indicates Durgin's affiliation with the "P. of H."—referring to the Patrons of Husbandry, or Grange, where Durgin was probably a member of Kezar Lake Grange No. 440 of North Lovell. Finally, in an oblong rectangle at the very top of the gravestone appear three intertwined loops—a sure signal to those in the know that Warren Durgin was affiliated with the Independent Order of Odd Fellows, no doubt as a member of Crescent Lodge No. 25 of North Lovell. Durgin and his fellow Grangers and brother Odd Fellows may have worn reversible ribbon-badges like the ones illustrated here, with beautiful colors and emblems

1. Durgin's occupations are listed on his "Soldier's Claim for Pension" of July 14, 1890, a copy of which was obtained from the Union veterans' records held in the U.S. National Archives in Washington, D.C.

2. These words are quoted from the 1865 "Special Order" appointing Durgin, as reproduced in the *Lewiston Journal*; see "Lovell was Home of Last Surviving Pall-Bearer (1933)."

3. Extensive quotes from the interview were later published in the *Lewiston Journal* (ibid.). According to that article, the original interviewer was "Don Seitz, well-known newspaper man, who, for many years, had a summer home in Norway, Maine."

for public displays on one side, and black and silver "In Memoriam" designs for funeral processions on the other side (see Figure 2-1).

The associational involvements of William Warren Durgin bring to mind historian Arthur Schlesinger's characterization of America as a "nation of joiners."[4] And Durgin's activities were not unusual. They exemplified widespread and persistent patterns documented by Gabriel Almond and Sidney Verba in *The Civic Culture: Political Attitudes and Democracy in Five Nations*, a study completed several decades after Durgin's death.[5] The United States, found Almond and Verba, had a cross-nationally distinctive "participant civic culture"—a remarkably widespread set of popular orientations to social and political life that served as a strong buttress for stable democracy. This conclusion was based on analysis of citizens' attitudes and self-reported behaviors in Britain, Germany, Italy, and Mexico, as well as the United States. In comparison with the citizens of the other nations, Americans were unusually positively oriented toward public affairs and confident of their ability to make a difference at both the national and the local level.[6] Americans also stood out for the range and quality of their participation in voluntary groups.[7] British and German men were about as likely as American men to report being members of at least one group, but the American respondents were frequently members of several associations. Very often they were active participants, serving as officers or members of committees.

The profile for American women was even more striking. They held many more memberships and were much more likely to be officers or committee activists than the other female citizenries Almond and Verba studied. As it happens, my chief source of reminiscences about Warren Durgin is his nearly ninety-year-old grandniece, Mrs. Hester McKeen Mann, a former school teacher.[8] After inquiring about Durgin—who lived as a Civil War pensioner in the household of Hester's mother during the final decades of his life and the first decades of hers—I asked Hester about her own associational activities. Hester participated in groups and events at the Lovell community church and was an active member of her local Grange and county (Pomona) Grange, attaining the highest, seventh, degree in the Patrons of Husbandry (which accepts both men and women as members). For a time Hester was a member of the Pythian Sisters (her husband was in

4. Schlesinger (1944); see also Hausknecht (1962).
5. Almond and Verba (1963).
6. Ibid. (p. 186).
7. Ibid. (chap. 11).
8. I spoke with Mrs. Mann several times by phone during July 1998.

Figure 2-1. *Ribbon badges for North Lovell lodges.* Left, *IOOF badge set on parade side;* right, *Grange badge set on funeral side.*

the Knights of Pythias); and she was devoted enough to the Eastern Star to become a vice matron. As Hester told me with evident pride, along with other local ladies she took the lead in founding the Lovell auxiliary to the Veterans of Foreign Wars. All in all, a very civically involved woman.

How Did America Become Civic?

Almond and Verba could describe the attitudes and forms of participation that made the United States an unusually participatory democracy, but they could not explain where these attitudes and patterns of participation originated. *The Civic Culture* was based on attitude surveys taken at a single point in time. U.S. voluntary associations might be less centralized and hierarchical in their operations than European voluntary groups, speculated Almond and Verba.[9] But they had no direct evidence about the structure and operations of associations. Evidence about the universe of U.S. voluntary groups and their nature and relationships to government and politics would have been a very useful complement to Almond and Verba's attitudinal data.

Social scientists who have continued to probe American civic engagement since the publication of *The Civic Culture* have relied even more exclusively on survey data. Today this methodological approach reigns supreme, as scholars mine survey data since the mid-1970s to explore whether and why Americans have become more distrustful of government and their fellow citizens and less likely to join voluntary groups.[10] This chapter, by contrast, relies on institutional and organizational evidence and looks backward all the way to the nation's beginning.

The longer-term issues that Almond and Verba left dangling are fascinating: How did Americans come to be so unusually civic in the first place? In particular, what was it about classic associational life in the United States that allowed widespread individual participation and local community involvement to be so closely married to engagement with national public affairs? This question is not merely of antiquarian interest. Many argue that big changes in American society and democracy have occurred since the 1960s (and I consider those developments in the closing chapter of this book). But we cannot really understand what is happening to our polity

9. Almond and Verba (1963, pp. 315–19).
10. For examples, see Putnam (1995a, 1995b); Ladd (1996); Verba, Schlozman, and Brady (1995); and Wuthnow (1998).

today, let alone prescribe appropriate remedies, unless we understand how Americans became unusually civically engaged in earlier eras.

Challenging Conventional Wisdom

Many people see little need to ponder the history of American civic engagement, because the overall contours of the story seem obvious. According to the standard wisdom, voluntary groups flourished locally in the United States in the absence of any strong national state. A weak state and autonomous religious institutions made it both necessary and possible for local groups of Americans to do things on their own. "Our reliance upon voluntary associations to achieve social goals stems from the widespread division and dispersal of authority in the United States" and on our dependence "on private religious associations to guide our public moral philosophy," declares a 1998 national commission report entitled "A Call to Civil Society," which offers nary a footnote to support this declaration, so self-evident does it seem to its authors.[11] Early U.S. voluntary groups are typically presumed to have been local, inward looking, and apolitical—perhaps involved with neighborhood and town affairs but otherwise "free" from any intertwinement with government or supralocal politics.

Of course everyone agrees that industrialization brought change. As the United States grew economically and expanded geographically, people became mobile and large-scale bureaucratic organizations took over many activities previously controlled by families and local communities. Vast cities and industries grew, bringing class divisions and social anomie. According to the standard wisdom, the associational life of Americans changed in a parallel fashion, moving from small, local, and informal to big, national, and bureaucratic.

A dark side to modernization is stressed by contemporary conservative theorists, who believe that voluntary groups were hurt by the growth of the national state—and especially by the rise of the modern "welfare state" with its social expenditures and market regulations. Conservatives adhere to a zero-sum logic, one that sees extralocal government and organization as almost automatically bad for the health of what George Will calls the "little platoons" of church, family, and neighborhood and community groups.[12] Clear-cut policy pronouncements flow from this presumption.

11. Council on Civil Society (1998, p. 9).
12. Will (1995).

In the words of Michael Joyce and William Schambra, "restoration of civil society [in America] will require nothing less than a determined, long-term effort to reverse the gravitation of power and authority upward to the national government and to send that authority back to local government and civil institutions."[13] Joyce and Schambra want America to return to what they presume was its original situation, as a country of families, churches, and neighborhoods acting through local associations outside of and apart from the state and politics.

But as we are about to see, empirical evidence sharply challenges received wisdom and conservative presumptions. From the very beginning of the American nation, democratic governmental and political institutions encouraged the proliferation of voluntary groups linked to regional or national social movements. Increasingly, groups were tied into translocal organizational networks that paralleled the local-state-national structure of the U.S. state. Moral-reform movements, farmers' and workers' associations, fraternal brotherhoods and sisterhoods, independent women's associations, veterans' groups, and many ethnic and African American associations all converged on this quintessentially American form of voluntary membership association. Local face-to-face participation complemented and went along with organized routes into county, state, regional, and national public affairs.

For most of U.S. history, politics and government encouraged rather than stifled organized civil society. Competition and contention among politically active groups, representative institutions and competitive elections, and many kinds of national government initiatives—all were conducive to the emergence and growth of voluntary associations with active memberships. Ironically, too, major American wars—from the Revolution of the late eighteenth century and the Civil War of 1861–65, through World Wars I and II—proved surprisingly beneficial for popularly rooted associations. As Americans mobilized for wars and other shared national endeavors, they also launched new voluntary associations and joined or revitalized previously established groups. Throughout most of American history, active democratic government and a vibrant civil society centered in federated associations went hand in hand.

To flesh out these arguments, I draw on a variety of sources. There is, unfortunately, no handy reference book or computer disk to which one can turn to map the rise and fall, the purposes and forms, of voluntary

---

13. Joyce and Schambra (1996, p. 29).

associations throughout U.S. history. The picture must be pieced together from in-depth social histories of particular places,[14] from accounts of individual associations,[15] from studies of specific types of associations,[16] and from directories that tally and describe large numbers of associations at specific points in time.[17] Valuable as all of these are, each genre and data source offers but fragmentary insights that are hard to add up. Fortunately, a few scholars have done broader studies, documenting the spread of associations of all types in many localities for half a century or more.[18] This chapter relies especially on such encompassing studies.

In addition, I report preliminary findings from a large-scale research effort I am coordinating called the "civic engagement project." As much out of curiosity as anything else, a group of student collaborators and I set out several years ago to map all large voluntary *membership* associations in U.S. history.[19] Leaving aside the obvious cases of major political parties and church denominations, we asked how many associations ever, at any time between 1790 and the present, enrolled 1 percent or more of American adults as "members" (according to whatever definition of membership each group used). If groups restricted membership to men or women, then 1 percent of the adult male *or* adult female population became the benchmark.[20] But no other relaxations of the demanding size criterion have been made. Groups restricted to particular occupational, racial, or ethnic groups are included in our master list only if they enroll 1 percent of the entire U.S. adult population. Representing every slice of the population is not our goal. Rather we seek a window into transformations in American society and democracy. Tracing very large voluntary membership associa-

14. Such as Blumin (1989); Doyle (1977); Glazer (1972); and Ryan (1981).

15. Including such fine scholarly works as Kaufman (1982); Macleod (1983); and McConnell (1992); as well as many official histories done by associational insiders.

16. Such as Carnes (1989); Clawson (1989); Dannenbaum (1984); Davies (1955); and Scott (1991).

17. Such as Schmidt (1980); Preuss (1924); and Stevens (1899).

18. These include Brown (1973); Brown (1974); and Gamm and Putnam (1999).

19. I stress *membership* associations, because many people use the term "voluntary group" to refer to contemporary nonprofit social service delivery agencies or, historically, to groups devoted to providing charity to the needy. In this chapter, and in the civic engagement project, I focus on voluntary associations of citizens, groups in which people do things together as fellow members, even if they also engage in some delivery of charitable aid to others and/or delivery of services to the broader community.

20. In most cases, gender restrictions are formal, often explicitly indicated in the name of an association. For certain groups, like major military veterans' associations, a gender restriction may not be explicit, but we recognize its overwhelming de facto existence. Of course, some associations change their rules about gender qualifications for membership; when that happens, we shift from, say, men-only to all U.S. adults in calculating, decade by decade, whether membership exceeds 1 percent.

tions seems a promising way to proceed, because these groups by definition were popular and widespread.

The list of fifty-seven groups the civic engagement project has identified so far appears as Table 2A-1 in the appendix at the end of this chapter. This list presents very large membership associations in the chronological order of their founding, *not* according to the dates at which they crossed the 1 percent membership threshold. Using the best long-term membership data available, Table 2A-2 shows the decades of U.S. national history from the 1790s to the present during which each group enrolled over 1 percent of eligible adults for at least one year.[21] A juxtaposition of Tables 2A-1 and 2A-2 reveals that many eventually large membership associations cross the 1 percent threshold within a few decades of their founding. But as Table 2A-2 indicates, a few, such as the National Rifle Association and the National Education Association, did not become truly large until a century or more after their founding.

For each association on our master list, we are developing a complete quantitative and qualitative profile, gathering information on origins and development, membership, activities and resources, and relationships to government, political parties, and religious institutions. We have also taken some steps to compare our set of large voluntary groups against lists of groups that other researchers have found in local settings. For this purpose, a systematic study being conducted by Gerald Gamm and Robert Putnam is of special interest. Using town and city directories, Gamm and Putnam count churches and voluntary groups present in twenty-six large, medium-sized, and small cities decade by decade from 1840 to 1940.[22] In one sense

21. So far, complete membership runs have not been discovered for every large association in our study. In some cases, we have made substantially informed judgments to indicate the decades in which an association exceeded 1 percent of men and/or women. Estimates had to be made for Christian Endeavor, the Modern Woodmen of America, the American Red Cross, the American Farm Bureau Federation, the Townsend movement, the March of Dimes, and Greenpeace USA. In all instances we are reasonably certain the associations did exceed 1 percent; our estimates address the span of decades during which this mark was passed.

22. The places in Gamm and Putnam's project are spread across the United States and classified by their populations in 1890 into three size categories: five big cities (St. Louis, Boston, San Francisco, Milwaukee, and Denver); ten medium-sized cities; and eleven small cities. Data come from official city directories published yearly to help people navigate their way within and among localities. Comparing some of these directories against other sources of information convinces me that they often left out (or delayed listing) labor unions or groups restricted to women or racial minorities. Not surprisingly, groups of most interest to employed mainstream men are the ones that appear soonest and most consistently in the directories. Still, keeping in mind the limitations of these data, we can still learn a lot about trends over time and across cities of various sizes.

the Gamm and Putnam and Skocpol studies are incommensurate. About a third of all the groups in Gamm and Putnam's twenty-six cities between 1840 and 1940 are religious congregations, a type of group not directly included in the Skocpol project. But roughly another third of Gamm and Putnam's groups are fraternal and veterans' groups (and their female equivalents), parts of translocal federations already well documented by previous analysts.[23] Fraternal and veterans' groups also constitute about two-fifths of the very large membership associations included in the list in Table 2A-1. Such voluntary associations devoted to brotherhood and sisterhood rituals, mutual aid, and community service were historically at the core of U.S. civil society. So it is not surprising that they are a large presence in both the Gamm and Putnam and the Skocpol studies.

Another way to calibrate the relationship of translocal federations and locally present groups is to see exactly which groups appeared in the city directories on which Gamm and Putnam relied for counts. So far, I have done this in detail using directories for Bath, Maine; Leadville, Colorado; and Portland, Oregon, for 1880, 1890, 1900, 1910, and 1920 (or the closest years with available directories).[24] Using national directories and studies that list translocal associations of various sizes, I found that, across all three of these cities and every decade, fully 75 to 90 percent of the churches and other associations listed were unambiguously linked to translocal federations.[25] If churches are set aside, then in any given place and decade from 33 to 60 percent of the remaining associations turn out to have been local units within the very largest U.S. membership federations listed in Table 2A-1; and most of the rest of the local groups were parts of smaller national or regional voluntary federations structured in much the same way as the very large federations. Few purely local associations, specific only to one city or its immediate surroundings, appeared in the city directories from 1880 to 1920. And those tended to be countywide professional associations or elite clubs

---

23. For systematic descriptions of many American fraternal groups, see Gist (1940); Schmidt (1980); and Stevens (1899).

24. I obtained the Bath directories, the same ones Gamm and Putnam used, from the Patten Free Library in Bath, Maine. Gamm and Putnam were kind enough to share with me photocopies of the directories they used for associational data on Leadville and Portland. Additional cities from their study will also be examined in due course, but patterns are clear cut, and I do not expect the general conclusions reported here to change.

25. Useful lists of associations appear in Breckinridge (1933); Gist (1940); Preuss (1924); Schmidt (1980); and Stevens (1899).

and cultural or recreational groups resembling counterparts in many other communities.

U.S. association-building was primarily a story of translocal as well as local efforts connected to broad movements and federal organizational frameworks. Let me suggest how and why this happened from the time of the American Revolution through the middle of the twentieth century. Then we can probe a bit more deeply into the consequences of federated membership associations for democratic participation in America.

The Roots of American Civic Voluntarism

An extensive and participatory civil society took shape from the start of U.S. nationhood, even as life for the vast majority of Americans proceeded on farms or in very small towns. In the era between the Revolution and the Civil War, voluntary groups multiplied and formed links across localities, spurred on by government activities and popular political contention in the new republic and by competitive religious evangelism in a nation without an established church.[26]

From Colony to Republic

The historian Richard Brown has traced the growth of voluntary groups of all sorts in Massachusetts, including the present state of Maine, which was part of Massachusetts until 1820.[27] Brown counts all sorts of groups decade by decade in hamlets, towns, and cities, tracing associational dynamics before and after the American Revolution—with the revolution understood as a process of political contention and institution-building that stretched from the 1760s through the 1790s.

Before truly voluntary groups could proliferate, there had to be concentrations of 200 to 400 families, with at least 20 percent of the men out of a total population of 1,000 to 2,000 persons engaged in nonagricultural occupations.[28] Still, there was nothing automatic about this socioeconomic threshold, which was surpassed by dozens of places in Massachusetts/Maine well before the Revolution. Despite this socioeconomic potential,

26. G. S. Wood (1996); Hatch (1989); and Finke and Stark (1992).
27. Brown (1973); Brown (1974).
28. Brown (1974, p. 47).

relatively few voluntary groups were created during colonial times. As Brown's statistics show, before 1760 there were only a few dozen voluntary groups apart from churches in all of Massachusetts/Maine; and more than a third of them were located in Boston, the colonial capital and only substantial city.

The story changed dramatically once the American colonies roused themselves to separate from Britain. Between "1760 and 1820 . . . over 1,900 voluntary associations were created" throughout Massachusetts/Maine, and during "the 1820s at least seventy were founded each year."[29] A wide variety of associations spread across Massachusetts and Maine, including charitable and missionary groups, political groups, lyceums, moral reform efforts, professional and trade associations, fraternal lodges, and new kinds of churches (especially Methodist and Baptist).

At first only groups such as the Masons and most churches were formally linked translocally. But many more spread as people in one locality modeled their efforts on similar undertakings elsewhere. Although women rarely organized separate translocal associations in this early period, recognizably similar female benevolent groups appeared in many towns.[30] And at least one translocal association, the American Female Moral Reform Society founded in New York City, eventually encompassed 445 auxiliaries across the middle states and greater New England.[31] Meanwhile, male promoters disseminated explicit models and instructions for founding and operating community associations. A prime example was Josiah Holbrook, who traveled, spoke, and published to promote "lyceums," that is, voluntary community institutions intended to promote adult education, sponsor traveling lecturers, and support the emerging "common" public schools and their teachers.[32] In the 1820s and 1830s, Holbrook published and periodically revised guidelines for the establishment of lyceums, along with detailed plans for local, county, state, and national lyceums, with all levels above the local to be based on representatives sent from below.[33]

More striking than the sheer rate of increase of voluntary groups in Massachusetts/Maine was the geographic pattern of foundings.[34] All kinds

29. Ibid. (p. 38).
30. Scott (1991, chap. 1).
31. Smith-Rosenberg (1985, p. 120).
32. Bode (1968); Monroe (1942).
33. For an elaborated version of lyceum plans, see Holbrook (1836–37).
34. Here I am working with data from Brown (1974, pp. 40–41, table 1).

of voluntary groups in Boston increased more than 650 percent between 1760 and 1830, yet the rate of increase was 920 percent for the rest of Massachusetts/Maine. The picture is even more clear cut when churches (as well as what Brown calls "profit-seeking" groups) are left aside. The number of such associations in Boston went from 14 before 1760 to 121 between 1760 and 1830 (a roughly 760 percent increase). However, the number in the rest of Massachusetts/Maine went from 24 before 1760 to 1,281 between 1760 and 1830—an increase of more than 5,000 percent. Between 1790 and 1830, as most of this associational proliferation occurred, the combined population of Massachusetts and Maine more than doubled, from 476,000 to 1,009,000.[35] Obviously, associational proliferation vastly outpaced population growth—and outran population most of all in the hinterland.

"In colonial America," Brown concludes, social patterns involving choice and extralocal awareness were "a highly restricted phenomenon, limited to port towns that were also administrative centers," places such as Boston, New York, Philadelphia, and (to a degree) Charleston. Such patterns penetrated parts of the hinterland only via elites "who were in touch with the [colonial] capital as an occupational necessity."[36] But throughout the countryside by the 1830s, "localism and insularity were being challenged, if not actually destroyed. People remained bound to the old organizations of family, church, and town, but now they possessed additional ties. . . . Sometimes the contact was direct, if they traveled to a meeting or convention or if outsiders came to them as part of a political campaign, lyceum, temperance or missionary association. More often, the contact was psychological, coming from memberships in countywide or statewide organization and the publications such activities produced."[37]

Civil Society Goes National

This remarkable transformation happened soonest and most intensively in the northeastern United States, yet similar changes soon spread across the expanding nation and involved people from many backgrounds.[38] By the time the Civil War broke out in 1861, the United States,

---

35. These population numbers come from U.S. Bureau of the Census (1975, part 1, p. 29, series A 195–209).
36. Brown (1974, p. 31).
37. Ibid. (p. 43).
38. Ibid. (p. 32).

amidst its contentiousness and enormous regional and ethnic diversity, had developed a recognizably national civil society.

From the 1830s through the 1850s, lyceums spread from New England into the upper South and (especially) into the Midwest east of the Mississippi River.[39] Vast moral crusades and temperance movements inspired the creation of thousands of interlinked local and state societies. Among the most prominent, the American Temperance Society by 1834 claimed some 5,000 societies and 1 million members in the East and Midwest. The Washingtonian crusade, which reached out for working-class members and reformed "drunkards," claimed some 600,000 members and 10,000 societies in the early 1840s. The Washingtonians were soon succeeded by the more institutionalized Order of the Sons of Temperance, which by 1860 was a truly continent-spanning federation boasting some 2,398 local "divisions" and 94,213 members in more than three dozen state divisions in the North, South, and across the Mississippi River into Iowa and California.[40] By the 1850s, the Independent Order of Good Templars (IOGT) began its climb to national prominence. Remarkably open to women as well as men for membership and leadership positions alike, by 1860 the IOGT claimed more than 50,000 members in 1,200 lodges spread across twenty states, including Alabama and Mississippi in the deep South.[41]

Fraternal orders also spanned the nation, despite the outburst of a temporary furor against patrician Masons and other "secret societies" that peaked in the 1830s.[42] From colonial times, Masonic lodges put down roots everywhere in America; indeed local lodges were founded immediately upon the arrival of military garrisons in each new territory and new "sovereign grand" lodges were chartered just as each state joined the U.S. union.[43] The Masons were a relatively elite fraternity, yet they became somewhat more accessible to a range of men after the anti-Masonic crisis and, more to the point, were soon followed by other fraternals open to working-class and white-collar Americans of various ethnic and racial backgrounds.[44] Sometimes diverse ethnic groups joined together in the

---

39. Bode (1968, sec. 2); Mead (1951).
40. Hodges (1877).
41. Turnbull (1901).
42. Kutolowski (1982); Ratner (1969).
43. Bullock (1996); Lipson (1977).
44. Bullock (1996, Epilogue); Clawson (1989, chap. 3).

same fraternal; at other times, they established separate groups with parallel structures and purposes.

Destined to become the model for many subsequent brotherhoods in the United States, the Independent Order of Odd Fellows (IOOF) spread from a lodge established in Baltimore, Maryland, in 1819. American Odd Fellows took an organizational step that the (basic "blue lodge") Masons never did. As the U.S.-centered IOOF broke away from British Odd Fellows between 1819 and 1843, it developed a three-tiered federal structure capped by a national-level "Sovereign Grand Lodge" formed from representatives sent from state-level grand lodges with jurisdiction over local lodges.[45] Perfectly suited to American conditions, this new IOOF structure allowed the originally eastern-seaboard fraternal to spread across the continent. By 1860 there were more than 170,000 U.S. Odd Fellows meeting in more than 3,000 local lodges in thirty-five states in all regions of the nation.[46] As the author of the 1852 edition of *The Odd-Fellow Text Book* proudly declared: "From town to town, from city to city, from state to state, has this Order spread, and thousands upon thousands of the best men of our nation have been gathered to its folds."[47]

Other U.S. fraternals also made rapid headway before the Civil War. Founded in 1834, the racially and ethnically exclusive Improved Order of Red Men (IORM) consisted of white Christians who dressed up like Native Americans and dated their order from 1492, when Columbus arrived in America. By 1860 almost 10,000 Red Men were meeting in 94 "tribes" spread across the "reservations" of Maryland, Pennsylvania, Virginia, Ohio, New Jersey, Missouri, Kentucky, Delaware, and the District of Columbia.[48] Not to be outdone, in 1836 Irish Americans founded the

---

45. T. A. Ross (1888, chaps. 1–3).

46. Ibid. (chap. 14).

47. Donaldson (1852, p. 9). By early in the twentieth century, according to Fuller (1913), the Odd Fellows had some 17,500 lodges dotted across communities of all sizes in the United States and British Canada. The Odd Fellows admitted only whites, yet like the Masons they built some bridges across religious denominations and across early Euro-American ethnic groups. Centered among native-born Protestants, the Masons, Odd Fellows, and Knights of Pythias accepted some Jews and allowed German-speaking and other immigrant local lodges to organize within their predominantly English-speaking orders. I base this on Dumenil (1984, pp. 10–13) and Clawson (1989, pp. 129–33), as well as on histories and constitutions I have found for Jewish or immigrant lodges. Catholics were not barred from the Masons and Odd Fellows, but the Church strongly opposed their joining. Later in the nineteenth century, when southern and eastern European immigrants arrived, native-Protestant-centered fraternals became less welcoming to ethnic members and lodges.

48. Lichtman (1901, pp. 314–15).

American branch of the Ancient Order of Hibernians, which was organized in eight states of the East, South, and Midwest by 1861.[49] During the 1840s, German Americans in New York City launched the Order of the Sons of Hermann and the Order of Harugari, two (eventually trans-state) beneficial and cultural federations dedicated to furthering German culture and defending German Americans from nativist attacks during widespread Know-Nothing agitations.[50] German Americans also launched their own "Independent" Order of Red Men in 1850, a fraternal that met in federated "stamms" rather than "tribes."[51]

In addition to Germans and the Irish, African Americans were the other very large minority from early in U.S. history. With the exception of some temperance orders, white-dominated U.S. voluntary associations shunned blacks as members. But African Americans built vast orders of their own, many of which paralleled the groups from which they were excluded. Prince Hall Masonry originated in 1775, when British Masons chartered a Negro Masonic lodge in Cambridge, Massachusetts.[52] Even before the Civil War, free blacks spread this fraternal empire across eighteen states, including "most of the Atlantic coastal states as far south as Virginia, and many midwestern states . . . [and] Maryland, Virginia, and Louisiana, the centers of the free Negro population" of the South.[53] In 1843, African Americans in New York City under the leadership of seaman Peter Ogden launched the Grand United Order of Odd Fellows, again with the aid of a lodge charter from England. By the early 1860s about 1,500 African American Odd Fellows were meeting in about fifty lodges scattered across more than half a dozen eastern states.[54]

Why Did It Happen?

Communities of all sizes established voluntary groups with remarkable simultaneity and many groups became linked in translocal organizations. Why was early American civil society so sharply and precociously transformed? Politics, religious freedom, and republican government lie at the heart of the answer.

49. Ridge (1986).
50. Stevens (1899, pp. 234–35, 282–84).
51. Ibid. (1899, p. 262).
52. Muraskin (1975).
53. Palmer (1944, p. 208). Palmer adds that the "three years following the end of the Civil War saw the inclusion of every southern state in the Negro Masonic ranks" after the slaves were freed.
54. Stevens (1899, pp. 236–37); Brooks ([1902] 1971).

Many ideological and material aspects of the American break from British imperial control fueled the growth of a democratic civil society.[55] "Above all," historian Nathan Hatch writes, "the Revolution dramatically expanded the circle of people who considered themselves capable of thinking for themselves about issues of freedom, equality, sovereignty, and representation."[56] The Revolution also gave ordinary Americans new tools for collective action, as the mobilization against Britain and subsequent struggles over a new U.S. Constitution disrupted taken-for-granted loyalties, brought geographically dispersed sets of Americans into contact with one another, and undermined prior city monopolies. During colonial times, for example, all Massachusetts print shops were based in Boston, but during the Revolution printers multiplied and dispersed to other parts of the region.[57]

Once victory and nationhood came, the ongoing political routines of the representative polity pulled Americans into broader, competitive political involvements. Elections were held for statewide and national offices, and fledgling political parties competed for support, linking some citizens in each place to fellow Federalists or Jeffersonians elsewhere. By the 1830s, virtually all adult white men had gained the right to vote; and transregional political parties were knitting together patronage machines and networks of grassroots associations capable of mobilizing popular votes in incessant rounds of elections.[58]

Surely it is no accident that both federated mass mobilizing political parties and federated popularly rooted voluntary membership associations emerged and became well institutionalized in the same era of American history, between the 1820s and the 1850s. Although parties and associations operated partly at cross-purposes—because most associations tried to be nonpartisan in order to attract people from competing electoral parties—they grappled with many of the same organizational dilemmas: how to inspire large numbers of people to participate while at the same time forging links across a growing and diverse new nation. Both parties and associations attempted to solve these dilemmas by linking interactive groups of local adherents into federated networks and decisionmaking structures.

Early America was also swept by the religious enthusiasms of the Second Great Awakening. Religious proselytization started during late

55. Brown (1974), G. S. Wood (1996).

56. Hatch (1989, p. 6).

57. Brown (1974, p. 43).

58. On early U.S. political parties, see Aldrich (1995, part 2); Kleppner (1982); Schudson (1998, chap. 3); and Shefter (1994, pp. 63–71).

colonial times and accelerated during the early national period. Here it is important to underline that the United States—in contrast to most other countries of that time—had no governmentally established church monopoly. "Beginning with Virginia in 1776 and ending with Connecticut in the 1840s, all American states eventually broke the traditional ties that had bound church and state together."[59] Under the Constitution and the Bill of Rights, competing denominations were free to preach and proselytize. Popularly oriented evangelical movements were encouraged to compete for members regionally and nationally.[60] Traveling organizers and preachers, especially Methodists and Baptists, spread out across the land. Established religious hierarchies were challenged and bypassed by wildfire movements that appealed to the religious passions and aspirations of ordinary Americans.[61] Religious fervor and expansion influenced American democracy and civil society by spreading values and models of organization across localities, states, and regions. Religion was not merely a matter of local congregations and charitable endeavors.

Early Methodist circuit-riding clergy, above all, pioneered new methods of associational organization.[62] They moved from place to place, inspiring local leaders to found and sustain new congregations, and then tied those bodies together into federations espousing a shared world view and moral purposes. As the Methodists spread their word and founded tens of thousands of local congregations in even the tiniest places, other religious denominations had to reach out and organize too, lest they shrink and die.[63] Through competitive emulation, a new model of association-spreading fanned across early America—one that assorted lay associations soon adopted, too.

Religious disestablishment and competition also facilitated the extraordinary civic empowerment of American women.[64] As the majority of churchgoers, women were likely to be drawn into reform crusades grounded in religious ideals and networks. Yet denominational divisions and competition left space for women association-builders to emerge. As historian Kathryn Kish Sklar explains, "beginning in the 1820s, women

59. Sklar (1998, p. 27).
60. Finke and Stark (1992).
61. Hatch (1989).
62. Mathews (1969).
63. Finke and Stark (1992); Hatch (1989).
64. For an overview of women's civic empowerment, see Baker (1984); Scott (1991); and Skocpol (1992, chap. 6).

were able to form vigorous pan-Protestant lay organizations, which challenged the authority of ministers and generated an autonomous social agenda."[65] Women members and leaders also quickly moved into prominence in temperance movements and organizations.[66]

The relentless westward expansion of the American nation, and the restless movement of its people, especially young men, likewise helped locally rooted yet translocally connected associations to spread.[67] Waves of migration spread across the continent, and newly arrived residents established familiar kinds of lodges or clubs at the same time that they built farms, businesses, and churches. Once settled, moreover, people visited or wrote to relatives and friends in their places of origin, learning in the process of new kinds of associations that they might help to establish in their new communities.

Indeed, unusually efficient and inclusive means of social communication allowed Americans, from early national times onward, to create interconnected groups for political, religious, and moral purposes. One indicator is especially telling: "Between 1790 and 1810 the United States witnessed an explosive growth in the number of newspapers—from 90 to 370."[68] Widespread literacy and newspaper reading facilitated communication, argues Richard Brown, echoing Alexis de Tocqueville's observation that "newspapers make associations, and associations make newspapers. . . . Of all countries on earth, it is in America that one finds both the most associations and the most newspapers."[69] But Tocqueville did not appreciate all of the conditions that facilitated communication and hence association-building. A very active and centralized arm of the early U.S. national state—the U.S. Postal Service— played the key role in this development.

Before the American Revolution, the colonies had a rudimentary postal system comparable to that in many European countries, with larger cities loosely tied together, especially along the Atlantic coast. This changed when Congress passed the Post Office Act of 1792, which "admitted newspapers into the mail on unusually favorable terms, . . . prohibited public officers from using their control over the means of communication as a surveillance technique, [and] established a set of procedures that facilitated the extraordinarily rapid expansion of the postal network from the Atlantic seaboard

65. Sklar (1998, p. 27).
66. Dannenbaum (1984); Epstein (1981).
67. Berthoff (1971, part 2).
68. Hatch (1989, p. 25).
69. Brown (1974, pp. 43–44); Tocqueville ([1835–40] 1969, p. 518).

into the transappalachian West."[70] "By 1828," historian Richard John points out, "the American postal system had almost twice as many offices as the postal system in Great Britain and over five times as many offices as the postal system in France. This translated into 74 post offices for every 100,000 inhabitants in comparison with 17 for Great Britain and 4 for France." In the 1830s and 1840s, the system accounted for more than three-quarters of U.S. federal employees, and most of the 8,764 postal employees in 1831 and the 14,290 in 1841 were "part-time postmasters in villages and towns scattered throughout the countryside."[71]

The postal network was shaped by U.S. government institutions. Congressional representation based in states and local districts gave members of the Senate and the House of Representatives a strong interest in subsidizing communication and transportation links into even the remotest areas of the growing nation—yet in a carefully calibrated way. Legislators wanted mail and news to be carried into even the smallest communities; and they also wanted to be able to travel to and from the national capital. Hence, they subsidized stagecoach travel and set cheap postal rates. Postal rules also allowed for the free exchange of newspapers among editors, so that small newspapers could pick up copy from bigger ones. But at the same time, rate structures were fine-tuned to prevent Eastern seaboard papers from outmarketing provincial newssheets.

To take advantage of postal subsidies, voluntary groups as well as political parties disseminated their messages in "newspaper" (and later magazine) formats. Translocal organizing was greatly facilitated. One of the first great moral reform movements in America—briefly embodied between 1828 and 1832 in the General Union for Promoting the Observance of the Christian Sabbath—was devoted to trying to stop the opening of post offices and transportation of the mails on Sundays. Ironically, this movement depended on the very federal postal system it sought to challenge because it relied on the mail to spread tens of thousands of pamphlets and petitions. The same was true of other great voluntary crusades in the pre–Civil War era, including the temperance movements and the popular drive against slavery that helped to spark the Civil War.[72] The early U.S. state, in short, created favorable conditions for associations, social move-

---

70. John (1995, p. 31).

71. Ibid. (pp. 5, 3).

72. On the General Union and other crusades, see John (1995, chaps. 6 and 7) and Dannenbaum (1984).

ments, and mass-mobilizing political parties—all of which, in turn, continuously roiled and transformed politics and the state.

The Federal Representative State as a Civil Model

There was a final way in which U.S. governing institutions influenced association-building: the structure of government served as an organizational model. The United States was put together as a federal republic, and both the nation and the states had written constitutions that spelled out rules for voting and representation; explicitly parceled out administrative, legislative, and judicial functions; and assigned levels of sovereignty to national, state, and local government. From early national times, American civil associations began to imitate this structure. Large and small voluntary membership federations of all sorts produced detailed constitutions, which they regularly debated and modified. Like the example from the Olive Branch local "division" of the Sons of Temperance illustrated here, members of local units might carry pocket "constitutions and by-laws" (see Figure 2-2).[73] And of course there were even more elaborate publications at the national and state levels.

Associations had detailed rules about eligibility for membership, payment of dues, the selection of leaders and representatives, and the adjudication of disputes.[74] The rules were hammered out in endless rounds of meetings at the national, state, and local levels. Local units were empowered to elect officers and representatives to state bodies, while local and/or state units sent representatives to national bodies—just as U.S. senators were originally appointed by state governments.

Associational constitutions included explicit rules about the establishment of state and local units and the flow of recruits into them. Unlike fraternal groups in other nations, for example, U.S. fraternals and their female partner groups required a potential member to apply to the lodge nearest his or her residence or have its written permission to apply elsewhere.[75] Traveling members had to have formal documentation from their local and

73. Published as Sons of Temperance (1854), this beautifully illustrated paper booklet comes from the author's personal collection. The reproduction here is about 93 percent of the original size.

74. Discussions in the remainder of this section are based on my reading of national group constitutions and literally dozens of state and local constitution booklets. I have also read numerous accounts of the founding of various lodges, posts, and local clubs.

75. The U.S. arrangements come into relief when one notices international fraternal disputes about fraternal jurisdictions such as those discussed in Pollard (1945, pp. 67–68).

Figure 2-2. *An 1854 constitution booklet from a local division of the Sons of Temperance*

CONSTITUTION.

To maintain uniformity, the Nationall Division of the United States ordain the following Constitution for the government of Subordinate Divisions, at the same time empowering them to make such By-Laws as do not contravene it or the Rules of the Order.

PREAMBLE.

We whose names are annexed, desirous of forming a society to shield us from the evils of intemperance, afford mutual assistance in case of sickness, and elevate our characters as men, do pledge ourselves to be governed by the following Constitution and By-Laws.

CONSTITUTION.

ARTICLE I.—*Name.*

This Association shall be known as OLIVE BRANCH DIVISION, No. 67, OF THE SONS OF TEMPERANCE, of the State of New York.

state units to be admitted as visitors away from home. Just as Americans had to establish their voting rights in their local communities and states, so too did they have to establish their memberships in translocal associations through their home communities. American associations may have encouraged outward ties, but no rootless cosmopolitanism was allowed.

The national and state jurisdictions of fraternals maintained elaborate zoning rules. New local lodges were required to have the endorsement of previously chartered units in their vicinity, as well as the approval of the relevant state jurisdiction. The point of these rules was to embed members in local groups and—perhaps even more significant—to manage the creation of local groups so as to avoid unnecessary fragmentation or duplication. State-level authorities encouraged would-be organizers of local units to meet and work together rather than competing. They also ruled against applications for new local lodges if they thought there was not a sufficient pool of potential members to sustain additional units.

Such rules meant that during the earliest stages of the development of an associational network, units were likely to be spread out, recruiting members across town lines. To attend early group meetings, Americans traveled amazing distances under poor transportation conditions. If and when an association matured and became popular, members from very small towns or urban neighborhoods could establish their own units. But new units could be added only with permission from higher authorities and only when majorities in neighbor units approved. Similarly, when associations went into decline, members of clubs or lodges that closed were allowed to join groups in neighboring areas or become "at-large" members of state associations. Classic American membership federations thus tended to be more cross-local in membership toward the beginning and the end of their life cycles and most locally rooted at their height.

Nevertheless, in all phases American association-building consisted of local undertakings linked to translocal movements and organizations. Local people took heart from regional and national exemplars; and they valued formal connections to higher-level representative governing institutions. Local group founders might be recruited and inspired by traveling "agents" sent out from state and national headquarters, or they might be people newly arrived in particular towns or regions who aspired to extend familiar associations. Either way, local founders proceeded within explicitly institutionalized "constitutional" rules of the game—rules that discouraged fragmentation and fostered cross-local contacts even as they protected state and local sovereignty within the unified whole.

Civic America in Modern Times

If waves of voluntary group formation occurred well before 1861, scholars agree that even greater bursts gathered force after the Civil War, expanding some older associations and launching many new groups destined to persist through much of the twentieth century. Established wisdom leads us to expect fundamental associational departures as the country was transformed from a society of farms and small towns into a metropolitan-industrial powerhouse. Some new types of groups did emerge while this great transformation was under way, but at the same time associational patterns established before the Civil War were renewed during the century after that conflict. Cross-class federated membership associations of many sorts continued to form the backbone of American civil society.

The Impact of Industrialization

Standard explanations for associational modernization focus on the responses of emerging actors to new stresses and opportunities offered by corporate industrialization and the growth of big cities. Scholars of a Marxian persuasion see industrialization and large-scale urbanization as motors of class differentiation and conflict. From this perspective, wage workers are likely to form unions and capitalists may band together in business groups. Associational innovation and expansion should follow lines of economic growth. Durkheimians, meanwhile, see voluntary associations as mechanisms of social integration, substituting for ties of family and neighborliness in pre-industrial villages.[76] One version of such reasoning appears in the historian Robert Wiebe's influential synthesis *The Search for Order, 1877–1920*, where the key actors are rising "new middle-class" professionals and businesspeople, who fashioned new associations and service groups in response to the unsettling transformations of immigration, industrialization, and urban concentration.[77]

In late-nineteenth and early-twentieth-century America, some changes did correspond to Marxian or Durkheimian expectations. New translocal associations were mostly launched from the more industrialized states of

---

76. Such arguments are elegantly made in Berthoff (1971, chap. 27) and Wirth (1938).
77. Wiebe (1967).

the Northeast and Midwest.[78] Such groups often spread into each state via the largest city or a highly commercialized region—into which professionals, businessmen, and mobile workers such as railroad men were often the carriers of new associational ideas. We also know from the research of Gerald Gamm and Robert Putnam that unions, professional associations, and other occupationally linked groups grew in relation to population in the late 1800s and early 1900s.[79] Gamm and Putnam's counts are confirmed by listings of statewide groups in the *Maine Register*. This annual directory documents a sharp increase of business and professional groups throughout the twentieth century, especially from 1920 on. The numbers of such associations rose steeply as ever narrower occupational and market segments organized themselves.

Elite "service" groups—chiefly Rotary clubs, Exchange clubs, and Lions clubs—also spread from city to city from the early through the mid-twentieth century.[80] Emphasizing fellowship and service to the broader community, such clubs accepted only a few leading people from each business or profession (although "professions" could be defined very narrowly to expand membership). Some argue that service clubs replaced cross-class fraternal associations because business and professional people grew tired of evening-long rituals, preferred shorter lunchtime meetings, and wanted to network among themselves rather than reaffirm "brotherhood" with blue-collar wage earners and white-collar employees.[81] But this cannot be the whole story, because as America industrialized, certain fraternal associations, including the omnipresent Masons, renewed themselves.[82] Still other fraternals—including the Knights of Columbus, the Loyal Order of Moose, the Benevolent and Protective Order of Elks, and the Fraternal Order of Eagles—grew to twentieth-century prominence with simplified rituals and emphasis on community outreach.

Tellingly, occupationally linked associations and elite service clubs were not the only kinds of groups that flourished as America modernized. For the period from the mid-1880s until around 1900 or 1910, Gamm and Putnam document sharp increases in city directory listings for reli-

---

78. This is based on information about the founding locations for large membership groups listed in Appendix 2A and also on an analysis done by Cameron Sheldon for fraternals listed in Schmidt (1980), which gives founding locations for 330 of the 528 entries.

79. Gamm and Putnam (1999, p. 526, figure 2).

80. Charles (1993).

81. Charles (1993) and Putney (1993) both suggest interpretations along these lines.

82. Dumenil (1984).

gious congregations, religiously connected associations, fraternal groups (and their female and youth auxiliaries), and independent women's groups.[83] Other sources also report sharp increases for national and local fraternal and women's groups.[84] Although Gamm and Putnam record a decline in the incidence of locally present fraternal and women's groups after the turn of the century, the numbers of such groups per 1,000 population remained much higher than the incidence of occupationally linked groups through the end of the Gamm and Putnam data series in 1940.

Statistical hypothesis-testing by Gamm and Putnam helps to pinpoint where associational growth occurred between the Civil War and the early twentieth century. They test the notions that foreign immigration, inflows of domestic migrants, industrialization, and/or urban expansion explain why the number of associations grew more in some cities than in others. They expected to find that bigger, more industrial, northeastern cities experienced sharper increases of associational incidence, and that cities experiencing rapid inflows of migrants might also show disproportionately more associational growth. But they found the opposite. Through 1910, associations proliferated beyond population growth in all twenty-six U.S. cities studied by Gamm and Putnam. Within this overall expansionary pattern, however, cities in the South and West added more associations per capita than those in the East; and small cities gained more associations per capita than medium-sized cities, which in turn gained more than the largest cities. Gamm and Putnam speculate that denizens of small and medium-sized cities may have created and maintained more associations because, in contrast to big-city dwellers around 1900, they did not have access to "industrialized" modes of entertainment such as movies or amusement parks.[85]

But a search for local entertainment cannot be the whole story. The vast majority of U.S. voluntary groups between 1870 and the mid-twentieth century were not merely local. They linked local groups into state, regional, and national networks and at the same time allowed people to meet close to home. Members of translocal associations could learn about and contribute to civic undertakings on a much broader scale than local units could on their own. The entertainment value of groups in towns and

83. Gamm and Putnam (1999, pp. 526–27, figure 2).
84. Stevens (1899); Breckinridge (1933).
85. Gamm and Putnam (1999, p. 549 and passim).

small cities was more than local too. Officers and members prized opportunities to travel to district, state, or national conventions. Important social and economic advantages likewise accrued to associations that managed to spread to many places. Insurance fraternals, for example, could reduce economic risk by including people from various places.

Perhaps most important, Americans, especially young men, changed residences and traveled constantly, so they were glad to find familiar groups in new places.[86] People transferred their memberships from place to place, founded new units of translocal associations where none existed, and visited clubs or lodges when they arrived for business or pleasure. City and associational directories recorded the days of the week or month when groups convened, precisely so that visitors from out of town could attend meetings. And nationwide associations had well-established procedures for helping traveling members. A 1908 Knights of Pythias directory, for example, included standardized telegraph codes that lodges could use to contact one another about visiting brothers in distress. So routinely burdened by eastern visitors seeking aid were Pythian lodges in the western cities of Denver and San Francisco that they banded together to establish bureaus for receiving and validating applications for help.[87]

By bearing in mind that local voluntary groups were usually part of translocal networks, we can better pinpoint the timing and causes of associational change during America's post–Civil War and industrial era. The Skocpol group data arrayed in Figure 2-3 highlight the periods when the (eventually) largest translocal membership associations were launched in unusual numbers. This figure also graphs the accumulation of large U.S. associations whose membership had surpassed 1 percent of the adult population by the given date. As Figure 2-3 shows, disproportionate numbers of eventually very large membership associations were created in the decades right after the Civil War. In large part, Gamm and Putnam's study records the eventual local proliferation of units connected to the new nation-spanning associations launched between 1860 and 1890. By the second decade of the twentieth century, more than twenty large membership associations coexisted. Many had been launched soon after the Civil War, and by the 1910s and 1920s the leaders and local and translocal

---

86. On the amazing mobility of nineteenth-century Americans, see Thernstrom (1973, pp. 220–32); Chudacoff (1972); and Kopf (1977).

87. For the communication codes and the indication of centralized bureaus, see Knights of Pythias (1908, pp. xi–xii, 13, 16).

Figure 2-3. *Foundings and Cumulative Incidence of U.S. Membership Associations*

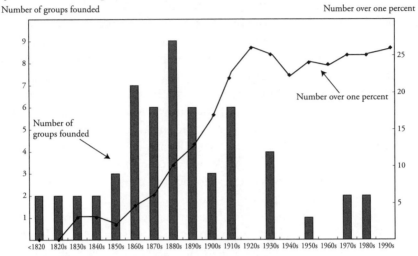

Number of groups founded   Number over one percent

Source: Civic Engagement Project, Harvard University; data as of July, 1999.

organizers of these federations had stimulated and linked together thousands of local groups in villages, towns, and cities of all sizes.[88]

War and Political Contention as Motors

Social observers often presume that the fundamental causes of change are economic. But wars and political contention also shape societies and cultures. For American civil society during the industrial era, wars and

88. Gamm and Putnam claim that association-building in modernizing America was mainly an urban phenomenon and did not occur to a comparable degree in nonurban towns and villages (with populations of less than 2,500). This claim conflicts with Richard Brown's (1974) empirical findings, as well as with the argument here that town and countryside in America were closely integrated. Gamm and Putnam fail to take into account that urban associations often recruited members from surrounding areas outside city limits. More important, Gamm and Putnam's claim that associations were predominately urban is based on skewed and incomplete data. To substantiate their claim, they compare the number of Masonic lodges and Episcopal churches per 1,000 population for their twenty-six cities with the number in the nation as a whole; since the density of these groups was greater in their urban sample than in the nation as a whole, Gamm and Putnam conclude that rural places were not very receptive to association-building. But the Masons and Episcopal churches were among the most elite and

periods of intense political contention brought more group foundings, growing memberships, and vital new undertakings.

America's most ambitious and ultimately successful associations were launched at the end of the Civil War and during the next quarter century; and this same period brought amazing growth to membership federations already in place before 1861. This fact seems counterintuitive. By far the largest and most destructive U.S. war, the Civil War tore apart preexisting federations like the Odd Fellows, the Sons of Temperance, and the Independent Order of Good Templars. It diverted adult energies and took millions of lives, leaving much of the South economically prostrate. Yet the Civil War also brought many "philanthropic results," as one contemporary observer celebrated.[89]

The Civil War unquestionably spurred translocal associationalism. During the conflict, fraternals like the Masons and Odd Fellows attracted many young men headed into or already enrolled in military service. These brotherhoods had well-established methods for aiding members away from home; and some Masonic grand masters allowed the establishment of special "military lodges" within the armed forces. Interestingly, Union military men languishing in Confederate prison camps may also have been aided by fraternal brothers.[90]

Immediately after the war's end, moreover, divided U.S. membership federations quickly reunited. Voluntary federations were, after all, better positioned to reknit North-South ties than the regionally polarized political parties. During the war, the Odd Fellows left chairs for southern grand lodge representatives sitting symbolically empty at each of their national conventions, calling the names and then mailing reports to the absent state delegations. Within months of the war's end, the southern grand lodge representatives returned to their waiting seats, reestablishing the unity of

---

urban-centered of hundreds of cross-class associations. One would expect Masonic lodges and Episcopal churches to be unusually concentrated in cities.

Had Gamm and Putnam looked at larger and more popular associations—like Methodist churches and the Independent Order of Good Templars (IOGT)—the picture would have been very different, as I have discovered using *Maine Registers*, which list associations for all kinds of local places. In the rural places surrounding the small city of Bath, Maine, for example, I found substantially higher concentrations per capita of Methodist churches and IOGT lodges than in Bath itself. For the Masons and Episcopal churches, however, the urban-biased pattern discovered by Gamm and Putnam holds true for Bath in relation to the rest of Sagadahoc County.

89. Brockett (1864).

90. For intriguing indications along this line, see Pollard (1945, pp. 77–79).

the Odd Fellows.[91] The U.S. government and political party system took years longer to pull back together.

Winning the Civil War was a tonic to associational efforts spurred from the North. Throughout the later nineteenth century, most new American voluntary associations were launched from the Northeast and Midwest. Late in the century, some spread from the West, but the defeated and economically distressed South was not a leader in postwar association-building. Launchings of new transregional associations rarely came from the South, and memberships and numbers of local units lagged there as well—except among African Americans.

The African American case is the exception that proves the rule, because the Civil War was a victory for African Americans as well as white northerners. From the Civil War on, African American voluntary associations proliferated at an accelerated pace. Many new membership federations, especially fraternal groups, were launched from cities in the upper-South and border states of Virginia, Kentucky, Tennessee, and Missouri.[92] And thousands of local units were added to old and new federations, with especially rapid and dense proliferation throughout the South.[93] That was where most African Americans lived and where newly freed men and women were able, along with their northern brothers and sisters, to join associations like the Prince Hall Masons and Heroines of Jericho; the Grand United Order of Odd Fellows and Household of Ruth; the Grand United Order of True Reformers; the Knights and Ladies of Tabor, the International Order of Twelve, and the Independent Order of Good Samaritans and Daughters of Samaria. In the late nineteenth century, therefore, both long-standing and newly launched African American associations built strong civic bridges between North and South—even as white associations in this era tended to expand along a predominantly East-West axis.

Whatever the regional contours of associational launchings and growth, though, post–Civil War American association-builders were determined to link people across regions. White leaders, especially, thought in terms of national unity and regeneration and worked hard to make this

---

91. T. A. Ross (1888, pp. 158–79).

92. This is based on founding places listed in Stevens (1899); Preuss (1924); and Schmidt (1980) for a dozen African American fraternal groups launched between the 1860s and 1920s.

93. See, for example, the proliferation documented in Brooks ([1902] 1971), Grimshaw ([1903] 1969); and Turner (1881), and the overall expansion of black fraternalism analyzed in Fahey (1994).

dream real. For many association-builders, the Civil War had an energizing and visionary effect, connecting them to one another and to a larger sense of purpose and possibility. During the conflict, men came together in great armies, and women and civilian men volunteered for war support or relief work.[94] Connections were forged within states and across states. As the war ended, the strengthened sense of national purpose and connections could be shifted—especially by the victorious northerners—toward bold efforts at nation-building and sectional reconnection.

A few prominent examples demonstrate close coupling between Civil War efforts and postwar association-building. Destined to quickly burgeon into America's third largest fraternal group, the Knights of Pythias was launched in 1864 by a group of young wartime federal clerks originally from different parts of the country, who adopted and undertook to spread a ritual about mutually sacrificial brotherhood inspired by the classical tale of the friendship of Damon and Pythias.[95] Similarly, the Patrons of Husbandry (or Grange) was the inspiration of a U.S. Department of Agriculture official who, on a postwar inspection tour into the ravaged South, imagined the benefits of a nationwide fraternity for farm families. Interestingly, Grange founder Oliver Kelley was able to open doors in the South by using his ties to fellow Masons.[96] The creators of the American Red Cross were women and men who had run the Union war-relief efforts of the U.S. Sanitary Commission and wanted to continue their efforts in new ways after the war.[97]

Similarly, former participants in the Sanitary Commission helped to launch the leading national women's association of the post–Civil War period, the Woman's Christian Temperance Union (WCTU). WCTU organizers were determined to create a nationwide association powerful enough to influence public opinion and government action at all levels.[98] Like other temperance groups right after the Civil War, the WCTU organizers were appalled by the drinking habits of ex-soldiers and worried that federal taxes on liquor, which helped finance the war, had become entrenched. The only way to develop sufficient power to fight these evils, temperance people thought, was through strong, federated voluntary or-

94. Brockett (1864); Maxwell (1956); Stille (1868).
95. The story of the Pythians' founding appears in Valkenburg (1886, pp. xvi, 17, 381–84).
96. Nordin (1974, p. 4).
97. Hurd (1959, chaps. 3–4); Maxwell (1956, chap. 13).
98. Bordin (1981).

ganizations that paralleled the government itself and reached into every congressional district.[99] During the 1880s, therefore, chief WCTU organizer Frances Willard traveled all over the country. She purposefully visited the Far West and repeatedly toured the South, leaving in her wake new local and state unions throughout the nation.[100]

Additional waves of association-launching came in the later 1880s and 1890s. One late-century dynamic was the emergence of many new national women's associations, some of which became very active in legislative as well as community affairs.[101] These included new female auxiliaries to the major male fraternal and patriotic groups, ethnic and professional women's associations, and such eventually giant independent women's membership federations as the National Congress of Mothers (later the PTA) and the General Federation of Women's Clubs. Where the Woman's Christian Temperance Union had pioneered soon after the Civil War, other activist, nationwide women's associations soon followed.

Also proliferating in this period were fraternal groups aiming to provide insurance to members. Many never grew very large because they were deliberately limited to potential memberships thought to be relatively healthy or were breakaways from previously established insurance orders (westerners frequently broke away from aging easterners). Still others, like the Order of the Iron Hall of 1881–91, were little more than thinly disguised Ponzi schemes that proved actuarially unsound and hence short-lived. Indeed, a considerable part of the sharp surge of fraternals that Gamm and Putnam record from their city directories for 1890, 1900, and 1910 may be due to such short-lived insurance experiments. Their method treats the sheer proliferation of locally present groups per capita as the leading indicator of civic vitality, which seems to be the reason Gamm and Putnam regard the 1880s and 1890s as an even more civically fertile period than the decades right after the Civil War. My interpretation is somewhat different, because I think that large-scale associations able to persist and grow may well be more significant than lots of short-lived failures.

Another, more civically relevant dynamic grew out of fierce ethnic and religious contention. The late 1880s and 1890s was a time of intense

99. For a clear argument along these lines by the Right Worthy Chief Templar of the Independent Order of Good Templars, see Turnbull (1901, p. 88).

100. Bordin (1986, chap. 8).

101. Breckinridge (1933); Clemens (1997); Clemens (1999); Croly (1898); Skocpol (1992, chap. 6); M. I. Wood (1912).

nativist agitation, as native-born Americans asserted Protestant folkways and defended public schools against new (or renewed) waves of immigration of Catholics and Jews from Europe.[102] In response, many federations of ethnic-American voluntary groups were pulled together in order to unite local groups for self-defense and assertion of American credentials. The new ethnic federations in turn stimulated the further spread of local and state ethnic associations. In general, large numbers of ethnic-American groups were launched or expanded during periods of nativist agitation in U.S. history—the 1840s and 1850s, the 1890s, and the 1920s.[103]

Despite fierce religious and cultural conflicts, ethnic-American groups tended to structure themselves and operate very much like the Protestant and native-born-dominated associations with which they were contending. Every group claimed to represent good Americans and godly people. Group badges and banners almost invariably featured U.S. flags (sometimes one U.S. flag crossed with the flag of the nation from which immigrants hailed); and group mottoes championed similar patriotic and ethical values. Almost every association sought to spread local and state units within regional or national federations. U.S. membership associations, in short, may have championed diverse racial, ethnic, and religious group identities. But they did so in ways that fostered similar experiences and expressed shared American citizenship.

World War I was yet another national crisis that proved good for much of America's organized civil society; and this war stimulated the bridge-building between North and South and among some ethnic groups. New, soon-to-be giant voluntary federations emerged right at the end of the war, including the nationwide American Legion, which grew as the northern-dominated Grand Army of the Republic (GAR) faded with the passing of the Civil War generation.[104] Meanwhile, previously established groups burgeoned through close partnership with federal wartime mobilizations. The Red Cross and the Young Men's Christian Association experienced explosions of membership, volunteering, and local chapter-building in conjunction with provision of war relief and services to soldiers.[105] Similarly, the Knights of Columbus cemented its Americanist credentials by

---

102. Lipset and Raab (1970, pp. 81–104).

103. This is based on an analysis of founding dates for various types of fraternals listed in Schmidt (1980), prepared by Cameron Sheldon.

104. Jones (1946); Pencak (1989).

105. Hurd (1959, chaps. 11–14); Hopkins (1951, pp. 485–504).

providing social services for military personnel.[106] During and soon after World War I, this Catholic fraternal federation used its new government partnership and legitimacy with the public to attract millions of members, gaining ground on Protestant rivals. Ever since, the Knights of Columbus has remained a leading American association.

Not all groups thrived during the war, of course. Identified with the foreign enemy, once vibrant and growing German American associations largely collapsed during World War I.[107] After America entered the war in 1917, the approximately one-tenth of the U.S. population who were of German descent switched to nonethnic-identified groups or relabeled previous groups in ostentatiously "American" ways. Obviously, each time a great war pulled many Americans together into stronger civic commitments, that same conflict also marginalized, and perhaps discouraged, other Americans. On balance, though, both the Civil War and World War I enhanced local and national solidarities in organized civil society, very much reinforcing the sway of federated membership associations.

Casting Wide Nets

Figure 2-4 offers an overview of the organizational process by which many of the large federated membership associations examined in the Skocpol civic engagement project grew in the period between the Civil War and the end of World War I. So many large associations were born in this period that not all can be included in one readable figure. Some large membership associations, such as labor unions, primarily married local units to economically defined intermediate units. But most large membership groups created between 1860 and 1920 took the form of local-state-national federations. For these, we can examine how quickly nationwide networks of state-level intermediate units were created. As Figure 2-4 suggests, the process was often rapid. Associations spread a virtually complete network of "grand lodges" or "state federations" or "state clubs" within fifteen to twenty-five years of their founding.

A more detailed examination of trends for individual associations reveals, moreover, that local groups and memberships tended to expand rapidly after the founding of a state-level organization. In other words, the promoters of nationwide American membership federations established

106. Kaufman (1982, chap. 8).
107. Thernstrom (1980, pp. 422–23).

Figure 2-4. *Establishment of State Units in Selected U.S. Voluntary Associations*

Number of states

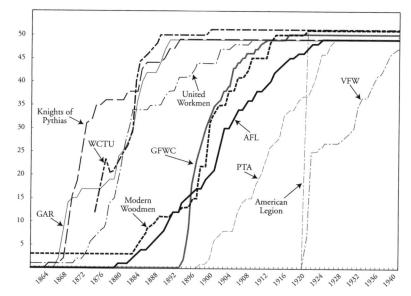

Source: Civic Engagement Project, Harvard University; data as of January 1999.

many state organizations and then worked to stimulate, encourage, and support networks of local groups in every town or community of any size within each state and spanning the United States. "Casting wide nets" is an apt label for this pattern of association-building. This was the usual strategy pursued by the leaders of voluntary membership groups in the seedbed period between the Civil War and 1920.

To make the casting-wide-nets strategy work, associational promoters were always on the move. Leaders fanned out across states and localities in order to stimulate "native" leaderships to create local clubs or lodges as quickly as possible. Everywhere leaders went, they tried to put state as well as local units in place. This method of organizational expansion was very reminiscent of the techniques used by Methodist and Baptist circuit-riding clergy to disseminate new congregations, like wildfire, across the pre–Civil War United States. It was also a method that took advantage of Americans' experiences during the Civil War, when mobilizations for military and civilian-support enterprises depended upon drawing local supporters into state-led organizations that were, in turn, assembled into the Confederate and especially the Union war efforts. Casting wide nets—stimulating organization and leadership across all the states and connecting community groups of all sizes within states—became the standard story of association-building in America between the Civil War and 1920. It was the strategy used by fraternal and women's groups, veterans' associations, moral-reform and political-reform movements, and community, religious, and recreational federations. Modern American civil society was constructed in this way.

The Twentieth Century

By the 1920s, the United States had become an industrial nation, and the data in Figure 2-3 document that about two dozen large-scale membership associations coexisted during each decade from then on. Of course, the mix of large (and smaller) membership federations changed over the decades. Some older groups like the Sons of Temperance, the IOGT, and the Grand Army of the Republic declined or went out of existence. Others were never more than temporary blips on the radar screen, perhaps because they died after reform crusades (abortive, as in the case of the Knights of Labor, or successful, as in the case of the National American Woman Suffrage Association). Still other groups—such as the American Protective Association, the Junior Order of United American Mechanics, the German-American Alliance, and the second Ku Klux Klan—became huge only briefly during periods of heightened ethnic or racial tension. Meanwhile, though, other groups emerged or flourished, often benefiting from junctures of welfare-state-building as well as wartime mobilization.

Today's conservatives claim that the growth of modern social provision has crowded out voluntary efforts. But many of America's membership associations pressed for public social programs in the first place and then prospered by helping government deliver benefits or services to millions of people. The Grand Army of the Republic grew along with generous state and national provision for Union military veterans and survivors.[108] The Grange and American Farm Bureau Federation were just as closely involved with government programs to aid farmers.[109] In-

108. McConnell (1992).
109. Hansen (1991); Nordin (1974).

dependent women's associations—including the WCTU, the General Federation of Women's Clubs, and the National Congress of Mothers (later the PTA)—were closely involved with local, state, and national efforts to help mothers, children, and families.[110] The Fraternal Order of Eagles and the Townsend Movement pressed for federal benefits for the elderly, and more recent associations of retirees have grown along with the resulting public programs.[111] Labor unions needed the U.S. government's help fully to establish themselves and in turn became champions of New Deal economic and social programs. And the American Legion championed the nation's most generous social program for young families, the G.I. Bill of 1944.[112] From the Civil War through the post–World War II era, voluntary membership associations have complemented the U.S. version of the modern welfare state. Associations have no doubt gained by being associated with bold national efforts that concretely helped millions of citizens; and the U.S. Congress and state legislatures have certainly responded to the capacity of widespread, federated voluntary associations to shape public opinion and mobilize social support for popular public programs.

The New Deal was a period of heightened electoral mobilization and new federal initiatives to help people and businesses during the Great Depression. The Townsend movement flourished at this juncture, demanding new efforts to aid America's elderly. And labor unions (including industrial as well as craft workers) finally gained a substantial foothold in U.S. civil society during the 1930s and 1940s. Yet this same period was stressful for other large groups. To cope with fiscal shortfalls as memberships aged, fraternal groups that had specialized in insurance merged, died, or were absorbed by profit-making companies. This started in the late 1910s and accelerated in the 1930s. Socially oriented fraternals also contracted, as Americans struggled to pay dues during the Depression and then young men went abroad to fight in Europe or the Pacific.

This hiatus could prove to be largely irreversible. One of the nation's oldest socially oriented fraternals, the Independent Order of Odd Fellows (along with its female partner, the Rebekahs) revived only slightly after 1945 and then continued to fade. But many other preexisting membership groups, including some fraternals, revived and flourished again after World

---

110. Croly (1898); Scott (1991); Skocpol (1992).
111. Pratt (1976).
112. Bennett (1996); Pencak (1946); D. R. B. Ross (1969); Skocpol (1997).

War II. The October 1956 issue of *Life Magazine* celebrated some 16 million U.S. Masons and pictured all fifty state Masters on its cover.[113] Despite shrinkage since the 1960s, the Masons remain, to this day, on the list of groups enrolling more than 1 percent of American adults; and the Eastern Star may still involve more American women than any other voluntary association. Overall, many U.S. associations launched from the 1850s through 1920 prospered during much of the first two-thirds of the twentieth century. These include fraternals such as the Elks, the Moose, the Eagles, and the Knights of Columbus (as well as the Masons and the Eastern Star); veterans' associations such as the Veterans of Foreign Wars and the American Legion; a variety of church-connected associations; male and female bowling federations; the American Federation of Labor (which united with the Congress of Industrial Organizations in 1955 to become the AFL-CIO); and community-oriented groups such as the Red Cross, the Boy Scouts, the YMCA, and the National Congress of Parents and Teachers (PTA).

As late as the mid-1970s, many large, chapter-based groups were still holding their own, as were hundreds of smaller federated membership groups with the same ways of doing things. The aftermath of World War II, like the end of previous major wars, re-energized scores of American membership groups. Taken together, a modernized set of federated membership associations still formed the integument of civil society for ordinary men and women after World War II—just as previous versions of such associations had structured community and extralocal civil participation for Americans through many previous generations.

What Difference Did Membership Federations Make?

The obvious question is: so what? Perhaps large numbers of federated associations flourished through much of American history. But what difference did they make in practice for ordinary Americans and for the health of U.S. democracy?

We cannot run national opinion surveys or do in-depth interviews to ask long-dead Americans what membership federations meant to them. Yet countless traces from the past suggest that such groups were intensely meaningful to many people. The evidence of William Durgin's gravestone

---

113. "The U.S. Masons" (1956, pp. 104–22).

is recapitulated in many old cemeteries, where graves are peppered with markers of their incumbents' ties to the Masons and Eastern Star, the Odd Fellows and the Rebekahs, and the Modern Woodmen and Royal Neighbors of America, in addition to the omnipresent markers for the major veterans' associations. Go into any slightly junky antique store, moreover, and you will find the material traces of lifetimes of membership, objects that people kept and treasured and passed to their children. Those objects stayed in families, until one day the grandkids, not remembering or caring what they were, unloaded them.

There are tiny, well-worn booklets spelling out the rules, procedures, ceremonies, and yearly programs of associations like the Odd Fellows, the Federated Women's Clubs, the Grand Army of the Republic, and the Independent Order of Good Templars. There are meticulously handwritten log books, documenting meetings, attendance records, and finances, week by week and month by month. There are dog-eared old song books for groups like the Grange and the Woman's Christian Temperance Union, full of hokey lyrics about associational efforts and values. And my favorite artifacts are the beautiful, reversible ribbon-badges that millions of club and lodge members wore in parades and funerals. Symbolic pins and medals were also given yearly to current and past officers at the local, state, and national levels.

What did people get out of participation in groups like the Grange or the GAR, the Odd Fellows or the Rebekahs, the Fraternal Order of Eagles, the (African American) Prince Hall Masons, the American Legion, or the Federation of Women's Clubs? Access to social insurance or other economic benefits was sometimes at stake. Entire families could be helped by economic aid channeled through group insurance or just given as fraternal charity in an emergency. Yet the effects of participation in these groups had to have been as much social, recreational, and civic as economic. After all, in many cases the dues and expenditures on regalia probably cost people a lot more than they ever got out, or expected to get out, in monetary terms. And the largest, most enduring groups were not centered on insurance.

People attended local meetings to socialize with others (usually men and women met separately). Many groups were also parts of interlocking complexes that encompassed the entire family. Male-only groups—including fraternals, veterans' associations, and union brotherhoods—had female partner groups for spouses, and sometimes junior affiliates for sons and daughters. Temperance associations reached out to youth and children.

The Grange and the American Farm Bureau Federation directly included fathers, mothers, and children in an integrated communal web of activities. Reinforcing family roles—while at the same time providing some distraction from everyday activities at home and in the labor market—was clearly a central mission for socially oriented associations.

Yet the reasons people participated and cared so much went beyond the local and the familial. Membership in local units of translocal federations offered connections to and organizational routes into broader social and political movements. People loved being part of larger "brotherhoods" and "sisterhoods" and often were inspired to join endeavors to which they knew thousands of others across their state and nation were also committed. Much excitement accompanied the sending of delegations from each local club or lodge or union or grange to attend district meetings, or annual state conventions, or annual national conventions. Internal newsletters and magazines covered the buildup to such meetings for months in advance. And after they were over, the officers and delegates from one's unit came back to tell everyone what happened at the big meeting—and about the sights in whatever city had hosted the meeting. During recurrent group conventions Americans from different parts of states and parts of the country met one another, learned about other people's homes, and exchanged ideas about group and civic affairs. Sometimes local branches of federations sponsored social visits, linking clubs or lodges together even apart from regular conventions. State and national officers and organizers were always on the move, visiting communities and carrying ideas from one to another.

Leaders and Members

America's classic three-tiered associations were special for the two-way links they established between members and leaders. Here we come to the heart of the difference these federations made for American democracy. In part, local-state-national federations constituted mobility ladders with rungs from the modest reaches of society to the national leadership. At the same time, they encouraged persons of high status or leadership rank to interact with a wide range of their fellow citizens.

Federated three-tiered groups had elaborate officer ladders. Each local club or lodge usually elected and appointed a complement of eight to a dozen or more officers and committee chairs each year. Several hundred thousand offices had to be filled each year in the largest voluntary membership associations alone; and many more openings existed in other federations that did not attract quite 1 percent of the U.S. adult population. Within each association, members could start small and move up. After successfully serving as the head of the local unit, a man or woman could climb the ladder of state offices and, with enthusiastic support from one's local and state colleagues, perhaps get onto the national ladder as well.

Empirical scrutiny shows what one would expect about social status and officerships in voluntary federations: the top posts were often held by white-collar, business, or professional men or women. But lowly clerks and farmers and skilled workers, or their wives, also attained such posts. Civic associations created status ladders that were not identical to the class hierarchies of the economy. A person of lesser occupational status could work his or her way up an associational ladder all the way to the top. Similarly, in the ritual-enacting fraternal groups, each individual could learn the roles and memorize the lines to earn higher degrees of membership—to be proudly displayed in elaborate badges and costumes.

The fact that high-status people were active participants in voluntary federations had important consequences for American democracy. Scholars often presume that higher-status people merely exert social control over others when they participate in, and lead, organizations. But we should not lose sight of the value of two-way interactions between higher- and lower-status people, especially in settings like churches and voluntary membership groups where there is a presumption of shared citizenship, of sisterhood and brotherhood.

Biographical sketches of prominent men and women of the past—businesspeople, politicians, professionals, prominent wives, society figures, and so forth—proudly proclaim their memberships and officer roles in a wide array of the same associations that also involved millions of their fellow citizens. In the past, prominent institutional leaders considered active participation in the Masons, the Odd Fellows, the Grange, the WCTU, the General Federation of Women's Clubs, the Elks, and the major veterans' groups to be a vital part of successful lives—or, for Catholics, it was the Ancient Order of Hibernians, the Knights of Columbus, and the Catholic Total Abstinence Union. As high-status (or eventually prominent) men and women worked their way up local-state-national leadership ladders, they had to interact with and mobilize ordinary members in the process. Because membership numbers and face-to-face meetings mattered in all the classic American voluntary associations, those who were leaders, or who wanted to use officerships in these groups to symbolize or validate broader societal leadership, had to care about mobilizing and inspiring large numbers of fellow members. Members counted. Leaders had to mobilize and interact with others, or they were not successful.

Fostering Citizenship and Political Engagement

Federated membership associations influenced the larger U.S. polity in a number of ways. Inside the clubs or lodges or posts, millions of people learned about group operations and collective debate and decisionmaking. They learned the "constitutional rules" that governed membership, dues-paying, and representation; they learned the rules of legislation and adjudication in their associations. Because mimicry of U.S. rules of taxpaying and representative governance was so central to group procedures, members gained knowledge very relevant to what they needed to know as American citizens.

People acquired and practiced organizational skills too.[114] Each year a new set of officers and committee members learned how to run meetings, keep record books, make speeches, and organize events. People going to the Grange or the weekly women's club gathering or the lodge on Wednesday night gained the kinds of organizational skills that, today, ordinary people are likely to gain only in church groups, if at all (see Chapter 12). At work, people in routine jobs may not have many chances to gain or practice leadership and organizational skills, so an associational world that offers such opportunities across class lines can be vital for democracy.

Moving from organizational side-effects to substantive political impacts, we can start with broad and indirect ways in which the classic membership federations promoted the culture of republican citizenship. In rituals, pledges, and programs, voluntary federations celebrated basic civic values of charity, community, and good citizenship. To be sure, only a minority of the federations were overtly politically partisan. But all celebrated "American" identity, republican governance, and service to the nation—including military service. "Our Order is no political association," declared Paschal Donaldson in the 1852 *Odd-Fellows Textbook*, but

---

114. On the importance of this, see Verba, Schlozman, and Brady (1995).

"we are bound by our obligations to perform all the duties which can be required of good citizens; and a violation of any of those laws, if proven against a member of our Fraternity, will subject him to immediate expulsion from our Society."[115]

Many federated membership associations went beyond celebrating and enforcing good citizenship to engage in legislative lobbying and efforts to shape public opinion. In what might be called transpartisan ways, they overtly sought to shape public decisions in communities, in states, and at the national level. In addition to American voluntary associations' involvement in national war mobilizations and the expansion and administration of major social programs, consider the efforts of the Woman's Christian Temperance Association and the National American Woman Suffrage Association on behalf of female suffrage; the efforts of labor unions to secure a range of social programs and economic regulations; and the championing of economic, educational, and family programs for farmers by the Grange and the American Farm Bureau Federation. Federated voluntary associations have been uniquely positioned to influence legislation and public opinion because their structures often parallel legislative and congressional districts. As American women's federations splendidly demonstrated in their campaigns for mothers' pensions and the Sheppard Towner Act in the 1910s, campaigns coordinated by many states at once can have a decisive impact on elected representatives, regardless of party.[116]

Voluntary membership federations, in short, have often rivaled political parties in affording organized leverage in civic and legislative affairs to large numbers of Americans.[117] Of course, the goals of membership associations have not always been good: the Ku Klux Klan was a temporarily large group that pursued racial domination, sometimes through violence; and there were nativist strands in the programs of many historically important American voluntary groups. I am not arguing that social tolerance and inclusive citizenship have invariably been furthered by associations with large memberships. Furthermore, many important things have been achieved by smaller, more agile groups, including elite advocacy groups willing to take a courageous stand on unpopular matters of principle. Nevertheless, large membership federations have recurrently

---

115. Donaldson (1852, p. 232).
116. Skocpol (1992, part 3).
117. Clemens (1997).

been a source of considerable popular leverage in American society and politics, especially during the century following the end of the Civil War.

Membership federations certainly helped to create a democratic civil society in which large numbers of ordinary people could participate, forge recurrent ties to one another, and engage in two-way relationships with powerful leaders. They institutionalized remarkable balances between intimate face-to-face activities and leverage in state, regional, and national affairs.

The story of American voluntarism has been clearly one of symbiosis between state and society—not a story of society apart from, or instead of, the state. Huge wars have stimulated the founding of associations and, in their aftermath, renewed associational memberships. Similarly, the growth of federal social spending, from Civil War pensions through Social Security and the GI Bill, has also been good for civic associations, which championed these programs and often grew along with them. Associational growth in tandem with expanding and active national government was not rigidly centralizing or bureaucratizing, because true membership federations remained rooted in local communities even as they were active at the higher levels of decision-making in the states and in Washington, D.C.

Let me conclude by coming back to Almond and Verba's 1963 celebration of American democracy in *The Civic Culture*. I cannot prove it, but I think that Almond and Verba saw, through the eyes of their respondents, many of the effects of America's still flourishing federated voluntary associations. When Almond and Verba found that Americans were more likely than other citizenries to serve as officers or committee leaders, they were glimpsing the classic voluntary federations in operation. When Almond and Verba noted that American women participated almost as much as men, they were registering the effects of PTAs and women's discussion clubs and female auxiliaries to fraternal and veterans' groups—groups that involved many millions of women in routines fully parallel to those of male associationalism.

Finally, when Almond and Verba found that Americans were confident they could influence both local and national affairs, surely they were picking up the dual engagement that federated associations afforded to so many ordinary Americans. People could be part of something immediate—with fellow locals they saw day to day—and part of grander endeavors at the same time. A historically evolved symbiosis of federal democracy and federated voluntary associations created a very special matrix for American citizenship and popular civic participation.

This conclusion might seem controversial to those who, pondering the ills of American democracy in the late twentieth century, presume that our country's civic past was aseptically local. But my conclusion would hardly be news to William Warren Durgin of North Lovell, Maine. In his own life, which spanned much of America's civically most generative era from the Civil War through the early twentieth century, Durgin personally took part in both nation-defining moments and everyday acts of membership. He not only fought for the union and served as Lincoln's pallbearer but was also a proud participant in three of America's most characteristic voluntary membership federations: the Odd Fellows, the Grand Army of the Republic, and the Grange. Humble though he was, a poor farmer and laborer, Warren Durgin knew firsthand what it meant to be an engaged participant in American democracy, a local and national citizen in peace as well as war.

Appendix 2A

Table 2A-1. *Large Membership Associations in U.S. History*

Common name	Founding date	Ending date	National, state, and local units
Ancient and Accepted Free Masons	1733		
Independent Order of Odd Fellows	1819		✓
American Temperance Society	1826	1865	✓
General Union for Promoting Observance of the Christian Sabbath	1828	1832	
American Anti-Slavery Society	1833	1870	✓
Improved Order of Red Men	1834		✓
Washingtonian Temperance Societies	1840	c. 1848	
Order of the Sons of Temperance	1842	c. 1970	✓
Independent Order of Good Templars	1851		✓
Young Men's Christian Association (YMCA)	1851		✓
Junior Order of United American Mechanics	1853		✓
National Teachers Association / National Education Association (NEA)	1857		✓
Knights of Pythias	1864		✓
Grand Army of the Republic	1866	1956	✓
Benevolent and Protective Order of Elks	1867		
Patrons of Husbandry (National Grange)	1867		✓
Ancient Order of United Workmen	1868		✓
Order of the Eastern Star	1868		✓
Knights of Labor	1869	1917	
National Rifle Assocation (NRA)	1871		✓
Ancient Arabic Order of the Nobles of the Mystic Shrine	1872		
Woman's Christian Temperance Union	1874		✓
Royal Arcanum	1877		✓
Farmers' Alliance	1877	1900	✓
Maccabees	1878		✓
Christian Endeavor	1881		✓
American Red Cross	1881		
Knights of Columbus	1882		✓
Modern Woodmen of America	1883		✓
Colored Farmers' National Alliance and Cooperative Union	1886	1892	✓
American Federation of Labor/ AFL-CIO from 1955	1886		

Table 2A-1. *(continued)*

Common name	Founding date	Ending date	National, state, and local units
American Protective Association	1887	c. 1911	✓
Loyal Order of Moose	1888		
Woman's Missionary Union	1888		✓
Woodmen of the World	1890		✓
National American Woman Suffrage Association	1890	1920	✓
General Federation of Women's Clubs	1890		✓
American Bowling Congress	1895		✓
National Congress of Mothers / National Congress of Parents and Teachers (PTA)	1897		✓
Fraternal Order of Eagles	1898		✓
German American National Alliance	1901	1918	✓
Aid Association for Lutherans	1902		
American Automobile Association (AAA)	1902		✓
Boy Scouts of America	1910		
Veterans of Foreign Wars of the United States (VFW)	1913		✓
Ku Klux Klan (second) (KKK)	1915	1944	✓
Women's International Bowling Congress	1916		✓
American Legion	1919		✓
American Farm Bureau Federation	1919		✓
Old Age Revolving Pensions (Townsend movement)	1934	1953	
Congress of Industrial Organizations (CIO)	1938	1955	
National Foundation for Infantile Paralysis/March of Dimes	1938		
Woman's Division of Christian Service/ United Methodist Women	1939		
American Association of Retired Persons (AARP)	1958		
Greenpeace USA	1971		
National Right to Life Committee (NRLC)	1973		✓
Mothers Against Drunk Driving (MADD)	1980		✓
Christian Coalition	1989		✓

Source: Civic Engagement Project, Harvard University; data as of July 1999.

Table 2A-2. *Large U.S. Membership Associations: Decades in which Membership Exceeded One Percent of Men, or Women, or Both*

Organization	<1820	1820s	1830s	1840s	1850s	1860s	1870s	1880s	1890s	1900s	1910s	1920s	1930s	1940s	1950s	1960s	1970s	1980s	1990s
Masons (1733–)	■																		■
Odd Fellows (1819–)															■				
American Temperance Society (1826–65)			■																
GUPOCS (1828–32)			■																
Anti-Slavery Society (1833–70)			■																
Red Men (1834–)											■								
Washingtonians (1840–46)				■															
Sons of Temperance (1842–73)					■														
Good Templars (1851–)						■	■												
YMCA (1851–)																			■
Jr. Order of United Amer. Mechanics (1853–)												■	■						
NEA (1857–)																			■
Knights of Pythias (1864–)										■	■	■							
Grand Army of the Republic (1866–1956)							■	■	■	■									
Elks (1867–)												■							■
Grange (1867–)							■			■	■								
Ancient Order of United Workmen (1868–)										■									
Eastern Star (1868–)												■							■
Knights of Labor (1869–1917)								■											
NRA (1871–)																		■	■
The Shriners (1872–)												■						■	
Woman's Christian Temperance Union (1874–)									■	■	■								
Farmers' Alliance (1877–1900)									■										
Royal Arcanum (1877–)										■									
Maccabees (1878–)										■									
Christian Endeavor (1881–)									■										
American Red Cross (1881–)											■	■		■		■	■	■	■
Knights of Columbus (1882–)											■								■
Modern Woodmen (1882–)										■	■	■	■						

AFL (1886–)/AFL–CIO after 1955
Colored Farmers Alliance (1886–1892)
American Protective Association (1887–1911)
Woman's Missionary Union (1888–)
Moose (1888–)
GFWC (1890–)
Nat. Amer. Woman Suffrage Assoc. (1890–1920)
Woodmen of the World (1890–)
American Bowling Congress (1895–)
PTA (1897–)
Eagles (1898–)
German American Natl. Alliance (1901–18)
Aid Association for Lutherans (1902–)
American Automobile Association (1902–)
Boy Scouts (1910–)
VFW (1913–)
KKK (second) (1915–44)
Women's Intl. Bowling Congress (1916–)
American Legion (1919–)
Farm Bureau (1919–)
Townsend Movement (1934–53)
CIO (1935–; merged with AFL in 1955)
March of Dimes (1938–)
United Methodist Women (1939–)
AARP (1958–)
Greenpeace USA (1971–)
NRLC (1973–)
MADD (1980–)
Christian Coalition (1989–)

Source: Civic Engagement Project, Harvard University; data as of July 1999.

References

Aldrich, John H. 1995. *Why Parties? The Origin and Transformation of Political Parties in America.* University of Chicago Press.

Almond, Gabriel A., and Sidney Verba. 1963. *The Civic Culture: Political Attitudes and Democracy in Five Nations.* Princeton University Press.

Baker, Paula. 1984. "The Domestication of Politics: Women and American Political Society, 1780–1920." *American Historical Review* 89(3): 620–47.

Bennett, Michael J. 1996. *When Dreams Came True: The GI Bill and the Making of Modern America.* Washington, D.C.: Brassey's.

Berthoff, Roland. 1971. *An Unsettled People: Social Order and Disorder in American History.* Harper and Row.

Blumin, Stuart M. 1989. *The Emergence of the Middle Class: Social Experience in the American City, 1760–1900.* Cambridge University Press.

Bode, Carl. 1968. *The American Lyceum: Town Meeting of the Mind.* University of Illinois Press.

Bordin, Ruth. 1981. *Woman and Temperance: The Quest for Power and Liberty, 1873–1900.* Temple University Press.

———. 1986. *Frances Willard: A Biography.* University of North Carolina Press.

Breckinridge, Sophinisba P. 1933. *Women in the Twentieth Century: A Study of Their Political, Social and Economic Activities.* McGraw-Hill.

Brockett, Linus Pierpont. 1864. *The Philanthropic Results of the War in America. Collected from Official and Authentic Sources by an American Citizen.* New York: Sheldon.

Brooks, Charles H. [1902] 1971. *The Official History and Manual of the Grand United Order of Odd Fellows in America.* Black Heritage Library Collection. Freeport, N.Y.: Books for Libraries Press.

Brown, Richard D. 1973. "The Emergence of Voluntary Associations in Massachusetts, 1760–1830." *Journal of Voluntary Association Research* 2(2): 64–73.

———. 1974. "The Emergence of Urban Society in Rural Massachusetts, 1760–1820." *Journal of American History* 61(1): 29–51.

Bullock, Steven C. 1996. *Revolutionary Brotherhood: Freemasonry and the Transformation of the American Social Order, 1730–1840.* University of North Carolina Press.

Carnes, Mark. 1989. *Secret Ritual and Manhood in Victorian America.* Yale University Press.

Charles, Jeffrey A. 1993. *Service Clubs in American Society: Rotary, Kiwanis, and Lions.* University of Illinois Press.

Chudacoff, Howard. 1972. *Mobile Americans: Residential and Social Mobility in Omaha, 1880–1920.* Oxford University Press.

Clawson, Mary Ann. 1989. *Constructing Brotherhood: Gender, Class, and Fraternalism.* Princeton University Press.

Clemens, Elisabeth S. 1997. *The People's Lobby: Organizational Innovation and the Rise of Interest Group Politics in the United States, 1890–1925.* University of Chicago Press.

———. 1999. "Securing Political Returns to Social Capital: Women's Associations in the United States, 1880s–1920s." *Journal of Interdisciplinary History* 29(3): 613–38.

Council on Civil Society. 1998. "A Call to Civil Society: Why Democracy Needs Moral Truths." New York: Institute for American Values.

Croly, Jennie June. 1898. *The History of the Women's Club Movement in America.* New York: Henry G. Allen.

Dannenbaum, Jed. 1984. *Drink and Disorder: Temperance Reform from the Washingtonian Revival to the WCTU.* University of Illinois Press.

Davies, Wallace Evan. 1955. *Patriotism on Parade: The Story of Veterans' and Hereditary Organizations in America, 1783–1900.* Harvard University Press.

Donaldson, Paschal. 1852. *The Odd-Fellows' Text Book.* 6th ed. Philadelphia, Penn.: Moss and Brother.

Doyle, Don H. 1977. "The Social Functions of Voluntary Associations in a Nineteenth-Century American Town." *Social Science History* 1(3): 333–55.

Dumenil, Lynn. 1984. *Freemasonry and American Culture, 1880–1939.* Princeton University Press.

Epstein, Barbara Leslie. 1981. *The Politics of Domesticity: Women, Evangelism, and Temperance in Nineteenth Century America.* Middletown, Conn.: Wesleyan University Press.

Fahey, David M. 1994. *The Black Lodge in White America.* Dayton, Ohio: Wright State University Press.

Finke, Roger, and Rodney Stark. 1992. *The Churching of America, 1776–1990.* Rutgers University Press.

Fuller, George H. 1913. *Directory of Subordinate Lodges of the Independent Order of Odd Fellows on the Continent of North America.* Boston: Grand Lodge of Massachusetts.

Galston, William A., and Peter Levine. 1998. "America's Civic Condition: A Glance at the Evidence." In *Community Works: The Revival of Civil Society in America,* edited by E. J. Dionne Jr. Brookings.

Gamm, Gerald, and Robert D. Putnam. 1999. "Association-Building in America, 1840–1940." *Journal of Interdisciplinary History* 29(3): 511–57.

Gist, Noel P. 1940. "Secret Societies: A Study of Fraternalism in the United States." *The University of Missouri Studies: A Quarterly of Research* 15(4): 1–184.

Glazer, Walter S. 1972. "Participation and Power: Voluntary Organization and the Functional Organization of Cincinnati in 1840." *Historical Methods Newsletter* 5(4): 151–68.

Grimshaw, William H. [1903] 1969. *Official History of Freemasonry among the Colored People in North America.* New York: Negro Universities Press.

Hansen, John Mark. 1991. *Gaining Access: Congress and the Farm Lobby, 1919–1981.* University of Chicago Press.

Hatch, Nathan O. 1989. *The Democratization of American Christianity.* Yale University Press.

Hausknecht, Murray. 1962. *The Joiners.* New York: Bedminster Press.

Hodges, Samuel W. 1877. "Sons of Temperance—Historical Record of the Order." In *Centennial Temperance Volume: A Memorial of the International Temperance Conference Held in Philadelphia, June, 1876.* New York: National Temperance Society and Publications House.

Hoffman, Alexander von. 1994. *Local Attachments: The Making of an Urban Neighborhood, 1890–1925.* Johns Hopkins University Press.

Holbrook, Josiah. 1836–37. "American Lyceum." *American Annals of Education* 6: 474–76; and 7: 183–84.

Hopkins, Charles Howard. 1951. *History of the Y.M.C.A. in North America.* New York: Association Press.

Hurd, Charles. 1959. *The Compact History of the Red Cross.* New York: Hawthorne Books.

John, Richard R. 1995. *Spreading the News: The American Postal System from Franklin to Morse.* Harvard University Press.

Jones, Richard Seelye. 1946. *A History of the American Legion.* Indianapolis: Bobbs-Merrill.

Joyce, Michael S., and William A. Schambra. 1996. "A New Civic Life." In *To Empower People: From State to Civil Society,* 2d ed., edited by Michael Novak. Washington, D.C.: AEI Press.

Kaufman, Christopher J. 1982. *Faith and Fraternalism: The History of the Knights of Columbus, 1882–1982.* Harper and Row.

Kleppner, Paul. 1982. *Who Voted? The Dynamics of Electoral Turnout, 1870–1980.* New York: Praeger.

Knights of Pythias. 1908. *The Official Pythian Lodge Directory.* Jacksonville, Fla.: Hugh H. Richardson.

Kopf, Edward. 1977. "Untarnishing the Dream: Mobility, Opportunity, and Order in Modern America." *Journal of Social History* 11: 202–27.

Kutolowski, Kathleen Smith. 1982. "Freemasonry and Community in the Early Republic: The Case for Antimasonic Anxieties." *American Quarterly* 34: 543–61.

Ladd, Everett C. 1996. "The Data Just Don't Show Erosion of America's 'Social Capital.'" *Public Perspective* (June/July): 1–6.

Lichtman, Charles H., ed. 1901. *Official History of the Improved Order of Red Men.* Rev. ed. Boston, Mass.: Fraternity.

Lipset, Seymour Martin, and Earl Raab. 1970. *The Politics of Unreason: Right-Wing Extremism in America, 1790–1970.* Harper and Row.

Lipson, Dorothy Ann. 1977. *Freemasonry in Federalist Connecticut, 1789–1835.* Princeton University Press.

"Lovell Was Home of Last Surviving Pall-Bearer of President Lincoln." 1933. *Lewiston Journal,* February 11, 1933, p. A1.

Macleod, David I. 1983. *Building Character in the American Boy: The Boy Scouts, YMCA, and Their Forerunners, 1870–1920.* University of Wisconsin Press.

Mathews, Donald G. 1969. "The Second Great Awakening as an Organizing Process, 1780–1830: An Hypothesis." *American Quarterly* 21(1): 23–43.

Maxwell, William Quentin. 1956. *Lincoln's Fifth Wheel: The Political History of the United States Sanitary Commission.* New York: Longmans, Green.

McConnell, Stuart. 1992. *Glorious Contentment: The Grand Army of the Republic, 1865–1900.* University of North Carolina Press.

McGerr, Michael E. 1986. *The Decline of Popular Politics: The American North, 1865–1928.* Oxford University Press.

Mead, David. 1951. *Yankee Eloquence in the Middle West: The Ohio Lyceum, 1850–1870.* Michigan State College Press.

Merz, Charles. 1927. "Sweet Land of Secrecy: The Strange Spectacle of American Fraternalism." *Harper's* 154: 329–34.

Monroe, John A. 1942. "The Lyceum in America before the Civil War." *Delaware Notes: Bulletin of the University of Delaware* 37(3): 65–75.

Muraskin, William Alan. 1975. *Middle-Class Blacks in a White Society: Prince Hall Freemasonry in America.* University of California Press.

Nordin, Sven D. 1974. *Rich Harvest: A History of the Grange, 1867–1900.* University of Mississippi Press.

Palmer, Edward Nelson. 1944. "Negro Secret Societies." *Social Forces* 23(2): 207–12.

Pencak, William. 1989. *For God and Country: The American Legion, 1919–1941.* Northeastern University Press.

Pollard, Ralph J. 1945. *Freemasonry in Maine, 1762–1945.* Portland, Maine: Grand Lodge of Maine.

Pratt, Henry J. 1976. *The Gray Lobby.* University of Chicago Press.

Preuss, Arthur R. 1924. *A Dictionary of Secret and Other Societies.* St. Louis, Mo.: B. Herder.

Putnam, Robert D. 1995a. "Bowling Alone: America's Declining Social Capital." *Journal of Democracy* 6(1): 65–78.

———. 1995b. "Tuning In, Tuning Out: The Strange Disappearance of Social Capital in America." *PS: Political Science and Politics* (December): 664–83.

Putney, Clifford. 1993. "Service over Secrecy: How Lodge-Style Fraternalism Yielded Popularity to Men's Service Clubs." *Journal of Popular Culture* 27: 179–90.

Ratner, Lorman. 1969. *Antimasonry: The Crusade and the Party.* Englewood Cliffs, N.J.: Prentice-Hall.

Ridge, John T. 1986. *Erin's Sons in America: The Ancient Order of Hibernians.* New York: AOH Publications.

Ross, Davis R. B. 1969. *Preparing for Ulysses: Politics and Veterans during World War II.* Columbia University Press.

Ross, Theodore A. 1888. *Odd Fellowship: Its History and Manual.* New York: M. W. Hazen.

Ryan, Mary P. 1981. *Cradle of the Middle Class: The Family in Oneida County, New York, 1790–1865.* Cambridge University Press.

Schlesinger, Arthur M., Sr. 1944. "Biography of a Nation of Joiners." *American Historical Review* 50(1): 1–25.

Schmidt, Alvin J. 1980. *Fraternal Organizations.* Greenwood Encyclopedia of American Associations. Westport, Conn.: Greenwood Press.

Schudson, Michael. 1998. *The Good Citizen: A History of American Civic Life.* Free Press.

Scott, Anne Firor. 1991. *Natural Allies: Women's Associations in American History.* University of Illinois Press.

Shefter, Martin. 1994. *Political Parties and the State: The American Historical Experience.* Princeton University Press.

Sklar, Kathryn Kish. 1998. "The 'Quickened Conscience': Women's Voluntarism and the State, 1890–1920." *Report from the Institute for Philosophy and Public Policy* 18(3): 27–33.

Skocpol, Theda. 1992. *Protecting Soldiers and Mothers: The Political Origins of Social Policy in the United States.* Belknap Press of Harvard University Press.

———. 1997. "The GI Bill and U.S. Social Policy, Past and Future." *Social Philosophy and Policy* 14(2): 95–115.

Smith-Rosenberg, Carroll. 1985. *Disorderly Conduct: Visions of Gender in Victorian America.* Knopf.

Sons of Temperance. 1854. *Constitution and By-Laws of Olive Branch Division, No. 67, of the Sons of Temperance of the State of New York.* New York: Oliver and Brother, Steam Printers.

Stevens, Albert C. 1899. *The Cyclopedia of Fraternities.* New York: Hamilton.

Stille, Charles J. 1868. *History of the United States Sanitary Commission, Being the General Report of Its Work during the War of the Rebellion.* New York: Hurd and Houghton.

Thernstrom, Stephen. 1973. *The Other Bostonians: Poverty and Progress in the American Metropolis, 1880–1970.* Harvard University Press.

————, ed. 1980. *Harvard Encyclopedia of American Ethnic Groups.* Harvard University Press.

Tocqueville, Alexis de. [1835, 1840] 1969. *Democracy in America.* Vols. 1 and 2. Edited by J. P. Mayer and translated by George Lawrence. Garden City, N.Y.: Doubleday, Anchor Books.

Turnbull, William W. 1901. *The Good Templars: A History of the Rise and Progress of the Independent Order of Good Templars.* N.p.

Turner, Howard H. 1881. *Turner's History of the Independent Order of Good Samaritans and Daughters of Samaria.* Washington, D.C.: R. A. Waters.

U.S. Bureau of Census. 1975. *Bicentennial Edition Historical Statistics of the United States, Colonial Times to 1970, Part 1.* Washington, D.C.: U.S. Government Printing Office.

"The U.S. Masons: A Pictorial Essay in Color." 1956. *Life,* October 8, pp. 104–22.

Valkenburg, Jno. van. 1886. *The Knights of Pythias Complete Manual and Text-Book.* Rev. ed. Canton, Ohio: Memento.

Verba, Sidney, Kay Lehman Schlozman, and Henry E. Brady. 1995. *Voice and Equality: Civic Voluntarism in American Politics.* Harvard University Press.

Wiebe, Robert H. 1967. *The Search for Order, 1877–1920.* New York: Hill and Wang.

Will, George. 1995. "Look at All the Lonely Bowlers." *Washington Post,* January 5, p. A29.

Wirth, Louis. 1938. "Urbanism as a Way of Life." *American Journal of Sociology* 44 (July): 1–24.

Wood, Gordon S. 1996. *The Radicalism of the American Revolution.* New York: Alfred A. Knopf.

Wood, Mary I. 1912. *History of the General Federation of Women's Clubs for the First Twenty-Two Years of Its Organization.* New York: General Federation of Women's Clubs.

Wuthnow, Robert. 1998. *Loose Connections: Joining Together in America's Fragmented Communities.* Harvard University Press.

3 | Organizational Repertoires and Institutional Change: Women's Groups and the Transformation of American Politics, 1890–1920

ELISABETH S. CLEMENS

IN THE DECADES surrounding the turn of the twentieth century, the institutions of American politics underwent "one of the more significant governmental transformations in American history," which included lasting changes in the nature and structure of political participation; party voting declined and interest-group politics became more important.[1] The center of gravity shifted from party-dominated elections to legislative and, increasingly, bureaucratic politics. These changes in the basic models of political participation came in the wake of efforts by agrarian groups and organized labor to secure greater leverage in a polity where the formal equality of white male citizens seemed increasingly irrelevant in the face of the power of economic corporations and party organizations. At the same time, women mobilized to secure the vote for the half of the adult population that was formally disenfranchised.[2] But

© 1993 by The University of Chicago. All rights reserved. A longer version of this paper was originally published in the *American Journal of Sociology* 98(4). The original elaborates both issues in organizational theory and the mechanisms of political co-optation. Fellowships from the Spencer Foundation and the Lilly Foundation Project on the Governance of Nonprofit Organizations at the Indiana University Center on Philanthropy provided support for this research.

1. McCormick (1986, p. 83).

2. Southern blacks were the great exception to this expansion of the polity as poll taxes and restricted registration were successfully used to remove African American males from the electoral rolls. McAdam (1986, pp. 68–69).

the connections between changing political institutions and the wave of popular political mobilization remain unclear. Did the activities of popular associations help to transform political institutions? If so, how?

These questions force us to think about the conditions under which those who are relatively weak or disadvantaged by a particular set of political rules can change those rules. The first step may be to reject the established conventions for political organization and to mobilize in ways that are not anticipated or constrained by the dominant rules and political actors. Fortunately for would-be political challengers, the social world presents multiple models of organization: an "organizational repertoire."[3] Such models comprise both templates for arranging relationships within an organization and scripts for action culturally associated with that type of organization; they carry cultural expectations about who can organize and for what purposes. The presence of alternative models in their organizational repertoire permits would-be challengers to make use of nonpolitical models of organization for political purposes. When deployed in novel ways by unfamiliar groups, even the most familiar organizational models can have unsettling consequences for political institutions.[4]

This model of institutional change underscores the importance of associational membership and civic engagement. Beyond providing opportunities for individuals to develop political skills and to cultivate social networks or social capital,[5] civic associations have often served as important sites for organizational experimentation. To the extent that such associations are public but not fully integrated with formal political institutions, they may provide platforms for the invention of new forms of political mobilization. These novel identities and strategies may give challengers an unexpected capacity to instigate institutional change.

In the decline of party politics in the United States,[6] nineteenth-century voluntary associations played a key role in elaborating a new style of politics focused on specific issues, interests, and legislative responses. Rather than adopting a single bureaucratic form, these groups made use of multiple models of organization—unions, clubs, parliaments, and corporations—each of which articulated in different ways with existing political institutions. Women's groups played a particularly important role in this

3. For an extended theoretical discussion of this concept, see Clemens (1997, pp. 45–52).
4. Tilly (1978, 1986).
5. Putnam (1993, 1995); Verba, Schlozman, and Brady (1995).
6. McGerr (1986); Shefter (1983).

process of organizational innovation precisely because women were formally disenfranchised (except in a few western states and in occasional local elections such as those for school boards) and culturally excluded from the fraternal world of electoral politics. A rapidly growing literature now documents the widespread involvement of women's groups in a political project that moved from the "municipal housekeeping" of the 1890s to the development of formidable state and national lobbies during the 1920s. While rarely producing a pure expression of womanhood, these efforts did span lines of race, ethnicity, class, and region.[7] Women's groups were not alone in this organizational innovation, but because of their marginal position in electoral politics, their efforts to create an institutional alternative are particularly clear.

Repertoires of Organization

For much of political sociology, organizations matter as resources; they make coordinated action possible and success more likely. But organization has consequences beyond the process of mobilization itself. When a group adopts a specific model of organization, it signals its identity both to its own members and to others. Consequently, the adoption of a model not usually linked to "that kind of group" repositions the group in relation to the field of other associations. The initial use of familiar forms by unfamiliar groups will have a destabilizing effect on existing conventions of organization. For example, the clubwomen, now quaint and moderate figures, named themselves in violation of established feminine conventions. The term "club" was rejected by some as a "masculine" label, but more daring groups such as the New England Women's Club "deliberately chose *club* to indicate a break with tradition; it did not want to be associated with good-works societies."[8] For outsiders, organizational form was a signal of these groups' novel qualities and aims: " 'What is the object?' was the first question asked of any organization of women, and if it was not the making of garments, or the collection of funds for a church, or philanthropic purpose, it was considered unworthy of attention, or injurious doubts were thrown upon its motives."[9]

7. Baker (1991); Frankel and Dye (1991); Muncy (1991); Scott (1991).
8. Quotations from Ruddy (1906, p. 24); see also Martin (1987, p. 63).
9. Croly (1898, p. 9).

By distancing themselves from religious associations and charitable societies, women's clubs constituted themselves as "absolutely a new thing under the sun."[10] And in defining itself through the appropriation of organizational models not traditionally associated with female groups, the women's club movement is a clear example of innovation grounded in the materials at hand. This process of organizational change through the rearrangement of existing repertoires characterized the nineteenth-century "woman movement" as a whole.

Once one group has pioneered the use of an organizational model in a new arena, it may then be adopted for use by other groups. Although the rationale for adoption may flow from momentary strategic advantages, widespread adoption is a source of fundamental change in the organizing categories of the political system. In the United States, the shift from the electoral regime of highly competitive parties to the legislative and administrative focus of interest group bargaining can be understood by examining the organizational experiments of groups that were comparatively disadvantaged under the first of these regimes. The subsequent shift in the available repertoire of organization—the recognized set of political options—then gave way to a system in which this form of mobilization became part of the taken-for-granted. Writing in 1900, John R. Commons, a prominent economist and social reformer, observed, "There is no movement of the past twenty years more quiet nor more potent than the organization of private interests. No other country in the world presents so interesting a spectacle."[11] With respect to the conventions of political action and organization, this new system entailed a focus on legislative rather than electoral politics and a consequent organization on the basis of stakes in particular issues rather than broad political philosophies. As one commentator complained by the 1920s, "The present unionized era of leagues, societies, alliances, clubs, combines and cliques offers confederation for mutual support of almost any interest conceivable except for the diversified interests of the humble in the application of general law. With united front the bankers, the brokers, the dairymen, the detectives, the sportsmen, the motorists, the innkeepers, the barbers, the mintgrowers, the Swiss bell ringers, *et al.*, may and do present their complaints to the legislature for adjustment."[12]

10. Wood (1912, p. 188).
11. Commons ([1907] 1967, p. 359).
12. Wismer (1928, p. 172).

Although manufacturers organized nonpartisan trade associations in both the United States and Europe, only in the United States did "interest"—rather than party, class, language, or religion—become the primary idiom of political life, a *legitimate* if not necessarily welcome form of political organization.[13] The making of specific claims on legislatures was not in itself new; it had previously taken the form of petitions, private bills directed at individuals, and bribery in the Gilded Age.[14] What was new was the exertion of issue-specific pressure through political education, public opinion, expert testimony, and the increasingly sophisticated legislative tactics of issue- or constituency-based organizations.

This new system of political organization grew out of an eclectic process of reorganization. Rather than accepting a single model for political action, groups drew on both traditional models and the most modern good-government groups and imitated what worked for their frequent opponents, the corporations and political machines.

This account of changes in the forms of political organization suggests that there will be a great deal of cultural work around the questions, What kind of group are we? and What do groups like us do? The links between organizational and cultural analysis are clear; models of organization are not only conventions for coordinating action but also statements of what it means for certain people to organize in certain ways for certain purposes.[15] In addition, both the substance of these debates and the subsequent patterns of mobilization should vary by the set of organizational models that are culturally and experientially available to a given group at a particular point in time. Finally, patterns of organization in response to novel or ambiguous situations should be shaped by a group's existing or desired ties to other groups committed to a particular model of organization. The selection of a specific organizational form should then strengthen ties between some organizations while weakening others.

This chapter explores each of these propositions using examples from the turn-of-the-century woman movement. I am not claiming that women's groups were unique in adopting new models of organization (indeed my argument suggests that available models of organization are likely to be noticed and used by multiple groups), only that women's

13. See also Clemens (1997); Maier (1981); McCormick (1986); Rodgers (1987).
14. Thompson (1985).
15. Kanter (1972).

groups were particularly well placed to explore the potential of organizational models newly introduced to the political arena.

The "Woman Movement": Scope and Sources

The "woman movement" of the late nineteenth and early twentieth centuries in the United States was rooted in the antebellum proliferation of female benevolent societies and abolitionist activities. When the Civil War amendments failed to provide for their enfranchisement, women gradually regrouped around the causes of temperance and woman suffrage, while constructing an impressive network of nationwide, federated women's organizations.[16] By the 1880s, women's organizations and causes were established alongside, but largely apart from, the nation's formal political institutions. The next decades saw increasing political mobilization of women as well as a series of legislative gains that compared favorably with the successes of women in other nations as well as with the victories of labor and agrarian insurgents in the U.S.[17] The ability of women's groups to enter the political arena without being fully co-opted suggests that processes of conservative organizational transformation are conditioned by both the social identity of those organized and the character of existing political institutions.[18]

The "woman movement" drew together women who were relatively privileged in terms of economic standing and education, yet suffered from formal and informal exclusionary practices that limited their ability to cultivate political skills or to exercise those skills if they were somehow acquired.[19] Notwithstanding their formal disenfranchisement in much of the nation (the Nineteenth Amendment was not ratified until 1920), middle- and upper-middle-class women constructed an impressive array of voluntary associations that were a significant force in the public life of the nation. Eighteen years after its founding in 1874, the Woman's Christian Temperance Union (WCTU) had 150,000 members and exerted influence on legislation ranging from temperance to woman suffrage.[20] The General Fed-

16. Scott (1991).
17. Clemens (1997); Skocpol and Ritter (1991).
18. Specific economic and political mechanisms are central to Max Weber's analysis of "the routinization of charisma" and Robert Michels's "iron law of oligarchy." On the relative insulation of nineteenth-century women's associations from these processes, see Clemens (1993, pp. 763–67).
19. Blair (1980); Sklar (1985).
20. Bordin (1981, pp. 3–4).

eration of Women's Clubs (GFWC) was founded in 1890 and had perhaps 500,000 members by 1905 and over a million by the end of the decade.[21] In addition to these groups, associated charities, civic clubs, auxiliaries of fraternal orders, and suffrage associations filled out a dense network of women's organizations. As a key element of the era's social reform constituency, these groups contributed to the founding of America's distinctively "maternalist" welfare state, a policy regime that emphasized programs such as mother's pensions rather than unemployment and old age insurance.[22]

Although women's organizations of the period realized that some form of political action would be needed to advance many of their causes, politics as usual was out of the question. In addition to their formal exclusion from electoral activity, women's associations joined in a broader cultural attack on political methods. According to Jennie June Croly, the first president of the GFWC: "If I were to state what seems to me to be the great hindrance to club life and growth, it would be the employment of political methods, of political machinery and wire-pulling to bring about results. Politics can never be purified until its methods are changed, while its introduction into our club life subverts the whole intention and aims of club organization."[23]

Politics itself was not rejected, only the existing forms of political organization, the models of the electoral party and patronage machines. To construct an alternative, women's groups drew on models of organization from other areas of social life. Borrowing from this broader repertoire of social organization, these groups helped transform patterns of political action in the Progressive Era.

No formal listing of such repertoires exists, but the range of culturally available models of organization can be reconstructed from the debates that groups conducted over what sort of organization they wanted to be. Convention proceedings are a rich source of this information because any change in organization or strategy usually entailed formal motions complete with statements of the facts (the "Whereas" clause) and an argument for some alternative model for group action. For example, factional divisions might be explained in terms drawn from the worlds of business and political

---

21. The calculation of exact membership figures is impossible because totals were typically given by clubs and some women held multiple memberships. Wilson (1979, pp. 100–01); Wood (1912, pp. 131, 154).

22. Gordon (1990); Skocpol (1992).

23. Croly (1898, p. 128).

reform. In 1911 one Wisconsin suffrage group proclaimed its intention to "bust the suffrage trust" (the national suffrage associations) and to found an alternative organization "with a commission form of government."[24] Business methods also defined new political strategies. Discouraging the use of public debates—a centerpiece of nineteenth-century political life—one California suffragist argued in 1913, "I think we must frankly acknowledge that people are not all convinced through reason, and that although the proposition that women should vote is seriously and profoundly true, it will, at first, be established with this class of people much as the virtues of a breakfast food are established—by affirmation."[25]

To reconstruct the repertoires of organization employed during this period, this study draws on an extensive reading of the proceedings of women's organizations. The material in this analysis is drawn primarily from a comparative study of political organization and strategies of labor, agrarian, and women's groups in three progressive states (California, Washington, and Wisconsin) between 1890 and 1920.[26] Because this analysis is concerned with innovation in political organization, these cases were selected from those states recognized for innovative political procedures in addition to substantive social policy. Though a number of eastern states did pass progressive social legislation, on the whole they were significantly slower to adopt procedural reforms such as the initiative, referendum, and recall that undermined the power of party organizations to control political agendas and outcomes.[27] Struggles within national organizations also frequently took the form of a regional split between an eastern leadership committed to established methods and midwestern or western factions more open to direct political action or state intervention. In addition to the convention proceedings and official publications of various state federations, I draw upon organizational debates as they were reported and analyzed in women's papers—including the *Wisconsin Citizen*, *Club Life* (San Francisco), the *Western Woman Voter* (Seattle), and the women's page of the *Wisconsin Equity News*—and in the histories published by and about different associations.[28] Throughout these accounts, groups' awareness of

24. Milwaukee *Evening Wisconsin*, October 10, 1911, Wisconsin Woman Suffrage Scrapbooks.
25. College Equal Suffrage League of Northern California [hereafter CESLNC] (1913, p. 11).
26. Clemens (1997).
27. Phelps (1914, p. xliv); Shefter (1983).
28. E.g., CESLNC (1913); Croly (1898); Gibson (1927); Park (1960); Ruddy (1906); Simpson (1909, 1915); Spencer [n.d.]; Williamson (1925); Winter (1925); Womans Parliament of Southern California (1892); Wood (1912).

others and mimicry of one another is clear. Rather than asserting that political innovation was grounded in the distinctive characteristics of individual states, this argument takes the process of organizational imitation and innovation as central to an understanding of the institutional changes of the period.

Focusing on repertoires of organization, the analysis seeks to identify mechanisms for such change by locating the interaction of popular associations and politics within a broader social system that embraces alternative models of organization and multiple institutions. When familiar organizational forms are deployed in unfamiliar ways, insurgent groups may destabilize existing institutions and ultimately contribute to the institutionalization of new conventions for political action.

Gender and Political Organization

Over the nineteenth century, the role of gender in defining political identity intensified. In the French "Declaration of the Rights of Man and Citizen" of 1791 and in the Fourteenth Amendment to the Constitution of the United States, voting was defined as the exclusive prerogative of adult men.[29] In the United States, these formal exclusions were reinforced by a dense web of political association. To the extent that political associations were based on workplace identities, the differing patterns of men's and women's involvement in the labor market ensured that these associations would be primarily single-sex groups. Similarly, insofar as turn-of-the-century political mobilization built on the fraternal organizations of nineteenth-century America, it perpetuated that period's distinctively male and female political cultures.[30] While organizations such as the Good Templars and the Patrons of Husbandry (the Grange) did embrace the moral issues of concern to women and at times allowed women to join, in all cases the political organization of men at the end of the nineteenth century powerfully influenced the participation of women.

But women's politics were not entirely derivative. Opening her massive overview of the women's club movement in the United States, Jennie June Croly proclaimed, "When the history of the nineteenth century comes to be written, women will appear as organizers, and leaders of great organized

29. Catt and Shuler (1926, pp. 32–45); Landes (1988, p. 122).
30. Baker (1984); Clawson (1985).

movements among their own sex for the first time in the history of the world."[31] In part, women's models of political action derived from their history of public participation; the revivalism of the Jacksonian era was echoed in the fervent calls for reform made by the Woman's Christian Temperance Union;[32] social reformers drew on a legacy of friendly visiting and personal service to the poor.[33] Middle- and upper-class women in particular adopted the models of the parlor meeting and charitable society, gradually adapting them as vehicles for a greater role in public affairs. Without directly challenging the fundamentally fraternal character of political life, women drew on domestic and religious models of action to begin crafting a public role for themselves. But the long-standing political exclusion of women meant that their activism would be particularly disruptive to the political order. The puzzle, then, is to explain how women's groups were able to transform their public identity in a way that largely sidestepped the culturally embedded equation of the political with masculinity.

In this enterprise, women activists drew on an organizational repertoire familiar to them as members of American society if not necessarily through their direct experience in women's groups: "The woman's club was not an echo; it was not the mere banding together for a social and economic purpose, like the clubs of men. It became at once, without deliberate intention or concerted action, a light-giving and seed-sowing center of purely altruistic and democratic activity."[34] Having appropriated a "male" model of organization, the clubwomen continued to transform their movement through further excercises in organizational imitation. One of Mrs. Croly's successors as president of the General Federation of Women's Clubs explicitly celebrated the innovation of the movement, while acknowledging its basis in imitation. Her "little book," *The Business of Being a Clubwoman,* "does not deal with purposes or programs, but with *ways* of running our affairs. We must learn to avoid our old mistakes and gain our ends by more direct paths. We can learn out of our own past. And no one but ourselves can give us much help. Colleges and social scientists and experts of various kinds can help us in the *matters* upon which we are working, but as to the *ways* of working we have to blaze our own trail."[35]

The need to invent new "ways of working" was a product of the

---

31. Croly (1898, p. 1).
32. Epstein (1981); Smith-Rosenberg (1985, pp. 129–64).
33. McCarthy (1982, pp. 3–24).
34. Croly (1898, p. 13).
35. Winter (1925, p. vi).

organizational repertoire that these economically privileged women inherited from the nineteenth century combined with their double exclusion from male organizations and partisan politics. Faced with these constraints, the clubwomen and their social peers were pushed to innovate.

Though club life was the form of many women's entry into public affairs, three other models of organization were central to the development of a more explicitly political strategy for women. First, women increasingly drew on corporate forms and cash exchanges to replace personal service as the preferred medium for social action. In addition, women's groups internalized the bureaucratic forms and methods of the modern state as they turned with greater frequency to state and federal governments, rather than their own communities, as the appropriate arenas for political action.[36] The final development involved the positive cultural revaluation of the model of the lobby. If these three organizational shifts are taken to an extreme, one arrives at a picture of the modern-day interest or issue group, with its use of educational literature and expert testimony to secure federal funding for some sort of program. As timeless as this form of political action may now seem, it was an invention of the Progressive Era, and women's groups played a central part in its elaboration and legitimation.

Organization as Business

All of these efforts at organizing women and their political activities took place during what is now widely recognized as a period of organizational revolution. Consequently, rather than confining the analysis to the relations between women's groups and politics, sweeping changes in the broader repertoire of social organization in nineteenth-century America must be considered. Of particular importance was the expansion of the market and the development of new forms of commercial relations.[37] Although the hierarchical relations of the corporation had mixed implications for women's self-presentation as independent citizens, the market appeared unambiguously modern.

For women's groups, however, the adoption of "business methods" had consequences that were not apparent in the activities of men already immersed in a system of market relations. Part of becoming a modern organization involved substituting cash exchanges for personal service.

36. Baker (1991).
37. Chandler (1977).

Speaking on "Woman's Work in the Church" to the 1892 Southern California Womans Parliament, the Rev. Lila F. Sprague declared: "The woman of to-day is inaugurating an epoch of belief; a belief that it is better in every way, for all concerned, to give five dollars in cash to the needs of the church, rather than ten dollars in poor cake, and poorer pie, which may, with a big crowd and plenty of hard work, yield a net return of one or two dollars."[38]

Throughout the Progressive Era, the conflict between traditional and activist women's groups continued to be expressed in terms of the role of money. The call for cash, however, had to confront the fact that many women had only limited access to funds of their own. Consequently, a reliance on the domestic production of baked goods and bazaar items continued alongside an effort to extract funds on the basis of a more "modern" female identity, that of the consumer. Mainstream suffrage associations sponsored "consumer fasts" in which women promised to forgo buying cosmetics and other luxuries for a week or so, sending the money saved to fund the fight for the vote. More radical organizations tried to sever the link between fund-raising and women's traditional roles, whether charity worker or consumer. In Wisconsin, the leader of the Political Equality League was quoted as declaring "that she will not conduct sales of cookbooks or postcards to raise a campaign fund and further declares that if it is to be that sort of a campaign she will seek a cool spot near Lake Superior and retire there. Promises, Miss Wagner points out, do not pay the bills and begging for money is humiliating."[39]

The shift to business methods characterized the delivery of services as well as their underwriting. Whereas personal contact between charitable women and their poor clientele had once been viewed as central to the project of moral uplift, this "friendly visiting" was increasingly under attack. From the perspective of scientific charity, this form of aid was inefficient; from the perspective of the disadvantaged and their advocates, it was frequently demeaning. In response to these complaints, volunteers in numerous cities sponsored Women's Industrial Exchanges where working women could sell homemade items such as baked goods and needlework, and charities joined together as "Charity Organization Societies" to coordinate both fund-raising and the delivery of services.[40] Indeed, part of

38. Womans Parliament of Southern California (1892, p. 8).
39. Racine *News*, July 11, 1911, Wisconsin Woman Suffrage Scrapbooks.
40. Sander (1998).

the mission of the new scientific charities was to move beyond a reliance on volunteers altogether.

The convergence of these trends toward cash support and paid supporters is evident in a novel program established by the Associated Charities of San Francisco, an organization in which women held considerable power. In the wake of the 1906 earthquake, the Associated Charities was the main conduit for both federal aid and private relief funds raised across the country and consequently developed the habit of operating on a cash basis. Later, in response to the plight of destitute women and children, these women established what one report described as "the most important sociological innovation ever made in San Francisco."[41] Continuing an earlier effort to deinstitutionalize the state's orphans, the Associated Charities simply boarded out babies for $12.50 a month. Like the later mothers' pensions, this program provided women with the money to support their own children. Unlike the mothers' pensions, however, women earned this money by entering into an explicit employment relationship with a public agency. For the charity volunteers of San Francisco, the potential of moral suasion or social control rapidly paled next to the demonstrated power of spending.

Spending was also a sign of full political citizenship. Recounting their contributions to the San Francisco Panama-Pacific Exposition of 1915, the Woman's Board explained: "Woman's co-operation in other world expositions has necessarily included an accounting of funds drawn from official sources. That is not the case with the Woman's Board which helped in the creation of San Francisco's Dream City of 1915 and in bringing it to a picturesque and notable obligation of stewardship; it financed all its own undertakings as well as those undertakings which it cheerfully assumed at the request of the Exposition directorate."[42]

The importance of this claim is underlined by its presence in the second paragraph of the preface, the first substantive claim in a book-length account. The political significance of financial autonomy is explained in the paragraph that follows: "There are in mind the men and women everywhere who may be interested in these achievements not merely for their intrinsic worth, but also for the reason that they bear eloquent witness to the success of a great human cause, for the reason that they are, in some sort, the first fruits of woman's emancipation in a state

41. Simpson (1909, p. 22).
42. Ibid. (p. ix).

newly made politically free, a practical thank-offering of woman's pride and woman's patriotism."[43]

By adopting "business practices," these activists diminished the role of distinctively gendered organizational forms in constituting their public identity. This adoption of business practices and cash exchanges simultaneously undermined the forms of intimacy, solidarity, and community traditionally associated with women's groups of the nineteenth century. In promoting the organization of working women, for example, elite clubs no longer sought to maintain the personal albeit supervisory ties of friendly visiting. In San Francisco, the prestigious California Club first sponsored the working-class Porteous Club and then left it to support itself. Once again, business practices signaled civic maturity: "That the little club is capable of managing its own affairs in a small way is sufficiently evidenced by the concert it gave in the early part of the year, when it was practically, though not yet nominally, on its own resources. . . . None the less was the affair organized and carried through in all business details by the Porteous members themselves, and so well did they manage that they netted $108.05 as their profit from the entertainment. After such a result none can doubt the business capacity of the baby Porteous."[44]

Such shifts toward business practices displaced the familial models of sisterhood and mother-daughter relations that had shaped both the organization and the self-image of women's organizations of the nineteenth century.[45] But if these changes made it possible for women's organizations to take public actions not directly linked to the domestic, the questions of how such actions could be made politically effective remained.

From Community to Bureaucracy

While the organization of activity around cash exchanges signaled personal dignity and political maturity, the move away from personal service as a primary public activity also had consequences for the ability of women to enter into politics and to stimulate the expansion of state agencies. To the extent that their activities were constructed around a cash nexus rather than personal service, experimental private programs could be adopted more easily by state agencies once sufficient public support had

43. Ibid. (pp. ix–x).
44. *Club Life* 5 (1902, p. 4).
45. DuBois (1991).

been generated. Without directly confronting the gendered opposition of home and electoral politics, the oblique embrace of business forms of organization resulted in an increasing isomorphism between women's associations and state agencies.

Yet if the reliance on cash facilitated such transfers, it was not the sole cause. Charitable programs for men had developed in much the same way; indeed, the reliance on work-based systems centered on employment exchanges or mandatory labor in coal yards was much more frequent for impoverished men. But there was a danger in distributing public monies to poor men, a danger beyond the threat that dependency posed to their moral character. Any such distribution might be easily turned to political purposes, to partisan advantage. Yet the same was not true for impoverished women. Because widows and unmarried women were unable to vote themselves and unattached to adult men as the very condition of their eligibility for aid, relief programs for these women were insulated from accusations of political corruption.[46] Given their relative immunity from the logic of political incorporation, the disenfranchised were culturally privileged as recipients of public largesse.

With respect to the organizational field of electoral politics, women's formal disenfranchisement insulated their associations from electoral incorporation, the onslaught of "predatory politics" that had undermined both agrarian and labor movements. But by adopting business practices as models of organization, women's groups could then accommodate themselves to the generic bureaucratic procedures common to both corporations and state agencies. These agencies were central to the new politics of interest groups and social programs. In many cases, women's groups played an important role in the establishment of these institutions. In the United States, many women demanded the vote not as a natural right but in order to secure specific reforms—child labor laws, temperance, protective legislation for working women. Frequently, women's groups not only demanded state intervention but then initiated it themselves by providing funds for kindergartens, probation officers, health inspectors, and other services later provided by public agencies.[47] Arguing that working women were without the protection of union contracts—owing to their incapacity

---

46. This characterization of aid recipients was, however, often merely a convenient construction since aid to indigent women could be used as a way of securing the support of male relatives, who might otherwise be called upon for financial support.

47. Gibson (1927, pp. 214, 216); Williamson (1925, p. 40).

to form contracts, the nature of the labor market, or the neglect of union organizers—women's labor reform groups called for state intervention to control both hours and wages for women, actions that often drew criticism from organized labor. These demands for economic regulation and social services mean that women's politics are of particular importance for understanding both the beginnings of the American welfare state and the entrenchment of interest group politics.

The creation of state agencies also had important implications for the future of women's politics in the United States. For just as the "business" transformations of women's organizations allowed for a measure of political success in the decades surrounding the turn of the century, those changes also undermined the strength of the organizations. By shifting to cash transactions, away from personal service and the creation of community, these organizational innovations eroded the personal networks and commitments that so often account for the success of a social movement.[48] The political effects of adopting "business practices" worked in opposite directions. The implementation of this model first served as a path by which women could sidestep the clearly gendered forms of the nineteenth-century polity. But once established in the polity, women's groups adopted increasingly hierarchical models of professionalism and expertise that ultimately made the widespread political mobilization of women less relevant for the determination of policy outcomes.[49] Although elite women reformers were much more likely than male bureaucrats to attend to and rely on their constituencies, more and more often a few well-placed experts and political insiders could accomplish as much as mass rallies and petition drives.

In this respect, Robert Michels's "iron law of oligarchy," which predicted an emerging gap between leaders and members of social movements, was fulfilled.[50] Insofar as women's groups had both created and captured state agencies, a smaller set of reformers and activists could

---

48. Before the recruitment of a cadre of wealthy supporters, for example, "the suffragette style drew on the militant traditions of the labor movement, and its protest tactics, such as outdoor rallies, were suitable to a constituency with little money." As money replaced effort as the medium of mobilization, suffragists were increasingly divided by class and pushed toward passive roles as donors and audiences: "Meetings went inside once there was money to hire halls" (DuBois 1991, pp. 169, 173).

49. Muncy (1991).

50. Michels ([1911] 1962). This distance did not necessarily translate into a conservative goal transformation because of the distinctive organizational context in which the leaders found themselves. During the 1920s, the leadership of the woman movement—particularly the suffragists—embraced the international peace movement and consequently endured attacks and red-baiting from conservative women's groups and politicians. Van Voris (1987, pp. 189–97).

successfully promote a political agenda that once required a mass movement. For example, in carrying out its infant health and birth registration campaigns, the newly established Children's Bureau relied on the cooperation of 1,500 clubwomen by 1914 and 11 million by the national Children's Year of 1918.[51] But the leaders of agencies were no longer leaders of movements and, as the woman movement was absorbed by parties and new voluntary associations during the 1920s, the new women bureaucrats were left vulnerable to conservative attacks and the dismantling of programs and agencies. But, in the meantime, women's groups had helped to legitimate new models of extraparty politics.

Politics without Parties

Because American women initially pursued their political goals without benefit of the vote, they developed methods of influence distinct from the electoral context of partisan politics. One opening was found in lobbying, the unsavory practice of the Gilded Age, "a constitutionally guaranteed right of all citizens . . . that nonetheless has no respectability unless it masquerades under euphemistic aliases." Unlike the vote, the right of petition was available to all; "minors, minorities, aliens, women, even idiots have always been able to employ it."[52]

In constructing their own "euphemistic alias," one that would distinguish them from aliens, idiots, and others with no claim on citizenship, women combined the tainted model of the lobby with educational strategies more conventionally associated with nineteenth-century women's organizations. As one clubwoman observed, "The earliest form of the woman's club was the study club, the 'Middle-aged Woman's University.'" But women did not immediately recognize education as a strategy of political influence. As of the First Biennial of the General Federation of Women's Clubs in 1892: "The educating of public opinion as the only permanent basis for welfare work seems not at the time to have become a part of the inner consciousness of the average General Federation worker."[53] Over the next decade, the links between women's politics and "educational strategies" were firmly secured. The woman suffrage movement embraced the model of education as a form for both internal mobi-

---

51. Ladd-Taylor (1991, p. 117); Muncy (1991).
52. Quotations from Thompson (1985, p. 27); see also Herring (1929, p. 36).
53. Wood (1912, pp. 26, 50).

lization, through a "Course of Study" on political science, and external cultivation of sympathizers among the male electorate.[54] Other women's groups linked education to social policy demands: "The method employed by the Consumers' League to better conditions invariably followed this rule: obtain facts through investigation, acquaint the public with the facts, and after educating public opinion, secure legislation."[55] This last step, the merging of educational and legislative strategies in a new model of political organization, proved most difficult.

The politics of education and public opinion ran into difficulty when women attempted to translate research and expertise into political influence. Having crafted a political role from a strategy associated with corporate bribes and illicit interests, women were vulnerable because this one political role could be easily attacked.[56] Despite these dangers, lobbying was one of the few models of political influence available to women, and they worked to legitimate this model by linking it to the conventions of professionalism and expertise. Before securing the right to vote, for example, members of the California State Federation of Women's Clubs replaced a loose Legislative Committee composed of six district representatives with one headed by a more powerful legislative chairman. The initial results were disappointing, but within two years the clubwomen claimed some credit for the passage of the eight-hour limit on the workday for women, the employers' liability law, and bills pertaining to child labor. By 1912, following the suffrage victory:

> The California Federation of Women's Clubs, through its Chairman of Legislation, invites all State organizations of women to cooperate with it in forming a central committee, a State Legislative Council of Women. . . . The purpose of this body will be to prevent duplication of this work and expense; to bring together experts from each society who can plan mutually for better work than would be possible alone; to decide how much legislation and what is wise to ask for, and to see that this is being prepared by responsible organizations; also to select a small committee to be in Sacramento during the session of the Legislature to look after all interests involved in such legislation.

54. Van Voris (1987, pp. 43–44).

55. Nathan (1926, p. 78). The political appropriation of education had been pioneered by the major parties themselves in an effort to cultivate the small but decisive group of independent voters that developed in the late nineteenth century (McGerr 1986). Within the woman suffrage movement, this strategy of education also resulted in demands for an education requirement.

56. Hichborn (1911, pp. 246–47).

One reform-minded journalist proclaimed that the California women had invented "the Scientific Management of Club Influence."[57]

The women's associations of California may have been somewhat precocious in establishing a formal lobby, but they were not alone. In Washington State, women's groups affiliated with the nonpartisan Joint Legislative Committee and eagerly joined in campaigns for labor legislation as well as women's issues more narrowly defined, forging important political alliances and developing considerable political skills.[58] Even the women's groups of Wisconsin, constrained as they were by nativism, dry sentiments, and a general cultural conservatism, were willing to venture into this new field of endeavor. The Milwaukee Consumer's League gave its support to women's hours legislation, although the primary advocates of these bills were the city's Social Democratic legislators.[59] The State Federation of Women's Clubs passed resolutions favoring mothers' pensions and child labor laws, sent officers to testify on bills, and created a Legislative Committee whose members "are finding the work decidedly educational, and are acquiring a knowledge of the methods used to pass or defeat bills never dreamed of in the philosophy of women's clubs."[60]

Having mastered these methods, women lobbyists effectively supported a wide range of legislation, which secured for the United States a reputation as a "maternalist" welfare state.[61] Tensions between the models for feminine and political identity lingered; women found that their choice of political techniques continued to draw comment. As Maud Wood Park of the National American Woman Suffrage Association wrote: "The Front Door Lobby was the half-humorous, half-kindly name given to our Congressional Committee in Washington by one of the press-gallery men there, because, as he explained, we never used backstairs methods."[62] Once women had secured bases of power within government, they sought to implement programs that would serve their constituencies but were increasingly constrained by their obligations to carry out programs promoted by other political coalitions. The women who led the Children's Bureau, for example, were torn between an infant health program favored by working women and the enforcement of child labor laws that threatened

57. Gibson (1927, pp. 181, 185, 188).
58. Tripp (1973, pp. 85–86).
59. Schmidt (1933, pp. 187–88).
60. Wisconsin Federation of Women's Clubs (1909, p. 83).
61. Skocpol and Ritter (1991); Skocpol (1992).
62. Park (1960, p. 1).

the tenuous family economies of those same women: "Female reformers in government functioned both as advocates for poor mothers and as administrators of the (sometimes injurious) policies that affected them, and their contradictory role made conflict with grass-roots mothers inevitable."[63] These organizational accomplishments won a grudging acceptance for politically active women, but they also transformed the relation between activists and the members of their self-adopted constituency.

Organizational Repertoires and Cross-Class Alliances

While these organizational innovations may have helped to undermine the solidarity of the woman movement—once rooted in the relatively intimate networks of clubs and parlors—they also made it possible to negotiate other class-based divisions among women. As long as privileged women drew on those models of organization closest to their own experience, their differences with working-class women and men were emphasized. But as their repertoire of organization expanded, so did the possibilities of cross-class alliances among women. The significance of changing organizational models is suggested by a comparison of the political development of privileged women with the experience of working-class women. Similarly excluded from formal political participation, working-class women confronted this situation with a different repertoire of organization. Although women rarely had equal standing within the labor movement, within two years of dropping its commitment to secrecy in 1878, the Knights of Labor did authorize the initiation of women.[64] In 1882, at the second convention of the Federation of Organized Trades and Labor Unions (the forerunner of the AFL), women were invited to participate. Thus, like the Patrons of Husbandry, these male-dominated organizations did not formally exclude women in the manner of the multiplying fraternal societies of the time.[65] But unlike the Patrons of

63. Ladd-Taylor (1991, p. 123).

64. The reasons that women could not join the Knights earlier were rooted in cultural beliefs about feminine character. The founder of the Knights, "though far in advance of many members of the early Knights, was so obsessed with the value of secrecy and with the sexist view that women could not keep secrets that, while he favored the inclusion of all male workers and mentioned women, he did not advocate opening membership to women" (Foner [1979, p. 185]). The model of organization thus identified those who could and should be organized. See also Delzell (1919, p. 10); Foner (1979, pp. 186–87); Levine (1983, pp. 324–25).

65. Clawson (1989, pp. 180–87).

Husbandry, who often found themselves claiming "some earnest Grangers and good workers, especially the sisters, who seem to take more interest in the grange than the brothers,"[66] the large nineteenth-century labor unions remained clearly the province of men. Women rarely accounted for more than 10 percent of the membership in the Knights of Labor and an even smaller proportion in the AFL.[67]

While this degree of openness compares favorably with that encountered by middle- and upper-middle-class women who sought to work alongside their fathers, husbands, and brothers, labor organizations were not free from more general cultural beliefs that women were not as amenable to organization as men. Reflecting on recent state-level suffrage victories, one socialist organizer asserted: "Many have contended that the work of propaganda among women requires essentially different methods than those used among workingmen. So it was said shortly ago that the work among agrarian populations must be carried on differently than for the town proletariat. This has been proven erroneous, and the same principles have been found to apply in both cases."[68]

Insofar as the labor movement was concerned, however, the conditions of employment of most working women made it difficult for them to organize effectively within the framework provided by the AFL. Although skilled women had joined craft unions in the late nineteenth century,[69] by the turn of the century the fastest-growing group of women workers were unskilled operatives working in industries such as textiles, garment manufacturing, and electrical goods. In these occupations, men and women alike proved difficult to organize; for women, this situation was aggravated by the AFL's repeated failure to hire women organizers.[70] But even these failures helped to reinforce the primacy of class rather than gender as the organizational basis of public identity for working women.

The tensions between models of political organization based on class solidarity and gender became evident in the policies of the Women's Trade Union League (WTUL), a cross-class alliance of wealthy, educated reformers and women activists who had made their way up through union movements and strike organizing. For the first decade of its existence, the WTUL adhered to the definition of working women as workers, overrid-

66. *California State Grange* (1887, p. 110).
67. Foner (1979, p. 188); Levine (1983, p. 325).
68. Simons ([1912?], p. 6).
69. Eaves (1910, pp. 314–15); Matthews (1913, pp. 40–50).
70. Dye (1980, pp. 13, 80).

ing the organizational experience that its elite sponsors brought from years of participation in the woman movement. Since the labor movement was technically open to women, an approach that emphasized craft-based organizing protected the sponsors from class-based attacks on their motives and the working women from charges of dual unionism. Dependent on the AFL for both financial support and legitimation as a labor organization, the WTUL was constrained from pursuing industrial models of labor organization or taking a more explicitly political approach that might aggravate the tensions between the AFL's official bipartisan stance and the independent electoral efforts of the socialist wing of the labor movement.[71] With the victory of craft unionism and the hegemony of the AFL only recently secured, any women's experiments in union form would inevitably challenge their most powerful allies. Only after years of disappointments and declining financial support from the AFL did the WTUL begin to draw on the models of political action developed within the middle-class bastions of the woman movement. Legislative campaigns began to replace union organizing and strikes.

This shift in strategy depended on the ongoing evolution of organization and strategy among middle- and upper-middle-class women. During the same years that the women's club movement began to grow rapidly among the middle class, women philanthropists had sponsored "Working Girls Clubs," which offered classes and lectures.[72] Although the clubs were popular in the Northeast, these attempts to build cross-class alliances relied on the public but prepolitical models of the women's club and were often a source of tension with working-class women, who were hostile to any patronizing, however well-intended. This hostility was echoed by the men of the labor movement. After certain "ladies of a philanthropic and religious turn of mind" established a "Girls' Union" in San Francisco in the late 1880s, the *Coast Seamen's Journal* complained, "While we believe they mean well, their mode of procedure is not such as will emancipate our sisters from the slavery and socially degrading position which they at present are placed in."[73] Club life did not appear to offer a path to significant economic improvement.

71. Ibid. (p. 87).
72. Montgomery (1987, p. 146). A decade or more later, the WTUL appealed to immigrant women by setting up clubs parallel to the men's fraternal benefit clubs, arguing that unionization could grow out of social solidarity. But, reflecting the ambiguous role of women in the work force, these clubs were caught in a controversy over whether to distribute marriage or strike benefits (Dye 1980, pp. 112–13).
73. Quoted in Matthews (1913, p. 5).

With the increasing turn of the women's club movement toward legislative activity, however, new parallels emerged between working-class and middle-class women's movements. Like their middle-class counterparts, working women risked censure when they ventured into the male world of politics. Surveying women's union activities in San Francisco, Lillian Matthews noted:

> The waitresses as a body and individually exhibit considerable more interest in municipal politics than do the women of other trade unions. . . . It is reported from numerous sources also that politicians of a certain class make use of the favor of waitresses because the publicity of their work throws them in contact with people whom they wish to influence. All this is mere rumor, however. But, whatever the reasons and whatever conclusions it may suggest, it is undoubtedly true that the waitresses mix into municipal politics, and that during some administrations they have received marked favors in the way of municipal positions.[74]

In a city governed by the allegedly corrupt Union Labor Party, participation in politics tarnished the reputation of the unionized waitresses at the same time that their activities suggested a further corruption of politics, a proletarian version of the "cunning spider-lobbyist" of the Gilded Age and her illicit mixing of the domestic and the political.[75] But if the waitresses were censured for their alleged appropriation of the clearly masculine model of patronage politics, other models of political action were culturally available. Faced with defeat at organizing workers, both the Knights of Labor and the AFL had sometimes turned to lobbying or legislative strategies, and at least potentially, this path was also open to working women and their more privileged allies.[76]

This shift in strategy is evident in the organizational development of the Women's Trade Union League. Between 1913 and 1915, the New York League switched its resources from supporting strikes to working for the

74. Matthews (1913, p. 81).

75. Herring (1929, p. 36). The reputation of the waitresses' union was also attacked because the "waitresses raise most of their funds for relief and sick benefits from their large annual ball. . . . One of the main features is a bar, and from the sale of drinks the receipts are $600 to $800. The sum thus derived goes into the benevolent fund." With these ill-gotten gains, the waitresses provided death benefits, supported a paid staff that was "not customary in other unions," established a minimum wage scale, and "molded together a class of workers who are notably hard to weld" (Matthews 1913, pp. 78–81).

76. Montgomery (1987, pp. 164–69).

passage of legislation and, above all, a woman suffrage bill: "The league's commitments to suffrage and protective legislation suggest that members had begun to cast their lot with women's organizations and feminist issues rather than with the male-dominated labor movement. . . . WTUL women also increasingly viewed their difficulties with organized labor as a fundamental conflict between men and women rather than as a conflict between workers and a predominantly upper-class organization."[77]

This shift required the organizational experiences and expertise that middle-class women had acquired over two decades of involvement first in the club movement and charitable associations, then in the politics of suffrage and social reform. As the contrasting fates of middle-class and working-class women's organizations demonstrate, the relationship between gender and politics is mediated by organizational form and capacity. For working-class women, the comparative openness of male unions to their participation lessened the incentive for organizational innovation at the same time that the hardships of their lives limited the time and resources available for independent organizing. For middle-class women, by comparison, the sharp ideological delineation between the separate spheres pushed them to invent new organizations.

The organizational developments within the far-flung woman movement support each of the propositions set forth above. Women's groups were constantly engaged in debates over the meaning of different organizational forms. Even when they adopted business models, they did so often not out of instrumental concerns but as an effort to demonstrate the status of the membership as autonomous, rational citizens eligible for an equal place in the American polity. Second, the organizational repertoires at stake varied both over time and by social position. An early generation of middle- and upper-middle-class women used the club to distinguish themselves from traditional female models of association, but later generations contrasted the solidary and still distinctively gendered women's study club with organizational models and practices (departments, cash exchanges, professionalism, and expertise) appropriated from business and bureaucracy. Over the same period, working-class women were frequently represented in—or at least by—work-based organizations that promoted identities based on employment or economic sector (e.g., the Knights of Labor and the Patrons of Husbandry).

77. Dye (1980, p. 123).

This class-related divergence of organizational repertoires created conditions in which the third proposition may be demonstrated: patterns of organization in response to novel or ambiguous situations should be shaped by a group's existing or desired ties to other groups committed to a particular model of organization. Faced with the task of creating organizations that would include working women, elite female reformers had to choose between models of organization based on work and gender. For as long as they were allied with and financially dependent on the AFL, the WTUL pursued organizationally conservative forms of workplace organizing. When this relationship became strained, the WTUL reconstituted itself around a more explicitly political model, strengthening its ties to other major women's associations. Through these efforts, the distinctively gendered models of organization dominant in the nineteenth century disappeared, only to give way to a political system in which the bureaucratically organized representation of women by women (experts and activists, usually privileged) emerged as the leading edge of social policy expansion in the United States. But even though the reorganization of gender and political identity was incomplete, these changes had far-reaching effects on the institutions of American politics.

Organizational Repertoires and Institutional Change

Through ongoing processes of organizational innovation—the constant search for political advantage or shared identity by trying something new, adopting some alternative model of organization—women's groups helped to create a new system of political institutions. In the place of a political system in which voting had been the central act and identity was grounded in the solidary networks of community and workplace, the beginning of the twentieth century saw the rise of a political regime in which groups claiming to represent categories of persons presented specific demands to legislatures, using the leverage of public opinion, lobbyists, and expertise rather than sheer numbers of votes. Although scholars may well differ over the conservative nature of these developments and their normative status, these changes stand as an important example of profound institutional transformations stemming from regular—not revolutionary—political processes.

Recognizing the importance of a multiplicity of organizational models, recent developments in organization theory and social movement studies help to explain such processes of political change. First, different models of movement organization (and differences in the identities of those organized) mean that some challengers may be more susceptible to the logics of incorporation that characterize a specific political regime. Second, in order to circumvent the disadvantages imposed by a specific regime, popular associations may import models of organization that are already culturally legitimate although not previously recognized as political. By using models of organization that are simultaneously familiar and novel, social movement groups may bring about changes in the taken-for-granted rules about what political organization is and what it is for.

In the United States, the loose-knit "woman movement" of the turn of the century provides an important example of this type of institutional change. Women's groups engaged in an eclectic process of copying and transforming multiple models of organization: "Colleges and social scientists and experts of various kinds can help us in the *matters* upon which we are working, but as to the *ways* of working we have to blaze our own trail."[78] Limited by their exclusion from the organization and practices of electoral politics, women's groups were particularly motivated to discover or invent new channels for their political activities. By drawing upon available alternative models of organization—business methods, state bureaucracy, and lobbies, along with models drawn from education and the professions—women's groups helped to pioneer a distinctively nonelectoral style of social politics. The success of their experiments was such that this new style was quickly appropriated by other political actors, and the historical origins of this model of political organization were forgotten as the system of interest group bargaining came to be seen as natural, indeed as constitutive of American politics.[79]

Women's associations were a source of political change because they were marginal to the existing electoral system, but not so marginal that they were ignored by other political actors. Together with the assumption of organizational heterogeneity—the assumption that a repertoire of organization exists—the presence of differences in political power is fundamental to this account of institutional change. The potential of a challenging group to produce changes in existing institutions is a joint product of the incentives to innovate produced by relative marginality as

78. Winter (1925, p. vi).
79. Moe (1980, p. 2).

well as the visibility and acceptability of those innovations to other political actors. This account of institutional change, however, does not imply that the challenging groups achieved all that they desired. The processes of organizational experimentation that can change the rules of political action do not necessarily alter the substance of political outcomes.

References

Baker, Paula. 1984. "The Domestication of Politics: Women and American Political Society, 1780–1920." *American Historical Review* 89(3): 620–47.

———. 1991. *The Moral Frameworks of Public Life: Gender, Politics, and the State in Rural New York, 1870–1930.* Oxford University Press.

Blair, Karen J. 1980. *The Clubwoman as Feminist: True Womanhood Redefined, 1868–1914.* New York: Holmes and Meier.

Bordin, Ruth. 1981. *Woman and Temperance: The Quest for Power and Liberty, 1873–1900.* Temple University Press.

California State Grange. 1887–1915. *Proceedings of the Annual Convention.*

Catt, Carrie Chapman, and Nettie Rogers Shuler. 1926. *Woman Suffrage and Politics: The Inner Story of the Suffrage Movement.* New York: Scribner's.

Chandler, Alfred D. 1977. *The Visible Hand: The Managerial Revolution in American Business.* Belknap Press of Harvard University Press.

Clawson, Mary Ann. 1985. "Fraternal Orders and Class Formation in the Nineteenth-Century United States." *Comparative Studies in Society and History* 27(4): 672–95.

———. 1989. *Constructing Brotherhood: Class, Gender, and Fraternalism.* Princeton University Press.

Clemens, Elisabeth S. 1993. "Organizational Repertoires and Institutional Change: Women's Groups and the Transformation of U.S. Politics, 1890–1920." *American Journal of Sociology* 98(4): 755–98.

———. 1997. *The People's Lobby: Organizational Innovation and the Rise of Interest Group Politics in the United States, 1890–1925.* University of Chicago Press.

Club Life. 1902–1906. Monthly.

College Equal Suffrage League of Northern California. 1913. *Winning Equal Suffrage in California.* National College Equal Suffrage League.

Commons, John R. [1907] 1967. *Proportional Representation.* New York: Augustus M. Kelley.

Connell, Carol, and Kim Voss. 1990. "Formal Organization and the Fate of Social Movements: Craft Association and Class Alliance in the Knights of Labor." *American Sociological Review* 55(2): 255–69.

Croly, Mrs. J. C. [Jennie June]. 1898. *History of the Women's Club Movement in America.* New York: Henry G. Allen.

Delzell, Ruth. 1919. *The Early History of Women Trade Unionists of America.* Chicago: National Women's Trade Union League of America.

DiMaggio, Paul J., and Walter W. Powell. 1983. "The Iron Cage Revisited: Institutional Isomorphism and Collective Rationality in Organizational Fields." *American Sociological Review* 48(2): 147–60.

————. 1991. "Introduction." In *The New Institutionalism in Organizational Analysis*, edited by Walter W. Powell and Paul J. DiMaggio. University of Chicago Press.

DuBois, Ellen C. 1991. "Harriot Stanton Blatch and the Transformation of Class Relations among Woman Suffragists." In *Gender, Class, Race, and Reform in the Progressive Era*, edited by Noralee Frankel and Nancy S. Dye. Lexington: University Press of Kentucky.

Dye, Nancy Schrom. 1980. *As Equals and as Sisters: Feminism, the Labor Movement, and the Women's Trade Union League of New York*. University of Missouri Press.

Eaves, Lucile. 1910. *A History of California Labor Legislation, with an Introductory Sketch of the San Francisco Labor Movement*. University of California Publications in Economics, 2. University of California Press.

Epstein, Barbara Leslie. 1981. *The Politics of Domesticity: Women, Evangelism, and Temperance in Nineteenth-Century America*. Middletown, Conn.: Wesleyan University Press.

Foner, Philip S. 1979. *Women and the American Labor Movement: From Colonial Times to the Eve of World War I*. Free Press.

Frankel, Noralee, and Nancy S. Dye, eds. 1991. *Gender, Class, Race and Reform in the Progressive Era*. University Press of Kentucky.

Geertz, Clifford. 1973. *The Interpretation of Cultures*. Basic Books.

Gibson, Mary S. 1927. *A Record of Twenty-Five Years of the California Federation of Women's Clubs*. California Federation of Women's Clubs.

Gordon, Linda, ed. 1990. *Women, the State, and Welfare*. University of Wisconsin Press.

Heclo, Hugh. 1974. *Modern Social Politics in Britain and Sweden*. Yale University Press.

Herring, Pendleton. [1929] 1967. *Group Representation before Congress*. New York: Russell and Russell.

Hess, Carla. 1990. "The Construction of Boundaries and Divisions of Labor: Teachers, Workers, and Professionals." Paper presented at the Annual Meetings of the American Political Science Association, San Francisco, Calif.

Hichborn, Franklin. 1911. *Story of the Session of the California Legislature of 1911*. San Francisco: Press of the James H. Barry Company.

Kanter, Rosabeth Moss. 1972. *Commitment and Community: Communes and Utopias in Sociological Perspective*. Harvard University Press.

Kingdon, John W. 1984. *Agendas, Alternatives, and Public Policies*. Boston: Little, Brown.

Ladd-Taylor, Molly. 1991. "Hull House Goes to Washington: Women and the Children's Bureau." In *Gender, Class, Race, and Reform in the Progressive Era*, edited by Noralee Frankel and Nancy S. Dye. University Press of Kentucky.

Landes, Joan B. 1988. *Women and the Public Sphere in the Age of the French Revolution*. Cornell University Press.

Levine, Susan. 1983. "Labor's True Woman: Domesticity and Equal Rights in the Knights of Labor." *Journal of American History* 70(2): 323–39.

Maier, Charles S. 1981. " 'Fictitious Bonds . . . of Wealth and Law': On the Theory and Practice of Interest Representation." In *Organizing Interests in Western Europe: Pluralism, Corporatism, and the Transformation of Politics*, edited by Suzanne Berger. Cambridge University Press.

March, James G., and Johan P. Olsen. 1989. *Rediscovering Institutions: The Organizational Basis of Politics*. Free Press.

Martin, Theodora Penny. 1987. *The Sound of Our Own Voices: Women's Study Clubs, 1860–1910*. Boston: Beacon Press.

Matthews, Lillian R. 1913. *Women in Trade Unions in San Francisco.* University of California Publications in Economics 3(1): 1–100. University of California Press.

McAdam, Doug. 1982. *Political Process and the Development of Black Insurgency, 1930–1970.* University of Chicago Press.

McCarthy, Kathleen. 1982. *Noblesse Oblige: Charity and Cultural Philanthropy in Chicago, 1849–1929.* University of Chicago Press.

McCormick, Richard P. 1986. *The Party Period and Public Policy: American Politics from the Age of Jackson to the Progressive Era.* Oxford University Press.

McGerr, Michael. 1986. *The Decline of Popular Politics: The American North, 1865–1928.* Oxford University Press.

Meyer, John, and Brian Rowan. 1977. "Institutionalized Organizations: Formal Structure as Myth and Ceremony." *American Journal of Sociology* 83: 340–63.

Michels, Robert. [1911] 1962. *Political Parties: A Sociological Study of the Oligarchical Tendencies of Modern Democracy.* Free Press.

Moe, Terry M. 1980. *The Organization of Interests: Incentives and the Internal Dynamics of Political Interest Groups.* University of Chicago Press.

Montgomery, David. 1987. *The Fall of the House of Labor: The Workplace, the State, and American Labor Activism, 1865–1925.* Cambridge University Press.

Muncy, Robyn. 1991. *Creating a Female Dominion in American Reform, 1890–1935.* Oxford University Press.

Nathan, Maud. 1926. *The Story of an Epoch-Making Movement.* Garden City, N.J.: Doubleday, Page.

Park, Maud Wood. 1960. *Front Door Lobby.* Boston: Beacon.

Phelps, Edith M., ed. 1914. *Selected Articles on the Initiative and Referendum.* 3d ed. New York: H. W. Wilson.

Putnam, Robert D. 1993. *Making Democracy Work: Civic Traditions in Modern Italy.* Princeton University Press.

———. 1995. "Tuning In, Tuning Out: The Strange Disappearance of Social Capital in America." *PS: Political Science and Politics* 28(4): 664–83.

Rodgers, Daniel T. 1987. *Contested Truths: Keywords in American Politics since Independence.* Basic Books.

Ruddy, Ella Giles, ed. 1906. *The Mother of Clubs, Caroline M. Seymour Severance: An Estimate and Appreciation.* Los Angeles, Calif.: Baumgardt.

Sander, Kathleen Waters. 1998. *The Business of Charity: The Woman's Exchange Movement, 1832–1900.* University of Illinois Press.

Schmidt, Gertrude. 1933. "History of Labor Legislation in Wisconsin." Ph.D. diss., University of Wisconsin.

Scott, Anne Firor. 1991. *Natural Allies: Women's Associations in American History.* University of Illinois Press.

Shefter, Michael. 1983. "Regional Receptivity to Reform: The Legacy of the Progressive Era." In *Political Parties: Development and Decay,* edited by Louis Maisel and Joseph Cooper. Beverly Hills, Calif.: Sage.

Simons, May Wood. [1912?]. "Woman and the Social Problem." Chicago: Charles H. Kerr and Co. Co-operative [Socialist Party imprint].

Simpson, Anna Pratt. 1909. "Story of the Associated Charities since the Fire of 1906." Reprinted from the San Francisco *Call.*

———. 1915. *Problems Women Solved: Being the Story of the Woman's Board of the Panama-Pacific International Exposition. What Vision, Enthusiasm, Work and Co-operation Accomplished.* San Francisco: Woman's Board.

Sklar, Kathryn Kish. 1985. "Hull House in the 1890s: A Community of Women Reformers." *Signs* 10: 658–77.

Skocpol, Theda. 1992. *Protecting Soldiers and Mothers: The Politics of Social Provision in the United States, 1870s–1920s.* Belknap Press of Harvard University Press.

Skocpol, Theda, and Gretchen Ritter. 1991. "Gender and the Origins of Modern Social Policies in Britain and the United States." *Studies in American Political Development* 5(1): 36–93.

Skowronek, Stephen. 1982. *Building a New American State: The Expansion of National Administrative Capacities, 1877–1920.* Cambridge University Press.

Smith-Rosenberg, Carroll. 1985. *Disorderly Conduct: Visions of Gender in Victorian America.* Oxford University Press.

Spencer, Mrs. Dorcas James. N.d. *A History of the Women's Christian Temperance Union of Northern and Central California.* Oakland, Calif.: West Coast Printing Company.

Swidler, Ann. 1986. "Culture in Action: Symbols and Strategies." *American Sociological Review* 51(2): 273–86.

Thompson, Margaret. 1985. *The "Spider Web": Congress and Lobbying in the Age of Grant.* Cornell University Press.

Tilly, Charles. 1978. *From Mobilization to Revolution.* Englewood Cliffs, N.J.: Prentice-Hall.

———. 1986. *The Contentious French.* Belknap Press of Harvard University Press.

Tripp, Joseph F. 1973. "Progressive Labor Laws in Washington State (1900–1924)." Ph.D. diss., University of Washington.

Van Voris, Jacqueline. 1987. *Carrie Chapman Catt: A Public Life.* New York: Feminist Press.

Verba, Sidney, Kay Lehman Schlozman, and Henry E. Brady. 1995. *Voice and Equality: Civic Voluntarism in American Politics.* Harvard University Press.

Western Woman Voter. 1911–13. Monthly.

Williamson, Mrs. Burton. 1925. "Ladies' Clubs and Societies in Los Angeles in 1892." Reported for the Historical Society of Southern California.

Wilson, Margaret Gibbons. 1979. *The American Woman in Transition: The Urban Influence, 1870–1920.* Westport, Conn.: Greenwood Press.

Winter, Alice Ames. 1925. *The Business of Being a Clubwoman.* New York: The Century Company.

Wisconsin Citizen. 1887–97. Monthly.

Wisconsin Equity News. 1911–17. Biweekly.

Wisconsin Federation of Women's Clubs. 1898–1913. *Proceedings of the Annual Convention.*

Wisconsin Woman Suffrage Scrapbooks. Wisconsin State Historical Society.

Wismer, Otto G. 1928. "Legal Aid Organizations: 'Lobbyists for the Poor.' " *Annals of the American Academy of Political and Social Science* 136 (March): 172–76.

Womans Parliament of Southern California. 1892. "A Magazine of Papers Read at the Womans Parliament Held at Los Angeles, California, November 15–16, 1892." Los Angeles, Calif.: Unity Church League of Los Angeles.

Wood, Mary I. 1912. *The History of the General Federation of Women's Clubs: For the First Twenty-Two Years of Its Organization.* New York: General Federation of Women's Clubs.

4 | National Elections as Institutions for Generating Social Capital

WENDY M. RAHN

JOHN BREHM

NEIL CARLSON

T HE CONCEPT OF social capital has proven to be enormously attractive to scholars in a wide variety of disciplines. Many political scientists have deliberated about how to identify a role for political institutions in the production of social capital. Effective institutions are not just one of the many unintended blessings of a vigorous civil society; rather, political authority that performs well and equitably contributes to the "trust, norms, and networks"[1] that enable people to solve collective action problems.[2] Institutions that require more citizen input may also provide an impetus for people to become engaged in something other than their private lives.[3] In this chapter, we examine national elections as political institutions that may contribute to the production of social capital.

Paper prepared for presentation at the 1997 annual meeting of the American Political Science Association, Washington, D.C., and the Civic Engagement and American Democracy Conference, Portland, Maine, Sept. 26–28, 1997. Data used in this paper can be retrieved from the National Election Studies website: (http://www.umich.edu/~nes). Brehm and Carlson acknowledge the support of the Arts and Sciences Research Council of Duke University. Neither NES nor ASRC bears responsibility for the analysis and interpretations presented.

1. Putnam (1993, p. 167).

2. Kenworthy (1997); Levi (1996); Tarrow (1996).

3. Schneider et al. (1997).

Elections and Social Capital

Once the ballots have been counted, do elections have any lingering effects on the American polity? One way in which the effects of elections persist is through the policy changes that may be enacted as a result of leadership turnover.[4] Our focus, however, is not the direct outcomes of elections, but rather the changes that may be wrought in the larger civic culture as a result of both the practical conduct of elections and their larger symbolic significance. After reviewing the empirical evidence for election-based change in civic attitudes, we present several hypotheses—which are not mutually exclusive—about ways in which elections may improve citizens' orientations toward the larger political community.

Our investigation is founded on two earlier empirical treatments of the origins of social capital in which we examined the reciprocal relationship between elements of the civic culture—namely civic engagement and abstract social trust—and political culture, defined by citizens' attitudes toward government.[5] We believe that some forms of social capital, particularly as manifested in widespread generalized trust, cannot be the product of purely social interaction among citizens. Instead, the performance of political institutions and people's confidence in them can play a large role in generating social solidarity.

We begin by observing that we are studying social capital in an advanced democracy: "A fundamental presumption of democracy is that citizens will feel that collectively, and sometimes even individually, they can intervene in public life to affect the course of their governance. Hence, in a democracy the individual's assessment of whether or not he and his fellow citizens have any influence in politics becomes in effect an assessment of whether or not a definitive feature of the regime is intact."[6] A sense of political efficacy signifies to citizens something about the nature of their society and its political authorities. The most visible sign to citizens that political authority is organized democratically, and hence that they have opportunities for influence, is the regular occurrence of competitive elections.[7]

People's feelings about authorities—in particular, whether these authorities can be trusted—depend in part on whether citizens believe they

4. Brady and Stewart (1991).
5. Brehm and Rahn (1997); Berger and Brehm (1997).
6. Madsen (1978, p. 869).
7. Madsen (1978).

can exercise influence over them. The real or anticipated consequences of citizen control provide democratic leaders with an incentive to behave in a trustworthy manner.[8] Feelings of their own inefficacy may lead citizens to doubt the trustworthiness of their authorities. To the extent that people use their beliefs about authorities to draw inferences about their own status in a group,[9] distrust of government officials undermines a sense of social identification with the larger group, an identification that facilitates trust in other group members. In addition, citizens may reason from their own lack of trust in authorities that other citizens have little incentive to obey the rules voluntarily and therefore that other people cannot be trusted. This is a self-fulfilling prophecy: as the legitimacy of authority erodes, it becomes a less credible third-party enforcer of contracts, its ability to punish "defectors" is reduced, and it is less able to secure voluntary obedience to group rules. In short, it becomes less capable of performing the functions that generate trust.[10]

How does our approach fit into the broader field of work on social capital? There are two central issues of concern: first, can individual responses to surveys convey information about social capital, which is by definition a property of collectives? Second, how does a large-scale institution like a national election produce social capital, which is usually discussed in terms of local or personal contact?

The answer to the first question is crucial if we are to avoid confusion about the concept of social capital. As it is defined by Coleman, "social capital inheres in the structure of relationships between persons and among persons. It is lodged neither in individuals nor in physical implements of production."[11] As Edwards and Foley point out, social capital is "context specific," and individual attitudes (like those measured by public opinion surveys) may not convey the extent to which the trust that is expressed can be "drawn upon" as a capital fund for action, as Coleman described it.[12] Social capital is clearly distinct from portable human capital like the civic skills identified by Verba, Schlozman, and Brady.[13] In recognition of this limitation, we want to stress that survey data indicate the possible presence

8. Levi (forthcoming).
9. Tyler (1997).
10. Levi (forthcoming).
11. James Coleman (1990, p. 302).
12. Edwards and Foley (1998, p. 131).
13. Verba, Schlozman, and Brady (1995).

of social capital; for example, individuals who express generalized trust in others may be able to draw on that trust in specific instances, and it may not be reciprocated. If one construes generalized social trust as a measure of what an ordinary person expects in ordinary interactions with others, then this indicator is a useful marker of general social capital. In this chapter we are interested in the national context, and the survey instruments in question are particularly useful as indicators of social capital in the structure of national polity. Finally, our inclusion of political efficacy as a social-psychological indicator of social capital tests precisely the availability of that capital to "fund" political action. Nevertheless, with our data, some additional error occurs in moving between individual and social levels of analysis.

This sets the stage for the second issue: how exactly can national elections generate social capital? Again, Coleman's analysis provides a useful analogy, characterizing social obligations as "credit slips" that individuals issue to each other. Institutions, such as Coleman's examples of the Cairo marketplace and Southeast Asian rotating credit associations, provide the "social context" and determine the exchange value of these slips. Institutions can diffuse obligations and render them available to a collective. We believe that elections produce a multitude of such obligations and thereby produce detectable quantities of social capital, albeit in a relatively diffuse manner.

Coleman used diagrams to demonstrate the properties of social relationships; we can do the same with elections. A simple diagram (Figure 4-1) represents the network of mutual obligations implicit in the democratic contract. It would be overly idealistic to claim that each link drawn here exists between every voter and every candidate, but such links are implicit in the democratic pact and are reinforced over time. The simplest links are obvious: Voter 1 issues Candidate 1 a "credit slip" for advocating policies Voter 1 supports or for being the kind of person Voter 1 considers a better prospective officeholder; Voter 2 does likewise for Candidate 2. Each link is reciprocal: the candidates likewise make promises and obligate themselves to the voters. But the key to generation of social capital in Coleman's treatment is "closure," the dotted-line relationships that connect triangles and larger shapes in a web of mutual obligation. These, too, exist by virtue of democratic norms of conduct; Voter 1 implicitly agrees to trust Candidate 2 to govern and confirms that Candidate 2 is obligated to respect Voter 1's constitutional rights. Meanwhile, simply by running for office Candidate 1 obligates Candidate 2 to acquiesce in the

Figure 4-1. *"Coleman Diagram" of an Election*

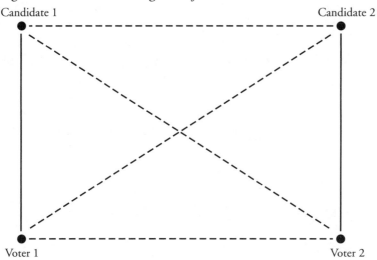

case of her victory and to play by the democratic rules of the game; she likewise implicitly recognizes Voter 2's right to vote against her without risk of retaliation. In effect, regular elections *depersonalize* and *institutionalize* these roles, creating a stock of social capital and making it possible for individuals to act with confidence that mutual obligations will be enforced.

This web of mutual obligations may be diffuse in comparison with those in the Cairo marketplace, but it functions to create a national identity, a "shared citizenship role" in an "imagined community."[14] Indeed, this community may not be restricted to voters and candidates; nonvoters, by virtue of their citizenship, may also be participants in mutual obligations if they abstain out of satisfaction. The web can be further strengthened by the intervention of political parties and civic organizations—to the extent that they act to create further ties of mutual obligation rather than to break them. Note that our approach embraces both of the roles for civic organizations discussed by Skocpol and Fiorina in the introduction to this volume; they may act both as the basis for "popular leverage" on the government and as stimulants of "dense," "apolitical" social ties.

14. Conover and Hicks (forthcoming).

We therefore postulate a model in which beliefs about one's own efficacy, the trustworthiness of political authority, and the trustworthiness of other people are tightly bound together in modern democracies. National elections, as arenas in which these beliefs are enacted, may provide an important institutional mechanism for undergirding the political-cultural attitudes associated with high levels of social capital, even in the absence of genuine face-to-face interaction. This is especially likely to be true in democracies, such as the United States, where political institutions and values are central components of citizens' national identities.[15]

The 1996 Election: Evidence for Significant Individual-Level Change

Fortunately, our account of elections can be studied using national survey data. In 1996, the American National Election Studies (NES) asked several questions relevant to our argument in both its pre- and postelection interviews (see Appendix 4A for coding of variables). Because these interviews were conducted with the same people, we can look for individual-level attitude change and its direction. Three questions dealt with respondents' perceptions of what most people are like—whether they were generally trustworthy, fair, or similar to themselves in basic values and beliefs. Another question asked about the respondents' level of influence in governmental decisionmaking, a sentiment that political scientists refer to as "external efficacy."[16] A fifth question asked again how often government could be trusted to do the right thing.[17] Tables 4-1a to 4-1e tabulate the pre- and postelection responses to these five questions.[18] There was some net change in a positive direction for four of the five questions, especially on general trust. Before the election, only 40 percent

15. Almond and Verba ([1963] 1989), Spillman (1997).

16. Craig, Niemi, and Silver (1990).

17. See Appendix 4A for exact question wording and variable numbers.

18. To simplify the presentation of the crosstabs, the government trust questions were recoded so that volunteered responses of "never" were included with the "only some of the time" responses. For the similarity questions, responses of "not very similar" and "not at all similar" were collapsed into one category, and for the external efficacy items, "strongly agree" and "agree" were collapsed into a single "inefficacious" category, while responses of "strongly disagree" or "disagree" were collapsed into one "efficacious" category. In our multivariate analysis, however, we retain the original categories of these variables.

of those interviewed reported that most people could be trusted, while over half of the postelection respondents offered a trusting response.[19] Most remarkable is that there was essentially no increase in distrust. Very few individuals who were trusting in the first wave changed their views, but over a quarter of initially cautious respondents were trusters in the postelection interview. The question about whether people are fair does not demonstrate as much net change, but the pattern is similar. The external efficacy and government trust items also show small net changes in a positive direction, with more pronounced improvement in people's perceptions of their own efficacy. Unlike the social trust questions, however, these two orientations show more substantial change in a "backward" direction; that is, a sizable minority of respondents who were initially trusting of government or believed their own efforts were efficacious became less so in the postelection interview. The level of perceived similarity of others to self remained virtually unchanged in the two interviews, though responses were less stable. Although the question does not demonstrate an election effect, we will later use the perceived similarity question to test specific hypotheses about the origins of social solidarity in modern democratic systems.

Election-Based Explanations for Change

The object of study for the present analysis is *change* in social trust, trust in government, and perceptions of external efficacy from the pre- to postelection interview.[20] Although it is impossible to fully isolate the election and campaign themselves as causes, the NES pre- and postelection data constitute a powerful quasi-experimental control. It is hard to imagine any other cause with impact wide and ubiquitous enough to account for broad shifts in social trust over a short two-month period

19. Among pre-election respondents, 38.7 percent trusted most people, while 61.3 percent were more cautious (unweighted). This compares to 33.9 percent and 60.9 percent, respectively, in the 1996 General Social Survey, another in-person national probability survey, which was conducted in the spring. The GSS codes a "depends" response, which was given by 5.2 percent of their sample. By comparison, in the 1992 NES postelection interview, almost 45 percent gave the trusting response. In the 1991 GSS, trusters were 40.5 percent of the sample, and in the 1993 GSS, 37.3 percent. In fact, the higher rates of trust recorded in the NES data inspired the idea that elections might have social-capital-enhancing effects.

20. Brehm and Rahn (1997).

Table 4-1. *Results of National Survey of People's Pre- and Postelection Views*[a]

1a. Social Trust of Others

| | Pre-election | | |
	Trusting	Cautious	Totals
Postelection			
Trusting	523	243	766
	86.9%	*26.8%*	*50.8%*
Cautious	79	663	742
	13.1	*73.2*	*49.2*
Totals	602	906	1,508
	39.9	*60.1*	*100*

Tau-b = .59   Pearson's r = .59

1b. Fairness of Others

| | Pre-election | | |
	Fair	Takes advantage	Totals
Postelection			
Fair	787	173	960
	84.9%	*30.4%*	*64.2%*
Takes advantage	140	396	536
	15.1	*69.6*	*35.8*
Totals	927	569	1,496
	62.0	*38.0*	*100*

Tau-b = .55   Pearson's r = .55

1c. Perceived Similarity to Others

| | Pre-election | | | |
	Very	Somewhat	Not	Totals
Postelection				
Very similar	70	100	21	191
	37.0%	*9.7%*	*7.3%*	*12.7%*
Somewhat similar	99	800	137	1,036
	52.4	*77.9*	*47.6*	*68.9*
Not similar	20	127	130	277
	10.6	*12.4*	*45.1*	*18.4*
Totals	189	1,027	288	1,504
	12.6	*68.3*	*19.1*	*100*

Tau-b = .31   Pearson's r = .33

Table 4-1. *(continued)*

1d. External Efficacy

	Pre-election			
	Efficacious	*Neutral*	*Inefficacious*	*Totals*
Postelection				
Efficacious	123	47	221	691
	71.6%	*35.1%*	*27.7%*	*45.3%*
Neutral	45	29	75	149
	7.6	*21.6*	*9.4*	*9.8*
Inefficacious	123	58	503	684
	20.8	*43.3*	*63.0*	*44.0*
Totals	591	134	799	1,524
	38.8	*8.8*	*52.4*	*100*
Tau-b = .40	*Pearson's r = .43*			

1e. Trust in Government

	Pre-election			
	Always	*Most*	*Only some*	*Totals*
Postelection				
Always	9	14	11	34
	23.1%	*3.5%*	*1.0%*	*2.2%*
Most	20	243	194	457
	51.3	*60.6*	*18.0*	*30.1*
Only some	10	144	872	1,026
	25.6	*35.9*	*81.0*	*67.6*
Totals	39	401	1,077	1,517
	2.6	*26.4*	*71.0*	*100*
Tau-b = .44	*Pearson's r = .44*			

Source: American National Election Study, 1996.

a. All percentages reflect the percentage of those from the pre-election category falling into the postelection category.

(the pre-election interview was administered from September 3 to November 4).[21]

Moreover, we believe that the relatively unexciting, low turnout election of 1996 provided a good opportunity to test the effect of elections in general, since there were neither powerful forces of social unrest to reduce the hypothetical benefits of elections nor a rampant political euphoria to boost them. Table 4-2 documents a number of measures of the most recent presidential elections, drawn from the NES. Respondents in 1996 reported being less interested in the campaign than in 1992, but more than in other recent years. Respondents reported watching slightly less TV coverage of the campaign, and a smaller percentage reported voting, but more reported being contacted by a political party, being better informed about politics, and having found at least one positive trait for each presidential candidate. The differences between the 1996 election and prior recent elections were generally small and inconsistent. In effect, the 1996 election may be as typical an election as possible until future cases with the same variables allow us to control for different election settings.

There are at least four classes of potential hypotheses accounting for change: political mobilization, campaign involvement, qualities of the campaign or candidates, and the election ritual.

Political Mobilization

Our hypothesis about the effects of political mobilization on political participation is somewhat different from the hypotheses of earlier examinations.[22] Like many others who write on social capital, we draw on Tocqueville's analysis in *Democracy in America* for inspiration. Discussions of Tocqueville often overlook the primacy of politics, politicians, and political associations as the engines of vigorous civil society in his think-

---

21. One possible spurious cause is the NES itself, of course: perhaps respondents become more trusting simply as a result of a pleasant experience with the survey interviewer. As a test for this reactivity effect, the model controls for the interviewer's pre-election assessments of the respondent's level of interest and cooperativeness. If the respondents were inclined to be primed by the pre-election survey to think more positively of others, we would expect greater changes among those who seemed more interested and cooperative in the pre-election interview. The results were generally disconfirming of such a reactivity effect (see Table 4-3). Apparent interest was positively related only to change in social trust and unrelated otherwise. Pre-election cooperation was *negatively* related only to change in social trust. Furthermore, none of the substantive coefficients were affected by the inclusion of the interviewer ratings.

22. See chiefly Rosenstone and Hansen (1993).

Table 4-2. *Comparison of 1996 Survey Responses with Those of Previous Elections*
Percent

Variable	Value	1996	1992	1988	1984	1980
Interest in campaign	Very much interested	31.9	38.9	27.9	28.4	29.8
	Somewhat interested	52.2	43.8	47.2	46.8	44.2
	Not very interested	15.9	17.3	25.0	24.8	26.0
Campaign TV consumption	Viewed one or more programs	75.7	88.9	n.a.	86.1	85.9
Turnout	Respondent reported voting	68.6	75.4	69.7	73.6	71.4
Did a party contact respondent?	Yes	29.2	20.1	23.6	23.7	24.4
Positive trait sum	Saw two positive traits in both major candidates	17.7	12.6			
	Saw at least one positive trait in both major candidates	84.8	60.1			
Political knowledge	Mean number of correct IDs	1.96	1.51			

Source: American National Election Studies, 1980–96.

n.a. Not available

ing.[23] Political associations were "the great free schools to which all citizens come to be taught the general theory of association."[24] And elections, despite "the dishonorable means often used by candidates and the calumnies spread by their enemies," were a means of bringing people together, which Tocqueville viewed as useful in combating individualism and the social isolation it encouraged: "Eagerness to be elected may, for the moment, make particular men fight each other, but in the long run, this same aspiration induces mutual helpfulness on the part of all; and while it may happen that the accident of an election estranges two friends, the electoral system forges permanent links between a great number of citizens who might otherwise have remained forever strangers to one another."[25]

In other words, political mobilization may contribute to social capital—not because it stimulates people to become involved in the political process (which it surely does)[26], but because it brings people into contact who otherwise would have no reason to meet. Thus, social capital may be created as a by-product of activities undertaken for other purposes, as Coleman argued;[27] if, for example, a party were added to Figure 4-1, it could close a triangle between Voter 1 and Candidate 1, creating additional mutual obligations and reinforcing the connection between citizen and government. The "permanent links" Tocqueville describes are not elucidated in his discussion, but we may assume that he was referring to the functional relationship supporters of candidates have to each other; they need each other in order to achieve the same goal.

This Tocquevillean hypothesis also presents the potential for reconciliation between Putnam and one of his most insightful critics, Sydney Tarrow. Tarrow proposes that the "operative cause" of differences in government performance between northern and southern Italy is "neither cultural nor associational but political," because "civic competence was deliberately developed after World War II as a symbol of the left-wing parties' governing capacity."[28] Our hypothesis suggests that political mobilization *is* a political-cultural phenomenon. Tarrow and Putnam are both right: political mobilization itself both directly affects institutional performance and creates and maintains social capital. We test this generic

---

23. Foley and Edwards (1997).
24. Tocqueville ([1835, 1840] 1969, p. 522).
25. Ibid. (p. 510).
26. See Rosenstone and Hansen (1993).
27. James Coleman (1990).
28. Tarrow (1996, p. 394).

mobilization hypothesis by including in our model whether respondents were urged to register or turn out to vote.

Political parties, in particular, forge links among people that are extensive both geographically and psychologically. Though this form of party mobilization, whose historic origins coincide with Tocqueville's travels to America, risks becoming anachronistic in today's candidate-centered political world,[29] still a substantial fraction of people (ranging 5–20 percent in other surveys to almost 30 percent in the 1996 NES data) are contacted by the political parties in election years. In fact, party mobilization was up considerably in 1996 (29.2 percent unweighted) over 1992 (20.1 percent), and resembled earlier peaks in 1972 and in two off-year elections, 1978 and 1982 (see Figure 4-2). And party contact may rise again in the future: the unexpected success of Democratic candidates in the 1998 midterm elections produced a resurgence of interest in grassroots, in-person mobilization, which many media observers credit with fueling the Democrats' gains. A general long-term trend is not readily discernible, but our statistical model provides some insight by testing the effects of party contact.

In the type of contact initiated by party representatives, people interact primarily on the basis of their *shared citizenship role*, which as a common political identity may facilitate a type of trust that does not depend on personal ties to specific group members, but rather is based on an "imagined community" of members.[30] Such depersonalized trust, which is reinforced by the institutionalized rules that govern elections, may be a prerequisite for democratic processes, given that the nature of the contacts between citizens and parties can involve conflicts of opinion. Nonparty forms of campaign contact may also have an impact on feelings of trust, but because contacts are often initiated by interests that are more narrowly drawn than the political parties, their potential to form "permanent linkages" among people may be limited. In our empirical model, we compare party and nonparty forms of campaign contact.

Campaign Involvement

We distinguish three ways in which campaigns may involve citizens: psychologically, behaviorally, and through the use of the ballot box.

29. See Aldrich (1995) on the development of the modern mass political party. See also John Coleman (1996).

30. Conover and Hicks (forthcoming).

Figure 4-2. *Party Contact in Election Years, 1956–96*

Percent contacted

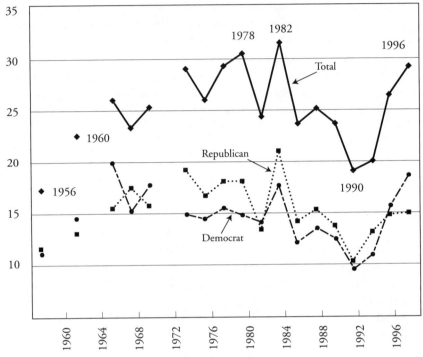

Source: American National Election Studies, 1956-96.

Campaigns aim to attract people's attention, and the more "noise" the better, according to some analysts.[31] Some campaigns do this better than others. For example, in 1992 interest in the campaign—due to the off-again, on-again Perot candidacy, the state of the economy, the closeness of the race, and innovations in campaign communication, among other things—grew steadily throughout the spring and summer, peaking right before election day and helping to reverse the two-decade slide in turn-out.[32] Interest in the 1996 campaign, as measured in the NES pre-election interview, was down considerably from 1992; only 27.2 percent reported being "very interested," whereas 39.5 percent had done so four years earlier

31. E.g., Popkin (1991).
32. Frankovic (1993); Nichols and Beck (1995); Rosenstone et al. (1993).

(see Table 4-2). We operationalize campaign interest as a latent variable, "psychological engagement," in our model (see Appendix 4-B for details on this and other latent variables).

By engaging people in the process of selecting leadership, campaigns may make people feel more connected to the political process. Election campaigns also provide people with ways to participate in politics, from placing a yard sign in their lawn to attending a rally for a favorite candidate. These activities may provide tangible evidence of one's potential to influence election outcomes and therefore contribute to more positive assessments of the political system. This variety of participation is constructed as the latent variable "behavioral engagement" in the model.

Finally, by providing people with the opportunity to vote, elections provide citizens with a means of influence, however blunt. Simply going to vote may remind people that they have that opportunity. In addition, to the extent that voting is also accompanied by social celebration, physically turning up at the voting place may also serve to integrate people into the community.[33]

QUALITIES OF THE CAMPAIGN, THE CANDIDATES, AND WINNING OR LOSING
Another way in which campaigns are not created equal is in their "quality," a purposely vague term that we use to encompass several different influences. For example, some contests are more vigorously contested than others. High-intensity campaigns provide voters with better information and allow them to base their choices on more substantive criteria. They also occasion more "noise" and so may engage voters in the process to a greater degree. In part, these qualities may be mediated through indicators of psychological and behavioral involvement discussed above, but they may also operate directly. We use an aggregate measure of the percentage vote margin between incumbent and challenging congressional candidates, imputed to the NES respondents by congressional district, to test this hypothesis.

Some campaigns may also feature "better" candidates. We focus on the presidential candidates, since the attitudes we are studying have the national political community as their focus. Rosenstone and Hansen find that turnout is stimulated when people have more favorable impressions of their preferred candidate,[34] and Marcus and MacKuen find that positive

33. Pomper and Sernekos (1989).
34. Rosenstone and Hansen (1993); see also Rosenstone et al. (1993).

feelings about both candidates lead to more interest in the campaign.[35] Also relevant is the work of Citrin and colleagues, which shows that the impressions citizens have of their political leaders' personal traits are linked to their overall trust in government;[36] more positive assessments of leadership qualities promote more faith that government is in capable hands. Just as a hard-fought game between good opponents may leave sports fans with more appreciation for the institution of the game itself, a presidential race may lead to more attachment to the institutions that govern the contest if citizens find that both contenders are worthy of respect at the end of the battle. The NES allows us to apply this hypothesis with trait evaluations of Bill Clinton and Bob Dole.

Finally, some have argued that citizens' sentiments about the political community are based on whether they are on the winning or losing side.[37] Anderson and Guillory argue, however, that institutional arrangements, in particular, systems that are characterized by consensual institutions, can act as a buffer to some of the discontent.[38] Although the United States has majoritarian rather than consensual institutions, we believe that elections are institutions in which differences are settled according to established normative rules and that therefore one of their chief functions is to bring the losers back into the community.[39] Thus, though we explicitly test for the potential that seeing one's preferred candidate lose can diminish support for the political community and its members, our expectation is that not getting what one wants is much less important than purely utilitarian accounts of civic support would suggest.

RITUAL OF SOLIDARITY   Some analysts have taken a more sociological perspective on elections, viewing them as rituals of social integration.[40] Campaigns, for example, can "bless" the winner, infuse a sense of hopefulness in the citizenry, restore institutional legitimacy, and bring people together.[41] Some view the "spectacular" aspect of elections darkly, as institutions that delude and hoodwink citizens. Edelman, for example, writes that the campaign "encourages acceptance of a myth by the masses of

35. Marcus and MacKuen (1993).
36. Citrin and Green (1986); Luks and Citrin (1997).
37. Clark and Acock (1989); Anderson and Guillory (1997).
38. Anderson and Guillory (1997); see also Lijphart (1984).
39. Nadeau and Blais (1993).
40. Edelman (1964, 1971); Bennett (1992).
41. Zullow (1994).

political spectators: a myth of protected status and of policies based upon an objective standard of equity rather than relative bargaining resources."[42] And Weissberg, finding no "reality-based" reason for feelings of political efficacy, concludes that such sentiments are illusionary, "a convenient set of beliefs protecting elites from mass dissatisfaction."[43] Our perspective on the ritualistic aspect of elections is different: theorists of decisionmaking argue that symbols allow individuals to come to believe that the decisions they make are important and worthy of their care.[44]

What would we expect to see if indeed elections functioned in part as rituals? We advance several hypotheses, drawing on some of Emile Durkheim's classic works on the nature of social cohesion: the idea that "representative rites" activate collective beliefs; that because individuals vary in the extent to which they are socially integrated their exposure to the ritual also varies; and that the interaction of people with others who occupy different social roles leads to "organic solidarity." Elections may function as religious rites, but we claim that the normative beliefs embedded in the enactment of the election "rite" will not affect everyone equally.

In *Elementary Forms of Religious Life*, Durkheim argued that religion was "more than the idea of gods or spirits."[45] In any society, even modern ones, he said, religion consists of a set of beliefs about the nature of the sacred, which he often called "collective representations," and a set of rites, which are "rules of conduct which prescribe how a man should comport himself in the presence of these sacred objects."[46] Durkheim divided religious rites into two categories, negative and positive, and further specified specific types of rites within each class. Elections, in our view, take the form of *representative rites*, the function of which is to activate the impor-

---

42. Edelman (1971, p. 22).

43. Weissberg (1975, p. 486); see also Ginsberg and Weissberg (1978). Clark and Acock (1989) attempt to distinguish between what they call the "pure participation" and "outcome-contingent" effects on political efficacy. Pure participation refers to the effects of participating per se on support for the political system. The argument is that people who participate (even if they do not get the outcome they desire) need to rationalize such behavior in terms of normative beliefs about citizen influence. On the other hand, people who participate *and* get what they want adjust their efficacy beliefs on the basis of having achieved their desired outcome. In our model, we include both of these effects. Our conclusions are somewhat at odds with theirs but are very consistent with Ginsberg and Weissberg 1978.

44. E.g., March and Olsen (1989); Feldman and March (1981).

45. Durkheim ([1915] 1976).

46. Ibid. (p. 41).

tant beliefs of the collective: "The mythology of a group is the system of beliefs common to this group. The traditions whose memory it perpetuates express the way in which society represents man and the world. . . . So the rite serves and can serve only to sustain the vitality of these beliefs, to keep them from being effaced from memory, and, in sum, to revivify the most essential elements of the collective consciousness. Through it, the group periodically renews the sentiment which it has of itself and of its unity; at the same time, individuals are strengthened in their social natures."[47]

As we discussed above, belief in political efficacy is the cornerstone of the psychology of democracy. The election rite, then, should act to increase social solidarity if it is effective in reinforcing these beliefs. As an indicator of social bonds, the "trust in people" questions do seem to evince the pattern (a unidirectional shift) that we would expect to see if some event, which we believe is the election, increased social cohesion.

We do not expect all election rituals to be equally effective or that all people are equally subject to the binding forces that rituals create.[48] The degree to which the ritual is able to promote a common focus of attention among participants will vary. With respect to elections, this means that some measures of campaign involvement, such as interest in the election, may also serve as indicators of the quality of the ritual. In other works (most notably *Suicide*),[49] Durkheim clearly recognizes that there is variation in the extent to which individuals are integrated into society. Some people internalize the beliefs that are represented in the election rite more than others, and these people will more likely have them reawakened by the pageantry of the process. What sorts of people are most likely to be stirred?

We must begin with education, for reasons that have been articulated by others and analyzed extensively by Durkheim himself. For example,

---

47. Ibid. (p. 375).

48. Our perspective on rituals departs somewhat from a Durkheimian tradition that emphasizes the physical gathering of a group of people and their common interaction, which culminates in a shared emotional feeling. Modern elections involve more of an "imagined community" than a face-to-face community (Anderson 1983). The mass media, however, may allow people to imagine their communion even though they are not assembled in the same location, and those psychological connections may allow people to participate in the ritual vicariously rather than directly (Dayan and Katz 1992). It may be, of course, that the resulting solidarity is less intense and more abstract than the bonding that occurs in real places such as sports stadiums and church sanctuaries, or even airplanes. But the citizen identity enacted through either real or vicarious participation is more extensive than these localized identities, and so the aggregate increase in solidarity is potentially great.

49. Durkheim ([1897] 1951).

Nie, Junn, and Stehlik-Barry argue that one of the chief functions of education is to produce what they call *democratic enlightenment,* "those qualities of citizenship that encourage understanding of and adherence to norms and principles of democracy. . . . Enlightenment signifies an understanding of and commitment to the rules of the democratic game and tempers the unbridled pursuit of self-interested political engagement."[50] One of the major outcomes of democratic enlightenment is increased knowledge about politics.[51] Therefore, more political knowledge should lead to greater sensitivity to the collective sentiments aroused by the election. We operationalize political knowledge with a measure constructed from the survey respondents' ability to identify the offices held by four major political figures.

For further hypotheses, we turn to Durkheim's opus *The Division of Labor in Society,* in which he advanced a theory of two types of societies, one based on mechanical solidarity, and the other on organic solidarity.[52] The former corresponds roughly to Granovetter's notion of "strong ties," the latter to "weak ties."[53] Strong ties involve individuals in relationships based on homogeneity, propinquity, and proximity. The ratio of common to uniquely held beliefs is very high, and thus it is relatively easy—"mechanical"—to link individuals to society as a whole because they share so much. Organic solidarity is a product of the division of labor: specialization leads individuals to recognize their need for others and to develop constructive relationships. This, of course, reflects the same basic theoretical mechanism as Tocqueville's thinking on political mobilization discussed above. Weak ties can enable communities to be cohesive even in the absence of the intimacy and emotional intensity found in close interpersonal relationships.[54]

Of course, these are ideal types. Social integration in real societies may involve mechanisms of both mechanical and organic solidarity. If elections produce higher levels of mechanical solidarity, then people whose social connections are more traditional, based on, for example, marriage or proximity, should exhibit more change in a trusting direction. In the model below, a latent variable of "social connectedness" tests this hypothesis. In

---

50. Nie, Junn, and Stehlik-Barry (1996, p. 6).

51. Nie, Junn, and Stehlik-Barry (1996); Delli Carpini and Keeter (1996).

52. Durkheim ([1893] 1984).

53. Granovetter (1973).

54. Ibid.; see also Newton (1997) for a similar discussion with respect to social capital and trust.

addition, people who perceive a great deal of similarity between themselves and others should be more susceptible to election influences.[55]

The opposing hypothesis is that elections produce the "advanced," organic variety of solidarity. This approach blunts to some extent the negative appraisal of elections by Edelman and others, since it predicts real, substantive interdependence among individual members of the voting public, based upon individual differences of opinion and ability and not upon mythical similarities—a sort of political division of labor. Durkheim's conceptions of solidarity are thus generally consistent with the web of mutual obligations that constitutes social capital as described by Coleman.[56] We operationalize this hypothesis by testing for the effects of civic engagement (membership in voluntary associations of many different types).

The Model

Before turning to the results, here is a brief review of our four classes of hypotheses, mechanisms through which national elections may stimulate improvements in attitudes reflective of social capital.

—Political mobilization: Elections stimulate participation and encourage interactions among people who may not ordinarily meet. Interaction helps to build trust in others and in government and to instill a greater sense of efficacy.

—Campaign involvement: Psychological or behavioral engagement with the campaign, or perhaps the simple act of voting itself, may cause people to feel more connected with politics, increasing both trust and feelings of efficacy.

—Qualities of the campaign: The positive (or negative) attributes of the candidates and/or the campaign may induce more (or less) confidence in the process.

—Campaigns as rituals: The ritualistic aspects of campaigns can lead to increases in abstract social trust by reinforcing mechanical or organic solidarity.

---

55. The fact that the election did not result in any net increase in people's perceived similarity to others (see Table 4-1c) suggests that its solidarity-enhancing effect did not operate through this mechanism. Nevertheless, those who see similarities between themselves and others may still show greater change in a trusting direction than those who do not.

56. James Coleman (1990).

Each of these hypotheses overlaps with the others. For example, mobilization is a means to stimulate greater behavioral engagement, and qualities of the campaign affect the extent to which people are psychologically engaged. If one observes high levels of trust among those who are engaged, one would want to know whether they were also mobilized. The only way to adjudicate among competing hypotheses is to measure and model the change explicitly. The remainder of this chapter engages in such a multivariate analysis, beginning in this section with an explication of the model. Subsequent sections contain a discussion of our findings.

The graphical equivalent of our statistical model appears in Figure 4-3. Estimating the model involves regressing each of the postelection measures on the equivalent pre-election measure (e.g., postelection trust in people regressed on pre-election trust in people), the contemporaneous measures of the remaining endogenous measures (in this example, postelection trust in government and postelection feelings of efficacy), and pre- and postelection measures of the causes we hypothesize might account for the increase in the dependent analysis. The coefficients on the lagged dependent variables measure the "stability" of the variable over the pre- to postelection interviews, and the coefficients on other variables in the model measure the extent to which each variable accounts for *change* in the dependent variable.[57]

This design has two advantages: first, and most relevant, the structure explicitly permits analysis of change in the variables. We already know that respondents, in general, became more trusting after the election; an explicit model of change is the best method to separate the effects of competing explanations. Second, we can better establish causal ordering. Our prior analysis demonstrated with cross-sectional data that individuals who trust others tend to trust government, and vice versa.[58] But it is impossible with the cross-sectional approach to demonstrate that change in social trust *causes* change in trust in government; one of the key requirements for a demonstration of causality is time-ordering of the variables, and only a panel approach, such as we present here, can establish the sequence of events for particular individuals.

We focus our remaining discussion on the results from the structural model. (The discussion of the measurement model analysis is in Appendix 4-B.)

57. Markus (1979); Finkel (1995).
58. Brehm and Rahn (1997).

Figure 4-3. *Model of Structural Equation Core Variables*

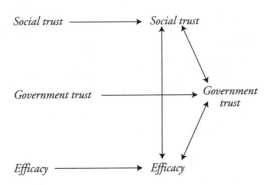

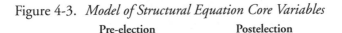

Results: Structural Equations Estimates

What accounts for the increase in trust discussed at the outset of this chapter? The structural equations estimates provide us with the ability to discriminate among the competing explanations. Table 4-3 displays the structural equations results for each of the postelection measures of trust and efficacy. The "stability" coefficients, or the coefficients on the lagged term for each model, confirm the impressions provided by Table 4-1. There is some stability from pre- to postelection, but also some change (i.e., the stability coefficients are all well under 1.0); explicating the sources of this change is of most interest to us.

Before we turn to an evaluation of our hypotheses, however, it is worth noting the coefficients that represent the endogenous relationships among the three dependent variables. In general, these relationships support the web of attitudinal connections that were sketched in the opening section of this chapter. Feelings of efficacy have a modestly strong and positive effect on social trust: the more that citizens believed that they could influence the actions of government, the more trusting of other people they became from the pre-election survey to the postelection survey. Government trust, too, had a positive effect on social trust. Trust in other people positively affects people's trust in government: people who were trusting of others became more trusting of government between the pre- and postelection surveys. Both trust in government and trust in people led to a significant increase in the respondent's sense of efficacy. All of the statistically significant coefficients were positive: trusters became more trusting and believed that they were more efficacious; those who felt efficacious became more trusting. As we argued, efficacy beliefs constitute the core normative apparatus of democracy, an essential component of Americans' civil religion. However, we did not find evidence that a high sense of efficacy affected the electoral change in trust in government—the only nonsignificant coefficient in the endogenous core of the model. Consistent with the notion that elections provide a ritual for renewing common bonds, those who more strongly adhered to the norms of democracy also became more attached to fellow members of the national political community. The reciprocal path was also true. Those who felt greater levels of social cohesion become more attached to the beliefs that underlie the political system. Government trust and social trust were in a similar feedback loop.

Evaluation of Hypotheses

We offered four different perspectives on the role of elections in generating social capital, and each of the three equations provides us with a further opportunity to assess what causes trust and feelings of efficacy to increase, independent of the endogenous relationships among the three. Rather than proceeding through every coefficient in the table, we summarize how each class of explanations fares, occasionally elaborating on relationships we find particularly interesting.

Campaign Mobilization

In general, mobilization does not appear to be particularly important for social capital, with one exception: contact by political parties. The effect of being contacted by a party is about half the size of trust in government and two-thirds the size of feelings of efficacy. Although the effect is smaller, it is nonnegligible, given that almost 30 percent of NES respondents reported that they were contacted by a political party during the 1996 campaign. Tocqueville's intuition about the importance of political parties in "forging links" among people appears to have been largely correct, as does Tarrow's speculation;[59] indeed, membership in political

59. Tarrow (1996).

Table 4-3. *Structural Equation Estimates for Models of Change in Trust and Feelings of Efficacy, 1996*[a]

	Social trust (postelection)	Government trust (postelection)	Sense of efficacy (postelection)
Lagged variables (stability coefficients)			
Social trust (pre-election)	0.54** (0.03)		
Government trust (pre-election)		0.34** (0.03)	
Sense of efficacy (pre-election)			0.42** (0.03)
Endogenous core			
Social trust (postelection)		0.14* (0.06)	0.19** (0.05)
Government trust (postelection)	0.10* (0.06)		0.13** (0.06)
Efficacy (postelection)	0.07* (0.06)	0.03 (0.08)	
Campaign mobilization			
Respondent was contacted by a party	0.05** (0.02)	−0.04 (0.03)	−0.01 (0.03)
Respondent was contacted by a non-party group	−0.02 (0.03)	−0.01 (0.03)	0.00 (0.03)
Respondent was encouraged to register or to vote	−0.01 (0.02)	0.02 (0.03)	0.05 (0.03)
Campaign involvement			
Respondent was behaviorally engaged	−0.03 (0.02)	.00 (0.03)	−0.02 (0.03)
Respondent was psychologically engaged	−0.06** (0.03)	0.07* (0.04)	0.07* (0.04)
Respondent voted	−0.05 (0.03)	−0.04 (0.04)	0.08** (0.04)
Qualities of the campaign			
Respondent voted for Dole	0.07** (0.03)	−0.04 (0.04)	−0.02 (0.03)
Respondent said both candidates had positive traits		0.11** (0.03)	
Vote margin between incumbent and challenging congressional candidates			0.02 (0.03)

Table 4-3. *(continued)*

	Social trust (postelection)	Government trust (postelection)	Sense of efficacy (postelection)
Ritual			
Civic engagement	0.09**		
	(0.04)		
Social connectedness	−0.02		
	(0.03)		
Similarity to others	0.04**		
	(0.02)		
Political knowledge	0.13**	−0.11**	0.06*
	(0.03)	(0.04)	(0.03)
Controls			
Is U.S. stronger?		0.07**	
		(0.03)	
Will standard of living improve?		0.05*	
		(0.03)	
Does government policy improve economy?		0.04	
		(0.03)	
Did Clinton increase deficit?		0.01	
		(0.03)	
Did Clinton increase taxes?		0.00	
		(0.03)	
Economic assessment		0.07*	
		(0.03)	
Personal finances		0.05	
		(0.03)	
Family income (thousands of dollars)			0.06*
			(0.03)
Days after election	−0.01	−0.01	0.02
	(0.03)	(0.03)	(0.03)
Cooperativeness (pre-election)	−0.06**	−0.01	−0.01
	(0.03)	(0.04)	(0.03)
Interest in interview (pre-election)	0.12**	−0.02	0.01
	(0.03)	(0.04)	(0.04)
Partisanship	0.00	0.00	0.00
	(0.03)	(0.03)	(0.03)

Source: American National Election Studies, 1996.

a. Cell entries are unstandardized coefficients from a structural equation model; latent variables were generated by a separate confirmatory factor analysis (see Appendix 4B). Standard errors appear in parentheses below coefficients. Asterisks mark coefficients where $p < .05$ in a one-tailed test (*) or a two-tailed test (**).

parties is itself a strong indicator of civic engagement (see Appendix 4-B). Party contact appears to strengthen community through the "apolitical" function of social trust, rather than by increasing trust in government or a sense of political efficacy; both of the latter have negative signs but are insignificant. These results are explicable. In the government trust equation, we controlled for people's perceptions of the major candidates and of the country's economic and foreign policy condition; the residual effects of party contact once those factors were removed may have to do with competition rather than national solidarity. Similarly, party contact had a negligible effect on efficacy once the effects of voting, engagement in the campaign, and political knowledge were controlled. The verifiable mechanism is the increased trust produced by personal interaction between the party representative and the citizen, consistent with the hypothesis.

Campaign Involvement

The second hypothesis to account for the change in trust and feelings of efficacy revolved around campaign involvement: when people are psychologically or behaviorally engaged in a campaign, or perhaps even to such a simple degree as by the act of voting itself, they feel more connected with the political process and thus more trusting and efficacious. The evidence in the present analysis provides only mixed and contradictory support for this hypothesis. As anticipated by earlier analyses,[60] turning out to vote did boost respondents' sense of efficacy. However, it did not increase either form of trust. Thus, while voting is desirable for many different reasons, it does not appear to be an important mechanism through which elections enhance social capital. Similar to the analysis of party contact above, once civic engagement and other indicators are controlled for, turnout may simply be an indicator of protest or discontent, thus slightly decreasing trust in others.

Psychological engagement in the campaign also appears to produce mixed effects. It led to greater trust in government and, not significantly, to feelings of efficacy, but it reduced social trust. It is impossible to discern from just one election whether this negative sign is due to the mostly negative campaign environment—both television news and the candidates' ads were the among the most negative in recent history.[61] Again, this

60. E.g., Clark and Acock (1989); Ginsberg and Weissberg (1978).
61. Bartels (1997).

may be explained by the fact that in this equation we are controlling for the participatory predisposition indicated by civic engagement; independent of this predisposition, psychological engagement's effects may be an indicator of a cautious individual or, as suggested, the result of the negative content of media coverage.

Qualities of the Campaign

The third hypothesis was that the qualities of the campaign would boost trust and feelings of efficacy: the attributes of the candidates and/or the campaign itself may induce greater confidence in the process. Our tests here were somewhat limited, but the results do provide partial support. Those who could identify multiple positive features of both Dole and Clinton did become more trusting in government from pre- to postelection. Cynics may view American elections as competitions among candidates lacking in positive qualities, and one would not expect cynics to become more trusting of their government. But one might expect those respondents who were able to recognize positive aspects of both of the major candidates for office to see the election as a contest between good alternatives and to become more trusting of their government. Despite consensus that the campaign was uneventful—Clinton's projected margin of victory remained remarkably stable over the nine months before the election—and despite small but significant percentages of poll respondents who truly disliked Clinton, the vast majority of NES respondents found something to like about both major candidates. Over 85 percent of the respondents found at least one positive trait for both Dole and Clinton, and 17 percent saw two positive traits in both candidates ("moral" and "gets things done").

Social trust was not affected by voting for the losing presidential candidates; in fact, losers acquired *more* social trust. Coleman's analysis might explain this as the recognition that the losing voter has incurred the obligation of others by losing gracefully,[62] thereby obligating others to reciprocate. However, the signs on trust in government and political efficacy are negative, though not significant, consistent with findings by other scholars that political attitudes can be adversely affected by losing. The margin of victory for the winning congressional candidate is not at all

---

62. James Coleman (1990).

significant, and the sign on this coefficient is in the wrong direction. Weakly contested races and wider margins for incumbents may not decrease feelings of efficacy much after all, all other things being equal.

Ritual

The fourth hypothesis is based on the notion that the American ritual of a presidential election provides an opportunity for building solidarity. The pre- to postelection changes observed in the two indicators of social solidarity suggest that solidarity did indeed increase, that large numbers of people with initially distrusting orientations exhibited more favorable views after the election. Our multivariate analysis adds some nuances to this election effect: the election rite apparently reinvigorated social cohesion more for some people than for others. As we expected, those who were already integrated into the norms and "collective representations" of the American political community, as measured by political knowledge, showed the most positive change. And elections lead to greater social trust for those who are strongly civically engaged. Ironically, our evidence suggests that elections do not lead to increased trust for those people who are well integrated into their local communities. The sign is negative, although not significant.

The former makes considerable sense and is eminently consistent with our earlier findings that increased civic engagement begets increased trust. As Putnam has recently argued, and Durkheim and Tocqueville stressed a century earlier, participation in groups reminds people of their interdependence, combats self-absorption, and teaches norms of reciprocity. In the specific context of our analysis of the change in trust over the course of the last month or so before the election, we argue that involvement in intermediate associations immerses participants to a greater degree than nonparticipants in the normative order, of which elections, as a means for coming to agreement about differences, play a particular role in the American civil religion.

The negative and weak coefficient for social connectedness speaks to the importance of the difference between rootedness and civic participation. One can easily be solidly rooted in a community without developing strong social connections or civic participation. Consider the southern Italian families of Putnam's classic study:[63] the majority of citizens experienced little mobility, residing always in the same locations, some with extremely strong

---

63. Putnam (1993, especially p. 114–15), or similar versions reported by Fukuyama (1995).

family and church ties; there was, however, little evidence of civic association, the difference that Putnam found to be singularly indicative of low levels of social capital. Residence in the community, *controlling for one's level of civic participation,* may well lead to greater distrust of others. These results, we believe, speak to the need to consider more carefully in theories of social capital production the difference between abstract social trust and more particular forms of trust in one's personal relationships and local community connections. These connections may well be forms of social capital, but they do not lead to the more abstract forms of social cohesion that are measured by questions about faith in "most people." Instead the "weak ties" of civic engagement rather than the "strong ties" of kinship and locality lead to greater trust of other people.

Our findings suggest that the fear that elections are "merely" rituals that repress or hoodwink citizens is overstated,[64] since the more-informed and more-involved segments of American society are the ones *most* vulnerable to the cohesion-producing properties of elections. Others who fear that the election ritual has become dysfunctional should be somewhat mollified by our results,[65] for we find substantial election effects on civic attitudes, both as a main effect and in the types of people who respond to the normative foundation of the ritual.

Finally, we note some interesting results among the controls in the model. Several measures of government performance suggest that respondents who see the United States as better off in several dimensions have more trust in government. This effect holds for most but not all of the measures of performance. An improved U.S. foreign policy position, improved economic conditions (standard of living, current economic assessment, personal finances), and a government perceived as being effective in handling the economy all led to more trusting assessments of government. Those who perceived major changes in federal taxes or in the deficit were unchanged in their trust of government.

Discussion

This analysis has shown that national elections—at least in the United States—can provide the context for increases in social capital, particularly

---

64. See Kertzer (1988); Edelman (1964, 1971); Ginsberg and Weissberg (1978).
65. See Bennett (1992).

in those sentiments that are indicative of national solidarity. Elections do this in part by stimulating improvements in political-cultural attitudes—a sense of political efficacy and trust in government. But elections also do this by engaging people in a rite that allows them to renew their attachment to national society, particularly those people who are well informed politically and already integrated into society via membership in voluntary associations. These associations are the mechanism through which Durkheim believed solidarity had to be achieved in post-traditional societies in which collective morality exerts a weaker pull on individuals.

How generalizable are our findings to other U.S. elections? As we noted earlier, several characteristics of the 1996 election were typical. But other elections could involve even more negativity, be more tightly contested, or involve more or less contact with the political parties. There is no particular reason to expect that changes in the variables would lead to changes in the patterns of effects observed in our analysis of the 1996 election. Nonetheless, an examination of the generalizability of our findings in future elections is possible, provided, of course, that we have similar pre- and postelection measures of social trust, trust in government, and feelings of efficacy.

The paramount independent variable for future consideration may be the presence or absence of elections themselves, a phenomenon that can be examined only in a comparative context. We may have unearthed a causal hypothesis for investigation in the extensive comparative democratic-economy debate:[66] do regimes that hold elections, all other things being equal, generate more social capital—and by extension, economic development (per Putnam)[67]—than nonelectoral regimes? Our model raises the possibility that it may be better to hold elections than not to, a finding with implications for foreign policy toward politically developing states and for others making portentous decisions about national politics in the developing world. The simple ritual of elections, given time to take hold, may be a crucial component in the development of the high quality of life represented by high levels of social capital. But perhaps the impact of elections is conditional upon their legitimacy; perhaps electoral rituals would not create social capital in one-party or authoritarian states where citizens' votes are widely perceived to be largely symbolic; perhaps the beneficial effects obtain only where elections have been repeated and uninterrupted.

66. E.g., Burkhart and Lewis-Beck (1994), Przeworski and Limongi (1993, 1997).
67. Putnam (1993).

Only further comparative analysis can tell whether the results reported here are a property of all elections per se, or only of decisive, effectual elections in advanced democracies.

Our chapter began with a discussion of the many connections between civic and political attitudes. Our analysis supports the general framework that there is a tight reciprocal relationship between social solidarity and political sentiments and confirms the inseparability of civil and political society in modern democratic systems. This intimate connection may ultimately be a source for optimism about the likely trajectory of American civic life. On one hand, regardless of whether one believes that social capital is declining,[68] Putnam's calls for efforts to increase civic engagement are vindicated:[69] civic engagement is clearly linked to social trust, independent of alternative causes. On the other hand, Tarrow's proposed alternative cause, political mobilization, has its own, independently beneficial effects:[70] we can improve our elections and make them more social-capital enhancing, by, for example, increasing mobilization by the political parties and enticing high-quality candidates to run; such efforts may redound to civil society with higher levels of political efficacy, more trust in government, and greater social solidarity.

68. Ladd (1996), Samuelson (1996).
69. Putnam (1994, 1995a, b).
70. Tarrow (1996).

Appendix 4A

Table 4A-1. *Wording and Coding of Questions Extracted from 1996 American National Election Studies*[a]

Variable	Question	Coding
Interpersonal trust (pre- and postelection)		
Can people be trusted?	Generally speaking, would you say that most people can be trusted, or that you can't be too careful in dealing with people?	*0;1; 1 = can be trusted*
Are people fair?	Do you think most people would try to take advantage of you if they got the chance, or would they try to be fair?	*0, 1; 1 = fair*
Civic engagement	*All group variables:* There are many types of organizations, groups, and charities that people might be involved with. We're interested in what kinds of groups you might be involved with. I'm going to read you a list of different types of organizations. For each type, could you tell me the name or names of the organizations you are involved with?	*0, 1; 1 = involvement in one or more groups of this type*
Nonpartisan civic organizations	Nonpartisan civic organizations interested in the political life of the community or nation—such as the League of Women's [sic] Voters or a better-government association?	

Labor unions

Our first type of group is labor unions. Are you involved with any labor unions? Which ones?

Professional associations

How about other organizations associated with your work such as a business or professional association or a farm organization?

Veterans' organizations

Veterans' organizations such as the American Legion or the Veterans of Foreign Wars?

Churches and synagogues

Are you a member of a local church, parish, or synagogue?

Other religious organizations

How about other organizations affiliated with your religion besides that, such as the Knights of Columbus or B'nai B'rith, or a Bible study group?

Elderly groups

Organizations for the elderly or senior citizens?

Ethnic associations

Organizations representing your own particular nationality or ethnic group such as the Polish-American Congress, the Mexican-American Legal Defense, or the National Association for the Advancement of Colored People?

Women's groups

Organizations mainly interested in issues promoting the rights or the welfare of women—an organization such as the National Organization for Women, or the Eagle Forum, or the American Association of University Women?

143

Table 4A-1. (continued)

Variable	Question	Coding
Political issue groups	Organizations active on any particular political issues such as the environment or abortion (on either side), or gun control (on either side) or consumers' rights, or the rights of taxpayers or any other issues?	
Ideological organizations	Organizations that support general liberal or conservative causes such as Americans for Democratic Action or the Conservative Caucus?	
Political parties	Organizations active in supporting candidates for elections such as a political party organization?	
Youth and sports groups	Groups in which children might participate, such as Girl Scouts, 4-H, youth sports leagues such as soccer or Little League?	
Literary and art groups Hobby and sports clubs	Literary, art, discussion, or study groups? Hobby clubs, sports or country clubs, bowling leagues, or other groups for leisure-time activities?	
Neighborhood associations	Associations related to where you live— neighborhood or community associations, homeowners' or condominium associations, or block clubs?	

Fraternal organizations	Service or fraternal organizations such as the Lions or Kiwanis or a local women's club or a college fraternity or sorority?	
Charitable organizations	Organizations that provide services in such fields as health or service to the needy—for instance, a hospital, a cancer or heart drive, or a group like the Salvation Army that works for the poor?	
Educational institutions	Educational institutions—local schools, your own school or college, organizations associated with education such as school alumni associations or school service organizations such as the PTA?	
Cultural organizations	Organizations that are active in providing cultural services to the public—for example, museums, symphonies, or public radio or television?	
Self-help groups	Support or self-help groups such as AA or Gamblers Anonymous?	
Any other groups	Any other organizations?	
Social connectedness		
Talk with neighbors regularly?	Do you have any neighbors that you know and talk to regularly?	*0,1; 1 = Yes*

Table 4A-1. *(continued)*

Variable	Question	Coding
Log (Years in residence)	How long have you lived in your present (city/town/township/county)?	*log of NES values from 1/52 [for 0] to 90; min −3.99, max 4.50*
Own home?	(Do you/Does your family) own your home, pay rent, or what?	*0,1; 1 = own house*
Married?	Are you married now and living with your (husband/wife)—or are you widowed, divorced, separated, or have you never married?	*0,1; 1 = married now*
Church attendance	If respondent attends religious services: Do you go to religious services every week, almost every week, once or twice a month, a few times a year, or never?	*0 to 1 by .25; 1 = every week*
Behavioral engagement Displayed a campaign button, sticker, or sign?	Did you wear a campaign button, put a campaign sticker on your car, or place a sign in your window or in front of your house?	*0,1; 1 = yes*

Attended political meeting	Did you go to any political meetings, rallies, speeches, dinners, or things like that in support of a particular candidate?	0,1; 1 = yes
Worked for party	Did you do any (other) work for one of the parties or candidates?	0,1; 1 = yes
Gave money to candidate	During an election year people are often asked to make a contribution to support campaigns. Did you give money to an individual candidate running for public office?	0,1; 1 = yes
Gave money to party	Did you give money to a political party during this election year?	0,1; 1 = yes
Gave money to group	Did you give any money to any other group that supported or opposed candidates?	0,1; 1 = yes
Psychological engagement		
Interest in campaign	Some people don't pay much attention to political campaigns. How about you? Would you say that you were very much interested, somewhat interested, or not much interested in following the political campaigns this year?	*0,.5,1; 1 = very much interested*
Campaign TV consumption	If respondent watched programs about the campaigns on TV: Would you say you watched a good many, several, or just one or two?	*0 to 1 by .33; 1 = a good many (0 is defined by "No" answer to v961002)*

Table 4A-1. (continued)

Variable	Question	Coding
Attention to campaign news	In general, how much attention did you pay to news about the campaign for president—a great deal, quite a bit, some, very little, or none?	0 to 1 by .25; 1 = a great deal
Attention to congressional campaign	In general, how much attention did you pay to news about the campaigns for election to Congress—that is, the House of Representatives in Washington—a great deal, quite a bit, some, very little, or none?	0 to 1 by .25; 1 = a great deal
Endogenous variables		
Government trust (pre-election)	People have different ideas about the government in Washington. These ideas don't refer to Democrats or Republicans in particular, but just to the government in general. We want to see how you feel about these ideas. For example: How much of the time do you think you can trust the government in Washington to do what is right—just about always, most of the time, or only some of the time?	0 to 1 by .33; 1 = just about always

	Question	Coding
Government trust (postelection)	How much of the time do you think you can trust the government in Washington to do what is right—just about always, most of the time, or only some of the time?	*0 to 1 by .33; 1 = just about always*
Efficacy (pre-election)	Please tell me how much you agree or disagree with this statement: "People like me don't have any say about what the government does."	*0 to 1 by .25; 1 = disagree strongly*
Efficacy (postelection)	People like me don't have any say about what the government does.	*0 to 1 by .25; 1 = disagree strongly*
Campaign mobilization		
Party contact	As you know, the political parties try to talk to as many people as they can to get them to vote for their candidate. Did anyone from one of the political parties call you up or come around and talk to you about the campaign this year?	*0,1; 1 = yes*
Nonparty contact	Other than someone from the two major parties, did anyone (else) call you up or come around and talk to you about supporting specific candidates in this last election?	*0,1; 1 = yes*

Table 4A-1. *(continued)*

Variable	*Question*	*Coding*
Talk about registration or turnout	During the campaign this year, did anyone talk to you about registering to vote or getting out to vote?	*0,1; 1 = yes*
Campaign involvement Voting	In talking to people about elections, we often find that a lot of people were not able to vote because they weren't registered, they were sick, or they just didn't have time. How about you—did you vote in the elections this November?	*0,1; 1 = yes, voted*
Qualities of the campaign Candidate supported	If respondent voted for a candidate for president: Whom did you vote for?	*0, 1; 1 = voted for Dole*
Positive trait sum	Think about Bill Clinton [Bob Dole]. In your opinion, does the phrase "(he [is]) [moral/gets things done]" describe Bill Clinton extremely well, quite well, not too well, or not well at all?	*0 to 4; 4 = positive evaluations of both candidates on both traits*
Congressional vote margin	Margin of victory of incumbent congressional candidate over nearest opponent, from FEC data.	*min − 25, max 100*

Ritual

Respondent's sense of similarity to others

In terms of general attitudes and beliefs, how similar would you say that other people are to you—very similar, somewhat similar, similar, not very similar, or not at all similar?

−.5 to 1;1 = very similar

Political knowledge

Now we have a set of questions concerning various public figures. We want to see how much information about them gets out to the public from television, newspapers, and the like. The first name is Al Gore[William Rehnquist/Boris Yeltsin/Newt Gingrich]. What job or political office does he now hold?

0 to 4; 4 = correct identification of all four figures

Controls

Strength of United States

During the past year, would you say that the United States' position in the world has grown weaker, stayed about the same, or has it grown stronger?

−1 to 1 by 1; 1 = stronger

Standard of living

Do you think that twenty years from now the standard of living for the people who are just children now will be better, about the same, or worse than it is today?

−1 to 1 by 1; 1 = better

Government policy and the economy

Over the past year would you say that the economic policies of the federal government have made the nation's economy better, worse, or haven't they made much difference either way? If better/worse, would you say much better or somewhat better?

−1 to 1 by .5; 1 = increased a lot

151

Table 4A-1. (continued)

Variable	Question	Coding
Clinton's effect on the deficit	Would you say that the size of the yearly budget deficit increased, decreased, or stayed about the same during Clinton's time as president? If increase/decrease, would you say it increased a lot or a little?	−1 to 1 by .5; 1 = increased a lot
Clinton's effect on taxes	Would you say that the federal income tax paid by the average working person has increased, decreased, or stayed about the same during Clinton's time as president? If increase/decrease, would you say it increased a lot or a little?	−1 to 1 by .5; 1 = increased a lot
State of the economy	What do you think about the state of the economy these days in the United States? Would you say that the state of the economy is very good, good, neither good nor bad, bad, or very bad?	−1 to 1 by .5; 1 = very good
Personal finances	What do you think of your personal financial situation these days? Would you say that your personal financial situation is very good, good, neither good nor bad, bad, or very bad?	−1 to 1 by .5; 1 = very good

Variable	Description	Coding
Family income (thousands of dollars)	Please look at page 21 of the booklet and tell me the letter of the income group that includes the income of all members of your family living here in 1995 before taxes. This figure should include salaries, wages, pensions, dividends, interest, and all other income.	*Low end of respondent's income bracket in thousands of dollars*
Days after election	This variable is based on the date of the interview. It counts the number of days after election day (November 5, 1996).	*1 to 58*
Cooperativeness (pre-election)	[Completed by interviewer] Respondent's cooperation was: very good, good, fair, poor, very poor. [Note: no respondents were rated "very poor."]	*.25 to 1; 1 = very good*
Interest in interview (pre-election)	[Completed by interviewer] Overall, how great was respondent's interest in the interview? Very high, above average, average, below average, very low.	*0 to 1; 1 = very high*
Partisanship	Combined 7-point partisanship scale recoded from −1 to 1, then folded at 0 so strong Democrat and strong Republican both equal 1.	*0 to 1 by .33; 1 = strong partisan*

a. The coding notation "min, max; value = response" denotes the range of the variable and response associated with the specified value of the variable.

Appendix 4B: The Measurement Model

The measurement model results, a confirmatory factor analysis, appear in Table 4B-1. We assume that each of the factors is correlated but that none of the measurement errors are correlated. We further assume that the variance of each latent variable is a free parameter. The fit for the confirmatory factor model is good, with a goodness-of-fit index of .88 and a root mean squared error of approximation of .05.

The first latent variables of interest are the measures for social trust pre- and postelection. Each is indicated by two variables, with the same question wording in each wave.

—Generally speaking, would you say that most people can be trusted, or that you can't be too careful in dealing with people?

—Do you think most people would try to take advantage of you if they got the chance, or would they try to be fair?

Both indicators are simple yes/no dichotomies. The first loading on each factor is, by convention, fixed to 1. The second, freed, loading (for "fair") is approximately 1, nearly on par with the scale factor, which means that the two indicators are tracking the same underlying factor to about the same extent. Both of the loadings are statistically significant beyond the $p<.05$ level.

The next latent measure of some interest is that for civic engagement. In our previous analyses, we examined whether individual membership in a list of civic organizations tracked the same latent variable.[71] The pattern of factor loadings is strikingly similar across the three studies. We fix the scale for this factor with membership in civic associations. Each indicator is coded 0 for no memberships and 1 for any membership. Although the 1997 NES ascertained the number of multiple memberships, as per analysis by Baumgartner and Walker,[72] in order to render the present analysis parallel with our previous work we collapse multiple memberships into a single code category. There is a theoretical reason in addition to the purpose of comparability: our concept of civic engagement should reflect the multiplicity of types of groups that individuals belong to, rather than the total number of groups. In other words, we regard activity in the PTA, a neighborhood watch, and coaching soccer as three indicators of civic involvement, whereas participation in soccer, softball, and bowling leagues

71. Brehm and Rahn (1997); Berger and Brehm (1997).
72. Baumgartner and Walker (1988).

Table 4B-1. *Scales for Trust and Engagement, 1996*[a]

Latent variable indicators	Loading	Standard error
Interpersonal trust (pre-election)		
Can people be trusted?	1.00	
Are people fair?	1.14	(0.14)
Interpersonal trust (postelection)		
Can people be trusted?	1.00	
Are people fair?	1.11	(0.07)
Social connectedness		
Talk with neighbors regularly?	1.00	
Log (years in residence)	1.05	(0.06)
Own home?	2.57	(0.16)
Married?	1.61	(0.08)
Church attendance	1.11	(0.05)
Behavioral engagement		
Displayed a campaign button, sticker, or sign?	1.00	
Attended political meeting	1.19	(0.06)
Worked for party	1.09	(0.06)
Gave money to candidate	1.26	(0.07)
Gave money to party	0.95	(0.06)
Gave money to group	0.54	(0.05)
Psychological engagement		
Interest in campaign	1.00	
Campaign TV consumption	0.74	(0.05)
Attention to campaign news	1.20	(0.07)
Attention to congressional campaign	0.99	(0.06)
Civic engagement		
Nonpartisan civic organizations	1.00	
Labor unions	0.62	(0.05)
Professional associations	1.68	(0.08)
Veterans' organizations	0.64	(0.05)
Churches and synagogues	1.33	(0.07)
Other religious organizations	1.35	(0.07)
Elderly groups	0.96	(0.06)
Ethnic associations	0.93	(0.06)
Women's groups	1.15	(0.06)
Political issue groups	1.64	(0.08)
Ideological groups	0.07	(0.04)
Political parties	1.88	(0.09)
Youth and sports groups	1.44	(0.07)
Literary and art groups	0.95	(0.06)

(continued)

Table 4B-1. *(continued)*

Latent variable indicators	Loading	Standard error
Hobby and sports clubs	1.27	(0.07)
Neighborhood associations	1.74	(0.09)
Fraternal organizations	1.12	(0.06)
Charitable organizations	1.65	(0.08)
Educational institutions	1.97	(0.10)
Cultural organizations	2.09	(0.10)
Self-help groups	0.55	(0.05)
Any other groups	0.92	(0.06)

Source: American National Election Studies, 1996.

a. Cell entries are factor loadings from a confirmatory factor analysis. All factor loadings are statistically very significant at $p < .001$ except Ideological Groups, where $p < .10$.

is one indicator of civic involvement. Moreover, loadings for the variable including the number of groups are very similar to those used here.

The high loadings are clearly associated with community (e.g., church and other religious organizations, sports groups, neighborhood associations, education groups) and purposive politics (e.g., professional associations, women's groups, political parties, and political issue groups). The weakest loadings are for membership in labor unions, ideological groups, and self-help groups. The weak loading for unions is because membership in a union is almost always compulsory within certain shops and hence does not represent a voluntary engagement in one's community. The weak loading for ideological groups is because of the explicitly divisive posture adopted by many of these groups.

The next latent measure of interest is social connectedness. Here, our purpose is to identify the extent to which an individual is well established within his or her local community. We fix the scale with a measure of whether the respondent talks with his or her neighbors regularly, coded as a dichotomy. Predictably, measures of whether a respondent owns his or her home, is married, and attends church regularly all scale close to 1, again suggesting a strong shared connection to the underlying factor. The number of years the respondent has resided in the community also loads in the predicted direction, and to a statistically significant degree, although the magnitude is not strong, so length of residence perhaps should not be used as a measure of connectedness.[73] (We employ the natural log of the

73. See, e.g., Teixeira (1992); Rosenstone and Hansen (1993).

number of years of residence in order to treat the small differences between relatively short stays in a community as intrinsically equivalent to large differences between relatively long stays in the community. At least one nonagenarian had resided in the same community for ninety years.)

We turn next to our construction of a latent measure for the extent to which a respondent is behaviorally engaged with politics. We have six dichotomous measures of political participation: whether the respondent wore a campaign button; attended a political meeting; worked for a party; and gave money to a candidate, party, or group. Note that each measure reflects activity on the part of the respondent, unlike the measures of political stimulation by others (contact by parties, by nonparties, and by people promoting voter registration). Our aim is to measure the now familiar concept of a respondent's involvement in the campaign[74] as distinct from general participation in civic life (measured by the civic engagement factor) or stimulation by the campaign. With the exception of giving money to groups, the remaining four freed loadings are all close to 1, again signifying strong connection to the concept. Even the loading for giving money to groups is reasonably strong, although small.

Our final latent measure is for the extent to which a respondent is psychologically engaged with the campaign.[75] The factor represents the amount of cognitive investment the respondent is willing to devote to politics. We fix the scale with the traditional question of whether the respondent is interested in the campaign, coded from 0 (not at all interested) through 1 (very interested). Three indicators are freed: whether the respondent watched news about the campaign on TV, how much attention the respondent paid to news about the presidential campaign, and how much attention the respondent paid to news about the congressional campaign. All three freed loadings are large and close to 1, again confirming the strength of the common factor.

References

Aldrich, John H. 1995. *Why Parties? The Origin and Transformation of Party Politics in America.* University of Chicago Press.

Almond, Gabriel A., and Sidney Verba. 1963. *The Civic Culture: Political Attitudes and Democracy in Five Nations.* Princeton University Press.

74. See, e.g., Verba and Nie (1972); Rosenstone and Hansen (1993).
75. See, e.g., Milbrath and Goel (1977).

Anderson, Benedict. 1983. *Imagined Communities.* New York: Verso.

Anderson, Christopher J., and Christine A. Guillory. 1997. "Political Institutions and Satisfaction with Democracy: A Cross-National Analysis of Consensus and Majoritarian Systems." *American Political Science Review* 91(1): 66–81.

Bartels, Larry M. 1997. "Campaign Quality: Standards for Evaluation, Benchmarks for Reform." Paper presented at the 1997 annual meeting of the American Political Science Association, Washington, D.C.

Baumgartner, Frank, and Jack L. Walker. 1988. "Survey Research and Membership in Voluntary Associations." *American Journal of Political Science* 32: 908–28.

Bennett, W. Lance. 1992. *The Governing Crisis.* New York: St. Martin's.

Berger, Mark, and John Brehm. 1997. "Watergate and the Erosion of Social Capital." Paper presented at the annual meeting of the Midwest Political Science Association, Chicago.

Brady, David W., and Joseph Stewart Jr. 1991. "When Elections Really Matter: Realignments and Changes in Policy." In *Do Elections Matter?* edited by Benjamin Ginsberg and Alan Stone. Armonk, N.Y.: M. E. Sharpe.

Brehm, John, and Wendy Rahn. 1997. "Individual-Level Evidence for the Causes and Consequences of Social Capital." *American Journal of Political Science* 41(3): 999–1023.

Burkhart, Ross E., and Michael S. Lewis-Beck. 1994. "Comparative Democracy: The Economic Development Thesis." *American Political Science Review* 88: 903–10.

Citrin, Jack, and Donald Philip Green. 1986. "Presidential Leadership and the Resurgence of Trust in Government." *British Journal of Political Science* 16(4): 431–53.

Clark, Harold D., and Alan C. Acock. 1989. "National Elections and Political Attitudes: The Case of Political Efficacy." *British Journal of Political Science* 19(4): 551–62.

Coleman, James S. 1990. *Foundations of Social Theory.* Harvard University Press.

Coleman, John. 1996. "Resurgent or Just Busy? Party Organizations in Contemporary America." In *The State of the Parties: The Changing Role of Contemporary American Parties,* 2d ed., edited by John C. Geen and Daniel M. Shea. Lanham, Md.: Rowman and Littlefield.

Conover, Pamela Johnston, and Barbara E. Hicks. Forthcoming. "The Psychology of Overlapping Identities: Ethnic, Citizen, Nation, and Beyond." In *National Identities and Ethnic Minorities in Eastern Europe,* edited by Ray Turan. Macmillan.

Craig, Stephen C., Richard C. Niemi, and Glenn E. Silver. 1990. "Political Efficacy and Trust: A Report on the NES Pilot Study Items." *Political Behavior* 12(3): 289–314.

Dayan, Daniel, and Elihu Katz. 1992. *Media Events: The Live Broadcasting of History.* Harvard University Press.

Delli Carpini, Michael X., and Scott Keeter. 1996. *What Americans Know about Politics and Why It Matters.* Yale University Press.

de Tocqueville, Alexis. [1835, 1840] 1969. *Democracy in America.* Vols. 1 and 2. Edited by J. P. Mayer and translated by George Lawrence. Garden City, N.Y.: Doubleday.

Durkheim, Emile. [1893] 1984. *The Division of Labor in Society.* Free Press.

———. [1897] 1951. *Suicide: A Study in Sociology.* Free Press.

———. [1915] 1976. *The Elementary Forms of Religious Life.* London: George Allen and Unwin.

Edelman, Murray. 1964. *The Symbolic Uses of Politics.* University of Illinois Press.

———. 1971. *Politics as Symbolic Action: Mass Arousal and Quiescence.* Chicago: Markham.

Edwards, Bob, and Michael W. Foley. 1998. "Civil Society and Social Capital beyond Putnam." *American Behavioral Scientist* 42(1): 124–39.

Feldman, Martha S., and James G. March. 1981. "Information in Organizations as Signal and Symbol." *Administrative Science Quarterly* 26: 171–86.

Finkel, Steven E. 1995. *Causal Analysis with Panel Data.* Thousand Oaks, Calif.: Sage.

Foley, Michael W., and Bob Edwards. 1997. "Escape from Politics? Social Theory and the Social Capital Debate." *American Behavioral Scientist* 40(5): 550–61.

Frankovic, Kathleen. 1993. "Public Opinion in the 1992 Campaign." In *The Election of 1992: Reports and Interpretations,* edited by Gerald Pomper. Chatham, N.J.: Chatham House.

Fukuyama, Francis. 1995. *Trust: The Social Virtues and the Creation of Prosperity.* Free Press.

Ginsberg, Benjamin, and Robert Weissberg. 1978. "Elections and the Mobilization of Popular Support." *American Journal of Political Science* 22(1): 31–55.

Granovetter, Mark. 1973. "The Strength of Weak Ties." *American Journal of Sociology* 78(6): 1360–81.

Kenworthy, Lane. 1997. "Civic Engagement, Social Capital, and Economic Cooperation." *American Behavioral Scientist* 40(5): 645–56.

Kertzer, David L. 1988. *Ritual, Politics, and Power.* Yale University Press.

Ladd, Everett C. 1996. "The Data Just Don't Show Erosion of America's 'Social Capital.'" *Public Perspective* 7(4): 1, 5–22.

Levi, Margaret. 1996. "Social and Unsocial Capital: A Review Essay of Robert Putnam's *Making Democracy Work.*" *Politics and Society* 24: 45–55.

———. 1998. "A State of Trust." In *Trust and Governance,* edited by Valerie Braithwaite and Margaret Levi. New York: Russell Sage.

Lijphart, Arend. 1984. *Democracies: Patterns of Majoritarian and Consensus Government in Twenty-One Countries.* Yale University Press.

Luks, Samantha C., and Jack Citrin. 1997. "Revisiting Trust in an Angry Age." Paper presented at the 1997 annual meeting of the Midwest Political Science Association, Chicago.

Madsen, Douglas. 1978. "A Structural Approach to the Explanation of Political Efficacy Levels under Democratic Regimes." *American Journal of Political Science* 22: 867–83.

March, James G., and Johan P. Olsen. 1989. *Rediscovering Institutions: The Organizational Basis of Politics.* Free Press.

Marcus, George E., and Michael B. MacKuen. 1993. "Anxiety, Enthusiasm and the Vote: The Emotional Underpinnings of Learning and Involvement during Presidential Campaigns." *American Political Science Review* 87(3): 688–701.

Markus, Gregory B. 1979. *Analyzing Panel Data.* Beverly Hills, Calif.: Sage.

Milbrath, Lester W., and M. L. Goel. 1977. *Political Participation.* 2d ed. Chicago: Rand McNally.

Nadeau, Richard, and Andre Blais. 1993. "Accepting the Election Outcome: The Effect of Participation on Losers' Consent." *British Journal of Political Science* 23(4): 553–63.

Newton, Kenneth. 1997. "Social Capital and Democracy." *American Behavioral Scientist* 40(5): 575–86.

Nichols, Stephen M., and Paul Allen Beck. 1995. "Reversing the Decline: Voter Turnout in the 1992 Election." In *Democracy's Feast,* edited by Herbert F. Weisberg. Chatham, N.J.: Chatham House.

Nie, Norman H., Jane Junn, and Kenneth Stehlik-Barry. 1996. *Education and Democratic Citizenship in America.* University of Chicago Press.

Pomper, Gerald M., and Loretta Sernekos. 1989. "The 'Bake Sale' Theory of Voting Participation." Paper presented at the annual meeting of the American Political Science Association, Atlanta.

Popkin, Samuel L. 1991. *The Reasoning Voter.* University of Chicago Press.

Przeworski, Adam, and Fernando Limongi. 1993. "Political Regimes and Economic Growth." *Journal of Economic Perspectives* 7: 51–69.

———. 1997. "Modernization: Theories and Facts." *World Politics* 49(2): 155–83.

Putnam, Robert D. 1993. *Making Democracy Work: Civic Traditions in Modern Italy.* Princeton University Press.

———. 1994. "Bowling Alone: Democracy in America at the End of the Twentieth Century." Manuscript, Harvard University.

———. 1995a. "Bowling Alone: America's Declining Social Capital." *Journal of Democracy* 6: 65–78.

———. 1995b. "Tuning In, Tuning Out: The Strange Disappearance of Social Capital in America." *PS: Political Science and Politics* 28(4): 664–83.

Rosenstone, Steven J., and John Mark Hansen. 1993. *Mobilization, Participation and Democracy in America.* Macmillan.

Rosenstone, Steven J., John Mark Hansen, Paul Freedman, and Marguerite Grabarek. 1993. "Voter Turnout: Myth and Reality in the 1992 Election." Paper presented at the 1993 annual meeting of the American Political Science Association, Washington, D.C.

Samuelson, Robert J. 1996. " 'Bowling Alone' Is Bunk." *Washington Post,* April 10, 1996, p. A19.

Schneider, Mark, Paul Teske, Melissa Marschall, Michael Mintrom, and Christine Roch. 1997. "Institutional Arrangements and the Creation of Social Capital: The Effects of School Choice." *American Political Science Review* 91(1): 82–93.

Spillman, Lyn. 1997. *Nation and Commemoration: Creating National Identities in the United States and Australia.* Cambridge University Press.

Tarrow, Sidney. 1996. "Making Social Science Work across Space and Time: A Critical Reflection on Robert Putnam's *Making Democracy Work.*" *American Political Science Review* 90(2): 389–97.

Teixeira, Ruy A. 1992. *The Disappearing American Voter.* Brookings.

Tyler, Tom R. 1997. "The Psychology of Legitimacy: A Relational Perspective on Voluntary Deference to Authorities." *Personality and Social Psychology Review* 1: 323–45.

Verba, Sidney, and Norman H. Nie. 1972. *Participation in America: Political Democracy and Social Equality.* Harper and Row.

Verba, Sidney, Kay Lehman Schlozman, and Henry E. Brady. 1995. *Voice and Equality: Civic Voluntarism in American Politics.* Harvard University Press.

Weissberg, Robert. 1975. "Political Efficacy and Political Illusion." *Journal of Politics* 37: 469–87.

Zullow, Harold M. 1994. "American Exceptionalism and the Quadrennial Peak in Optimism." In *Presidential Campaigns and American Self-Images,* edited by Arthur H. Miller and Bruce E. Gronbeck. Boulder, Colo.: Westview.

PART TWO

Civic Life in a Changing Society

5 | Professions and Civic Engagement: Trends in Rhetoric and Practice, 1875–1995

STEVEN BRINT
CHARLES S. LEVY

IN *Democracy in America,* Tocqueville placed great importance on the "art of association" as a key to the strength of
American democracy: "Americans of all ages, all stations of life, and all
types of disposition are forever forming associations. There are not only
commercial and industrial associations in which all take part, but others of
a thousand different types—religious, moral, serious, futile, very general
and very limited, immensely large and very minute."[1] Since the mid-
1980s, a number of commentators have expressed unease about trends in
community and civic involvement in the United States.[2] Many have contrasted Americans today with those described by Tocqueville a century and
a half ago. Virtually all of the contemporary discussion has focused on

We would like to thank the following people from the professional associations in our sample for
help in the preparation of this paper: Jean Bonwill, Rena Calabrese, Rhea Farberman, Ann Kurzius,
Daryl Limpus, Darmea S. McCoy, Kimya Morris, Tracy Moxley, Rosemary Rathz, June Scangarello,
Robert Tenuta, Phil Simon, and Tony Wrenn. We would also like to thank the following people from
colleges and universities in our sample: Curtis Ayres, Cory Bowman, Irene Hegarty, Sidney Holmes,
Debra S. Levine, Don Pattison, William Roberts, Jack Shannon, Bonnie Wallis, and Henry S. Weber.
We are grateful for comments we received on the paper from Thomas Brante, Marshall Ganz, Peter
Dobkin Hall, Virginia Hodgkinson, Robert Putnam, Theda Skocpol, and Robert Wuthnow. Jerry A.
Jacobs offered assistance in data collection at the University of Pennsylvania.

1. Tocqueville ([1840] 1961, Vol. 2: p. 128).
2. Bellah et al. (1985); Etzioni (1993); Putnam (1995); and Putnam (1996).

trends in the participation of individuals—in political activities,[3] in community organizations (such as the PTA and the Rotary Club),[4] in charitable giving,[5] and in institutions of religious worship. A few related studies have examined individuals' understandings of the relationship between commitments in their own lives and the lives of their communities.[6]

In view of the current focus on individual participation, it is worth recalling that Tocqueville's discussion of voluntary association was only one part of his analysis of civic engagement in American democracy. In Tocqueville's view, the energies generated in associational life supported democratic society at least in part because institutional forces restrained and channeled those energies in supportive ways. If we stretch the everyday meaning of the term "civic engagement" a little, it is possible to think of Tocqueville as having been interested in two types of civic engagement: one based on the participation of individual citizens in the associations of civil and political society, and the other based on normative orientations sustained, above all, by institutions and institutional leaders.[7]

In several chapters of the first volume of *Democracy in America*, Tocqueville considered institutional forces that provided guidance for American democratic society and restraint against both the passions of the majority and the biases of powerful minorities. The structure of government itself is a major topic, taking up six early chapters of the first volume. In addition, institutional forces in society are carefully discussed for their role in providing intellectual and moral support for democratic

3. Rosenstone and Hansen (1993); Verba, Schlozman, and Brady (1995).

4. Putnam (1995); Ladd (1996); Putnam (1996).

5. Hodgkinson (1996, pp. 24–33).

6. Bellah et al. (1985); Wuthnow (1996); Wolfe (1998).

7. The terms "civic" and "engagement" have primary and secondary meanings. The primary usage of the term "civic" has to do with the activities of citizens, particularly with their rights and duties in relation to this legal status. Civic activity requires no absence of partisanship or self-interest, and indeed nearly all proponents of civic life applaud the play of partisanship and self-interest as a reflection of the healthy contention necessary to democratic government. A secondary, but also frequent meaning of the term "civic" emphasizes a normative position, a broad (rather than narrow) and objective (rather than self-interested) orientation to the needs of the civilized political community. It has connotations of a broad, nonpartisan perspective when, for example, someone is referred to as having a "civic spirit." In its primary meaning, the term "engagement" suggests active participation—in this case, active participation in civic life. A secondary, but still frequent meaning of the term "engagement" emphasizes depth of involvement. In this sense, the opposite of engagement is a superficial or reflex reaction. Thus, someone engaged with a public issue gives it deep and careful consideration, while someone less engaged reacts more reflexively.

societies. The legal profession and the judiciary, he argued, served to safeguard the long-range interests of society against the short-run passions of popular opinion.[8] Similarly, Protestant religious doctrine provided essential moral restraints to balance the freedoms guaranteed by the liberal state.[9] And the culture of democracy itself helped to regulate social relations through their extensions into everyday activities—from the honoring of parliamentary forms around the dinner table to the respect for others' opinions in childhood games.[10] Even in his discussion of voluntary associations, Tocqueville emphasized the importance of intellectual and moral associations over other types. "Nothing," he wrote, "is more deserving of our attentions than the intellectual and moral associations of Americans."[11]

From Individuals to Institutions

Although institutional life has received relatively little attention in recent discussions of civic engagement in American democracy, it has not been entirely ignored. Ann Swidler has argued pointedly against the idea that a civic community can be created through increasing emphasis on voluntary associations. These usually devolve, she argues, into "lifestyle enclaves." Instead, to "create a civic community—a community that can link us to those unlike ourselves . . . we must place greater emphasis on strengthening American institutions—including families and schools, governments and universities." And, she observes, while "America still has vibrant community participation . . . our institutional life is a shambles."[12]

This chapter shares Swidler's premise that discussions of community and civic engagement should pay more attention to institutions. We suggest that one reason commentators so often feel a sense of unease about the strength of "civic America" is that important institutions in American society rarely represent themselves publicly as having larger social or civic purposes. The paper does not entirely share Swidler's conclusions, however.

8. Tocqueville ([1835] 1961, Vol. 1: chap. 16).
9. Ibid. (chap. 17).
10. Ibid. (chap. 14).
11. Tocqueville ([1840] 1961, Vol. 2: p. 133).
12. Swidler (1997, p. B4). Discussions of the role of particular institutions in building and sustaining "civic life" in the United States can be found in Bryk, Lee, and Holland (1993); Popenoe (1993); Brint (1994, chaps. 1, 2); Skocpol (1996); and Vallely (1996).

A focus on the absence of public-oriented voices in American institutions can be misleading if it leads us to overlook a conflicting (and at least equally important) trend: the incorporation of community and civic impulses in the bureaucratic structure of those same institutions.

In this chapter we concentrate on professions and professional associations. The professions are a strategically important focus for discussions of civic engagement in American democracy. In the late nineteenth and early twentieth centuries, professional elites saw themselves as guardians of important social values. By encouraging a link between community welfare and professional authority, their ideology of "social trustee professionalism" provided a salient and visible contrast to the more exclusively economic orientations of farmers, businessmen, and organized workers.[13]

We provide evidence that expressions of connection to community and civic life began in the 1920s to decline markedly among leaders of the major professions. In this respect, we agree with those who see the 1920s and 1930s as a key turning point in the tenor of professionals' connection to American civic and community life. We also show that community and civic activities are embedded in the organizational life of the professions to a greater degree than they were in the past. The historical trajectory suggests less a decline of social purpose in the professions than a bureaucratization of social purpose. Our interpretation of the causes of this change emphasizes the role of professionals in the status politics of the late nineteenth and early twentieth centuries and the influence of organizational developments in the professions since that time. We conclude by discussing the implications of our analysis for contemporary discussions of civic engagement in American democracy.

Sampling and Data Collection

Our sample includes both professional associations and colleges and universities. We selected ten professional associations and five colleges and universities to study.

We attempted to find professional associations that are representative of the full range of professional life—those that represent major and minor professions, predominantly humanistic and predominantly scientific/technical occupations, and occupations both close to and remote from the

13. Haskell (1984); Brint (1994, chaps. 1, 2).

state.[14] Four of the professional associations we studied can be described as mainline professional associations: the American Bar Association (ABA), the American Institute of Architects (AIA), the American Medical Association (AMA), and the American Society of Mechanical Engineers (ASME). Two others, the American Chemical Society (ACS) and the American Psychological Association (APA), are part mainline professional associations and part academic discipline associations. In both cases, most members are practitioners rather than academic researchers. For this reason, we treat them as mainline professional associations. Three other organizations are academic discipline associations: the American Historical Association (AHA), the American Political Science Association (APSA), and the Modern Language Association (MLA). One of the organizations, the National Education Association (NEA), has a mixed history. For more than 100 years it was a mainline professional association, but it was remade as a trade union in the 1960s.

We have two reasons for including colleges and universities in the sample. First, they are gatekeepers for and conduits into the professions, and in this sense they are central to the organization of professional labor markets. Second, they are comparatively active in community and civic affairs. Most organizations that employ professionals are rather single-mindedly concerned with practical, business-related activities. This is somewhat less true of colleges and universities. Including colleges and universities, therefore, provides a sense of the maximum extent of community and civic engagement in professional work settings other than churches and social service agencies that are explicitly devoted to social welfare activities. Two of the colleges and universities in our sample are liberal arts colleges: Dartmouth and Pomona. Three are research universities: the University of California, Berkeley (UCB), the University of Chicago (Chicago), and the University of Pennsylvania (Penn).

We collected three types of information on each of the organizations in the study. First, we collected presidential inaugural speeches. It is our view

14. We had hoped to include new as well as older professional associations. However, professional associations founded in recent decades are often organized more like trade associations than like the classic professional associations of the past. They provide job- and product-related information but eschew scientific and scholarly communications, investigations of standards, mechanisms for collegial control, and other structural characteristics of the classical nineteenth-century associations. New professional associations in computer software engineering, such as the Association of Computer Professionals (founded in 1982) and the American Computer Scientists Association (founded in 1993), are examples of the trade association form of professional organization.

that content analysis can be an invaluable tool for understanding patterns of cultural change, and we have used these speeches to measure trends in the discourse of professional leaders. In the case of the professional associations, these speeches were collected at the time of founding and at ten-year intervals beginning as early as 1875 and continuing through 1995.[15] We collected speeches from the middle of each decade—that is, from presidents of the associations in 1875, 1885, 1895, 1905, and so on.[16] For colleges and universities, we collected all presidential inaugural speeches from 1875 onward.

Second, we collected information on the community and public service activities of the organizations. This included information on such matters as the existence and volume of business of speakers' bureaus, the date of founding and activities of public affairs offices, the date of founding and activities of government relations offices, institutionalized relationships with charitable organizations, sponsorship of voluntary help for people in need of professional services, and the beginning date of any annual visitors' days. It also included information about committees, commissions, and research units explicitly concerned with community and civic affairs. Because much of this information was not available longitudinally, we had to settle in many cases for current or recent catalogues of community and civic activities. Some catalogues contained information on the longevity of the programs; others did not. A few histories were available to provide supplementary information on the civic and community activities of the organizations.[17] We also conducted interviews with several community and public affairs officers about the history of their organizations' involvement with community activities.

Finally, we collected information on changes in the structure and size of the organizations over time. This organizational information included

15. In the twentieth century, the professional associations in our sample elected new officers annually. In the nineteenth century, presidents sometimes served multiyear terms. In a few cases, a speech for the designated year could not be located or consisted of only a short report on the activities of the association. Short reports were typically given by presidents in the middle of their terms or at the end of multiyear terms. In these cases, we substituted an inaugural speech from the next year available in the series. The first important president of the University of California, Daniel Gilman, was inaugurated in 1872, and the first president of the American Bar Association, James O. Broadhead, assumed office in 1879. We included the speeches of Gilman and Broadhead in the sample.

16. The year 1875 is an appropriate starting point. The formal organization of professional life in the United States began for the most part in the decade after the Civil War. Only five of our fifteen organizations (Dartmouth, the University of Pennsylvania, the American Medical Association, the National Education Association, and the American Institute of Architects) were founded before 1875.

17. See, e.g., Campion (1984) on the activities of the American Medical Association.

the membership (or for colleges and universities, the enrollment), the budget, the staff size, and the number of sections or departments in the organization and the dates of their incorporation.

The Rhetoric of Organizational Leaders, 1875–1995

We begin by looking at the changing character of professional concerns and commitments as expressed in the speeches of leaders of the fifteen organizations in our sample. We have analyzed the content of some 160 speeches given by professional association and college and university presidents over the 120-year period covered in our study.[18] We have grouped the data into four time periods of comparable length and acceptable correspondence to distinctive periods in the history of the American professional middle class: 1875–99, 1900–29, 1930–69, and 1970–95.[19]

Presidential speeches are, of course, only one possible source of data on changing patterns of professional concerns and commitments. A complete study of professional ideology would necessarily examine editorials in leading professional publications, the writings of highly regarded thinkers

18. Not all speeches that would fall into our sampling framework could be obtained for coding. Some were never published or appeared in obscure and difficult-to-obtain publications. When we could not obtain a specific speech, we substituted presidential speeches from an adjacent year where possible. For this paper, we were able to code thirteen presidential speeches for the ABA, thirteen for the AIA, twelve for the AMA, twelve for the MLA, twelve for the NEA, eleven for the APA, eleven for ASME, eleven for the AHA, ten for the APSA, and nine for the ACS. Speeches of college and university presidents were in some cases also difficult to obtain. Some presidents did not participate in inaugurals and some inaugural speeches were not preserved. Substitutions were not generally possible for inaugurals of college and university presidents, although in some cases the first convocation represented a substitution in the president's own mind for an inaugural speech that under the press of circumstances was never given. In these cases, we substituted first-convocation speeches for inaugural speeches. For this paper, we were able to code sixteen speeches for presidents and chancellors of UCB, ten for Chicago, eight for Dartmouth, six for Pomona, but only five for Penn. The total number of speeches is 159. However, we excluded the speeches from Penn in reporting the findings because we could only find a small number of presidential speeches relative to the potential pool of presidential speeches from this institution. Therefore, the effective total number of speeches is 154, not 159.

The primary virtue of our method of sampling is that it allows us to cover a wider range of organizations than would otherwise be possible. We have enough speeches to see patterns of variation over time in the themes of speeches given in each professional organization. However, because we must rely on a relatively small number of speeches in each era, we inevitably run the risk of giving too much weight to an unrepresentative speech that happens to fall in our sample. For a few institutions, we have been able to draw on more comprehensive studies of presidential speeches. These studies tend to confirm the trends we have found. See Ausubel (1950); Parker (1953); and Murphy and Bruckner (1976).

19. On distinguishing periods of American middle-class politics, see Brint (1994, chap. 2).

in the profession, the speeches and writings of rank-and-file professionals, and other sources. Such a comprehensive study is beyond the scope of this chapter.

At the same time, presidential speeches have important advantages as a source of data on the concerns and commitments of the leaders of professional organizations. It is at ceremonial occasions that leaders are empowered to speak ex cathedra about the purposes of their organizations and the issues that affect those purposes. The presidential speeches are both more detached from passing events and more likely to concentrate on the evolving interests of leading professionals than other kinds of speeches or articles usually are. In addition, the highly focused ceremonial context requires presidents to use rhetoric that will elicit a positive response from the assembled membership. Most speeches, therefore, are about issues that speakers believe their audiences will find appropriate and important to think about. We believe that most of these speeches are authentic records of the concerns and commitments of professional elites. However, even if our findings reported *only* the changing nature of socially acceptable pieties among professionals, they would be of considerable interest for what they would tell us about the climate of socially acceptable thought surrounding the professions in different eras. Some methodological advantages also exist in the choice of presidential speeches as data for the study of professional ideologies. Because presidential speeches represent similarly situated, naturally occurring historical series, we are able to eliminate many selection problems that could otherwise bias a content analysis of professional discourse.[20]

Measuring Presidential Discourse

In each speech, we have coded the incidence of more than a dozen types of expressed concerns and commitments.[21] These expressed concerns

---

20. Presidential speeches do also have certain limitations as a source for data. These speeches can be highly conventional in content and style. Indeed, some association presidents have analyzed the rhetorical form of the genre as part of their speeches. See Wright (1976) and Ziowolkowski (1986). Moreover, organizational leaders are not always motivated to discuss their more controversial priorities or act on the priorities they do discuss.

21. We coded thematic movements in the speeches and distinct new mentions within and between thematic movements, not every specific reference. These thematic movements usually covered several paragraphs, but they sometimes covered only a sentence or two. Thus, we marked a page-long discussion of the role of law in the history of civilization as one reference to a value function of the profession, but we also coded a sentence on the need for recruiting more women into the legal profession as one social reform reference.

and commitments refer to purposes of the professional organization and to forces within and outside the professional organization that affect its activities. Together, these references cover nearly all of the themes developed in the speeches.

In our discussion, we aggregate these references into four primary content categories: (1) the sociocultural and (2) instrumental purposes of the organization or profession, (3) the internal activities and issues of the organization or profession, and (4) the external forces of regulation that are seen as influencing the organization or profession. These neutral-sounding terms should not obscure the meaningful concerns they represent. *Sociocultural purposes* are the animating ideal purposes of the organization—the role leaders expect members to play in the life of the society. *Instrumental purposes* are the technical achievements of members of the professions—advances in expertise that have, for example, cured new diseases or created new technologies. *Internal activities* are the lifeblood of the organization: the priority projects, committees, task forces, and internal factions that absorb the energies and interests of most members. *External forces* refers to pressures in the environment—from interpretations of the meaning of changing client demographics to issues posed by new forms of government regulation.

Because sociocultural references are particularly relevant to discussions of the civic engagement of institutions, we examine that content area in a more disaggregated way. The four sociocultural reference categories we discuss are: (1) the civilizational purposes of the professional activity (e.g., a reference to the diffusion of knowledge for the good of society or to the benevolence of the medical profession); (2) community-serving purposes (e.g., a reference to the contributions of the profession to the improvement of community life); (3) civic purposes (e.g., a reference to the contributions of the profession to the health of the state or to the creation of good citizens); and (4) social reform purposes (e.g., a reference to the advancement of women or racial and ethnic minorities or a reference to the housing needs of the poor).[22]

---

22. Altogether we coded fourteen reference categories. The four categories related to the sociocultural purposes of the organizations and professions are discussed in the text, leaving ten other reference categories. The second set of reference categories has to do with the instrumental and technical purposes of the organizations and professions: (1) purposes involving the practical application of science (e.g., a discussion of the use of scientific knowledge to purify water and thereby prevent disease); (2) purposes involving responsiveness to a relevant market (e.g., responding to the need for more trained legal manpower); and (3) other instrumental and technical purposes (e.g., standardizing civil law across

From Social to Organizational Concerns

Table 5-1 provides a breakdown of the thematic content of the speeches for the four primary content categories in four time periods.[23] The data show that the number of references to broad sociocultural purposes declined over time. As references to sociocultural purposes declined, they were replaced by discussions of internal affairs and to a lesser extent by discussions of the instrumental and technical achievements of members.[24]

A clear example of this pattern can be found in speeches by presidents of the American Bar Association. In the first two periods, nearly all the

---

jurisdictions). The third set of reference categories has to do with internal forces of organization. Specifically, these included: (4) internal constituencies and their relations, including appeals for cooperation among these constituencies (e.g., a reference to the leader's hope that faculties of science and humanities can each see what the other contributes to the institution); (5) the rules, practices, and assumptions of the organization, including discussions of the need for reform or validation of these rules, practices, and assumptions (e.g., a reference to the mechanisms by which members of committees are chosen or to the rules regulating charges of misconduct); and (6) the institution's resource needs and plans for the use of resources (e.g., calls for new facilities or new types of financial help). The final set of reference categories has to do with external forces of regulation: (7) the state or its representatives as a regulating force (e.g., a reference to the importance of appreciating the role of a governing board or a discussion of a change in the federal law regulating the profession); (8) other occupations or organizations as a regulating force (e.g., a reference to the need of a university to coordinate with other four-year colleges); (9) a relevant market as regulating force (e.g., a reference to the number of practitioners in a field as compared to the market demand); and (10) all other external regulating forces (e.g., wealthy benefactors, public opinion, war, or other historical circumstances).

23. In most cases, a number of reference categories are represented throughout the 120-year period studied. Early leaders of the bar may, for example, at once extol the civilizational purposes of their profession while advocating that lawyers "reduce the law to a science to develop its usefulness" and mention in passing the need to overcome sectional and political rivalries within the association. See Carter (1895). Some rhetorically gifted presidents managed to cover most of the reference categories in a single speech.

24. Speeches in several of the associations did not fit these two major patterns of change. Presidents of two of the academic discipline associations closely associated with civic life (the American Historical Association and the American Political Science Association) largely resisted the trend away from expressions of broad sociocultural concerns. In those two academic discipline associations, civilizational and civic references remained relatively constant (and rather high) throughout the period. By contrast, the presidents of two scientific-industrial societies (the American Chemical Society and the American Society of Mechanical Engineers) began with little interest in sociocultural matters and continued (so far as we can say from the limited data) to have little interest in them throughout most of the period studied. (Several presidents of ASME in the years between 1930 and 1970 did become interested in the intersection of technology and social life, leading to a temporary surge in themes concerning the civilizational and civic values of engineering.) In the APA, sociocultural references increased somewhat over time as clinicians and academics interested in humanistic and social psychology entered the association in larger numbers after World War II; they soon outnumbered the behaviorists and replaced them as leaders. See Crawford (1992). The speeches of presidents of the AIA and UCB included themes of both conservation and development throughout the period studied.

Table 5-1. *Themes of Speeches by Presidents of Selected Professional Organizations, 1875–1995*[a]

Percent

Organization	Sociocultural purposes				Internal organization				Instrumental purposes			
	1879–99	1900–29	1930–69	1970–95	1879–99	1900–29	1930–69	1970–95	1879–99	1900–29	1930–69	1970–95
Mainline professional organizations												
American Bar Association	93	83	43	28	4	13	38	57	4	4	13	9
American Chemical Society	...	12	36	9	...	10	21	53	...	72	33	13
American Institute of Architects	41	73	10	34	44	16	57	18	0	0	18	25
American Medical Association	46	38	33	20	36	42	26	22	14	10	16	16
American Psychological Association	9	33	47	38	18	13	4	30	64	0	33	4
American Society of Mechanical Engineers	24	21	56	29	18	7	17	0	57	71	23	71
National Education Association	80	94	32	41	8	3	48	34	0	3	8	10
Academic discipline associations												
American Historical Association	...	64	76	81	...	7	9	4	...	0	6	0
American Political Science Association	...	52	62	52	...	29	10	0	...	16	5	36
Modern Language Association	41	46	37	27	15	11	50	43	30	14	0	7
Colleges and universities												
Dartmouth College	50	57	34	33	50	30	59	60	0	0	3	0
Pomona College	...	69	58	...	...	0	0	...	...	24	22	...
University of California, Berkeley	42	22	37	22	27	50	37	58	16	22	12	8
University of Chicago	...	53	41	6	...	41	37	65	...	6	4	10

Source: Authors' presidential speech files.

a. Percentages reported only where more than one speech was available for coding in each time period.

speeches had to do primarily with the contribution of the profession to improving civilization or civic life. James Broadhead, the first president of the ABA, for example, evoked a common theme of wise guidance in the light of liberal principles: "It is the business of those who have studied [the law] . . . to see that public sentiment springs from a pure fountain and flows in an unobstructed channel, and [that] pursuance of its mandates shall secure to each citizen the fulness of individual existence and impose so much restraint on each as is necessary for the good of all."[25] By the last period, these kinds of broad sociocultural references constituted only about a quarter of the themes in presidential speeches of the ABA. Issues related to membership concerns and internal activities, particularly task groups and committee work, assumed a correspondingly larger share of attention. ABA President James D. Fellers used his speech in the mid-1970s, for example, to describe the formation of fifteen commissions and projects to examine controversies in such areas as information technology and the law, accounting practices, media law, and medical malpractice.[26]

The same general pattern—decreasing emphasis on broad sociocultural purposes and increasing emphasis on internal affairs—is evident also in two of the other major professional associations (the American Medical Association and the National Education Association), four of the five colleges and universities (Dartmouth, Pomona, Chicago, and Penn), and one of the academic discipline associations (the Modern Language Association). As in the ABA, the emphasis is no longer on the special thing the profession or institution does in society, but rather on the special place it is for those who are a part of it. A speech by a president of the American Psychological Association in the mid-1990s illustrates one kind of internal issue—what to do about divisions that arise in the association. The speech criticizes two groups of members—research scientists for using science as "a cudgel to pummel practitioners" and practitioners who "besmirch the image" of the profession by marketing superficial advice in pursuit of personal celebrity.[27] Most themes in this area, however, focus on the accomplishments of task forces and committees of the organization or on new membership services.

We also found some increase over time, though less striking, in references to instrumental and technical purposes. Closely tied to industrial

25. Broadhead (1879, p. 70).
26. Fellers (1975).
27. Fox (1996).

advance, leaders of the ACS focused on the practical scientific achievements of their discipline from the beginning. Shifts in this direction were evident in five other of the professional associations (the American Bar Association, the American Institute of Architects, the American Medical Association, the American Society of Mechanical Engineers, and the National Education Association), one of the colleges and universities (the University of California, Berkeley), and one of the academic discipline associations (the American Political Science Association). Recent presidents of the NEA have, for example, more often talked about changing school practices on the basis of research results. Emblematic of this trend, one recent president of the APSA used as the central trope of his speech the idea that the founding fathers of the United States were not learned visionaries but social engineers.

The Content of Professional Ideals

We have shown that references to the broad sociocultural purposes of professional life declined over time in this sample of professional speeches. But what specific sociocultural purposes have organizational leaders had in mind when they did express a sense of connection to the broader society?

Figure 5-1 compares the number of references to civilizational, civic, and social reform and community-serving concerns by leaders of each of the organizations over the 120-year period. The data show that references to the civilizational purposes of professions have been the most common rallying point of leaders concerned with the relationship between professions and the larger society. References to civilizational functions were three times as common in the speeches as references to civic life, and they were four to five times as common as references to the community-serving purposes of professions or to social reform concerns.

What did professional elites mean by serving civilization? This varied from profession to profession. College and university presidents emphasized the importance of the diffusion of knowledge, the creation and perfection of "a higher vision" of life, and the cultivation of desirable qualities of mind. Leaders of the bar emphasized the ideals of justice, the protection of individual freedoms, and the improvement of human abilities to meet social needs in an orderly and nonviolent fashion. Presidents of the American Institute of Architects evoked the spiritual and social benefits of beauty in the built environment. Presidents of the American

Figure 5-1. *Sociocultural References in Presidential Speeches, by Type of Organization, 1875–1995*

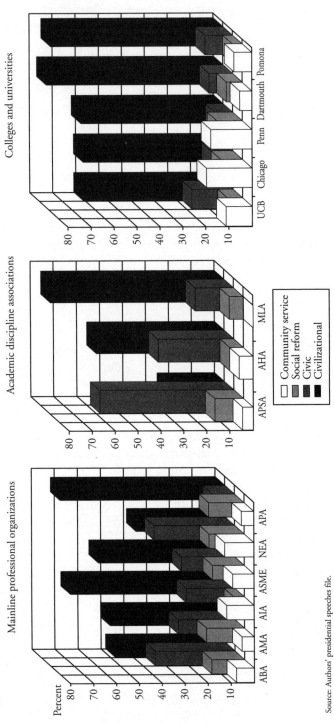

Source: Authors' presidential speeches file.

Medical Association focused on the application of scientific intelligence to the humane project of curing disease. Although references to sociocultural purposes are most evident in the years before 1930, they rarely disappeared entirely in this set of organizations. So, for example, in 1945 the speaker of the AMA's House of Delegates, H. H. Shoulders, proclaimed, "Let us again concern ourselves with advancing the science of medicine, with meeting the standards of medical education and with delivering a higher quality of medical service, ever mindful that science without a soul may be cruel and inhumane, whereas science possessed of a soul is the very highest achievement, the apotheosis of humanity."[28]

References to civic ideals were less frequent. As many historians of middle-class progressivism have emphasized, tensions have periodically flared between "nonpartisan" experts and deal-making politicians comfortable with the give and take of partisan politics. It should not be surprising therefore that leaders of professional associations in our sample often took a dim view of government and politics.[29] Among leaders of the mainline professional associations, government was depicted as a threat to the aspirations of the professions nearly as often as it was depicted as a legitimate object of the professions' civic concern. Both disdain for low governmental standards and fear of the state as a heavy-handed and biased regulator are evident in the speeches of leaders of the organized legal, medical, and architectural professions. Civic purposes were hardly ever mentioned by presidents of private colleges and universities or by leaders of the more humanistic academic associations.[30]

Presidents of the American Political Science Association were, by some measure, more likely than others to see the work of their association as serving civic purposes. They were followed by leaders of the bar, public school teachers, and academic historians. Thus, in the presidential speeches of the ABA, the bar was frequently depicted as the enemy of corruption and slipshod legislation and the protector of individual rights. The ideal of well-crafted law was frequently connected to the health and strength of the state. In the words of James C. Carter: "Considerable mischief arises from a passion for ill-advised and ill-considered law making."[31] Presidents of the

28. Shoulders, quoted in Fishbein (1947, p. 483).

29. Hofstadter (1955, chaps. 5, 6); Tyack and Hansot (1982, pp. 129–80); Schudson (1996); and Wiebe (1995).

30. For a provocative epistemological approach to interprofessional differences, see Halliday (1985).

31. Carter (1895).

American Historical Association saw lessons for government and public choices in the historical record, and presidents of the National Education Association often spoke of the public schools as the cornerstone of republican virtue and democratic fellowship. Among the colleges and universities, only presidents of the public University of California, Berkeley, showed a relatively high level of explicit concern about civic life. Most often this concern was expressed as an expectation that the university would help to create thoughtful and productive citizens who could contribute to the resolution of public problems.

In spite of the social reform ferment of the Progressive and New Deal eras, social reform references were almost completely absent from presidential speeches until the 1960s, and even in the 1970–95 period they were rare. In the 1960s, minority representation became a significant topic in the colleges and universities and the NEA. During the same period, the health and legal needs of disadvantaged populations began to emerge as concerns in the American Medical Association, the American Psychological Association, and the American Bar Association. Otherwise, only a small number of scattered references exist to such matters as antipoverty activity, the design of good housing for workers, and opportunities for women in the profession. References to the community-serving purposes of professional life were rarer still.

The Disappearing Presidential Voice

A narrowing of concerns can be measured not just in the themes of presidential speeches. Presidential speeches also grew shorter and in many cases more peripheral to the main focus of professional meetings.

One measure can be found in the diminishing time allotted to presidential speeches. Between 1875 and 1929, speeches that ran fifteen or twenty pages in print (or longer) were the norm for presidents of institutions like the American Bar Association and Dartmouth College, both places where oratory has historically been highly valued. Even in the ABA and at Dartmouth, presidential speeches in recent decades were more likely to run three to seven pages in comparable print. Even briefer speeches were typical in some of the organizations.

One reason for this change is that over the course of the century association leaders began to specialize in administrative work, and celebrity authors and public figures stepped in to provide a sense of larger purpose and inspiration. Presidents became hosts rather than intellectual leaders.

Only two of the five post-1960 chancellors of the University of California, Berkeley, for example, gave full-scale inaugural orations. Celebrity speakers became the center of attention at these "Charter Day" events, even when a new chancellor was installed. One chancellor, Edward Strong, self-consciously cut short his already brief acceptance speech to give more time to the guest speaker, President John F. Kennedy. Similarly, in the 1980s presidents of the American Institute of Architects ceded pride of place to celebrity guest speakers. In the American Bar Association from the late 1970s onward, presidents became publicly responsible only for the business affairs of the association. Presidential speeches in the American Society of Mechanical Engineers also came to focus on business affairs. The ASME presidents' speeches apparently came to be considered so peripheral to the life of the organization that they were no longer preserved in the 1980s and 1990s.

The Bureaucratization of Civic Engagement, 1930–95

As themes related to civic engagement receded from the speeches of professional leaders, activities connected to civic engagement became institutionalized in the formal bureaucratic structure of most of the professional organizations in our sample. However, the scope of this institutionalization was highly variable. Only two of the organizations show markedly high levels of activity in civic and community life. In the American Bar Association and the University of California, Berkeley, the public ethos of professionalism may have diminished, but practices of civic engagement have flowered through bureaucratic channels. In those two institutions, civic engagement through bureaucratic means began in the 1930s but grew substantially after the activist 1960s. Although a late starter, the University of Pennsylvania is now nearly as civically engaged as the ABA and Berkeley. The University of Chicago, the American Chemical Society, the American Institute of Architects, and the American Medical Association show somewhat less activity in civic and community life, but they are far from entirely enclosed in their own cocoons. In the other eight organizations, civic engagement does not appear to be a high priority.

From these data, we draw two tentative conclusions: first, resources are a major influence on civic and community activity in professional organizations—the resource-rich organizations are more able to be engaged.

Second, among these resource-rich organizations a close connection to the state is associated with high levels of activity.[32]

For the purposes of this chapter, we consider activity to have a civic or community orientation if time, talent, or money is donated by members of the organization to activities that primarily serve people outside the organization. We also count activities in which time and talent are heavily subsidized by individuals or by the organization for these purposes. Even so, in some cases, it is impossible to separate professional from community-serving activities. When the ABA makes judgments about the qualifications of judges nominated to the federal judiciary, it serves professional and public interests simultaneously. Similarly, a good case can be made that the American Medical Association has been active in public health throughout its history through the dissemination of research findings to clinicians and in setting standards for medical education and procedural terminology within the profession. Here we therefore focus on activities for which individuals gain no important *professional* distinction other than recognition as contributing members of a community outside the profession.

In the cases we know most about, our sense is that the growth of community and civic activity dates from the 1960s and especially the 1970s. This activity increased in the 1980s and 1990s, particularly in the universities and the well-to-do professional associations.[33] In many respects, this growth appears to have followed and compensated for the problems of the federal welfare state. But we must be tentative about the dating of trends toward increasing civic and community engagement. It is entirely possible that at least some of the organizations were more active earlier but simply did not retain evidence of their activities. For this reason, we do not make strong statements about trends in civic engagement. We

32. A third conclusion is still more tentative: Apart from the universities, many of the more active organizations—including the ABA, the AIA, and the AMA—are professional associations composed largely of independent business people in private and group practice rather than in corporate or government employment. Some mirroring may exist at the national level of the long-standing relation between small business people and leadership in local civic and community affairs.

33. It is impossible to know precisely what proportion of budget and time these organizations devote to community and civic activities. Budget categories often mix programs that are and are not pertinent. Much time is volunteered and so are some property resources that, if counted as potential income, would inflate the total going to these activities. Our best estimate is that community and civic activities account for no more than 2 percent of the total budget in any organization, and in most cases substantially less. The American Bar Association may be an outlier in this regard, higher both in budget and time volunteered than the other organizations in our sample.

concentrate instead on the current profile of civic engagement in the fifteen organizations.

Highly Engaged Organizations: The ABA and UCB

From the beginning, the ABA saw itself as engaged in community improvement primarily through activities to standardize law in the various states. These efforts led to a number of uniform laws and model codes, including the Uniform Commercial Code. From the beginning, the ABA was also involved in numerous community and civic activities. These increased in the 1930s when the ABA became involved in assisting with the provision of legal services for indigent defendants. In 1942, it instituted its first self-described public service activity, the traffic court program to improve laws related to drunk driving.[34] Today, the ABA is engaged in literally thousands of community and civic activities, the great majority of them instituted since 1960. These activities are of four types: committees that allow ABA members to engage in action on public issues, civic education projects, activities that assist in the legal representation of persons in need, and community activities in and around the ABA's Chicago-area community.

The ABA has more than fifty committees and commissions that allow members to be involved in a wide range of issues connected to the law. Many are concerned with strictly professional issues—rules of conduct, discipline, continuing education, and the like. Approximately one-third, however, treat issues that are more relevant to the public at large than to the profession itself. These include committees on bioethics, domestic violence, drugs and substance abuse, campaign finance, the environment, homelessness and poverty, immigration, literacy, national security, the mass media, the elderly, and the legal needs of children.

One of the major civic education activities of the association is Law Day, which began in the 1950s. As part of Law Day, the ABA provides interested teachers throughout the country with lesson plans appropriate to different grade levels. These introduce processes of conflict resolution, the American legal system, and constitutional law; and they outline scenarios for mock trials. More recently developed civic education projects include efforts to bring lawyers into classrooms and work settings to talk

---

34. American Bar Association, Division for Media Relations and Public Affairs (1997).

about the law and legal issues as well as more comprehensive instructional programs for school use.

The ABA's committee on legal aid for indigent persons began in the 1930s. Several other ABA committees—all constituted since 1960—help organize legal representation for people in need, including children, the elderly, the homeless, victims of disasters, lower-ranking military personnel, and immigrants. ABA statistics indicate an increase since 1985 in the number of lawyers who participate in pro bono activities through organized programs. According to these statistics, which may overstate participation, some 150,000 lawyers (17 percent of all attorneys) are reported to have donated an average of twenty hours to pro bono activities in 1995. Nearly a quarter-million legal matters were handled in this way.[35] The ABA publishes a directory of pro bono projects, helps young lawyers make connections to public interest organizations, and holds conferences on pro bono and public interest law. In the 1990s it also organized donations of computer equipment and training activities by large law firms to resource-poor public service organizations.

Activities in the Chicago area include the ABA's "adoption" of South Loop School on Chicago's South Side, the provision of ten speakers a year for the Chicago public schools, the organization of charitable giving of food, clothes, and toys to the local community around the December holidays, and participation in local walkathons, marathons, and other fundraising activities. The ABA also allows employees to support charities of their choosing through deductions from their paychecks.

The University of California, Berkeley, currently lists some 300 public and community service activities.[36] Nearly every department and every professional school in the university is involved in community outreach and public service activities. These activities can be divided into five types: (1) facilities and performances open to the public; (2) volunteer and charity work and charitable donations; (3) educational outreach; (4) research specifically designated as oriented to public service; and (5) community economic development activities. The first two have a long history, but they became stronger and better organized after 1960. The last three are products of the period since 1970.

Since its founding in 1868 the campus has opened some of its facilities to the public and invited the public in for performances, lectures, and

---

35. American Bar Association, Division of Legal Services (1998).
36. University of California, Berkeley, Office of Community Relations (1997).

symposiums. A number of "community resources" in the city of Berkeley and adjoining areas are, in fact, owned and operated by UC Berkeley. Some of these facilities (the University Herbarium, Sather Tower carillon, the Phoebe Hearst Anthropology Museum) date to the early years of the university, a few others (e.g., the Lawrence Hall of Science) are products of the Cold War, but many others (e.g., the Berkeley Art Museum, the Pacific Film Archive, KALX, the Blackhawk Automotive Museum) are recent additions. The university also donates playing fields and rents buildings at $1 a year for a homeless shelter and to house city offices.

Students and faculty at Berkeley have a long history of volunteering in causes. Volunteering as an institutionalized feature of university activity began, however, only during the activist 1960s. The campus volunteer center founded in 1967 now places some 2,000 students a year in volunteer activities. Other volunteer activities provide medical and legal services through community clinics. The university also participates in the AIDS walkathon, charity events for the Special Olympics, and fundraising for the United Way. A small element of this volunteer effort (e.g., Clinica de la Raza) remains oriented to ideals of self-determination for minority communities that were popularized by ethnic nationalists in the 1960s.

The university is involved in more than three dozen educational outreach programs, nearly all of which began in the 1970s or later. The major activity involves a pledge of the university to improve K–12 education in the Bay Area. The pledge has three components: a K–12 partnership with four Bay Area school districts, an academy that brings school children onto campus during the academic year and the summer, and an "interactive university project" designed to build an information infrastructure for area schools through the Internet and other media. Some outreach programs involve specific departments (such as the Chemistry Scholars and Young Musicians programs), others are organized efforts to improve low-performing schools (in one case, through the "adoption" of a local middle school), and still others incentive programs aimed at encouraging high-ability, low-income high school students (such as the Incentive Awards Program and the Pre-Collegiate Academy). The university also operates a large continuing education program for adults.

The most recent programs connected to civic engagement are publicly oriented research centers and community development centers. Many research centers combine scholarly and public service activities. Others are predominantly oriented to improving community and civic life. The latter, founded since the 1970s, include the Center for Environmental Design, the PACE Center (Policy Analysis for California Education), the Center for Family and Community Health, and the Center for Occupational and Environmental Health. In the 1980s and 1990s, UCB became involved in a variety of economic community development programs to revitalize impoverished neighborhoods and towns near the university. These programs operate in the East Bay communities of Oakland and Richmond and in south Berkeley. Some involve aid to small business; others provide funds and organization for residents interested in improving the safety, attractiveness, and economic vitality of areas near the university.

Moderately Engaged Organizations: Private Universities and High-Revenue Professional Associations

The moderately engaged organizations are financially as strong (or nearly as strong) as the ABA and UCB, but they are not as closely connected to the public sector. These moderately engaged organizations include the two private universities in the sample (Chicago and Penn) and three mainline professional associations (the American Chemical Society, the American Institute of Architects, and the American Medical Association).

Penn is not far behind Berkeley as a center of community and civic activism in academe. Quite a bit of its activity is related to programs that serve both institutional and community interests. According to Penn's director of economic development, the university expects to spend $50 million between 1998 and 2003 on community economic development activities. This money will be used for joint planning with local leaders, to create a loan fund for strategic acquisitions, to help existing and new businesses gain access to capital, and to attract businesses to the neighborhoods surrounding the campus. Penn is also working with local businesspeople to make a nearby commercial corridor a "keystone" (or tax-free) zone. It is encouraging faculty and staff to live in and revitalize the surrounding neighborhoods through highly subsidized mortgage plans. Penn has also started a targeted job training program to provide employment opportunities to local residents. In 1998 it employed twelve program graduates in construction work.

Penn's primary educational outreach program creates courses for West Philadelphia schools. Seventy-two of the courses are currently being taught by Penn students. Each of the courses aims to combine teaching, research, and service. The courses are in such subjects as diet and nutrition, urban planning, and environmental improvement. Penn also sends nearly 2,000 students into local schools to volunteer as recreation and teachers' aides. In addition, each of the professional schools at the university operates clinics in the community that provide services ranging from dental screening to conflict mediation to opportunities for developing artistic skills.

Community and civic activity at Penn also involves a large number of "bite-sized" programs: small-scale computer and furniture donations, a panhandling program that places containers in stores for donations to be used by homeless shelters and other social service organizations, the provision of extra street-sweeping and "safety ambassadors" in the surrounding Spruce Hill neighborhood, and a graduation ceremony for a job training program for single mothers.

Like Berkeley and Penn, the University of Chicago has worked with community leaders to improve the poor neighborhoods surrounding it. The university provides substantial financial support for the Southeast Chicago Association, which is involved in crime prevention, business recruitment, and retention and code enforcement in neighborhoods adjacent to the university. The university has also been involved in a number of educational outreach programs, including its long-established Laboratory School and a new charter school. It has also provided modest subsidies for academic enrichment programs in Chicago, such as Saturday science classes and operates a program that sends some 160 volunteer teachers' aides into community schools. Like UCB, it provides Internet instruction and an Internet curriculum for a number of local public schools. Three research units at the university can be characterized as oriented to public issues. The Center for School Improvement is intimately connected to ongoing reform in the Chicago schools and provides policy-relevant resources for the school system. Chapin Hall is a center for research on children that works to strengthen networks of social service providers. The Chicago Health Policy Research Program, which is largely foundation-sponsored, investigates critical health issues in the region.

The American Chemical Society, a very well supported professional association, has also taken an active role in public and community affairs in recent years. In 1995 it spent some 4.2 million dollars on community and public affairs activities (nearly 2 percent of its budget). These activities include educational materials and workshops for children, fellowships for college and graduate students, production of television and radio shows on chemistry-related topics, and relations with the Smithsonian Museum. One office of the ACS organizes community outreach projects and provides speakers for schools and community groups. These activities date from the mid- and late 1970s.

The primary activities of the American Institute of Architects are in the areas of public education and city neighborhood renewal. None of these activities began before the 1960s. The AIA supports and operates its own philanthropic foundation, which concentrates on providing resources for improving architectural education in grades K–12. The association recently participated in a Carnegie Foundation evaluation of architecture education in grades K–16, one aspect of which was to raise student consciousness about how architecture contributes to the quality of community life. It also created a public television series, "Back from the Brink," about the revitalization of downtown areas in American cities. For a number of years, the AIA has fielded regional disaster assistance teams to help in the reconstruction of disaster areas. More recently, the association has fielded regional urban design assistance teams that provide three-day intensive consultations for community groups. In 1995 the AIA initiated the "Legacy Project," which is designed to leave a lasting architectural contribution to the city that hosts its annual meeting. These contributions have included building homes with Habitat for Humanity, designing and building homeless shelters and employment centers, and submitting new designs for one city's public housing. The AIA is organized in a decentralized way and, like the ABA, its hundreds of local chapters sometimes mount their own public service activities.

During the Progressive Era, the American Medical Association was very active in public health reforms, and it even looked sympathetically on government "sickness insurance" plans. However, since the end of World War I, the AMA has been active primarily in representing its members' scientific and political-economic interests.[37] Considering the membership and budget of the AMA, its involvement in civic and community activities is relatively modest. Much of the public service work of the AMA has been hortatory—resolutions passed by the association and disseminated to physicians and policymakers. These resolutions began in 1876 when the association urged communities to adopt sanitary water supplies. They continued through the early twentieth century on such issues as smallpox vaccinations (1901), health fraud and quackery (1913), milk standards (1914), and sharing the burden of care for the poor (1937). In 1924 the

37. Burrows (1963); Campion (1984, pp. 50–54).

AMA began making radio broadcasts with health messages, and it added televised messages in 1946. It continued its advocacy of health and safety legislation in 1954 by recommending that seat belts be required equipment in all automobiles.

The association began to take a more activist stance in public health in 1960 when it helped to organize a countrywide polio prevention program using the Sabin oral vaccine. In its public service activities since that time, the AMA has continued to favor large-scale campaigns that it pursues simultaneously on the national and state levels. In 1972 it launched a campaign to educate the public on health risks associated with tobacco. In the 1980s it began efforts to raise the legal drinking age to twenty-one and opposed all forms of discrimination against AIDS patients. In 1991 it helped to create a grassroots program against family violence in 700 communities. Like the ABA, its committee structure allows members to become involved in public issues such as control of tobacco and domestic violence, women's health issues, and health insurance reform. The association has developed a series of "physician guidelines" on public health issues, including recognizing and treating substance abuse, confronting media violence, and AIDS prevention. These guidelines are distributed to physicians free of charge. The AMA is also involved in patient education programs, such as Partners-in-Care, and has sold millions of consumer health books, videos, and brochures on topics ranging from child care and first aid to an encyclopedia of medicine. The AMA does not keep track of charitable medical work, although a majority of doctors apparently do some charitable work.

Less-Engaged Organizations: Academic Discipline Associations, Liberal Arts Colleges, and Others

Eight of the fifteen organizations are only minimally involved in civic and community activities. These eight include the three exclusively academic discipline associations (the American Historical Association, the American Political Science Association, and the Modern Language Association), one association whose membership includes both academics and clinicians (the American Psychological Association), the lower-budget professional association in science (the American Society of Mechanical Engineers), and the teachers' association (the National Education Association). The two liberal arts colleges, Dartmouth and Pomona, are also in this group of less-engaged organizations.

The American Political Science Association was involved in the 1930s and 1950s in "citizenship training" activities with Carnegie Foundation support. It also operated a Government Affairs Institute in the 1950s directed toward service and public affairs. Scientifically minded political scientists often strongly opposed these activities.[38] Today, none of the three academic discipline associations contribute to charities, work with their local communities in any way, or even operate speakers' bureaus. The only current public service activity of any of the academic discipline associations is the AHA's involvement in National History Day. It is, of course, not surprising that academic discipline associations are relatively disengaged from public life. Neither their function nor their status-allocating structures nor their level of discretionary resources leads in the direction of an active public presence. As learned societies, their primary purpose is to publish scholarly materials and to assemble once a year for a scholarly meeting. Their members' public service activities are connected not to the discipline but to the procedures used by colleges and universities for evaluating candidates for promotion. Even if the academic discipline associations were motivated to be engaged in civic and community affairs, they would not have the resources to engage in many of these activities and at the same time attend to their priority activities. Their budget-to-membership ratios are among the lowest of the organizations in our sample (see Table 5-2).

The American Psychological Association is a hybrid organization—part academic discipline association and part mainline professional association representing the interests of mental health clinicians and psychologists in corporate and private employment. Only one-third of APA members, however, work in colleges and universities. (Three-fifths work in clinical settings.) The APA is more involved in public service activities than the purely academic discipline associations, but it is not as active in the mental health area as the AMA is in other health areas. It has published and distributed public service brochures on topics related to mental health, and it has also developed a website that provides information on a variety of topics connected to psychology and mental health. Its main contribution to public affairs and civic action is through the research of its members on topics such as behavioral health, smoking cessation, and promotion of good teaching and parenting skills.

---

38. Somit and Tanenhaus (1962).

Table 5-2. *Operating Budget of Ten Professional Associations, 1995*

Association	Ratio of budget (in dollars) to members	Budget (in millions of dollars)
Mainline professional associations		
American Chemical Society	1,599:1	231.1
American Medical Association[a]	685:1	193.9
American Psychological Association	450:1	53.1
American Institute of Architects	561:1	32.0
American Bar Association	339:1	127.0
National Education Association	74:1	147.5
American Society of Mechanical Engineers	n.a.	n.a.
Disciplinary associations		
Modern Language Association	219:1	7.0
American Political Science Association	125:1	1.5
American Historical Association	75:1	1.5

Sources: American Medical Association (1995, p. 49); Calabrese (1998); Gale Research (1996).
a. AMA data are for 1994.
n.a. = not available.

ASME also has only a small involvement in civic and community activities. Nearly all of ASME's activity is related to engineering education. Its members have been involved in promoting precollegiate engineering education through an annual robotics competition and through collaboration with the Girl and Boy Scouts and the Junior Engineering Technical Society (JETS). It has also provided instructional and guidance materials to middle schools for engineering-related units in science classes.

The two liberal arts colleges provide entertainment and lectures that are open to the public, but they are otherwise quite uninvolved in civic and community life. Dartmouth's Rockefeller Center brings politicians and policymakers to speak on campus, and it operates study groups on issues of public interest. However, the presence of the institutions in public affairs is minimal. These colleges see their task as highly focused on the education of their students. This purpose is supported by the major resource providers for the colleges—parents who prefer a focused educational experience for their children over the diversity of experiences available at larger schools.

The National Education Association is a special case. Although it operated for its first hundred years as a mainline professional association, it converted to a trade union–style organization in the 1960s. Since that time, its primary mission has been to lobby for support of public education and to promote the economic well-being of its members. It also weighs in on issues of controversy surrounding the public schools. But it is no longer organized like the mainline professional associations to raise standards, disseminate research, and represent a "disinterested" body of occupational specialists. Its relative inactivity in civic and community life follows from its primary identity as a trade union.

Interpreting Patterns of Civic Engagement

Our findings show a decline in the expression of public-oriented themes in the speeches of leaders of most professional organizations, relatively little in the way of civic and community engagement until the 1960s and 1970s, and the development of specialized offices and committees concerned with civic and community life in many (although by no means all) of the organizations since that time. Our interpretation of the causes behind this pattern of change combines an emphasis on the external political environment and the internal characteristics of the organizations themselves. In particular, we emphasize: (1) the status politics of early industrializing America, (2) the shifts in professionals' orientation to public life occasioned by the rise of consumerism and pluralism in the 1920s and the growth of the federal welfare state in the 1930s, and (3) the increasing bureaucratic capacities of professional organizations due to their growth, institutionalization, and growing internal complexity. Each of these developments has tended to redirect professionalism away from its patrician roots and its original ideal interests in protecting and improving society. As the professional associations' interest in public service declined, the organized professions gave way to the welfare state as the primary legitimate guardian and improver of society. At the same time, as professional associations grew in membership and resources, they developed the organizational capacity to engage in civic and community life. Since the 1960s, this capacity has been exercised in varying degrees by the professional associations according to their constitutive identities and self-defined purposes, their degree of connection to the public sector, and the size of their budget. An important context for this activity is the perceived end of "the era of big government" and the resulting sense that other organizations must contribute more than they have to social progress and the amelioration of social ills.

The Political Environment as a Source of Change

Historians of late-nineteenth- and early-twentieth-century America have emphasized the distinctive role of middle- and upper-middle-class professionals in the politics of the period. During this age of tremendous industrial growth, increasing urban problems, and frequently violent class conflict, many professionals came to see themselves as guardians of the public interest against the more purely partisan interests of businessmen, workers, and farmers. Richard Hofstadter emphasized status competition as an underlying force, arguing that members of old, respectable families rebelled inwardly against the social prominence of the crude and ruthless businessmen and urban politicians they saw dominating the landscape.[39] Other historians, such as Robert Wiebe and David Tyack, have emphasized the underlying interests of the new professionals in carving out a place for themselves as nonpartisan experts in the new areas of economic and social organization opening up in the advanced sectors of an industrializing society. These historians have argued that professionals found in organization and expertise an alternative foundation for social order appropriate to a world of large urban centers rather than small village communities.[40]

Men like Daniel Coit Gilman and Arthur D. Little shared a genius for organization-building. To use a phrase popular in the American Chemical Society, they saw themselves at the head of an "advancing front of science." Even so, the leading interpretations of "the search for order" in late-nineteenth- and early-twentieth-century America may give too much weight to organization and expertise as the dominant expressions of professionalism. Businessmen and professionals were clearly not the only organization builders during the period. Instead, the evidence suggests a general wave of associationalism and organizational development beginning as early as the 1840s.[41] Nevertheless, we have been unable to detect a comparable level of interest in nonmaterialistic values expressing "the public good" in the associations that represent either more- or less-privileged groups.[42] Thus our findings suggest that the professional middle class asserted itself as much through ideological as through organizational means. Its substitute for religious idealism was not so much organization and expertise as a different kind of "religion"—the religion of occupational activity in the

---

39. Hofstadter (1955, chap. 4).
40. Wiebe (1967, chap. 5); Tyack and Hansot (1982, part 2).
41. Gamm and Putnam (1999).
42. See, e.g., Wilentz (1984); Hattam (1993); and Clemens (1997).

name of civilization. As a foundation for professionals' claims to priority in the social order, expertise played a secondary role in most of the professional associations we studied. (The two associations representing professionals in scientific-industrial occupations were exceptions to this rule.) Over and over again, professionals put themselves forward as the agents of civilization and civic improvement. Individuals, not organizations, were the agents of social improvement, and these motivated individuals were to be directed both by cultural aspirations and by expertise.

The regularly repeated injunction to serve civilization appears to have had at least three cultural sources: the strictures of an activist Christianity,[43] the optimism of Enlightenment currents in philosophy,[44] and the law and culture of fiduciary relationships.[45] Each of these cultural currents helped during the course of the nineteenth century to transform the inwardly turned guild and aristocratic values of earlier professional elites.

Although one sees some lingering fidelity to this "social trustee professionalism" in the 1920s and 1930s, the overall tenor of professionalism clearly began to change. Others have argued that the market for patrician stewardship gradually declined by the end of the Progressive Era. The causes of the decline are numerous, but three of the more important were the disenchantments of war, the consumerism of the prosperous 1920s, and the growing acceptance of cultural pluralism among educated elites.

World War I created a deep sense of resentment and alienation among younger intellectuals, attitudes that later reverberated in professional life. To younger intellectuals, the war seemed to have nothing grand about it—it was marked by power politics, national dissensus, and carnage—and it sapped the enthusiasm of many. As Henry Allen has written, "the war would make cynicism a sort of etiquette and irony a motive and tone in art and literature right up through the present day.[46] Many intellectuals,

---

43. From the presidential speeches of the period, see, e.g., van Brunt (1875), Campbell (1885), Holden (1886), and Blaisdell (1911). The Christian motifs in these speeches are consistent with the outward-looking, society-reforming upper-class Christianity promulgated by New England theologians, such as Henry Ward Beecher, from the 1820s on. See Hall (1994).

44. From the presidential speeches of the period, see, e.g., Gilman (1872), Carter (1895), Wheeler (1899), and Hughes (1925).

45. From the presidential speeches of the period, see, e.g., Kellogg (1893) and Meldrim (1915). After an absence in the 1920s and 1930s, the imagery of professionals as social fiduciaries returned in several speeches from the Cold War and Civil Rights eras. See, e.g., Yarnell (1947); Kerr (1952); Silcox (1955); and Alexander (1969).

46. Allen (1998, p. 26).

supported by the cosmopolitanism of the cities, grew tired of a middle-class culture they considered stifling and patronizing. By the end of the Progressive Era, an important minority began to consider professional elites less guardians of all society than of Anglo-Protestant hegemony. Randolph Bourne spoke for many in his generation when he criticized middle-class men for making "pleasant children" out of their wives and fumed that "the whole of Anglo-Saxon culture" would have to be over-thrown if the world was "ever to have any freedom or any life or honesty or sensitiveness of soul."[47]

Depleted from within, the old ideals of professional stewardship were buffeted from without by the successes of consumer capitalism. In the prosperous 1920s consumer sovereignty became a watchword not only in merchandising but also in government, education, popular culture, and other spheres of American life.[48] Profiles in popular magazines of "heroes of production" (business, scientific, and political leaders) gave way to profiles of "heroes of consumption."[49] Sports and then other extracurricular activities (band, glee club, drama, etc.) became focal points for high school students in the 1920s and 1930s. As one high school principal of the period put it, extracurricular activity "pulsates with life and purpose," whereas the formal curriculum "owes its existence to a coercive regime, loosely connected and highly artificial."[50]

When the demand for socially responsive leadership returned after the Great Depression, the organizational focus of civic engagement shifted from professional institutions (and the political leaders influenced by them) to the federal welfare state. The professions were left, for the most part, standing on the sidelines as the Roosevelt administration took the initiative to mount a massive federal assault on economic and social problems. Some of the professional associations added activities in harmony with the New Deal, such as the ABA's committee on legal aid for the indigent, but most resisted on the grounds that the federal government threatened to intrude on the capacity of private associations to regulate their own affairs. Only after the welfare state was fully institutionalized after World War II did the organized professions and the private colleges and universities fully make their peace with it.

47. Bourne, quoted in Lasch (1965, pp. 92–93).
48. Fox and Lears (1983); Olney (1991); and Lears (1994).
49. Lowenthal (1961, chap. 4).
50. Quoted in Cohen (1985, p. 257).

The Organization as a Source of Change

Organizational developments paralleled and reinforced the changes in the political environment. When progressivism reigned, professional organizations had structural incentives to mobilize their members' normative commitments. By the 1920s, most professional associations had become well institutionalized. Growth in membership led to an increasing number of sections, committees, and offices and encouraged a tendency to focus on internal concerns. Finally, however, continuing growth after World War II enhanced the capacity of organizations to respond to a wide range of environmental demands through specialized, bureaucratic offices. As we have shown, in many professional organizations, this capacity has been used (in limited ways) since the 1970s for activities aimed at civic and community improvement.

It must be remembered that professional elites in the nineteenth and early twentieth centuries were for the most part leaders of small and struggling bands of practitioners. In the 1880s, only the National Education Association and the American Medical Association had more than 500 members. Issues of legitimacy were necessarily salient. Many of the new national associations faced periodic battles to secure their position against other organizations hoping to supplant them. Critics still saw professionalism as a kind of conspiracy against the laity, and liberal economists were suspicious of professional association as a means of monopolizing job opportunities in particular fields. Scientists had established material bases of legitimacy (and were often well supported by industry), but other professionals mobilized their own constituencies in part by projecting a familiar set of "high-minded" values in relation to the large problems of community and civic life. Like D. Everett Waid, president of the American Institute of Architects in 1925, they insisted that "the highest form of leadership is not money or power but professional service" and that by holding fast to the highest professional standards, architects "contribute to the future welfare of the race."[51] In statements such as Waid's, sociologists often read a bid for preeminence on the part of men of culture against the economically powerful who dominated a practically minded and commercial age. But we should not forget that these expressions were also proven political tools for organization builders. They helped to mobilize members and to mollify outside critics.

51. Waid (1925, p. 12).

All of the professional associations experienced strong growth in the early twentieth century see Figure 5-2.) This growth was accompanied, predictably enough, by substantial internal differentiation. In the interwar period, professional associations added many of the sections and committees that remain important to them today. The American Chemical Society, for example, is more than 100 years old, but one-third of its sections were founded in the twenty years between 1919 and 1940. During the same period, several of the associations reorganized in response to the increasing size of their memberships and the increasing complexity of their activities. The ACS stopped publishing reports of its annual meetings in 1934 owing to their increasing distance from the concerns of rank-and-file members, which then numbered more than 20,000.[52] Many introduced new layers of bureaucracy. The NEA, with a membership already over 80,000, created its Representative Assembly in 1921. The AMA founded or acquired seven new specialty journals in the decade after the end of World War I, and it officially recognized specialty boards in medicine in 1934.[53] The ABA created a representative structure, the House of Delegates, in 1936.[54] Even when growth was not a pressing matter until the 1950s and 1960s (as it was not for the AIA and the APA), the models of the age proclaimed that professional associations could not be efficient and respectable if they were not well staffed and organized into appropriate offices, sections, and committees. The APA reorganized in 1946, greatly expanding its number of divisions.[55]

Under the circumstances, it is not surprising that professional elites tended to focus on the inner workings of their own organizations. Five of the professional associations already had more than 5,000 members by 1920 and even the academic discipline associations had that many members by 1955. In contrast to the founding generations, professional elites in the mid-twentieth century became leaders of large and successful organizations. The inner workings of organizations were complicated and challenging, as well as of great interest to the majority of members who found a niche in sections and committees and the interests these generated and set in play.

52. Skolnik and Reese (1976, pp. 236–37).

53. American Medical Association Archives (1996).

54. American Bar Association, Division for Media Relations and Public Affairs (1997).

55. On the APA, see Evans, Sexton, and Cadwallader (1992, pp. 187–89). On the AIA, see Saylor (1957).

Figure 5-2. *Membership in Professional Associations, 1880–1995*

Number of members

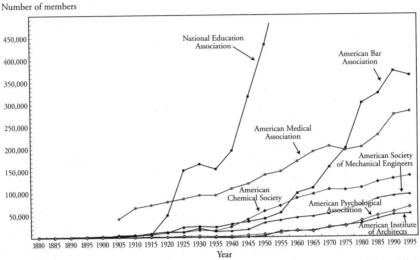

Sources: Gale Research (1957-1995); Saylor (1957, p. 30); Skolnik and Reese (1976, p. 456); American Bar Association, Division of Marketing Research (1998); American Medical Association, Department of Database Services (1998); American Psychological Association (1998); American Society of Mechanical Engineers Archives (1998); National Education Association, Business and Financial Department (1998).

In his presidential speech of 1935, Ernest Russell, president of the AIA, noted with regret the triumph of organizational interests over the institute's original cultural mission. "The programs of conventions," he observed, "are criticized because of the time consumed by organization or internal matters, and because the practice of architecture as a profession and as an art receives too little attention. The criticism is justifiable, but it is difficult to correct." In what seems to be (but probably was not) a self-consciously ironic commentary on the problem, Russell goes on to suggest that an organizational device be used to solve the problem of organizational dominance: "I will strongly recommend that this question of convention programs be given special study by a committee appointed for the purpose."[56] Howard Mumford Jones, president of the Modern Language Association, lamented, "The central problem . . . has two faces: gigantism and multitudinousness. Can the giant of 1980 continue to wear the clothes, however stretched and patched, of the pygmy of 1883?"[57]

56. Russell (1935, p. 3).
57. Jones (1966, p. 5).

During this period of growth and differentiation, the presidencies themselves became much more clearly political offices. Men who were interested in office had to make the rounds of the constituencies. Campaigning and horse-trading became a part of organized professional life. Donald E. Wood, an unsuccessful candidate for president of the AMA in 1964, recalled: "As I made my rounds of the hospitality suites and the caucuses, I recognized that at least the major states—California, New York, Illinois, Texas—all had their own axes to grind, their own candidates to get elected. It was just as it is at the national Republican or Democratic convention. You back my candidate. I'll support yours."[58] Professionals themselves developed a sense that the president was as much a favorite of a faction as the representative of the whole body.

While growth and institutionalization led professional organizations away from a focused concern with their occupations' contribution to public life, these forces eventually also brought new resources and structures that could, in time, be used for civic and community activities. As the leaders of professional organizations focused on internal dynamics and lost touch rhetorically with public life, they created specialized offices and programs to represent the organizations concretely in their efforts to contribute to public life. Colleges and universities created public affairs and community relations departments as early as the 1920s. By the 1930s, the ABA had organized a number of committees and projects connected to public issues. The AMA and ASME began to develop such a presence around 1960. Other organizations (the ACS, the APA, the AIA) did so for the first time in the supportive climate of the 1970s at a time of continued rapid growth.

In the 1980s and 1990s the budgets of several of the professional associations grew to an impressive size. The American Chemical Society is a particularly notable example. Its 1997 budget topped $300 million. Most of its income comes from publications rather than membership dues (the latter representing less than 5 percent of revenue). *Chemical Abstracts* abstracts and indexes the world's chemistry-related research and provides access to the resulting scientific database in electronic and hardcopy formats. This division alone generated $163 million in 1997, primarily through charges for electronic services. Another large contributor ($82 million in 1997) was the Publications Division, which publishes a wide range of scientific journals, periodicals, and books. Other well-supported

58. Wood, quoted in Campion (1984, p. 95).

associations, such as the AMA and the ABA, are much more dues-dependent. Dues are more than $400 per year in these associations.

These resources, encouraged by a supportive political climate, have helped foster an expectation for *some* civic and community involvement among the leaders and staff of the mainline professional associations. This expectation is no doubt related also to the perception that the federal role in social policy has diminished and that government should not attempt to solve all social problems. Instead of relying on the federal government to solve social ills, private and public institutions have moved toward collaborative and partnership models. Some associations that speak frequently about the need for civic activism do relatively little themselves—the National Education Association and the American Psychological Association are two examples—but only academic discipline associations, chartered for scholarly purposes and limited by small treasuries, have so far been entirely exempt from this climate of expectations promoting civic engagement.

Implications

How one evaluates the transformation we have described depends on the degree of importance one attaches to ideology. Those who attach great importance to ideology can plausibly interpret our findings as showing decline in the connection of the professions to public life. Those who attach importance to practices alone will interpret our findings as showing that professional associations are actively engaged in civic and community life, in all likelihood more than ever before. Accepting neither of these two interpretations, in this last section we discuss the implications of our findings for the question of civic engagement in American democracy.

We do not believe our findings should be interpreted as a paean to the civic virtue of professional leaders of the past or as a criticism of the organizational concerns of today's professional elites. Professional leaders may have expressed themselves more consistently and more eloquently in the past about their civilizational and civic roles, but they did not necessarily act successfully on their expressed ideals.[59] Moreover, the ideals of the

---

59. Strong ideals can mask weak positions. The early presidents of the University of California were, for example, notoriously weak and subject to the direct intervention of the Regents in everyday university affairs. The first strong president of the university, Benjamin Ide Wheeler, was less given than his predecessors to eloquent rhetoric about the social role of universities, but he diminished the role of the Regents and raised buildings and programs out of previously fallow soil. See Stadtman (1970, pp. 88–106).

past showed characteristic weaknesses and blind spots, even when they were effective. They often encouraged arrogance and purism in dealings with the public, and they coexisted, as is well known, with a nearly total exclusion of minorities and women from positions of leadership—and indeed from membership in many cases.[60]

In the broader political culture, too, social trustee professionalism left an ambiguous political legacy. In the nineteenth century, professionals supported a conservative politics of nation-building, opposed in many ways to the populist impulses of Catholics and Jews, poor farmers, urban workers, and Democrats.[61] And yet by the turn of the century the professional ideology of civilization-building clearly also nourished the Progressive movement.[62] The consequences of professional ideology depended on the level of mobilization of more-advantaged and less-advantaged groups in society and on the kinds of political alliances made between middle-class professionals, upper-class businesspeople, and lower-status groups. When lower-status groups were highly mobilized, professionals' concerns about civilizational values could be a progressive force in political life, one that tended to support populist energies for change, while encouraging them along a reformist rather than a radical path. When professionals acted alone or were allied primarily with business elites, civilizational concerns usually supported the existing social and political order.[63]

Civic engagement through bureaucratic means has had equally ambiguous implications. There are reasons for professional organizations to feel proud of their recent civic record—many of their civic and community activities have had an important impact. But most of the professional organizations we studied are only minimally engaged, and even the most involved devote but a comparatively small proportion of resources to civic activities. Clearly, professional organizations cannot hope to substitute for institutions that are more directly and continuously involved in civic and community life. Insofar as the professions are perceived to be a major vehicle for the "new volunteerism" or "new communitarianism" in American society, they are likely to prove a poor form of transportation.

More important, the bureaucratization of civic engagement encourages a compartmentalization of consciousness. If organizations have special

60. On the racist views of representative figures of the professional elite of the late nineteenth and early twentieth centuries, see Lagemann (1989, pp. 30, 46, 48, 74, 79–80 ff.).

61. Ladd and Hadley (1976); and Meyer, Tyack, Nagel, and Gordon (1979).

62. Hostadter (1955); and Wiebe (1967).

63. Brint (1994, pp. 104–5, 112–14).

offices of community and public affairs, members may feel that their community and civic responsibilities are "taken care of." Instead of fostering a culture of connection to the broader society, the bureaucratization of civic engagement frees many professionals from any marked sense of connection to the life of their society. It thereby aids in the transformation of professionalism from an ideology linking community and authority into an ideology linking markets and skills. A paradox results: for all of the increased civic and community activity of professional organizations, the cultural connection of professionals to public life may in fact be declining.

However we may feel about these developments, it would be unwise to indulge in feelings of nostalgia for the old professionalism. Its day has passed. The watchwords today are participation and responsiveness, not authority. John Busby put this shift in cultural expectations well in his 1985 presidential speech to the AIA: "The architect today doesn't—and can't—work in a vacuum. Those days are gone. . . . Paternalism is out. Responsiveness is in."[64] Undoubtedly, any new professional ideology that emphasized community and civic engagement would have to combine its normative priorities and expert skills with a genuine respect for dialogue and pluralism. No such ideologies may emerge as alternatives to today's more purely expert forms of professionalism, but it is impossible to envisage the professions once again becoming coherent vehicles for civic engagement without the development of a new ideology of professionalism similar in some respects to the old, but better adapted to the demands of contemporary democratic society.

Appendix 5A: The Presidential Speeches File

This appendix lists the presidential speeches coded in the content analysis. The speeches are grouped by the president's organization and are in chronological order.

American Bar Association

1879, James O. Broadhead, "Address of James O. Broadhead."
1885, John W. Stevenson, "The Address of the President, John W. Stevenson."

---

64. Busby (1985, p. 17)

1895, James C. Carter, "Address of the President, James C. Carter."

1905, Henry St. George Tucker, "Address of the President, Henry St. George Tucker."

1915, Peter W. Meldrim, "Address of the President, Peter W. Meldrim."

1925, Charles Evans Hughes, "Annual Address. Liberty and Law."

1935, Scott M. Loftin, "Independence of the Judiciary. Annual Address."

1945, David A. Simmons, "The Supremacy of the Law. Annual Address."

1955, Lloyd Wright, "Milestone and Concepts of the Lawyer-Citizen. Annual Address."

1965, Lewis F. Powell, "The State of the Legal Profession."

1975, James D. Fellers, "State of the Legal Profession."

1986, William W. Fallsgraff, "A Year in the Life of the ABA: Remarks to the House of Delegates."

1996, Roberta Cooper-Ramo, "President's Statement to the ABA House of Delegates."

American Chemical Society

1894, Henry W. Wiley, "Synthetic Food of the Future."

1913, Arthur D. Little, "Industrial Research in America."

1924, L. H. Baekland, "Prospects and Retrospects."

1932, L. V. Redman, "Stabilized Research—A National Asset."

1945, Bradley Dewey, "The Chemist and the Public."

1966, William J. Sparks, "President's Message."

1976, Glenn T. Seaborg, "What's Past Is Prologue."

1986, Ellis K. Fields, "President's Message."

1996, Ronald C. Breslow, "Interesting Times for Chemistry."

American Historical Association

1895, George B. Hoar, "Popular Discontent with Representative Government."

1906, J. B. McMaster, "Old Standards of Public Morals."

1916, H. M. Stephens, "Nationality and History."

1926, C. M. Andrews, "The American Revolution: An Interpretation."

1936, Michael I. Rostostovtzeff, "The Hellenistic World and Its Economic Development."

1946, Carlton J. H. Hayes, "America and Europe."

1956, Lynn Thorndike, "Whatever Was Was Right."
1966, Franklin C. Lane, "At the Roots of Republicanism."
1976, Gordon Wright, "History and Morality."
1986, William H. McNeill, "Mythistory or Truth: Myth, History and Historians."
1996, John Coatsworth, "Welfare."

American Institute of Architects

1875, Henry van Brunt, "Annual Address."
1886, Thomas U. Walters, "President Walters' Address."
1895, Daniel Hudson Burnham, "Address of the President."
1907, Frank Miles Day, "Address of the President."
1915, R. Clipston Sturgis, "Address of the President."
1925, D. Everett Waid, "Address of the President."
1935, Ernest J. Russell, "The President's Address."
1945, Raymond J. Ashton, "Address of the President."
1955, Clair William Ditchy, "President Ditchy's Convention Address."
1965, Arthur Gould Odell, "Bright Future of the Profession."
1976, Louis DeMoll, "The President's Report: Louis De Moll, FAIA."
1985, John A. Busby, "Report of the President."
1995, Chet Widom, "Welcome to Day 1. . ."

American Medical Association

1875, W. K. Bowling, "Address of W. K. Bowling, MD, President of the Association."
1885, Henry F. Campbell, "Address of the President."
1904, John H. Musser, "Address. Some Aspects of Medical Education."
1915, Victor C. Vaughan, "Remarks by the President, Dr. Victor C. Vaughan."
1925, William Allen Pusey, "Address of the President, William Allen Pusey."
1935, Walter L. Bierring, "Address of the President, Walter L. Bierring."
1945, Herman L. Kretschmer, "Address of the President, Dr. Herman L. Kretschmer."
1955, Walter B. Martin, "Address of the President, Dr. Walter B. Martin."
1965, James Z. Appel, "We the People, Are We Sheep?"

1975, Malcolm C. Todd, "Address of the President."
1985, Joseph F. Boyle, "Address of the President."
1995, Robert E. McAfee, "A Modern Fable."

American Political Science Association

1907, Albert O. Shaw, "Presidential Address."
1916, Ernest Freund, "Principles of Legislation."
1926, Charles Merriam, "Progress in Political Research."
1936, Francis W. Coker, "American Traditions Concerning Property and Liberty."
1946, John M. Gaus, "A Job Analysis of Political Science."
1955, Charles McKinley, "The Constitution and the Tasks Ahead."
1965, David B. Truman, "Disillusion and Regeneration: A Quest for a Discipline."
1976, Austin Ranney, " 'The Divine Science': Political Engineering in American Culture."
1985, Philip E. Converse, "Power and the Monopoly of Information."
1996, Sidney Verba, "The Citizen as Respondent: Sample Surveys and American Democracy."

American Psychological Association

1896, J. McKeen Cattell, "Address of the President before the American Psychological Association."
1906, Mary W. Calkins, "A Reconciliation between Structural and Functional Psychology."
1916, J. B. Watson, "The Place of Conditioned Reflex in Psychology."
1926, Madison Bentley, "The Major Categories of Psychology."
1937, Clark Hull, "Mind, Mechanism, and Adaptive Behavior."
1946, Henry E. Garnett, "A Developmental Theory of Intelligence."
1956, E. Lowell Kelly, "Consistency of Adult Personality."
1965, Jerome S. Bruner, "The Growth of Mind."
1975, Donald T. Campbell, "On the Conflict between Biological and Social Evolution and between Psychology and Moral Tradition."
1985, Janet T. Spence, "Achievement American Style: The Rewards and Costs of Individualism."
1996, Ronald Fox, "Charlatanism, Scientism, and Psychology's Social Contract."

American Society of Mechanical Engineers

1881, Robert M. Thurston, "Our Progress in Mechanical Engineering."
1884, John E. Sweet, "President's Address 1884."
1894, Eckley B. Coxe, "Technical Education."
1904, James M. Dodge, "The Money Value of Technical Training."
1914, James Hartness, "The Human Element: The Key to Economic Problems."
1924, Fred R. Low, "Power Resources, Present and Prospective."
1935, Ralph Flanders, "Neglected Elements of Recovery."
1947, D. Robert Yarnell, "The Public Responsibility of Engineers."
1955, Lewis K. Silcox, "Pathway of Progress."
1966, James H. Harlow, "Chief Mechanical Engineer."
1974, Richard B. Robertson, "America the Beautiful."

Dartmouth College

1877, Samuel Colcord Bartlett, "President Bartlett's Inaugural."
1893, Wiliam Jewett Tucker, "Inaugural Address."
1909, Ernest Fox Nichols, "The President's Address."
1916, Ernest Martin Hopkins, "The President's Inaugural Speech."
1945, James Sloan Dickey, "Convocation Address."
1970, James G. Kemeny, "Inaugural Address."
1980, David T. McLaughlin, "Inaugural Address."
1987, James O. Freedman, "Inaugural Address."

Modern Language Association

1886, Franklin Carter, "Study of Modern Languages in Our Higher Institutions."
1896, James Morgan Hunt, "English as a Living Language."
1907, Henry Alfred Todd, "The Genesis of Speech."
1916, Jefferson Fletcher, "Our Opportunity."
1926, Hermann Collitz, "World Languages."
1936, Carlton Brown, "The Attack on the Castle."
1946, Ernest Hatch Wilkins, "Petrarchan Byways."
1956, Louise Pound, "Then and Now."
1966, Howard Mumford Jones, "The Giant and the Pygmy."
1976, Germaine Bree, "Presidential Address."

1986, Theodore Ziolkowski, "A Rhetoric of Ritual: Or Crisis and Community."

1996, Sander L. Gilman, "Habent Sua Fata Cibelli; or, Books, Jobs, and the MLA."

National Education Association

1885, F. Louis Soldan, "Address of the President."

1890, James Canfield, "Response."

1907, Nathan Schaeffer, "What Can Schools Do to Aid the Peace Movement?"

1915, David Starr Jordan, "President's Address: The Teacher and War."

1926, Mary McSkimmon, "The Challenge of Childhood."

1935, Henry Lester Smith, "Looking Ahead in Education."

1945, F. L. Schlage, "Significant Achievements."

1955, Waurine Walker, "A Call to Greatness."

1965, Lois V. Edinger, "Education for World Responsibility."

1975, James A. Harris, "Report of the President."

1985, Mary Hatwood Futtrell, "Report of the President."

1995, Keith Geiger, "Allies for Education: 1995 Representative Assembly Keynote."

Pomona College

1901, George Augustus Gates, "Inaugural Speech of President George Augustus Gates."

1911, James A. Blaisdell, "Inaugural Speech of President James A. Blaisdell."

1928, Charles K. Edmunds, "Inaugural Speech of President Charles K. Edmunds."

1941, Elijah W. Lyon, "Inaugural Speech of President Elijah W. Lyon."

1969, David Alexander, "Inaugural Speech of President David Alexander."

1991, Peter W. Stanley, "Inaugural Speech of President Peter W. Stanley."

University of California

1875, Daniel Gilman, "Inaugural Speech of President Daniel Gilman."

1881, W. T. Reid, "Inaugural Speech of President W. T. Reid."

1885, Edward S. Holden, "Inaugural Speech of President Edward S. Holden."

1888, Horace Davis, "Inaugural Speech of President Horace Davis."

1893, Martin Kellogg, "Inaugural Speech of President Martin Kellogg."

1899, Benjamin I. Wheeler, "Inaugural Speech of President Benjamin I. Wheeler."

1920, David P. Barrows, "Inaugural Speech of President David P. Barrows."

1923, William Wallace Campbell, "Inaugural Speech of President William Wallace Campbell."

1930, Robert G. Sproul, "Inaugural Speech of President Robert G. Sproul."

1952, Clark Kerr, "Inaugural Speech of Chancellor Clark Kerr."

1953, Glenn Seaborg, "Inaugural Speech of Chancellor Glenn Seaborg."

1961, Edward W. Strong, "Charter Day Speech of Chancellor Edward W. Strong."

1965, Roger Heyns, "Inaugural Speech of Chancellor Roger Heyns."

1972, Albert Bowker, "Charter Day Speech of Chancellor Albert Bowker."

1980, I. Michael Heyman, "Inaugural Speech of Chancellor I. Michael Heyman."

1990, C. L. Tien, "Inaugural Speech of Chancellor C. L. Tien."

University of Chicago

1892, William Rainey Harper, "First Convocation Speech of William Rainey Harper."

1907, Harry Pratt Judson, "Acceptance."

1923, Ernest Dewitt Burton, "First Convocation Speech of Ernest Dewitt Burton."

1930, Robert Maynard Hutchins, "Inaugural Address of Robert Maynard Hutchins."

1951, Lawrence A. Kimpton, "Inauguration Banquet Speech."

1961, George Wells Beadle, "The University of X: An Academic Equation."

1968, Edward W. Levi, "Inaugural Address."

1976, John T. Wilson, "Inaugural Address of John T. Wilson."

1978, Hanna Holborn Gray, "Inaugural Address of Hanna Holborn Gray."

1993, Hugo Sonnenschein, "Inaugural Address of Hugo Sonnenschein."

University of Pennsylvania

1881, William Pepper, "Inauguration of William Pepper, M.D."

1931, Thomas G. Gates, "Address of Thomas G. Gates, President of the University of Pennsylvania."

1970, Martin Meyerson, "Text of Commencement Address Given by Martin Meyerson, President-Designate of the University of Pennsylvania."

1981, Sheldon Hackney, "Inaugural Address."

1994, Judith Rodin, "The Inaugural Address."

References

Alexander, David. 1969. "Inaugural Speech of President David Alexander." Honnold-Mudd Library Special Collections, Pomona College, Claremont, Calif.

Allen, Henry. 1998. "Strand's Great Moment." *The New York Review of Books* 45(8): 26–28.

American Bar Association, Division of Legal Services. 1998. "Pro Bono Activity through Organized Programs." Mimeo.

———, Division of Media Relations and Public Affairs. 1997. *ABA Overview.* Chicago: American Bar Association.

———, Division of Marketing Research. 1998. "Membership Table I." Chicago: American Bar Association. Mimeo.

American Medical Association. 1995. *Proceedings of the House of Delegates.* Chicago: American Medical Association.

———, Archives. 1996. *Highlights in AMA History.* Chicago: American Medical Association.

———, Department of Database Services. 1998. "AMA Membership and Market Share, 1847–1989." Chicago: American Medical Association. Mimeo.

American Psychological Association. 1998. "American Psychological Association Member Totals, 1892–1997." Washington, D.C.: American Psychological Association. Mimeo.

American Society of Mechanical Engineers Archives. 1998. "Statistics on ASME Membership Data." New York: American Society of Mechanical Engineers. Mimeo.

Ausubel, Herman. 1950. *Historians and Their Craft: A Study of Presidential Addresses of the American Historical Association, 1884–1945.* Columbia University Press.

Bellah, Robert N., Richard Madsen, William M. Sullivan, Ann Swidler, and Steven M. Tipton. 1985. *Habits of the Heart: Individualism and Commitment in American Life.* University of California Press.

Blaisdell, James A. 1911. "Inaugural Speech of President James A. Blaisdell." Honnold-Mudd Special Collections, Pomona College, Claremont, Calif.

Brint, Steven. 1994. *In an Age of Experts: The Changing Role of Professionals in Politics and Public Life.* Princeton University Press.

Broadhead, James O. 1879. "Address of James O. Broadhead." *Annual Report of the ABA* 2: 51–70.

Bryk, Anthony S., Valerie E. Lee, and Peter Holland. 1993. *Catholic Schools and the Public Good.* Harvard University Press.

Burrows, James. 1963. *AMA: Voice of American Medicine.* Johns Hopkins University Press.

Busby, John A. 1985. "Report of the President." American Institute of Architects Library and Archives, New York. Mimeo.

Campbell, Henry F. 1885. "Address of the President." *Journal of the American Medical Association* 4: 477–86.

Campion, Frank D. 1984. *The AMA and U.S. Health Policy since 1940.* Chicago Review Press.

Carter, James C. 1895. "Address of the President, James C. Carter." *Annual Report of the ABA* (Chicago) 18: 185–236.

Clemens, Elisabeth S. 1997. *The People's Lobby: Organizational Interests and the Rise of Interest Group Politics in the United States, 1890–1925.* University of Chicago Press.

Cohen, David K. 1985. "Origins." In Arthur G. Powell, Eleanor Farrar, and David K. Cohen, *Shopping Mall High Schools: Winners and Losers in the Educational Marketplace.* Boston: Houghton-Mifflin.

Crawford, Meredith P. 1992. "Rapid Growth and Change at the American Psychological Association: 1945 to 1970." In *The American Psychological Association: An Historical Perspective,* edited by Rand B. Evans, Virginia Staudt Sexton, and Thomas C. Cadwallader. Washington, D.C.: American Psychological Association.

Evans, Rand B., Virginia Staudt Sexton, and Thomas C. Cadwallader, eds. 1992. *The American Psychological Association: An Historical Perspective.* Washington, D.C.: American Psychological Association.

Etzioni, Amitai. 1993. *The Spirit of Community: Rights, Responsibilities and the Communitarian Agenda.* New York: Crown.

Fellers, James D. 1975. "State of the Legal Profession." *American Bar Association Journal* 61: 1053–59.

Fishbein, Morris. 1947. *A History of the American Medical Association, 1847–1947.* Philadelphia: W. B. Saunders.

Fox, Richard Wightman, and T. J. Jackson Lears, eds. 1983. *The Culture of Consumption: Critical Essays in American History, 1880–1980.* Pantheon.

Fox, Ronald. 1996. "Charlatanism, Scientism and Psychology's Social Contract." *American Psychologist* 51: 777–84.

Gale Research. 1957–1995. *Encyclopedia of Associations.* Detroit: Gale Research. Annual series.

Gamm, Gerald, and Robert D. Putnam. 1999. "The Growth of Voluntary Associations in America, 1840–1940." *Journal of Interdisciplinary History* 29: 511–57.

Hall, Peter Dobkin. 1994. "Religion and the Origin of Voluntary Associations in the United States." Working Paper 213, Program on Non-Profit Organizations. Yale University.

Halliday, Terence C. 1985. "Knowledge Mandates: Collective Influence by Scientific, Normative and Syncretic Professions." *British Journal of Sociology* 36: 421–27.

Haskell, Thomas L. 1984. "Professionalism versus Capitalism." In *The Authority of Experts,* edited by Thomas L. Haskell, 180–225. Bloomington: Indiana University Press.

Hattam, Victoria C. 1993. *Labor Visions and State Power: The Origins of Business Unionism in the United States.* Princeton University Press.

Hodginson, Virginia A. 1996. *Nonprofit Almanac, 1996–97: Dimensions of the Independent Sector.* San Francisco: Jossey-Bass.

Hofstadter, Richard. 1955. *The Age of Reform: From Bryan to FDR.* Knopf.

Holden, Edward S. 1885. "Inaugural Speech of President Edward S. Holden." Bancroft Library Special Collections, University of California, Berkeley.

Hughes, Charles Evans. 1925. "Annual Address. Liberty and Law." *Annual Report of the ABA* 50: 183–98.

Jones, Howard Mumford. 1966. "The Giant and the Pygmy." *Publications of the Modern Language Association* 81: 3–11.

Kellogg, Martin. 1893. "Inaugural Speech of President Martin Kellogg." Bancroft Library Special Collections, University of California, Berkeley.

Kerr, Clark. 1952. "Inaugural Speech of Chancellor Clark Kerr." Bancroft Library Special Collections, University of California, Berkeley.

Ladd, Everett C., Jr. 1996. "The Data Just Don't Show Erosion of America's 'Social Capital.'" *Public Perspective* 7 (June/ July): 1, 5–22.

Ladd, Everett C., Jr., and Charles Hadley. 1976. *Party Systems in American Politics.* W. W. Norton.

Lagemann, Ellen Condliffe. 1989. *The Politics of Knowledge: The Carnegie Corporation, Philanthropy, and Public Policy.* Middletown, Conn.: Wesleyan University Press.

Lasch, Christopher. 1965. *The New Radicalism in America, 1889–1963: The Intellectual as a Social Type.* Knopf.

Lears, T. J. Jackson. 1994. *Fables of Consumption: A Cultural History of Advertising in America.* Basic Books.

Lowenthal, Leo. 1961. *Literature, Popular Culture and Society.* Englewood Cliffs, N.J.: Prentice-Hall.

Meldrim, Peter W. 1915. "Address of the President, Peter W. Meldrim." *Annual Report of the ABA* (Chicago) 40: 313–28.

Meyer, John W., David Tyack, Joanne Nagel, and Audri Gordon. 1979. "Public Education as Nation-Building in America, 1870–1930." *American Journal of Sociology* 85: 591–613.

Murphy, William Michael, and D. J. R. Bruckner, eds. 1976. *The Idea of the University of Chicago.* University of Chicago Press.

National Education Association, Business and Financial Department. 1998. "NEA Membership, 1857–1997." Washington, D.C.: National Education Association. Mimeo.

Olney, Martha L. 1991. *Buy Now, Pay Later: Advertising, Credit and Consumer Durables in the 1920s.* University of North Carolina Press.

Parker, W. R. 1953. "The MLA, 1883–1953." *Publications of the Modern Language Association* 68 (Sept. supplement): 3–39.

Popenoe, David. 1993. "American Family Decline, 1960–1990." *Journal of Marriage and the Family* 55: 529–40.

Putnam, Robert D. 1995. "Bowling Alone: America's Declining Social Capital." *Journal of Democracy* 6: 65–78.

———. 1996. "The Strange Disappearance of Civic America." *American Prospect* 24 (Winter): 34–48.

Rosenstone, Steven, and John Mark Hansen. 1993. *Mobilization, Participation and Democracy in America.* Macmillan.

Russell, Ernest J. 1935. "The President's Address." *Octagon* (June): 3–4.

Saylor, Henry Hodgman. 1957. *The AIA's First Hundred Years*. Washington, D.C.: American Institute of Architects.

Schudson, Michael. 1996. "What If Civic Life Didn't Die?" *American Prospect* 25 (March–April): 17–28.

Silcox, Lewis K. 1955. "Pathway of Progress." *Mechanical Engineering* 77: 4–5.

Skocpol, Theda. 1996. "The Tocqueville Problem: Civic Engagement in American Democracy." Presidential Address at the annual meeting of the Social Science History Association, New Orleans.

Skolnik, Herman, and Kenneth M. Reese. 1976. *A Century of Chemistry: The Role of Chemists and the American Chemical Society*. Washington, D.C.: American Chemical Society.

Somit, Albert, and Joseph Tanenhaus. 1962. *The Development of Political Science*. University of California Press.

Stadtman, Verne A. 1970. *The University of California, 1868–1968*. McGraw-Hill.

Swidler, Ann. 1997. "To Revitalize Community Life We Must First Strengthen Our National Institutions." *Chronicle of Higher Education*, May 17, pp. B4–5.

Tocqueville, Alexis de. [1835–40] 1961. *Democracy in America*. Vols. 1 and 2. New York: Schocken.

Tyack, David B., and Elizabeth Hansot. 1982. *Managers of Virtue: Public School Leadership in America, 1820–1980*. Basic Books.

University of California, Office of Community Relations. 1997. *Cal in the Commuity: A Guide to Community Partnerships and Campus Resources*. University of California, Berkeley.

Vallely, Richard M. 1996. "Couch-Potato Democracy?" *American Prospect* 25 (March–April): 25–26.

van Brunt, Henry. 1875. "Annual Address." *Proceedings of the Annual Meeting* (American Institute of Architects) 9: 5–9.

Verba, Sidney, Kay Lehman Schlozman, and Henry E. Brady. 1995. *Voice and Equality: Civic Voluntarism in American Politics*. Harvard University Press.

Waid, D. Everett. 1925. "Address of the President." *Proceedings of the Annual Meeting* (American Institute of Architects) 58: 9–12.

Wheeler, Benjamin I. 1899. "Inaugural Speech of President Benjamin I. Wheeler." Bancroft Library Special Collections, University of California, Berkeley.

Wiebe, Robert H. 1967. *The Search for Order, 1877–1920*. New York: Hill and Wang.

———. 1995. *Self-Rule: A Cultural History of American Democracy*. University of Chicago Press.

Wilentz, Sean. 1984. *Chants Democratic: New York City and the Rise of the American Working Class, 1788–1850*. Oxford University Press.

Wolfe, Alan. 1998. *One Nation, After All: What Middle-Class Americans Really Think About: God, Country, Family, Racism, Welfare, Immigration, Homosexuality, Work, the Right, the Left, and Each Other*. Viking/Penguin.

Wright, Gordon. 1976. "History and Morality." *American Historical Review* 81: 1–11.

Wuthnow, Robert. 1996. *Poor Richard's Principle: Recovering the American Dream through the Moral Dimension of Work, Business and Money*. Princeton University Press.

Yarnell, D. Robert. 1947. "The Public Responsibility of Engineers." *Mechanical Engineering* 69: 5–6.

Ziolkowski, Theodore. 1986. "A Rhetoric of Ritual: Or Crisis and Community." *Publications of the Modern Language Association* 101: 314–21.

6 | Vital Signs: Organizational Population Trends and Civic Engagement in New Haven, Connecticut, 1850–1998

PETER DOBKIN HALL

CONTEMPORARY DEBATE on civic engagement has directed attention to the associational life of communities as an indicator of the vitality of civil society. Some, like Robert Putnam, argue that declining membership in such traditional voluntary associations as bowling leagues, fraternal societies, and "mainline" religious congregations is symptomatic of diminished civic capacities.[1] Others, like Peter Drucker, say the remarkable growth in the population of nonprofit organizations, which they see as creating new "spheres of effective citizenship" in which individuals can "exercise influence, discharge responsibility, and make decisions," indicates a renewal of civic vitality.[2] Still others point to

The research on which this chapter is based was supported by the AAFRC Trust for Philanthropy, the Aspen Institute's Nonprofit Sector Research Fund, the Lilly Endowment, and the Program on Non-Profit Organizations, Yale University. I am grateful to my students Rachel Kleinfeld, Patricia Reixach, and Christine Janis for sharing their valuable work on New Haven congregations and to Phuc Tran for his insightful study of the reorganization of New Haven's charities in the Progressive Era. Earlier versions of this work were presented at the annual meetings of the Society for the Scientific Study of Religion / Religion Research Association, Nashville, Tennessee, November 1996; the Association for Research on Nonprofit Organizations and Voluntary Action, New York, November 1996; the Religious Institutions Workshop, Program on Nonprofit Organizations, Yale University, January 1997; and the Russell Sage Conference on Civic Engagement, Portland, Maine, September 1997.

1. Putnam (1994, 1995).
2. Drucker (1989, p. 205).

211

churches and other religious bodies as primary transmitters of civic values and competencies.[3]

This study of long-term trends in associational life in New Haven, Connecticut, evaluates these conflicting hypotheses about the impact of different forms of organizational activity on civic engagement over the past century and a half. Because New Haven was one of the primary nurseries for the invention and diffusion of voluntary associations early in the nineteenth century and has, since the 1920s, been the subject of many landmark studies of civic life, it is an appropriate setting in which to evaluate the links between associational trends and civic vitality.[4]

Although scholarship on civic engagement has tended to focus on voluntary associations and nonprofit organizations, this chapter broadens that discussion by giving attention to market organizations of various types (what Tocqueville called "commercial associations"), which at times have provided many of the goods and services that we conventionally associate with nonproprietary entities. The study not only illuminates the extent to which both proprietary and nonproprietary organizations may foster civic engagement but also, in doing do, attempts to refine the language and concepts used in describing the entities Americans use to define and pursue shared values and purposes.

Definitional Issues

When Alexis de Tocqueville in the 1830s noted the propensity of Americans "of all ages, all conditions, and all dispositions" to "constantly form associations," he cast a wide net that included "not only commercial and manufacturing companies, in which all take part, but associations of a thousand other kinds, religious, moral, serious, futile, general or restricted, enormous or diminutive."[5] Although contemporary neologisms like "nonprofit organization" and "nonprofit sector" lay claim to part of the domain described by Tocqueville, they are clearly not equivalent terms,

3. Verba, Schlozman, and Brady (1995).

4. These include the National Bureau of Economic Research's pioneering study, *Trends in Philanthropy: A Study in a Typical American City* (King and Huntley [1928]), Robert Warner's important early study of urban blacks (1940), and Robert Dahl's *Who Governs? Democracy and Power in an American City* (1961), as well as classic studies by Nelson Polsby (1980) and August Hollingshead and Frederick Redlich (1958).

5. Tocqueville (1945, Vol. 2, p. 114).

since his associational universe included both political parties and commercial enterprises that subsequent organizational development clearly distinguished from the eleemosynary entities now considered to compose the nonprofit sphere. Further, though "nonprofit organization" is commonly used as a catch-all term, because it has very specific meanings derived from taxonomies in the Internal Revenue Code and state corporation statutes of the post–World War II decades, its usefulness as a descriptor of earlier voluntary entities is limited; few of these were incorporated, and the largest and most important component of the nonprofit universe—religious bodies—have never had to register as tax-exempt.[6]

For the sake of clarity, I use the term "nonproprietary entity" to refer to any organization or association not established for the personal financial inurement of its principals. I use the term "voluntary association" only to refer to membership organizations. The term "nonprofit organization" is used only to refer to entities that enjoy that status by virtue of IRS registration—and the term is used inclusively to describe both charitable tax-exempt and noncharitable agencies. In preference to the terms "church" and "religious organization," I use the more nuanced designations "congregation," "denomination," and—when referring to nondevotional enterprises with religious ties or missions—such terms as "faith-based" or "religiously tied" organization.

Although primarily concerned with changes in the population and the purposes of nonproprietary entities, this study also focuses on changes in the division of tasks among business, government, and nonproprietary agencies in the production and provision of goods and services. Although firms operating in certain industries and areas of activity such as the arts, education, health care, and human services are today predominantly nonprofit, in the past the balance between nonproprietaries, commercial enterprises, and government differed significantly.[7] Examining changes in the allocation of ownership and the forces that drove those changes provides valuable insight into the nature of civic vitality.[8]

6. John G. Simon (1987) provides the best and most concise overview of the tax taxonomy of charitable tax-exempt and other nonprofits; Burton Weisbrod (1989) includes detailed information on organizational establishment and registration trends within the federal taxonomy.

7. Legal scholar and economist Henry B. Hansmann (1997) provides the best conceptual framework for understanding the range of ownership forms.

8. The construction of the population of organizations involved three steps: first, using city directories, lists were made of all organizations providing goods and services in categories set forth in the National Taxonomy of Exempt Entities; second, those organizations that were clearly proprietary

New Haven's Organizational Population:
An Overview of Trends

The number of nonproprietary entities in New Haven grew dramatically between 1850 and 1910 (see Table 6-1). That period was followed by an eighty-year period of overall stability during which the organizational population hardly varied, despite fluctuations in the population of the city.

Subtrends within particular categories suggest that significant turbulence roiled beneath the apparent stability: although fraternal and sororal

---

were separated—but not eliminated—from the sample. (Thus, for example, under the category of arts organizations, entities like the Silver Moon Orchestra, a popular dance band, were omitted from the population of nonproprietary entities, while others, like the New Haven Military Band were included. Even though the latter was neither incorporated nor tax-exempt—and hence not a nonprofit in the technical sense—it was clearly a nonproprietary voluntary association.) Third, all entities that were clearly government agencies were separated—but not eliminated—from the nonproprietary population. Finally, "religion" was taken to mean only entities with devotional or liturgical purposes (such as congregations and convents), not service organizations established by or supported by religious groups (thus, for example, the St. Francis Orphan Asylum and the Center Church Home for Distressed and Indigent Women, though both faith-based, are treated as firms providing human rather than religious services; similarly, parochial schools are treated as educational rather than religious entities).

What remained after these screenings and sortings was a broad sample of voluntary, mutual benefit, charitable, educational, and religious entities grouped according to a simplification of the twenty-six NTEE (National Taxonomy of Exempt Entities) "major areas" into seven categories: culture/arts, education, health, human services, mutual benefit / membership benefit, and religion.

Because of the significance attached to "national associations," entities operating as chapters of national franchise-form entities—ranging from Boy Scouts and the Red Cross to most veterans', fraternal, and sororal organizations—were identified from standard reference works on the subject. Although included in the general analysis of the local organizational population, trends in their growth and decline were separately noted. Despite the fact that many religious entities are units of national associations—denominational bodies—they were not included in tallies of national associations because of the difficulty in comparing these complex and variable structures with one another or with secular counterparts. Nonetheless, whether congregations were denominationally affiliated, free-standing, or members of loosely coupled "faith families"—which became a highly important issue in the second half of the twentieth century—is noted when appropriate.

A second body of data, consisting of charitable tax-exempt organizations registered with the IRS in 1996, is also referred to. This information, which includes the names, revenues, areas of activity, and locations of 501(c)3 and 501(c)4 organizations, was obtained from agency files. The activities coded in the NTEE include the following (from Hodgkinson, Weitzman, Toppe, and Noga [1992]): arts, culture, humanities; education; environment; animal-related; health, general; mental health; disease, disorder-related; medical research; crime, legal-related; employment, job-related; food, agriculture; housing, shelter; public safety; recreation, sports; youth development; human services; international, foreign affairs; civil rights; community improvement; philanthropy, voluntarism; science; social science; public affairs; religion-related; mutual benefit / membership benefit; unknown/unclassified.

Table 6-1. *Nonproprietary Organizations (NPOs) in New Haven, 1850–1990*

Year	Population of New Haven	Number of NPOs	Number of congregations	Congregations as a percentage of NPOs	Number of fraternal/sororal organizations	Fraternals/sororals as a percentage of NPOs	NPOs per 1,000 population
1850	20,345	42	21	50	1	2	2.1
1860	36,267	81	35	43	16	20	2.3
1870	50,840	130	53	41	41	32	2.6
1880	62,882	249	57	23	61	32	4.0
1890	86,045	326	72	22	155	48	3.8
1900	108,027	458	65	14	204	45	4.2
1910	133,605	605	90	15	257	43	4.5
1920	162,537	602	111	18	224	37	3.7
1930	162,655	676	102	15	156	23	4.2
1940	160,605	604	98	16	108	18	3.8
1950	164,443	649	118	18	85	13	4.0
1960	162,048	595	136	23	81	14	3.9
1970	137,707	614	120	20	69	11	4.5
1980	126,109	587	190	32	15	3	4.7
1990	130,474	630	183	33	10	2	4.8

Source: Population data are from State of Connecticut, *Register and Manual* (Hartford: Secretary of State, State of Connecticut, 1998). Organizational data are from various editions of the New Haven city directory.

entities and churches roughly followed the increase in the organizational population until 1910, after that the trends diverged. National associations—the bulk of which were lodges and chapters of fraternal and sororal entities and labor unions—declined steadily and virtually disappeared by 1990. Congregations, in contrast, dipped slightly in number in the wake of the Great Depression and steadily increased in number until, by 1980–90—an era generally supposed to be one of increasing secularization—they constituted one-third of the nonproprietary organizations in the city.

In some ways these trends are unsurprising. The declining number and significance of fraternal and sororal associations doubtless mirrors the assimilation of ethnic groups (who, by the 1950s, were rapidly blending into the general population) and the flight of whites to the suburbs, which began in earnest after 1960.

It should be noted, however, that fraternal and sororal, veterans', and other mutual benefit organizations that flourished in the city seldom followed their members to the suburbs. In fact, many of the communities surrounding New Haven—Branford, East Haven, Guilford, Hamden, and West Haven—already possessed their own social organizations of this type, all of which, by the 1970s, were also suffering declining membership, despite the towns' rapidly growing populations. (The sole exception was the YM-YWCA, which adapted to changing demographics by changing its mission from faith-based social service to secular recreation and youth activities and reorganized itself as a local franchise-form entity with branches in the growing suburbs.)

Because the suburbanization of surrounding towns was fueled by the developing transportation infrastructure, particularly the interstate highway system (I-95, completed in 1958 and I-91, completed in 1963), easy access to urban amenities actually discouraged the growth of new social and service organizations. Rather than establishing their own private day schools, for example, suburbanites—often eschewing their own public schools—sent their children to Foote, Hamden Hall, and Hopkins. The New Haven Lawn Club and the New Haven Country Club drew on growing suburban constituencies. Other well-established youth organizations like the Boy and Girl Scouts and the "Y" regionalized their organizational structures and continued to prosper, despite the declining fortunes of the center city.

The fact that these trends mirror those found by Robert Putnam and Gerald Gamm in their study of organizational populations in twenty-one

American cities from 1850 to 1940 suggests that the New Haven numbers are reliably representative. It also suggests two interesting hypotheses about the dynamics of associational populations:

—that the rise of bureaucratic institutions, particularly municipal and state educational, health, and human services organizations in the decades after 1900, did not negatively affect organizational populations. Indeed, the population of nonproprietary entities, religious and secular, appears to have grown most rapidly with the expansion of government at all levels after World War II; and

—that the conventions that equate modernism, urbanism, and activist government with secularization are not manifested in declines in the number or proportional significance of churches in the population of nonproprietary organizations. Indeed, quite the contrary, the number of churches grew steadily throughout the whole period 1850–1990—and with particular intensity after 1950.

These organizational trends take on further significance when viewed in terms of shifts in New Haven's human population. As Table 6-1 shows, New Haven's human population reached its peak in the period 1920–30 and began to decline after 1950. Although the city lost one-fifth of its 1950 population in the ensuing forty years, the population of nonproprietary entities remained relatively stable, and the density of these organizations increased significantly, from one organization for every 253 people in 1950 to one organization for every 207 people in 1990. These entities seem to have become steadily more important to the life of the city.

The implications of the increasing density of nonproprietary entities are suggested by important economic trends of the decades after 1950, particularly the decline of New Haven's industrial base and its loss of stature as a regional commercial center. In 1950, the city was the regional transportation hub of southern New England, with the New York, New Haven, & Hartford Railroad employing thousands of residents of New Haven and nearby communities. Manufacturing establishments—including Winchester (the world's largest maker of ammunition and firearms), A. C. Gilbert (producer of Erector sets, American Flyer trains, and other educational toys), the New Haven Clock Company, and a host of hardware manufacturing firms—employed 50,000. In addition, the city boasted ten commercial banks, three savings banks, and three building and loan associations—all of them locally owned and controlled.

Table 6-2. *Nonproprietary Organizations in New Haven, by Industry,*
1850–1990

Percent

	Year				
	1850	*1900*	*1930*	*1960*	*1990*
Arts and culture	5	1	2	1	2
Education	6	2	5	6	7
Health care	2	1	2	4	10
Human services	11	5	7	7	18
Mutual benefit	8	75	53	49	15
Religion	46	14	21	26	33
Other	22	1	10	7	15

Source: New Haven city directories.

By 1990, a largely nonprofit service economy had risen in place of
the once mighty New Haven Railroad, myriad manufacturing establishments, the three department stores, and sixteen banks. The four largest employers were nonprofit entities—Yale University, Yale–New Haven
Hospital, the Hospital of St. Raphael, and the Knights of Columbus.
Together they employed one-third of the city's work force—more than
double the number employed by New Haven's four largest surviving
for-profit firms. At the same time, the city had become a major catch-
ment area for clients of public welfare agencies and nonprofit human
services providers—as well as the regional center for services relating to
arts, culture, and health care.[9]

Closer examinations of organizational population, especially in the
more recent past, give a clear idea of the shifts underlying its apparent
stability. Table 6-2 shows that despite relative stability in the population of
nonproprietary organizations, the purposes of these entities changed considerably in the sixty-year period between 1930 and 1990:

—Mutual benefit organizations—fraternal and sororal, ethnic, and
membership—which accounted for more than half the organizational
population in 1930, constituted only 15 percent of the organizational
population by 1990, and the fraternal/sororal entities, which had made up
the bulk of the mutual benefit category, all but disappeared.

9. New Haven Chamber of Commerce (1994).

—The number and proportional significance of congregations increased dramatically, from 18 percent of the nonproprietaries in 1930 to 33 percent in 1990.

—The number of organizations providing human services grew from 7 percent in 1930 to 18 percent of the organizational population in 1990; the number providing health care grew from 2 percent in 1930 to 10 percent in 1990.

The numbers do not tell the whole story, however: for even within areas that do not loom large in numerical or proportional significance, major shifts were unfolding.

Conversions of Ownership and the Expansion of the Nonproprietary Domain

Among the most important shifts in the 1930–90 period was the migration of important areas of service provision across the boundary between the proprietary and the nonproprietary sector. This trend was related to a major expansion in the range of activities considered appropriate to eleemosynary organizations, from the traditional "charitable, educational, and religious" to nearly any kind of activity not resulting in the distribution of profits to owners or proprietors. In 1930 the vast majority of arts, cultural, educational, and health organizations were proprietary entities; by 1990 most were nonprofits or public agencies.

In only a few instances were these shifts the result of the kinds of ownership changes that became common nationally in the health care industry during the 1990s. The more common pattern was the elimination of for-profit enterprises and their replacement by nonprofits or public agencies:

—In 1930, every legitimate theater (that is, nonmovie theater) was a commercial enterprise; by 1990 these had been replaced by a host of nonprofits—the Shubert Center for the Performing Arts, the Palace Performing Arts Center, the Long Wharf Theater, Yale Repertory Theater, and a host of small professional theater companies.

—In 1930, in addition to the city-run (but privately endowed) New Haven Free Library and the venerable voluntary association the Young Men's Institute, New Haven boasted a half-dozen "circulating" and "subscription" libraries operated for-profit, often by bookstores. By 1990 the latter had entirely disappeared.

—In 1930, in addition to three major hospitals, the religiously tied Hospital of St. Raphael and the secular Grace and New Haven Hospitals, a variety of for-profit enterprises served New Haven's health care needs, including Carlson's Private Hospital, Joseph H. Evans Private Hospital, Jack's Private Hospital, and the Whitney Hospital. By 1990 all the proprietary hospitals had disappeared.

—In 1930, in addition to an assortment of trade schools (secretarial, hairdressing, physiotherapy, pharmacy, and so on), New Haven supported sixteen proprietary schools that offered regular academic courses. By 1990 a handful of these—Mrs. Foote's School, Mrs. Clive Day's School, the Rosenbaum Tutoring School, and Larson School—had converted to nonprofit ownership. The rest had been replaced by new nonprofits or public institutions.

The switch from for-profit to nonprofit service provision was only one of several conversion patterns. For example, care for orphans changed from a private nonproprietary service to a public one. In 1930 the city's orphaned were served by four nonproprietary institutions—the Jewish Home for Children, the New Haven Orphan Asylum, the Sacred Heart Charitable Institution for Children, and the St. Francis Orphan Asylum—and a single public agency, the New Haven County Home. By 1990, private provision had been completely replaced by a state-run system of foster care and a major public entity—the Children's Center—a nonresidential facility whose primary activity was the provision of services to children with special needs. (The St. Francis Orphan Asylum also survived as a corporate entity, but had been transformed into a residential facility for the profoundly retarded rather than orphans.)

In addition to changes in ownership, there was a major secularization of service provision. In 1930 the needs of the elderly were served by twelve nonproprietary organizations, ten of which were religiously tied. By 1990 all of the faith-based service providers had been replaced by five for-profit and two large nonprofit regional agencies located outside the city. The two older secular nonprofits, the Hannah Gray and Mary Wade Homes, survived. With the closing of the county's almshouse in the 1940s, public provision for the elderly became a thing of the past.

The transformation of eldercare was part of a broad withdrawal of congregations and other religious entities from traditional arenas of service provision. Although four of the six settlement houses extant in 1930—the Church of the Redeemer's Welcome Hall, St. Paul's Church's Neighborhood Music School Settlement, Lowell/Farnam House, and the Yale Hope Mission—survived into the 1990s, neither of the survivors continued under religious auspices.[10] Although there was still a notable religious presence in education in 1990, of the fourteen church-run schools operating in 1930, seven had gone out of business and been replaced by newer institutions.

Another notable trend involved the growth of entirely new areas of activity dominated by nonprofit firms. In 1930 the city's only museums (an art gallery and a museum of natural history) were operated by Yale University. By 1990, in addition to Yale's museums, there were seven nonprofit museums and art galleries. Grantmaking was nonexistent in the city in 1930; by 1990 there were nine grantmaking foundations of sufficient size to be listed in the *Foundation Directory*, and their assets totaled more than $130 million. In 1930 all but one of the city's seven nonuniversity-affiliated musical bands and orchestras were for-profit; by 1990 only two proprietaries were sufficiently well established to be listed in the city directory—but they had been joined by an impressive array of nonprofits, including the New Haven Symphony and Orchestra New England.[11] Child care, an industry that barely existed in 1930, had grown from three to eleven agencies, ten of them nonprofit.

Finally, referring again to Table 6-1, local chapters of national associations, which had constituted 223 of New Haven's 676 nonproprietary organizations in 1930 (33 percent) had declined to 66 (11 percent) of the organizational population by 1990. Though the overall organizational population remained stable (at 676 in 1930 and 630 in 1990), there was a massive die-off of traditional voluntary and membership associations. They were replaced by charitable tax-exempt nonprofit service entities operated by credentialed professionals of one sort or another.

Entities of almost every type disappeared—fraternal/sororal, patriotic, veterans', labor, PTAs, and religious (Knights of Columbus, Lutheran League, Epworth League). Even denominationally affiliated churches suffered major declines after 1930. The sole exceptions to this trend were advocacy groups (e.g., Greenpeace, the National Association for the Advancement of Colored People (NAACP), and the Urban League) and disease or disability-related health charities (e.g., American Cancer Society,

10. Everett Hill's history of New Haven County, written at the high tide of Progressivism, gives a fine overview of settlements and other charitable activities (1918). Detailed histories of New Haven settlements include Clarence A. Grimes's history of the Neighborhood Music School Settlement (1957) and Joan Crouse's paper on the Yale Hope Mission (1992).

11. Perhaps the best case study of the "nonprofitization" of the performing arts is Paul J. DiMaggio's essay on cultural entrepreneurship in late-nineteenth-century Boston (1986).

Easter Seals, Red Cross, national health charities). The PTA chapters, which had coordinated national, state, and local education policies and constituencies, were replaced by local parent-teacher organizations (PTOs) anchored in particular schools.

The Dynamics of Change

There does not appear to have been any single driving force behind these changes. In most instances, the chronology, scale, and scope of change seems to have affected industries in which public agencies and commercial and nonproprietary firms coexisted, rather than nonprofits. In some instances, changes were caused by shifts in public policy, in others by demographic or economic trends, in others by technology.

A switch from proprietary to nonprofit form frequently took place in several stages. The mass audience for the legitimate stage suffered first from the introduction of "talkies" to movie theaters in the late 1920s and, in the 1950s, from the introduction of television. The shrinkage of the market for stage performances to an upper-class niche audience coincided with the rise of foundation and corporate funding for the arts in the 1950s and, in the 1960s, the establishment of federal agencies (including the National Endowment for the Arts and the National Endowment for the Humanities) willing to fund activities that would otherwise be unable to sustain themselves—all of which restricted their grantmaking to nonprofit or public agency recipients.

In the health care industry proprietary hospitals (which had accounted for 33 percent of the national hospital population in 1930) were virtually eliminated in favor of "voluntary" nonprofit firms and public agencies (which together accounted for 87 percent of all hospitals by 1970).[12] These trends were driven locally and nationally by federal government policies, particularly the Hill-Burton Act of 1946, a major program to provide federal grants to states for construction of local hospitals. Such legislation, together with the rise of grantmaking foundations and private health insurance, was "tailor-made" for the rise of "voluntary hospitals as a sector."[13]

12. U.S. Department of Commerce (1975, p. 79).

13. The shifting ownership forms in health care have been the subject of extensive study, particularly because of "conversions" of nonprofits to for-profit ownership since the 1980s. On this, see Stevens (1989, p. 201); see also Starr (1982), Fox (1986), Rosenberg (1987), and Gray (1991).

The shift in library ownership, in contrast, had little to do with government policies. Rather, it was driven by changes within the library industry, particularly changing visions of the library's public role. Through the 1950s, libraries, like museums, conceived of themselves as guardians and definers of cultural standards. As such, they devoted their resources to preserving and circulating the Great Works, not to purchasing current best sellers. This practice created the niche that gave rise to for-profit "circulating" and "subscription" libraries. As the authority of traditional cultural elites declined with the cultural and economic empowerment of the masses after World War II, the public libraries were forced to defend their budgets to an increasingly resistant and skeptical public—and, as they did so, they began acquiring more popular works and eliminated the market for proprietary libraries.

Shifts in education, like those in health care, were driven by public policies and expenditures. Before World War II, few municipalities attempted to offer either comprehensive secondary education to an entire population or specialized vocational training. Indeed, as late as 1940, fewer than half the national population of seventeen-year-olds were high school graduates—in contrast to 1970, when more than three-quarters were.[14] Even at its peak population in 1950, New Haven had but a single high school to serve the entire city, and students seeking specialized vocational training had to acquire it either through apprenticeships or from proprietary institutions. By 1990, however, state and local governments in Connecticut and elsewhere had not only made high school education available to anyone who wanted it, but had also created a system of regional vocational-technical high schools and community colleges that co-opted the market in which proprietary schools had flourished.

This did not eliminate the market for private education, however. Indeed, the accommodation of the public schools to the needs of a far more diverse and less well prepared population of students created niches for nonprofit schools that could offer advanced levels of preparation for college entrance (which had become more competitive with the democratization of secondary education). At the same time, changes in federal tax policies favorable to nonprofit firms and philanthropic giving encouraged proprietary entities like Mrs. Foote's, Mrs. Clive Day's, and the Rosen-

14. U.S. Department of Commerce (1975, p. 379).

baum Tutoring School to convert to nonprofit form.[15] A few proprietaries, like the elite Gateway School for Girls, hung on into the 1960s, but as secondary education increasingly required libraries, laboratories, and higher levels of teaching expertise that, in the private sector of education, were only likely to receive support from donors seeking tax savings, they were eventually forced to close their doors.

Higher education was also transformed in the years after World War II. Before the 1960s, Connecticut, like most New England states that had developed infrastructures of private colleges and universities before the Civil War, had limited its commitment to public higher education to a single agricultural school (the University of Connecticut) and three teachers' colleges. As the post–World War II baby boomers came of age in the 1960s, this commitment was significantly expanded: the teachers' colleges became substantial universities, and a community college system was established. Public sector growth was paralleled by enormous expansion of private higher education: proprietary institutions like New Haven's Larson College reorganized as the nonprofit Quinnipiac College—which by the 1990s offered professional degrees in law, communications, and other areas, as well as a full undergraduate curriculum. Older two-year urban institutions like the University of Bridgeport and the University of New Haven likewise transformed themselves into nearly full service entities offering postgraduate degrees in several areas. Catholic institutions—Fairfield and Sacred Heart Universities, the University of Hartford, and New Haven's Albertus Magnus College—experienced tremendous growth. All in all, between 1930 and 1990, higher education, which had been almost entirely nonprofit, had become a classic mixed economy, with nonprofit, public, and even proprietary institutions (e.g., Tarkio-Post University) competing for students.

Secularization and nonprofitization of service provision, particularly care for the elderly, was a product of several factors. On the government side, the availability of social security and public grants reshaped the market in favor of nonprofit firms, as it did for hospitals. However, with these subventions came oversight and monitoring by public agencies for whom, especially after 1970, greater efficiency and economies of scale were of increasing importance. As private insurers joined governments in pur-

---

15. Whitlock (1994) and Castrol (1988) provide detailed histories of two of the schools that converted from proprietary to nonprofit form. I am grateful to Elise Weissenbach for sharing with me archival materials on the Gateway School.

suit of these goals, it became increasingly difficult for small facilities, most of which were church-run, to qualify for reimbursements at levels that could sustain their operations.[16] On the private side, the urban mainline Protestant and Catholic congregations and religious orders were entering a period of crisis: as congregations shrank with the flight of city residents to the suburbs after 1960, maintaining the "old ladies' homes" became an expensive luxury. For the Catholic institutions, which had depended on the low-cost labor of members of religious orders, declining recruitment into religious vocations required the employment of a far more expensive lay labor force. This took its toll on both Catholic nursing homes and schools when the number of convents in the city (a good proxy for the population of women religious) declined: five shut their doors between 1960 and 1990.

Increased individual giving and the availability of foundation and corporate support for nonprofits in the post–World War II decades seem not to have benefited faith-based service providers. Anecdotal evidence suggests that this was no accident. The Neighborhood Music School Settlement (NMS), founded by St. Paul's Episcopal Church as a nonproselytizing ministry, had served children of every faith since the turn of the century with such effectiveness that, by the 1920s, the Community Chest and its successor, the United Fund, had become its largest single source of revenue. In 1946 the United Fund board informed NMS that it would curtail future support if the school retained its ties to the church. Faced with extinction, NMS reorganized and reincorporated as a secular nonprofit. It seems likely that the treatment of NMS was typical of the treatment of faith-based service providers in the postwar period, reflecting on the one hand the growing judicial sensitivity to church establishment issues and, on the other, the efforts of federated agencies like the United Fund (and its successor, the United Way), to capture the financial loyalty of Catholics and Jews, who were becoming increasingly influential in the city's economic and political life. (By the 1920s, Jews and Catholics had established federated fundraising entities paralleling the Protestant-dominated but nominally nonsectarian Community Chest. By the 1950s, these had joined forces with the Chest's successor, the United Fund.)

The decline of the fraternal/sororal bodies, most of them chapters of national associations, was due in large part to the creation of government-

16. Jafferis (1996).

run social insurance, since most of these organizations provided a variety of sickness, funeral, and life insurance benefits for their members.[17] Assimilation and the erosion of ethnic identities through intermarriage undoubtedly helped to undermine the basis for these organizations; virtually every ethnic and religious group except the Jews practiced extensive exogamy after the second World War.[18] In some cases politics, particularly the rise of anti-German sentiment during World War II, discouraged membership.[19] Declining immigration also limited the number of potential new recruits: as Wiedersheim notes in his history of New Haven's chapter of the Harugari Singing Society, when the German "economic miracle" of the 1960s reduced the flow of immigrants to New Haven, the club, for the first time in its eighty-five year history, found its membership declining and aging.[20] Some of these entities, like the Jewish women's organization, the United Order of True Sisters, survived, but only by shifting its activities from voluntary service and personal charity to targeted fundraising for hospitals, rehabilitation programs, and other nonprofit service providers.[21] Others, like the Masonic lodges, reduced the number of lodges and consolidated their activities at a single location—the Masonic Temple on Whitney Avenue. (Half a century earlier, there had been three such temples in the city.)

Finally, it is useful to place the turbulence of the last forty years of the twentieth century in broader historical perspective—particularly because some of the more mythic and ideologized accounts of organizational mortality and morbidity have attempted to portray the growth of the modern nonprofits as responsible for the near extinction of traditional voluntary associations. Table 6-3 shows the mortality of New Haven's nonproprietary organizations at thirty-year intervals between 1870 and 1990. In each interval, between half and three-quarters of all nonproprietaries died off, regardless of the rate at which new organizations were created. In fact, the two periods of greatest organizational growth (1870–1900 and 1961–89) were also the periods of highest organizational mortality. They are also notable as the ones in which there were major

17. Kauffman (1982) and Johnston (1979).
18. Barbara Coyle (1980) provides a detailed study of interethnic marriages in central Connecticut during the first half of the twentieth century.
19. Wiedersheim (1992).
20. Ibid. (p. 39).
21. Ratner (1981).

Table 6-3. *Births and Deaths of New Haven Nonproprietary Organizations (NPOs), 1870–1989*

Number unless otherwise noted

	1870–99	1900–29	1930–59	1960–89
NPOs at start of period	130	458	676	427
NPOs at end of period	458	676	595	630
Deaths per period	85	256	427	310
Deaths per period (percent)	65	56	63	72
New NPOs per period	415	474	276	513
New NPOs per period (percent)	91	70	6	81

Source: New Haven city directories.

shifts in organizational type: in the period 1870–1900, locally based community-serving entities were eclipsed by national mutual benefit associations; in the period 1960–89, national mutual benefit associations were replaced by locally based charitable tax-exempt nonprofit service provider organizations.

Given the diversity and complexity of the forces driving organizational birth and death, it is impossible to attribute the die-off of traditional associations to any single factor. It is also not entirely clear that the new nonprofit organizations of the postwar decades have been any less dependent on or productive of social capital—though it is indisputable that the social and human capital with which they are associated is of a very different kind than that which produced the Tocquevillian associational universe.

New Haven's Nonprofit Economy

Although the forces that drove the transformation of New Haven's nonproprietary entities were diverse, their aggregate impact was, indisputably, the creation in the decades after 1950 of conditions that favored the growth of a charitable tax-exempt nonprofit domain of extraordinary strength and vitality. Indeed, by 1990 the nonprofit service economy had all but replaced both the older industrial and commercial economy and the rich and varied domain of voluntary nonproprietary organizations.

By the last decade of the twentieth century, four large nonprofits had become the city's largest employers, and nonprofits owned nearly 70 percent (in value) of the city's real estate. In addition to the nationally renowned educational and health care institutions, New Haven's theaters, museums, and galleries served as major magnets for cultural tourism and brought thousands of visitors and millions of dollars into the city's economy. While many of these were connected to Yale University (the Yale Art Gallery, the Yale British Art Center, the Yale Repertory Theater, the Peabody Museum of Natural History), many others were free-standing entities (the Connecticut Children's Museum, the Creative Arts Workshop, the Neighborhood Music School, the John Slade Ely House, the Long Wharf Theater, the New Haven Symphony Orchestra, the Palace Performing Arts Center, the Performance Studio, the Shubert Theater, Orchestra New England) resulting either from conversions of older commercial or voluntary enterprises or, more frequently, the wave of foundings of charitable tax-exempt firms after 1960.

Although New Haven had always been a regional center for human services delivery, the new nonprofits differed in important ways from their predecessors. To begin with, they occupied a far more significant place in the organizational population. Representing only 5 percent of the city's nonproprietaries in 1900 and 7 percent in the period 1930–60, by 1990 their share of the nonprofit population had grown to 18 percent—and this is very likely an undercount, since it neither includes the rapidly expanding group home industry nor takes into account the increasing importance of churches as venues for social service delivery.[22]

Unlike traditional voluntary institutions supported by donations, like New Haven Associated Charities (the city's charity organization society) or the church-run orphanages, old folks' homes, and settlement houses, the new nonprofits were professionally staffed and managed and derived their revenues from a mix of foundation and corporate grants, earned income, and government grants, contracts, and vouchers.[23] The services they offered were far more specialized. In place of the general array of relief, education, and counseling available from an institution like Welcome Hall—the settlement house run by the Church of the Redeemer—or Associated Charities, entrepreneurial social activists established separately

22. Studies of service provision by religious congregations in New Haven include Williams, Griffith, and Young (1993); Chang, Williams, Griffith, and Young (1994); and Hall (1995). Ram Cnaan's forthcoming book provides an excellent national overview of the subject.

23. On government contracting with nonprofits, see Smith and Lipsky (1993), Gronbjerg (1994), and Salamon (1996).

incorporated enterprises to deal with drug and alcohol abuse, mental illness, mental retardation, child and spousal abuse, job training, and home medical, social, and psychiatric services; and many of these targeted particular racial and ethnic groups.

Community Organizations and Community-Serving Organizations: Who Benefits?

Locational patterns suggest that a distinction developed between older types of community organizations and new types of community-serving organizations. The former tended to be located in or near the neighborhoods they served. Welcome Hall and Associated Charities, for example, were situated on State Street, adjacent to the industrial and immigrant working-class residential neighborhoods that stretched from the tracks of the New York, New Haven, & Hartford Railroad (which paralleled State Street) to the Mill River and the harbor. In addition, this area boasted an astonishing concentration of fraternal, labor, and other mutual benefit associations representing every nationality: forty organizations listed the Swedish Fraternal Building at the corner of Elm and State Streets as their meeting place; twenty-two others met at 117 Court Street, which was just around the corner; another sixteen convened at 28 Crown, just off State Street. This was one of half a dozen similar clusters: twenty black voluntary associations met at 76 Webster or 139 Goffe; Catholic organizations were concentrated in the 400 block of Orange Street; twenty-eight labor unions and fraternal/sororal organizations listed 210 Meadow Street as their address; sixteen Masonic organizations listed 285 Whitney Avenue as their meeting place. All in all, 20 percent of the city's nonproprietary entities in 1931 met in just six places!

By 1990 the locational relationships between organizations and their constituencies had largely disappeared: there were no clusters of agencies comparable to those of half a century earlier and, to the extent that they clustered at all, their location was determined by the nature of the services they offered. Thus, for example, the major funders of social services and some of the key service providers (United Way, the New Haven Foundation, the Visiting Nurses Association, the Girl Scouts, and Family Counseling of Greater New Haven) were located in the Community Services Building at 1 State Street; health care agencies tended to cluster in the vicinity of the city's two major hospitals; social service agencies serving the

African American community were concentrated in and around Dixwell Plaza at 200–226 Dixwell Avenue; arts agencies were clustered on Audubon Street, in or around the Greater New Haven Community Foundation building; the surviving Masonic lodges had made the Masonic Temple at 285 Whitney their headquarters; the rest of New Haven's nonprofits occupied a variety of usually rented offices around the city—primarily in the Central Business District and the East Rock, Prospect Hill, and Yale neighborhoods (which together contained 35 percent of the city's nonprofits).

Most of the major new nonprofit clusters, 1 State Street (the Community Services Building), Audubon Street, and 220–226 Dixwell Avenue / Dixwell Plaza, were, as products of the city's zeal for urban renewal, the result of intentional efforts by urban planners to create centers of community activity. Unfortunately, one consequence of the planners' zeal was the destruction of the older clusters of neighborhood–based locations for community life. The old Elm-Court-State-Crown area that had once housed nearly a hundred largely voluntary associations was razed and turned into subsidized housing and parking lots; the Meadow Street cluster, once home to thirty labor and fraternal/sororal entities, vanished under the Oak Street Connector, the major approach to I-95; 76 Webster Street, which provided shelter to a dozen African American associations, vanished in the renewal of the Dixwell ghetto. Other clusters, like the concentrations of fraternal/sororal entities in Westville (at the Masonic Temple at 903–907 Whalley Avenue) and in Fair Haven (126 Grand), fell prey to the Depression, white flight, and aging membership.

By the 1990s the city's nonprofits were unlikely to be located in or near communities in need. The most important of them—the hospitals, colleges and universities, and arts organizations—had come to serve largely suburban regional constituencies (and even their employees tended to live in the suburbs). The small to midsized agencies serving at-risk populations appeared to locate in the middle-class neighborhoods where their executives and staff lived—or, if suburban, felt less threatened.

By 1996 there was an inverse relationship between the neighborhoods in which nonprofits were located and the areas in which their clients were likely to reside: only 23 percent of New Haven's nonprofits were located in the five neighborhoods whose black populations exceeded 50 percent and that together contained 58 percent of the city's African American population (see Table 6-4). In contrast, 40 percent of New Haven's nonprofits are located in the six neighborhoods with the lowest proportion of

Table 6-4. *Nonprofit Organizations (NPOs) in New Haven Neighborhoods with High and Low African American Populations, 1996*

Neighborhood	Total population of neighborhood	NPOs in neighborhood	Black population of neighborhood (percent)	Total NPOs in city (percent)	Total blacks in city (percent)
High African American population					
Newhallville	7,798	14	94	2	17
Dixwell	6,298	28	85	5	13
Long Wharf	1,655	29	60	5	2
Dwight	6,799	19	50	3	7
Hill	17,420	47	50	8	19
Total	...	137	...	23	58
Low African American population					
Central business district	997	74	28	12	0.05
Yale	5,383	34	14	6	2
East Rock	9,290	93	7	15	1
Westville	6,904	32	10	5	1
Annex	5,362	5	8	0	1
Morris Cove	5,115	12	0.5	2	0.001
Total	...	250	...	40	5
Total African Americans in city	130,000	622	...	100	63

Source: Population data are from the New Haven City Room website: http://statlab.stat.yale.edu/cityroom/NHOL.html. Organizational data are from the Internet Nonprofit Center website: http://www.nonprofits.org.

black residents (totaling a mere 5 percent of the city's African Americans).
The locations of nonprofits most likely to serve the needs of low-income
African Americans—organizations in the fields of civil rights, employment, health, and housing—reveal this pattern even more clearly: the four
neighborhoods that were more than 50 percent African American (New-
hallville, Dixwell, Long Wharf, and Dwight) were home to only two of the
city's six civil rights organizations, eleven of sixty-nine employment-related
organizations, thirteen of fifty-six health care agencies, and seven of thirty-
two housing agencies.

These data suggest that the new service-provider nonprofits, rather
than being community organizations in the sense of being "of, for, and by"
the communities they served, were community-serving organizations run
by credentialed professionals, funded by public agencies, foundations, and
corporations, and pursuing agendas set by constituencies other than those
being served.

The only significant exceptions are religious organizations. Of the
fifty-five New Haven entities classified as religious by the 1996 IRS lists of
charitable tax-exempt organizations, nearly 20 percent were located in the
four predominantly black neighborhoods. Of the more inclusive listing of
congregations in the 1990 City Directory, one-third (eighty-one out of
183) were located in the city's four predominantly black neighborhoods.
This (and the fact that only 10 percent of the city's secular nonprofits were
located there) suggests that the community organizations (as opposed to
community-serving organizations) remaining in the city's poorest areas
were, by the 1990s, overwhelmingly likely to be churches or other faith-
based agencies.

Religious Countertrends

Patterns of birth, death, duration, and location involving congregations and other faith-based entities run counter to secular trends in several
important ways. First, despite the supposedly increasingly secular character
of society, religious organizations grew steadily in number and proportional significance in New Haven, increasing from 15 percent of the
nonproprietary population in 1930 to 33 percent in 1990—a period in
which the overall organizational population remained relatively stable.
Second, in contrast to earlier periods, the proliferation of congregations
did not give rise to networks of secular associations.

Table 6-5. *New Haven Congregations by Period of Establishment*

Denomination	Congregations in 1989	Established before 1930	Established after 1930
UCC (Congregational)	8	8	0
Protestant Episcopal	8	8	0
United Methodist	5	2	3
Lutheran	4	3	1
Baptist	13	5	8
Presbyterian	2	1	1
Christian Science	2	1	1
Roman Catholic	17	14	3
Jewish	5	0	5
African Methodist	2	1	2
Free Will Baptist	8	1	7
Pentecostal	6	1	5
Jehovah's Witness	2	0	2
Nondenominational	58	6	52
Other	17	4	13
Total	158	56	102

The character of the churches established after 1930 may help illuminate the meaning of these trends. As Table 6-5 shows, the vast majority of new church establishments in New Haven were nondenominational (64 percent). Of the nondenominational congregations, almost all were located in the African American or Hispanic communities, and most were spin-offs of theologically conservative Baptist, Methodist, or Pentecostal faith families.[24]

Studies of communities, associations, and civic engagement suggest that there are significant differences in the forms of public participation of religious groups. The Yankee City study of Newburyport in the 1930s found not only that religious affiliation, rather than economic or political connections, constituted the most important cross-cutting link between the city's secular associations, but also that liberal Protestant groups (Congregationalists, Unitarians, and Episcopalians) were associationally involved to a far greater extent than either the conservative Protestants (Baptists and Meth-

---

24. On nondenominational congregations, see Trueheart (1996); on their role in the African American community, see Hall-Russell (1996).

odists) or the Roman Catholics. The liberal Protestants, moreover, were more likely to sponsor organizations that served the whole community (like the YMCA and the Boy Scouts) rather than their own members (like the Catholic temperance and devotional societies). Overall, Warner and Lunt found that liberal Protestants alone accounted for over one-third of the city's 357 associations, while Catholics were tied to only 33 (11 percent). Protestant groups, moreover, were far more likely to include Catholics and Jews as members than the other way around (174, or nearly 40 percent of the city's associations—most of them connected to liberal Protestant congregations—had Catholic and Jewish members). Associations of this type included the Yankee City Women's Club, the Yankee City Country Club, the Rotary, the Chamber of Commerce, and the Boy Scout troops.[25]

Warner's findings are paralleled by the work of other scholars, who have found compelling links between religious and organizational demography.[26] E. Digby Baltzell's 1979 study of leadership and authority in Boston and Philadelphia attributed Philadelphia's failure to build a cultural and educational infrastructure commensurate with its extraordinary financial resources to the religiously rooted anti-institutionalism of the city's Quaker leadership, which tended to focus its energies and resources inward on the Quaker community rather than outward on the development of an inclusive, institutionally based civic life.[27] Economist Laurence Iannacone's study of fundamentalist congregations found that while they drew impressive financial and volunteer support from their members, they directed these resources inwardly toward their own faith communities rather than outwardly in broader forms of civic engagement.[28] Sociologist David Swartz's study of the religious affiliations of hospital trustees found that members of theologically conservative congregations were far less likely to be found on the boards of secular community-serving organizations than liberal Protestants, even in communities where liberal Protestants were in the minority, that conservative Protestants and Catholics were overwhelmingly more likely to sit on the boards of hospitals with ties to their own denominations, and that these boards were unlikely to include trustees who were not members of their faith communities.[29]

25. Warner and Lunt (1941, pp. 324, 328, 346, 348).

26. On the regional character of institutional and philanthropic cultures, see Hall (1982, 1992); Wolpert (1989, 1993); Bowen, Nygren, Turner, and Duffy (1994); and Schneider (1996).

27. Baltzell (1979).

28. Iannacone (1998). See also Hoge, Zech, McNamara, and Donahue (1996).

29. Swartz (1998).

These findings are powerfully affirmed by recent studies of civic engagement based on national surveys and in-depth interviews.[30] These found that religion, rather than income, education, workplace, or school, accounted for the acquisition of basic civic skills and that there was significant variation between denominations in imparting these skills; liberal Protestant denominations were found to be far more effective than conservative Protestants or Catholics. Verba, Schlozman, and Brady also found race and religion to be significant in the acquisition of civic skills and political participation. Churches attended by African Americans, regardless of denomination, were more likely both to impart civic skills and promote political participation, and "the churches that African-Americans attend have special potential for stimulating political participation."[31]

While Verba, Schlozman, and Brady do not directly address whether denominational affiliation affects participation in secular voluntary associations, their findings, when linked to earlier studies, suggest that theologically conservative congregations are likely not only to direct their voluntary and financial resources toward their own faith communities, but also to prefer political rather than secular forms of collective action in the public sector, including the use of congregations as direct actors in the political arena.

The 1996 IRS data on New Haven's tax-exempt organizational population seem to affirm these findings. Of 310 exempt entities located in the 06511 and 06519 zip code areas—which include the Hill and Dixwell neighborhoods, where New Haven's African American population is concentrated, forty-eight (15.4 percent) were identifiably black organizations (identified as such either by their names, locations, or histories); of these, thirty (9.7 percent) were secular nonpolitical organizations and eighteen were churches or religious organizations. Of the thirty secular nonpolitical organizations, nine were quasi-governmental entities, organizations (such as tenants' councils) formed to influence government action or (as in the case of Head Start and community development corporations) to carry out government policies. Of the seventeen exempt entities in the 06519 zip code area, seven (41 percent) were secular nonpolitical entities and 10 were churches. Of the seven secular nonpoliticals, five were quasi-governmental organizations.

30. Verba, Schlozman, and Brady (1995).
31. Ibid. (pp. 325-27, 383–84).

The clustering of public agencies, nonprofits, and faith-based organizations in and around the Dixwell Plaza—an effort by city planners and foundations to create a community center for the city's oldest black neighborhood—expresses the distinctive relationships of public sector activism. As described by *Inside New Haven's Neighborhoods*, a publication jointly sponsored by the city's Office of Housing and Neighborhood Development, the Redevelopment Agency of the City of New Haven, Yale University, the Science Park Corporation (a public-private industrial development partnership), the New Haven Colony Historical Society, and the George Dudley Seymour Foundation, "the entire triangle made by Dixwell Avenue and Goffe and Webster Streets is almost entirely commercial or service oriented."[32] In 1996 the area contained the following public, nonprofit, and religious agencies:

Dixwell Avenue (East side, between Sperry and Admiral Streets)
Elm Haven Houses (public housing)
Isadore Wexler School (public school)
Dixwell Avenue United Church of Christ
Dixwell Community House
Dixwell Children's Creative Art Center (church-run nonprofit)
Dixwell Pre-School and Day Care Center (church-run nonprofit)
Hannah Gray Home (nonprofit eldercare facility)

Dixwell Avenue (West side, Bristol to Charles Street)
United House of Prayer for All People
St. Martin de Porres Roman Catholic Church
East Rock Lodge, Improved Benevolent Order of Elks
Greater New Haven Business and Professionals Association
New Haven Free Library—Stetson Branch
Christ Chapel New Testament Church
Literacy Volunteers of Greater New Haven
New Haven Board of Education/Head Start Center
Dixwell Neighborhood Corporation
Youth Business Enterprises
Community Children and Family Services
Connecticut Outreach Center
Young Ministers' Alliance

32. *Inside New Haven's Neighborhoods* (1982, p. 116).

Varick African American Methodist Episcopal Church
Varick Family Life Center
VWA Drop-in Center/National AIDS Brigade

Sperry Street, Dixwell to Goffe
St. Martin de Porres Roman Catholic Church
Little Rock Church of Christ's Disciples
Mount Bethel Missionary Baptist Church
Fire House

Goffe Street, Sperry to Broadway
Agape Christian Center
St. Mary's United Free Will Baptist Church

This impressive cluster was not, as noted, created by accident. It was very much the intention of the city's leaders and the foundations and federal agencies that lavishly funded their activities both to create new public spaces and to forge partnerships between community and municipal agencies. The prominence of churches as anchors for the effort—particularly Dixwell United Church of Christ, whose ultramodern edifice is part of the integrated complex that includes public housing, a public school, and a nonprofit (but publicly funded) community center housing an assortment of day care, arts education, and recreation activities and services—testifies to the essentially political orientation (and effectiveness) of the city's African American congregations.

These findings are consistent with Verba, Schlozman, and Brady's conclusions about the capacities of African American churches to generate political skills and stimulate political participation. The small number of exempt organizations in neighborhoods where African Americans make up roughly 50 percent of the population is a strong indicator that associations are not a major vehicle of collective action for the city's African Americans. Moreover, they suggest that New Haven's African Americans, overwhelmingly members of doctrinally conservative congregations, have been impressively responsive to their churches' teachings and have, in consequence, directed their voluntary energies into congregational life—while generally avoiding spheres of nonpolitical voluntarism. This might explain why, while the impressive growth in the number of African American congregations over the past half-century has brought black clergy into increasing prominence as political leaders, it has not been matched either by a comparable proliferation of community-based voluntary organizations or by notable increases in voter participation.[33]

It is worth noting that these anti-institutionalist tendencies were not characteristic of the African American residents of New Haven in the pre–World War II period.[34] In the nineteenth and early twentieth centuries, New Haven's small black community (which in 1940 was only 4 percent of the city's population) created a wide range of religious congregations (Baptist, Congregational, Episcopal, and Methodist), fraternal and sororal groups (including six Masonic and two Odd Fellows lodges), and an assortment of charitable and benevolent societies (including the Hannah Gray Home) and social clubs.

That contemporary African American congregations have not produced a comparable number of secular voluntary nonprofit organizations may be an illustration of the alternative model of civic participation suggested by sociologist John Stanfield in his 1993 article on African American traditions of civic responsibility:

> If we are going to come to terms with the rich civic cultures in African-American Communities, we must first revise our thinking about civic responsibility. Sociological studies of civic responsibility in particular and of philanthropy in general explore the ways in which such processes, such as socialization and social change, and structures, such as institutions and communities, influence human propensities to engage in civil stewardship. Conventional philanthropic studies with sociological foci tend to be grounded in structural-functional notions of social organization (institutions, communities, task organizations, social movements, societies), social processes (socialization), and stratification (class, gender, race). This grounding has encouraged a monocultural perspective in sociological philanthropic studies . . . [which] interprets American society as a mode of social organization with one value system, a system in which conflict is dysfunctional. Social and cultural diversity in monocultural social systems is presented either as a temporary antecedent to total assimilation or as pathological.[35]

Giving and volunteering, Stanfield points out, have different cultural meanings in different settings.[36] If so, the high levels of civic competency

33. Zaretsky (1997) gives detailed information on declining voter participation in New Haven elections.

34. Bailey (1913) and Warner (1940) provide detailed accounts of the geographical origins, economic circumstances, and associational involvements of New Haven blacks before World War II.

35. Stanfield (1993, p. 140).

36. On this, see also Hall-Russell (1996).

found by Verba and his associates in studying African-Americans suggest that, in identifying associational activity as the desideratum of community vitality, there is a need for less-ethnocentric approaches to analyzing communities.

Conclusion

The history of New Haven's associational and organizational entities makes a strong case for the need to redefine the terminology and concepts used to describe nongovernmental and nonproprietary associations and organizations:

—*Voluntary associations* appear to be distinct in many respects from the charitable and tax-exempt nonprofit organizations that proliferated in the decades after World War II. Voluntary associations were primarily subunits of national associations and membership organizations with significant mutual benefit characteristics (which would preclude their being registered, under the current IRS Code, as 501(c)(3) charitable entities).

—*Nonprofit organizations* are distinct in many respects from voluntary associations. They are seldom membership organizations run by volunteers and supported by donated moneys; more often they are professionally staffed and subsist on a mixture of earned, donated, and grant and contract revenues from governments, foundations, and corporations.

—*Religious entities*, while sharing characteristics of both voluntary associations and nonprofit organizations, are different from both. They are, in most cases, membership organizations and, in the case of denominationally affiliated congregations, subunits of national associations. Unlike nonprofits, they remain largely dependent on donations. These characteristics, however, may be changing, since the last half of the twentieth century was notable for the proliferation of nondenominational congregations and—thanks to the social policies of the Great Society and late-1990s "welfare reform"—increasingly dependent on government funding for their social ministries.

The differences between major types of nonproprietary entities may have important implications for those who seek to use associational population trends as indicators of the vitality of civil society, levels of social capital, or the intensity of civic engagement.

First and foremost, it seems clear that the post–World War II charitable tax-exempt nonprofits have the weakest association with vital polities and economies. As professionally staffed, entrepreneurially managed enterprises, these nonprofits, despite the wide range of services they offer to clients, have few ties to the communities they serve. Seldom located in the same neighborhoods as their clients and supported, managed, staffed, and funded by outside agencies, and seldom inviting community participation in decision-making or fund-raising, they do little to contribute to the ability of city residents to develop or exercise civic skills. At best, they serve as civic arenas for the stratum of professionally credentialed "knowledge workers" who are becoming increasingly responsible for running the nation's service economy.

Second, it seems clear that voluntary associations of the traditional type have been powerfully associated with the efficacy and vitality of a wide range of economic and political institutions. Together with congregations and the rich extracurricular offerings of the public schools, voluntary associations provided abundant arenas for learning and practicing civic skills—which were carried over into a public domain that supported half a dozen daily newspapers, a wide assortment of advocacy groups, and a rich array of political and civic clubs and associations.

Third, evidence of ties between religion and civic engagement is more ambiguous. Despite the historic association between congregations and secular associations, the most recent wave of congregational growth seems to be producing civic outcomes characterized neither by a proliferation of secular associations nor by increased political participation and activism.[37] This may be due to the theological conservatism of the congregations that constitute the majority of new religious bodies in the city, which traditionally focus on participation within themselves rather than outwardly into the community. It may also be due to diminished opportunities for more public forms of engagement resulting from the decline of inclusive voluntary associations (such as PTAs) and the increasing dominance of nonprofit firms and public agencies that provide services to but are not rooted in the community.

In addition to suggesting that voluntary associations, nonprofits, and religious entities are quite different types of organizations despite their superficial similarities, this study points to significant differences in the character of public life according to which kinds of organizations serve as the major vehicles of civic engagement. Moreover, there is evidence that the predominance of one or another organizational type may be the product of political agendas rather than historical accident.

37. Zaretsky (1997).

Epilogue: Nonprofits and the Privatization
of Civic Engagement

The most illuminating—but most frequently overlooked—aspect of Tocqueville's observations on the nature of civic engagement in American democracy is his analysis of the links between the formal processes of democratic government and the informal institutions of democratic culture. He describes the role of voluntary intermediary bodies in the political process in a way that connects two very different domains: the private spheres of belief, expression, and association and the public spheres of electoral activity and governance. He breaks these connections into three components: "the public assent which a number of individuals give to certain doctrines and in the engagement which they contract to promote in a certain manner the spread of those doctrines"; "the exercise of the right of association is the power of meeting" in civil associations that establish "centers of action at certain important points in the country" by which activity in regard to ideas "is increased and its influence extended"; and the formation of political associations through which "the partisans of an opinion may unite in electoral bodies and choose delegates to represent them in a central assembly." In a nutshell, "civic associations . . . facilitate political association" while "political association singularly strengthens and improves associations for civil purposes."[38]

This insight—which Putnam updated in form but not in substance in *Making Democracy Work* (1993) and "Bowling Alone" (1994)—suggests that the ultimate measure of civic vitality is not merely participation in private civic organizations, but public engagement in democratic processes of voting, electioneering, and governing.[39]

From this perspective, the absence—unique among Connecticut's major cities—of an organized political opposition to the political regime that has controlled city government for half a century merits examination.[40]

---

38. Tocqueville (1945, Vol. 2, pp. 123–24).

39. Putnam's attention to associational activity is keyed to his interest in the "efficacy" of democratic institutions, including levels of voter participation.

40. In New Haven in 1999, registered Democrats outnumber registered Republicans ten to one—with a significant number of independents absenting themselves entirely from opportunities to participate in party nominating processes and to serve on municipal boards and commissions. In 1997, Republicans did not run a candidate to oppose the Democrat incumbent—who polled 79 percent of the votes cast; the remainder went to four independent candidates in an election in which only 30 percent of registered voters voted—a decline of 5 percent from the previous mayoral canvass (Zaretsky [1997]). In 1998 Republicans held only two of the thirty seats on the city's Board of Aldermen.

The rise of one-party rule, the emergence of nonprofits as the dominant vehicle of collective action, and the disappearance of traditional voluntary associations appear to be related. Specifically, there is evidence that Democratic hegemony was built on urban renewal and redevelopment programs that used federal government and private foundation funds to construct a system of political patronage that has wielded extraordinary power over the lives of average citizens.

Raymond Wolfinger's classic 1974 study of urban renewal, *The Politics of Progress*, suggests that redevelopment programs selectively razed neighborhoods whose residents opposed urban renewal and supported candidates who challenged the political machine.[41] Dan Humphrey's 1992 study of foundation initiatives in New Haven during the 1960s suggests that political leaders used nonprofit rather than public redevelopment agencies because the former enabled them to ignore competitive bidding and civil service rules. The mayor and his redevelopment administrator, Humphrey argues, "used the growing redevelopment bureaucracy and the potential patronage involved in each renewal project to infuse political concerns with those of redevelopment." Directly controlled by the mayor and staffed by political loyalists, Humphrey writes, "practically every stage in the renewal effort provided an opportunity to include or exclude those who might benefit." Accordingly, the mayor's decisions about selecting renewal areas, bailing out struggling businesses, compensating property owners, and hiring consultants, legal and appraisal firms, insurance companies, architects, construction companies, and labor unions were shaped by "a self-absorbed obsession with his own political longevity." Superimposed on this was the Ford Foundation's own model of urban change as a top-down process, which favored cooperative interagency and intergovernmental action on the executive level but discouraged community involvement in decisionmaking in order to minimize the influence of ethnic enclaves resistant to redevelopment policies.[42]

Between 1953 and 1968, the city razed more than 6,300 housing units, displacing more than 18 percent of New Haven's population, the majority of them Jews, Italians, Poles, and other potential challengers to Irish political hegemony. Very little urban renewal money went to relocating these people within the city (a mere 722 low-income residential units were built over this fifteen-year period), while huge sums were spent on

41. Wolfinger (1974) is a finely textured study of urban renewal in New Haven.
42. Humphrey (1992, pp. 66, 65–66, 15).

highway, commercial, and office construction that served the interests of suburban professionals and managers.[43]

Although aging infrastructure, obsolescent industrial plants and equipment, the assimilation of immigrants, and the influx of southern blacks all influenced the transformation of political and economic life in New Haven, the urban renewal efforts of the 1950s and 1960s appear to have played a particularly important role in fostering the growth of non-profit service industries and the development of what Joseph Galaskiewicz has called an "urban grants economy"—a system of reciprocal exchanges of financial, political, and legitimacy resources between the influentials in government, big businesses, and the major nonprofit agencies.[44]

The growth of the service economy and its distinctive configuration of political and economic relationships profoundly altered the character of civic engagement and political participation, on the one hand, fueling the decline of organizations and activities (like the PTA, scouts, and the fraternal and sororal entities) that invited broad communitywide partici-pation while, on the other, encouraging the growth of new organizations that operated within a setting of increasingly stratified interests and oppor-tunities.

Peter Drucker links the expansion of "the nonprofit organizations of the so-called third sector" to the growth of a new class of "knowledge workers" who reject traditional arenas of public participation in favor of a privatized "sphere of effective citizenship" in which they can "exercise influence, discharge responsibility, and make decisions." "In the political culture of mainstream society," Drucker argues, "individuals, no matter how well educated, how successful, how achieving, or how wealthy, can only vote and pay taxes. They can only react, can only be passive. In the counterculture of the third sector, they are active citizens. This may be the most important contribution of the third sector."[45]

The stratification and privatization of civic life is not merely being driven by the desire of monied and educated elites to forge a sense of community and social efficacy. The proliferation of nondenominational congregations standing outside the religious mainline expresses the same desires, although they draw on very different constituencies. Unlike tradi-tional religious bodies, which drew their membership from neighbor-

43. Ibid. (pp. 62–63).
44. On urban grants economies, see Galaskiewicz (1985).
45. Drucker (1989, p. 9).

hoods, the new congregations tend to recruit on the basis of doctrinal and ethnic affinities that do not necessarily correlate with geographical proximity.[46] Indeed, Drucker's portrayal of the knowledge workers' attraction to nonprofits as "spheres of effective citizenship" strikingly parallels the description of African American congregations as settings in which blacks who were denied opportunities to vote and hold office in public institutions could vote and elect officers, advocate, deliberate, and make decisions—characteristics that led E. Franklin Frazier to characterize the "Negro church" as a "nation within a nation" and an institution that had specifically political, as well as religious, meaning to adherents.[47]

The privatization of civic life, whether reflected in the shift of education, health, and social service provision to nonprofit agencies, in the segmentation of faith communities, or in the displacement of genuinely public space by malls, office centers, and cultural complexes, appears to be both pervasive and stratified, affecting society as a whole, as well as its subcultures.[48] While the religious communities have been slower to formalize their nonprofit status, they too are increasingly being drawn into the privatized institutional system. Between 1996 and 1998, the number of New Haven congregations that had incorporated and received charitable tax-exempt status nearly doubled, while the number reporting active involvement in social service provision increased between 1984 and 1997 from 7 to 35.[49]

Contemporary patterns of civic life in New Haven, characterized by increasing organizational density, segmented participation, and declining political engagement, does not offer direct answers to the questions posed by Putnam and Drucker. On the one hand, the disappearance of traditional forms of civic engagement does not merely threaten the efficacy of public institutions, but their very existence. Voter nonparticipation and the

46. The members of venerable African American congregations like Varick A.M.E., who used to come from its immediate neighborhood, now—because of the expansion of social and economic opportunities for African Americans since the 1960s—live all over the greater New Haven area, though they return to worship on Sundays with old friends and acquaintances. St. Stanislas and St. Boniface Churches, which served the Polish and German Catholic enclaves that once clustered around them, now serve almost entirely suburban members. Many of the new evangelical congregations, located in industrial structures entirely isolated from residential areas, serve similarly dispersed constituencies.

47. On the inward civic orientation of black religious groups, see Paris (1985, p. 7). For more extended treatments of this issue, see Frazier (1964) and Lincoln and Mamiya (1990). For a detailed study of varieties of civic engagement by New Haven's black religious communities, see Hall (1998).

48. On the privatization of public life, see Sorkin (1992).

49. *Infoline* (1984, 1997) and Hall (1998).

increasing reluctance of citizens to run for office or serve on public boards and commissions challenges both the legitimacy and the functionality of government. On the other hand, the proliferation of private nonprofit entities whose aggregate scope embraces every aspect of activity once undertaken either by government or by inclusive voluntary associations suggests the emergence of a new architecture of public life, the configuration of which we can, at this point, only dimly envision.

References

Bailey, William B. 1913. *Living Conditions among Negroes in the Ninth Ward, New Haven.* New Haven, Conn.: New Haven Civic Federation.

Baltzell, E. Digby. 1979. *Puritan Boston and Quaker Philadelphia: Two Protestant Ethics and the Spirit of Class Authority.* Free Press.

Bowen, William G., Thomas I. Nygren, Sarah E. Turner, and Elizabeth A. Duffy. 1994. *The Charitable Nonprofits: An Analysis of Institutional Dynamics and Characteristics.* San Francisco: Jossey-Bass.

Castrol, Michael. 1988. "The Rosenbaum Tutoring School." *Jews in New Haven* 5: 147–52.

Chang, Patricia M. Y., David R. Williams, Ezra E. H. Griffith, and John Young. 1994. "Church-Agency Relationships in the Black Community." *Nonprofit and Voluntary Sector Quarterly* 23(2): 91–106.

Cnaan, Ram. Forthcoming. *Social Services and the Religious Community in an Era of Devolution.*

Cnaan, R. A., with S. C. Boddie and R. J. Wineburg. 1999. *The Newer Deal: Social Work and Religion in Partnership.* Columbia University Press.

Coyle, Barbara A. C. 1980. "An Investigation of the Marriage Patterns of Middletown, Connecticut's Four Principal White Ethnic Groups: The Italians, Polish, Irish, and Jews in Terms of Ethnicity and Religion, 1900–1979." In *Ethnic Heritage Studies Journal 1980.* Middletown: Graduate Liberal Studies Program, Wesleyan University.

Crouse, Joan M. 1992. "Student Initiated Social Outreach: The Yale Hope Mission." Paper presented at the annual meeting of the Association for Research on Nonprofit Organizations and Voluntary Action (ARNOVA). New Haven.

Dahl, Robert A. 1961. *Who Governs? Democracy and Power in an American City.* Yale University Press.

Demerath, N. J., III, and Rhys Williams. 1993. *A Bridging of Faiths: Religion and Politics in a New England City.* Princeton University Press.

Demerath, N. J., Peter Dobkin Hall, Rhys Williams, and Terry Schmitt, eds. *Sacred Companies: Organizational Aspects of Religious and Religious Aspects of Organizations.* Oxford University Press.

DiMaggio, Paul J. 1986. "Cultural Entrepreneurship in Nineteenth Century Boston." In *Nonprofit Enterprise in the Arts: Studies in Mission & Constraint,* edited by Paul J. DiMaggio, 41–61. Oxford University Press.

Drucker, Peter F. 1989. *The New Realities in Government and Politics / in Economics and Business / in Society and World View.* Harper and Row.

Fox, Daniel M. 1986. *Health Policies, Health Politics: The British and American Experience, 1911–1965.* Princeton University Press.

Frazier, E. Franklin. 1964. *The Negro Church in America.* New York: Schocken Books.

Galaskiewicz, Joseph. 1985. *Social Organization of an Urban Grants Economy: A Study of Business Philanthropy and Nonprofit Organizations.* Orlando, Fla.: Academic Press.

Gray, Bradford H. 1991. *The Profit Motive and Patient Care.* Harvard University Press.

Grimes, Clarence A. 1957. *They Who Speak in Music: The History of the Neighborhood Music School, New Haven, Connecticut.* New Haven, Conn.: Neighborhood Music School.

Gronbjerg, Kirsten. 1994. *Understanding Nonprofit Funding.* San Francisco: Jossey-Bass.

Hall, Peter Dobkin. 1982. *The Organization of American Culture, 1700–1900: Institutions, Elites, and the Origins of American Nationality.* New York University Press.

———. 1992. *Inventing the Nonprofit Sector and Other Essays on Philanthropy, Voluntarism, and Nonprofit Organizations.* Johns Hopkins University Press.

———. 1995. "There's No Place Like Home: Contracting Human Services in Connecticut, 1970–1995." Working Paper. Program on Nonprofit Organizations. Yale University.

———. 1997. "Apples and Oranges: Definitional Dilemmas in Assessing the Place of Religion in the Organizational Universe." Paper presented at Independent Sector's Spring Research Forum, Alexandria Virginia.

———. 1998. "Two Models of Interorganizational Fields: African American Voluntary Associations, Congregations, and Nonprofit Organizations in New Haven, Connecticut, 1900–1996." Paper presented at the annual meeting of the Association for Research on Nonprofit Organizations and Voluntary Action, Seattle.

———. 1999. "Blurred Boundaries, Hybrids, and Changelings: The Fortunes of Nonprofit Organizations in the Late Twentieth Century." In *Critical Anthropology Now: Unexpected Contexts, New Constituencies, Changing Genres,* edited by George E. Marcus and Paul Rabinow. Santa Fe, N.M.: American College of Research.

Hall-Russell, Cheryl. 1996. "Evolving Philanthropic Trends in African American Mega-Churches and Their Impact on the American Context." Paper presented to the Silver Anniversary Conference of the Association for Research on Nonprofit Organizations and Voluntary Action (ARNOVA), New York.

Hansmann, Henry B. 1997. *The Ownership of Enterprise.* Harvard University Press.

Hill, Everett G. 1918. *A Modern History of New Haven and Eastern New Haven County.* New York: S. J. Clarke.

Hodgkinson, Virginia A., Murray S. Weitzman, Christopher M. Toppe, and Stephen M. Noga. 1992. *Nonprofit Almanac, 1992–1993.* San Francisco: Jossey-Bass.

Hoge, Dean R., Charles Zech, Patrick McNamara, and Michael J. Donahue. 1996. *Money Matters: Personal Giving in American Churches.* Louisville, Ky.: Westminster John Knox Press.

Hollingshead, August, and Frederick C. Redlich. 1958. *Social Class and Mental Illness.* New York: John Wiley and Sons.

Humphrey, Daniel C. 1992. "Teach Them Not to Be Poor: Philanthropy and New Haven School Reform in the 1960s." Ph.D. diss., Teachers College, Columbia University.

Iannacone, Laurence R. 1998. "Why Strict Churches Are Strong." In *Sacred Companies: Organizational Aspects of Religious and Religious Aspects of Organizations,* edited by N. J. Demerath, Peter Dobkin Hall, Rhys Williams, and Terry Schmitt. Oxford University Press.

Infoline Directory of Community Services—South Central Region. 1984 and 1987. New Haven: United Way of Connecticut.

Inside New Haven's Neighborhoods: A Guide to the City of New Haven. 1982. New Haven, Conn.: New Haven Colony Historical Society.

Jeavons, Thomas. 1998. "Identifying Characteristics of 'Religious' Organizations: An Exploratory Proposal." In *Sacred Companies: Organizational Aspects of Religious and Religious Aspects of Organizations,* edited by N. J. Demerath, Peter Dobkin Hall, Rhys Williams, and Terry Schmitt. Oxford University Press.

Jafferis, Aaron. 1996. "Eulogy for a Home." *New Haven Advocate,* July 4, p. 7.

Johnston, Michael. 1979. "Italian New Haven: Building an Ethnic Identity." *New Haven Colony Historical Society Journal* 26(3): 23–26, 30–31.

Kauffman, Christopher J. 1982. *Faith and Fraternalism: The History of the Knights of Columbus.* Harper and Row.

King, Willford I., and Kate E. Huntley. 1928. *Trends in Philanthropy: A Study in a Typical American City.* New York: National Bureau of Economic Research.

Lincoln, C. Eric, and Lawrence H. Mamiya. 1990. *The Black Church in the African American Experience.* Duke University Press.

McClendon, David. 1996. "Local Jaycees Chapter in Crisis over Membership." *New Haven Register,* July 1, p. A3.

New Haven Chamber of Commerce. 1994. *The Source, 1994–95.* New Haven, Conn.: Greater New Haven Chamber of Commerce.

Paris, Peter J. 1985. *The Social Teaching of the Black Churches.* Philadelphia: Fortress Press.

Polsby, Nelson. 1980. *Community Power and Political Theory: A Further Look at Problems of Evidence and Inference.* Yale University Press.

Putnam, Robert D. 1993. *Making Democracy Work: Civic Traditions in Modern Italy.* Princeton University Press.

———. 1994. "Bowling Alone: America's Declining Social Capital." *Journal of Democracy* 6(1): 65–78.

———. 1996. "The Strange Disappearance of Civic America." *The American Prospect* 24 (Winter): 34–48.

Ratner, Sadie S. P. 1981. "United Order of True Sisters, New Haven Number 4: 117 Years of Sisterhood and Beneficence." *Jews in New Haven* 3: 50–63.

Rosenberg, Charles E. 1987. *The Care of Strangers: The Rise of America's Hospital System.* Basic Books.

Salamon, Lester M. 1996. *Partners in Public Service: Government-Nonprofit Relations in the Modern Welfare State.* Johns Hopkins University Press.

Schneider, J. C. 1996. "Philanthropic Styles in the United States: Toward a Theory of Regional Differences." *Nonprofit and Voluntary Sector Quarterly* 25(2): 190–210.

Simon, John G. 1987. "The Tax Treatment of Nonprofit Organizations: A Review of Federal and State Policies." In *The Nonprofit Sector: A Research Handbook,* edited by W. W. Powell. Yale University Press.

Smith, Steven R., and Michael Lipsky. 1993. *Nonprofits for Hire: The Welfare State in the Age of Contracting.* Harvard University Press.

Stanfield, John H. 1993. "African American Traditions of Civic Responsibility. *Nonprofit and Voluntary Sector Quarterly* 22(2): 137–53.

Starr, Paul. 1982. *The Social Transformation of American Medicine.* Basic Books.

Stevens, Rosemary. 1989. *In Sickness and in Wealth: American Hospitals in the Twentieth Century.* Basic Books.

Swartz, David. 1994. "Secularization, Religion, and Isomorphism: A Study of Large Nonprofit Hospital Trustees." In *Sacred Companies: Organizational Aspects of Religious and Religious Aspects of Organizations,* edited by N. J. Demerath, Peter Dobkin Hall, Rhys Williams, and Terry Schmitt. Oxford University Press.

Tocqueville, Alexis de. [1835–40] 1945. *Democracy in America.* 2 vols. Translated by Henry Reeve. Knopf.

Trueheart, Charles. 1996. "Welcome to the Next Church." *Atlantic Monthly,* August, pp. 37–58.

United States Department of Commerce. 1975. *Historical Statistics of the United States, Colonial Times to 1970.* Washington, D.C.: U. S. Government Printing Office.

Verba, Sidney, Kay Lehman Schlozman, and Henry E. Brady. 1995. *Voice and Equality: Civic Voluntarism in American Politics.* Harvard University Press.

Warner, Robert A. 1940. *New Haven Negroes: A Social History.* Yale University Press.

Warner, W. Lloyd, and Paul S. Lunt. 1941. *The Social Life of a Modern Community.* Yale University Press.

Weisbrod, Burton. 1989. *The Nonprofit Economy.* Harvard University Press.

Whitlock, Reverdy. 1994. *History of the Foote School.* New Haven, Conn.: Foote School.

Wiedersheim, William A. 1992. "The Harugari Singing Society: German-American Ethnicity in New Haven." *New Haven Colony Historical Society Journal* 39(1): 33–42.

Williams, David R., Ezra E. H. Griffith, and John Young. 1993. "Study of the African American Clergy in Greater New Haven." New Haven, Conn.: Program on Non-Profit Organizations and School of Epidemiology and Public Health.

Wolpert, Julian. 1989. "Prudence and Parsimony: A Regional Perspective." *Nonprofit and Voluntary Sector Quarterly* 18(3): 223–36.

———. 1993. *Patterns of Generosity in America: Who's Holding the Safety Net?* New York: Twentieth Century Fund.

Zaretsky, Mark. 1997. "New Haven Mayor Pulls in 79% of Vote." *New Haven Register,* November 5.

7 | Social Change and Civic Engagement: The Case of the PTA

SUSAN CRAWFORD

PEGGY LEVITT

The greatest of the changes we face are those that have been transforming the American family. Divorce, two-career parents, stepfamilies . . . the list goes on, familiar to all of us. We must do more, across every level of the PTA, to reach out, to include, to do everything possible to serve the needs of the evolving family and its children.

—Joan Dykstra, *1997 National PTA president*

THE SOCIAL CHANGES of the late twentieth century, particularly changes in family structure, pose unique challenges to voluntary organizations. Groups in which women play key roles as leaders and members are especially affected. Sharp increases in female-headed households and in labor-force participation by women with children since the 1950s have changed the nature of women's civic engagement. In order to

We gratefully acknowledge the support of Professor Theda Skocpol and Children's Studies at Harvard, whose financial assistance made this research possible. We thank Robert Putnam for his extensive comments on earlier drafts and for allowing us to cite his forthcoming book *Bowling Alone* (Simon and Schuster, forthcoming 2000). We thank Brandon Haller and Christopher Winship for helpful comments on our statistical analysis. We thank Kristin Goss for providing us with relevant articles and other data. We are grateful for the assistance of the National PTA Headquarters, particularly archivist Annie Wang and membership chairperson Michelle Byrnes, as well as the principals we interviewed in the Brookline, Boston, Concord, Dorchester, Medford, and Winchester public schools. We also thank Joyce Epstein, Christopher Jencks, Karen Mapp, and Christine Woyshner for useful conversations about various aspects of this research. We take full responsibility for any omissions or inconsistencies, and the opinions contained in this paper are strictly our own.

249

remain viable, organizations must adapt their missions and operations to accommodate changing family arrangements. Furthermore, in an increasingly diverse and multicultural society, voluntary organizations must reach out to members of different racial, ethnic, and economic backgrounds. Organizations that operate as if their membership continues to be the predominantly white, middle-class, stay-at-home mothers of previous decades find themselves increasingly irrelevant in today's world.

In this chapter, we explore how social and demographic changes have affected one of the oldest and most influential women's organizations in the United States, the National Parent-Teacher Association (PTA). We use the PTA as a case study to help explain how changing women's roles have influenced participation in certain types of organizations and to illustrate a broader story about civic engagement and the decline of national federated organizations.

Demographic changes prove particularly critical for school-support groups, as single and working mothers face multiple demands on their time that limit their ability to participate. According to the U.S. Department of Education, lack of time is the major problem preventing parents from becoming more involved in their children's education.[1] In 1996, 76.7 percent of married mothers, 80.6 percent of divorced or widowed mothers, and 71.8 percent of never-married mothers with school-age children were in the labor force (see Figures 7-1 and 7-2).[2] A substantial number worked full time; in 1990, 40 percent of married mothers with children age six to seventeen worked full time, year round.[3]

The National PTA's membership dropped precipitously in the late 1960s and 1970s. Membership declined from a high in the early 1960s of almost fifty members per 100 families with children under eighteen to fewer than twenty members per 100 families with children under eighteen in the early 1980s.[4] Although participation rebounded somewhat in the

---

1. U.S. Department of Education (1994, p. 3).

2. U.S. Department of Commerce (1997).

3. Spain and Bianchi (1996, p. 152). The number of single mothers has increased sharply in recent decades. Looking at families with own children under age eighteen, the number of female-headed families has increased from 2,099,000 (8 percent of families with children) in 1960 to 7,874,000 (23 percent of families with children) in 1997 (U.S. Bureau of the Census, March 1997 and earlier reports).

4. Note that this ratio uses the number of families with own children under eighteen as the denominator, which is larger than the number of families with only school-age children (thus underestimating PTA membership per 100 families with school-age children). The numerator would include nonparent PTA members, such as teachers (thus overestimating PTA membership for families). We use these readily available figures to provide estimates, acknowledging their limitations. Throughout the chapter, "families with children" refers to families with own children under age eighteen.

Figure 7-1. *Percentage of Mothers with Husbands
in the Labor Force, by Age of Children, 1948–70*

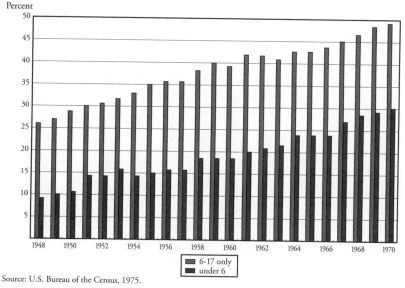

Source: U.S. Bureau of the Census, 1975.

1980s and the early 1990s, the organization never recaptured its membership heights of the late 1950s and early 1960s.

A decrease in the number of families with children does not explain the large post-1960 drop. While the number of families with children decreased relative to the total population in this time period, the absolute number of families with children increased. The PTA lost 5 million members between 1959 and 1975 alone, while the number of families with children increased by almost 5 million and public school enrollment increased by over 9 million. Between 1990 and 1997, the PTA lost a half-million members, even though the number of families with children under eighteen grew by over 2 million and public school enrollment grew by over 5 million.[5]

Since women entered the labor force in large numbers at the same time that the PTA suffered its sharpest membership losses, it is tempting to assume a straightforward causal relationship between maternal employment and organizational decline. Analyses of survey data reveal that full-time working mothers and single mothers are less likely to participate in

5. National PTA membership statistics; National Center for Education Statistics (1997, table 3).

Figure 7-2. *Percentage of Mothers in the Labor Force*
with Children Age Six to Seventeen, by Marital Status, 1960–96

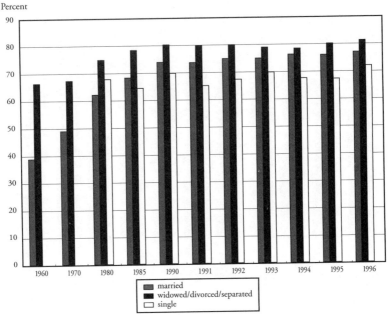

Percent

Source: *Statistical Abstract of the United States 1997*, no. 631.

school service groups than married stay-at-home mothers. The PTA literature itself discusses the stresses experienced by two-career families and
single mothers that make participation in these types of organizations more
difficult. However, although the labor-force participation rate of married
mothers with school-age children rose from 39 percent in 1960 to 61
percent by 1980, it seems unlikely that this increase would have caused
such a large membership decline. In fact, the labor-force participation rate
of women with school-age children rose steadily between 1948 and 1960,
which were years of dramatic growth for the PTA.

Furthermore, some studies find that part-time employment may actually increase the likelihood of participation in school service groups. There
is also some evidence that PTA membership among nonworking married
women has declined at a greater relative rate than that of other women.[6]
Thus the changing family is a factor in the PTA's decline, but it is not the

6. Putnam (1995b, p. 30).

whole story. In this chapter we examine additional factors that contributed directly to the decline of the PTA, including competition from other parent-teacher organizations, the racial integration of the National PTA, and national dues increases.

Competition from other parent-teacher organizations is a factor worth highlighting. The number of local parent-teacher organizations (PTOs) grew substantially during the period of the PTA's largest decline, for reasons we discuss later. These are organizations that may look similar to the PTA at the local school level but are not affiliated with the National PTA. Most are not integrated into a state or national organizational network, unlike their PTA counterparts.[7] There has been much debate about the relationship between declines in PTA membership and growth in these other PTOs. Though there are few data that allow us to assess this relationship with surety, we do not believe that the massive decline in PTA membership can be entirely explained by shifts in membership to PTOs.[8] Rather, we believe participation in parent-teacher groups has declined overall since 1960, in part because of the social and demographic changes discussed above. The PTA lost over 5 million members between 1959 and 1997, while the number of families with children grew by over 9 million and public school enrollment increased by over 11 million. The number of parents involved in alternative school-based groups would need to be enormous to fully account for the PTA's decline, not to mention the larger number of parents who should be involved given the increase in number of families with children. Robert Putnam uses recent survey data to argue that it is not numerically possible for PTOs to have fully absorbed the PTA's post-1960 membership loss.[9]

7. Most of this chapter concerns the National PTA and its affiliated state and local units. When we talk about groups that are not affiliated with the National PTA, we use the term "parent-teacher organization," or PTO. When discussing survey data that encompass both the PTA and PTOs, we use the term "parent-teacher group."

8. Unlike the National PTA, which has a national headquarters, archives, and membership records spanning back a century, membership figures for other parent-teacher groups are very difficult to ascertain. No one keeps statistics on nationwide PTO membership, and most surveys do not offer comprehensive trend data or distinguish between PTOs and the National PTA. Most of the education researchers and practitioners we consulted, however, believe that participation in parent-teacher groups in general has declined since the PTA's heyday, primarily because of changes in work and family life. Others stress the lack of relevant data and call attention to new forms of parental participation that do not involve group membership, which must also be taken into account.

9. Putnam (forthcoming, 2000). Putnam cites a 1993 *Newsweek*-commissioned survey which found that two-thirds of parents involved in any type of school-based group were members of National PTA-affiliated local units. He states that even if the PTA were the only parent-teacher group in 1960, newly emerging PTOs could not have fully accounted for the PTA's large membership defection.

Even if the number of parents participating in parent-teacher groups were equal to that during the PTA's heyday, the decline of a nationwide organization with state and local affiliates and the simultaneous rise of autonomous local groups is significant. The drop in PTA membership needs to be understood within the context of membership declines in other large federated voluntary organizations since the 1960s. Much has been written about large membership losses in fraternal groups (Elks, Shriners, Masons, and others), labor unions, church-related groups, traditional women's groups (such as the League of Women Voters and the Federation of Women's Clubs), and others (such as the Red Cross and the Boy Scouts).[10] In the case of public schools, the new participatory arenas replacing the National PTA tend to be local parent-teacher groups, school-based management teams and parent-run after-school programs. In an attempt to accommodate busy parents, other new forms of participation focus on parents helping children at home and do not require attendance at meetings at all.

This trend raises interesting questions. What is lost when a broad, multipurpose national federation declines in favor of numerous local parent-teacher groups? What is lost when parental involvement shifts from involvement in a school-based group to helping the individual child more at home? Throughout its history the National PTA has had significant impact on state and national policy issues broadly affecting children. The PTA structure connects local units to each other and to state and national-level bodies. In contrast, many new forms of participation focus solely on the individual school or child. When parental participation shifts toward more individualistic, localized concerns that are not connected to broader organizational networks, how does that speak to changing conceptions of citizenship and civic engagement?

In this chapter we pose the following questions: (1) How have the changing role of women and changes in family structure affected the PTA's membership figures, members' levels of participation, and the types of participatory structures available to them, (2) how have the functions of the organization changed as a result, (3) what other factors, besides changes in family structure, influence rates of participation in the PTA, (4) how has the organization responded to these changes, and (5) how does the decline of the PTA speak to broader debates about the changing nature of civic engagement? Another question that we consider very briefly is why the PTA grew so much (controlling for numbers of families with children)

10. Putnam (1995a, pp. 68–70); Skocpol (1997, p. 473).

between 1940 and 1960. Although we are primarily concerned about questions of decline, the very rapid growth of the PTA and other civic organizations in the post-World War II years is worth examining.

To address these questions, we reviewed PTA convention proceedings, magazines, and other materials at the National PTA archives, analyzed survey data, and conducted interviews with school principals in the Boston area in 1997. We chose principals from a variety of school settings, ranging from an upper-middle-class school serving a predominantly white population to a more ethnically mixed school where 30 percent of the families live below the poverty line. Approximately half of the schools we visited had parent-teacher groups that were affiliated with the National PTA. We selected principals who had been in the school system for many years so that they could address the issue of changes over time.

We begin by briefly reviewing the PTA's history and development and discussing the historical effect of family structure on the organization. We then look at the impact of current family demographics on participation by summarizing research on parental involvement and presenting our own analysis of General Social Survey data.[11] We next discuss other factors that contributed to the PTA's decline in the late 1960s and 1970s. We look at the PTA's response to changing family structures and a more diverse society by analyzing its literature and interviewing school administrators. We conclude with a discussion of the relevance of changes in the PTA to broader debates about civic engagement.

Organizational Development and the Structure of the PTA

Alice McLellan Birney established the National Congress of Mothers in 1897. The Congress initially emerged not from grass-roots activism but from the organizing efforts of a few prominent women.[12] It aimed to spread maternal influence or "mother thought" throughout the country. It encouraged "civic" motherhood as a way to right societal ills and encouraged "scientific" mothering by teaching parents to take better care of their own children. As Birney stated: "Men have a thousand imperative outside interests and pursuits, while nature has set her seal upon woman as the caretaker of the child; therefore it is natural that woman should lead in

11. Davis and Smith (1972–1994).
12. Skocpol (1992, p. 334).

awakening mankind to a sense of the responsibilities resting upon the race to provide each newborn soul with an environment which will foster its highest development."[13]

National Congress of Mothers convention speaker Sallie Cotton called for the development of a national training school in domestic sciences for women, similar to military academies that prepared men for national service: "The crown of womanhood is motherhood, and the glory and pride and hope of a nation all concentrate in its mothers. . . . Her [woman's] greatest value to a nation must ever be in the capacity of a mother. . . . When the duties of home life are invested with the dignity of Government recognition, woman herself will feel more impressed with their value."[14]

The new organization grew rapidly. Although Birney had not initially envisioned state-level associations, plans were soon under way to build them. Organizers reached out to existing mothers' clubs, kindergarten associations, and other women's organizations: "It was primarily to these groups that effective appeal was made, since for the most part they represented the locally organized but nationally still unorganized womanhood of America. . . . The idea of a National Congress acted as a powerful magnet, drawing all the scattered groups into a common program of endeavor."[15] By 1900, six state branches of the National Congress of Mothers had been established; by 1915, there were thirty-three such branches representing 60,000 individual members. Concerted membership drives or "Mothers' Crusades" in the next two years doubled the membership, and in 1917 the organization employed a paid fieldworker to coordinate the growth effort.[16]

The National Congress of Mothers undertook a diverse set of activities that included organizing discussion groups about the ideas of child study, opening baby clinics, supporting local schools, and advocating for legislative changes. Participants were generally middle- to upper-class mothers. Lower-income families were beneficiaries of "friendly visiting" and other forms of charitable service that had been a significant part of the organization's early mission. In subsequent years, the National Congress played a major role in shaping state and national social policies on child labor, mothers' pensions, child health and nutrition, and juvenile justice.[17]

13. National Congress of Mothers (1897, p. 9).
14. Ibid. (pp. 217–19).
15. Overstreet (1949, pp. 43–44).
16. National Congress of Parents and Teachers (1947, p. 72).
17. Skocpol (1992, chaps. 6 and 8).

The organization changed its name to the National Congress of Mothers and Parent-Teacher Association in 1908 and to the National Congress of Parents and Teachers (NCPT) in 1924. After the Progressive Era, the NCPT became increasingly active in public schools. In 1926 it helped form the National Congress of Colored Parents and Teachers (NCCPT) for segregated schools. The founder and first president of the NCCPT, Selena Sloan Butler, is now considered a cofounder of the National PTA.[18] PTA activities over the years addressed important child welfare issues of the day, as well as public school education. During the Depression the PTA ran supplementary nutrition and emergency-service programs. During World War II it ran a weekly radio series, "The Family in War." In the 1950s the PTA helped organize the testing and dissemination of the polio vaccine. Membership also soared during this time, topping the 12 million mark from 1960 through 1963.

After the 1960s the National PTA continued to divide its attention between broader child-welfare issues and school support. In the 1970s it focused on smoking, alcohol, and drug-abuse prevention. In the 1980s it created drug-abuse-prevention and HIV/AIDS education programs. In the 1990s it convened a national summit on parent involvement in education.[19] Owing to a convergence of factors that we discuss below, the PTA experienced a drastic membership decline in the late 1960s and 1970s. By 1980, membership had dropped below 6 million, more than 50 percent from its peak in the early 1960s. Participation rebounded slightly to 7 million in 1990–91. However, the PTA lost 500,000 members between 1990 and 1997, despite a national increase of over 2 million families with children in this period.

Mission and Organizational Structure of the Modern PTA

The PTA's stated mission is threefold: (1) to support and speak on behalf of children and youth in schools, in the community, and before governmental bodies and other organizations that make decisions affecting children, (2) to assist parents in developing the skills they need to raise and protect their children, and (3) to encourage parent and public involvement in the public schools of this nation.[20]

18. National PTA (1997).
19. Ibid.
20. Ibid. (1995b, p. 6).

The PTA has a federated structure, operating at the local, state, and national levels. There are also two "intermediate" levels—a regional level added in 1936 that encompasses several states, and a council level composed of several local units. The National PTA holds an annual convention and sets national agendas and priorities. It works with other child-advocacy organizations to establish program and legislative initiatives to benefit child welfare. The organization is governed by a board of directors composed of national officers elected at the annual convention, regional directors elected by their regions, state PTA presidents, participants in two national commissions, two youth representatives, and the immediate past PTA president.[21] Although there is a paid administrative staff of approximately sixty people in Chicago (in the National Headquarters Office) and Washington (in the Governmental Relations Office), the national president and all other officers at all levels serve as volunteers.

The PTA is divided into eight regions. Regional directors, who are elected by the states of their region, provide support to state-level offices. The role of the state-level PTA is to "provide advice, support, and field service; interpret PTA policies, plans, and practices; promote publications and programs; bring non-PTA parent-teacher groups into PTA membership, and perform other functions as the state PTA may determine."[22] Each state writes its own by-laws and sets its own dues structure. State branches are responsible for developing leadership at the council level and organizing new local PTAs. They also collaborate with other statewide child advocacy organizations and promote understanding of the PTA's mission.

PTA councils lie between the state and local levels of the organization. Each state can organize into districts represented by councils, which coordinate local PTA programs and act as a conduit for information about state and local activities. At the local level, there are more than 25,000 units that carry out the grass-roots activities of the organization. These are the groups the public associates most commonly with the PTA. They are based at local schools and address educational and health concerns of children through programs and advocacy. According to the 1995–96 *National PTA Handbook*: "The local unit builds. It builds coalitions to better serve the needs and interests of children, families, and other members of the community. It builds skills and leadership in its members, to help them become more

---

21. Ibid. (p. 13).
22. Ibid. (p. 14).

effective, whether they are dealing with parenting issues, the media, or the state legislature."[23]

Thus, the PTA has a sophisticated organizational structure. Ideas and programs are disseminated downward from the national level and upward from the local level. State and local branches determine their own dues; one dollar per local unit member goes to the National PTA. Approximately 85 percent of the national organization's funding comes from membership dues. The remaining portion of its budget comes from the PTA's permanent endowment fund, grants, publications, and convention and conference attendees. State and local units support themselves financially through dues and fund-raising, although there are limited grants available from the national organization for certain programmatic initiatives.

Leadership at lower levels of the PTA appears to be a prerequisite for national leadership. The 1997 National PTA president, Joan Dykstra, was involved with the PTA for more than twenty years before becoming president. She served as the vice president and president of the Wisconsin State PTA and was the vice president for Region Four, which includes Wisconsin. She also had ten years of service as a member of the National Board of Directors and chaired several key national committees.[24] Similarly, past presidents served the majority of their adult lives as leaders in numerous voluntary organizations and boards rather than in paid careers. Many presidents also taught school. They generally served in progressively responsible PTA positions at the local, state, and national levels before their election to national president. Ann Lynch, national president from 1989 to 1991, was the first president to hold a full-time professional job during her term in office.[25]

The 1998 National PTA president, Lois Jean White, is the first African American president in the PTA's history. Before becoming national president, she had a twenty-five-year career as a music teacher and symphony principal flutist. She served as the president of the Tennessee State PTA, as a member of the National PTA's Education Commission, and in numerous other PTA positions.[26] White began her two-year term as president determined to bring more racial and economic diversity to the PTA. Although the organization became fully integrated in 1970, the image that it is a predominantly white, middle-class, suburban organization persists. We

23. Ibid. (p. 18).
24. Ibid. (1995a).
25. Ibid. (1991).
26. Ibid. (1997).

discuss White's efforts to open the PTA to a broader range of participants later in this chapter.

Family Structure and the PTA from a Historical Perspective

The founders of the National Congress of Mothers conceived of the organization as spreading maternal love and "mother thought" outside of the immediate family to the larger community. Alice McLellan Birney and other early leaders stressed that they were "women of the home." They clearly believed that women belonged at home unless they were compelled by unfortunate circumstances to support themselves. They aimed to make motherhood more of a professional occupation and to spread its influence via "municipal housekeeping."[27] Stated Alice Birney, "It is because most women have not had the knowledge and training which would enable them to evolve the beautiful possibilities of home life that they have in many instances found that sphere narrow and monotonous."[28]

A brief look at the backgrounds of some of the early National Congress leaders reveals that they too may have found the home sphere "narrow and monotonous." Although they described themselves as "women of the home," they were generally well educated, well traveled, and publicly visible. After finishing high school at fifteen, Alice McLellan Birney spent a year at Mount Holyoke, where she wanted to study medicine. She married at age eighteen but was widowed a year later, while pregnant with her first child. She then worked in the advertising business to support herself and her daughter for thirteen years. She had two more children by her second husband, a prominent Washington, D.C., lawyer who died shortly after the founding of the National Congress of Mothers. Alice Birney focused on the new organization after his death and cared for her young daughters with the help of her mother.[29]

Other early leaders also claimed to be "women of the home." Birney's immediate successor, Hannah Kent Schoff, traveled extensively during her eighteen years as president and played a major role in the growth of the new organization, despite having seven children. Margaretta Willis Reeve, the fourth president (1923–28), was described as "having an unusually fine

27. Skocpol (1992, p. 337).
28. Ladd-Taylor (1994, p. 45).
29. Ibid. (p. 48).

educational background" and read and spoke several languages fluently. Before her election as president she served as a state vice president and president, chair of a key national committee for three terms, and editor of the organization's *Child Welfare Magazine*.[30] The fifth president, Ida Caddell Marrs (1928–30) no longer claimed to be merely a "woman of the home." She had ten years of teaching experience and nine years of increasing leadership responsibilities with the PTA before attaining her presidency.[31]

The rank and file of the early PTA were primarily middle- and upper-class mothers who did not work outside their homes. The organization viewed itself as a mainstay and preserver of family life. In 1906, for instance, the organization held a "Divorce Congress" with the aim of tightening divorce laws and reducing the incidence of divorce.[32] During the Progressive Era, leaders advocated pensions for poor mothers so they would not have to "neglect" their children by working outside their homes. A 1921 PTA magazine article entitled "Should Mothers Accept Outside Work?" spoke out forcefully against mothers leaving their children in the care of "hirelings" in order to take a job.[33]

Societal changes precipitated by World War II created institutional tensions between a commitment to stay-at-home motherhood and a desire to support women working for the war effort. In a number of magazine articles in the early 1940s the PTA used war imagery to describe the role of homemaker:

Reveille sounds at five or six in the morning, when the alarm clock goes off. The homemaker rises as promptly as the soldier in camp, dresses as quickly and as neatly. She puts on a fresh house dress, and, instead of standing at attention as a flag goes up, she steps out for a moment into her flower garden.... New skills are required to build defense within the modern home.... If she is a good defense major, she know her canned-goods code.[34]

To attention, Homemakers! Yes, the alert has been sounded, and the homemakers of America have awakened and stand ready to do their part! Never has there been such a demand for well-informed family leaders.[35]

30. National Congress of Parents and Teachers (1947, p. 94).
31. Ladd-Taylor (1994, p. 65); also see the PTA's website: http://www.pta.org.
32. National Congress of Mothers (1906, p. 25).
33. Willis (1921, pp. 127–28).
34. Smith (1941, pp. 4–5).
35. Calvert (1942, p. 18).

Favorable articles on women's employment outside the home also appeared during this period: "The opening up of new opportunities for women to work outside the home, whether on a volunteer basis or for pay, raises many important questions regarding family life and child welfare. . . . The quality of the relationship between a child and his mother is more important than the number of hours a mother is at home. . . . We cannot deny that these new opportunities for work outside the home will give a feeling of increased significance to some women. They will find new outlets for their energies . . . there will probably be an increased buoyancy of spirit."[36]

During World War II the PTA addressed the still controversial issue of child care for working women. A 1943 article in the organization's magazine, *National Parent-Teacher*, examined how communities could best develop day-care facilities and other support systems needed by working mothers: "In a very real sense, the provision of extended school services for children of working mothers is an adaptation and an extension of the regular parent-teacher program. . . . The provision of adequate care and guidance for children of working mothers is one of the pressing problems that must be solved in many American communities."[37]

As the war drew to a close, however, PTA literature mirrored social trends that encouraged women to resume their roles as homemakers. A 1945 PTA President's Message on the postwar needs of the country ran: "WANTED—38,000,000 skilled homemakers to give full time to the care of their homes, their husbands, their . . . children, and several million old people and dependent relatives. HOMEMAKING IS A BIG AND IMPORTANT BUSINESS."[38] Though some PTA literature written during the war highlighted the benefits of women working outside the home, the postwar transition articles urged women to return to their old ways and focus on welcoming their husbands home. "Above all, wives and mothers, act and *be* normal. Expect the best to happen and it usually will. Don't try to show your hero off. . . . Welcome Father home, and make it the kind of home he wants and you want."[39] The PTA postwar literature also revisited the "civic motherhood" themes of the early National Congress of Mothers: "[Woman] has been forced by circumstances to change her way of life. . . . Woman's place is still in the home, but let us give a broad definition to

36. Stolz (1942, p. 6).
37. Goodykoontz (1943, p. 10).
38. Hastings (1945, p. 3).
39. Kabat (1946, p. 6).

that word home. . . . May we glory in our role as women. May we assume responsibility for community, national, and international homemaking."[40]

The 1950s and 1960s

In the decades immediately following World War II, PTA membership soared from just under 3½ million in 1945 to over 12 million by 1960. The organization reaped the rewards of a societal emphasis on traditional families, the postwar baby boom, and concerted membership drives. It actively recruited members through door-to-door canvassing, newspaper and radio advertisements, publicity drives, and letters and phone calls to nonparticipating parents. Promotional materials were directed at middle-class wives and mothers who did not work outside the home. Though a 1953 handbook encouraged local units to hold some meetings at night so that fathers could attend, it made no mention of reaching out to single and working mothers.

Who Participates?

After 1963 the PTA began a period of membership decline that persisted for nearly twenty years. By 1975 membership had dropped by nearly 50 percent; by 1985 there were only 5½ million PTA members in the country. The number of local chapters decreased from a high of 47,000 in the early 1960s to a low of 24,400 in 1984. These declines are similarly dramatic even when we control for changes in the numbers of families with children. A slight recovery in the 1980s brought membership back up to about 7 million by 1990, but the organization lost a half-million members and almost 2,000 local chapters between 1990 and 1997, even though the number of families with children increased by over 2 million. In 1997–98 the PTA had 6,461,895 members belonging to 25,533 chapters (see Figures 7-3 through 7-7).

The PTA's decline corresponds to the period in which large numbers of middle-class mothers entered the paid labor force and the number of female-headed households increased. However, we believe that several factors together contributed to the PTA's decline during this period. Before we turn to a discussion of these, we take a closer look at the actual

40. Hastings (1946, p. 3).

Figure 7-3. *National PTA Membership, 1900–97*

Millions

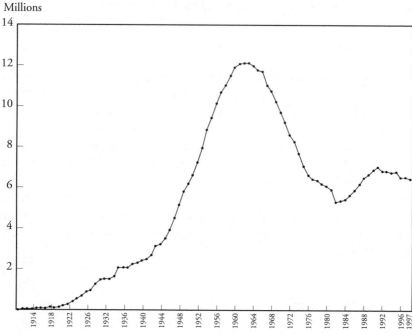

Source: National PTA membership statistics, various years.

relationship between maternal employment, marital status and participation in school-support organizations.

In the following section we briefly review the extensive literature on parental involvement in children's education.[41] We then present our analysis of General Social Survey data. We stress one important caveat. All of the studies we review in upcoming paragraphs do not distinguish between the PTA and other PTOs. Although we are primarily concerned with the National PTA, we use these studies as a proxy for understanding the impact of demographic characteristics on membership. To avoid confusion, we use the term "parent-teacher groups" to refer to PTOs and the PTA together.

41. There is a growing body of literature about parental participation in education that tries to ascertain how parental involvement benefits children and to examine creative ways that schools can involve busy parents. See Epstein (1995 and 1996) for an excellent overview of this subject. In this brief review we focus specifically on characteristics that influence likelihood of participation in parent-teacher groups.

Figure 7-4. *National PTA Membership per 100 Families*
with Children under Eighteen, 1900–97

Members per 100 families

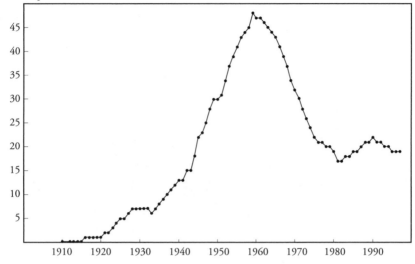

Source: PTA membership figures are from National PTA membership statistics. Number of families with children 1950 and later is from U.S. Bureau of the Census. March 1997 and earlier; pre-1950 figures are estimates from Putnam (forthcoming 2000).

Findings from Previous Research

The National Education Longitudinal Study (NELS:88) revealed that approximately 32 percent of the parents surveyed participated in parent-teacher groups. Parental participation increased with parental education, for all racial and ethnic groups.[42] A National Center for Education Statistics report based on NELS:88 data also highlighted the relationship between participation and parental education. It reported that only 10 percent of two-parent families with no high-school diploma were members of parent-teacher groups; 60 percent of two-parent families with college degrees were members of parent-teacher groups. Of single mothers, only 9.7 percent of those without a high-school degree were members, but almost 50 percent of college-educated single mothers were members.[43]

42. NELS:88 is a national random sample of 26,000 eighth graders and their parents; the PTA and PTOs constitute one category. Cited in Kerbow and Muller (1993, p. 35).

43. National Center for Education Statistics (1988, table 2-9).

Figure 7-5. *Change in National PTA Membership, 1951–98*[a]

Percent change

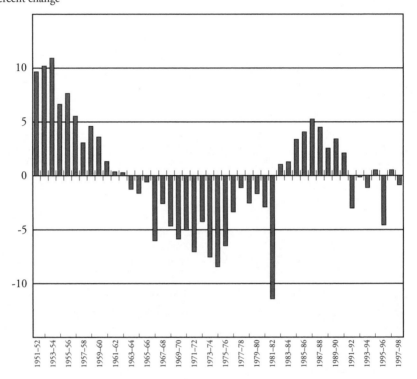

Source: Calculated from National PTA membership figures. This shows the membership change from one school year to the next. For example, in the 1953–54 school year, membership increased 11 percent from the 1952–53 school year.
a. Dues were increased in 1966–67, 1973–74, 1981–82, 1991–92, and 1995–96.

Participation in parent-teacher groups also varied by race and ethnicity. Muller and Kerbow found that controlling for education and socioeconomic status (SES), African American and to a lesser extent Hispanic parents were more likely to belong and to attend meetings regularly than their white and Asian counterparts.[44] College-educated African Americans were the most likely to participate. Middle- and high-SES African American parents were more likely to be members than white parents with similar characteristics.[45] These findings are contra-

44. Muller and Kerbow (1993, p. 35).
45. National Center for Education Statistics (1988, table 2-9).

Figure 7-6. *Local Units of the National PTA, 1950–98*

Number of local units

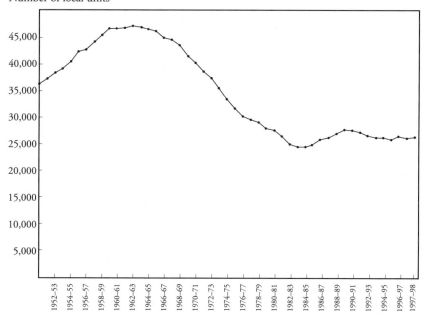

Source: National PTA membership statistics, various years.

dicted by Nicholas Zill, who used the 1993 National Household Education Survey to predict levels of parent involvement in schools (though not necessarily parent-teacher group membership) by family characteristics.[46] He found that being African American, Hispanic, and especially Asian decreased the odds of high participation.

Several studies found that single mothers and mothers working full time were less likely to participate in parent-teacher groups. Interestingly, in some studies, part-time working mothers displayed higher rates of participation than either full-time employed mothers or full-time homemakers. Zill found that single mothers and mothers employed full time were less likely to be active, but women employed part time were more likely to be highly active than stay-at-home mothers.[47] Although Muller's findings corroborate Zill's for full-time workers, she found no clear differ-

46. Zill (1996, p. 23).
47. Ibid.

Figure 7-7. *PTA Members per 1,000 Public Elementary and Secondary School Children, 1960–97*

Members

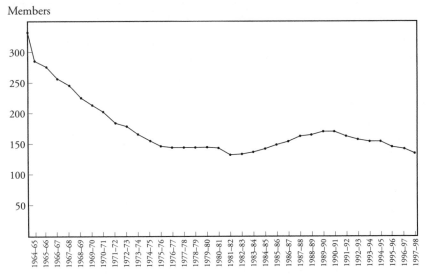

Source: Calculated from National PTA membership figures and National Center for Education Statistics.

ences in parent-teacher group participation between part-time working mothers and stay-at-home mothers.[48] She did, however, find that mothers working part time were more likely than stay-at-home mothers to be involved in their children's education in other ways. Muller hypothesized that mothers working part time have more community ties and opportunities for involvement than nonworking mothers but that they do not face the same time constraints as full-time working mothers. Putnam found that working full time diminished community involvement for women working both out of necessity and by choice. However, women working part time, especially those doing so by choice, were more likely to volunteer, join clubs, and engage in informal socializing than full-time working women or full-time homemakers.[49]

Parent-teacher group membership also varied by the type of school. Parents of children in private schools were more likely to participate than those enrolled in public schools (57 percent and 29 percent respectively).[50]

48. Muller (1993, p. 96).
49. Putnam (forthcoming, 2000).
50. National Center for Education Statistics (1988, chap. 4).

In addition, school characteristics were highly influential. Children in schools with "minimal student problems, high teacher engagement, or strong academic pressure" were much more likely to have parents involved in parent-teacher groups than were children in more troubled schools. Parents in schools that initiated frequent contact with parents were also more likely to be parent-teacher group members than parents in schools with little school-initiated contact (73 percent and 27 percent).[51] Racial and ethnic composition of the school was also relevant. Kerbow and Bernhardt found that, controlling for socioeconomic status, schools with high percentages of Hispanic and African American parents had higher levels of parent-teacher group involvement.[52]

It is important to distinguish between levels of participation. Much of the research summarized above simply examines membership. Membership, however, can encompass everything from paying dues to active leadership. A study of 1,400 white and African American junior high school students and their parents revealed that while 61 percent of the parents held nominal membership in parent-teacher groups, only 5 percent held leadership positions or participated actively.[53] When asked why they were not more involved in their children's school, 62 percent of the parents replied that lack of time constrained them the most.

The principals we interviewed offered several differing accounts of the relationship between changing family structures and parent-teacher group involvement. In one school, membership declined as more women went to work. Nonworking women assumed most of the leadership roles. Some men were active, but they tended to take on traditionally male tasks such as serving on the computer or technology committee. In another school, participation shifted with changing family structures. New organizations created to meet the needs of dual-career families diverted participation into other arenas, such as after-school program boards. New kinds of extended-care services that needed support from volunteers competed with traditional school-support groups for parents' time and attention. In a third school, participation thrived because the principal successfully created new participatory opportunities that were "user-friendly" for both working and nonworking parents. And finally, in a special developmentally based program that attracted the more educated, middle-class parents in a primarily

51. Ibid.
52. Kerbow and Bernhardt (1993, p. 126).
53. Eccles and Harold (1996, p. 23).

working-class town, the principal felt there was too much parent involvement. He described his task as having to limit parental participation and to channel it appropriately.

In sum, research on parent characteristics and parent involvement reveals that parental education and socioeconomic status, as well as type of school, matters for parent-teacher group membership. Mothers working full time and single mothers are less likely than homemakers to participate in such organizations, though some research finds part-time employment to predict greater involvement. While some research finds that, controlling for socioeconomic status, African American and Hispanic parents are more likely to participate in parent-teacher groups than their white or Asian counterparts, other studies contradict these findings.

Analyses from the General Social Survey

To explore these questions further, we analyzed parental involvement in school service organizations using the General Social Survey (GSS) from 1974 to 1994.[54] Using logistic regression analysis, we explored how various factors influenced the likelihood of school service group membership.

In preliminary analysis of a data set of 5,589 men and women with school-age children, we found that marriage, higher levels of education, higher family income, and being female were associated with greater likelihood of membership in school service groups. The effect of marriage on participation varied by income. Working full time decreased the likelihood of participation, as did being of race "other." Being African American or working part time had no significant effect in these models. Eighteen percent of men in this sample reported membership in a school service group; marriage, higher educational levels, and higher family income predicted a greater likelihood of men's involvement. (See Table 7A-1 in the technical appendix for regression results.)

The subset of women with school-age children included 3,650 women, 18 percent of whom were African American. Our analyses support the claim that married women and women with higher educational levels are more likely to belong to school service groups. Women of "other" races

---

54. In the data analysis, we assume that the respondents with children in the household who answer yes to the school service membership question are referring to groups such as the PTA, although this is not always the case. See the appendix for a discussion of this and other issues and for a more detailed discussion of the statistical analysis.

were significantly less likely to participate in these organizations, and race had no effect for African Americans in the initial basic models. Language and cultural barriers may partially explain lower participation rates among "other" race respondents. Full-time work diminished the likelihood of participation, and not working increased the likelihood of participation. These data showed no effect on participation of working part time. The impact of income on participation varied by labor-force status. (See Tables 7-A2 and 7-A3 for regression results.)

Interestingly, the impact of race did not emerge until we analyzed the effects of race by income. We found that at all income levels whites were more likely to participate than African Americans. Holding education and marital status constant, more family income increased the odds of membership for whites, while for African Americans, higher family income decreased the odds of membership. Thus lower-income African Americans were more likely to be members of school service groups than higher-income African Americans of similar education and marital status.[55]

An analysis of the differential impacts of labor-force attachment revealed further complexities. Married women were more likely to participate than single women. Among married women, full-time employment diminished the likelihood of participation. Labor-force participation, however, did not affect single women. A single mother working full time was as likely to participate as a single mother who did not work full time (although single women overall participated less than married women of any labor-force status). The effect of labor-force attachment also varied by income. Women working full time were less likely to participate as their family income increased. Women not in the labor force or working part time were more likely to participate as family income increased.

These results provide interesting food for thought for theorists of civic engagement and PTA leadership. The leaders of the PTA are right to be concerned about the impact of two-career families and single motherhood on membership rates. The data show that single mothers participated in school service groups at lower rates than married mothers. The impact of

55. Holding education and marital status constant, high-income whites in these models were most likely to be members of a school service group, followed by low-income whites, low-income African Americans, and finally high-income African Americans. See appendix for predicted probabilities from logistic regression models that gave us these results. Predicted probabilities were calculated using Model 5c.

full-time work was negative for married mothers. Minority group members participated at lower rates than whites. Since higher levels of education predict a greater likelihood of parent-teacher group involvement, the fact that PTA membership declined so significantly in recent decades despite rising overall educational levels is noteworthy. We believe that the combination of more mothers in the full-time labor force and an increasing number of single mothers is partially responsible for the PTA's current membership difficulties. This is, however, only one part of the story. In the following section, we discuss additional factors that help to explain the PTA's decline.

Additional Factors Affecting PTA Membership

Several other factors contributed to the decline of the PTA in the 1960s and 1970s. In addition to the general trend toward membership retrenchment in large federated voluntary organizations after the early 1960s, there are several additional influences that bear directly on the PTA. These include the rise of competing organizations, busing and racial integration, school consolidations in the late 1970s, and dues increases.

The data available for evaluating these issues are limited. The National PTA has not kept records on the demographic characteristics of its membership. The PTA did not conduct surveys of exiting members to determine why they left during the period of rapid decline. There are no good data allowing us to evaluate how much membership declines in the 1960s and early 1970s were related to parents' joining competing parent-teacher organizations rather than leaving school service groups altogether. There are also no comprehensive longitudinal national data about membership in non-PTA parent-teacher groups.[56]

56. The General Social Survey (GSS) provides trend data back to 1974, although it does not distinguish between the PTA and other school service groups. Among the GSS respondents with school-age children, membership in any school service organization dropped substantially in the early 1980s, had recovered by the early 1990s, and by 1994 had returned to its 1974 levels. Because the GSS did not begin asking the school service group membership question until 1974, we cannot use it to assess trends in the PTA's period of large decline. Other surveys on the topic of participation in parent-teacher groups, such as the Gallup / Phi Delta Kappan polls on the public's attitude toward education, lack long enough trend data and conflate the PTA with PTOs. The term "PTA" is often commonly understood in surveys to mean any parent-teacher group, whether it is affiliated with the National PTA or not.

The Rise of PTOs and Other Organizations

The National PTA stresses the increase in comparable competing organizations in the late 1960s and 1970s as a key reason for its decline. A 1976 management audit of the National PTA states: "Membership in the National PTA declined by 23% in the four year period ending in 1975. While no statistics are available, it is known that local PTOs have been growing in numbers every year."[57]

PTOs emerged as an alternative for individuals who became dissatisfied with the National PTA. As the 1967 National PTA president put it, "Extremists have infiltrated PTAs and persuaded some to withdraw from the State and National Congresses."[58] Many parents in the 1960s found the PTA too conservative and nonconfrontational in debates around issues such as busing and teacher collective bargaining. The PTA's stated policy of "nonintervention" in school administrative matters limited its role. Other parents saw the organization as too liberal and feared it would impose agendas to promote school-based sex education or the federalization of public schools. To stave off decline, the PTA tried to keep its members aware of the advantages of affiliation with a federated organization. A 1970s PTA brochure entitled "Why a PTA instead of a PTO," for example, explained how the structure of the PTA allowed local unit members to have a voice at the state and national levels. It stressed that local PTOs did not provide this broader representation and did not receive assistance from state or national organizations.[59]

Since the 1970s, other types of groups have emerged that also compete with the PTA for parents' energies. In some of the schools we visited, participation in the PTA dropped as members joined other school-based organizations. This was in part the result of changes in statewide education legislation that altered the relationship between communities and schools. For example, Massachusetts Special Education Law 776, which expanded services to special-needs children, gave parents the right to advocate for their children to ensure they received services to which they were entitled. The 1993 Educational Reform Act also altered the relationship between parents and schools by requiring parents' input into more substantive areas of school activities. Thus at each school a School Advisory Council (SAC)

57. William M. Young and Associates (1976, p. 115).
58. National Congress of Parents and Teachers (1967, p. 24).
59. National PTA (1976).

was established consisting of parent, teacher, and community representatives. Through these and other channels, parents became involved in curriculum and budget decisions and in evaluating achievement standards.

As a result, interested parents could choose between participation in PTAs or SACs. Most principals felt that the two groups attracted different kinds of individual. As one principal put it, "Parents interested in more real issues veer toward the school council." He felt that the PTA was weaker because more capable parents, interested in curriculum issues, worked for the SAC. In some schools, principals found this a fruitful division of labor because more active, sophisticated parents worked on substantive issues, while others participated in traditional PTA activities where general parent involvement was more appropriate. In other schools, the principal felt trapped in the role of mediator, trying to preserve a central role for the PTA without compromising the SAC functions.

In some schools, parent involvement was also diverted by new organizations that emerged to meet the need of families with working parents. After- and before-school care programs, which are increasingly common, require a great deal of parent involvement and seemed to absorb the energies of those once involved in the PTA.

We think that competing groups cannot fully account for the post-1960 decline of the PTA. Putnam argues that it is not numerically possible for PTOs to have fully absorbed those who left the PTA.[60] The PTA's membership dropped from over 12 million in 1959 to 6.5 million in 1997, while over the same period the number of families with children increased by 9 million. Competing organizations would have acquired enormous memberships encompassing the large majority of parents participating in school-based groups if they alone accounted for the PTA's decline.[61]

60. Putnam (forthcoming, 2000). Putnam uses a 1993 *Newsweek*-commissioned survey: "The Third PTA National Education Survey," which found that two-thirds of parents belonging to any school-based group were PTA members. A total of 53 percent of parents surveyed belonged to one or more group. Thirty-five percent were PTA members, 22 percent PTO members, 12 percent belonged to booster clubs, and 15 percent belonged to another parent group. He notes that even under the unlikely assumption that all parent-teacher group members in 1960 were affiliated with the National PTA, competitor organizations would not account for the full decline.

61. At its heyday of 12 million members in the early 1960s, there were forty-seven PTA members per 100 families with children. Assuming an equal proportion of parent-teacher group members to the number of families with children today, there would be at least 16 million members of parent-teacher groups now. (This figure is a lower bound, since it assumes the PTA was the only parent-teacher group in 1960, which is improbable). Since the PTA now has only 6.5 million members, other groups would have to have almost 10 million members, or more.

There is also some anecdotal evidence of membership decline in PTOs. A 1993 *New York Times* article discussed the large membership drop since the early 1960s in the United Parents Associations (UPA), New York City's federation of parent-teacher groups (which did not appear to include the PTA). In fact, most of the education professionals and researchers we spoke with did not believe that membership in competing groups could fully account for declining participation in the PTA.

Perceptions of the PTA's Efficacy

Closely tied to the rise in alternative parent-teacher groups was the growing perception that the PTA was not effective at its task. The general public seemed to see the PTA as an increasingly irrelevant "punch and cookies" group: "Too often, PTA programs have been conceived along lines similar to the programs of some women's clubs: primarily as entertainment, secondarily as uplifting fare, and incidentally as educational stuff in the broadest sense of the term."[62] In response to this criticism, the PTA revised its long-standing nonintervention policy in 1972 and began encouraging parents to play a more active role in school policy: "There can be no doubt that the PTA should seek to be involved in the collective bargaining process."[63] The organization also passed a national resolution supporting busing in 1972.

Taking a more activist stance appears to have both hurt and helped the PTA. Some parents felt that the organization did not become confrontational enough and gave teachers' unions too much voice. Parents who wanted to pursue educational reform often chose to do so through other organizations. This reputation as a supporter of the status quo continues to plague the PTA today. For example, the author of a 1995 *Policy Review* article wrote, "In the last twelve months, I have attended two national PTA meetings and five state conventions, and I cannot recall a single instance in which any policy contrary to the interests of teachers unions was given a proper hearing. . . . It is virtually impossible for parent members [of the PTA] to develop parent-friendly policies that may conflict with the interests of teachers unions."[64]

Other members became alienated when local PTA units chose a more activist stance. For example, Ohio PTA official Barbara Sprague attributed

62. Mok (1963, p. 127).
63. National PTA (1978).
64. Haar (1995, p. 87).

the 1970s membership decline in her state at least partially to the PTA's opposition to a collective-bargaining law that allowed teachers to strike. In Montgomery County, Maryland, the county council of PTAs "upset its longtime allies in the county teachers association [in 1992] when it refused to support a teacher pay raise."[65] The Texas PTA believes it lost members in the 1990s by lobbying against the carrying of concealed weapons and by promoting sex education.

Busing

School busing was another factor that contributed to PTA membership decline. Some dissatisfied parents left the organization not because they disagreed with the PTA's support for busing but because their children no longer attended local schools. Because busing sent many children to schools outside their local neighborhoods, it became more difficult for parents to participate. A former National PTA president said in a 1977 interview, "Many of the parents still want to come to the schools, but the schools aren't close by and they just can't drop in. Sometimes it takes so long to get there that it's difficult to become involved."[66]

Racial Integration of the National PTA

Another factor contributing to membership drop in the South was the racial integration of the PTA. After the Supreme Court ruled in *Brown* v. *Board of Education,* the National PTA delegated the responsibility for its integration with the National Congress of Colored Parents and Teachers (NCCPT) to state-level organizations. In the mid-1960s, only nine states remained segregated. Meetings between the PTA and NCCPT to discuss desegregation began in 1966, and in 1970 the National PTA mandated the desegregation of all state organizations. Although the PTA should have grown by approximately 250,000 members (the number of NCCPT members) after its integration, membership declined significantly in most of the nine states that continued to resist integration until 1970.[67]

65. Stephen Buckley, "As Schools Cut Back, PTAs Trade Cookies for Clout," *Washington Post*, April 9, 1992.
66. Lawrence Feinberg, "PTA Seeks to Reverse Decline with Activism," *Washington Post*, December 5, 1977.
67. Donovan (1997, p. 15).

We calculated the membership change in the nine "holdout" states—Alabama, Arkansas, Florida, Georgia, Louisiana, Mississippi, North Carolina, South Carolina, and Texas—each year from 1963 to 1972 to see how the desegregation policy affected membership (see Table 7-1). In 1970–71 there were major declines in most of these states' memberships. All but two of the nine states that had resisted integration experienced declines that were significantly larger than the nationwide declines that year. Whereas the National PTA membership declined by 5 percent in 1970–71, Mississippi lost 40 percent of its members, South Carolina and Louisiana almost 13 percent, and Alabama and North Carolina 11 percent. Twenty-eight percent of the total national membership loss in 1970–71 came from just seven southern states; close to 18 percent came from Mississippi, Florida, and North Carolina alone.[68]

Dues Increases

Analyses of membership changes between 1960 and 1997 also reveal interesting relationships between membership declines and dues hikes. National dues are collected as part of local organization dues. They rose from five cents per member in 1960 to one dollar per member in 1997. We found that small national dues increases were associated with significant membership decreases. Although the actual financial increases seem small, they appear to have caused local units and individuals to question their PTA membership.[69] When dues were raised from five to ten cents in 1966–67, membership dropped over 6 percent; the decline in the previous year had been less than 1 percent. The dues increase from ten to twenty cents in 1973–74 sparked a drop of close to 8 percent nationally, whereas the decline in the previous year had been only 4 percent. During that same year, membership shrank in almost every state, with several states experiencing huge losses. California alone lost over 85,000 members and 149 local chapters in 1973–74. The PTA literature of the period reveals the organization's concern about dues-related membership loss. Numerous

68. Donovan posits that since black and white parents in southern states were unlikely to belong to the same churches, social circles, and residential areas, perhaps integrated PTAs lost some of their community atmosphere and made members feel less strongly connected to the group. Ibid. (p. 16).

69. Small financial increases may, in fact, not be perceived in the aggregate as small by local chapters. A ten cent increase in national dues per member might have been viewed as a significant increase in the cost of national affiliation for some local units.

Table 7-1. *PTA Membership Loss in Key Years of Racial Integration, 1963–73*

Percent

Year	Alabama	Arkansas	Florida	Georgia	Louisiana	Mississippi	North Carolina	South Carolina	Texas	National
1963–64	4.41	2.06	0.09	1.42	–8.96	0.19	–1.49	0.08	–1.08	–1.16
1964–65	–1.27	1.32	0.12	–1.27	–4.13	–5.93	0.43	1.73	1.56	–1.71
1965–66	0.14	–1.75	0.95	–2.76	–6.10	–2.73	0.21	–1.52	1.40	–0.69
1966–67[a]	–10.52	–4.28	–4.42	–2.58	2.72	–10.78	–5.14	–3.62	–9.51	–6.17
1967–68	–2.67	–1.64	–1.41	–1.86	–6.27	–6.43	–0.58	–1.08	–2.15	–2.71
1968–69	–4.04	–1.40	–6.36	–2.54	–1.02	–5.77	–5.21	–1.76	–0.12	–4.77
1969–70	–7.12	–6.06	–5.58	–3.07	–11.81	–9.09	–3.75	–14.02	–3.20	–5.87
1970–71[b]	–11.07	–7.38	–7.60	–3.91	–12.80	–39.66	–11.50	–12.95	1.42	–5.11
1971–72	–5.02	–1.80	–6.28	–1.61	6.62	–8.60	–10.36	1.69	–2.97	–7.22
1972–73	–12.94	–11.14	–3.39	–7.27	7.04	25.80	2.75	3.27	–1.43	–4.30

Source: Calculated from National PTA membership figures.

a. Racial integration talks begin.

b. National PTA mandates desegregation in all states.

PTA magazine articles touted the benefits of membership and urged local units and individuals not to leave on account of rising national dues.[70]

The "dues increase as catalyst" hypothesis receives even clearer support from the changes in the 1980s and 1990s. Because there were so many factors driving membership declines in the 1960s and 1970s, it is difficult to differentiate the effect of dues increases from other factors. In the 1980s and 1990s, the relationship between dues increases and membership drops is strikingly clear. In the years immediately preceding the 1981–82 national dues increase from twenty to fifty cents, membership decline had slowed to approximately 2 percent a year. In 1981–82, however, membership dropped over 11 percent—more than 2,500 local units and 600,000 people.[71] Membership figures began to increase in the following year and grew throughout the 1980s. When dues rose again in 1991–92, however, membership dropped 3 percent despite ten previous years of sustained growth. The most recent dues increase in 1995–96—which raised national dues from seventy-five cents to one dollar per member—sparked a greater than 4 percent membership decline despite membership increases in the previous year (see Figure 7-5, p. 266).

The Changing Social and Political Context

Finally, other explanations reflect the larger school climate. When student enrollment declines and schools consolidate (as occurred in the late 1970s), fewer PTA chapters are needed.[72] Our interviews with principals indicated that the nature and strength of parental participation in different communities reflects the larger political context in each town. Two of the principals we interviewed worked at schools in urban settings with long histories of community activism. They had strong legacies of political mobilization around issues such as rent control. The PTA and SAC members in these schools felt entitled to a say in how their schools were run and

---

70. The significance of the dues increases was that they appeared to cause local chapters and individual members to reevaluate the value of their affiliation with the National PTA. It seems unlikely that such small monetary increases would have caused individual members to leave the organization, yet the decline in local units does not account for all of the individuals who left in dues increase years. One possibility is that dues increases galvanized splinter groups of dissatisfied parents into breaking off from the local PTA unit; that is, individuals dropped out but local chapters remained in the school.

71. The local chapter loss occurred between 1981 and 1983.

72. However, PTA chapters and membership numbers recovered somewhat in the 1980s, when school enrollment remained low.

were accustomed to expressing it. In several of the other schools we visited, the principals claimed that the town's limited experience with civic engagement carried over into parental involvement in the schools. Parents were not accustomed to active participation and felt that school governance was the domain of paid professionals.

Discussion

Given this evidence, what can we conclude about the role of changing family structures in the PTA's membership decline? We believe that multiple factors led to declines in PTA membership, only one of which was changing family demographics. Competing participatory arenas, increases in dues, desegregation, busing, and the politics of educational reform have all played a role in reshaping the organization. The larger social and political context, which contributed to the decline in many large federated organizations, is another critical factor. Clearly, however, increases in the number of full-time working mothers and female-headed households have strongly affected voluntary organizations such as the PTA.

Our review of PTA magazines, National convention proceedings, and other documents suggests that the organization did not pay sufficient attention to these demographic changes as they emerged. The PTA did not seek to meet the changing needs of its constituents in the early years of family transformation. It continued to operate as if its members were primarily stay-at-home mothers, despite the growing number of two-career and female-headed families. However, during the 1980s and 1990s, embracing, supporting, and accommodating family changes became a major PTA concern.

The PTA's Current Response to Changing Family Needs

The "parental time crunch" is a reality for many families: "With the rise in two-breadwinner families, one-parent families, and the need for family members to hold more than one job, families have many demands on their time. . . . Teachers are also strapped for time. Although some would like to make home visits to families or talk more with students' parents, many teachers are parents themselves and have families to attend

73. U.S. Department of Education (1994, p. 3).

to."[73] PTA literature reflects a growing concern about how time pressures affect parents' ability to participate. In 1993 the National PTA published *The Busy Parent's Guide to Involvement in Education,* a booklet that provides suggestions for time-effective involvement in children's education: "Start first with the ideas that appeal to you most and will easily fit into your schedule, and then add others as time permits. The good news is that no matter how little time you have, you will find a number of things in these pages that you can do to help your children."[74]

A 1995 special back-to-school section published by the PTA in *Good Housekeeping* magazine included suggestions for busy working parents who wanted to play an active role in their children's education. The PTA suggested that they team up with stay-at-home mothers to do tasks that could be done in small blocks of time. It encouraged parents to volunteer at school during their lunch hour or to conduct a tour of their workplace. Some parents have formed PTAs in workplaces, where they meet during lunch to discuss concerns about their children's education, even though their colleagues' children may attend different schools.[75]

Local PTA units have mounted various strategies to aid working parents. Many PTA units hold meetings in the evening and during breakfast hours to accommodate parents' schedules. The Shawnee Mission East PTA in Shawnee Mission, Kansas, provides baby-sitting for parents during parent-teacher conferences. In Portland, Oregon, Happy Valley Elementary PTA members read books to children during office lunch hours.[76]

Federal legislation passed in 1994 promotes parental involvement in education. The Goals 2000: Educate America Act received considerable input and legislative support from the National PTA. It calls for the Department of Education and other federal agencies to encourage parents to become involved in their children's education. It calls for the creation of family resource centers and parental involvement at the grass-roots level. A Department of Education bulletin suggests that employers can support school involvement by providing flexible lunch hours for visiting or volunteering at schools and time off for PTA meetings and parent-teacher conferences.[77]

Some of the schools we visited went to great lengths to ensure that working parents could still play a role in their children's education. They

74. Albert (1993).
75. *Good Housekeeping* and the National PTA (1995).
76. Cutright (1989).
77. U.S. Department of Education (1994).

scheduled meetings during the school day, before school, and in the evenings. "Our idea is," said one principal, "to let parents know that we are available to them at all hours of the day or night." Schools serving diverse populations developed a range of volunteer tasks that required different levels of skill and involvement so that all parents could feel they were making a contribution and feel competent in doing so. Said the principal: "We have lowered the stakes to encourage involvement."

In most of the schools we visited, the PTA was still, as one principal put it, "a milk and cookies organization," responsible for fund-raising, field trips, and enrichment activities. In other schools, the PTA assumed new functions in response to changing family needs. For example, in a suburban school serving primarily middle-class families, the PTA now runs an after-care program that serves more than 100 families. The road to its establishment was rocky. There was much discussion about whether the PTA should get into the business of providing after-school care, especially since only a portion of the school's families would benefit from the service. Eventually, however, it became clear that the school served an increasing number of families with two working parents and that the PTA needed to address their child-care needs.

Social Change, the PTA, and Civic Engagement

The use of the National PTA as a case study provides insight into how large voluntary organizations are affected by and try to adapt to new demographic and social trends. Although change in family structure is not the only factor contributing to PTA decline, married mothers working full time and single mothers are substantially less likely to participate in school support organizations. Lack of time militates against parental involvement.

Throughout its history, the PTA has adapted to new social trends by making changes in its functions and operations. During World War II it supported day care and other activities for mothers working in the war effort. In the 1970s it adopted a more activist stance in response to politically tumultuous times in public education.

To maintain its relevance and efficacy, the PTA leadership knows it must reach far beyond its traditional constituency of white middle-class women who do not work outside their homes. Since the 1980s, the organization has devoted significant resources to accommodate two-career and single-parent families. The organization has also made a serious attempt to reach out to a more diverse group by incorporating cultural and language diversity into local units in schools with large immigrant populations. Lois Jean White, 1998–99 National PTA president, wants the PTA to break into communities where it has not been present in the past. The focus of her two-year term is reaching out to urban families. In addition to seeking greater racial and economic diversity, she continues to emphasize the involvement of working parents: "Come in for just a day. . . . Working parents have technical skills they could share with the classroom."[78] Mindful of busy families, the PTA formally expanded its notion of participation by putting forth six "national standards" in 1997. Its new national standards for parental participation in education connect advocacy and school governance efforts to a broader framework of parental volunteering and encouraging children's study habits.[79]

Taking measures to include two-career and multicultural families will help the PTA maintain its relevance in today's society. Other steps are important as well. First, the PTA must continue to attract more men. This chapter has focused on women because they are the traditional constituency of the PTA, and their participation has been strongly affected by the changes in labor-force participation and family life in recent decades. The PTA, however, now strives to involve men as key participants. Continued emphasis on recruitment of fathers as well as mothers is necessary for a modern PTA. The PTA also will need to work cooperatively with new groups promoting parental involvement in education. For example, the PTA supports the promising National Network of Partnership Schools, an organization begun in 1995 to improve parental participation and that in 1998 had more than 1,000 affiliated schools.[80] Finally, the

---

78. "Contemporary Black Women," *Ebony*, March 1998, p. 90.

79. The six national standards were developed from the framework of parental participation expert Dr. Joyce Epstein. They are: "(1) Communicating between home and school on school programs and child's progress; (2) Strengthened parenting or improved child-rearing skills; (3) Student learning, such as helping with homework; (4) Volunteering; (5) School decisionmaking and advocacy; and (6) Collaborating with community involving universities, businesses, and other community members in school issues." PTA Website: http://www.pta.org.

80. The National Network of Partnership Schools operates at district, state, and national levels to assist member schools via newsletters, training workshops, and other means to implement comprehensive parental participation programs. According to the director, Dr. Joyce Epstein, the Network desires to work in partnership with the PTA, not as a competitor. Since most non-PTA parental participation is local and individual, the fact that the Network operates as a network of schools and collaborates with the National PTA is noteworthy.

National PTA may need to broaden some of its legislative advocacy positions in order to continue meeting the needs of modern families. The organization adamantly opposes school-choice voucher programs and generally supports initiatives favored by teachers' unions. In a 1996 document the National PTA stated, "post baby boomers are issue oriented, diverse, and visionary . . . and parents wish to give family time priority."[81] The ways in which the organization redefines its mission and enhances the effectiveness of membership outreach activities will determine the PTA's future viability.

The very nature of what constitutes parental participation in education, however, is changing. As one education researcher explained it, parents want to help their children succeed but they do not necessarily want to join an organization to do so. Busy parents are often interested primarily in their own child's welfare. Dr. Joyce Epstein, a Johns Hopkins University professor and leading expert on parental involvement in education, finds that while few parents are involved frequently in the school building, most want to know how to help their children at home.[82] Survey data back up this claim, revealing that 95 percent of parents talk to their children about school once a week and three-fourths of parents help with homework once a week.[83] Parents also seem willing to work with teachers in order to help their children. Ladd cites a 1992 survey that found that 90 percent of parents of first-grade children had attended a conference with their child's teacher, but only 8 percent had served on a parent advisory committee.[84]

Within the political and social context that shaped the general decline of large voluntary cross-class federated associations, the PTA faces substantial challenges. The PTA organized intensive membership drives at its height; however, it also benefited from a social context in which membership in civic organizations was growing at a phenomenal rate. But times have changed. States Skocpol, "In the center and the 'left' (such as it is) of the U.S. associational spectrum virtually no great federations have either appeared or gained a clear-cut new lease on life. Instead, the pattern is a profusion of staff-led, narrowly-focused advocacy groups, representing relatively particular sociocultural identities or advocating positions on

81. National PTA (1996, p. 3).
82. Epstein (1996, p. 218).
83. *Newsweek* (1991, p. 22).
84. Ladd (1988).

narrow hot button policy issues."[85] This same narrowing toward particular interests has occurred with respect to schools, as evidenced by the rise in local groups focused solely on individual schools and an increased emphasis on parents focusing on their own children.

What is lost when a broad-based, cross-class, nationwide organization declines and is partially replaced by autonomous local groups that are not tied to larger networks? What does the decline of the PTA say about notions of citizenship and civic engagement? To address these questions adequately, we need to make a distinction between volunteerism, parents' involvement in children's education, and civic engagement. Helping children with homework or talking to them about school is necessary and important. However, when these forms of parental involvement in education do not take place within an organizational structure that addresses issues pertinent to both the local school and a broader network, they should not be misread as civic engagement. Local parent-teacher groups, school boards, and after-school programs all benefit individual schools, parents, and children. But there are important costs when these groups rise at the expense of a broad-based national participatory framework. As schools become increasingly homogeneous, the need for an organization that can connect local units to each other and to state and national bodies is even more pressing. State and national PTA meetings and conventions bring together representatives of very different types of schools. They strive for a broad nationwide vision of effective educational practice. We believe that the decline of the National PTA does indicate a decline in civic mindedness, despite the usefulness of other forms of parental participation.

The National PTA has also been instrumental in helping to pass laws to protect children. In 1998 alone, the National PTA's legislative program supported the expansion of the Family and Medical Leave Act, supported federal legislation to enhance parental participation in education, and advocated increased drug-abuse prevention funding.[86] In addition, the organization publishes a legislative newsletter on current issues and advocacy strategies and operates a toll-free hotline that provides information about federal legislation affecting children. Its Website provides links to congressional representatives, model letters members can send to Congress, and information on becoming more involved in advocacy. State-level PTAs

85. Skocpol (1997, pp. 473–74).
86. National PTA website: http://www.pta.org.

have their own extensive legislative programs. The PTA helps effect important legislative changes and provides a forum for debating higher-level state and national policy issues.[87]

We return to the question of whether a National PTA can be viable in the current social and political climate. Or have parents' and teachers' interests become so fragmented and narrow that they cannot be addressed through a broad-based organization? Can the PTA be flexible enough to meet diverse parent needs? If common ground can be found, are parents and educators interested in working in their local schools from within a larger organizational network? An education researcher put the question to us succinctly: can the National PTA model still work in current times?

It is clear that the PTA must continue its efforts to meet the needs of today's families. And in certain situations the PTA may not be the appropriate participatory framework, despite its efforts to accommodate change. In general, however, we feel that if the majority of parents and teachers cannot achieve some broad consensus on issues as fundamental as public education or see the inherent value in belonging to a broad-reaching network, our nation's civic life will be diminished.

Like many large voluntary organizations, the PTA initially responded slowly to societal changes. Although the organization has begun to make major accommodations that reflect new social trends and family realities, it still faces many challenges. Membership levels may very well never reach their earlier heights, in part because of larger trends in civic participation. However, as the PTA continues to embrace modern families and to work in cooperation with new groups, it will continue its historic legacy as a strong advocate for all children.

In the 1970s, when the PTA was losing members to local PTOs, it published a brochure highlighting the advantages of affiliation with the National PTA: "Sometimes in working to improve conditions in 'my' school, parents lose sight of the fact that their children will grow up with and live with *all* children. Only by belonging to a local unit of the National PTA, instead of a PTO, can you work for a better environment in which all children can grow and learn."[88] Twenty-plus years later the implications of this statement for civic engagement are clear.

87. Ibid.
88. National PTA (1976).

Appendix 7A

Sample Selection

To create a data set, we began with all individuals who were asked the question "Are you a member of a school service group?" in the General Social Survey (GSS) between 1974 and 1994. We selected the subset of respondents with school-age children in the household and then specifically women with school-age children. Since our research question primarily concerns women with school-age children, most of our analysis was performed on this group of 3,650 people. Note that these respondents were individuals with school-age children living in the house; they were not necessarily the parents of the children. We assumed that the adult household members responding (most of whom were the head of household or spouse of head of household) were responsible for the children living in the household.

In the overall data set of all men and women asked about school service group membership ($N = 19,113$), 9.8 percent of the men and 16.6 percent of the women were members. School service group membership composition in the GSS was 69 percent female and 31 percent male. Interestingly, 29 percent of the people who answered "yes" to the question about school service group membership had no children under age seventeen. While approximately 20 percent of those were accounted for by school professionals such as teachers, other respondents likely interpreted this question to mean something other than belonging to a PTA-type group. For example, perhaps 18–25 year olds interpreted this question as inquiring about membership in some type of college group; others may have read it as inquiring about some type of alumni club membership.

Table 7A-1 gives the logistic regression coefficients for our brief analysis of the sample of men and women with school-age children.

Discussion of the Logistic Regression Models for Women with School-Age Children

Model 4a (see Table 7A-2) shows that marriage and higher levels of education are robust predictors of membership. Model 4b shows that for married women, likelihood of membership increases as income increases,

Table 7A-1. *Impact of Demographic Variables and Labor-Force Status on Membership of Men and Women with School-Age Children in a School Service Group*[a]

Coefficient results of logistic regression analysis

Dependent variable	Model 1 a	Model 1 b	Model 2 a	Model 2 b	Model 3 a	Model 3 b
Constant	-4.60**	-3.13**	-4.50**	-4.41**	-4.48**	-4.48**
	(.42)	(.62)	(.43)	(.43)	(.43)	(.44)
Female	1.17**	1.16**	1.18**	1.18**	1.05**	1.05**
	(.07)	(.07)	(.08)	(.07)	(.07)	(.08)
Marriage	.60**	-1.9*	.59**	.59**	.55**	.55**
	(.08)	(.83)	(.08)	(.08)	(.08)	(.08)
ln (family income)	.13**	-.02	.12**	.11**	.14**	.14**
	(.04)	(.06)	(.04)	(.04)	(.04)	(.04)
Education (coded 1–4)	.47**	.46**	.47**	.47**	.49**	.50**
	(.03)	(.03)	(.03)	(.03)	(.03)	(.03)
Marriage × family income		.25**				
		(.08)				
Black			-.08	-.10	-.08	-.08
			(.09)	(.10)	(.09)	(.09)
Other race				-.50*	-.48*	-.48*
				(.21)	(.22)	(.22)
Working full time					-.32**	-.34**
					(.07)	(.07)
Working part time						-.07
						(.10)
Log likelihood	-3,015.54	-3,010.94	-3,015.17	-3,012.22	-3,001.98	-3,001.74
Chi square	593.31	602.50	594.05	599.95	558.80	558.96

Source: General Social Survey, 1974–94.

*$p < .05$; **$p < .01$.

a. Standard errors in parentheses. $N = 5,589$ men and women with school-age children.

while income has no effect on likelihood of participation for single mothers. As income increases, the impact of marriage grows larger.[89]

Because coefficients on logistic models can be difficult to interpret, we calculated some sample probabilities on basic background factors to illustrate their effects. To calculate predicted probabilities, we selected a model and used various base categories in order to calculate the predicted Y's.

Effect of marriage: base category of woman with high-school education (model 4a)
Single: 11 percent probability of membership
Married: 20 percent

Effect of education: base category of married woman (Model 4a)
Less than high school: 13 percent probability of membership
College graduate: 40 percent

Model 5a shows no effect for being African American; however, being of race "other" substantially decreases likelihood of membership. The following example illustrates the effect (model 5a).[90]

Effect of race: base category of single woman, high-school graduate
White: 21 percent probability of membership
Other: 11 percent

Model 5b shows that the effect of education does not vary by race for African Americans: the impact of education on likelihood of participating is the same for whites and African Americans. Being African American has no effect on participation until we analyze the impact of race by income. A higher family income has a positive effect on the likelihood of membership for whites. For African Americans, the income effect on participation is reversed: African Americans are less likely to participate as their income increases. Low-income African Americans are more likely to participate

89. We tried adding the interactions between income and education and between education and marriage, which were not significant and are not reported. The interaction between income and marriage was significant and is reported in Table 7A-2.

90. The coefficient on black in Model 5a is negative, however the coefficient is not statistically significant. Note that one cannot compare probabilities across models; different models predict different probabilities.

Table 7A-2. *Impact of Demographic Variables on Membership of Women with School-Age Children in a School Service Group*[a]

Coefficient results of logistic regression analysis

Dependent variable	Model 4		Model 5				
	a	b	a	b	c	d	e
Constant	−3.06**	−1.58*	−2.32**	−2.34**	−2.46**	−2.34**	−2.32**
	.46	.66	.14	.14	.15	.14	.14
Marriage	.65**	−2.21*	.63**	.64**	.65**	.64**	.64**
	(.09)	(.95)	(.09)	(.09)	(.09)	(.09)	(.09)
ln (family income)	.08	−.06					
	(.05)	(.07)					
Family income (coded 1–3)			.07	.08	.13*	.08	.06
			(.06)	(.06)	(.06)	(.05)	(.05)
Education (coded 1–4)	.50**	.49**	.51**	.51**	.50**	.51**	.51**
	(.04)	(.04)	(.04)	(.05)	(.05)	(.04)	(.04)

	(1)	(2)	(3)	(4)	(5)	(6)
ln (family income) × marriage	.28** (.10)					
Black		−.13 (.11)	−.02 (.27)	.47 (.32)	−.13 (.11)	−.14 (.11)
Other race		−.72** (.25)	−.72** (.26)	−.71** (.26)	−.19 (.59)	−.85 (.77)
Black × education			−.05 (.11)	.05 (.12)		
Black × family income				−.42** (.15)		
Other × education					−.21 (.22)	−.38 (.25)
Other × family income						.51 (.34)
Log likelihood	−1,990.92	−1,990.40	−1,990.30	−1,986.46	−1,989.96	−1,988.82
Chi square	290.54	291.57	291.78	299.47	292.46	294.74

Log likelihood −1,995.47
Chi square 281.44

Source: General Social Survey, 1974–94.
*p < .05; **p < .01.

a. N = 3,650 women with school-age children.

than high-income African Americans of similar educational and marital status. By computing predicted probabilities, we also see that whites at all income levels are more likely to participate than African Americans.

Effect on income varying by race: base category of married with some college (model 5c):
Lower-income white: 45 percent
Lower-income African American: 35 percent
Higher-income white: 52 percent
Higher-income African American: 24 percent

In this analysis, the impact of education and income did not vary by race for respondents of race "other." Small sample sizes are likely a problem here.

With respect to labor-force status, model 6a shows that full-time work is negatively associated with participation. We cannot, however, draw conclusions about the effect of part-time work, probably because of the small sample size of part-time working women. Model 6c shows that women who are not working outside of their homes are more likely to be members of a school service organization. Model 7a shows how the impact of labor-force participation varies by marital status. For married women, full-time work diminishes the odds of membership. For single women, full-time workers are as likely to participate as non-full-time workers. Overall, however, married women are still more likely to participate than single women. We illustrate this result with another calculated sample probability of membership, using a high-school graduate with $20,000 income as a base category (model 7a) (see Table 7A-3):

Single, working full time: 23 percent
Married, working full time: 29 percent
Single, not working full time: 23 percent
Married, not working full time: 39 percent

Here we see that single women are as likely to participate when they work full time as when they do not. Full-time working married women participate at higher rates than single women, and married women not working full time participate at even higher rates.

In model 7b, we see how the effect of income on participation varies by labor-force status. A woman working full time is less likely to participate as income increases, while a woman not working full time is more likely

Table 7A-3. *Impact of Labor Force Status on Membership of Women with School-Age Children in a School Service Group*[a]
Coefficient results of logistic regression analysis

Dependent variable	Model 6			Model 7		
	a	b	c	a	b	c
Constant	−3.26**	−3.27**	−3.46**	−3.25**	−3.81**	−3.21**
	(.46)	(.46)	(.48)	(.47)	(.54)	(.49)
Marriage	.56**	.56**	.60**	.78**	.57**	.55**
	(.09)	(.09)	(.09)	(.12)	(.09)	(.09)
Education (coded 1–4)	.52**	.52**	.52**	.52**	.52**	.52**
	(.04)	(.04)	(.04)	(.04)	(.04)	(.04)
ln (family income)	.12*	.12*	.11*	.10*	.17**	.11*
	(.05)	(.05)	(.05)	(.05)	(.06)	(.05)
Working full time	−.37**	−.38**		−.06	1.75	−.33**
	(.08)	(.09)		(.14)	(.99)	(.08)
Working part time		−.02				
		(.11)				
Not working			.27**			
			(.08)			
Marriage × full-time work				−.44**		
				(.17)		
ln (income) × full-time work					−.21*	
					(.10)	
Black						.02
						(.14)
Black × full-time work						−.24
						(.21)
Log likelihood	−1,984.91	−1,984.89	−1,989.78	−1,981.60	−1,982.64	−1,983.99
Chi square	302.56	302.61	292.83	309.19	307.10	304.39

Source: General Social Survey, 1974–94.

*p < .05; **p < .01.

a. Standard errors in parentheses. N = 3,650 women with school-age children.

to participate as income increases. We found no statistically significant results on how the impact of full-time work varied by race.

References

Albert, Linda. 1993. *The Busy Parent's Guide to Involvement in Education*. Chicago: National PTA.

Calvert, Maude. 1942. "To Attention, Homemakers!" *National Parent-Teacher* (April): 18–20.

"Contemporary Black Women." March 1998. *Ebony*.

Cutright, Melitta. 1989. *The National PTA Talks to Parents: How to Get the Best Education for Your Child*. New York: Doubleday.

Davis, James, and Tom W. Smith. *General Social Surveys, 1972–1994* [machine-readable data file]. Chicago: National Opinion Research Center [producer], 1994; Storrs, Conn.: Roper Center for Public Opinion Research, University of Connecticut [distributor].

Dillon, Sam. 1993. "A Surge in Advocacy within Parent Groups; PTAs Shift from Bastions of the Status Quo to Challengers of Authority." *New York Times*, October 13.

Donovan, Brooke. 1997. Unpublished term paper, SOC 194. Harvard University.

Eccles, J., and R. Harold. 1996. "Family Involvement in Children's and Adolescents' Schooling." In *Family-School Links: How Do They Affect Educational Outcomes?*, edited by A. Booth and J. Dunn. Mahwah, N.J.: Lawrence Erlbaum.

Epstein, Joyce. 1995. "School/Family/Community Partnerships: Caring for the Children We Share." *Phi Delta Kappan* (May): 701–12.

———. 1996. "Perspectives and Previews of Research and Policy for School, Family, and Community Partnerships." In *Family-School Links: How Do They Affect Educational Outcomes?*, edited by A. Booth and J. Dunn. Mahwah, N.J.: Lawrence Erlbaum.

Good Housekeeping and the National PTA. 1995. *How to Get the Best for Your Child: Back to School Special 1995*.

Goodykoontz, Beth. 1943. "Women at Work." *National Parent-Teacher* (February) : 8–10.

Haar, Charlene. 1995. "Cutting Class: The PTA Plays Hooky from Educational Reform." *Policy Review* (Summer 1995): 86–90.

Hastings, Minnetta. 1945. "The President's Message: Wanted—38,000,000 Skilled Homemakers." *National Parent-Teacher* (March): 3.

———. 1946. "The President's Message: The World Needs Women." *National Parent-Teacher* (May): 3.

Kabat, George J. 1946. "Welcome Home, Father." *National Parent-Teacher* (April): 4–6.

Kerbow, David, and Annette Bernhardt. 1993. "Parental Intervention in the School: The Context of Minority Involvement." In *Parents, Children, and the Schools*, edited by Barbara Schneider and James Coleman. Boulder, Colo.: Westview.

Ladd, Everett. 1998. "Bowling with Tocqueville: Civic Engagement and Social Capital." Bradley Lecture, American Enterprise Institute for Public Policy Research. September 15, 1998. Website: http://www.aei.org/bradley/b1091598.htm.

Ladd-Taylor, Molly. 1994. *Mother-Work: Women, Child Welfare, and the State, 1890–1930*. University of Illinois Press.

Marshall, R., and B. Paulin. 1987. "Employment and Earnings of Women: Historical Perspective." In *Working Women: Past, Present, Future,* edited by Karen Shallcross Koziara, Michael H. Moskow, and Lucretia Dewey Tanner. Washington, D.C.: Bureau of National Affairs / Industrial Relations Research Association.

Mok, Paul. 1963. *Pushbutton Parents and the Schools.* Dell.

Muller, Chandra. 1993. "Parent Involvement and Academic Achievement." In *Parents, Their Children, and Schools,* edited by Barbara Schneider and James Coleman. Boulder, Colo.: Westview.

Muller, Chandra, and David Kerbow. 1993. "Parent Involvement in the Home, School, and Community." In *Parents, Their Children, and Schools,* edited by Barbara Schneider and James Coleman. Boulder, Colo.: Westview.

National Center for Education Statistics. 1988. *Statistical Analysis Report NELS: 88.*

———. 1997. *Digest of Education Statistics 1997.* Website: http://nces.ed.gov.

National Congress of Mothers. 1897. *The Work and Words of the National Congress of Mothers (First Annual Session).* Washington, D.C.: National Congress of Mothers.

———. 1898. *Second Annual Convention Proceedings,* 1898.

———. 1900. "Woman and the New Century." *Quarterly Report* 1(2): 113–14.

———. 1906. "The Divorce Congress." *National Congress of Mothers Magazine* (December): 25–27.

National Congress of Parents and Teachers. 1947. *Golden Jubilee History, 1897–1947.* Chicago: National Congress of Parents and Teachers.

———. 1953. *Parent-Teacher Manual for Parent-Teacher Associations in Membership with the National Congress of Parents and Teachers.* Chicago: National Congress of Parents and Teachers.

———. 1958. *Annual Convention Proceedings Volume 62.* Chicago: National Congress of Parents and Teachers.

———. 1960. *Annual Convention Proceedings Volume 64.* Chicago: National Congress of Parents and Teachers.

———. 1962. *Annual Convention Proceedings Volume 66.* Chicago: National Congress of Parents and Teachers.

———. 1967. *Annual Convention Proceedings Volume 71.* Chicago: National Congress of Parents and Teachers.

———. 1970. *Annual Convention Proceedings Volume 74.* Chicago: National Congress of Parents and Teachers.

———. 1972. *Annual Convention Proceedings Volume 76.* Chicago: National Congress of Parents and Teachers.

National PTA. 1976. *Why a PTA Instead of a PTO?* Chicago: The National PTA.

———. PTA. 1981. Unpublished Executive Committee minutes. May 10, 1981.

———. 1989. Biographical information sheet on Ann Lynch, National PTA President, 1989–91.

———. 1995a. Biographical information sheet on Joan Dykstra, National PTA President, 1995–97.

———. 1995b. *National PTA Handbook, 1995–96.* Chicago: National PTA.

———. 1997. *National PTA at 100 Years.* Website: http://www.pta.org.

Newsweek. 1991. "The Second PTA/Chrysler National Parent Survey: A Study of Parental Involvement in Children's Education."

Oguntoyinbo, Lekan. 1994. "The PTA in Need of Punch, Not Cookies." *Cleveland Plain Dealer*. April 11.

Overstreet, Harry and Bonaro. 1949. *Where Children Come First: A Study of the PTA Idea*. Chicago: National Congress of Parents and Teachers.

Putnam, Robert. 1993. *Making Democracy Work: Civic Traditions in Modern Italy*. Princeton University Press.

———. 1995a. "Bowling Alone: America's Declining Social Capital." *Journal of Democracy* 6(1): 65–77.

———. 1995b. "Bowling Alone, Revisited." *The Responsive Community* (Spring): 13–33.

———. 1995c. "Tuning In, Tuning Out: The Strange Disappearance of Social Capital in America." *P.S.: Political Science and Politics* 28 (December): 664–68.

———. 2000 (forthcoming). *Bowling Alone*. Simon and Schuster.

Schoff, Hannah. 1910. "The President's Desk: Present Tendencies of College Education for Girls." *Child Welfare Magazine* 4(7): 189–90.

Skocpol, Theda. 1992. *Protecting Soldiers and Mothers: The Political Origins of Social Policy in the United States*. Belknap Press of Harvard University Press.

———. 1996. "Unraveling from Above." *American Prospect* (March–April): 20–25.

———. 1997. "The Tocqueville Problem: Civic Engagement in American Democracy." *Social Science History* 21(4): 455–76.

Smith, Afton. 1941. "The Homemaker Takes Over." *National Parent-Teacher* (September): 4–5.

Spain, Daphne, and Suzanne Bianchi. 1996. *Balancing Act: Motherhood, Marriage, and Employment among American Women*. New York: Russell Sage Foundation.

Stolz, Lois Meek. 1942. "War Invades the Children's World." *National Parent-Teacher* (May): 4–6.

U.S. Bureau of the Census. 1975. *Historical Statistics of the United States, Colonial Times to 1970, Bicentennial Edition*. Series D63-74. Part 2. Washington, D.C.

———. March 1997 and earlier. "Household and Family Characteristics." Current Population Reports, Series P20-495. Washington, D.C.

U.S. Department of Commerce. 1997. *Statistical Abstract of the United States*. 117th ed. Washington, D.C.

U.S. Department of Education. 1994. *Strong Families, Strong Schools*. Washington, D.C.

Welch, Linda Latham. 1995. "It's Not Your Mother's PTA: Group Evolves, but at What Cost?" *Austin American-Statesman*, September 29.

Willis, Mary M. 1921. "Should Mothers Accept Outside Work?" *Child Welfare Magazine* 10(6): 127–28.

Zill, Nicolas. 1996. "Family Change and Student Achievement: What We Have Learned, What It Means for Schools." In *Family-School Links: How Do They Affect Educational Outcomes?*, edited by Alan Booth and Judith Dunn. Mahwah, N.J.: Lawrence Erlbaum.

8 | *Technological Change and Associational Life*

MARCELLA RIDLEN RAY

PUBLIC DISCOURSE OFTEN focuses on the disadvantages or the potential threats to democratic community posed by the influences and misapplications of technology. In particular, we fear that the impact of technology will deenergize, depersonalize, and atomize the individual. We worry that technology makes it easier for the individual to voluntarily abandon community. We are apprehensive about the control that technology has over people's lives, but we also hope that resistance to necessary technological developments will not be too great. And we are uneasy about the vulnerability of the public to sophisticated technological manipulation by the mass media and by government. These are the understandable anxieties of a free and dynamic society.

The newest technologies, with potential to absorb the time and attention of individuals in socially isolated circumstances, seem to easily complement a tenacious love of privacy for which Americans are known. We are faced with unease about the influence of the Internet, joined with renewed attention to a persistent argument about the detrimental effects of television on social connectedness. Full consideration of the effects of technology is incomplete unless it addresses what works, as well as what is problematic. For this reason, I asked how technologies might augment associational life. It is somewhat counterintuitive to suggest that technol-

297

ogy enhances social connectedness. The idea is contrary to the commonly, and historically, articulated "suspicion [of] the printing press, the automobile, the telephone, and the television as solvents of the glue that binds people together. Each new technology brings a warning: to fall under its spell will be to sacrifice not only simplicity but also community, to metamorphose into alienated, isolated, sedentary blobs."[1] Yet, such skepticism appears unfounded. The direst predictions of dissolution of social ties remain unrealized.[2]

Another prevalent belief is that people are resistant to using new technology.[3] If this were a prevalent response, it is unlikely that we would find technologies serving social connectedness in a significant way. Yet the majority of Americans today actually seem at ease with new technologies. Thus, in 1996, 73 percent of a national adult sample interviewed by Yankelovich Partners said that new technologies make life easier.[4] Most respondents to a 1995 *Time*/CNN/Yankelovich poll, provided with various adjectives to describe their feelings about using new technology, were comfortable (72 percent), confident (60 percent), and in control (55 percent). A clear majority also said that they were not overwhelmed (63 percent), not ill-at-ease (61 percent), and not anxious (63 percent) about using new technologies.[5] This level of sanguinity suggests that resistance to technology is not an overriding sentiment.

Indeed, Americans readily draft technology to perpetuate a pattern of social connectedness. This use of resources is a pattern increasingly characterized by choice, diversity, and integration. The following describes the interface of newspapers and magazines, the telephone, the automobile, television, and the Internet with the links Americans forge among themselves. These adaptations of technology reflect motivation and appreciation for connecting with others—even as these connections assume varying forms.

---

1. Kupfer (1995, p. 95); also see Boorstin (1978, pp. 10–11, 29–30).

2. See, for example, Guterbock and Fries (1997); Ladd (1999); Thelen (1996); Verba, Schlozman, and Brady (1995, pp. 43–96); and Rosenblum (1998, pp. 5, 349–63).

3. See report of the Subcommittee on Technology to the U.S. National Resources Committee in Stern ([1937] 1972, p. 66); Hollander (1981, pp. 316–17).

4. Roper at University of Connecticut (1996).

5. The question asked, "For each of the following, please tell me if this describes or does not describe how you feel about using new technology products and services, such as computers, the Internet, fax machines, and cellular phones . . . Describes; Does not describe; Not sure." Roper at University of Connecticut (1996).

The Newspaper and Periodical: Loose Connections

Newspapers provided an early means for establishing and maintaining common ties among Americans through broad distribution of general information. Tocqueville noted during his visit to this country in the 1830s that the press fostered a sense of connectedness.[6] The newspaper bridges physical distances by enlarging the arena of public discourse and providing links that are necessary for collective behavior and thought. Commonly shared information is therefore an important underpinning of associational life. Indeed, the reason given most often in a 1985 Times Mirror survey for "following the news" was "to feel more involved in what's going on in the world" (59 percent).[7]

A decline in the number of newspapers throughout the twentieth century in the United States might seem to suggest that some disintegration of these common ties has occurred. In 1997 there were 26 percent fewer daily papers listed by the *Editor and Publisher International Yearbook* than in 1921.[8] Per capita circulation also changed from 0.26 to 0.21 during the same time period. This means that in 1921 a daily newspaper circulated for every 3.8 Americans. From 1945 to 1955, every 2.9 persons could share a daily paper if they liked. But by 1960 the per capita rate was falling, notwithstanding the effects of transportation improvements, advanced production technology, economy of scale and other management strategies. That decline steadily progressed to its lowest point ever in 1997, when one daily newspaper circulated for every 4.7 Americans.[9]

This pattern reiterates itself in a drop of 27 percentage points in self-reported daily newspaper reading, from 69 to 42 percent, in the General Social Survey from 1972 to 1996. No significant change occurred in the small portion (an average of 5 percent) of survey respondents who

6. Tocqueville ([1835] 1945, pp. 1:195, 2:342).

7. The complete question stated, "Here is a list of reasons some people give for following the news. Which one of these reasons best describes why you, yourself, watch, read, or listen to the news?" Other reasons: learning about useful things (36 percent), learning about something exciting or interesting (12 percent), having something to discuss with friends (8 percent), entertainment (7 percent), passing the time (6 percent), relaxation (4 percent), to help with work (3 percent). Roper at University of Connecticut (1989).

8. Calculated from Bureau of the Census (1975, p. 809; 1998, p. 580). Data for years 1945–1993 were provided by the research department of the Newspaper Association of America from annual editions of the *Editor and Publisher International Yearbook* (New York: Editor and Publisher.).

9. Calculated with the sources in note 8 above and total population figures reported by the United States Bureau of the Census (1975, p. 10; 1998, p. 8).

never read the paper, but a larger proportion of respondents paced their newspaper reading to several times a week, once a week, or less than once a week.[10] A similar trend in daily newspaper reading is reported by the Pew Research Center, which found in 1998 that 47 percent of Americans read a newspaper yesterday, compared to 71 percent in 1965.[11] Sunday papers do not reflect these patterns. Per capita circulation for Sunday papers averaged 0.24 from 1970 to 1997, showing little change for a quarter of a century.[12]

The newspaper, then, is not disappearing from the lives of Americans, but neither does it possess the day-to-day immediacy that it once held. Perhaps this change would indicate a deterioration of links among Americans—if it were their only news source. The newspaper, always an important source of general news and information, loosely binds a diverse network of Americans who have a variety of ways of tapping into that pool of information shared by all. A 1995 Gallup Poll in which respondents could refer to eighteen different sources that included headline news services, public television news programs, and talk shows emphasizes the growing assortment of choices that Americans have for obtaining news and information.[13] Two recent reviews of empirical evidence about how citizens obtain political information note that individuals differ in their information requirements. Individuals selectively seek sources that meet their needs, which vary over time.[14] At least since the arrival of radio, there is a tendency to combine, customize, and explore the menu of media possibilities.

In response to a Roper question about using multiple sources of news, respondents said they used an average of 1.54 sources in 1959 but only 1.38 in 1992.[15] Pew found that the percentage of respondents who did not

10. Question: "How often do you read the newspaper—every day, a few times a week, once a week, less than once a week or never?" Davis and Smith (1995); Roper at University of Connecticut (1997).

11. Pew (1998a).

12. U.S. Bureau of the Census (1998, p. 580).

13. Half of the sample were asked the following question: "As you know, people get their news and information from many different sources, and I would like to ask you where you get *your* news and information. I will read a list of sources, and for each one, please tell me how often you get your news from that source: very regularly, somewhat regularly, occasionally, or never." The question for the other half was the same, except the gradients were "every day, several times a week, occasionally, or never." Moore (1995).

14. Chaffee and Frank (1996, pp. 48–58); Weaver (1996, pp. 34–47).

15. Question: "I'd like to ask you where you usually get most of your news about what's going on in the world today—from the newspapers, or radio, or television, or magazines, or talking to people or where?" Multiple responses were permitted. Mayer (1993, p. 603).

get news yesterday from the TV, newspaper, *or* radio doubled from 8 percent in 1994 to 15 percent in 1996.[16] Americans are either narrowing their selections for news input *or* diversifying them beyond the bounds of the survey question. Although both may be true, the aforementioned Gallup question that recognizes numerous choices suggests that the array of news and information resources is broadening. Consequently, one goes to the Internet for headline news and to the newspaper for detail; tunes in to National Public Radio while jogging; turns on network news if home at the right time; and relies on Cable News Network (CNN) to stay in touch with major events when traveling or at home. Respondents in a recent Pew Research Center poll agreed they had no need to worry if they missed their usual news programs since "there are so many ways to get the news these days."[17]

A small number of Americans also get news and information electronically. In four surveys conducted by Louis Harris between August 1995 and January 1996, an average of 9 percent of American adults reported logging on to the World Wide Web for political information.[18] In 1998, 36 percent went online and over one-half (55 percent) of online users surveyed by the Pew Research Center used the Internet to obtain news at least once a week. Most participants continued to rely primarily on print and broadcast. Three-fourths of online news users in the same poll indicated there was no change in the rate with which they drew upon other information sources, suggesting little "crowding out" by the online resource.[19]

Periodicals reflect more particular interests of like-minded individuals and groups, often stemming from the activities of voluntary organizations.[20] Magazine circulation reinforces smaller sets of common ties that cut across distance and other barriers within the larger social context. The

16. Pew (1996a).

17. Pew (1998a).

18. Questions: "Do you ever access the World Wide Web, or not?" and "Do you ever use the World Wide Web to get information about politics or political candidates or not?" Birdsell, Muzzio, and Taylor (1996).

19. Questions: "How frequently do you go online to get news . . . would you say every day, 3 to 5 days per week, 1 or 2 days per week, once every few weeks, or less often?"; "Would you say you get more of your news from online sources, or from traditional sources such as TV news, newspapers, and magazines?"; "Since you started getting news online, are you using other sources of news MORE often, LESS often, or about the same as you used to?" Pew (1998a).

20. Guidelines provided by the United Nations Educational, Scientific, and Cultural Organization (UNESCO) for its annual statistical yearbook define a periodical as a publication concerned with general or specialized subjects published in a continuous series for an indefinite period.

Research Committee on Social Trends recognized this use of print media as a means to associate less intimately than in face-to-face interaction:[21] "'House organs,' trade journals, fraternal bulletins, and publications with purposes covering the entire range of contemporary interests, have multiplied. They are important as bonds keeping together those with common objectives."[22]

Periodicals have a somewhat different history than newspapers. This type of publication, no matter the list examined, has multiplied. Titles in *The Union List of Serials* and *The International Directory of Little Magazines and Small Presses*, for example, continue to increase annually.[23] The Ayer/Gale database, with the longest history, carried 2,869 titles in 1900 and slowly expanded to 11,408 in 1997.[24] Two contemporary databases show increases even in the short term. The *National Directory of Magazines* lists 28,105 entries in 1998, nearly doubling in ten years. The *Standard Periodical Directory* shows an increase of 34 percent between 1991, when it listed 70,383 periodicals, and 1998, when it listed 94,413.[25]

The frequency with which periodicals are published has slowed, at least since 1935. Then, over half (55 percent) of the periodicals in the Ayer/Gale database were monthly publications; only 30 percent were published that frequently in 1997. A similar pattern occurred in the publication of weekly periodicals—23 percent of the total in 1935 fell to 4 percent in 1997. Over one-fourth (28 percent) were published quarterly in 1997

21. The Research Committee on Social Trends was a group of scientists appointed by President Hoover in 1932 to establish a baseline for social indicators in American society. Research Committee (1933, p. v).

22. Willey and Rice (1933a, p. 159).

23. The *Union List of Serials* and its supplement, *New Serials Titles* (Washington, D.C.: Library of Congress) began in 1913 as an initiative by the American Library Association. A conservative estimate of the total universe of titles in this work, proffered by a representative of the Library of Congress, is 950,000. Now in its thirty-second edition with more than 6,000 entries, the *International Directory of Little Magazines and Small Presses* (Paradise, Calif.: Dustbooks Publishing) was first published in 1964 with fewer than 200 titles.

24. This is a mix of weekly, semimonthly, bimonthly, quarterly, and other U.S. and Canadian periodicals. Subject areas covered include agriculture, ethnic, fraternal, college, religious, and women's publications, general interest magazines, and trade, technical, and professional serials. Willey and Rice (1933a, p. 157); U.S. Bureau of the Census (1975, p. 810; 1998, p. 580).

25. Annual editions of *The National Directory of Magazines* (New York: Oxbridge Communications) lists U.S. and Canadian magazines, journals, tabloids that carry advertising, and some specific-interest newspapers. Annual editions of *The Standard Periodical Directory* (New York: Oxbridge Communications) list U.S. and Canadian publications published at least every twenty-four months; included are directories, consumer magazines, newsletters, trade journals, scientific society transactions and proceedings, etc. I subtracted a classification for newspapers in my treatment of the data.

in contrast to a minuscule 8 percent sixty years earlier.[26] There is a point at which more issues do not result in more readers, one consultant in the industry explains, referring to the drop in the average annual number of issues, per Standard Rate and Data Services (SRDS), from 12.2 in 1988 to 11.8 in 1993.[27]

Periodical readership is difficult to pinpoint. One source, using the consumer periodical population listed with SRDS, found that the average household bought 4.9 of these magazines in 1963 and 5.9 in 1988.[28] Time-use studies indicate that, between 1946 and 1985, at least one-fourth of Americans were reading magazines yesterday.[29] Survey results vary with the questions posed. Princeton Survey Research found that nearly one-third (31 percent) of respondents in 1995 reported reading a magazine yesterday;[30] in a 1990 Gallup poll, a slightly higher proportion (36 percent) reported doing so.[31] In the 1970s, several surveys suggest that 62–67 percent of the adult population read magazines regularly; one in 1979 found that the 61 percent who described themselves as regular magazine readers averaged 2.3 subject types of periodicals.[32] Two surveys in 1990 found that roughly similar proportions of American adults had read magazines in the previous week.[33] The periodical industry has more optimistic data on readership. In audience research results of the 1940s, 69 percent of Americans age fifteen and older were regular consumers of 4.6 periodicals per reader.[34] In the 1980s, 94 percent of adults in the United States were reading, on average, 11.6 magazines per month, according to the Magazine Publishing Association.[35] Whatever the source—time studies,

26. Willey and Rice (1933a, p. 157); U.S. Bureau of the Census (1977, p. 810; 1998, p. 580).

27. SRDS lists approximately 2,800 titles, according to an account executive there. The magazines listed in this source rely on advertising, keep SRDS informed of circulation information, and generally are not found on newsstands. Examples found in this database include *Reader's Digest* and *The Nation*; some not found here are *Highlights for Children* and *Guideposts*. Kobak (1994, p. 235).

28. Kobak (1990, p. 82).

29. Robinson (1980; 1990).

30. Roper at University of Connecticut (1996).

31. Gallup (1992, p. 49).

32. The Roper Organization repeated a question that asked, "On the average weekday, about how much time do you spend reading magazines?" Respondents reported amounts of time ranging from less than fifteen minutes daily up to five hours as follows: in 1973, 62 percent; in 1974, 67 percent; in 1977, 63 percent. The 1979 national survey of adults was conducted by the Institute for Survey Research for the National Science Foundation. Roper at University of Connecticut (1989).

33. Gallup (1992, p. 49); Mayer (1994, p. 139).

34. Peterson ([1964] 1975, p. 56).

35. Taft (1982, p. 314).

surveys, industry research—each implied that reading magazines was a regular part of American lives that showed no sign of waning.

The subject matter of periodicals grew increasingly diverse at the same time. The United States Census of Manufactures, a source of partial trends in periodical consumption between 1947 and 1977, revealed some shifts in prevalent subject matter.[36] At midcentury, a simple set of categories existed. There were magazines classified as business news, general news, and "other." Interest grew in specialized periodicals, women's and home services magazines, and general entertainment magazines. Circulation of farm periodicals and comics fell. The special-interest magazine burgeoned in the 1960s, fueled by rising levels of education, affluence, and leisure interests and cutting-edge technology that made niche marketing cost-effective for the first time: "Leisure activities merely whetted the appetite of many for more printed information about their avocational pursuits."[37]

Reader interests continue to expand, and titles come and go. In the space of six years, from 1988 to 1993, Standard Rate and Data Services listed 900 new titles and 760 disappeared.[38] *The Standard Periodical Directory* demonstrates the dramatic diversification and volatility of interests. This directory listed nearly 92,000 titles in 1996, organized under 255 subjects. Some categories were renamed, combined with others, or dropped between 1991 and 1996. Nineteen completely new subjects appeared during the same period. I arbitrarily selected subject categories that contained 800-plus entries and found twenty-nine varieties of periodicals that were that large in one or more years between 1991 and 1996. These large categories accounted for approximately half of the total number of publications annually. An appreciable amount of flexing occurred within this group in addition to the renaming, attrition, and diversification noted. First, the number of subject categories with 800-plus entries expanded from seventeen to twenty-nine during the six-year period (see Table 8-1). Second, three patterns emerged when the original seventeen categories were ranked in size from one to sixteen. Twelve subjects remained at the top of the list, characterizing a stable set of priorities and interests underlying periodical consumption, but others were more transitory. Four moved up into the largest sixteen subject categories, while five fell from this group. Periodicals on religious, education, and sports topics retained

36. U.S. Department of Commerce (1947–1977).
37. Abrahamson (1996, pp. 25–27, 74, 77).
38. Kobak (1994, p. 236).

their high position and presumably people's interest. The rise in rank of publications of regional interest and those on the environment and ecology reflects people's growing interest in those areas. The meteoric fall of genealogy magazines from ninth to twenty-third in rank shows a downturn in interest, at least in sharing this information via print media. Perhaps online sources are replacing the periodical for genealogy enthusiasts.

New forms of connectedness seem to continually stimulate the periodical market. A current phenomenon is the very small homemade publication termed the 'zine, "an outlet for the eccentric preoccupations of the people who publish them."[39] An example is *Office and Art Supply Junkie*, one of thousands of 'zine titles collected by one source by mid-1997. 'Zines are a variation on the mimeographed sheet of earlier times, whose production was made so much easier with the computer. In yet another variation of the periodical, the large electronic online magazine, sometimes called a Webzine, makes interaction among writers, editors, and readers possible. More than 8,300 readers dropped in to post messages, send e-mail, or chat online on the first day of the electronic edition of *Time Online*. The editor's comments a year later are noteworthy: "Most gratifying has been the improvement in the quality of discussion since the days when the message boards were dominated by Lizard NC and the Gun Guys. We've become a gathering place for thousands of literate, well-informed, plugged-in readers who can also write. Painful as it has been at times, I think being so directly accountable to our online readers has made us better journalists—and *Time* a better magazine."[40] In this case, it appears that electronic communications have effectively established new paths of social connectedness.

The Telephone: Pervasive Connections

The penetration of residential service indicates that the phone is a basic element of associational infrastructure. Over one-third (35 percent) of American households had a phone by 1920. This figure rose to 41 percent in 1930, fell to 31 percent during the Great Depression, and bounced back to 42 percent by 1942. The rate continued to rise until phone service reached 94 percent of households in 1991. Household

39. Brown (1997).
40. Elmer-DeWitt (1994).

Table 8-1. *Size and Rank of Large Subject Categories of Periodicals, 1991 and 1996*

	1991		1996		
Subject category	*Rank*	*Number*	*Rank*	*Number*	*Percentage change*
College students	1	5,339	1	4,507	−16
House organ	2	2,715	9	1,482	−45
Medicine	3	2,338	2	2,918	25
Religion and theology	4	2,244	6	2,152	−4
Ethnic issues	5	2,034	21[a]	925	−55
Education	6	1,807	4	2,541	41
Law	7	1,798	3	2,859	59
Computers and automation	8	1,478	7	1,915	30
Business and industry	8	1,478	5	2,505	69
Genealogy	9	1,202	23[a]	895	−26
Health	10	1,167	8	1,778	52
Investment	11	1,151	13	1,174	2
Agriculture	12	929	19[a]	994	7
College alumni	13	890	22[a]	897	1
Sports and sporting goods	14	819	10	1,436	75
History	15	810	12	1,314	62
Poetry and creative writing	16	808	22[a]	897	11
Categories that rose in rank	*from*		*to*		
Environment and ecology	19	730	11	1,377	89
Regional interest	25	607	14	1,131	86
Politics	17	796	15	1,106	39
International affairs	22	703	16	1,072	34
Total		31,843		35,875	

Source: Compiled from annual editions of the *Standard Periodical Directory* and information provided by the publisher, Oxford Comunications, New York.
a. Fell from ranking among the sixteen largest subject categories.

phone service saturation remains at that level.[41] With its arrival, the persistent immediacy of the telephone ring pierced insulated life-styles. "The telephone is clearly the most obtrusive of agencies, and local calls are an accepted part of daily routine," observed the Research Committee on Social Trends in 1933.[42] In 1907 an individual received, on average, an incoming local call every three days and a toll call every fifteen days; twenty years later those intervals had shortened to 1.5 and ten days. Committee members concluded that, largely owing to the telephone, individuals were in continual contact with others: "Personal isolation—inaccessibility to the demands of others for access to one's attention—is increasingly rare, or, when desired, increasingly difficult to achieve." Recent evidence supports this early thesis about the impact of the telephone in reducing isolation. Smith examines the characteristics of General Social Survey respondents who do not own a telephone and finds that, as a group, they seem more socially isolated than phone owners: "They tend to be residentially mobile, not to read newspapers and not to have voted in the last presidential election, not to attend church nor belong to other voluntary organizations, have low confidence in banks and high social alienation, and be skeptical of human nature. While most of these associations are modest, they collectively describe the non-telephone owner as one with few ties to society in general. . . . In many regards, people with no telephone in their households are outsiders."[43]

The phone first presented a unique opportunity to manage the quality of contacts with various degrees of personal distancing in which gradients of social interaction can be added and refined. Face-to-face discussion is optional. The phone visit may supplement or supplant the act of "calling," "visiting," or "dropping in."[44] It is therefore possible to develop associational life further afield and to intensify social interaction close to home with the phone. Accelerated contact by phone seemed to strengthen and reinforce local attitudes, behavior, and social controls.[45] In his social history of the telephone, Fischer called it a "technology of sociability."[46] This was particularly true where party lines existed.[47] The party line in my

41. U.S. Bureau of the Census (1975, pp. 776, 783; 1998, p. 573).
42. Willey and Rice (1933b, p. 201).
43. Smith (1990).
44. Lynd and Lynd (1929, pp. 140, 275); Willey and Rice (1933a, pp. 134–54).
45. Willey and Rice (1933a, p. 151).
46. Fischer (1992, p. 266).
47. Allen and Dillman (1994, pp. 30, 180).

childhood community fostered neighborhood networks and connections, rural-town exchanges, and contacts beyond local boundaries as well. These links strengthened cooperation and solidarity and gave party-line subscribers a sense of collective identity.

The continual diversification and innovation that surrounds the telephone keeps the potential for social connectedness at a high level of readiness. Recent developments in telephone technology reflect a progressive push toward making it amenable to connecting with others, even as life-styles change. When a 1992 Roper Organization survey asked respondents if they had any of twelve optional features such as call-waiting, a speakerphone, memory dialing, etc., each feature was in use by at least a small portion. Five years earlier four of the listed features—the portable cellular phone, caller ID, video telephone, and the permanent phone number—were not in use by any respondent.[48]

Cordless units were reportedly in the possession of one-third of the adult population in 1992, allowing freedom of movement within a certain circumference around the base unit.[49] That range of communication convenience was extended further with the cellular phone. Twenty-four percent of a national sample owned car or cellular phones in 1995, according to a Times Mirror survey.[50] Others, the Wirthlin Group and Gallup, found that 22 percent and 25 percent of national adult samples reported owning a cellular phone that same year.[51] Also in that year, 29 percent of those surveyed who drove, and nine out of ten did, informed Gallup that yes, they had "talked on the telephone while driving."[52] In a 1997 survey conducted by Luntz Research Company, 38 percent reported they "currently use a cellular phone."[53] The Federal Communications Commission reports that the number of cellular phone subscribers at the end of 1996, over 44 million, had ballooned from 91,600 subscribers in 1984.[54] In the home, an increase in working, faxing, and using computers has sparked new growth in the number of phone lines. Almost 15 percent of households had second phone lines by 1995, up from 2.7 percent in just eight years.[55] The decision to get

48. Mayer (1994, p. 132).
49. Ibid.
50. Times Mirror (1995).
51. Roper at University of Connecticut (1995).
52. Gallup (1996, p. 180).
53. Roper at University of Connecticut (1998).
54. Federal Communications Commission (1997, pp. 74–75) .
55. Ibid., p. 27.

an additional line, it is reasonable to assume, is made to protect access to the rest of the world when one line is tied up with work matters or an Internet connection.

The telephone has become so well integrated into the fabric of society that it would be a challenge to definitively catalogue its functions. We use it to "reach out and touch someone" and to provide emotional support. We organize meetings and social events via the phone. We construct phone trees to disseminate information quickly throughout a network. We recruit volunteers and charitable donations by phone and mobilize support for particular causes.[56] We also use it to manage a major resource that facilitates associational life—our time—more effectively.

Little documentation actually exists on how Americans use the phone. Fischer concluded that by the 1920s home phones were used primarily for social purposes. It was then that the phone industry began to focus its marketing on relationships with friends and family.[57] Self-reports also point to the phone as an important conduit to social connectedness. Although fewer than 5 percent of people in a 1935 time-study sample reported telephoning as an activity, reasons supplied for talking on the phone suggested, even at that early date, that 64 percent of calls were social; three-fourths of these conversations occurred between friends.[58] Visiting by phone persists to the present. A national survey of adult leisure activities in 1982 found that 45 percent of respondents spoke by phone with friends or relatives daily, and another 32 percent did so once or twice a week.[59] Pew Research reported that 67 percent of respondents surveyed in 1998 said they had called a friend or relative yesterday just to talk.[60] We can surmise from these items that the phone is frequently used to maintain social connectedness.

---

56. Having received a phone solicitation was very or somewhat important to 23 percent of charitable contributors in a recent Independent Sector survey. *Giving and Volunteering* (1996, p. 105).

57. Fischer (1992, pp. 75, 253).

58. Sorokin and Berger (1939, pp. 106, 191, 197).

59. Question: "Now I'll read you a list of activities and ask how often you engaged in them during the past year. Some activities you may do only in the winter or the summer, for example. When answering how often you participate in those activities, think of how often you did them during the season: Every day or almost every day; About once or twice a week; About once or twice a month; Less than once a month; Never . . . Talk on the phone with friends or relatives." Watching television and reading the newspaper were choices, as well. United Media Enterprises (1983, p. 30).

60. Question: "Yesterday did you (a) visit with family or friends and (b) Call a friend or relative just to talk?" Pew (1998a).

Other sources of information, in the absence of direct data, help to characterize telephone usage. A rough estimate of conversation minutes per phone line reached by the Federal Communications Commission averaged twenty-five minutes a day from 1980 to 1995.[61] When Gordon S. Black interviewed a national sample of adults in 1986 for *USA Today*, 46 percent reported spending an hour talking by phone every day; another 37 percent spent less time than this on the phone, and 13 percent talked for two or three hours a day.[62] Neither tells if the conversation was for business or for other purposes. However, between 1920 and 1980 there were, on average, 2.28 residential phones for each business phone.[63] A similar pattern of one nonresidential to 2.23 residential lines existed from 1988 through 1995.[64] Distribution of phone capacity between homes and businesses is more heavily residential, although its allocation for business, household maintenance, and social purposes remains undocumented.

Despite the ubiquity of the phone, the individual finally has control over its intrusive nature. With the arrival of the telephone answering machine, which was adopted quickly, it is no longer necessary for incoming calls to cause arbitrary disruption at an inopportune time. In 1981, only 3 percent of a national Roper Organization sample reported owning an answering machine; eight years later, 25 percent reported ownership.[65] In yet another eight years, only 23 percent of a national adult sample surveyed by NBC News/ *Wall Street Journal*/Hart Teeter stated their households did *not* have answering machines.[66] In a 1992 Roper Organization poll of answering-machine owners, nearly half (48 percent) reported "frequent or often" use of the device "to listen to who is calling and then decide whether to talk to them or call them back."[67] One-fourth (26 percent) of answering-machine owners in a *Washington Post*/Kaiser/Harvard poll described the answering machine as a necessity when asked if they thought of it that way or "as a luxury you could do without."[68]

61. Federal Communications Commission (1997, pp. 33, 36).

62. Question: "I would like to ask you a few questions about your everyday activities. On an average day, how many hours do you . . . talk on the telephone?" The choice of 0, 1, 2, or 3 hours is too imprecise to determine actual time spent on the phone. Roper at University of Connecticut (1993).

63. U.S. Bureau of the Census (1975, pp. 776, 783; 1980, p. 584; 1984, p. 560).

64. Federal Communications Commission (1997, p. 27).

65. Mayer (1994, p. 128).

66. Roper at University of Connecticut (1996).

67. Mayer (1994, p. 146).

68. *Washington Post* (1996, p. 13).

The Automobile: Conveyor and Catalyst of Connections

Adaptation of the automobile was rapid, as was its remarkable impact on associational life. The Research Committee on Social Trends established that in the eighteen-year period from 1913 to 1931 private motor-vehicle registrations multiplied twenty times and the motor vehicle and gas tax became one of three major sources of government revenue.[69] The first automobile seen in Middletown, Indiana, arrived early in the century and became an integral part of the life and leisure style of the community by 1925.[70] By the 1930s the car was a necessity, a view that persisted despite slower sales of new and replacement cars during the Great Depression.[71] Development of suburban residential divisions, already apparent in 1933, was expedited by the automobile.[72]

Cars parked in the driveways of numerous Americans brought new freedom of movement. Although the car made it easier for many people to socialize and intensified local contacts, it had the capacity to detract from local community involvement. Those with greater mobility could, if they chose, more easily detach themselves from civic matters.[73] This development prompted broad concern about the impact on church attendance in Middletown. The local paper once estimated that "10,000 persons leave Middletown by automobile for other towns and resorts every fine Sunday."[74] One pillar of the church interviewed in the original study acknowledged a decision to forgo worship services to embark on an eighty-mile trip to a lake he had never seen. His comments reflect a personal choice between expanding his experiences on one hand, and fulfilling a social responsibility on the other: "It's a fine thing for people to get out that way on Sundays. No question about it. They see different things and get a larger outlook. . . . You can't do both. I never missed church or Sunday School for thirteen years and I kind of feel as if I'd done my share. The ministers ought not to rail against people's driving on Sunday. They ought just to realize that they won't be there . . . during

69. Research Committee (1933, pp. 172, 1366–67).

70. Middletown is a small industrial city in Indiana that Robert and Helen Lynd studied in 1924–1925 and again in 1935; Lynd and Lynd (1929, pp. 251–53; [1937] 1965). A follow-up study was done between 1976 and 1978 by Caplow et al. (1982).

71. Lynd and Lynd ([1937] 1965, p. 267).

72. McKenzie (1933, pp. 464–65).

73. Willey and Rice (1933b, pp. 179–80).

74. Lynd and Lynd ([1937] 1965, p. 307).

the summer, and make church interesting enough so they'll want to come."[75]

The locus of association activity, its flavor, and its geographic reach shifted with the automobile. Sunday dinners and get-togethers lost favor.[76] Visiting in the parlor and courting rituals, once centered in the home, faded as activities increasingly relied on the automobile.[77] It was not unusual for a drive or an event accessible by wheel to replace an evening gathering on the porch.[78] A dampening effect on neighboring occurred, even as neighborhoods became voluntary in a truer sense.[79] Old neighborhoods, town celebrations of holidays, and church attendance competed with the day trip, the vacation, and access to resources from an ever widening social space.[80]

Additional options for who, how, and when people got together evolved around the car. It became a focal point of socializing for small groups and made larger gatherings a more frequent occurrence. Motoring, for instance, was a popular social activity, and drives often included groups of friends.[81] Social events, once occasional, became regular occurrences with access by car.[82] Middletown residents attended gatherings more frequently, organized impromptu affairs such as picnics, and followed high-school ball games at home and away.[83] Visits to relatives living at some distance became more frequent.[84]

Often combined with spending time with friends and family, tourism and travel for pleasure developed into a new variant of association. Today, the most frequent reason for pleasure travel is to visit friends and family—the means of getting there is the automobile over three-fourths of the time.[85] Yet another instance of the car as a catalyst for association is the existence of 1,100 automobile hobby and recreational groups at local, state, regional, national, and international levels listed in 1997 by the *Encyclo-*

75. Lynd and Lynd (1929, pp. 259–60).

76. Ibid., p. 153.

77. Caplow et al. (1982, p. 164).

78. Lynd and Lynd (1929, p. 254).

79. Kolb and Brunner (1952, pp. 167–68).

80. Lynd and Lynd (1929, pp. 260–63); Kolb and Marshall (1944, p. 2); Kolb and Polson (1933, esp. p. 27).

81. Steiner (1933, p. 922); Sorokin and Berger (1939, pp. 69, 104, 191).

82. Lynd and Lynd (1929, p. 265).

83. Ibid., pp. 260, 485–87.

84. Caplow et al. (1982, pp. 198, 260–62).

85. This is the average of nine measures taken between 1984 and 1996 (*National Travel*).

pedia of Associations.[86] Other voluntary groups such as the American Automobile Association were influential early on in shaping public policy through their efforts to improve streets and roads.[87]

Only 9 percent of all households in 1990 were without a car, according to the Federal Highway Administration, and a majority (58 percent) of domiciles had two or more vehicles.[88] Most respondents (93 percent) polled in 1996 by *Washington Post*/Kaiser/Harvard considered the automobile a necessity.[89] The physical arrangement of contemporary communities has made the personal vehicle the linchpin of many aspects of American life outside the home. The coordination of work, chores, and leisure made possible by the automobile continues to give rise to innovative ideas like drive-in movies, drive-in worship services, and drive-through funeral home visitations. Travel time to organizational, religious, and social events amounted to more than one-fifth (22 percent) of total commuting time in 1985.[90] National Personal Transportation Surveys show the number of trips Americans reported taking for social and recreational reasons grew by 12 percent between 1969 and 1990. Over the same period of time, the length of these trips grew shorter by 10 percent and the number of miles traveled remained about the same, suggesting an increase in density of associational life.[91]

The Television: Connections and Disconnections

Television was "on the threshold" of American daily life in the early 1930s.[92] Introduced at the 1939 New York World's Fair, it rapidly diffused as World War II ended.[93] It entered the Middletown community in 1946 with two hours of daily programming.[94] Three decades later, Middletown had eight television channels, including four that were cable. Almost everyone, 98 percent of the households, owned at least one TV set. Nationally, the household saturation rate has matched this since 1980.[95]

86. *Encyclopedia of Associations* (1997).
87. Cowan (1997, p. 233).
88. U.S. Bureau of the Census (1997, p. 630).
89. *Washington Post* (1996, p. 13).
90. Robinson and Godbey (1997, pp. 322–23).
91. U.S. Bureau of the Census (1998, p. 636).
92. Keppel (1933, p. 993).
93. Mayer (1993, p. 594).
94. Caplow et al. (1982, pp. 22–23).
95. Bureau of the Census (1998, p. 573).

Viewing options have multiplied. The 862 television stations on air by 1970 grew to 1,532 by 1995.[96] The allocation of viewing time across broadcast network stations, independent stations, public television, basic cable, and pay cable is also becoming more selective. The network stations' leading share of viewer attention fell from 69 to 46 percent between 1983 and 1996; pay cable services absorbed this decline with a 23 percentage point increase in share, bumping independent stations into third place.[97] Sixty-seven percent of TV households subscribed to cable in 1996, up from 7 percent in 1970.[98] The larger portion of cable subscribers (58 percent) in 1994 chose from thirty to fifty-three channels; fifty-four or more channels were available to 38 percent.[99] In contrast, the average viewer in 1985 had access to only nineteen channels, according to Nielsen Media Research.[100] Television poses two choices that leave their imprint on associational life. One involves the use of TV as a source of general news and information that reinforces social connectedness. The other involves using TV as a leisure pursuit. This is seen in responses to a 1994 Roper-Starch national survey.[101] The three most salient reasons for watching television programs were for information (46 percent), entertainment (47 percent), and relaxation (35 percent).[102]

The manner in which Americans gather their news and information demonstrates the importance of the information function of TV. Repeated questioning by Roper between 1959 and 1994 indicates that, for consumers, television surpassed the newspaper as a major source of news in 1963.[103] Regular news viewing outpaced newspaper reading by an average of ten per-

96. Ibid.

97. *World Almanac* (1999, p. 260); Wright (1995, p. 232).

98. Nielsen Media (1997); Wright (1995, p. 232).

99. *Television and Cable Factbook* (1994, p. S239).

100. Roper (1992, p. 6).

101. Roper Starch Worldwide (1995, p. 31).

102. Question: "People have given us various reasons why they watch television. Here are some of them. Please tell me if you think each of them explains your use of television very well, somewhat, or hardly at all: To obtain information about what is happening in the world; To spend time with your family and/or friends; To forget about the worries of everyday life; To be entertained; To fill your spare time; For companionship when you are alone; Simply to relax; To be able to talk to others about programs; To see what happens to my favorite characters on TV; To get ideas on how to deal with real-life situations." Roper Starch (1995).

103. Question: "First, I'd like to ask you where you usually get most of your news about what's going on in the world today—from the newspapers, or radio, or television, or magazines, or talking to people or where?" Respondents could name more than one choice. Data for 1994 were provided by courtesy of the Roper Organization. Mayer (1993, pp. 593–611).

centage points in fourteen measures taken by Times Mirror between 1990 and the summer of 1995. An average of 82 percent reported watching TV news programs regularly; an average of 72 percent said they regularly read newspapers.[104]

A smattering of single surveys also suggest a preference for television news. Sixty percent of a national adult sample surveyed by Minnesota Opinion Research in 1984 said they would choose TV or radio to get their news in preference to a newspaper or magazine.[105] Kane, Parsons and Associates conducted a national survey of adults in 1987 who identified their main source of news as follows: television (56 percent), newspapers (28 percent), radio (11 percent), and magazines (2 percent).[106] In 1995 a Hart and Teeter Research survey asked which news sources respondents used regularly; television (87 percent) overshadowed newspapers (60 percent).[107] A national survey conducted by Ohio University in June 1995 found that local and network television news took precedence over reading the daily newspaper for regular users of these media.[108]

Leisure viewing poses an additional choice between two contexts—solitary viewing or as a social activity. The personal choices exercised (or not) in the use of television, which so complements the strain of individualization in American society, raise concerns about an imbalance between private and public interests. If television curtails the variety of attachments of individuals to associational life in a large way, the health of a pluralistic democratic society may be at risk. Putnam argues that television has indeed been a liability to associational life. This resonates with many Americans' dissatisfaction with how responsibly we have used television and the choices that its use entails.[109]

104. Questions: "Do you happen to read any daily newspaper or newspapers regularly, or not?" and "Do you happen to watch any TV news programs regularly, or not?" Times Mirror (1995, p. 65).

105. Question: "Some people prefer to read their news in newspapers or magazines, and some people prefer to get news on TV (television) or radio. If you had to choose one way of getting news and information, would you rather read it in a newspaper or magazine, or would you rather get it on TV or radio?" Roper at University of Connecticut (1989).

106. Question: "What would you say is your main source of news . . . TV (television), newspapers, magazines, or radio?" Roper at University of Connecticut (1989).

107. Question: "Which of the following sources of news, if any, do you use on a regular basis—television, radio, newspapers, or news magazines?" Roper at University of Connecticut (1995).

108. Regular users were those who watched or read the news four or more days each week. Stempel and Hargrove (1996, pp. 551–52).

109. Putnam (1995).

The greater part of leisure is dedicated to individual pursuits, which television viewing can be, especially with 2.3 sets per household.[110] Time-usage research indicates that watching television was the largest single free-time expenditure between 1965 and 1985.[111] In 1960, Gallup added watching television to a list of activities that a respondent could identify as "your favorite way of spending an evening."[112] When that question was asked in 1938, reading received the most mentions (21 percent), but television prevailed in 1960 for 28 percent of those polled. This pattern continued in four subsequent years, although it rose and then fell: 1966 (46 percent), 1974 (46 percent), 1986 (33 percent), and 1990 (24 percent). Television viewing was the most popular of two dozen activities in 1979 when the Roper Organization asked, "When you have free time, which of these things do you frequently do?"[113] A 1979 Leisure Development Center/Gallup survey asked, "How do you spend your free time? Please name as many [activities] as you like on the card."[114] Of the twenty-four possibilities, the activity choice that included television, "Getting relaxed at home such as TV-watching, listening to radio or records, playing with children, just doing nothing, etc.," was selected by four-fifths of the respondents. In 1982, United Media Enterprises found that watching television and reading a newspaper were the leisure activities reported as most often engaged in during the prior year.[115] Almost three-quarters, 72 percent, stated they had watched TV every day or almost daily, and 70 percent recalled reading the newspaper that frequently. Finally, in 1995 and 1997, Louis Harris and Associates asked national samples, "What are your two or three most favorite leisure time activities?"[116] The open-ended question produced thirty-six different responses. In both years, TV watching was second only to reading, named by 25 percent of survey participants in 1995 and 19 percent in 1997.

"People don't visit anymore." One resident in a rural community studied by Allen and Dillman thus explained the impact of television on

---

110. For data on leisure-time pursuit, see Robinson and Godbey (1997, pp. 126, 322–23); Sorokin and Berger (1939, pp. 148–60, 194–95); Almond and Verba ([1963] 1993, pp. 209–11); Ferge (1972); Hastings and Hastings (1982, pp. 483–84, 496); United Media Enterprises (1983, pp. 30–32). For the number of sets per household see U.S. Bureau of the Census (1998, p. 573).

111. Robinson and Godbey (1997, pp. 322–23).

112. Gallup (1987, pp. 104–5; 1991, p. 130).

113. Roper at University of Connecticut (1989).

114. Hastings and Hastings (1982, pp. 483–84, 496).

115. United Media Enterprises (1983, p. 31). See note 59 for the question.

116. Taylor (1997).

the once popular activity of talking and strolling about town on a summer evening.[117] It is not self-evident, however, that a shift from the sidewalks to the television set was necessarily a retreat from associational life. On the contrary, in the rural community of my childhood, TV became a reason for social gatherings. My first exposure to television was in the living room of a neighbor in 1949. After several families had eaten a potluck supper together, I helped to arrange chairs in rows facing the TV set with its tiny window to world affairs. Friends and acquaintances with television were generous in inviting the rest of us to join them. Regular meetings of the Methodist Youth Fellowship, coupled with Sunday-night viewing at a group leader's home, kept carefully to the agenda so we could watch Ed Sullivan afterward. Watching television together, especially late movies, was a teenage social event. Television stimulated conversation, as well. We were eager to discuss what we were seeing and learning as our world view expanded through this medium.

Researchers who returned to Middletown in the late 1970s expressed astonishment to find people watching so much television (a median of twenty-eight hours per week). They also found a richer and fuller associational life than in 1935. Clubs and associations had proliferated, and voluntary association membership rates were high. The ratio of churches to people had increased, along with attendance. Sports participation, reading, movie-going, and listening to the radio had grown more popular. More time was being spent with family. Unemployment was about the same.[118] So where had the time to watch television come from?

Part of the answer was in the gain of fifteen leisure hours per week attributable to shorter work days and weeks. However, estimates suggested that viewing time far exceeded that gain. Another part of the answer was surely in time saved by the labor-saving conveniences found in most Middletown homes in 1978. Especially noteworthy, however, is the researchers' observation that homework, housework, and family conversation frequently coincided with watching television. Middletowners were "deepening" time—that is, compounding the number of tasks done simultaneously. Participants in a 1982 nationwide poll also attended to more than just the television set; less than half (41 percent) reported that they "usually pay close attention."[119]

---

117. Allen and Dillman (1994, pp. 180–81) .
118. Caplow et al. (1982, esp. pp. 22–25).
119. United Media Enterprises (1983, p. 55).

The finding in Middletown that associational life did not lose out to watching television—that folks had found a way to do both—was similar to behavior reported by United Media Enterprises in 1982. Heavy TV watchers of four hours per day tended to be involved in fewer leisure activities than light viewers of one hour per day. There was no significant difference, however, between heavy and light viewers in the amount of leisure time spent at home. Fewer heavy TV watchers were volunteers, but those who did volunteer contributed larger amounts of time each month. A little over one-fourth of heavy and light TV users alike participated once a week or more in clubs or community affairs.[120] These findings suggest that television is not necessarily anathema to associational life.

Socializing around televised sporting events and elections has become commonplace. Sports bars are regular gathering places. When Roper Starch asked Americans about their motivation(s) for viewing television, 57 percent reported that spending time with family and/or friends described their motivation somewhat or very well; 46 percent said that being able to talk with others about programs motivated them to watch television. Others (36 percent) said that they watched TV to get ideas for how to deal with real-life situations.[121] These rationales are not unlike the motivation for watching how-to and religious programs, participating in Oprah Winfrey's Book Club, or communicating with the broader public via televised talk shows.[122] Television programs also spark the organization of nonprofit membership organizations. The *Encyclopedia of Associations* carries entries for such groups at the regional, state, local, and national levels. These widely diverse lists include cable television associations, the Boston Society of Vulcans of Mass, the Rin Tin Tin Fan Club, and the Riverton-Fremont TV Club.[123]

Clearly, television does not inevitably detract from associational life. It does enrich and add dimensions to social experience. World views and cognitive understandings expand with television, often with unclear effects on social and community relationships. Frequently discussed and criticized while it remains at the core of daily life, it acts as a catalyst for public, moral discourse. Perhaps this is one of television's more important contributions to associational life. The televised congressional hearings in 1987 about the

120. Ibid., pp. 60–63.
121. See note 102 above.
122. For discussion of the latter see Gamson (1998).
123. *Encyclopedia of Associations* (1997).

Iran-contra affair were a vivid example. These hearings prompted an out-pouring from Americans who joined the public debate by contacting committee members. An analysis of these communiques by historian David Thelen indicated that Americans "have created their own sources and authorities for fact and viewpoint by which to evaluate what appears on television. . . . In the course of talking about the hearings, Americans transformed themselves from television watchers into active citizens and patriots. By writing or calling a legislator, they defined citizenship in practice."[124]

The Internet: Connections in Cyberspace?

The Internet is a new frontier for associational life. Individuals and groups are rapidly crossing the Internet threshold to link, via computer, with others throughout the world. Less than 2 percent of Americans were using the Internet in 1994.[125] Two years later surveys began to show that more than 35 percent of adults go online for some reason.[126] The phenomenon resists accurate measurement in three ways: (1) it is decentral-ized; (2) its patterns change too quickly for measures to hold; and (3) the measures and definitions used are not standardized. The debate that swirls around results produced by Nielsen Media Research on use of the Internet is fueled by the latter problem. "Nielsen and its academic advisers . . . appear hopelessly split on how to interpret the numbers; depending on whom and when one asks, there were 22 million adult Americans on [the] Internet last August, or 19.4 million, or 16.4 million."[127] The Internet, the Information Superhighway, the World Wide Web, online services, and information services are all terms used in surveys. These are not mutually

124. Thelen (1996, p. 9).
125. Swisher (1996).
126. Hart and Teeter Research learned from 38 percent of a national adult sample in December 1996 that they "regularly use the Internet or other online computer information services, either at home or at work" (Roper at University of Connecticut [1996]). In November 1997, 37 percent of those interviewed by the Pew Research Center said they "use a computer at work, school, or home to connect with other computers over the Internet, with the World Wide Web, or with information services such as America Online or Prodigy." Thirty-six percent reported similarly in April and May of 1998 (Pew [1998b; 1998a]).
127. Lewis (1996).

exclusive, their meaning is fuzzy to many, and measures of Internet usage must be considered in this context.

Nevertheless, the Internet's suitability and potential for associational life is under exploration. Experimentation largely centers on blending this medium into known forms of association. Times Mirror interviewed a subset of online users that constituted 14 percent of a national sample in June 1995.[128] They were exploring the potential for association online in typical ways. Almost one-quarter (23 percent) had an "online buddy" they had never met. Over one-third (35 percent) had received an electronic news clipping or story from a friend. Almost one-fourth (23 percent) were communicating regularly with others via online forums, discussion lists, or chat groups from one to five days a week, others less often. (This rose to 35 percent in 1998.)[129] One-tenth of the users had discussed politics or had participated in political activity online. Fifteen percent had expressed an opinion on a political or social issue to a bulletin board, online news-group, or electronic mail list. Thirty-six percent of those who used the World Wide Web learned "about new Websites to visit" from friends and relatives.

Online users interviewed by Times Mirror in 1995 readily embraced electronic mail.[130] Nearly three-fourths (72 percent) of them communi-cated with others in this manner; the majority used it several times a week, if not daily. One year later, 83 percent were using e-mail.[131] One-half of the e-mailers in 1995 checked their electronic mailboxes once or more every day. Over two-thirds described their online mail as personal or a mix of personal and work subject matter. Eighty-three percent communicated in this way with family and friends. Fifty-nine percent found that access to e-mail resulted in more frequent contacts with family and friends.

Groups also form on the Internet. A small portion of e-mailers have joined "list servs" in which participants, presumably with a common interest, can simultaneously send the same message to everyone; 62 percent of these "joiners" are on more than one list service.[132] Forums for continu-ous thematic online discussion number in the thousands. Usenet, a large cooperative electronic bulletin board service that organizes postings by

128. Times Mirror (1995). Twenty-two percent of a national sample were online users by March 1996. Pew (1996a).
129. Pew (1998a).
130. Times Mirror (1995).
131. Pew (1996b).
132. Times Mirror (1995).

subject matter, carries 50,000 newsgroups—up from 40,000 in July 1997 and 5,000 in 1993.[133] For a random sample of 745 Compuserve and Prodigy subscribers in 1992, various social reasons (24 percent) were second only to seeking non-work-related information and education (38 percent) as rationales for using online bulletin boards.[134] As participants explore these new modes of interaction, written rules for communicating on the Internet are emerging. This "netiquette" relies upon "respecting the rights and desires of others, setting an example of how you want strangers to treat you, and acknowledging that the Internet is very different from face-to-face communication."[135] The way is thus paved for civil online interaction.

Social connectedness in cyberspace spills over into familiar arenas. Students at the Institute of Public Policy of George Mason University elicit online help just as one might from a neighbor in the classic sense. A student's call for help with typing a hat (^) over a Y in a mathematical formula elicited four different suggestions during a recent afternoon. Churches use home pages to recruit members and to publicize planned events. Six thousand religious congregations listed World Wide Web addresses in September 1994.[136] In another example of old and new institutional blends, thousands of volunteers "met" on Net Day in California on March 9, 1996, to wire schools across the state with Internet connections. Complaints heard in a series of meetings led one scientist at Sun Microsystems to organize an initiative to connect every school in the state to the Internet. This individual developed endorsements, home pages, and electronic presentations for schools to use on the Net to mobilize community support. Columnist Robert Kuttner describes the subsequent chain of events "as a kind of statewide high-tech barn-raising . . . a new way of building community support for institutions that are necessarily public."[137] Net Day illustrates how computer-mediated communication reduces the costs of association. In an analysis of seven similar cases of grass-roots political initiatives, Bonchek found that computer-assisted interactions cost less than more traditional methods, provided more accurate information, and were more efficient.[138]

133. Baym (1995, p. 138); Usenet (1997, 1998).
134. James (1992, pp. 88–94).
135. Hoffman (1995, p. 336).
136. Broadway (1996).
137. Kuttner (1996).
138. Bonchek (1995).

Net Day demonstrates grass-roots, ad hoc voluntary associations of the nature remarked upon by Tocqueville, who noted that greater achievement is possible when the initiatives of individuals and public officials are combined.[139] Formally organized groups also mediate the interface of Information Age technology into society. A recent example of this role in the *Los Angeles Times* describes the problems encountered by the New Main Public Library in San Francisco. In this new high-tech facility, outraged patrons had difficulty finding books, and many books were inaccessible in closed stacks. The surge of indignation paled, however, in the shadow of public reaction to the discovery of 100,000 books culled and buried in a nearby landfill. A local chapter of a nonprofit membership association, the Gray Panthers, subsequently organized a rescue of books from the landfill and, as one member stated, is "keeping them in trust for the library until they come to their senses. . . . These were the books that librarians had preserved for generations."[140]

Used to blend new with old forms of association, the Internet offers additional choice and gradients to the quality of interaction, bringing people into new configurations of interaction. How the applications of this technology will ultimately enhance or negatively influence and alter associational activity is obviously unknown. Its compatibility with associational life, however, is questionable to some. Mendelson articulates the concern echoing through discussions of the Internet: "In a world where connections are everywhere but are mostly meaningless, transient, fragile and unstable. . . . In a world without tangible bodies or enduring memories, no one can keep promises. No one can even remember why they might be worth keeping. . . . Words written on the transient phosphorescence of a computer screen . . . will soon be effaced by others."[141]

Discussion

I show in this chapter that Americans put technology to work on behalf of social connectedness. They do so with interest, creativity, and alacrity. Pragmatic decisions made by individuals about conducting their associational lives—who, what, where, when, why, and how to connect

---

139. Tocqueville ([1835] 1945, p. 1: 98).
140. Curtius (1997).
141. Mendelson (1996).

with others—incorporate technology. Applications of technology are embedded in daily life, ease the integration of private and public activities, and add endurance and resilience to associational life. Clearly the technologies reviewed here have been and are resources of great utility for building and maintaining social connectedness. Interests and activities that make up associational life continue to multiply and diversify, stimulating interpersonal interaction and participation in associational life. This is not inconsistent with demonstrations that a heightened flow of information-sharing and interest in affiliation prompts involvement in politics *and* augments the political skill of individuals.[142] Nor is it contrary to other current streams of research that document a vital contemporary pattern of citizen activity.[143]

Technologies are used to develop gradients of connectedness. One way of thinking about systems of interconnectedness is in terms of weak and strong ties. Granovetter explained that density of social ties affects the diffusion of information; strong, or overly dense, ties curtail the flow of communication and weaker ties facilitate the flow.[144] It now seems more accurate to speak of ties of varying degrees between weak and strong. The array of print media illustrates the difference between weaker and weak ties. Newspapers, a source of general news and information, have the widest general coverage and sustain the weakest ties. Periodicals that pursue particular interests appeal to more limited segments of the population, helping to maintain ties that are somewhat stronger than the weakest ones. A prepublication reviewer of this volume rightly pointed out that books are also a means to sustaining this web of connectivity. A broad interest in sharing what others read is reflected by the regularly published lists of the bestsellers—fiction and nonfiction, paperback and hardcover. Such ties would fall somewhere between newspapers and periodicals on a scale of weak to strong ties. Book topics also become very specialized; they then reinforce stronger bonds between smaller and particular portions of the population.

Safeguarding the privacy that Americans value highly leads to other applications of technologies that shape associational life. This is most evident in the way in which television is used to pursue both private *and*

---

142. Lipset, Trow, and Coleman ([1956] 1977, pp. 79–105, 367–71); Guterbock and Fries (1997, pp. 99–115).
143. See note 2 above.
144. Granovetter (1973).

associational interests. Uses made of the telephone, in particular, illustrate how Americans negotiate between protecting their privacy from intrusion and ensuring their accessibility to others. At the same time the phone is used assertively to keep in touch with people, thereby short-circuiting social distances. The consumption of general news and information through a customized package of media resources is yet another way of balancing private and nonprivate interests. It is a means to acknowledge others and stay in tune with the larger group while individualizing one's mode of association.

Change in associational life is intimately linked with applications of technology. Adaptations of technology expand social space and make it denser at the same time, a phenomenon first noted early in this century. Changes in the locus of associational life—from the front porch to the automobile to the sports bar to cyberspace—are brought about with technologies. Traditional forms of association, such as neighboring, are sustained yet transformed with new technologies like the Internet.

Technologies offer choice in shaping associational life, and Americans have clearly exercised this choice. Association as a matter of individual choice, preference, and selection is more truly voluntary than ever before. The discretion to shape one's own associational life, in contrast to having it prescribed by social pressure and custom, is inherent with responsibility. This brings us to the question about decisions made by the individual less bound by customary social constraints, like the parishioner in 1920s Middletown who chose a drive to the lake over going to church. We know that Americans love their privacy; will they use new technologies to neglect their duties to one another, and thus to themselves? The question is a reminder of the risk that accompanies new freedoms to associate. The answer, thus far, seems to be both yes and no.

Undoubtedly, there is more of what Selbourne calls "random forms of human association," what Gellner projects as a greater sense of fragmentation or alienation, and what Manent denotes as the anxiety of democratic man.[145] But when choice comes into play, values also come into focus.[146] American values have traditionally embraced both individualism *and* social connectedness, which exist in tension with one another. The technologies examined here are used for both ends; television is a particularly poignant illustration of a dual-purpose technology. Struggle to maintain an appro-

145. Selbourne (1997, p. 5); Gellner (1994, pp. 7–8); Manent (1996, pp. 53–65).
146. Berlin (1969, pp. 171–72).

priate balance between private and public interest is part of the American tradition. We are often dissatisfied with our own performance, as seen in the acute concern of many Americans about excessive individualism. Yankelovich tells us that this perceived imbalance may be shifting. Polls over the past several decades reflect a move by Americans away from a self-centered orientation toward a larger view of themselves as part of a network of reciprocity and interdependence.[147] As Americans continue to value both privacy and social connectedness, they apply technology to shaping, transforming, and coordinating their private and associational lives. Guidance in making informed choices about the balance between the two, once provided by what Gellner calls the "tyranny of cousins, and of ritual,"[148] must now come from within, from freely adopted social constraints, and from the forum of public discourse.

References

Abrahamson, David. 1996. *Magazine-Made America*. Cresskill, N.Y.: Hampton.

Allen, John C., and Don A. Dillman. 1994. *Against All Odds*. Boulder, Colo.: Westview.

Almond, Gabriel A., and Sidney Verba. [1963] 1993. *The Civic Culture: Political Attitudes and Democracy in Five Nations*. Newbury Park, Calif.: Sage.

Baym, Nancy K. 1995. "The Emergence of Community in Computer-Mediated Communication." In *Cybersociety*, edited by Steven G. Jones. Thousand Oaks, Calif.: Sage.

Berlin, Isaiah. 1969. *From Four Essays on Liberty*. Oxford University Press.

Birdsell, David, Douglas Muzzio, and Humphrey Taylor. 1996. "17 Million American Adults Use World Wide Web." *Harris Poll* 11 (February 15).

Bonchek, Mark S. 1995. "Grassroots in Cyberspace: Using Computer Networks to Facilitate Political Participation." Working Paper 95-2.2, Political Participation Project, MIT Artificial Intelligence Laboratory. Presented at the annual meeting of the Midwest Political Science Association, Chicago.

Boorstin, Daniel J. 1978. *The Republic of Technology*. Harper and Row.

Broadway, Bill. 1996. "Flocking to the Web." *Washington Post*, September, 18, sec. B, p. 7.

Brown, Ed. 1997. "Extreme Publishing: Supply Room Confidential." *Fortune*, May 12, p. 26.

Caplow, Theodore, Howard M. Bahr, Bruce A. Chadwick, Reuben Hill, and Margaret Holmes Williamson. 1982. *Middletown Families: Fifty Years of Change and Continuity*. University of Minnesota Press.

Chaffee, Steven, and Stacey Frank. 1996. "How Americans Get Political Information: Print versus Broadcast News." *Annals* (July): 48–58.

Cowan, Ruth Schwartz. 1997. *A Social History of American Technology*. Oxford University Press.

147. Yankelovich (1998).
148. Gellner (1994, pp. 7–8).

Curtius, Mary. 1997. "Libraries Write New Chapter." *Los Angeles Times*, February 1, sec. A, p. 1.

Davis, James Allan, and Tom W. Smith. 1995. General Social Surveys, 1972–1994. [Cumulative file]. Chicago: National Opinion Research Center [producer], 1994. Ann Arbor, Mich.: Interuniversity Consortium for Political and Social Research [distributor].

Elmer-DeWitt, Philip. 1994. "Beyond Shovelware." *Folio* 23(17): 54–55.

Encyclopedia of Associations. 1997. Detroit, Mich.: Gale Research.

Federal Communications Commission. 1997. "Trends in Telephone Service." Industry Analysis Division, Common Carrier Bureau, Washington, D.C.

Ferge, Susan, ed. 1972. "Part III: Statistical Appendix." In *The Use of Time: Daily Activities of Urban and Suburban Populations in Twelve Countries*, edited by Alexander Szalai. The Hague: Mouton.

Fischer, Claude S. 1992. *America Calling.* University of California Press.

Gallup, George, Jr. 1987–1996. *The Gallup Poll: Public Opinion.* Wilmington, Del.: Scholarly Resources.

Gamson, Joshua. 1998. *Freaks Talk Back.* University of Chicago Press.

Gellner, Ernest. 1994. *Conditions of Liberty: Civil Society and Its Rivals.* Penguin.

Giving and Volunteering in the United States: Findings from a National Survey. 1996. Washington, D.C.: Independent Sector.

Granovetter, Mark S. 1973. "The Strength of Weak Ties." *American Journal of Sociology* 78(6): 1360–80.

Guterbock, Thomas M., and John C. Fries. 1997. *Maintaining America's Social Fabric: The AARP Survey of Civic Involvement.* Washington, D.C.: American Association of Retired Persons.

Hastings, Elizabeth Hann, and Philip K. Hastings, eds. 1982. *Index to International Public Opinion, 1980–1981.* Westport, Conn.: Greenwood.

Hoffman, Paul E. 1995. *Netscape and the World Wide Web for Dummies.* Foster City, Calif.: IDG Books Worldwide.

Hollander, A. N. J. 1981. "Science, Technology, Modernization and Social Change." In *The Social Implications of the Scientific and Technological Revolution.* Paris: UNESCO.

James, Michael Lynn. 1992. "An Exploratory Study of the Perceived Benefits of Electronic Bulletin Board Use and Their Impact on Other Communication Activities." Ph. D.diss., Florida State University.

Keppel, Frederick P. 1933. "The Arts in Social Life." In *Recent Social Trends in the United States: Report of the President's Research Committee on Social Trends*, Research Committee on Social Trends. McGraw-Hill.

Kobak, James B. 1990. "25 Years of Change." *Folio* 19 (March): 82–89.

———. 1994. "Magazine Trends." *Folio* 22 (Special Sourcebook Issue): 235–38.

Kolb, J. H., and Edmund deS. Brunner. 1952. *A Study of Rural Society.* Westport, Conn.: Greenwood.

Kolb, John H., and Douglas G. Marshall. 1944. "Neighborhood-Community Relationships in Rural Society." *Bulletin* 154 (November). Agricultural Experiment Station of the University of Wisconsin.

Kolb, J. H., and R. A. Polson. 1933. "Trends in Town-Country Relations." *Research Bulletin* 117 (September). Agricultural Experiment Station of the University of Wisconsin and United States Department of Agriculture.

Kupfer, Andrew. 1995. "Alone Together: Will Being Wired Set Us Free?" *Fortune*, March 20, pp. 94–96.

Kuttner, Robert. 1996. "Net Day: A Lesson in Logging On." *Washington Post*, February 19, sec. A, p. 25.

Ladd, Everett Carll. 1999. *The Ladd Report.* Free Press.

Lewis, Peter. 1996. "In a Recount, Cyber Census Still Confounds." *New York Times*, April 17, sec. D, p. 1.

Lipset, Seymour Martin, Martin A. Trow, and James S. Coleman. [1956] 1977. *Union Democracy: The Internal Politics of the International Typographical Union.* Free Press.

Lynd, Robert S., and Helen Merrell Lynd. 1929. *Middletown: A Study in American Culture.* New York: Harcourt, Brace.

———. [1937] 1965. *Middletown in Transition: A Study in Cultural Conflicts.* New York: Harcourt Brace Jovanovich.

Manent, Pierre. 1996. *Tocqueville and the Nature of Democracy.* Boulder, Colo.: Rowman and Littlefield.

Mayer, William G. 1993. "Trends in Media Usage." *Public Opinion Quarterly* 57(4): 593–611.

———. 1994. "The Rise of the New Media." *Public Opinion Quarterly* 58(1): 124–46.

McKenzie, R. D. 1933. "The Rise of Metropolitan Communities." In *Recent Social Trends in the United States: Report of the President's Research Committee on Social Trends*, Research Committee on Social Trends. McGraw-Hill.

Mendelson, Edward. 1996. "The Word and the Web." *New York Times Book Review*, June 2, p. 35.

Miller, Warren E. 1994. National Election Studies, American National Election Studies Cumulative Data File 1952–1992 [computer file]. 6th release. University of Michigan, Center for Political Studies [producer]. Ann Arbor: Interuniversity Consortium for Political and Social Research [distributor].

Moore, David W. 1995. "Americans' Most Important Source: Local TV News." *Gallup Poll Monthly* (September): 3–4, 6.

National Travel Survey. 1985–1995. Washington, D.C.: United States Travel Data Center.

Peterson, Theodore. [1964] 1975. *Magazines in the Twentieth Century.* University of Illinois Press.

Pew Research Center for the People and the Press. 1996a. Media Consumption Survey. Website: April; http://www.people-press.org/tec96que.htm [accessed March 16, 1997].

———. 1996b. Survey of Technology. Website: October; http://www.people-press.org/tec96que.htm [accessed March 16, 1997].

———. 1998a. Biennial News Consumption Survey. Website: http://www.people-press.org/med98que.htm [accessed January 7, 1999].

———. 1998b. November 1997 Values Update Survey. Website; http://www.people-press.org/valuetop.htm [accessed January 7, 1999].

Putnam, Robert D. 1995. "Tuning In, Tuning Out: The Strange Disappearance of Social Capital in America." *PS: Political Science and Politics* (December): 664–83.

Research Committee on Social Trends. 1933. *Recent Social Trends in the United States: Report of the President's Research Committee on Social Trends.* McGraw-Hill.

Robinson, John P. 1980. "The Changing Reading Habits of the American Public." *Journal of Communication* 30 (Winter): 147–57.

———. 1990. "Thanks for Reading This." *American Demographics* (May): 6–7.

Robinson, John P., and Geoffrey Godbey. 1997. *Time for Life.* Pennsylvania State University Press.

Roper Center at University of Connecticut. 1989–98. Public Opinion Online. Available in LEXIS, Market Library, RPOLL File.

Roper Center. 1992. "Mass Communications." *Public Perspective* (September/October): 5–6.

Roper Starch Worldwide. 1995. "America's Watching: Public Attitudes toward Television." New York.

Rosenblum, Nancy L. 1998. *Membership and Morals.* Princeton University Press.

Selbourne, David. 1997. *The Principle of Duty.* London: Little, Brown.

Smith, Tom W. 1990. "Phone Home? An Analysis of Household Telephone Ownership." GSSDIRS Methodological Report 50. Website: http://www.icpsr.umich.Edu/GSS/home.htm [accessed July 1997].

Sorokin, Pitirim A., and Clarence Q. Berger. 1939. *Time-Budgets of Human Behavior.* Harvard University Press.

Steiner, J. F. 1933. "Recreation and Leisure Time Activities." In *Recent Social Trends in the United States: Report of the President's Research Committee on Social Trends.* Research Committee on Social Trends and McGraw-Hill.

Stempel, Guido H., III, and Thomas Hargrove. 1996. "Mass Media Audiences in a Changing Media Environment." *Journalism and Mass Communication Quarterly* 73(3): 551–52.

Stern, Bernhard J. [1937] 1972. "Resistances to the Adoption of Technological Innovations." In *Technological Trends and National Policy.* New York: Arno Press.

Swisher, Kara. 1996. "There's No Place Like a Home Page." *Washington Post.* July 1, sec. A, p. 1.

Taft, William H. 1982. *American Magazines for the 1980s.* New York: Hastings House.

Taylor, Humphrey. 1997. "Fishing, Gardening, Golf and Team Sports Are America's Most Popular Leisure Activities—Apart from Reading, TV Watching, and Spending Time with Family." *Harris Poll* 31 (July 7).

Television and Cable Factbook. 1994. Washington, D.C.: Warren.

Thelen, David P. 1996. *Becoming Citizens in the Age of Television.* University of Chicago Press.

Times Mirror Center for the People and the Press. 1995. "Technology and On-Line Use." Princeton Survey Research Associates.

Tocqueville, Alexis de. [1835–40] 1945. *Democracy in America,* Vols. 1 and 2. Knopf.

United Media Enterprises. 1983. *Where Does the Time Go?* New York: Newspaper Enterprise Association.

United States Bureau of the Census. 1975. *Historical Statistics of the United States, Colonial Times to 1970.* Washington, D.C.: U.S. Government Printing Office.

———. 1980–1998. *Statistical Abstract of the United States.* Washington, D.C.: U.S. Government Printing Office.

United States Department of Commerce. 1947–77. *Census of Manufactures.* Washington, D.C.: U.S. Government Printing Office.

Usenet Information Center. 1997–98. Website: http://sunsite.unc.edu/usenet-i/home.html [accessed July 29, 1997, and February, 7, 1998].

Verba, Sidney, Kay Lehman Schlozman, and Henry E. Brady. 1995. *Voice and Equality: Civic Voluntarism in American Politics.* Harvard University Press.

Washington Post/Kaiser Family Foundation/Harvard University Survey. 1996. "Survey of Americans and Economists on the Economy." Menlo Park, Calif.: Kaiser Family Foundation.

Weaver, David H. 1996. "What Voters Learn from Media." *Annals* (July): 34–47.

Willey, Malcolm M., and Stuart A. Rice. 1933a. *Communication Agencies and Social Life.* McGraw-Hill.

———. 1933b. "The Agencies of Communication." In *Recent Social Trends in the United States: Report of the President's Research Committee on Social Trends,* Research Committee on Social Trends. McGraw-Hill.

World Almanac and Book of Facts 1999. 1998. Mahwah, N.J.: Funk and Wagnalls.

World Values Study Group. 1994. World Values Survey [computer file]. ICPSR version. Ann Arbor, Institute for Social Research [producer]. Ann Arbor, Interuniversity Consortium for Political and Social Research [distributor].

Wright, John W., ed. 1995. *Universal Almanac 1996.* Kansas City, Mo.: Andrews and McMeel.

Yankelovich, Daniel. 1998. "How American Individualism Is Evolving." *Public Perspective* (February/March): 3–6.

9 | Mobilizing Civic Engagement: The Changing Impact of Religious Involvement

ROBERT WUTHNOW

Throughout american history, civic involvement has been deeply influenced by the nation's preponderant commitment to its religious organizations. When Tocqueville visited, new denominations were moving westward with the rapidly expanding population, helping to promote a sense of obligation to fellow citizens as much as to God. The benevolent and temperance societies born in that era, the craft guilds and ladies' auxiliaries that so often met in church basements, and subsequent waves of labor organizations and women's clubs and Masonic orders all depended significantly on the leadership skills and social networks that people developed at their places of worship.[1] But questions are now being raised about religion's capacity to mobilize civic involvement.

Since the 1960s, American religion has undergone a dramatic series of changes. The 1950s, which at the time were hailed as a period of religious revival, appear in retrospect to have been an exceptional period, rather than a harbinger of the future. Family-oriented religion prompted by the postwar baby boom and insecurities generated by the Cold War encouraged religious participation in record numbers but also produced what observers recognized as a shallow, customary style of participation rather than a deep or theologically grounded commitment. The turmoil

---

1. Hall (1992); Hewitt (1984); Jolicoeur and Knowles (1978).

of the 1960s, especially the Civil Rights and antiwar movements, led many younger Americans to abandon their parents' houses of worship. Liberal and mainline Protestant and Roman Catholic churches sustained heavy losses. Indeed, by the 1980s, the center of gravity in American religion appeared to have shifted toward more conservative evangelical and fundamentalist organizations.

At the turn of the century, the changing composition of American religion has left many questions unanswered about its capacity for mobilizing civic engagement. For some observers, religion is simply too divided to provide a strong basis for social cohesion in the wider society; other observers recognize religion's potential, both as a source of beneficial collective values and as a supplier of social services, but wonder if the present configuration of religious loyalties is promising or worrisome. Particularly at issue is the question of whether those forms of religious expression that were most conducive to civic engagement in the past may be declining in strength while other forms are growing stronger. The reason this question is central to any discussion of civic renewal can be illustrated by considering two examples of contemporary religious commitment provided by two men interviewed in 1997.

Edward Nelson, age sixty, is a certified public accountant who runs his own business in a town of approximately 12,000 people in rural Pennsylvania. Ed and his wife are members of the local Presbyterian Church, a congregation of 300 people who meet in a stylish building constructed in the 1960s. They have been members for more than thirty years. Ed says he makes it to Sunday services at least twice a month (less often during tax season), and he has served on the church's executive council, its search committee, and several denominational committees. His involvement in the church is a way of keeping in touch with people in the community. When he was on the search committee, he became closely acquainted with the Kiwanis president, who was also on the committee. Through his contacts at church, he was invited to join Rotary, which he has now belonged to for nearly two decades. He also became active in the YMCA and has served for the past several years on its board. Ed has his doubts about some of the stories in the Bible, but he believes he has an obligation to serve other people as much as he can.

Gary Rush manages a bookstore a few blocks from Ed Nelson's accounting office. Gary and his wife, both in their late thirties, attend an independent evangelical church called Faith Fellowship. On most Sundays, attendance runs close to 400 people, and the numbers have been climbing steadily in recent years. Gary likes the biblical preaching and the way people care for one another. "We're the body of Christ," he explains, "that's why we call ourselves a fellowship." He faithfully attends Sunday school and the worship service each Sunday morning, a Bible study group on Sunday evening, and prayer meeting on Wednesday. In recent years he has taught Sunday school, served as a deacon, and been on the board of elders. He especially enjoyed his stint as a deacon. Because of the growing "needs" in the community, he helped set up a "benevolence committee." He wants the church to be a "resting place" where people in need can "find hope." Like Ed Nelson, he believes God wants him to care about others.

Both men illustrate how religious commitment can encourage civic engagement, albeit in quite different ways. But recent discussions about the decline of such engagement raise questions about how typical these men are. Perhaps American religion is losing its capacity to mobilize civic involvement. Or perhaps involvement in religion itself is weakening. To address these possibilities we need to examine a variety of evidence.

I begin with a brief review of what we know about recent trends in American religion and then examine the relationships between participation in religious organizations and involvement in other kinds of civic activity. This evidence suggests the importance of distinguishing among several major categories of religious expression in the United States. It also suggests the need to consider new ways in which religious organizations may be stimulating civic involvement.

The Religion Factor

The relationship between religious participation and civic engagement has been documented in other research. Surveys conducted by the Gallup Organization for Independent Sector since the late 1980s consistently show that active church attenders are more likely to give money and time to voluntary organizations, including ones that have no evident connection to churches.[2] The work of Sidney Verba and his coauthors on political mobilization demonstrates that church is one of the most important places in which people learn transferable civic skills.[3] Some comparative research

2. Hodgkinson et al. (1995).
3. Verba, Schlozman, and Brady (1995).

also suggests that the higher level of volunteering in the United States than in other advanced industrial societies may be the result of Americans' more active religious participation.[4] People like Ed Nelson and Gary Rush exemplify the reasons for these connections. Active church members are likely to be exposed to religious teachings about loving their neighbor and being responsible citizens, they are more likely to have social capital in the form of ties to fellow congregants that can be used to mobilize their energies, and they are more likely to be aware of needs and opportunities in their communities as a result of attending services in their congregations.[5]

Religious participation appears to have remained relatively constant over the past several decades. In "Bowling Alone," Robert Putnam reports that, according to Gallup surveys conducted between 1972 and 1992, the percentage of people who attended church during the previous seven days varied only between 40 percent and 42 percent; similarly, NORC General Social Survey (GSS) data showed a variation of 34 to 37 percent during the same period.[6] These are precisely the years during which Putnam claims that other forms of civic engagement declined.

Closer examination of data on religious participation also indicates a lack of change. Table 9-1 reports detailed responses to the GSS question about church attendance for 1974 and 1991 (the years most relevant to our subsequent analysis).[7] The patterns in the earlier and more recent surveys are virtually the same. Other research that compares different time periods shows a temporary increase in religious participation during the 1950s, but otherwise indicates little change, perhaps for as long as five decades.[8] And Putnam's observation that membership in "church-related groups" *fell* during the 1970s and 1980s does not seem to contradict these conclusions; as I have discussed elsewhere, evidence shows that responses to this question are ambiguous because some people take the question to

4. Ibid. (p. 80); Greeley (1997).
5. Wuthnow (1991).
6. Putnam (1995).
7. I use the 1974 and 1991 General Social Surveys because 1974 was the first year in which questions about voluntary associations were asked and 1991 because this is the most recent year in which these questions were asked of a majority of respondents (in 1994, only one-third of respondents were queried about voluntary associations and in 1996 these questions were not included); voluntary association membership is one measure of civic engagement to which religious participation can be related.
8. Hout and Greeley (1987).

Table 9-1. *Church Attendance in 1974 and 1991*

Percent

Frequency of attendance at religious services	1974	1991	Change
More than once a week	8	6	−2
Every week	22	23	1
Nearly every week	6	6	0
Two to three times a month	9	10	1
Several times a year	13	12	−1
Once a year	15	14	−1
Less than once a year	7	9	2
Never	12	13	1
Number in survey	1,481	1,492	

Source: General Social Surveys, 1974 and 1991.

mean church membership while others take it to mean membership in groups or committees connected with churches.[9]

The lack of change in religious participation in recent decades means that any decline in other forms of civic participation cannot be understood simply as a function of an eroding base in religion. Instead, the possibilities that must be entertained are (a) that the *relationship* between religious participation and civic engagement is weakening, or (b) that certain changes in the *composition* of religious participation are taking place that may signal problems for civic engagement in the future.

The first of these possibilities appears not to be supported. The GSS data include a list of voluntary associations (such as service groups, youth groups, and fraternal orders) of which respondents are asked to indicate whether they are members. It is among these memberships that Putnam finds evidence of decline, at least when controlling for changes in levels of education. My analysis of the 1974 data (leaving out the item about church-affiliated groups) shows that the odds of participating in a voluntary association were about 21 percent greater among respondents who attended religious services regularly (at least twice a month) than among those who attended religious services less often. In the 1991 data the odds

9. Wuthnow (1997).

were almost exactly the same. And when different levels of education were taken into account, the results did not change.[10]

The second possibility—about change in the composition of religious participation—requires discussing what some of these changes may have been. The most significant change has been the decline of so-called mainline Protestant denominations and the relative rise of some evangelical and independent churches. The largest mainline Protestant denominations are Methodist, Presbyterian, Episcopal, Lutheran, American Baptist, and United Church of Christ churches. Starting in the early 1960s, all of these denominations lost members, some as much as a quarter of their memberships by the early 1980s; since then they have shown no growth relative to the total U.S. population. In contrast, the Southern Baptist Convention, National Baptist Convention, various independent Baptist churches, and such evangelical denominations as Pentecostal, Holiness, Assemblies of God, Evangelical Free, and Christian and Missionary Alliance churches have all grown rapidly. Unlike Catholics, Protestants as a whole compose a somewhat smaller proportion of the population than they did in the early 1970s, but this change is not as great as that within Protestantism itself. Thus, among respondents in the GSS surveys (leaving aside Jews, other non-Christians, and those with no religious preferences), 71 percent were Protestants in 1991 (72 percent had been in 1974), but among Protestants, 63 percent were in evangelical denominations by 1991; only 56 percent had been in 1974.[11]

The relative decline of mainline denominations is generally understood to have been rooted in demographic change more than in public rejection of the teachings or practices of these denominations. Mainline denominations were populated by better-educated people and by larger proportions of middle-class families. Starting in the 1960s, birth rates in these segments of the population fell sharply; fewer offspring meant fewer potential members;

---

10. In logit regression models where the dependent variable was a dichotomous variable indicating membership in at least one of the fifteen nonreligious voluntary associations, the odds-ratio for church attendance (dichotomized at twice monthly or more rather than once a month or less) was 1.215 in 1974 and 1.206 in 1991; and with education in the models, the respective odds-ratios were 1.207 and 1.200 (all coefficients were significant at or beyond the .01 level of probability).

11. The NORC data do not permit detailed classification of respondents, especially in earlier years; thus, I classified Presbyterians, Episcopalians, Methodists, and Lutherans as mainline, and Baptists, Other Protestants, and Protestant—No denomination as evangelical. Readers are cautioned to understand the operational meaning of these terms in the present context. The distinction corresponds more with polity type in these data than with differences in personal belief.

in addition, later marriage and child-bearing created greater spacing between generations, a change that also resulted in fewer potential members. In contrast, evangelical churches were populated by larger numbers of working-class families, and these families tended to have more children; evangelical churches also placed higher expectations on children about retaining the religious loyalties of their parents; and some of these churches benefited from the growing number of new immigrants after 1965.

National studies show that some of these demographic differences are likely to have a continuing effect on the composition of American religion. In 1974 the average number of children among evangelicals was 2.57; it was 2.32 among mainline Protestants and 2.30 among Catholics. By 1991 these differences were still pronounced: 2.28 children among evangelicals, 1.71 among mainline Protestants, and 1.86 among Catholics. In the recent period, the differences in generational spacing were also evident: among evangelicals age eighteen to twenty-nine, 50 percent had at least one child, whereas among mainline Protestants only 39 percent had children (among Catholics, 37 percent did). The likelihood of couples having no children or fewer children also showed strong differences: among evangelicals age thirty to forty-nine, 17 percent had no children, whereas among mainline Protestants 32 percent did not have children (16 percent of Catholics had no children).

The smaller likelihood that evangelicals would lose the religious loyalties of their children is evident in results from a national survey of teenagers. Among twelve- to fifteen-year-olds, a small and virtually similar proportion of evangelicals, mainline Protestants, and Catholics did not attend church more than a few times a year (24, 22, and 25 percent, respectively). But among respondents ages sixteen or seventeen, this proportion remained small among evangelicals (22 percent), whereas it rose markedly among mainline Protestants (39 percent) and Catholics (36 percent).[12]

The greater likelihood of evangelicals' perpetuating themselves can also be seen in the results of studies among adults. In one national survey, 91 percent of those who had grown up in an evangelical denomination were still affiliated with an evangelical denomination as adults, whereas

12. My analysis of data collected in 1991 from approximately 1,400 teenagers; see Hodgkinson and Weitzman (1992) and Wuthnow (1995). Using the same denominational definitions as in the other studies, 326 of the respondents were classified as Evangelical Protestants, 267 as Mainline Protestants, and 331 as Catholics.

only 79 percent of those from mainline backgrounds were still in a mainline denomination (85 percent of Catholics continued to be Catholics). The same study also demonstrated that people from mainline denominations were more likely to become evangelicals than the reverse (and more Catholics were likely to become evangelicals than mainline Protestants).[13]

Although the relative shift from mainline to evangelical Protestants should not be exaggerated, its importance to civic engagement lies in the different religious traditions represented by the two. Mainline denominations grew out of the Protestant Reformation and were for this reason territorial churches that were deeply implicated in civic affairs from the start. In North America they formed regional and national federations that kept local congregations in contact with one another and that encouraged the formation of benevolent associations, Bible societies, and temperance unions. Evangelical churches emphasized the autonomy of the local congregation to a greater extent. Whereas the mainline churches participated in progressive social betterment programs during the first half of the twentieth century, evangelical churches focused more on individual piety.

During the 1980s, many evangelical Protestants became interested in political issues, especially in response to *Roe* v. *Wade* and earlier court rulings concerning school prayer. Under the leadership of Jerry Falwell, Pat Robertson, and others, evangelicals forged what was known as the Religious Right and through organizations such as the Moral Majority and the Christian Coalition became more actively involved in partisan politics. At the local level, many evangelicals nevertheless continued to focus on personal piety and were intensely involved in the activities of their local churches. Denominational affiliations often remained intact, but evangelical pastors also found that the growth of their own congregations was often associated with appeals other than denominational backgrounds.

Gary Rush illustrates some of these developments. He was raised as a Wesleyan Methodist, had attended several Baptist churches, and had taken courses at a Bible Institute. In the course of shopping for a church, his ties to any particular denomination diminished. Indeed he mentions several

13. In the 1991 General Social Survey, 91 percent of those who were in evangelical denominations at age sixteen continued to be affiliated with an evangelical denomination; 79 percent of those in a mainline Protestant denomination at age sixteen continued to be in a mainline denomination; and 85 percent of Catholics at age sixteen continued to be Catholics. Among those from mainline backgrounds, 15 percent became evangelicals, whereas among those from evangelical backgrounds only 7 percent became mainliners; among those from Catholic backgrounds, 10 percent became evangelicals and 4 percent became mainline Protestants.

times that denominations are not important and should be deemphasized. In their place he attaches great significance to the local church, letting it subsume almost all of his spiritual interests. In the background of his thinking, however, is an awareness of evangelicalism as a national movement. He recalls that he first became aware of this movement when it was popularized by Jimmy Carter, and he mentions Pat Robertson as a national leader he admires. Like many evangelicals, he is personally uninterested in politics, but he also believes that the nation is experiencing a moral crisis.

Before turning to a comparison of the civic activities of evangelicals, mainline Protestants, and Catholics, it will be helpful to understand some of the social characteristics of each group and how these characteristics have been changing. On some of these characteristics, evangelical and mainline Protestants are actually further apart in the 1990s than they were in the 1970s.

Evangelicals are much more likely to be African Americans than either mainline Protestants or Catholics are. For instance, the 1991 General Social Survey shows that 28 percent of evangelicals are African Americans, but only 8 percent of mainline Protestants and 9 percent of Catholics are evangelicals. This difference is largely attributable to the fact that African Americans overwhelmingly belong to Baptist denominations and Pentecostal churches. It nevertheless suggests the importance of considering possible differences in social characteristics between evangelicals who are white and evangelicals who are African American.

Among white evangelicals the most distinctive social change has been in educational achievement. Whereas only 11 percent in the 1974 General Social Survey had graduated from college, in 1991 the figure had risen to 17 percent. The other notable change was in the proportion of white evangelicals who described their political views as "conservative" or "extremely conservative"—from 16 percent in 1974 to 23 percent in 1991 (like other respondents, most described themselves as middle of the road or slightly conservative). Otherwise, white evangelicals showed few changes.

African American evangelicals differed dramatically from white evangelicals. Whereas white evangelicals improved markedly in the proportion who had graduated from college, African American evangelicals showed no change (5 percent were college graduates in 1991, 6 percent in 1974). A lack of change or worsening conditions were evident in several other measures as well. For instance, in 1991, 22 percent described their families of origin as "far below average" financially, virtually the same proportion

(21 percent) as had done so in 1974. In addition, fewer in 1991 described themselves as working full time (34 percent) than did so in 1974 (41 percent). In contrast, 23 percent said they were working only part time or were unemployed in 1991, up from 15 percent in 1974. And, despite the fact that 65 percent in both periods said they had two or more children, the proportion who were currently married dropped from 53 percent in 1974 to 31 percent in 1991. Not surprisingly, the vast majority of African American evangelicals agreed that "the lot of the average person is getting worse," and this proportion was somewhat higher in 1991 (83 percent) than it had been in 1974 (76 percent).

Mainline Protestants are overwhelmingly white, but they differ in several important respects even from white evangelicals. On education, for instance, mainline Protestants were considerably more likely than white evangelicals to have earned college degrees by 1974 (18 percent and 11 percent), and this difference was still evident in 1991 (26 percent and 17 percent). Whereas white evangelicals had become more politically conservative, mainline Protestants showed no change (18 percent in both surveys said they were conservative or extremely conservative). Mainline Protestants were also slightly older (an average age of fifty) than evangelicals (an average of forty-six). And mainline Protestants were somewhat less likely than evangelicals to attend church regularly (40 percent of mainline Protestants, 50 percent of evangelicals), but in neither group had this proportion changed significantly between 1974 and 1991.

Catholics fall between mainline Protestants and evangelicals on many social characteristics, according to these surveys. In terms of higher education, they were similar to evangelicals in 1974 (11 percent had college degrees), but by 1991 had improved more than evangelicals (20 percent of Catholics had college degrees, 17 percent of evangelicals). They were *least* likely to describe themselves as political conservatives, and this proportion did not change significantly (11 percent and 12 percent, respectively). Although Catholics were predominately white (like mainline Protestants), the impact of immigration was evident in the fact that the proportion who described their race as "other" rose from less than 1 percent in 1974 to 5 percent in 1991 (although comparable data were not gathered on Hispanic origin, some estimates suggest that as many as a quarter of American Catholics may now be Hispanic). Catholics were younger on average than Protestants (an average age of forty-four in 1991). They were also more likely to attend religious services regularly (57 percent in 1974 and 54 percent in 1991).

Further detail on the religious characteristics of evangelicals, mainline Protestants, and Catholics is available in other surveys. Although the three groups do not differ substantially in the percentages who are members of particular congregations, evangelicals are much more likely than mainline Protestants (who are in turn more likely than Catholics) to belong to *small* congregations, and they are the most likely to say their close friends belong to the same congregation. By substantial margins, evangelicals were more likely than the others to say that the Bible should be taken literally (more than half did, only one-fifth of the others). Evangelicals were also the most likely to attend Sunday school classes and participate in Bible study groups.[14]

Membership in Associations

The question of greatest interest is whether the level of civic engagement differs among evangelicals, mainline Protestants, and Catholics. One way of answering this question is simply to compare how likely members of each group are to be a member of any nonreligious voluntary association. With Catholics as a comparison group (and controlling for differences in education and differences between 1974 and 1991), the General Social Survey data show that the odds of being a member of any such organization if one is an evangelical are approximately 20 percent lower than if one is a Catholic. If one is a mainline Protestant, these odds are about 30 percent higher than they are if one is a Catholic.[15]

14. These results are obtained from my Economic Values Survey, a 1992 survey of approximately 2,000 nationally representative men and women who were working full or part time (the questions are included in the appendix of Wuthnow (1994). Evangelical and mainline Protestants were categorized in the same way as in the General Social Surveys. There were 525 evangelical Protestants, 569 mainline Protestants, and 543 Catholics. The percentages of each (respectively) who had the following characteristics were as follows: members of congregations with fewer than 200 members, 39, 27, and 7; attend services every week, 44, 34, 42; regularly attend Sunday school classes, 35, 20, 6; believe that the Bible should be taken literally, word for word, 55, 22, 21; currently participate in a Bible study or fellowship group, 31, 21, 13; have five or more close friends in their congregation, 42, 35, 39.

15. Results are from logit regression models in which being or not being a member of any nonreligious voluntary organization is the dependent variable, type of religion is the independent variable (with Catholics as the comparison category), and year and education as control variables. The odds-ratio for evangelicals is .809; for mainline Protestants it is 1.299 (both significant at or beyond the .01 level of probability).

A better answer comes from considering the effect of church attendance on civic engagement within the different religious communities. As mentioned previously, the odds of being a member of a nonreligious group are about 20 percent higher among regular church attenders than among infrequent attenders. We can now see whether this relationship is stronger or weaker in certain contexts (see Table 9-2).

Among all evangelicals, church attendance was *not* significantly associated with being a member of some other civic group in either 1974 or 1991. The same lack of a relationship was evident when only white evangelicals were examined. Among black evangelicals, there had been a relationship in 1974, but this relationship had virtually disappeared by 1991.

Mainline Protestants showed a consistent and strong relationship between church attendance and membership in other civic organizations both in 1974 and in 1991. In both surveys, the odds of being a member of a civic organization were almost 50 percent greater among those who attended church regularly than among those who did not attend regularly.

Catholics fell in between. In both years, regular attenders were about 20 percent more likely than less frequent attenders to be members of some other civic organization. But further analysis revealed that this effect was present only for women. Indeed, women who attended religious services regularly were about 40 percent more likely than women who attended less regularly to be members of civic organizations, whereas there was no significant difference among men who did or did not attend regularly.

Our interview with Gary Rush provides some insight into the lack of external civic involvement among evangelicals. His Sundays and evenings are taken up with church activities to the point that he has little time to be involved in anything outside the church. More important, he regards the church as a place unlike any other. Almost all of his close friends belong to the church, and he values the fellowship with them as a kind of utopian experience. They model "the love of Jesus," making decisions by consensus and going out of their way to avoid personal conflicts. In comparison, Gary dislikes the abrasive encounters he sometimes has in other contexts. His view of the wider community also influences how he responds to it. He does not aggressively proselytize his neighbors, but he believes the community can only be served one person at a time. Thus he prefers to work with the few individuals who come to the church seeking help, rather than cooperating with other organizations, because he can tailor his responses to the particular needs of these individuals.

Table 9-2. *Odds-Ratios for the Effect of Church Attendance on Membership in Any Nonreligious Group*[a]

Sample	Evangelical Protestants	Mainline Protestants	Catholics
Controlling for education			
All respondents			
1974	1.118	1.475***	1.194
1991	1.017	1.481***	1.285*
White respondents			
1974	1.065	1.506***	1.160
1991	1.019	1.463**	1.347**
Black respondents			
1974	1.357	...	...
1991	1.100	...	...
Controlling for education and sex			
All respondents			
1974	1.161	1.485****	1.254**
1991	1.058	1.505***	1.337**

Source: General Social Surveys, 1974 and 1991.

a. Logit regression models for a membership in any of fifteen nonreligious organizations by church attendance, controlling for education; significance calculated using the Wald test.

*$p < .10$ percent; **$p < .05$ percent; ***$p < .01$ percent; ****$p < .001$ percent.

People like Gary Rush are subject to several forces that keep their voluntary involvement within the bounds of their own religious community. One is that their churches expect a great deal more of them. In one national survey, for example, evangelicals who attended church regularly were more than six times as likely as evangelicals who did not attend regularly to be involved in doing volunteer work for their church exclusively; in comparison, mainline Protestants who attended regularly were only about twice as likely as those who did not attend regularly to be involved in this way.[16] A related factor is that evangelical churches offer more internal activities in which to be involved. For instance, they are more likely to have active

16. The results in this paragraph are from my Economic Values Survey. Exclusive volunteering at church was operationalized as saying yes to a question asking about having "done volunteer work at your church" in the past year and saying no to a question asking about having "donated time to a volunteer organization." The odds ratio from a logit regression analysis relating this variable to church attendance was 6.459 among evangelical Protestants, 2.550 among mainline Protestants, and 2.357 among Catholics.

adult Sunday school programs and small group ministries, and their members are more likely to have friends within the church. Of course many evangelical congregations in the past have been limited by their small memberships, thus demanding more of their members but being able to offer fewer programs. But as evangelical churches have grown larger, they appear to be even more capable of dominating their members' activities. In the study cited in note 16, for instance, evangelicals who regularly attended churches of more than 200 members were almost five times as likely as those who did not attend regularly to be exclusively involved in church volunteering, whereas members of evangelical churches with fewer than 200 members were only about three times as likely to volunteer.[17] Finally, many evangelicals attend churches that emphasize separation from "the world" or distinctive beliefs that may discourage them from mingling with outsiders. The impact of these beliefs can be seen in the same study. Among biblical literalists there was a significantly stronger relationship between church attendance and exclusive volunteering for church activities than there was among people who rejected biblical literalism.[18] The behavior of Gary Rush thus appears to be typical of many evangelicals.

In contrast, Ed Nelson is encouraged by his attendance at a mainline Protestant church to become involved in other community organizations, such as Rotary and the YMCA board. Indeed, the General Social Survey data suggest that he is quite typical in this respect. When specific *kinds* of civic organizations were examined, those that showed the strongest relationships with church attendance among mainline Protestants were service groups, youth organizations, and school service groups.

The finding that attendance among Catholics reinforced civic engagement only among women was unanticipated. Further examination of the data suggests a possible explanation. When specific kinds of civic groups were examined separately, church attendance among Catholic women was positively associated only with school service groups, youth groups, and "literary, art, discussion, or study groups."[19] Also, the relationship between

17. The respective odds ratios were 4.763 and 3.122.

18. Among all Protestants, logit regression models for exclusive church volunteering as the dependent variable, church attendance as the independent variable, with evangelical and mainline controlled, yielded an odds ratio of 4.195 among biblical literalists and 2.826 among nonliteralists.

19. Among Catholic women, logit regression models (with year and education controlled) yield odds-ratios of 2.184 for the relationship between church attendance and membership in a youth group, 1.941 for membership in a school service group, and 1.968 for membership in a literary-discussion group (all significant at or beyond the .01 level).

membership in a civic group and church attendance was stronger for married Catholic women than for single Catholic women and for women who have children.[20] These results are consistent with what is known about child-rearing practices in many traditional Catholic families: mothers are more likely to attend church than fathers and to take responsibility for the religious upbringing of children. By implication, these mothers may also be more active in school, youth, or study groups that benefit their children.

A young woman we talked to in Massachusetts illustrated these findings as she talked about her parents. Both were Irish and devoutly Catholic. Her father usually went to Mass but worked long hours supporting his wife and four children. Her mother valued church and family above everything else, often combining the two. She served on a committee that cleaned the church each week, often enlisting the children to help, and she volunteered regularly at the parochial school where the children attended. She also belonged to a women's guild at the church and through it met women with whom she sometimes played cards or went bowling. Beyond these activities and her relationships with her extended family, she felt little need to join other clubs.

Of course being a member of a church organization is only one kind of civic engagement. That it is important is evident, nevertheless, in the research that Putnam and others have done, showing that such memberships are positively related to trust, voting, and other measures of community involvement. Most people who hold such memberships, surveys show, also say they give time to these organizations, and other studies show that volunteering and philanthropy are much more common among people who belong to such organizations than among people who do not belong. It is worth noting, too, that the differences observed here between evangelicals and mainline Protestants also pertain to some of these other activities. For instance, mainline Protestants are more likely than evangelicals to say they are currently involved in charity or social service activities, to have donated time in the past year to a voluntary organization, and to have worked on a community service project.

The differences between evangelicals and mainline Protestants should not be exaggerated. On a church-by-church basis, many mainline Protes-

20. Logit regression models (with year and education controlled) for the likelihood of being a member of any nonreligious civic organization by church attendance yielded odds-ratios of 1.444 among married Catholic women and 1.406 among Catholic women with children; the comparable odds-ratios for never-married Catholic women and Catholic women without children were not significant.

tant congregations are vibrant, while many evangelical congregations are experiencing stagnation. The shift from one state to the other has nevertheless been sufficiently pronounced to have received widespread attention. Some observers argue that evangelical churches will continue to grow because they offer more distinctive beliefs and require greater commitment. Others argue that evangelicalism has adapted better to a commercial, entrepreneurial culture, whereas mainline denominations hark too strongly to the national traditions from which they originated.

What has not been sufficiently emphasized is the fact that mainline Protestant churches encourage civic engagement in the wider community, whereas evangelical churches apparently do not. This is not to suggest that evangelical churches are ineffective at generating social capital. Indeed, they do better than mainline churches in getting members to attend services, creating friendships among these members, and mobilizing them for Bible studies and other church meetings. But the social capital they generate is more likely to be kept within their own organizations.

To the extent that social capital is a way of creating the volunteer labor to get important tasks done, evangelical churches may be growing because they do a better job of guarding their own social capital. But to the extent that they grow, they may also contribute to the depletion of the society's wider stock of social capital.

Civic Skills

Apart from membership itself, participation in civic organizations is often thought to be beneficial to the functioning of American democracy because it generates civic skills. People learn how to work together on committees, lead meetings, and serve as officers; they may also develop networks or be encouraged to write news stories or contact public officials. Many of these skills are transferable, meaning that they can perhaps be learned in churches and then used in other settings as well. Churches may generate such skills, perhaps especially among Protestants, and perhaps with greater benefit to lower-income people than is often the case in other civic organizations.[21]

Data from the 1987 General Social Survey permit an examination of the ways in which participation in the religious traditions we have been

21. Verba, Schlozman, and Brady (1995).

considering may facilitate the attainment of civic skills. In addition to being asked whether they belonged to any of the voluntary associations included in other General Social Surveys, this study asked respondents whether they had "ever done any active work" for each organization, such as "been a leader, helped organize a meeting, been an officer, or given time or money." One measure of civic skill, therefore, is whether a person said he or she had been active in these ways in *any* of the organizations listed. To determine whether religious participation mobilizes any of these activities, we again compared the civic activities of regular church attenders with those of infrequent church attenders. To ensure that the relationships were not attributable to other differences, we controlled for level of education, race, and the total number of organizations in which people claimed to be members (see Table 9-3).

Among evangelicals, church attendance was *not* statistically related to a greater likelihood of being active in at least one of the fifteen nonreligious organizations listed. Among mainline Protestants, regular church attenders were about 28 percent more likely to have done active work in nonreligious organizations than irregular attenders. And among Catholics, there was a statistically significant relationship about like that among mainline Protestants. In other words, the pattern was somewhat similar to that seen previously for memberships. In contrast, active work in church-affiliated groups was significantly more likely among regular attenders than among irregular attenders in evangelical churches, just as it was in mainline Protestant and Catholic churches.

The study also permitted comparisons of the likelihood of respondents having engaged in particular activities. These activities were not asked about for each kind of group, thus making it impossible to determine whether they took place in religious or nonreligious settings. Because the activities fostered transferable skills, though, it is interesting to know that they took place in many contexts. The particular activities asked about included: serving on committees, serving as an officer, attending conferences or workshops, writing to newspapers or magazines for the organization, contacting government officials on behalf of the organization, and giving money in addition to regular dues.

Among evangelicals, regular church attenders were significantly more likely than irregular attenders to have engaged in four of these activities: serving on committees, serving as an officer, attending conferences or workshops, and giving money; regular church attenders were no more likely to have written to newspapers or contacted government officials.

Table 9-3. *Odds-Ratios for the Effect of Church Attendance on the Development of Civic Skills*[a]

Civic activity	Evangelical Protestants	Mainline Protestants	Catholics
Did active work in any nonreligious group	1.021	1.278*	1.336
Did active work in a church-affiliated group	2.951****	2.642****	4.349****
Served on committees	1.422****	2.126****	1.281**
Served as an officer	1.517****	1.855****	.989
Attended conferences or workshops	1.368****	1.460***	1.112
Wrote to newspapers or magazines for the organization	1.003	1.350*	1.116
Contacted government officials on behalf of the organization	.812	1.151	.771
Gave money in addition to regular dues	1.402****	1.665****	1.049

Source: General Social Survey, 1997.

a. Logit regression models for each dependent variable by church attendance, controlling for education, race, and total memberships; significance calculated using the Wald test.

*$p < .10$ percent; **$p < .05$ percent; ***$p < .01$ percent; ****$p < .001$ percent.

Among mainline Protestants, similar results were evident, with two exceptions: there was also a marginally significant relationship between church attendance and having written to newspapers, and all of the other relationships were *stronger* than they were among evangelicals. Among Catholics, attendance was largely unrelated to these specific activities: only serving on committees was significantly more likely among regular attenders than among irregular attenders.

These results are consistent with Verba et al.'s conclusions about the differences between Protestants and Catholics in generating civic skills. They interpret the differences by suggesting that Protestants are more likely to be drawn into lay-led activities, whereas Catholics may attend large parishes in which there is little lay activity other than participating in weekly Mass. These results are also consistent with the previous discussion about differences between evangelicals and mainline Protestants. They qualify that discussion by showing that evangelicals do learn certain skills, such as working together on committees and serving as officers. These are transferable skills. The only problem is that evangelicals are less likely to hold memberships in nonreligious organizations to which they can transfer these skills.

Volunteering

The best data with which to assess the impact of religious involvement on volunteering is the 1994 Giving and Volunteering Survey, a nationally representative study conducted among approximately 1,500 respondents by the Gallup Organization for Independent Sector.[22] The advantage of this study is that it asks respondents about volunteering for specific kinds of organizations. Although some kinds of organizations elicit too few responses for separate analysis, those that can be examined specifically include the following:

Religious organizations: Religion-related, spiritual development organizations (including churches, synagogues, monasteries, convents, seminaries, etc., but not church-affiliated schools that offer broad educational curricula, nursing homes, Catholic Charities, Jewish federations, etc.).

Public/society benefit organizations: Civil rights, community and social action, and advocacy groups (includes those that deal with minority and women's equity issues); community improvement and community capacity planning committees; science, technology, and technical assistance programs; volunteer organizations; philanthropic and charitable organizations such as Rotary, Kiwanis, etc.; consumers' organizations, advocacy organizations such as antinuclear groups, antipoverty boards, etc.

Human services organizations: Day care centers; foster care services; family counseling centers; consumer protection agencies; legal aid; crime and delinquency prevention programs; homelessness agencies; employment/jobs programs; food assistance programs; housing, shelter services; public safety, emergency preparedness, and relief efforts; recreation, sports, athletics; Red Cross, YMCA, and other similar multiservice organizations such as United Way, Catholic Charities, Protestant welfare agencies, United Jewish Appeal, etc.

22. See Hodgkinson et al. (1995).

Health (including mental health) organizations: General and rehabilitation organizations, including those that provide services for and assistance with mental health, mental retardation, and the developmentally disabled; substance abuse programs; disease research and public education programs; hospitals, nursing homes, hospices, clinics, crisis counseling centers, hotlines, etc.; fund drives or private health associations such as the American Heart Association, American Cancer Society, March of Dimes, etc.

Educational/instructional organizations (formal and informal): Elementary and secondary schools or colleges (public or private, which may be church-affiliated or nonsectarian); libraries; research and educational institutions; adult education programs; informational education programs; fund drives for educational associations.

Youth development organizations: Boy and Girl Scouts; Camp Fire groups; 4-H clubs; youth groups with religious affiliations such as the Catholic Youth Organization, Little League, and other athletic groups engaged in youth development.

Arts, culture, and humanities groups: Architecture, design, performing arts groups; cultural/ethnic awareness groups; historical preservation groups; humanistic societies; museums; operas; symphony orchestras; photography groups; theaters; public television and radio.

Informal/independent assistance: Helping neighbors, friends, or organizations on an ad hoc basis; spending time caring for elderly persons or babysitting the children of a friend, but not as part of an organized group or for pay (this excludes helping relatives for no pay).

Not surprisingly, there is a strong relationship between church attendance and volunteering for religious organizations, and this relationship is especially strong for evangelicals. Evangelicals who attended church regularly were almost four times as likely as irregular attenders to have volunteered within the previous year for a religious organization; in comparison, regularly attending mainline Protestants were about three times as likely as irregular attenders to have done so, and Catholics were between two and three times as likely to have done so (see Table 9-4).

Volunteering for nonreligious activities tends to follow the same pattern as seen previously for membership in civic associations. Among evangelicals, the only relationship that reached a marginal level of statistical significance was that between church attendance and youth development activities. In contrast, mainline Protestants showed significant relationships between church attendance and the following kinds of volunteering: public/society benefit, health, education, the arts, and informal volunteer-

Table 9-4. *Odds-Ratios for the Effect of Church Attendance on Volunteering*[a]

Type of volunteer activity	Evangelical Protestants	Mainline Protestants	Catholics
Religion-related	3.983****	3,084****	2.656****
Public or society benefit	1.064	1.677***	1.089
Human services	1.358	1.220	1.126
Health	1.063	1.405**	1.294*
Education	1.164	1.476***	1.478****
Youth development	1.356*	1.206	1.071
Arts	1.295	1.520	.921
Informal or alone	1.218	1.329**	1.441**

Source: Hodgkinson (1995), 1994 Giving and Volunteering Survey.

a. Logit regression models for the likelihood of having volunteered in each area within the past year by church attendance, controlling for education; significance calculated using the Wald test.

*$p < .10$ percent; **$p < .05$ percent; ***$p < .01$ percent; ****$p < .001$ percent.

ing. In each instance, the odds of regular church attenders volunteering were between 30 and 60 percent higher than the odds of irregular church attenders volunteering. Among Catholics only two kinds of volunteering were significantly related to church attendance: volunteering for education-related activities and for informal activities (health activity was marginally related).

It is worth noting that the presence of statistical relationships between church attendance and volunteering does not necessarily mean that the rate of volunteering was always higher among mainline Protestants than among evangelicals (especially when differences in education and race are taken into account). Nevertheless, it is the case that mainline Protestants were significantly more likely than evangelicals to do volunteer work in all of the following areas: public/society benefit, human services, education, and the environment, as well as informal volunteering. Because evangelical volunteering is concentrated to a greater degree within religious organizations themselves, it is also worth noting the kinds of specific activities of which this volunteering was composed. According to a follow-up question in the survey, nearly 60 percent of it was concerned with maintaining the religious life of the congregation itself, such as teaching Sunday school, assisting the pastor, singing in the choir, serving as a deacon, or ushering at worship services.

These results suggest the need for caution in interpreting general statements, such as those that often appear in the media or in religious settings, about the positive role of religion in mobilizing volunteer efforts. Much of this volunteering, especially among evangelicals, was concentrated within congregations themselves and devoted to the maintenance of those congregations. As for wider connections between church attendance and volunteering in other kinds of activities or agencies, mainline Protestants (followed by Catholics) were considerably more likely to mobilize such links than were evangelicals. Of course the role of maintaining religious organizations themselves should not be minimized. We shall want to consider in a later section what these organizations do and how they relate directly to other organizations.

Political Participation

A number of political participation measures were included in the 1987 General Social Survey. The items covered standard measures such as voting, but also made it possible to compare participation in local activities with that in national politics and to see what people did besides show up at the polls. The specific questions were: whether respondents had voted in the two previous presidential elections (1980 and 1984), whether they voted regularly in local elections, whether they had "ever worked with others in this community to try to solve some community problems," whether they had "ever taken part in forming a new group or a new organization to try to solve some community problems," whether during elections they had ever tried "to show people why they should vote for one of the parties or candidates," whether they had "done work for one of the parties or candidates," whether they had "attended any political meetings or rallies" in the previous three or four years, whether they had ever "personally gone to see, or spoken to, or written to some member of local government or some other person of influence in the community about some needs or problems," and whether they had contacted or written to "representatives or governmental officials outside of the local community."

Of the ten measures of political participation, among evangelicals there was a significant relationship between church attendance and four of the measures (see Table 9-5). These were having voted in the two presidential elections, having voted regularly in local elections, and having worked to solve local community problems. Among mainline Protestants the pat-

Table 9-5. *Odds-Ratios for the Effect of Church Attendance on Political Activity*[a]

Political activity	Evangelical Protestants	Mainline Protestants	Catholics
Voted in 1980 election	1.346****	1.595****	1.826****
Voted in 1984 election	1.294****	1.568****	1.914****
Almost always vote in local elections	1.386****	1.406****	2.123****
Worked with others to solve community problems	1.224****	1.268**	1.106
Took part in forming a new group	1.154	1.148	1.247
Contacted officials outside local community	1.030	1.175	1.161
Contacted local officials	.927	1.051	1.259**
Attended political meetings or rallies	1.130	1.127	1.007
Worked for parties or candidates in elections	1.049	1.211*	1.087
Tried to show people why they should vote for one party or candidate	1.059	1.022	1.083

Source: General Social Survey, 1987.

a. Logit regression models for each dependent variable by church attendance, controlling for education and race; significance calculated using the Wald test.

*$p < .10$ percent; ***$p < .05$ percent; ***$p < .01$ percent; ****$p < .001$ percent.

tern was virtually identical. Regular attenders were more likely than irregular attenders to have voted in presidential and local elections and to have worked on community problems; they were also marginally more likely to have worked for parties or candidates. Among Catholics, too, the results were similar. Attendance was significantly related to having voted in presidential and local elections; it was not associated with having worked on community problems, but it was related to having contacted local officials.

These results, then, deviate in several important respects from those in previous sections. They can be interpreted to indicate that evangelicals are just as likely as mainline Protestants or Catholics to be mobilized by their religious involvement to participate in politics. Or they can be interpreted to say that mainline Protestants are no more likely to exhibit a relationship between church attendance and political participation than evangelicals. In either case, the differences in civic engagement seen in previous sections are not evident here. These results also suggest an important qualification to the literature that has stressed the political mobilization of conservative Christians. To the extent that one would expect this mobilization to be more characteristic of evangelicals than of mainline Protestants, it does not appear to be particularly profound. To be sure, evangelicals are more likely to register and to vote than they did before the early 1970s, and this propensity is partly because their church participation encourages them to vote and partly because more of them have social characteristics that are associated with voting (such as higher education or living in the suburbs). But these data show no support for the idea that church attendance among evangelicals has also mobilized them to attend political rallies, lobby, and work to sway elections. Of course some of those activities became more pronounced after 1987, especially with the presidential candidacy of Pat Robertson in 1988 and the subsequent formation of the Christian Coalition. But the Moral Majority, Religious Roundtable, and other conservative Christian movements that emerged between 1978 and 1980 appear in retrospect to have mobilized more attention in the media than they did energy among evangelical church members. This conclusion, it is worth noting, is also supported by the fact that none of the other studies—in which specific questions were asked about membership in, active work for, or volunteering for political groups—showed any relationship between church attendance and political activity among evangelicals.

Changing Modes of Organization

Thus far we have concentrated on the statistical relationships between participation in churches and other kinds of civic involvement. In such relationships the actual connections generally remain unspecified. Individuals presumably make friends, hear about opportunities, and learn transferable skills when they attend churches, and this "social capital" then permits them to participate more easily in other organizations. But the connections may also be structured more formally.

In our interviews we found many people whose civic involvement had been facilitated in strictly informal ways by their participation in churches. For example, one woman recalled going to the Presbyterian church with her husband when they first moved to their suburban home near Sacramento, meeting some other women, and through them becoming involved in the PTA. Another woman talked about becoming active in an environmental organization; it was completely separate from the Methodist church she often attended, but she said her church's teachings about stewardship had motivated her involvement: "While you're here in this life," she said, "it's nice if you try to contribute as much as you as a human being can to the betterment of all mankind to make it a little bit better place to be." Some of these activities are ones that would be missed in surveys about volunteering. For instance, a chiropractor who attends a Mennonite church says he often charges patients less than the insurance companies would permit him to charge. He perceives this as a kind of "statement" that reflects his church's stance against greed and materialism.[23]

Beyond these informal connections, a number of people took part in activities wholly or largely contained within their congregations that were meant to be of benefit to the wider community. These were generally committees such as Gary Rush's "benevolence committee." At an evangelical church in New Jersey, for instance, a lay leader told us she was a member of a committee that supervised the "Sunshine Fund." This was a special collection that the congregation took up each Sunday to purchase food and clothing for people in need who might come to the pastor. She said there was also a committee that raised support for missionaries in other countries. She counted this as a way that the church helped the poor.

A national study of congregations suggests that charitable activities performed formally or informally within local churches are quite common.[24] For instance, 50 percent of congregation officials reported that they offered meal services or operated food kitchens, 39 percent provided shelter for the homeless, 30 percent operated programs for abused women, 28 percent had programs to prevent teen pregnancy, and 20 percent provided tutoring or literacy programs.

---

23. A national survey I conducted in 1989 (Values Survey, discussed in Wuthnow [1991]) showed that church attendance also motivated certain kinds of individual volunteering. Specifically, with education, age, and gender controlled for, logit regression models showed that those who attended church at least several times a month were 1.167 times more likely than those who attended less often to have visited someone in the hospital in the previous year; 1.166 times more likely to have taken care of an elderly relative in their home; and 1.179 times more likely to have taken care of someone who was very sick; there were no significant relationships, however, between church attendance and loaning money to someone, helping someone through a personal crisis, or giving money to a beggar.

24. Hodgkinson and Weitzman (1993).

In addition, we found examples of churches teaming up with other religious organizations in order to mobilize their members more effectively for civic activities. Eastside Ministries in Cleveland is an example. It is a coalition of six congregations (United Church of Christ, Episcopal, Methodist, Roman Catholic, and two Lutheran), all composed mainly of white Anglos, that was initiated in the 1980s to provide social services in a low-income section of the city that is largely Hispanic. Its annual budget is approximately $20,000 (not counting the salary of its full-time coordinator, which is paid by one of the churches), most of which comes from individual donations and from a grant from one of the sponsoring congregation's denominational headquarters. Approximately 200 volunteers help run its regular programs, including a youth center, a tutoring program in local schools, and a used-clothing store.

Nationally, 39 percent of congregation officials reported in 1993 that their church participated in, supported, or was affiliated with programs involving other organizations for providing meals to needy families; 36 percent were involved in such coalitions to provide shelter to homeless people; 31 percent were in cooperative arrangements to prevent alcohol and drug abuse; and 16 percent had cooperative arrangements to provide tutoring.[25]

Then there were a number of temporary alliances between churches and secular nonprofit agencies.[26] In East Harlem a small citizens' advocacy group worked with local churches to hold public meetings to educate young people in the community about police brutality, ways of gaining access to legal assistance, and how to help mobilize voters during elections. In Allentown, Pennsylvania, a woman who became concerned about caring for people with AIDS received temporary office space free of charge in a church office building for a few months before she was able to organize a separate nonprofit agency with space of its own. Other examples include church committees working with neighborhood associations or block-watch efforts, churches providing meeting space for independently sponsored symposiums on teen violence, and churches adopting parks for clean-up projects or remodeling a battered women's shelter.

Finally, we found an increasing variety of complex, formal partnerships between religious and nonreligious organizations. Among the most common are partnerships with community development corporations (CDCs).

25. Ibid. (pp. 31–33).
26. These and the following examples are from my Civic Involvement Project; see Wuthnow (1998).

For instance, a CDC in inner-city Philadelphia was a nonprofit organization that coordinated the efforts of a number of other agencies in order to provide low-income housing. One of these agencies was a financial accountability committee headed by representatives of twelve suburban congregations, each of which contributed money to the project, and four of which received matching funds from their denominations for the effort. This committee reported back to the individual churches; its members also worked closely with the central nonprofit operations committee in charge of getting the work done. This committee worked with officials from the municipal government, which donated the land; with representatives from HUD in Washington and from its state-level counterpart in Harrisburg; with a nonprofit organization set up by local banks to handle the day-to-day financing; and with a nonprofit organization established by local contractors who did the actual construction work at cost. The representative from one of the local churches told us that the $1 million his denomination had contributed was a small part of the $60 million the project was spending in its first phase alone; yet this contribution gave the congregation a stake in the wider community, and he personally had significantly extended his network of first-hand contacts in the community.

Looking Ahead

None of the research discussed here suggests that religion has a negative effect on civic engagement. Despite their apparent emphasis on their own congregations, evangelical religious involvement does not discourage participation in other voluntary associations; with the exception of voting, it just does not encourage it. Evidence that religious involvement among Catholics encourages civic participation is also limited, but there is some evidence that it does. The clearest relationships between religious involvement and civic engagement are among mainline Protestants. The fact that mainline Protestant churches have declined in recent decades, therefore, means that civic engagement is probably not as strong as it would have been if these churches had not declined.

More than the possibility of decline (or growth) in civic engagement, however, the ways in which American religion may influence the character of civic engagement in the future are important to consider. Evangelicals, mainline Protestants, and Catholics all practice well-institutionalized forms of religious expression in the United States, and they are likely to remain important to the well-being of civil society. Nevertheless, these religious communities are also subject to the social forces that influence their members and that bear on their established modes of organization. Each one will refract these social forces in a distinctive way.

Evangelical Protestants are perhaps in the strongest position to resist broader social influences, and yet the success of their churches has in many ways come at the price of cultural accommodation. Unlike their predecessors at the end of the nineteenth century, most evangelicals live in suburbs (rather than on farms or in small towns), and a growing proportion of them have some higher education. Their concerns about work, layoffs, career changes, burnout, and conflicts between work and family life are indistinguishable from those of mainline Protestants and Catholics. More of them are remaining single, experiencing divorce, or postponing marriage and child-rearing. The large minority of evangelicals who attend African American churches are also especially subject to racial discrimination and the continuing problems of poverty and unemployment. In all these ways, evangelicals face the same complexity and porousness that influences the American population in general.

The response from evangelicals has been to face these challenges by devoting large shares of time and energy to their local congregations. These congregations have benefited as a result, growing in size, expanding into new locations, and enlarging their share of the churched population. Higher levels of education among their members and a focus on family issues has helped to enlarge the resources needed to administer attractive church programs. But studies of better-educated evangelicals also show that they have become more like nonevangelicals in their willingness to engage in "cognitive bargaining" with the wider society. To the extent that particular interpretations of the Bible have helped to erect sectarian defenses between them and the wider society, the erosion of these "distinctives" also means that evangelicals may find it harder in the future to shield themselves from cultural influences.

The impact of broader social influences on evangelical civic engagement is clearly a matter of speculation, but the evidence considered here suggests the following, perhaps paradoxical, possibilities. On the one hand, the accommodation of evangelicals to the wider culture will probably result in their civic participation becoming more like that of mainline Protestants and Catholics—that is, more dispersed among social agencies than concentrated in churches themselves. On the other hand, this same accommodation may result in slower growth among evangelical churches and more sporadic connections to other civic organizations. Declining growth rates have already been observed in some evangelical fellowships (for example, among Baptist and Assembly of God churches). Many evangelical churches are also facing hard times financially. In the short term, the response of clergy to these developments may be to place greater emphasis on loyalties to the congregation. In the longer term, such loyalties may diminish relative to other activities that are of greater interest to evangelical families. But evangelical families will also have to work around busy schedules, volunteering for a few hours here and there, rather than devoting themselves fully to an organization over a long period of time. Insofar as they have national leaders to play symbolic roles in the political arena, they may also limit their political participation to voting or giving vocal support to a few selected issues, rather than becoming seriously involved in grass-roots political movements.

The recent histories of the Moral Majority, Christian Coalition, and other religiously conservative political interest groups suggest the ambiguities of evangelical civic involvement. These groups have capitalized on evangelicals' sense that something is wrong with mainstream culture. Evangelicals frequently express high levels of concern about materialism, the messages conveyed by the entertainment industry, and specific topics such as abortion, pornography, and homosexuality. Yet the percentage of evangelicals who are actively involved in conservative interest groups has remained quite small. Most are more committed to their churches than to larger political interest groups. And, although they try to distance themselves from the wider culture, they seldom do so with much success.

The likelihood of cultural accommodation is also enhanced by the fact that evangelical Protestants are compelled by their own beliefs to draw connections between themselves and the outside world. Many of the ones we talked to expressed ambivalence about the fact that their churches seemed to be doing so little in the wider community. An African American woman who is a divorced mother of two put it well as she talked about the Baptist church she attends. "It's like a support system," she said, referring to the group for single parents in which she participates. But she said the church was also like a "club" that focused too much of its energies on its own members. "Doctors should be out there healing patients," she observed in response to a question about churches helping the poor, "not just helping other members of their club."

Mainline Protestants refract social forces through a lens of declining loyalties to particular denominations, some emphasis on the local experience of "community" that attracts evangelicals, and diminishing resources for the broad social programs they were able to sponsor a few decades ago. The fact that attendance at mainline churches continues to facilitate involvement in a wide variety of civic and voluntary organizations poses an encouraging scenario for the future of civic engagement. At least critics who charge that mainline Protestantism has become too privatized to have any discernible consequences appear to be wrong; only the declining number of mainline Protestants gives cause for a pessimistic assessment of the future of civic engagement.

But mainline Protestants are exposed to all the social forces that undermine long-term memberships in hierarchical civic organizations and that encourage more intentional, short-term forms of involvement. A person like Ed Nelson who stays involved in Rotary for decades as a way of fulfilling his responsibilities as a Christian citizen may become rarer, while those who spend an hour helping with Habitat for Humanity, who do no volunteer work at the peak of their professional careers, and who then participate in volunteer activities as retirees may be more typical. In addition, mainline Protestants are adapting to a broader institutional environment that consists of the many nonprofit organizations that came into being in the second half of the twentieth century, often with strong backing from Protestant clergy and laity. Mainline churches are likely to work increasingly with these secular agencies, forming short-term partnerships, rather than encouraging members to join traditional civic groups on their own.

In the past, mainline Protestant churches were often able to inspire civic engagement by locating their buildings near the town square and attracting prominent citizens who were often predisposed to take part in civic activities anyway. People like Ed Nelson could become involved in Rotary and the YMCA mostly through the people they met at church. But mainline churches have had to work harder when they were located in cities and suburbs where their memberships were more geographically dispersed. In case after case, we found that mainline members who were involved in outside civic activities had also been a part of deliberate efforts within the church to cultivate those connections. One woman had served on her church's "Church and Society" committee for several years before she initiated a violence-prevention program in the community. Another woman went from serving as director of her church's Christian-education committee to serving on a learning task force in the local schools. Others had been sent to work in low-income neighborhoods when they were teenagers involved in the church youth group or had helped with a food distribution program in the church basement. These examples show that the health of church programs themselves is an important factor in thinking about how civic engagement may be mobilized in the future. As many mainline churches shrink in membership and experience financial difficulties, it is unclear whether they will be able to do as effective a job in nurturing other civic activities as they did in the past. If anything, they are likely to depend increasingly on coalitions with secular and faith-based nonprofit agencies in their communities, and on the fact that some mainline churches (especially in the suburbs) have grown and remained prosperous, even while others have ceased functioning entirely.

The research presented here is least satisfactory in suggesting scenarios for the future of civic engagement among Catholics. In part, this is because Catholics are more diverse than either mainline Protestants or evangelicals and, to this extent are likely simply to mirror the wider population. Critics who charge that Catholicism has accommodated to the dominant Protestant culture of the United States by encouraging privatized convictions appear to be correct insofar as attendance at Catholic churches does not encourage civic participation to the same extent as attendance at mainline Protestant churches. Still, Catholic parishes have in the past been able to work through a wide variety of Catholic institutions, such as parochial schools and church-related colleges and hospitals, thereby having an effect on the wider society that depended little on the personal volunteering of laity.

In personal interviews, a number of the Catholics we talked to described a spiritual journey that gives some perspective on the statistical results. When they were children, Catholicism was more a way of life than a religious practice—embedded in family networks and in the material culture of the home. As they grew older, they remained Catholic but became dissatisfied with formal aspects of the church. Their spirituality increasingly expressed itself in personal explorations and in deeds of service. Volunteering emanated from their world view but was not connected to church participation or the lack thereof. As a Catholic man who volunteers three hours each week at a shelter for runaway teenagers told us, "I strive at every moment to be true to my spirituality, and volunteering is just a part of what I do." For people like this, service to others is an aspect of their spirituality, but it may be mobilized more by their work or their involvement in social movements than by their participation in church.

The Catholic population is also becoming more diverse as a result of immigration, suggesting that its role as an agent of assimilation in civil society may be especially important in the future. Whereas Protestant congregations recruit members voluntarily and thus divide readily along racial and ethnic lines, the territorial basis of Catholic parishes means that direct interaction among racial and ethnic groups cannot be as easily avoided.

Apart from these speculations about future possibilities, the data that can be assembled on religion and civic participation point mainly to the importance of asking questions about the extent to which religious involvement actually helps to mobilize participation in other civic organizations. Religion may have a salutary effect on civil society by encouraging its members to worship, to spend time with their families, and to learn the moral lessons embedded in religious traditions. But the impact of religion on society is likely to diminish if that is the only role it plays. What interested Tocqueville about voluntary organizations was not just their ability to provide friendships or to teach people civic skills; more important was their ability to forge connections across large segments of the population, spanning communities and regions and drawing together people from different ethnic backgrounds and occupations. The denominational structures and benevolent associations that grew out of religious impulses in Tocqueville's time were examples of such organizations. At the end of the twentieth century, with the decline of many of these traditional organizations, the ability of religious people to create innovative partnerships with nonreligious community agencies, volunteer centers, and nonprofit corporations may be the greatest test of their role in mobilizing civic engagement.

References

Greeley, Andrew M. 1997. "The Other Civic America: Religion and Social Capital." *American Prospect* 32 (May–June): 68–73.

Hall, Peter Dobkin. 1992. *Inventing the Nonprofit Sector: And Other Essays on Philanthropy, Voluntarism, and Nonprofit Organizations.* Johns Hopkins University Press.

Hewitt, Nancy A. 1984. *Women's Activism and Social Change: Rochester, New York: 1822–1872.* Cornell University Press.

Hodgkinson, Virginia A., and Murray S. Weitzman. 1992. *Volunteering and Giving among American Teenagers 12 to 17 Years of Age: Findings from a National Survey.* Washington, D.C.: Independent Sector.

———. 1993. *From Belief to Commitment: The Community Service Activities and Finances of Religious Congregations in the United States.* 1993 edition: *Findings from a National Survey.* Washington, D.C.: Independent Sector.

Hodgkinson, Virginia A., Heather A. Gorski, Stephen M. Noga, and E. B. Knauft. 1995. *Giving and Volunteering in the United States, 1994.*Vol. 2: *Trends in Giving and Volunteering by Type of Charity.* Washington, D.C.: Independent Sector.

Hout, Michael, and Andrew M. Greeley. 1987. "The Center Doesn't Hold: Church Attendance in the United States, 1940–1984." *American Sociological Review* 52 (June): 325–45.

Jolicoeur, Pamela M., and Louis L. Knowles, "Fraternal Associations and Civil Religion: Scottish Rite Freemasonry." *Review of Religious Research* 20 (1978): 3–22.

Putnam, Robert. 1995. "Bowling Alone: America's Declining Social Capital." *Journal of Democracy* 6 (January): 65–78.

Verba, Sidney, Kay Lehman Schlozman, and Henry E. Brady. 1995. *Voice and Equality: Civic Voluntarism in American Politics.* Harvard University Press.

Wuthnow, Robert. 1991. *Acts of Compassion: Caring for Others and Helping Ourselves.* Princeton University Press.

———. 1994. *God and Mammon in America.* Free Press.

———. 1995. *Learning to Care: Elementary Kindness in an Age of Indifference.* Oxford University Press.

———. 1997. "The Shifting Character of Social Capital in the United States." Unpublished paper, Princeton University.

———. 1998. *Loose Connections: Joining Together in America's Fragmented Communities.* Harvard University Press.

PART THREE

The Ironies of Contemporary Activism

10 | *The Rise of Citizen Groups*

JEFFREY M. BERRY

A STRONG TRADITION in political theory values participatory democracy over representative democracy. To the most feasible degree possible, we should engage in face-to-face democracy, working with our neighbors to govern ourselves rather than relying on elected representatives to make decisions on our behalf.[1] Face-to-face participation will make us better citizens by educating us about our communities and teaching us to be tolerant and cooperative. These benefits from participation do not come just from what is overtly political but from all types of cooperative civic activity where the goal is to make the neighborhood or city a better place to live. In this sense, declining community participation represents more than a loss of interest in civic affairs; it also reflects a weakening of the very foundation of democratic politics.[2] This alleged decline of community is controversial because there are also those whose measurements indicate that community participation is stable or even rising.[3] It is clear, though, that rank-and-file Ameri-

I was very fortunate that Jennifer Rich and Tracy Turner agreed to help me with the research that serves as the basis for this paper. They were exceptionally skilled and dedicated assistants, and this work could not have been completed without their help.

1. See Barber (1984); Berry, Portney, and Thomson (1993); and Mansbridge (1980).

2. Putnam (1995a); Putnam (1995b).

3. See, for example, Ladd (1996).

cans sense a loss of community in the neighborhoods and cities where they live.[4]

This preoccupation with community involvement has pulled scholars away from any sustained examination of national interest groups. Although membership in national associations is one measure of involvement and participation, it is treated as almost incidental to more demanding forms of participation. After all, one's participation in a national interest group might not require more than a few minutes a year—the time it takes to write a check for one's annual dues. In Benjamin Barber's terms, such participation is characteristic of "thin" democracy rather than "strong" democracy.[5]

Although there is little agreement on how to interpret the data on community-level involvement, or even on what constitute the most meaningful indicators of strong democracy, there is no dispute about the trend line for national interest groups. Since the 1960s the number of interest groups has skyrocketed.[6] A good deal of this growth has come from organizations that do not have individuals as members, such as corporations, nonprofits, and trade associations; yet membership organizations have boomed as well. In particular, citizen groups have grown sharply in number and expanded greatly in size. Organizations with memberships in the hundreds of thousands are not unusual. Among environmental groups, for example, the Sierra Club, the National Audubon Society, the National Wildlife Federation, and Greenpeace USA all have more than a half-million members. This in turn gives the groups substantial financial resources to hire large staffs of lobbyists and researchers. The entire environmental movement generated $4 billion in revenue in 1996. Between 1987 and 1996, donations to environmental groups increased by 91 percent. All other charitable giving grew by just 67 percent during the same period.[7] Groups on both the right and the left have proved extraordinarily adept at identifying constituencies who are willing to open up their wallets to support them.

Since national citizen groups are just one type of organization through which individuals may participate in civic life, analyzing how these groups have fared in recent years may seem to offer a rather limited insight into

4. An eloquent plea for community can be found in Bellah et al. (1985).
5. Barber (1984).
6. Berry (1997); Schlozman and Tierney (1986); Walker (1991).
7. Allen (1997).

the political health of the United States. There is good reason, though, to look at these organizations, because their fortunes over time are a mirror of changing interests and values in society at large.[8] What is particularly important about national citizen groups is that they are avowedly political organizations. (By citizen group I mean a political interest group whose basis of organization is not built on the vocational or professional aspirations of its members or financial supporters.) People join these organizations, believing that they will *represent* them in the political process. Although a small proportion of these groups engage in political activity as a by-product of other membership inducements—the American Association of Retired Persons (AARP), for example—most national citizen lobbies offer few selective incentives significant enough on their own to attract members.[9] People join groups like the National Rifle Association, the National Organization for Women, Public Citizen, the Eagle Forum, or the Environmental Defense Fund because they know those groups will speak to policymakers on their behalf. Indeed, there is usually no other reason to join these groups—lobbying is what they do, and those who join understand that.

Whatever the virtues of face-to-face democracy, America cannot rely entirely on institutions built around self-governance. Most governing is done by representatives who act for us rather than by participatory institutions. When we think of representatives in the political process, it is usually in the context of elected legislators and the work they do on behalf of their constituents. Nevertheless, representation in the political process takes many forms, and theorists have cast a wide net in analyzing how representation is transacted.[10] The representation that is carried out by national citizen groups is more than a complement to people's civic engagement in their own communities. People who join a national citizen group are making a declaration about their political identity. They are defining who they are politically and consciously choosing to increase their commitment to that identity through the financial contribution that is required. Such participation is not divorced from the motives that lead people to take part in community-based organizations.

Membership in a national interest group is, in its own way, a search for community. It is not, of course, the same kind of community that

8. Skocpol, this volume.
9. Berry (1977).
10. See Pitkin (1972).

face-to-face interaction offers, but by identifying with a cause, people also identify with others who join the same group. For example, one might think of oneself as an environmentalist and know and admire people who are even more actively involved in environmental affairs. For a variety of reasons, though, it may not be feasible to become active in a group on the local level. At the same time, paying $35 or $50 to join a national organization may make one feel united with others who feel the same way. Alternatively, people who become active in a local group may over time come to recognize that solving the problems the local group is working on also requires action at the national level. Thus they may donate money to a lobbying group in Washington so that it will speak for them and represent them in national policymaking.

The success of citizen groups in mobilizing large numbers of supporters has worked to make our national interest group system more representative of the interests of the American population. Yet the segments of the American population that are most effectively represented by these groups hold values that are sometimes at odds with the interests of those further down the economic ladder. Liberal groups sometimes place environmental or consumer protection ahead of economic development that might benefit working-class Americans. More broadly, as labor has declined, citizen groups advocating quality-of-life concerns have become the dominant voice of American liberalism.

Group Participation

To understand how well citizen lobbies represent their constituents in national policymaking, we turn to data on interest group participation in the legislative process. How effectively are people connected to national policymaking through these organizations? How does the participation of citizen groups in national politics compare with that of other types of lobbies?

There is little consensus among scholars on the role played by citizen groups. The dominant theoretical framework, derived from Mancur Olson's *The Logic of Collective Action*, demonstrates that these groups shouldn't exist. Olson's formal theory, which has had a dramatic influence on interest group scholarship, says that such groups that do exist are "characterized by a low degree of rationality."[11] He washes his hands of this

11. Olson (1968, p. 161).

irrationality and says that explaining participation in these kinds of groups in the real world is more the province of social psychologists than of economists.

The data used here come from a larger study of citizen groups and postmaterialism in American politics. To try to understand how the representative role of these advocacy organizations may have changed over time, I divided the postwar history of citizen groups into three distinct periods. The first period, from 1948 through 1963, is a time when we would expect to find relatively little citizen group advocacy. The literature on interest groups from that era barely mentions such organizations.[12] There was some civil rights advocacy and a bit of environmental lobbying, but citizen groups appear to have been bit players on the interest group stage. During the second period, from 1964 through 1980, there was an explosion in the number of liberal citizen groups.[13] These organizations worked on a variety of issues—environmental protection, civil rights, equality for women, consumer affairs, the Vietnam War, and so on. In the last period, the Reagan-Bush years (1981–92), conservative citizen lobbies became much more visible. Thus, in this final era, Washington was full of both liberal and conservative advocacy groups.

The congressional agenda was carefully measured for a single year in each period. The political world is a messy place, and there is no pretense that everything aside from citizen group activity was held constant in those three separate years. Still, there was constancy in a few key respects. Each year, 1963, 1979, and 1991, was the third year of a first-term president. The third year was chosen to avoid both the honeymoon of the first months of a new presidency and the exigencies of election-year politics in the Congress. The Democrats controlled Congress in the three different years studied. (The White House was controlled by Democrats in 1963 and 1979 and by a Republican in 1991.) Finally, each of the years also falls toward the end of the selected period so that there are not wide disparities in the time elapsed between the data points.

In this first pass at the data, the primary unit of analysis is the congressional hearing. I used hearings rather than bills introduced for a number of reasons. Most important, it is simply not practical to examine a sample of the thousands of bills introduced into the Congress each year.

---

12. See the two leading scholarly texts of the era, Key (1964) and Truman (1951).
13. Berry (1977).

A large proportion are relatively trivial private bills, and there is little hope of uncovering information in the press or through congressional documents on all but the most salient of issues.[14]

The issue purview extends to all domestic social and domestic economic policy hearings. Excluded were appropriations, which largely parallel statutory authorizations, oversight hearings, nominations, and foreign and defense policy. (Foreign trade, however, is included because it is typically no less a domestic economic issue than a foreign policy problem.) A yearly index of all hearings published by the Congressional Information Service (CIS) provided the comprehensive list of hearings to investigate. For each entry in the index we conducted a preliminary investigation to see if there was enough information to undertake a legislative history. Data were drawn from five sources: *Congressional Quarterly Weekly Report*, the *New York Times*, the *Wall Street Journal*, published congressional hearings, and summaries in the CIS index itself. The process continued until all possible cases were reviewed. In the end, seventy-four cases were completed for 1963, fifty-seven for 1979, and seventy-four for 1991 (total $N = 205$).

What of those issues that do not receive hearings? There are some bills that proceed to the floor without a hearing, but they surely represent a small percentage of those issues generally considered to be politically significant. Hearings on important issues are difficult to bypass because of committee prerogatives and because committee deliberations offer a relatively efficient process for mediating disagreements within and between the parties. Clearly, the more controversial a proposal, the more likely it is to receive a hearing. Does this mean that the cases generally exclude hearings on routine and noncontroversial matters? In reading through the narratives and coding sheets of all 205 cases, one would quickly conclude that many of these issues were fairly routine and that the level of controversy surrounding them varied greatly.

Population Baseline

To properly interpret how representation by interest groups may have changed over time, some sort of baseline is necessary so that the degree to which group participation exceeds or falls short of their presence in the

---

14. Hearings were also used because a key part of the larger study dealt with agenda-building. By definition, a hearing means that a problem is on the agenda, the issue is of at least modest significance, and there is some record of what went on. See Berry (1999).

population can be determined. To measure representation by interest groups is, of course, to measure bias as well. Ideally, the proportion of interest groups participating in the political process could be compared with a population of interests held by citizens. To call such a comparison unwieldy does not do justice to the methodological complexity of such an undertaking. This kind of endeavor would require highly sophisticated and nuanced public opinion polling on an extensive array of issues. Less ideal, but still difficult, is to measure actual group participation against a baseline of organizations that, presumably, want to be extensively involved in the policymaking process. Broad judgments can certainly be made about the general direction of bias in such organizational population figures, and data on participation can be evaluated to determine whether bias in this population is exacerbated or diminished by participation rates.

Unfortunately for scholars studying interest groups, there is no standard database that includes the population of lobbying organizations over time. Although Congress passed a law in 1946 to require that lobbyists register with it, it was a toothless piece of legislation and was widely ignored by interest groups. In 1995 a new lobbying registration law was passed, and though it may help contemporary scholars, its narrow conception of what constitutes lobbying makes it a problematic source of data.[15] Even measuring the participation of groups in a single year is difficult. There are no official lists of who participates in individual policy conflicts. Scholars do not even agree on what an interest group is. Some study only voluntary organizations, thereby excluding corporations and other institutions that lobby.

The single best study of the contours of the interest group community is Kay Lehman Schlozman and John Tierney's *Organized Interests and American Democracy*. Drawing on a commercially published directory, *Washington Representatives*, Schlozman and Tierney examined each entry in the 1981 edition and classified the roughly 7,000 organizations included into twelve basic types of interest groups.[16] Although there were surely groups missing from the directory, Schlozman and Tierney's study is carefully crafted, and there is no reason to doubt the basic patterns that emerged from their data. Luckily, the year they chose to study, 1981, corresponds closely to the middle year of this study (1979), so some direct comparisons can be made with the case history data.

15. On the problems with the law and the resulting data, see Furlong (1997).
16. Schlozman and Tierney (1986). The directory they drew on is Close (1981).

Combining some of their categories to approximate the definition of citizen group used in this study, the Schlozman and Tierney data show that roughly 7 percent of all interest groups with some representation in Washington in 1981 were citizen groups.[17] Some organizations had their own lobbying office in Washington; others hired lobbyists from law firms or public relations firms to represent them. Schlozman and Tierney also use a second measure restricted to organizations that had their own lobbying office. Using that measure, the proportion of citizen groups with Washington representation rose to about 14 percent because most of the interest groups using lobbyists from law firms and public relations firms are corporations who find it more economical to hire lobbyists as the need dictates rather than to fund a Washington office of their own. The first measure is the more comprehensive one because it recognizes the different forms that Washington representation can take; the second measure, restricted to organizational offices, sharply underestimates business representation.

Who Testifies?

Schlozman and Tierney's 1981 data offer a rigorous measurement of who is represented in interest group politics. Being represented in Washington is the first step toward influencing public policy. For an interest group, just being informed about what is going on in specific policy areas and having the capability to monitor events so that organizational leaders are well informed is important.[18]

To actually exert influence, however, groups must act on the information that their representatives collect. A beginning point for studying influence is to see which groups actually participate. To measure participation, each of the congressional hearings for the 205 cases in this study was reviewed to see which groups testified. Although there are groups that participate in the legislative process without making an attempt to testify, there is reason to believe that hearings capture much of the overall roster of lobbying participants. Testifying at hearings helps to legitimize a group's

17. I have combined Schlozman and Tierney's (1986, p. 67) categories for "Citizens' groups," "Civil rights groups/Minority organizations," "Social welfare and the poor," and "Elderly/women/handicapped." Some of these organizations would fit into my category of nonprofits (which eventually got lumped together with "other" in my figures), but this grouping of their organizations is roughly comparable to my classification of citizen groups.

18. Heinz et al. (1993, pp. 3–7).

participation in the policymaking steps that follow. Lobbyists like to use the opportunity that hearings afford to involve the organization's leaders, who typically deliver the testimony. For membership organizations, hearings are an opportunity for a photo and an article in the newsletter demonstrating the importance and effectiveness of the Washington office. Schlozman and Tierney's survey of Washington lobbyists showed that 99 percent of their respondents indicated that their organization testified before the Congress.[19]

One assumes that the more important a group is perceived to be on the issue at hand, the more likely it will be allowed to testify. Groups more sympathetic with the committee or subcommittee chair's position are probably also favored, but since the Democrats controlled the Congress in all three years studied, there is some constancy on this point. The minority side on committees also influences the list of participants.

The findings in Table 10-1 are striking. As a proportion of all groups participating, citizen groups increased from 23.5 percent in 1963 to 31.8 percent in 1991. In all three years citizen groups were overrepresented in the legislative process, although the 1981 baseline population figures offer the only true statistical comparison. If the actual proportion of citizen lobbies was around 7 percent, the comparable 1979 data indicate that they testified at a rate of almost four times their number in the interest group population. For 1963, the percentage of citizen groups in the population is unknown, but it is inconceivable that it was equivalent to the 23.5 percent of the testimony offered that year.

The lack of a firm population baseline for 1991 may raise some question about the trend line in the magnitude of overrepresentation. Since the proportion of testimony from citizen groups increased from 1979 to 1991, can we assume that citizen groups were overrepresented at an even greater rate by the end of this period? If citizen groups grew as a proportion of the lobbying population, the magnitude of overrepresentation may not have increased during that time. Although there is no one baseline to use for 1991, there is strong evidence to suggest that the proportion of citizen lobbies decreased during this decade. The legislative case histories for 1991 reveal that the number of groups started in the previous decade was small. This stands to reason—many of the citizen group "markets" had already matured by 1981. The environmental market, for example, was saturated

---

19. Schlozman and Tierney (1986, p. 150).

Table 10-1. *Interest Group Testimony at Hearings as a Percentage of All Interest Groups Testifying during the Year, 1963, 1979, and 1991*[a]

Interest group	1963[b]	1979[c]	1991[d]
Citizen groups	23.5	26.2	31.8
Corporations	18.1	22.0	19.1
Trade associations	31.8	28.9	25.5
Professional associations	12.9	11.8	14.5
Labor unions	6.3	4.4	3.8
Other[e]	7.4	6.7	5.3

a. Comparing the rate of change over time for citizen groups with the rate of change of all other interest groups, $t = .004$.

b. For 1963, N for hearings examined = 74; N for number of groups that testified = 1,373.

c. For 1979, N for hearings examined = 57; N for number of groups that testified = 947.

d. For 1991, N for hearings examined = 74; N for number of groups that testified = 922.

e. Veterans' organizations, nonprofits, churches, and other groups.

by advocacy groups working on a wide variety of issues. Between 1970 and 1980 the number of environmental groups in the United States listed in the *Encyclopedia of Associations* grew from 221 to 380. In 1990, however, there were only sixteen more, for a total of 396.[20] In contrast, the Washington representation of some business sectors had boomed. In health care, for example, there were around 100 health-related lobbies operating in Washington in 1979; in 1991 there were more than 700.[21] These additional 600 health groups in Washington surely exceeded the total number of new citizen groups that opened up shop in Washington during the same time. Business developments in fields like telecommunications, computers, and biotechnology make it highly likely that Washington representation expanded greatly for these industries as well.

It is fair to conclude that by 1991 citizen groups constituted less than the 7 percent of all Washington representation that was found in 1981. Similarly, using Schlozman and Tierney's narrower gauge for organizations with Washington offices, citizen groups would have constituted less than the 14 percent of offices in the 1981 population figures. By whatever standard used, the overrepresentation of citizen groups grew between the 1979/1981 period and 1991. Even allowing for some imprecision in the

20. Baumgartner and Jones (1993, p. 186).
21. Rauch (1994, p. 91).

data, the inescapable conclusion is that this overrepresentation was enormous: by the early 1990s, this relatively small proportion of organizations lobbying in Washington provided roughly one-third of all congressional testimony from interest groups. All the more impressive is that citizen groups increased their share of the hearings limelight at a time when the opportunities to testify were becoming a scarcer resource. The average number of groups to testify at a hearing in 1979 was 16.6; in 1991 it was 12.5. And while the opportunity to testify was becoming scarcer, the overall number of interest groups in Washington was, of course, increasing.

Why have citizen groups been so successful in gaining a disproportionate share of these attractive opportunities to gain publicity for their policy stands? There appear to be a number of reasons. First, citizen groups have historically depended on an information strategy in their legislative lobbying. They firmly believe that if they can get the "facts" out to the public, opinion will swing their way. Business did not traditionally rely as much on an outside strategy, though this has changed over the years as sectors of industries have found themselves in more competitive situations. Impressionistic evidence suggests that business is relying more on public relations campaigns. The "Harry and Louise" ads against the Clinton health care proposal sponsored by the Health Insurance Association of America are perhaps the best-known example of a business or industry going public. Second, and relatedly, citizen groups have allocated their resources to emphasize research and the dissemination of information. Jobs and work assignments are designed to maximize publicity for their cause through low-cost outlets. Third, as has been demonstrated elsewhere, citizen groups were primary initiators of many of the proposals about which these committees were holding hearings.[22] It stands to reason that the groups pushing an issue onto the congressional agenda, and working with sympathetic legislators and their staffs to make that happen, would be given substantial opportunity to testify.

Who Counts?

Measuring congressional testimony is, of course, only a first step in assessing the role of interest groups in the legislative process. One way to test these initial findings is to determine not simply who participates but whose participation counts the most. Who are the most important actors in these legislative struggles? There is no one accepted way of determining

22. Berry (1999).

this, but one approach is to use press accounts. Although the measurements are not definitive, the available space for each story dictates that journalists mention only the most important participants. Given the large number of cases, that they go back as far as 1963, and that most of these bills were never the subject of any published scholarly research, press accounts are really the only practical option for determining which groups were, at the very least, the most visible participants in the process.

The virtues of this approach extend, however, beyond its availability. Stories in the *New York Times*, the *Wall Street Journal*, and *Congressional Quarterly Weekly Report* offer the judgments of some of the nation's most experienced and competent beat reporters. The assumption is that the beat reporters for these publications have some sophisticated understanding of the issues they are covering—or at least of the politics surrounding the issue—and that their stories reflect reasonable conclusions about which groups deserve mention in their descriptions and analyses. In the articles about the 1963 debate over the Domestic Cotton Price Equalization Bill, reporters repeatedly cited the American Textile Manufacturers Association, the National Cotton Council, and the American Farm Bureau Federation but only occasionally mentioned regional groups headquartered outside of Washington. These reports are taken to be informed assessments of who the most important spokespeople are for the interests involved. Possibly the regional groups were a little more important and the National Cotton Council a little less important, but it seems a good bet that experienced journalists for these respected publications can determine which groups are most involved on an issue.

The data in Table 10-2 reveal a pattern similar to that found for congressional testimony. Citizen groups are more than a quarter of all interest groups mentioned in print coverage of these issues in 1963 and 1979. By 1991, citizen group citations grow to four out of every ten mentions of lobbying organizations.[23] Again, there is a pattern of enormous overrepresentation of citizen groups when compared against a population baseline. It may be that these groups proportionally represent public opinion, but their participation in the legislative process is far in excess of

23. As indicated in Table 10-2, the rate of change for citizen groups over time is not statistically significant from that for all noncitizen groups. However, our primary concern is not with the rate of change between citizen and noncitizen groups, but with the magnitude of difference between the rate of citation for citizen groups and their actual proportion of the population of interest groups. Since that comparison is indirect, with a summary statistic for 1981 and an estimate for 1991, there is no significance test to be used.

Table 10-2. *Press Coverage of Interest Groups as a Proportion of All Interest Groups Mentioned, 1963, 1979, 1991, and 1995*[a]
Percent

| Interest group | Print media coverage | | | Television coverage |
	1963[b]	1979[c]	1991[d]	1995[e]
Citizen groups	28.9	26.9	40.2	45.6
Corporations	10.7	17.2	1.8	24.3
Trade associations	31.1	26.5	23.7	13.0
Professional associations	15.5	11.6	26.7	3.8
Labor unions	9.7	15.5	5.6	4.0
Think tanks	n.a.	n.a.	n.a.	4.3
Other[f]	4.1	2.3	2.1	5.1

Source: For 1963, 1979, and 1991 citations in the *New York Times*, the *Wall Street Journal*, and *Congressional Quarterly Weekly Report*. For 1995, author's calculations from 295 newscasts on ABC, CBS, CNN, and NBC.

n.a. Not available.

a. Comparing the rate of change over time for citizen groups with the rate of change of all other interest groups (print media years only), $t = .16$.

b. For 1963, N for issues covered = 55; N for groups mentioned = 1,194.

c. For 1979, N for issues covered = 49; N for groups mentioned = 691.

d. For 1991, N for issues covered = 49; N for groups mentioned = 766.

e. For 1995, N for groups mentioned = 847.

f. Veterans' organizations, nonprofits, churches, and other groups.

their proportion in the interest group universe. Since citizen groups in Washington in 1991 are estimated to have constituted less than 7 percent of total group representation, the 40 percent of all print citations to interest group activity that year is an overrepresentation of at least six to one. If organizations with their own offices in Washington are the baseline, the overrepresentation is still substantial. If for the sake of argument citizen groups were 10 percent of all offices in 1991—a very generous estimate—the overrepresentation is of a magnitude of four to one. Whichever standard is used, it is clear that these groups participated in legislative politics at a rate far in excess of what their numbers would suggest and that they were at the center of debate in Washington over public policy.

The Nightly News

The extent of the overrepresentation of citizen groups is impressive, but skeptics might argue that these measures cover only part of the policymaking process. The pluralist critics taught us long ago that what gets on the agenda may be a more accurate reflection of political influence than of the influence of groups on the limited range of alternatives that are offered during formal consideration of legislation.[24] The impact of interest groups on agendas is not altogether clear. Some studies have found interest groups to be a major influence, and others have concluded that they play a much more modest role.[25]

One way to extend the research beyond what was on the formal agenda of Congress is to look at media coverage of public policy in general. To accomplish this, I analyzed television network news to see what kinds of stories involving interest groups appeared during a single year. Exposure on the network news is a crucial resource for most interest groups because the long process of getting government to respond to their priorities must often begin with an effort to build awareness of the problems they are concerned about. With the huge increase in the number of interest groups, the competition among lobbies for a spot on the congressional agenda has become ever more intense. Each group must try to rise above the din to gain the attention of policymakers and of the public.[26]

With the explosion of "new media," gaining attention may seem easier than ever. With diverse options, all groups can presumably find an outlet for themselves. Yet for all the discussion and excitement about Websites on the Internet, chat rooms, cable television, and talk radio (a rather old technology), there is not much evidence that these venues have enhanced the prowess or even the visibility of interest groups. Furthermore, while these new media may qualify as "media," what interest groups really crave is coverage by respected and widely followed news organizations. No interest group in Washington would prefer coverage on a top-notch Website to coverage on the CBS Evening News.

The network news shows were chosen because of their large national audiences, their prestige, and their perceived importance among Washingtonians. The data set that was created used 1995 as the window on TV coverage of lobbying groups. For 295 days during that year, I watched a network news broadcast, alternating among ABC, CBS, CNN Headline News, and NBC. No year can be said to be typical, and how usual or unusual this one was is not known. This was the year of the O. J. Simpson

24. Bachrach and Baratz (1962).
25. See Baumgartner and Jones (1993); and *contra*, see Kingdon (1984).
26. Salisbury (1990).

trial, the Oklahoma City bombing, and the Contract with America. It is hoped that the large number of observations—548 stories that included mention of at least one interest group—minimizes bias from any short-term anomalies in what made the network news in 1995.[27]

The results are striking. Although they were but a small part of the lobbying population, citizen groups constituted 45.6 percent of all the interviews with interest group representatives, mentions of specific lobbying organizations, and references to interest group sectors. No specific coding of issue areas was undertaken, but citizen groups were largely featured commenting on environmental and consumer issues, and there were numerous stories on abortion and civil rights (see Table 10-2).

Gaining Respect

In evaluating the stories that ran, an assessment was made of how citizen groups were portrayed in them. In a study of television network news coverage of interest groups between 1969 and 1982, Lucig Danielian and Benjamin Page found that half of all stories about citizen groups involved demonstrations or protests of some type. Such stories commonly cast the citizen groups in an unfavorable light because they came across as unruly, rebellious, radical, or simply out of the mainstream. As Danielian and Page concluded, "Citizens' action groups can penetrate the media, but often only at the cost of alienating the public, corrupting the groups'

27. Given the brevity of most stories, only a limited number of variables could be coded. I concentrated on which specific organizations were covered and on general references to interest group sectors. Thus, I recorded references to both the "American Association of Retired Persons" and "senior citizen organizations." There had to be an obvious public policy context in the story for any groups involved to be counted. If there was a story on price-cutting on diapers that mentioned Procter and Gamble, this story would not be included and Procter and Gamble would not be coded as an interest group; if, however, there was a story on disposable diapers as an environmental problem and a Procter and Gamble spokesperson appeared to defend the company, then that story would count and the company would be coded as one of the interest groups receiving coverage. A story did not have to show specific instances of lobbying since the simple act of a group representative talking to the reporter is an attempt to influence public opinion. The data do not distinguish between national lobbies and those on the state and local level because differentiating a national story from a state or local one was frequently difficult to do. A typical story might start with a correspondent reporting from Washington on some action EPA was contemplating. Then, after the issue was described, it would be illustrated by giving a specific example of a conflict in Denver or Albuquerque or Duluth. Spokespeople for the environmentalists and the business interests might come from this local conflict, or they might be mixed in with advocates from Washington. From the viewers' point of view, what is important is which sides of the controversy get articulated, not where a group is headquartered.

purposes, and presenting only the most cryptic policy reasoning—with questionable persuasive effects."[28]

Danielian and Page's study included the years with the most serious protests against the Vietnam War. Although the 1995 TV data included fewer stories featuring protests and demonstrations, still some citizen groups used demonstrations and some did outlandish things for the specific purpose of attracting TV coverage (such as Operation Rescue and Act Up). As it turns out, citizen groups—at least liberal citizen groups—were treated more respectfully in 1995 than in the earlier period. Only 18 percent of the 1995 stories involving citizen groups included footage of some type of demonstration. And even when they did, it was pretty tame stuff. A typical example was senior citizens protesting proposals by congressional Republicans to cut back on Medicare. Over time, it is evident that journalists have come to view citizen groups as a conventional and responsible part of the establishment, not as radicals.

When all references to citizen groups were divided into those where a group was advocating a conservative position and those where a group was advocating a liberal one, another strong pattern emerged. Specific references to liberal organizations or generic references to sectors comprising liberal citizen groups were 60.5 percent of the total. For conservatives, the comparable figure was 27.6 percent. This same pattern emerged when stories with the most frequently cited interest groups were isolated. Of the twenty-one lobbying organizations receiving the most coverage, eight were liberal citizen groups and four were conservative citizen lobbies (see Table 10-3). For comparison's sake, the top twenty from Danielian and Page's sample are set next to the 1995 leaders. Only four citizen groups were included in the 1969–82 set, and they were all liberal (the Moratorium Committee, the NAACP, the ACLU, and the constellation of groups operated by Ralph Nader).

For 1995 the disparity in the way conservative and liberal groups were treated was actually greater than the statistics indicate. Virtually all of the references to liberal citizen groups had a neutral or positive spin. Not so for conservatives. The conservative citizen group that received the most coverage was the National Rifle Association (NRA). Many of the references to the NRA had a negative connotation. A CBS story in October featured a Pasadena citizens' group fighting guns on the street. The scenes of street

---

28. Danielian and Page (1994, p. 1074).

Table 10-3. *Lobbying Organizations That Received the Most TV News Coverage, 1969–82 and 1995*

Rank	Organization, 1969–82	Number of appearances	Rank	Organization, 1995	Number of appearances
1	AFL-CIO	40	1	National Rifle Association	17
2	Moratorium Committee	21	2	Million Man March	15
3	Exxon	18	3	Christian Coalition	13
4	American Petroleum Institute	16	4	American Civil Liberties Union	11
5	Gulf Oil	15	5	National Organization for Women	10
6	United Auto Workers	14	6	Philip Morris	9
7	OPEC	11	7	American Medical Association	8
8	U.S. Olympic Committee	10		Major League Baseball (owners)	8
	NAACP	10	9	American Airlines	5
10	International Olympic Committee	8		Catholic Church	5
	General Motors	8		Dow Chemical/Dow Corning	5
12	Society of Friends	7		NAACP	5
	Texaco	7		TimeWarner	5
	American Civil Liberties Union	7	14	American Association of Retired Persons	4
15	Palestine Liberation Organization	6		Center for Responsive Politics	4
	Ralph Nader	6		Consumer Federation of America	4
	Teamsters Union	6		Empower America	4
	U.S. Chamber of Commerce	6		Family Research Council	4
	U.S. Steel	6		Greenpeace	4
20	Mobil Oil	5		Major League Baseball Players' Union	4
				Reynolds Tobacco	4

Source: For 1969–82, Danielian and Page (1994, p. 1068); for 1995, author's calculations from 295 newscasts by ABC, CBS, CNN Headline News, and NBC.

crime clearly suggested that the citizen group was on the right track, while the NRA, which was mentioned as an opponent of gun control, was cast in a less favorable light. Among generic references to interest group sectors or types, the greatest number were to state militias. In the wake of the Oklahoma City bombing, this coverage was negative in the extreme. (Some may wonder why organizations whose membership is composed of grown men who march around in the woods playing soldier qualify as an interest group. They are certainly not conventional lobbies, but some of the state militias did testify before Congress after the bombing, and they do make attempts, lame as they may be, to influence public opinion.) If the negative references to the NRA and all the references to state militias are removed from these calculations, the ratio of coverage becomes roughly three to one in favor of the liberal citizen groups.

Bad for Business

The news for liberal citizen groups is doubly good. Not only did news stories strongly favor them over conservative citizen groups, but business lobbies received the worst treatment of all. Since the greatest proportion of lobbying by liberal citizen groups is on consumer and environmental policies, their adversaries are usually corporations and business trade associations. In fully two-thirds of the 1995 network news stories involving corporations, the corporation was defending itself against some kind of accusation. Business trade groups responded to accusations 44 percent of the time.

The prototypical business story was something like CBS's March report on the safety problems of Chrysler minivans, complete with grisly footage of accidents. A December story on CBS noted that Costco was being sued by the Consumer Product Safety Commission for selling unsafe baby cribs. ABC ran a story in October noting that Citibank and Chemical Bank had lowered the minimum due on credit payments. The critical story warned that this led to more interest being assessed on consumers who paid only the monthly minimum.

The coverage of business in 1995 contrasted starkly with the way business was treated on the nightly network news between 1969 and 1982. Business organizations were the subject of 36.5 percent of all interest groups mentioned in the stories for those years, comparable to the 1995 percentage (37.3) for corporations and trade groups combined. Danielian and Page found that business was treated quite respectfully. One striking finding was that 99.2 percent of "straight statistical material in interest group source stories came from business groups." Business was often presented by the networks as if it offered an unbiased opinion on policy: "All this suggests that business sources were portrayed as presenting sober, factual, dispassionate positions in contrast to the emotional and often disorderly demonstrations by citizens' action groups."[29]

By 1995, of course, it was the citizen groups who were being presented as sober and factual sources of information about public policy, while business was no longer to be trusted. This unfavorable coverage of business fits with a larger pattern of television journalism that has developed over the years. As media expert Thomas Patterson writes, "The notion that 'bad news makes for good news' has long been a standard of American journalism, but the media have raised it to new heights in recent decades. Negativity in the news increased sharply during the 1970s, jumped again during the 1980s, and continues to rise."[30] Emphasis is often placed on failure, scandal, and ineptness. Because journalists especially like to emphasize conflict, stories about competing interest groups are often framed as good guys versus bad guys. This works to the disadvantage of business groups, who are often portrayed as the heavies fighting public-spirited citizens who have organized to fight to protect their community. Business is also hurt by the brevity of reporting in an age where public policy is so complex. In his study of reporting on environmental issues, Robert Entman notes, "The real media biases favor simplicity over complexity, persons over institutional processes, emotion over facts, and, most important, game over substance."[31] Such a system of journalistic norms favors environmental and consumer groups who can warn of dire health and safety consequences, putting the onus of proof on corporations to prove that the charges are false. And that "proof" is often quite complicated and unsuited for a minute-and-a-half report on the network news.

Research

When lobbyists approach policymakers or journalists, they hope to persuade them that they have something new and important to add to the debate at hand. More broadly, lobbyists try to develop a reputation for

29. Ibid. (p. 1072).
30. Patterson (1996, p. 17).
31. Entman (1996, p. 78).

expertise and to become recognized by those they deal with on a recurring basis as a trusted source of reliable information. They are aided in this when their organizations devote significant resources to research support staffs or outside consultants, or both.

Sometimes the research that groups take with them to Capitol Hill or to an administrative agency is a synthesis or repackaging of research done elsewhere that the group itself had nothing to do with. However, offering up original work is absolutely essential to gaining press attention for research. A summary of what academics have said over the years is not nearly as likely to generate a story in the *New York Times* as a brand new study of the subject. Advocacy groups try to design studies that are both substantively important and rigorous enough to get past an educated, skeptical audience who will rightfully wonder if the findings are compromised by a research design structured to produce specific results.

How the press treats interest group research is an excellent test of a group's credibility. Although each research report released to the press and the public receives a separate judgment, measuring the broader pattern of whose research makes the papers offers an indication of how successful different sectors are in preparing studies judged to be scientifically (or social scientifically) credible. For the 295 days included in the 1995 media research, the daily and Sunday *New York Times* and weekday *Wall Street Journal* were read with an eye toward identifying stories in which research was a central topic.[32] Research from any source was included in the results and, as Table 10-4 indicates, the government produced the greatest volume of newsworthy research. The government has enormous resources, and it should come as no surprise that it is the source of a great deal of important research. For example, a Labor Department report that "glass ceilings" and "concrete walls" still block women and minorities from positions in top management stimulated considerable news coverage.[33] More surprisingly, perhaps, colleges and universities were only the third largest producer of newsworthy research. Research is their business, though in fairness much of that work is basic research that is not intended to have immediate

32. If it was not directly mentioned in the headline, there at least had to be a hint in the headline that research might be discussed in the body of the article. Stories did not have to have any immediate lobbying context, but did have to have some public policy relevance. This is certainly not as exact a method as used for some of the other tests detailed here, but despite a larger margin for error, any broad patterns that emerge from the data should tell us how different interest group sectors do in comparison with each other. Stories that were exclusively New York City–related were excluded.

33. Kilborn (1995).

Table 10-4. *Research Featured in the Newspapers, by Source, 1995*
Percent

Source	Frequency
Government	30.6
Citizen groups	19.4
Academe	17.6
Independent research institutions	10.2
Corporations	9.3
Think tanks	5.6
Trade associations	2.8
Other advocacy groups[a]	2.8
Professional associations	.9
Labor unions	.9

Source: Author's calculations from 108 stories in the *New York Times* and the *Wall Street Journal* that appeared during 295 days in 1995.

a. Veterans' organizations, nonprofits, churches, and other groups.

relevance to policy questions. Still, there are many professional schools, especially those in public policy, public health, and business, where newsworthy, policy-relevant research by faculty is highly valued. Citizen groups were responsible for about one out of every five research-related stories. These groups did better than business—surprising, perhaps, because of the substantial resources at the disposal of corporations and trade groups. Labor unions were all but invisible.

What is not known is what level of resources was needed to yield the coverage that these different types of groups received. Although the liberal citizen groups—who produced virtually all the citizen group research that was cited in these 1995 articles—like to portray themselves as Davids fighting Goliaths, the reality is that many of them have substantial resources with annual budgets in the tens of millions of dollars. Of twenty-four liberal citizen groups active on the 1991 legislation and for which budgetary information was available, the average annual budget was $14 million. The average size of the liberal groups' staffs was 132 ($N = 22$). These organizations have the resources to underwrite studies that are substantial enough to attract press coverage. Whether it was Public Citizen's report that NAFTA is not producing the jobs promised, the Fair Housing Alliance's study concluding that insurance companies redline even middle-class black and Hispanic neighborhoods, the ACLU's documentation of spying by the FBI on gay and lesbian groups, or Children Now's study of how children are portrayed on television, liberal advocacy groups were able to gain coverage for their work.[34] The articles focused on the content of the research, not on the political motivations behind the sponsorship.

The ultimate impact of these studies is not known, but it is clear that liberal citizen groups have a significant influence on what people read when they read about politics. What is particularly important about the articles in the national press concerning research is that such stories suggest a direction that public policy should follow. Policymakers may ignore that with which they disagree, but the cumulative impact of policy-relevant research that gains publicity is to influence how problems are defined and options understood. Citizen groups are aided in their efforts to shape the political agenda by their extreme overrepresentation on network television news, the reports of their research in the newspapers, and the other media exposure their ideas receive.

Scholars have not developed a precise social science model detailing the process by which interest group advocacy leads to agenda change. The efforts that lobbies make to influence policymakers to take up their issues are relatively straightforward and not difficult to observe. Nevertheless, agenda-building is a complex process because there are so many different parts to the puzzle. We do know, however, that press coverage influences what ends up on the nation's political agenda.[35] Interest groups are by no means a dominant influence on the press, but among all lobbies, liberal citizen groups do especially well in getting the media to pay attention to their issues.[36]

Conclusion

When people ask how they can influence policy on an issue that is important to them, the answer for millions of Americans has been to join

---

34. Cooper (1995); Herbert (1995); Wilke (1995); Dunlap (1995); and Lewin (1995).

35. See Behr and Iyengar (1985); Iyengar and Kinder (1987); and Page, Shapiro, and Dempsey (1987).

36. Page, Shapiro, and Dempsey's (1987) study of the press and public opinion found that advocacy by interest groups per se was negatively correlated with attitudinal change, but that there were strong differences between different types of groups. "In general, the public apparently tends to be uninfluenced (or negatively influenced) by the positions of groups whose interests are perceived to be selfish or narrow, while it responds more favorably to groups and individuals thought to be concerned with broadly defined public interests. The best examples of the latter in our data are environmental groups and perhaps also general 'public interest' groups like Common Cause" (p. 37).

a citizen group. The irony of this is that the enormous popularity of these groups comes at a time when Americans are said to be increasingly disengaged from civic activities. Membership in national citizen groups has not figured prominently in this debate because social scientists place much greater value on more demanding, face-to-face forms of political participation. These organizations require no active involvement on the part of their members.

Yet citizen groups are an instrumental part of modern American democracy, and they engage their members in the political process in a meaningful way. They are not the hallmark of "thin democracy" but a reflection of people's abiding concern for the health of their society.[37] Robert Putnam argues that the declining membership in local associations is alarming because it reflects a disengagement from civic life and thus a weakened commitment to working for the betterment of society.[38] If we accept this, then the same logic dictates that the growing membership in Washington-based citizen lobbies be seen as an encouraging sign of people's engagement with social and political problems addressed at the national level. People who join the Christian Coalition care passionately about the health of the nation. Donors to Common Cause are not merely concerned; they are angry about a government corrupted by a broken campaign finance system. These are not thin citizens but full-bodied activists, and the nation needs more of them, not fewer.

More problematic, perhaps, is the concern that membership in national groups does not generate social capital to the same degree that participation in local groups does. There is little doubt that this is true, and ideally, grass-roots participation would generate all the social capital that is necessary. Fortunately, people who join national groups are likely to participate in other ways in the political process. Verba, Schlozman, and Brady found that 65 percent of people who are affiliated with a civic or political organization attend some of its meetings.[39] For the very same types of organizations the authors ask about, many members do nothing more than write a check. Yet these are not two separate segments of the population. There is not one sector that goes to meetings and another that writes checks. Rather, people choose among the organizations that they are affiliated with and participate at different levels in

37. Barber (1984).
38. Putnam (1995a).
39. Verba, Schlozman, and Brady (1995, p. 63).

each. A woman who joins the National Organization for Women (NOW) might do nothing more than write an annual check and put it in the mail. That same individual, however, may belong to a group of women that meets regularly to discuss issues pertaining to women in their profession, may also donate to Emily's List, may work for an occasional woman running for office, may vote only for pro-choice candidates, and may at some point decide to respond to communications from NOW asking her to write to her congressional representative. As part of this broader array of feminist activism, membership in NOW is no trivial act—it is part of a larger political identity.

Some of these national groups offer members opportunities to participate through chapters at the state and local level. And members who belong to organizations without local chapters will likely have no trouble finding analogous groups where they live. Regardless of any linked participation with state or local groups, the national lobbies are, by themselves, a means by which people search for community. When people identify with a cause, they also identify with the people who join the same group.

Another reason for viewing membership in a national citizen group as a meaningful type of political participation is that the national groups can do things that local groups cannot. If one's principal political concern is stopping abortion, it makes more sense to join a national citizen group than a local one. There is no real local solution to abortion; basic policy governing the availability of abortion is made in Washington. Even on those issues for which there are both local and national solutions to the same broad issue, such as the environment, only the politically naive could think that working exclusively at the local level will solve the underlying problems. We do not know if the growth of national citizen groups came at the expense of local ones, but if so it was a perfectly rational response on the part of the politically active. The number of these groups surged during the 1960s and 1970s as the federal government grew, the number of programs run out of Washington rose, and the nation began to focus on a set of issues that could not be resolved without the involvement of Congress, the president, and the federal courts.

In a controversial passage in his masterful *A Preface to Democratic Theory*, Robert Dahl defined the "normal" democratic political process in the United States as "one in which there is a high probability that an active and legitimate group in the population can make itself heard effectively at some crucial stage in the process of decision."[40] Citizen groups are "heard" in many important ways in the policymaking process. They are singularly impressive in their rate of participation before congressional committees, in their disproportionate share of network news stories featuring interest group opinions, and in their ability to get newspapers to report on research they have sponsored. Although the data reviewed here do not bear directly on the question of how effective these organizations have been in influencing public policy, that matter has been taken up elsewhere, and citizen groups prove to be strong and successful advocates in Congress, both in getting their issues on the agenda and in getting legislation passed.[41]

The successes that these groups have enjoyed make it all the more rational for Americans to direct some of their political resources toward Washington-based citizen lobbies. Although members for the most part share only in collective goods, they take individual satisfaction that their contributions are working to support these groups. Just how closely members monitor their groups is unclear, but supporters are more politically involved than the average American. The high public visibility of these groups certainly contributes to people's sense that they are getting their money's worth by supporting them.

These groups have enhanced the representation of many diverse and important constituencies in national policymaking, but they do little to address the fundamental inequalities of political participation. By and large these groups represent middle-class and upper-middle-class citizens. As Schlozman, Verba, and Brady point out in this volume, those who recruit people to join or participate in organizations seek out those who are already well represented in the political process. On the liberal side we have seen the rise of environmental groups, consumer groups, rights groups, and good government groups—organizations that stress quality-of-life issues that appeal to the more affluent in society. While these groups have prospered, labor unions and groups focused on economic inequality have declined. The problem with national citizen groups is not that they manifest an erosion of civic engagement or social capital, but that they empower only part of the population.

---

40. Dahl (1956, p. 145). Many years later, in a response to critics of pluralist theory, Dahl reflected on this definition and concluded that "the intent of the sentence is readily misunderstood" (1982, p. 208).

41. Berry (1999).

References

Allen, Scott. 1997. "The Greening of a Movement." *Boston Globe.* October 19.

Bachrach, Peter, and Morton S. Baratz. 1962. "Two Faces of Power." *American Political Science Review* 56 (December): 947–52.

Barber, Benjamin. 1984. *Strong Democracy.* University of California Press.

Baumgartner, Frank R., and Bryan D. Jones. 1993. *Agendas and Instability in American Politics.* University of Chicago Press.

Behr, Roy L., and Shanto Iyengar. 1985. "Television News, Real-World Cues, and Changes in the Public Agenda." *Public Opinion Quarterly* 49 (Spring): 38–57.

Bellah, Robert N., Richard Madsen, William M. Sullivan, Ann Swidler, and Steven M. Tipton. 1985. *Habits of the Heart.* New York: Perennial.

Berry, Jeffrey M. 1977. *Lobbying for the People.* Princeton University Press.

———. 1997. *The Interest Group Society.* 3d ed. New York: Longman.

———. 1999. *The New Liberalism: The Rising Power of Citizen Groups.* Brookings.

Berry, Jeffrey M., Kent E. Portney, and Ken Thomson. 1993. *The Rebirth of Urban Democracy.* Brookings.

Close, Arthur C. 1981. *Washington Representatives—1981.*Washington, D.C.: Columbia Books.

Cooper, Helene. 1995. "Consumer Group Says NAFTA Claims Haven't Been Met." *Wall Street Journal,* September 5, p. B7B.

Dahl, Robert A. 1956. *A Preface to Democratic Theory.* University of Chicago Press.

———. 1982. *Dilemmas of Pluralist Democracy.* Yale University Press.

Danielian, Lucig H., and Benjamin I. Page. 1994. "The Heavenly Chorus: Interest Group Voices on TV News." *American Journal of Political Science* 38 (November): 1056–78.

Dunlap, David W. 1995. "F.B.I. Kept Watch on AIDS Group during Protest Years." *New York Times,* May 16, p. B3.

Entman, Robert M. 1996. "Reporting Environmental Policy Debate." *Harvard International Journal of Press/Politics* 1 (Summer): 77–92.

Furlong, Scott R. 1997. "Interest Group Lobbying: Differences between the Legislative and Executive Branches." Paper delivered at the annual conference of the American Political Science Association, Washington, D.C..

Heinz, John P., Edward O. Laumann, Robert L. Nelson, and Robert H. Salisbury. 1993. *The Hollow Core.* Harvard University Press.

Herbert, Bob. 1995. "NAFTA's Bubble Bursts." *New York Times,* September 11, p. A15.

Iyengar, Shanto, and Donald R. Kinder. 1987. *News That Matters.* University of Chicago Press.

Key, V. O., Jr. 1964. *Politics, Parties, and Pressure Groups.* 5th ed. New York: Thomas Y. Crowell.

Kilborn, Peter T. 1995. "Women and Minorities Still Face 'Glass Ceiling.' " *New York Times,* March 16, p. A22.

Kingdon, John W. 1984. *Agendas, Alternatives, and Public Policies.* Boston: Little, Brown.

Ladd, Everett C. 1996. "The Data Just Don't Show Erosion of America's 'Social Capital.'" *Public Perspective* 7 (June/July): 1 ff.

Lewin, Tamar. 1995. "Children on TV out of Touch, Study Finds." *New York Times,* February 27, p. B8.

Mansbridge, Jane J. 1980. *Beyond Adversary Democracy*. Basic Books.

Olson, Mancur, Jr. 1968. *The Logic of Collective Action*. New York: Schocken.

Page, Benjamin I., Robert Y. Shapiro, and Glenn R. Dempsey. 1987. "What Moves Public Opinion?" *American Political Science Review* 81 (March): 23–43.

Patterson, Thomas E. 1996. "Bad News, Period." *PS* 29 (March 1996).

Pitkin, Hannah Fenichel. 1972. *The Concept of Representation*. University of California Press.

Putnam, Robert D. 1995a. "Bowling Alone: America's Declining Social Capital." *Journal of Democracy* 6 (January): 65–78.

———. "Tuning In, Tuning Out: The Strange Disappearance of Social Capital in America." *PS* 18 (December): 664–83.

Rauch, Jonathan. 1994. *Demosclerosis*. New York: Times Books.

Salisbury, Robert H. 1990. "The Paradox of Interest Groups in Washington—More Groups, Less Clout." In *The New American Political System*, edited by Anthony King. Washington, D.C.: AEI Press.

Schlozman, Kay Lehman, and John T. Tierney. 1986. *Organized Interests and American Democracy*. Harper and Row.

Truman, David B. 1951. *The Governmental Process*. Knopf.

Verba, Sidney, Kay Lehman Schlozman, and Henry E. Brady. 1995. *Voice and Equality: Civic Voluntarism in American Politics*. Harvard University Press.

Walker, Jack L., Jr. 1991. *Mobilizing Interest Groups in America*. University of Michigan Press.

Wilke, John R. 1995. "Study Finds Redlining Is Widespread in Sales of Home-Insurance Policies." *Wall Street Journal*, September 12, p. A6.

11 | Extreme Voices: A Dark Side of Civic Engagement

MORRIS P. FIORINA

T HE ONGOING DISCUSSION of civic engagement includes something for everyone. At the programmatic level, conservatives applaud a means of addressing societal problems that does not involve the coercive power of government, while liberals appreciate voluntaristic approaches as the principal ones available at a time when popular support for activist government is at a low ebb. At the philosophical level, communitarians are gratified by any increased recognition of the need for people to meet their civic obligations, while their liberal adversaries can acknowledge civic engagement as a means of generating the social capital that furthers the welfare of individuals. Finally, those of us who work on the intermediate social scientific level are intrigued by hypotheses relating temporal changes in social relations to the welfare of societies. Moreover, there is room in the discussion for more of us than usual: the relevance of history, sociology, and to a lesser degree political science is clear, but even economists—like liberal political philosophers—can recognize an argument for enlightened self-interest buried beneath the unfamiliar terminology.

To be sure, some look skeptically on the current preoccupation with civic engagement and social capital. Where are the dependent variables,

I wish to thank Bill Bianco, Kristin Goss, Bill Mayer, Robert Mickey, Theda Skocpol, and Sid Verba for helpful comments.

they ask? Has anyone demonstrated that variations in civic engagement are related to welfare measures of any interest? Thus far, plausible argument substitutes for hard evidence. Others are dubious about the purported decline of civic engagement in America, believing that even the independent variable has not been accurately characterized.[1] The chapters in this collection explore some of these issues.

This chapter too reflects a skeptical stance, but of a somewhat different sort. While many have questioned whether purported declines in civic engagement have had identifiable adverse consequences, only a few curmudgeons have suggested that civic engagement may not necessarily be a good thing.[2] That is what I argue here. Put simply, at least in the political realm I am doubtful that the relationship between civic engagement and social welfare is generally positive. For present purposes we can stipulate that high levels of civic engagement are optimal,[3] but I think that intermediate levels of civic engagement may well lead to outcomes that are inferior not just to outcomes produced by higher levels of civic engagement but also to those produced by lower levels.[4]

I begin by presenting a brief case study to illustrate the argument. Then I discuss an ironic development—that Americans have grown increasingly unhappy with government at the same time that government has grown ever more open to their influence. I believe that these trends are causally related, because people who take advantage of increased opportunities to participate in politics often are unrepresentative of the general population. Then I consider some of the normative arguments about civic engagement in light of the unrepresentativeness of those so engaged. In particular, how might society dilute the extreme voices that dominate political participation? Finally, an appendix explores the more social scientific question of why participators are unrepresentative.

1. For the views of one skeptic see Ladd (1996).

2. Do those whose engagement takes the form of joining the Ku Klux Klan or a militia make a net positive contribution to social capital? Clearly, one group can deploy its social capital to the detriment of other groups or of society as a whole.

3. But only for present purposes. There are reasons for doubting this claim as well. The classic example in the literature is the high voter turnout in Austria and Germany at the time their democracies were crumbling; Tingsten (1937, pp. 225–26). These high levels of political engagement apparently represented anger, desperation, and other motivations that normally are not viewed as things societies should seek to maximize.

4. Verba and Nie (1972, chap. 18) offer an earlier version of this argument. Their discussion seems to have been forgotten during the intervening years.

My Home Town

Just outside historic Concord Center lies a four-square-mile area known as the Estabrook Woods.[5] Harvard University is the dominant landholder, with approximately 670 acres administered by its Museum of Comparative Zoology (MCZ). The Middlesex School, an elite private high school with approximately 300 acres, is the second largest landholder.[6] Harvard has a reputation for doing whatever is best for Harvard with its properties, so the town was pleasantly surprised in 1994 when the university offered to preserve its land in perpetuity, providing that 400 adjacent acres could be similarly protected in order to guarantee the continued integrity of the MCZ land as an ecological research area. Led by the Concord Land Conservation Trust (CLCT) a campaign to meet Harvard's challenge began. The Middlesex School promised to donate fifty acres on completion of its long-range development plan.

Middlesex had formally begun its expansion planning in 1990. A shift to coeducational status in the 1970s had strained the capacity of its athletic fields. In addition, given escalating housing costs in the surrounding area, the school wished to add to its existing stock of faculty housing. Over the course of the next few years the school voluntarily held two public meetings in cooperation with the town's Natural Resources Commission, four meetings in cooperation with the town's Planning Board, and four ad hoc meetings with interested members of the community. During this period the opposition began to form. The CLCT receded from view, taking no formal part in what followed. The opposition was led by a relatively new group, the Thoreau Country Conservation Alliance, which had supported a major recent campaign by Don Henley to preserve the Walden Woods.[7] Substantively, the opposition reflected preservationist concerns—Thoreau and Emerson had written about the woods—as well as the obvious environmentalist sentiments.

---

5. The following case is based on my reading of the files held in the offices of the Concord Natural Resources Commission, the reports of the controversy contained in various issues of the *Concord Journal*, and conversations with representatives of the town, the school, and involved citizens. Because Concord is a small town and the controversy was recent and painful for many of those involved (several interviewees made references to unpleasant encounters in grocery stores), I do not cite those interviewed by name.

6. The 1992 movie *School Ties* was filmed on the Middlesex grounds.

7. Don Henley is the lead singer for the Eagles, a California rock group (known, e.g., for the song "Hotel California"). He nationalized the campaign to preserve land around Walden Pond.

Figure 11-1. *Map of Estabrook Country, Middlesex School Properties*

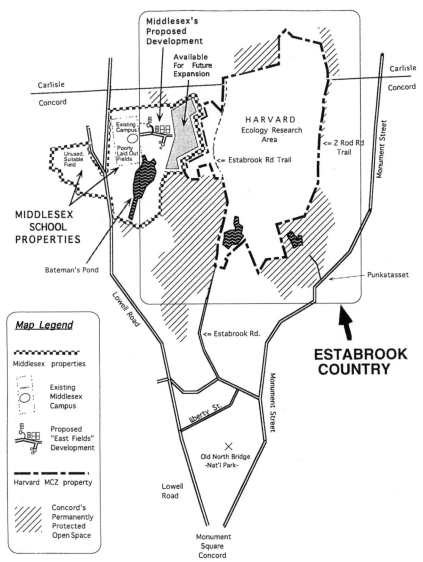

Source: Amended Middlesex proposal as of September 1997. Distributed by the Thoreau Country Conservation Alliance.

Middlesex submitted a plan in June 1993, providing for two soccer/la-crosse fields, eight tennis courts, six faculty housing units, and thirty-three parking spaces to occupy about twelve acres of its land (see Figure 11-1). Several points should be noted before continuing. First, Middlesex is a progressive institution responsible for a significant part of the ethnic diversity that might be said to exist in Concord. Moreover, the school has been a longtime protector of the Estabrook Woods; over the years it had purchased adjoining land to prevent development, and in the 1960s the school's trustees were among the leaders in the drive to acquire the large tract that was donated to Harvard.

Second, Middlesex was not proposing a toxic waste dump. Most of the area to be developed would consist of athletic fields. The school promised to use environmentally friendly grass treatments to minimize impact on the bordering woodlands. And although the new area would require a wetland crossing to reach, the school worked with town officials to mini-mize this impact.

Third, the area in dispute was not an old-growth redwood forest. There are stands of old-growth trees within the MCZ tract, but the disputed land lies to the settled side of the old Estabrook road, a path still used by mountain bikers and horse riders and easily passable by four-wheel drive vehicle. Plows and cows had been over much of this peripheral part of the "woods" many times in Concord's past.

For fifteen years I lived with my family about half a mile from Middlesex—close enough to hear the spectators cheering at the athletic contests. To us and our neighbors the school's proposal seemed reasonable in itself, and part of an all-around good deal for the town. The more important question, of course, is how the rest of the town felt, and on that score I have little doubt that we were more conservation-minded than average. Between deer eating the rhododendrons and coyotes eating the cats, there is a general feeling that nature is doing quite well in Concord. The fall air carries the sound of chain saws, and the spring breezes carry the smoke from open burning of brush. A sizable minority of the town feel that Thoreau was something of a ne'er-do-well. And it was a Californian, after all, who led the campaign to save Walden Woods (an earlier generation of Concordians sited the town dump a quarter-mile from the shore of the pond). In separate interviews with two town officials who were involved in the controversy, I conjectured that the Middlesex plan would have passed two or three to one in a town-wide vote; neither disagreed. This community sentiment was not apparent in the ensuing politics, however. On the contrary, the subsequent proceedings were dominated by a small group of citizens implacably opposed to the Middlesex plan.

The town's Planning Board is generally responsible for evaluating the engineering and safety aspects of proposed developments. In practice the board also advises on some of the environmental questions projects are likely to encounter at later stages. Over the course of fifteen months the board worked with Middlesex to scale down the plan and change the design of the wetland crossing to mitigate its impact. In October 1994, sixteen months after the school's application, the board approved a revised six-acre plan.

The application then went to the Natural Resources Commission (NRC), a five-member board created in the 1960s charged with administering the Massachusetts wetlands laws. Like other town boards, the NRC consisted of volunteers and those co-opted by town officials and sitting members of this and other boards. At the time, the NRC was composed of a retired environmental lawyer, a wildlife biologist, the conservation administrator of another town, a self-described environmental activist, and the director of the MCZ land, who recused himself from the proceedings because MCZ land abutted the property in question.

A year of intense controversy followed the Middlesex submission to the NRC. At eight public meetings activists and commission members repeatedly raised objections to the school's plan. By every indication the activists were sincere in their opposition, contributing impressive quantities of their own time and money. To some extent they saw the Estabrook Woods as an organic entity; the question was not the marginal one of "how much additional impact," but the much starker one of "preservation versus destruction." Moreover, the heavier-than-necessary infrastructure proposed in the initial plan gave rise to suspicions that Middlesex harbored additional future expansion plans. Although I am confident that the existing plan was not controversial outside the narrow circles of the activists, a more ambitious proposal to increase the size of the school and expand the campus deep into the woods would likely have been another story. To the outside observer the natural compromise appeared to be approval of Middlesex's current plan on condition that land located deeper in the woods be permanently protected, but this suggestion was rejected by Middlesex in 1993 and did not surface again until very late in the process after the contending parties had gridlocked.

Over the course of the year Middlesex representatives argued with the NRC and the activists about nesting goshawks, dragonflies and beetles, and indian corn hills. The NRC files contain attendance sheets for five of these meetings, with a median attendance of fifty-five, although the local newspaper reported that one meeting was attended by more than 100 people. There are approximately 10,800 registered voters in Concord, so ½ to 1 percent of the citizenry took an active role in these proceedings.

A year after taking up the Middlesex proposal the NRC denied the permit. To no one's surprise, Middlesex announced that it would appeal the decision to the state Department of Environmental Protection. More surprising was the school's announcement that it would withdraw its not-yet-final donation of fifty-six acres to the campaign. Opponents were surprised and disappointed; the school's donation had been assumed to be a fait accompli.

Matters soon got worse. The town's counsel recommended to the Board of Selectmen that the town not contest the appeal. The NRC decision was based on three grounds, none of which was defensible on appeal. The first was the NRC's claim—denied by Middlesex—that the project would affect more than 5,000 square feet of wetlands. This is considered a "does so—does not" kind of argument that the school would eventually win by making further modifications to its wetlands crossing. The second was the threat to critical habitat, but a few days after its decision the NRC received official notification from the state's Natural Heritage and Endangered Species Program that the project raised no serious questions. There is some disagreement about whether this decision came as a complete surprise.

The third basis on which the NRC denied the appeal was less tangible: in its capacity as custodian of the town's natural heritage and resources the commission did not think that the project should go forward. But the law does not empower local conservation boards with this kind of wide-ranging discretionary authority, so absent any merit in the first two claims, the commission's decision was what in an earlier era might have been termed "arbitrary."

Thus, after five years of activity, two years of intense politics, and thousands of dollars of expenditures, the land conservation drive had regressed. It was not just back to square one, but even further back: the Middlesex project would go forward, and the drive was fifty-six acres poorer than it once had been.

At this point cooler heads finally intervened. The Selectmen—elected town officials—who had taken no visible role in the proceedings, proposed that the parties go to mediation. Middlesex and the town agreed to split the cost of three sessions, but when no agreement was reached, the school agreed to pay for additional sessions. The mediation included the League of Women Voters and representatives of the activists, along with Middlesex and the NRC. Ultimately, after eight sessions, agreement was at hand. In a last-ditch effort some of the activists filed desperate lawsuits, but the courts declined to intervene.[8] In April of 1997 the NRC unanimously approved the agreement, but not before being condemned by one of their erstwhile supporters: "[Your] integrity has been compromised . . . you will go down in history as destroyers of the earth."[9]

In May of 1997—seven years after Middlesex began the planning process, and four years after its first official submission—the town signed the agreement, which goes into effect if the school's appeal is denied (which at the time of this writing has still not been decided). Middlesex sources report that they had budgeted $75,000 for the permitting process, but have spent $400,000 on consultants, lawyers, and mediation. Being mostly in-house, the town's expenditures are difficult to estimate, although it has spent about $10,000 on outside legal fees. The pending final settlement amounts to a slightly scaled-down version of what emerged from the Planning Board stage in 1994. The school agrees to place 100 acres of peripheral land under a permanent conservation restriction and accepts a twenty-year restriction on a tract of land deeper in the woods.

To some, the preceding case illustrates grass-roots democracy: concerned citizens actively participated in the affairs of their community and materially affected the outcome. To others, the preceding case illustrates the opposite of grass-roots democracy: a few "true believers" were able to hijack the democratic process and impose unreasonable costs—fiscal and psychological—on other actors as well as the larger community. In the eloquent words of one citizen who monitored the proceedings: "As a taxpayer, these extensive debates only dishearten those of us who place their trust and confidence in the institutions, processes and representatives that give structure to our town, states, and country."[10]

---

8. Among other things, the unreconciled activists charged that clearing trees for soccer fields would diminish the earth's capacity to cleanse the air and that use of synthetic building materials for faculty housing would harm chemically sensitive residents of Concord.

9. Quoted in Bryan Davis, "NRC Votes to Sign Middlesex Pact," *Concord Journal,* April 24, 1997, p. 16.

10. Letter of Thomas Doe, September 26, 1995, contained in the files of the Natural Resources Commission.

I acknowledge that my sympathies lie with the second camp. In recent years many academics have exalted civic engagement, seeing in it the solution to social problems and conflicts that have resisted the application of expertise and money. But civic engagement can be expected to have such salutary consequences only if those engaged are representative of the interests and values of the larger community. That is true by definition if *everyone* is engaged, but when engagement is largely the domain of minority viewpoints, obvious problems of unrepresentativeness arise. When they do, civic engagement has a dark side that is not sufficiently recognized by its proponents. Unfortunately, as a brief survey will suggest, over the course of the previous generation developments in American politics have cumulated to increase the conflict between civic engagement and representative democracy.

From JFK to WJC

As a starting point, consider the much-discussed decline in trust in government. There is a great deal of evidence on this subject, but the best time series are those contained in the American National Election Studies (see Figure 11-2). From the mid-1960s to the mid-1990s people's trust in government declined dramatically: a generation ago two-thirds to three-quarters of the population expressed high levels of trust; under one-third did so in 1996.

Three observations. First, those who write on this subject generally assume—at least implicitly—that the decline in trust is bad. I am agnostic on this point. Patrick Henry, Thomas Jefferson, and other American luminaries probably would have been more disturbed by the 1960s figures than the 1990s ones. Second, there also is a tendency for analysts to assume that the early figures are representative and the later ones aberrant. That seems a dubious assumption. Anyone reasonably familiar with American history should have no trouble thinking of eras when popular attitudes probably looked more like they do today than they did in the 1960s. Rather than 1994 Americans being a bunch of angry cynics, 1964 Americans may have been a bunch of deluded optimists. Third, many observers have pointed out that declines in trust are not limited to government or to the United States.[11] As a social scientist committed to generalization I recognize the

11. See, for example, Lipset and Schneider (1983).

Figure 11-2. *Americans' Level of Trust in the National Government,*
1964–96[a]

Percent

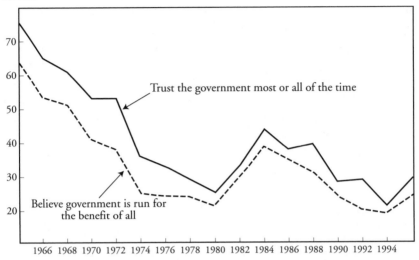

Source: American National Election Studies, website: www.umich.edu/~nes.
a. The original questions read: (a) "How much of the time do you think you can trust the government in Washington to do
what is right—just about always, most of the time, or only some of the time?" and (b) "Would you say that the government is
pretty much run by a few big interests looking out for themselves or that it is run for the benefit of all the people?"
Responses to the first question in this figure include those who answered "just about always" or "most of the time." Data on
1986 responses to the second question do not exist.

validity of that observation, but it has not affected the analyses and
theorizing of most students of the subject, so I claim a similar privilege, at
least for now.[12]

Why has trust declined? There are a number of possible explanations.
One is the economy. Inflation soared in the late 1960s, and the great
postwar expansion came to an end in the early 1970s. Trust headed south
during this period, recovering somewhat during the prosperity surrounding Ronald Reagan's reelection and again during the Clinton prosperity of
the 1990s. Analyses that focus specifically on economic correlates of the
trust series conclude that economic conditions matter but fall considerably
short of a complete explanation.[13]

---

12. The argument to follow may well have relevance to other institutions and countries, but I am
not prepared to attempt such generalizations at this time.
13. For a recent survey of the evidence see Lawrence (1997).

A second explanation might be called the Smith-Barney explanation (from their slogan, "we make money the old-fashioned way—we earn it!"): government is distrusted because it has *earned* the citizenry's distrust. Vietnam and civil disorders, Watergate, stagflation and the Ayatollah, $200 billion deficits and Iran-contra, Whitewater, Lewinsky—the list is long and implicates both parties. Political scientists have argued about whether the trust items reflect evaluations of the regime, or only particular office-holders, with at least some evidence for the latter.[14] Surely government incompetence and malfeasance has something to do with the decline in trust, but, unfortunately, how much is impossible to say, given that we cannot measure such variables in any temporally comparable way.

Some observers think a third explanation is relevant either by itself or as a supplement to the first two. By objective standards American politics is no worse today than in earlier eras, but people may perceive it as worse because of increasingly cynical media that are relentlessly negative in their coverage of politics. Setting aside the first century and a half of American history, that claim seems to be true for the previous two generations or so.[15] And it is at least suggestive that surveys regularly show people to be far more positive about their local schools, local environment, local race relations, and so forth than about their national counterparts, where their impressions must be based heavily on unrepresentative reports in the mass media.[16]

Quite likely each of the preceding explanations contributes to the decline in trust in government. But I propose still another hypothesis that is not inconsistent with the preceding ones: the rise of participatory democracy has contributed to the decline in trust. There are two components to this hypothesis—that participatory democracy has advanced, and that this advance has turned Americans off. The first claim is easy to document; the second requires a bit more explanation.

The Rise of Participatory Democracy

No one would claim that the United States today has anything approaching the kind of politics advocated by prominent participatory

14. Citrin (1974).
15. Sabato (1991).
16. See the data reported in "My Town, The Nation," *Public Perspective* (July/August 1992): pp. 94–96.

democratic theorists, but I do claim that changes in the past half-century have cumulated to strip away much of the insulation from political and institutional processes.[17] The political system today is far more exposed to popular pressures than was the case at midcentury.[18] Consider a partial listing of the changes.

In the electoral arena, John Kennedy entered a few primaries in 1960 to demonstrate to party professionals who controlled the delegates that a Catholic could win in Protestant states. Four years later Barry Goldwater's "purist" or "amateur" supporters rolled over the Republican establishment in the caucuses and primaries, and George McGovern's followers did the same on the Democratic side in 1972.[19] While the parties declined, the advantage of incumbency in congressional elections surged. The literature began to use the terms "candidate-centered" politics and "entrepreneurial" politics to describe the new reality of candidates communicating directly with constituencies rather than relying on the traditional party organizations and encompassing interest groups.

On the institutional side Congress made its proceedings—both committee and floor—more public in the early 1970s. Judicial processes were opened up by expanded rules of standing promulgated from within, as well as by legislation giving citizens greater access to the courts.[20] Similarly, bureaucratic processes were opened up, both by new legislation mandating expanded public notice and participation and by the aforementioned actions of the courts. At the local level, "maximum feasible participation" was the watchword of the 1960s, and ensuing decades saw the proliferation of local government bodies such as planning boards, resource boards, and so forth—many of them filled by volunteers.[21] Concord's NRC is one of thousands of similar bodies created since the 1960s.

In political science jargon, these are changes on the supply side of the political system—office-holders and institutions that supply public policies are far more exposed to popular pressure today than a generation ago.

17. Well-known works in the participatory democratic tradition include Barber (1984) and Pateman (1970).

18. This is the organizing theme of a textbook, *The New American Democracy* (1998) that I have written with Paul Peterson. The book provides a comprehensive survey of the changes.

19. James Q. Wilson distinguished "amateurs" from "professionals" in his 1962 work *The Amateur Democrat.* The term "purist" seems to have come into common use in the mid-1960s, especially in connection with the Goldwater campaign.

20. For a detailed discussion see Stewart (1975).

21. Burns (1991) documents these local government trends.

But there were also important changes on the demand side of the system. As various observers have documented, the 1960s and 1970s saw an "advocacy explosion."[22] The number of organized interests exploded in those decades. No doubt there was some interaction between the formation of interests and the supply-side changes: the easier it was to participate in electoral and institutional processes, the more incentive there was to do so, but political scientists have not yet worked out the dynamic. At any rate, relative to a generation ago, a strikingly more open political process now faces a strikingly larger number of interest groups.

Organized interests are not the only actor on the demand side, of course. Even the potential influence of the ordinary unorganized citizen increased. Opinion polls and attention to them burgeoned in the 1970s (see Figure 11-3), giving politicians more accurate and up-to-date information about public opinion than they had ever had before. Instant reaction to political events and decisions has become commonplace.

Other technological innovations closed the distance between the demand and supply sides. Individual politicians developed direct-mail appeals for funds and support and took advantage of other communications advances to get their messages out. But groups and individuals were able to use the same innovations to press their demands and get their messages in. Today aroused constituents can communicate their views to politicians almost instantaneously. In 1994, for example, an aroused home-schooling movement stampeded the House of Representatives with half a million communications in a matter of days, overwhelming Capitol Hill switchboards and fax machines.[23]

In sum, the political system of John Kennedy's America was far different from that of Bill Clinton's America. The "elitist" democracy of the 1960s Yale pluralists has been supplanted by the "populist" democracy of today, as Robert Dahl himself recently has argued.[24] Contemporary Americans have far more opportunities to influence their government directly than did Americans of midcentury. And therein lies the irony: contemporary Americans are far more distrustful of, cynical about, and hostile toward that government. Americans trusted their government more when party bosses chose nominees, when Southern committee barons dominated Congress, when legislatures and boards conducted their business

22. Important studies include Schlozman and Tierney (1986) and Walker (1991).
23. This episode is described in Fiorina and Peterson (1998, pp. 199–200).
24. Dahl decries this development in *The New American Political (Dis)Order* (1994).

Figure 11-3. *Media Coverage of Poll Results, 1950–88*[a]

Number of public opinion stories

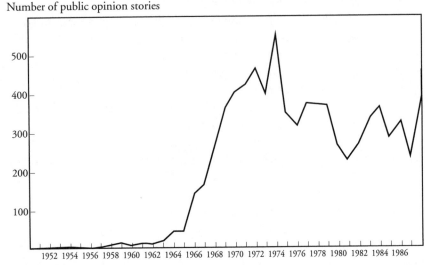

Source: John Brehm, *The Phantom Respondents* (University of Michigan Press, 1993), p. 4.

a. Figure shows the number of stories cited under "public opinion" in *The New York Times* index. According to John Brehm, the cited public opinion stories "by and large report poll results, and only rarely reflections on public opinion in the broader sense."

behind closed doors, when access to the courts and bureaucracy was restricted, and when big business, big labor, and big agriculture dominated the interest group universe.

Why Participatory Democracy Makes Americans Unhappy

"Clowns to the left of me, jokers to the right"
from Stealer's Wheel, "Stuck in the Middle with You"

There are several reasons why Americans who have more opportunities than ever before to influence the actions of their government trust their government less than before. One explanation—popular two decades ago—is "overload." Noting the increase in interest group activity and popular participation described above, some democratic theorists expressed their concern that with encompassing organizations such as parties and unions declining, interest-aggregating structures were being overwhelmed by the rise in interest articulation.[25] Moreover, if the scope of government has expanded, so that expectations are higher than in the past, the problem would be compounded.[26] Although the relevant evidence is mostly circumstantial, this explanation has a good deal of plausibility.[27]

More recently, Hibbing and Theiss-Morse have resurrected Bismarck's caution against watching the production of sausages or laws.[28] Considering the low standing of Congress in relation to the presidency and the Supreme Court, Hibbing and Theiss-Morse argue that Congress is despised precisely because of its openness. Congress allows citizens to see democracy in all its messiness—interest groups lobbying, parties posturing, members dealing and compromising. Generalizing this argument, the more open American politics becomes, the less citizens can maintain the fiction of public-spirited officials working cooperatively to solve social problems and defuse social conflicts. Again, this explanation certainly is plausible.

While seeing merit in both of the preceding hypotheses, I propose a third that is not inconsistent with either: the transition to a more participatory democracy increasingly has put politics into the hands of unrepresentative participators—extreme voices in the larger political debate. Consider another brief listing of research findings.

Back in the 1960s political science students studied Anthony Downs's exposition of the centrist logic of two-party competition.[29] A generation later intellectual inheritors of the Downsian tradition were working to develop models in which the candidates did *not* converge to the center.[30] A changed reality caused this shift in the modeling agenda.[31] During the 1980s pundits and scholars alike remarked on the (electorally) unhealthy influence of "cause groups" in the Democratic primaries who exerted a "left shift" on popular perceptions of Democratic candidates.[32] With a "new Democrat" in titular control of his party for most of the 1990s, the problem has become more serious in the Republican Party, where observers

25. Crozier, Huntington, and Watanuki (1975) offer a representative statement.

26. As noted by May (1997).

27. I indicated some sympathy for this position in an earlier article: "Through a complex mixture of accident and intention we have constructed for ourselves a system that articulates interests superbly but aggregates them poorly"; Fiorina (1980, p. 44).

28. See Hibbing and Theiss-Morse (1995).

29. Downs (1957, chap. 8).

30. For examples, see Alesina and Rosenthal (1995, chap. 2).

31. For recent empirical work on the divergent nature of candidate competition see Ansolabehere and Snyder (1988), and King (1988).

32. Brady and Sniderman (1984). Regrettably, this fascinating study never has been published.

judge that the religious right controls two-thirds of the state party organizations.

Party activism today is ideologically motivated to a much greater extent than in the past. The demise of the spoils system, public sector unionization, conflict-of-interest laws, changes in our political culture, and other factors have cumulated to diminish the material rewards for party activism and the associated incentive to compromise abstract principles in order to maintain material benefits. Today's activists are more ideologically motivated, and whatever the sample studied—state convention delegates, national convention delegates, financial contributors, campaign activists (see Figure 11-4), or candidates themselves—those so motivated come disproportionately from the extremes of the opinion distribution.[33]

The situation is similar with interest groups. At one time groups were viewed as moderating influences in politics.[34] Because people had multiple memberships they were subject to cross-pressures that led them to moderate their stands. On some important issues groups were so heterogeneous internally that they could not take clear positions or exert political influence.[35] Contrast those stylized facts with the contemporary ones. The economic groups formed in the previous generation are more focused and specialized than the older groups people joined before that. They represent single industries, not large sectors. Moreover, there has been a proliferation of "single-issue groups." In the 1960s the NRA was everyone's example of the latter; today, people have their choice of hundreds, many involving matters far more esoteric than guns. Scholars today are more likely to view interest groups as a divisive force in politics, not a moderating one.

If the polarization of political activists were purely a partisan phenomenon or one limited to the national political level, devotees of civic engagement might dismiss it as an exception to the axiom that the more civic engagement the better. Voting in a primary or attending a pro-choice rally may not be the best examples of what they mean by civic engagement. But anyone who has followed a variety of nonpartisan community conflicts in recent years—sex education, land use, leash laws, the organization of

---

33. On state delegates see McCann (1996). On national delegates see Miller and Jennings (1986). On contributors see Brown, Powell, and Wilcox (1995). On candidates see Erikson (1990).

34. The locus classicus is Truman (1958).

35. As discussed by Bauer, Poole, and Dexter (1968) in the context of trade legislation.

Figure 11-4. *Ideology Thermometer Scores of Party Identifiers and Activists, 1968–96*[a]

Liberal-conservative thermometer

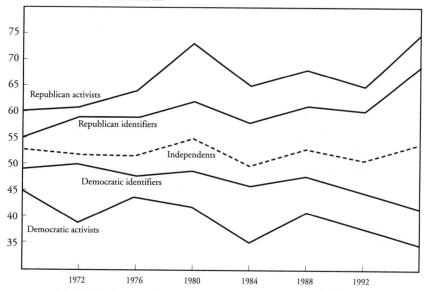

Source: American National Election Studies, website: www.umich.edu/~nes.

a. Activists are defined as respondents who engaged in three or more campaign activities. Partisan identifiers do not include leaners. The liberal-conservative thermometer score measures the respondents' relative thermometer ratings of "liberals" and "conservatives."

children's activities, and so forth—can testify to the generality of the phenomenon. One group of activists may propose something outside the mainstream of community sentiment only to be countered by another group's proposal equally far off in another direction. Or opponents may simply exercise their "exit" option and withdraw from the discussion. In most such conflicts my strong suspicion is that a handful of people picked randomly off the street could have offered proposals that would have beaten the formal contenders in majority votes of the community.

What is going on here? The answer is clear enough. Ordinary people are by and large moderate in their views—relatively unconcerned and uninformed about politics most of the time and comfortable with the language of compromise, trade-offs, and exceptions to the rule. Meanwhile, political and governmental processes are polarized, the participants self-righteous and intolerant, their rhetoric emotional and excessive. The moderate center is not well represented in contemporary national politics—and often not in state and local politics either.[36]

The abortion issue provides a noteworthy illustration. Survey after survey finds that the majority of Americans are "pro-choice buts." They endorse the principle of choice and oppose the overturning of *Roe* v. *Wade*, but blithely approve of numerous restrictions such as parental consent, mandatory counseling, viability testing, and denial of public funding. As Colin Powell, among others, has discovered, however, the debate is dominated by people who condemn as pro-choice someone who would abort a fetus without a brain, and people who denounce as pro-life someone who would outlaw the abortion of a healthy eight-month fetus. Irony of ironies, it took an unelected Supreme Court to impose the kind of broadly acceptable compromise that elective politics had been unable to achieve for two decades, although it had long been evident in the public opinion polls.[37]

In sum, another reason people are frustrated with government is that all too often they see the participants in government locked in battle over unattractive and unrealistic alternatives. The result is unnecessary conflict and animosity, delay and gridlock, and a public life that seems to be dominated by "quarrelsome blowhards," to borrow Ehrenhalt's apt terminology.[38]

Other aspects of political activism exacerbate the problem. Verba and Nie, and Verba, Schlozman, and Brady report that participants care about somewhat different issues than nonparticipants.[39] Thus, not only do the activists debate extreme alternatives, but they also talk about issues nonactivists care less about. Moreover, purist "true believers" have a style different from that of ordinary people. They place more weight on symbols (dubbed "principles"), reject what appear to be reasonable compromises, draw bright lines where many people see only fuzzy distinctions, and label those who disagree with them as enemies.[40] Changes that empower or even

---

36. On the polarization of national politics see McCarty, Poole, and Rosenthal (1998).

37. For polling data on abortion showing majority support for various restrictions, see Ladd (1990), "The Pro-Choice Label" (1992). Those citations, along with "Abortion" (1995), also show that after the substance of the court decisions was explained, comfortable majorities approved of them, with figures for Democrats, independents, and Republicans not differing significantly. We should recognize, of course (with Justice Ginsberg), that an earlier Court probably helped to polarize the issue by institutionalizing a pro-choice position in *Roe*, rather than allowing normal politics to compromise the issue.

38. Ehrenhalt (1998).

39. Verba and Nie (1972, chap. 15); Verba, Schlozman, and Brady (1995, chap. 16).

40. As noted by the common man's philosopher Eric Hoffer (1951) many years ago. For a more contemporary statement see Glendon (1991).

enhance the visibility of these "extreme voices" help to explain "why Americans hate politics"[41] and distrust government.[42]

Civic Engagement and Social Welfare

Much of the debate on civic engagement implicitly presumes that it is a good: the more of it there is, the better off we are. I have argued that such an assumption is invalid, at least in the political realm. In the old order, when ordinary Americans had less opportunity to engage in politics, they apparently were happier with government and what it did than they are today, when they have more opportunities. The reason, I suggest, is that the composition of those who participate has changed. Those willing to compromise policies in order to control offices, jobs, and other tangible benefits have been replaced by those who are motivated largely by policy and ideological commitments. To compromise these is to remove the very motive for participating in the first place. Moreover, these committed activists have less need to broaden their appeals in order to mobilize a mass following than previously. In today's America the courts, the media, and money can substitute for sheer numbers. Thus, only small minorities of highly motivated citizens take advantage of the new participatory opportunities, minorities who are by and large extreme voices in the context of American politics and who have less reason to moderate their commitments than in the past.

What Is to Be Done—Party Renewal?

If the reader is willing to entertain the notion that over at least some of its range civic engagement is socially harmful, what is to be done? Many political scientists trace a variety of problems in contemporary politics to the weakening of traditional political parties. At least since the 1930s many in our profession have believed that parties dominated by professionals

41. Dionne (1991) argues that the country is stuck in a political debate that is foreign to the concerns and beliefs of the larger population, but he describes the discrepancy without explaining why the political order is out of step with the larger population. I am suggesting a mechanism that could help explain the gap he decries.

42. In fact, a recent study by King (1997) shows that people who are far from the position of the strong partisans of either party are more mistrustful. Given the data in Figure 11-4 and variants of it that I have constructed, I suspect that the relationship King finds would be even stronger if positions of political activists were considered.

interested primarily in control of office, patronage, and honest graft had a strong incentive to appeal to the center of the body politic. In that way lay the path to victory and attainment of the associated material goals. Even with a largely inactive citizenry, competitive parties would achieve socially satisfactory conditions—at least relative to conceivable alternatives. When party competition failed, social suffering was often the result.[43] Many in our profession continue to take a positive view of parties, and calls for party renewal periodically resound.

But today's parties are part of the problem, not the solution. Primary elections, civil service coverage, unionization of government workers, conflict-of-interest laws, investigative journalism, and other developments have combined to diminish the material incentives for party activism. Ideological incentives appear to have filled the void. But only a minority are so motivated, and this minority is unrepresentative: "maximum feasible participation" turns out to be pretty minimal, and "power to the people" means power to minorities of extremists.

What Is to Be Done—New Modes of Participation?

If strengthening political parties is not the answer, what is? Perhaps surprisingly, I think the answer may lie in going further down the path of popular participation. To paraphrase John Dewey, the answer to the problems created by increased civic engagement is even more civic engagement. In part, I am led to this position because there is no turning back; any argument to restrict popular participation would be met with incredulity, if not ridicule. One of the more interesting observations of Hibbing and Theiss-Morse is that although voters rarely participate, they value the opportunity to participate in the abstract and would oppose any restrictions on that opportunity.[44]

Thus, the only possibility is to go forward and raise various forms of civic engagement to levels where extreme voices are diluted. Studies of voter turnout have concluded that despite its older, whiter, and wealthier character the actual presidential electorate does not differ significantly in partisanship or presidential preference from the potential universal voting electorate.[45] Given that the actual electorate is about half its potential size,

43. This is Key's classic argument in *Southern Politics* (1949).
44. Hibbing and Theiss Morse (1995, p. 19).
45. Wolfinger and Rosenstone (1980, chap. 6); Teixeira (1992, chap. 3).

these findings suggest that a reasonably representative politics can be achieved with levels of participation somewhere between the 10 and 20 percent levels now measured by most indicators and the 50 percent turnout in presidential elections.

That will not be easy. Consider Concord again, one of the minority of New England towns with a traditional town meeting—as close to direct democracy as occurs in the United States. Although the meeting is no more than a fifteen-minute drive for anyone, average turnout is less than 10 percent of registered voters, with a modern high of 14 percent.[46] It is doubtful that another 30 or 40 percent of the residents could be induced to give up several evenings each year. The problem is that classic forms of participation like this are far too costly for today's citizens. New England town meetings are traditionally scheduled for early spring, after the snows have melted but before the fields are dry enough to plow. For the eighteenth- and nineteenth-century participators, town meeting must have been a welcome diversion after a long lonely winter, especially in an era with no television and little reading material. In contrast, consider the situation of today's two-worker commuter families. Spend several evenings a week listening to your fellow citizens debate issues?[47] That's bonkers. Spend your precious Saturday afternoon at a caucus? Oh, right. Give up dinner out in order to make a contribution? Let them get their money from the PACs.

It is time to abandon the notion of political participation as part of human nature. It is not; it is an unnatural act. The experience of the city-states of antiquity where the civic engagement of the political class was supported by slave labor cannot serve as the model for today's complex mass democracies.[48] Nor can the experience of a nineteenth-century agricultural society where alternative forms of entertainment were unavailable.[49] Contrary to the suggestions of pundits and philosophers, there is

46. Figures reported in Stephens (1995). Mansbridge (1983, pp. 131–32) reports mid-nineteenth-century attendance rates for Concord of about 40 percent, but they soared as high as 70 percent on occasion.

47. Another study concluded that the Concord town meeting was demographically representative, except that the proportion of attendees from households with children under eighteen was only 65 percent of their proportion of registered voters (Bracco and Frasier, 1997). I suspect similar underrepresentation would be found for residents who commute to Boston, for single parents, and for couples who work full time.

48. While Jones discounts the extent to which Athenian democracy was dependent on slavery, he also notes that at times police literally had to rope citizens into the Assembly in order to get a quorum (1957, p. 109). Evidently participation was problematic at times even in ancient Athens.

49. For a discussion of the Lincoln-Douglas debates as entertainment see Holzer (1993).

nothing wrong with those who do not participate; rather, there is something unusual about those who do. All too often they are the people "nobody sent."[50]

Of course, I am overstating the case in order to underline the point, which is that the kinds of demands on time and energy required to participate politically are sufficiently severe that those willing to pay the costs come disproportionately from the ranks of those with intensely held extreme views. Given that people cannot be forced to participate, the alternative is to get the costs down.

Thus, we should give a fair hearing to proposals for newer, lower-cost forms of political participation. In particular, we need to reconsider the notion that people must be physically present, or must invest large blocks of their time. Ross Perot's talk of electronic town halls was met with derision among academics, but the possibilities offered by modern communications deserve investigation, if only because they may be the only practical remedies.

The standard objection to movement in this direction is that making participation easier raises its quantity but lowers its quality. People who do not invest their time and engage in deliberation will be less informed, or indeed will be badly informed, expressing their stereotypes and prejudices in low-cost participatory acts. This objection is less compelling than it might seem.

In the first place, the statistical law of large numbers works against it. Empirically, recent research on public opinion shows that however uninformed and inconsistent individual attitudes may appear to be, in the aggregate public opinion seems to be reasonable and rational.[51] Similarly, despite periodic gay-rights initiatives and other popular attempts to deny rights to minorities, studies of direct democracy find little indication that it produces outcomes any worse than those produced by legislatures.[52]

As the various jury theorems remind us, aggregation is an enormously powerful process.[53] For example, even if we assume that an average U.S. senator has a .75 probability of being right on a particular policy question

50. From the classic anecdote about the Chicago machine's attitude toward self-selectors, as related by Rakove (1979, p. 318).

51. See the important studies of Page and Shapiro (1992) and Stimson (1991).

52. Cronin (1989, p. 229).

53. Condorcet (1976) generally is credited with the basic result. For extensions see Grofman and Owen (1986) and Ladha (1992).

(a generous assumption in the view of this congressional scholar), and that an average citizen's probability of being right is .51 (a conservative assumption in the view of this neopopulist), the probability that a Senate *majority* makes the wrong decision is greater than the probability that a national referendum of 100 million voters does. Both probabilities are quite small, but the point is simply that large numbers can more than compensate for less information.

In the second place, it is not at all clear that ordinary people *are* more badly informed than activists, for ideology often masquerades as information. The activists on various issues may be more informed about those issues, but their information is typically selective, exaggerated, and biased in various ways. Some recent studies have compared the views of various political "elites" with those of equally expert but not politically active control groups. For example, leaders of environmental groups were asked to rate various environmental cancer risks. Their ratings were then compared with those of a sample of cancer researchers. Unsurprisingly, relative to expert but disinterested opinion, the environmental activists significantly overstated the risks of environmentally caused cancer.[54] Such findings are not at all surprising, but they seriously undercut arguments that informed minorities make better—as contrasted with "different"—decisions than uninformed majorities.[55] It is not clear that empowering "informed" extremists and letting them fight it out produces better public policies than a politics in which ordinary uninformed citizens have more influence.

Conclusion

While the far-ranging debate about civic engagement and social capital is full of disagreements, few have questioned the basic premise that civic

54. For all risk factors, environmental activists considered the cancer risk to be greater than the scientists did: e.g., on a scale of 1 to 10, activists rated dioxin 8.1, scientists rated it 4.7; for DDT, activists 6.7 and scientists 3.8; for nuclear power, activists 4.6 and scientists 2.5. Rothman and Lichter (1996, pp. 234–35).

55. One of the Concord activists I spoke with believed that he had acted in the enlightened interest of the larger community. He bemoaned the impossibility of sitting down with uninformed residents who favored the Middlesex plan and explaining how destruction of a vernal pool would harm the reproduction of salamanders. He had no persuasive answer to the question: "What if they were to reply 'I understand all that, but I'll trade the salamanders for soccer fields.'"

engagement is a good thing, or at least that it does no harm. I do—at least when attention focuses on civic engagement in the political realm. There are plenty of political scientists, politicians, and journalists who believe that American democracy worked better when the only participation expected of citizens was that they vote early and often. Today, when citizens have far more opportunities to determine the choice of candidates and policies, small and unrepresentative slices of the population disproportionately avail themselves of those opportunities. Too often the consequence is "clowns to the left and jokers to the right"—a politics that seems distant from the views of ordinary people. When future research attempts to relate civic engagement to welfare measures, it should bear in mind that the relationship between political engagement and social welfare may well be U-shaped, with societies better off with either "a little" or "a lot" than with "some."[56]

Appendix 11A: Why Are Extremists Disproportionately Represented in Politics?

Social scientists often puzzle over things that normal people consider to be self-evident. Here is another example: why are people with extreme views disproportionately likely to be represented in politics? I begin with the more general question: why does *anyone* participate?

Why Participate?

The tradition I represent customarily views actions as instrumentally motivated. Thus, investing time, effort, or money in politics is like any other investment; you do it if the expected benefit exceeds the cost. The more individuals value the benefit—a smoke-free society, for example—the more likely they are to participate. The more costly is participation—transportation to the site of an antismoking demonstration, for example—the less likely they are to participate. Of course, the expected benefit must also incorporate the likelihood that the individual's participation determines whether the benefit occurs. So, the basic calculus of participation takes the following form:

$$(1) \qquad\qquad E(P) = p(B) - c,$$

56. Verba and Nie (1972, chap. 18).

where E(P) = the individual's expected utility of participating,
   p = the probability the individual's action is decisive for the
      outcome,
   B = the individual's evaluation of the proposed alternative versus
      the status quo, and
   c = the individual's costs of participating.

The limitation of such an instrumental explanation of participation is well known from the notorious "paradox of not voting."[57] In many settings the probability that an individual's participation makes a difference is objectively so small that an instrumental explanation of participation is incredible. Why should a rational individual vote in a national election, join tens of thousands of other people in a pro-choice or pro-life demonstration, or give $20 to a million-dollar campaign? In cases like these the marginal impact of an average individual is objectively too small to explain his or her participation.[58]

Thus, a second type of explanation sometimes is brought to bear: actions may have intrinsic value—rather than means to other ends, actions may be ends in themselves. A philistine may pay $1 million for a painting because he believes it will be worth $2 million next year, at which time he will sell it, but an art lover may pay $1 million for a painting for the simple joy of owning it. Naturally enough, economists refer to the latter sort of behavior as "consumption" behavior, as distinct from the former, "investment" behavior. Political scientists find the term "expressive" behavior more descriptive than consumption behavior, since in the political context individuals are often expressing a preference for some political outcome rather than a desire to consume some product.

Of course, one can trivially explain any action by saying that the individual likes doing it. Thus, claims that citizens vote in national elections in order to express their sense of citizen duty may well be true, but that hardly supports an instrumentalist conception of participation.[59] Still, it is not true that adding expressive benefits to the basic calculus of participation necessarily results in degenerate explanations. Such exercises

---

57. Ferejohn and Fiorina (1974).

58. Any self-respecting rational-choice scholar would reject the argument that people systematically overestimate how much their actions matter. Such an argument is tantamount to destroying the theory in order to save it.

59. Barry (1970, pp. 15–18).

have produced nonobvious propositions consistent with empirical evidence.[60] In the present context consider the consequences of adding an expressive benefits term, E, to (1):

$$(2) \qquad\qquad E(P) = p(B) - c + E.$$

Far from being empirically vacuous, (2) gives rise to at least four propositions. Notice that p, the probability of individual impact, determines the balance between instrumental and expressive motivations (e.g., if $p = 0$, any participation *must* be expressively motivated). Thus, if individuals decide whether or not to participate based on (2), the following propositions would hold (ceteris paribus):

—Numbers proposition: Mass arenas will be dominated by those participating for expressive reasons, whereas elite arenas will have more instrumental participators. This proposition is simply the generalized paradox of not voting. In a presidential election, for example, the probability that one's vote determines the outcome is so infinitesimal that only the deluded would vote for instrumental reasons. But in a small government board or legislative subcommittee each participant could well have the deciding vote.

—Level proposition: Participation in national arenas will be more expressive than participation in local arenas. The logic underlying this proposition is similar to that underlying the previous one, assuming that local arenas generally have fewer participants. Two dozen dog lovers who pack the monthly meeting of the local recreation board to oppose a leash law may reasonably believe they can change the outcome, but those tens of thousands who travel to Washington to march for some cause must be primarily expressing their preferences.

—Resource proposition: When resources are unequally distributed, those with more of them are more likely to be instrumentally motivated than those with fewer. Money is the obvious example. The senior citizen who sends $10 in response to a direct-mail appeal warning of the diabolical intentions of Ted Kennedy or Jesse Helms is more likely to be expressing a preference than is the $200,000 soft-money contributor who expects something more tangible for his or her investment.

—Dynamic proposition: In sequential processes, when the final outcome becomes obvious, only expressive participants will be left in the

60. Fiorina (1976).

arena. To say that the handwriting is on the wall is also to say that further activity no longer has any impact on the outcome; hence, such activity must be expressively motivated. Over time, the ratio of diehards to instrumentalists increases.

These four propositions suggest that incorporating expressive benefits of participation in a rational-choice framework does not result in tautology or even ad hocery. On the contrary, the extremely simple formulation summarized in (2) generates a number of propositions with empirical content.

Why Do Extremists Participate?

Although it goes part way toward answering our question, the formulation in (2) falls short. Specifically, (2) implies disproportionate extremist participation *only where participation is instrumentally motivated.* That is, the greater the difference (B) between the values one attaches to a proposed alternative and the status quo, the greater the expected value of participating. Thus, people with extreme views about moves away from the status quo have higher expected values.

But what of arenas in which instrumental benefits are not the primary or even a significant motivation for participation? As argued above, in such arenas participators must be motivated by expressive benefits. But if participation has intrinsic value, then disproportionate extremist participation in such arenas logically requires that extremists get more expressive benefits from participation. Why should this be true? Why are there not comparable proportions of wishy-washy moderates who enjoy voting and attending mass demonstrations, who love to work in national campaigns, and who take satisfaction in writing small checks to obscure causes? Why should the "taste" for political participation be distributed so nonrandomly?

The common-sense answer is that extremists "care" more than moderates. But what does that mean, exactly, and can it be measured independently of the behavior it is thought to explain? Extremist is a relative term, commonly referring to someone whose preferences lie distant from the mainstream, which often will include the status quo. So, someone deeply dissatisfied with the status quo will take greater satisfaction in expressing his or her dissatisfaction than someone not comparably dissatisfied. Alternatively, someone upset by some other extremist's proposal to move away from the status quo will take greater satisfaction in expressing disagreement than someone not so upset. If so, the intrinsic value of an action—its "expressive" value—is directly related to the distance of the actor from the status quo or another contending alternative.

In short, what needs to be added to (2) is an assumption that expressive benefits vary directly with instrumental benefits. Formally, $E = f(B)$, where $f' > 0$. This is a powerful assumption that is sufficient to produce a relationship between extremism and participation for both instrumental and expressive reasons. I believe the assumption is empirically correct, but within my own tradition I am not aware of any deep theoretical justification for it, although there is a social-psychological literature on the empirical relationship between intensity of preferences and extremism of preferences that may be relevant.[61]

Selection or Polarization?

When do extremists select into politics, as presumed in the preceding discussion, and when does politics transform ordinarily uninvolved citizens into activist extremists, as the older community-conflict literature suggests was often the case?[62] My observations of contemporary American politics lead me to believe that selection is the dominant process, but I know of no work aimed squarely at the question.

If political processes seem to become more polarized, even when they do not begin that way, there are at least two explanations. One is another selection process, although one of selecting out rather than selecting in. Johnson has proposed a model of "unraveling" in voluntary groups.[63] Assume that the members of a group can be arrayed along some policy dimension. Then a standard median voter model identifies the most preferred position of the median member as the outcome of a majority vote in the group. But any dissatisfied member who considers the median position unsatisfactory has the option of quitting the group. In particular, if moderates find the group median too extreme and resign, then the new median will be even more extreme, and more relative mod-

61. Early discussions can be found in Allport and Hartman (1925) and Cantril (1946). Rational-choice scholars have sought to represent intensity of preferences mathematically (Rabushka and Shepsle, 1972, pp. 43–53), but I am not aware of any effort to derive a relationship between extremism and intensity.

62. For a discussion, see Coleman (1957).

63. Johnson (1990).

erates may resign. Thus, groups may polarize by shedding their less extreme members.[64]

An alternative possibility is that people with moderate preferences are transformed into extremists during the process of group conflict, as described in sociological literatures such as those dealing with the fluoridation controversies of the 1950s. Such a process appears to involve preference change, which will require the application of different models.

All in all, the empirical side of the study of participation is somewhat more advanced than the theoretical side, at least in this instance. People with relatively more extreme preferences are more likely to participate, other things being equal, but a full explanation of that claim appears to require some synthesis of ideas from different theoretical traditions.

References

"Abortion." 1995. *American Enterprise* (July/August): 107.

Alesina, Alberto, and Howard Rosenthal. 1995. *Partisan Politics, Divided Government, and the Economy.* Cambridge University Press.

Allport, Floyd, and D. A. Hartman. 1925. "The Measurement and Motivation of Atypical Opinion in a Certain Group." *American Political Science Review* 19: 735–60.

Ansolabehere, Stephen, James Snyder, and Charles Stewart. 1998. "Candidate Positions in Congressional Elections." Manuscript.

Barber, Benjamin. 1984. *Strong Democracy.* University of California Press.

Barry, Brian. 1970. *Sociologists, Economists, and Democracy.* London: Collier-Macmillan.

Bauer, Raymond, Ithiel de Sola Pool, and Lewis Anthony Dexter. 1968. *American Business and Public Policy.* New York: Atherton.

Berelson, Bernard, Paul Lazarsfeld, and William McPhee. 1954. *Voting.* University of Chicago Press.

Bracco, Donato, and Cline Frasier. 1997. "Voting in Concord in 1997." Report on file in the Concord Free Public Library.

Brady, Henry, and Paul Sniderman. 1984. "Floors, Ceilings, Guessing, and Other Pitfalls in Survey Research—The Case of Left Shift." Manuscript.

Brown, Clifford, Lynda Powell, and Clyde Wilcox. 1995. *Serious Money.* Cambridge University Press.

Burns, Nancy. 1994. *The Formation of American Local Governments.* Oxford University Press.

Cantril, Hadley. 1946. "The Intensity of an Attitude." *Journal of Abnormal and Social Psychology* 41:129–35.

64. Of course, if the most extreme members are more likely to resign, then the group would tend to become more moderate. The process can produce either polarization or moderation, depending on which members find the median position of the group intolerable

Citrin, Jack. 1974. "Comment: The Political Relevance of Trust in Government." *American Political Science Review* 68: 973–88.

Coleman, James. 1957. *Community Conflict*. Glencoe, Ill.: Free Press.

Condorcet, Marquis de. 1976. *Condorcet: Selected Writings*. Edited by Keith Baker. Indianapolis: Bobbs-Merrill.

Cronin, Thomas. 1989. *Direct Democracy*. Harvard University Press.

Crozier, Michael, Samuel Huntington, and Joji Watanuki. 1975. *The Crisis of Democracy*. New York University Press.

Dahl, Robert. 1994. *The New American Political (Dis)Order*. Berkeley, Calif.: IGS Press.

Dionne, E. J., Jr. 1991. *Why Americans Hate Politics*. Simon and Schuster.

Downs, Anthony. 1957. *An Economic Theory of Democracy*. Harper and Row.

Ehrenhalt, Alan. 1998. "The Increasing Irrelevance of Congress." *Legislative Studies Section Newsletter* (January): 16.

Erikson, Robert. 1990. "Roll Calls, Reputations, and Representation in the U.S. Senate," *Legislative Studies Quarterly* 15: 630.

Ferejohn, John, and Morris Fiorina. 1974. "The Paradox of Not Voting: A Decision Theoretic Analysis." *American Political Science Review* 68: 525–36.

Fiorina, Morris. 1976. "The Voting Decision: Instrumental and Expressive Aspects." *Journal of Politics* 38: 390–415.

———. 1980. "The Decline of Collective Responsibility in American Politics." *Daedalus* 109: 25–45.

Fiorina, Morris, and Paul Peterson. 1998. *The New American Democracy*. Boston: Allyn and Bacon.

Glendon, Mary Anne. 1991. *Rights Talk: The Impoverishment of Political Discourse*. Free Press.

Grofman, Bernard, and Guillermo Owen, eds. 1986. *Information Pooling and Group Decision Making*. Greenwich, Conn.: JAI.

Hibbing, John, and Elizabeth Theiss-Morse. 1995. *Congress as Public Enemy*. Cambridge University Press.

Hoffer, Eric. 1951. *The True Believer*. Harper.

Holzer, Harold. 1993. *The Lincoln-Douglas Debates*. HarperCollins.

Johnson, Paul. 1990. "Unraveling in Democratically Governed Groups." *Rationality and Society* 2: 4–34.

Jones, A. H. M. 1957. *Athenian Democracy*. Johns Hopkins University Press.

Key, V. O., Jr. 1949. *Southern Politics*. Knopf.

King, David, 1997. "The Polarization of American Parties and Mistrust of Government." In *Why People Don't Trust Government*, edited by Joseph Nie, Philip Zelikow, and David King. Harvard University Press.

———. 1998. "Competition and Polarization in American Politics." Manuscript.

Ladd, Everett C. 1990. "Abortion: The Nation Responds." *Ladd Report* 8. W. W. Norton.

———. 1996. "The Data Just Don't Show Erosion of America's 'Social Capital.' " *Public Perspective* 7 (June/July): 1, 5–22.

Ladha, Krishna. 1992. "The Condorcet Jury Theorem, Free Speech, and Correlated Votes." *American Journal of Political Science* 36: 617–34.

Lawrence, Robert. 1997. "Is It Really the Economy, Stupid?" In *Why People Don't Trust Government*, edited by Joseph Nie, Philip Zelikow, and David King. Harvard University Press.

Lipset, Seymour Martin, and William Schneider. 1983. *The Confidence Gap*. Free Press.

Mahtesian, Charles. 1997. "Tooth Squads." *Governing* (June): 40.

Mansbridge, Jane. 1983. *Beyond Adversary Democracy*. University of Illinois Press.

May, Ernest. 1997. "The Evolving Scope of Government." In *Why People Don't Trust Government*, edited by Joseph Nie, Philip Zelikow, and David King. Harvard University Press.

McCann, James. 1996. "Presidential Nomination Activists and Political Representation: A View from the Active Minority Studies." In *In Pursuit of the White House*, edited by William Mayer. Chatham, N.J.: Chatham House.

McCarty, Nolan, Keith Poole, and Howard Rosenthal. 1998. *The Polarization of American Politics*. Manuscript.

Miller, Warren, and M. Kent Jennings. 1986. *Parties in Transition*. New York: Russell Sage.

Page, Benjamin, and Robert Shapiro. 1992. *The Rational Public*. University of Chicago Press.

Pateman, Carole. 1970. *Participation and Democratic Theory*. Cambridge University Press.

"The Pro-Choice Label." 1992. *Public Perspective* (September/October): 99.

Rabushka, Alvin, and Kenneth Shepsle. 1972. *Politics in Plural Societies*. Columbus, Ohio: Merrill.

Rakove, Milton. 1979. *We Don't Want Nobody Nobody Sent*. Indiana University Press.

Rothman, Stanley, and S. Robert Lichter. 1996. "Environmental Cancer: A Political Disease." *Annals of the New York Academy of Sciences* 775: 231–45.

Sabato, Larry. 1991. *Feeding Frenzy*. Free Press.

Schlozman, Kay Lehman, and John C. Tierney. 1986. *Organized Interests and American Democracy*. Harper and Row.

Stephens, David. 1995. "Town Meeting Revisited." Report on file in the Concord Free Public Library.

Stewart, Richard. 1975. "The Reformation of American Administrative Law." *Harvard Law Review* 88: 1669–1813.

Stimson, James. 1991. *Public Opinion in America*. Boulder, Colo.: Westview.

Teixeira, Ruy. 1992. *The Disappearing American Voter*. Brookings.

Tingsten, Herbert. 1937. *Political Behavior: Studies in Election Statistics*. London: King and Son.

Truman, David. 1958. *The Governmental Process*. Knopf.

Verba, Sidney, and Norman Nie. 1972. *Participation in America*. Harper and Row.

Verba, Sidney, Kay Schlozman, and Henry Brady. 1995. *Voice and Equality*. Harvard University Press.

Walker, Jack. 1991. *Mobilizing Interest Groups in America*. University of Michigan Press.

Wilson, James Q. 1962. *The Amateur Democrat*. University of Chicago Press.

Wolfinger, Raymond, and Steven Rosenstone. 1980. *Who Votes?* Yale University Press.

12 | Civic Participation and the Equality Problem

KAY LEHMAN SCHLOZMAN
SIDNEY VERBA
HENRY E. BRADY

IF CIVIC ENGAGEMENT is on the skids, does it really matter? Discussions about the health of civil society are ordinarily conducted as if the reasons for concern are self-evident. When we bother to ask why we care about civic engagement, however, several answers suggest themselves. Participation in voluntary activity matters for three broad categories of reasons: the development of the capacities of the individual, the creation of community and the cultivation of democratic virtues, and the equal protection of interests in public life.[1] In this chapter, we focus on the last of these and explore the implications of patterns of citizen participation in American politics for equal protection of interests.

---

1. Robert Putnam (1996, p. 27) makes the point that many discussions of the decline in civic engagement proceed from the unstated assumption that civic engagement is beneficial to society and that its decline is to be regretted. There are, however, a number of helpful discussions about why we care about civic engagement; among them are Mansbridge (1980, chap. 17); Parry, Moyser, and Day (1992, chap. 1); Putnam (1993); Skocpol (1996); Newton (1997); Edwards and Foley (1997); and Warren (1998). Different authors use different rubrics to categorize the salutary consequences of civic involvement. In proposing tripartite benefits from voluntary activity, we make no claims of either novelty or definitiveness. Rather we seek to position our work within an ongoing dialogue.

Why Care about Civic Engagement?

Of the three broad justifications for concern about civic engagement, the first—that it develops the capacities of the individual—derives from John Stuart Mill. According to the various versions of this perspective, voluntary action is educational, and those who take part become in many ways better human beings—more independent, efficacious, and competent, larger in their capacities for thought, greater in their respect for others and their willingness to take responsibility, better able to appraise their own interests and those of the community.[2]

The second argument made on behalf of civic engagement, its salutary implications for the creation of community and democracy, is in many ways a corollary to the first. In this case the educational effects of civic participation are valued not for their meaning for the individual but for their consequences for community and democracy. The heirs to Tocqueville who make this argument stress several themes. They point to the democratic orientations and skills that develop when people work together voluntarily: social trust,[3] norms of reciprocity and cooperation, and the capacity to transcend narrow points of view and conceptualize the common good. In short, when there is a vigorous sector of voluntary involvement—and the strong associational foundation that underlies it—it becomes easier for communities, and democratic nations, to engage in joint activity and to produce public goods.[4] Moreover, a vital arena of voluntary activity between individual and state protects citizens from overweening state power and preserves freedom.

The third rationale for concern about civic engagement shifts the emphasis from shared community interests to the conflicting interests of individuals and groups and focuses on equal protection of interests. Interestingly, this perspective draws nourishment from Madison's fundamental insight in *Federalist* No. 10 that differences of opinion are sown in the nature of humankind, especially in the unequal acquisition of property. Through the medium of political participation, citizens communicate information about their preferences and needs for government action and

2. See, for example, Bachrach (1967); Pateman (1970); and Parry (1972).

3. This perspective clearly draws from Coleman's (1988) concept of social capital.

4. Many commentators point out that the inevitable result of collective action is not necessarily to foster community and democracy. Some groups—for example, militias—hardly promote democratic values. Moreover, organizations of like-minded individuals beget conflict as well as cooperation. See, for example, the arguments and references contained in Foley and Edwards (1997) and Berman (1997).

generate pressure on public officials to heed what they hear. Of course, we know that public officials act for many reasons, only one of which is their assessment of what the public wants and needs. And policymakers have ways other than the medium of citizen participation to learn what citizens want and need from the government. Nonetheless, what public officials hear clearly influences what they do. Therefore, as long as citizens differ in their opinions and interests, the level playing field of democracy requires that we take seriously the fact that citizens differ in their capacity and desire to take part politically. The democratic principle of one-person, one-vote is the most obvious manifestation of the link between voluntary participation and equal protection of interests. However, for forms of voluntary political participation beyond the vote—for example, writing letters to public officials, attending protests, or making political contributions—there is no such mandated equality of participatory input.

The questions raised by an emphasis on equal protection of interests are somewhat different from those raised by a focus on the development of the individual or the nurturance of community and democracy. First, the cooperative voluntary activity that fosters individual faculties or promotes community and democracy need not be explicitly political. Indeed, some versions of the neo-Tocquevillian argument about community and democracy focus explicitly on voluntary activity in the zone between state and market. In contrast, when equal protection of interests is at stake, the voluntary activity that counts is necessarily political. Furthermore, when it is a matter of the education of individuals or the cultivation of democratic habits, the aggregate quantity of civic engagement is critical. When we move from a conception of congruent community interests to one of clashing individual and group interests and, thus, to a concern with equal protection of interests, questions of representation come to the fore. What matters is not only the amount of civic activity but also its distribution, not just how many people take part but also who they are. In short, concern for democratic equality forces us not only to inquire how many people are bowling and whether they do so solo or in leagues, but also to ask who bowls.

Animated by our concern with equal protection of interests, in this chapter we probe the contours of citizen participation in American politics. We investigate from a variety of perspectives the issue of participatory equality—asking what and from whom the government hears.[5]

5. This chapter draws heavily from the findings of our jointly authored book (Verba, Schlozman, and Brady [1995]), as well as subsequent investigations reported in Brady, Schlozman, and Verba (1999).

The Citizen Participation Study

We employ data from the Citizen Participation Study, a large-scale, two-stage survey of the voluntary activity of the American public. The first stage consisted of over 15,000 telephone interviews of a random sample of American adults that we conducted during the last six months of 1989. These twenty-minute screener interviews provided a profile of political and nonpolitical activity as well as basic demographic information. In the spring of 1990, we conducted much longer, in-person interviews with a stratified random sample of 2,517 of the original 15,000 respondents chosen so as to produce a disproportionate number of those active in politics as well as of African Americans and Latinos. The data in this chapter are from the 2,517 respondents in the follow-up survey.[6] The data presented are weighted to produce an effective random sample.

Understanding Political Participation

Through their activity, citizens in a democracy seek to control who will hold public office and to influence what the government does. Political participation provides the mechanism by which citizens can communicate information about their interests, preferences, and needs—and generate pressure to respond. In a meaningful democracy, the people's voice must be clear and loud—clear so that policymakers understand citizen concerns and loud so that they have an incentive to pay attention to what is said. Since democracy implies not only governmental responsiveness to citizen interests but also equal consideration of the interests of each citizen, democratic participation must also be equal.

In thinking about why some people are active and others are not, we find it helpful to invert the usual question and to ask instead why people do *not* take part in politics. Three answers immediately suggest themselves: because they can't; because they don't want to; or because nobody asked.

"They can't," suggests a paucity of necessary *resources*—time to take part, money to contribute to campaigns and other political causes, and skills to use time and money effectively. "They don't want to," focuses

---

6. A more detailed description of the sample, the sample weights that allow the sample to be analyzed as a random sample, and a listing of the relevant measures can be found in the appendixes to Verba, Schlozman, and Brady (1995).

attention on the absence of political *engagement*—lack of interest in politics or little concern with public issues, a belief that activity can make little or no difference, little or no knowledge about the political process, or other priorities. "Nobody asked," implies isolation from the networks of *recruitment* through which citizens are mobilized to politics. These three components—resources, engagement, and recruitment—form the backbone of an explanatory model of citizen participation that we call the Civic Voluntarism Model. Our discussion of participatory inequalities in this chapter focuses on the first and last of this trio of participatory factors.

Participatory Inequality in America

As it is in so many other ways, American politics is special when it comes to citizen participation. That voter turnout in the United States lags behind voter turnout in other democracies is well known. What is less frequently acknowledged is that in other forms of political activity—for example, campaigning, being active in the local community, or contacting government officials—Americans are as active as, or substantially more active than, citizens elsewhere. What is distinctive about political participation in America, however, is that it is so unequally distributed, hewing more closely to the fault lines of social class. In the United States the skew introduced by the relationship between high levels of education or income and high levels of political activity—a bias characteristic of political participation in democracies around the world—is especially pronounced.

Recent trends in American politics have significant consequences for the nature of political activity and the extent of participatory inequalities. The nationalization and professionalization of both our political parties and organized interests have redefined the role of citizen activist as, increasingly, a writer of checks and letters. The rise of mass mail and electronic communications and the concomitant rise of citizen groups and political action committees dovetail with media-intensive and increasingly costly election campaigns to enhance the relative importance of cash as a medium of participatory input. This development has profound implications for political equality among citizens. A participatory system in which individual financial contributions figure so importantly is characterized by extreme inequalities of participatory input. The range of people whose voices are heard and the range of issues articulated are narrowed with the result that the democratic ideal of the equal representation of the needs and preferences of all citizens is jeopardized.

Of Time and Money

If we compare the distinctive properties of time and money as forms of participatory input, we can understand why, as money gains in relative importance, the participatory system becomes less equal. As resources for politics, time and money differ in that time is both more constrained and more evenly distributed than is money. Time, unlike money, cannot be banked for later use if not expended today. Furthermore, in contrast to money, there is a fixed upper bound on time: the best-endowed of us has only twenty-four hours in a day. Because time is inherently limited, disposable time is more evenly distributed among individuals than is disposable income. Even allowing for the difference in the metrics, the gap in dollars between the richest and poorest is far wider than the gap in hours between the busiest and most leisured. Indeed, of all the resources that facilitate political involvement, money is the most stratified.[7]

Who enjoys the luxury of excess money or time to devote, if desired, to political participation? In case it was not apparent before Hemingway's famous observation, we now know that the rich have more money. What is more, it is well known that income and wealth are distributed more unequally in the United States than they are in other developed democracies. With respect to the question of whether those who are financially well off also have more free time, we might have contradictory expectations. On one hand, we might guess that the rich would have more free time because they can hire others—gardeners or accountants, for example—to do what most people have to do for themselves. On the other hand, we might expect the rich to have less free time because they manage to accumulate wealth by dint of the long hours they log at work.[8] In fact, our data demonstrate that income and other measures of socioeconomic status are not related to the availability of free time. Instead, what determines how

7. On the multiple resources that are useful for political participation, see Verba, Schlozman, and Brady (1995, chaps. 10–11).

8. In fact these conjectures reflect the contradictory predictions of economic theory, which holds both that an income effect would produce more leisure for the wealthy because they are able to purchase it and that a substitution effect would produce less because their wages raise the opportunity cost of free time. See Mincer (1962).

much time is available are such life circumstances as having a job, a spouse who works, or children, especially preschool children. Thus, unlike all other politically relevant resources—not only money but also education and various kinds of civic skills—free time does not hew to the fault lines of social stratification.

Because those who are financially well off are more likely than the less well heeled to take part, the increased emphasis on making financial contributions as a form of political activity has potential consequences for participatory equality. Figure 12-1 compares two income groups at the extremes, roughly the bottom fifth (who had family incomes below $15,000 at the time of our survey in 1990) and the top tenth (who had family incomes above $75,000), and shows that, with respect to all forms of activity, the former are much less active than the latter. They are less likely to vote, only half as likely to go to a protest or to get in touch with a government official, only one-third as likely to engage in informal activity within the community, and only one-tenth as likely to make a campaign donation.

It matters not only whether citizens take part politically but also how much they do. Earlier we mentioned that, as the only act for which there is mandated equality in each citizen's input, the vote is unique among political acts. For other acts, the volume of activity—letters written, dollars contributed, meetings attended, and so on—can be adjusted according to the willingness and wherewithal of the activist. Although the affluent are more likely to be active as both campaign workers and campaign donors, their relative advantage grows when we consider not simply the fact of their activity but also the amount of their activity. Figure 12-2 presents data only for those who were active and shows that, among those who worked as volunteers in campaigns, those in the lowest income group actually gave more time—an average of four hours a week more—than those in the highest income category. Among those who gave money to campaigns, however, the situation is, not unexpectedly, very different. Among givers, those at the top of the income ladder gave, on average, nearly fourteen times as much as those at the bottom.

We can push this line of reasoning one step further by using units of participatory input rather than individuals as our metric. Figure 12-3 gives us a politician's-eye view of what the citizenry would look like if each income group's visibility depended on the amount of political activity it produced. The upper-left section of Figure 12-3 presents as a baseline the distribution of various family income groupings within the population.

Figure 12-1. *Percentage Active in Various Activities:*
High- and Low-Income Groups

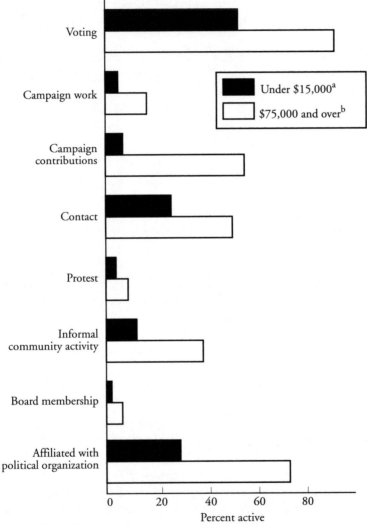

a. *N* = 483 weighted cases.
b. *N* = 224 weighted cases.

Source: This and subsequent figures and tables have been adapted from Verba, Schlozman, and Brady (Harvard University Press, 1995) and Brady, Schlozman, and Verba (*America Political Science Review*, 1999).

Figure 12-2. *Mean Hours and Dollars Given to Political Campaigns, by Family Income*

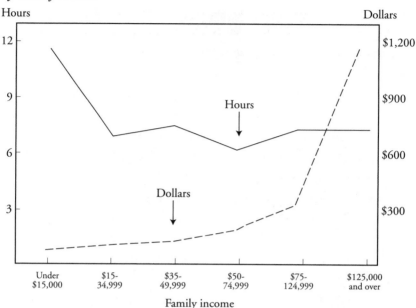

The other graphs show the proportion of the population in various income categories weighted by the amount of activity produced by that income group: by the votes citizens cast, the number of hours they work in campaigns, and the number of dollars they contribute to candidates, parties, and campaign organizations. For comparison, we provide information about voluntary activity in nonpolitical domains: the proportion of hours and dollars contributed to charity and to religious institutions by different family income groups.

The activist population provides a very different income perspective from the population as a whole. Those at the top of the income hierarchy produced more than their proportionate share of votes, campaign hours, and campaign dollars. However, the distortion is much less pronounced for votes than for campaign time and, in turn, less for campaign time than for campaign money. The 3 percent of the sample with family incomes over $125,000 are responsible for 4 percent of the votes, 8 percent of the hours devoted to campaigning, and fully 35 percent of the money contributed. Indeed, the top two income groups, who constitute less than 10

Figure 12-3. *Volume of Political and Nonpolitical Activity: Percentage from Various Family Income Groups*

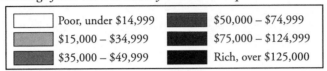

Poor, under $14,999	$50,000 – $74,999
$15,000 – $34,999	$75,000 – $124,999
$35,000 – $49,999	Rich, over $125,000

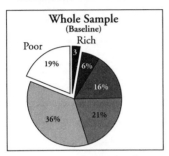

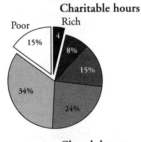
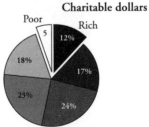
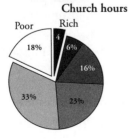
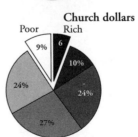

Whole Sample (Baseline); Votes; Campaign hours; Campaign dollars; Charitable hours; Charitable dollars; Church hours; Church dollars

percent of the sampled population, donated more than half of the money used to conduct campaigns. At the other end of the family income scale are those with family incomes under $15,000, who constitute 19 percent of the sample. They were responsible for 14 percent of the votes and 13 percent of the hours volunteered in campaigns. However, they are barely visible in electoral contributions—donating only 2 percent of the campaign dollars.

Figure 12-3 also shows comparable figures for the hours devoted to charitable activity and to educational, social, or charitable activities associated with a church (beyond attendance at services), as well as for the dollars contributed to charity and to religious institutions. In terms of the volume of voluntary activity, the poor are underrepresented and the affluent overrepresented. Further, the distortion is generally greater in the domain of politics than in other arenas and much greater for money than for time. With respect to hours, the poor are underrepresented in all three domains, but by the largest amount for campaign activity. The affluent are overrepresented by a substantial amount in campaigning, and by a smaller amount in charitable hours. They are proportionately represented in the number of hours devoted to church work. Note, in fact, that both the highest- and lowest-income groups contribute a proportional share of the church hours, suggesting that the religious domain is the one of greatest relative equality. In terms of dollars, the affluent are overrepresented and the poor underrepresented in the money contributed in all three domains. However, the bias is much less pronounced for donations to religious institutions than for donations to charities.[9] And the bias is greatest for campaign contributions.

It is hardly surprising that those with higher family incomes are more generous in their financial contributions, but not necessarily in the amount of time they give. After all they have more money—and, in comparison with the poor, they are relatively better off with respect to money than with respect to time. It is less obvious why they should be relatively more generous than those who are less well off in their contributions to politics than in their contributions to charity or church—especially since democratic politics is the arena of voluntary activity with the strongest underly-

9. Among those who contributed, those with family incomes under $15,000 gave on average of $97 per year to charity; those with incomes over $125,000 gave on average $1,176. The figures for church giving were $373 and $1,662 respectively. For giving time, activists among the poor actually gave somewhat more hours per week to charitable and church work than the rich.

ing egalitarian commitment. In an age when candidates rely ever more heavily on campaign contributions, the extent to which campaign dollars come from the wealthy has implications for equality in a democracy.

Participatory Equality and Government Benefits

Why should we care that some people are much more active than others and, therefore, that government officials hear much more from some quarters than from others? If those who do not take part in politics are distinctive—in their political opinions and concerns or their need for government action—then the equal protection of interests may be in jeopardy. Our data show clearly that those who are especially active in politics do not necessarily represent the views or the priorities of those who are more quiescent. The government hears different messages from members of groups that are not especially active. In particular, when those who are disadvantaged by virtue of low levels of education or income do participate, they express distinctive sets of concerns, needs, and opinions.

In the Citizen Participation Study, all respondents who indicated that they, or any family member in the household, received a particular government benefit were asked whether they had been active *in relation to* that benefit: Had they taken that program into account in deciding how to vote? Had they given a campaign contribution based, at least in part, on concern about it? Had they contacted an official to complain about the program? Did they belong to an organization concerned about that program? Recipients of benefits targeted at the poor (such means-tested benefits as Aid to Families with Dependent Children (AFDC), food stamps, or Medicaid) are less likely than recipients of non-means-tested benefits (for example, veterans' benefits, Social Security, or Medicare) to have been active.[10]

The data in Figure 12-4 show the proportion of the recipients of each benefit who reported an activity related to the benefit program for each

---

10. Note that the referent in the questions about government benefits was the respondent or any immediate family member living in the household. In the text when we refer to "food stamp recipients" or "those who received veterans' benefits," the recipient may in fact have been a family member in the household of the survey respondent.

We should also note that, although there is a means test for student loans, we are categorizing them with non-means-tested benefits. The level of permissible income for student loans is much higher than for other means-tested benefits such as food stamps or AFDC, and the beneficiaries are not located primarily among the poor.

Figure 12-4. *Activities of Benefit Recipients Directly Related to Benefit Programs*

Percent of benefit recipients

a. Less than 1 percent.

kind of activity: voting, contributing, contacting, and membership in an organization. Clearly, recipients of non-means-tested benefits were more likely to have been active than recipients of means-tested benefits. The difference is especially striking with respect to campaign donations and membership in an organization associated with the benefit—with the American Association of Retired Persons (AARP) and veterans' organizations presumably playing a major role. Thirty-five percent of the recipients of veterans' benefits and 24 percent of the recipients of Social Security, in contrast to 2 percent of AFDC recipients and none of the food-stamp recipients, belonged to an organization concerned about the program. However, the distinction between recipients of means-tested and non-means-tested benefits also applies to voting decisions.[11] The data on contacting a public official are interesting. We might expect that inclusion in the non-means-tested programs would be more or less automatic and thus would require people to have fewer contacts with public officials. Nevertheless, Medicare recipients were more likely than Medicaid recipients to communicate with officials about their medical benefits; Social Security recipients were more likely than AFDC recipients to contact a public official about their benefits.[12] Clearly, the government hears more from those on some programs than on others, and the ones it hears from are the more advantaged citizens.

What Messages Do They Send?

Our concern with understanding the voice of the people led us to do something novel in our survey. We asked about the issues basis of activity—what activists actually say when they take part. Every time someone indicated having undertaken some kind of political activity, we inquired whether there were particular issues or problems associated with their

11. It has been suggested to us that the seeming salience of entitlement programs for voting decisions is only a reflection of the fact that political leaders have drawn attention to these programs in campaigning and thus tells us more about political leaders than about citizens. That candidates make promises about protecting Social Security or veterans' benefits but not about means-tested benefits, however, is itself a political fact worth noting and may reflect what they are hearing from citizens and the organizations to which they belong.

12. Student loans are an exception. There is relatively little activity in relation to student loans. However, there is still more activity in relation to student loans than there is in relation to most means-tested programs.

participation.[13] Thus we were able to establish the substantive content of what public officials hear from political activists.

Table 12-1 summarizes the subject matter behind the political activity in which an issue concern was expressed and compares advantaged and disadvantaged respondents with respect to the issue concerns that animated their participation.[14] In order to ensure that we are dealing with isues that were actually communicated to public officials, we focus solely on those activities in which an explicit message can be sent: contacting an official, protesting a policy, campaign work, or contributions accompanied by a communication, informal community activity, or voluntary service on a local board. The issue-based political act is the unit of analysis, and the figures represent the proportion of all issue-based activities for which the respondent mentioned, among other things, a particular set of policy concerns.

Although both the advantaged and the disadvantaged had wide-ranging policy concerns, the distribution of their concerns differs. Compared with the issue-based activity of the advantaged, that of the disadvantaged is more than twice as likely, and that of respondents in families receiving means-tested benefits four times as likely, to have been animated by concerns about basic human needs—poverty, jobs, housing, health, and the like. Moreover, their activity was more likely to have been motivated by concern about drugs or crime. The activity of the advantaged, in contrast, was more likely to have been inspired by economic issues such as taxes, government spending, or the budget or by social issues such as abortion or pornography.

When we consider the actual number of communications, however, a very different story emerges. Because the disadvantaged are so much less active than the advantaged, public officials actually hear less about issues related to basic human needs from the disadvantaged than from the slightly smaller group of advantaged respondents—even though references

13. For discussion of how these data were collected and coded, see Verba, Schlozman, and Brady (1995, pp. 84– 91, 220–25).

14. Both to generate additional cases for analysis and to purge the lowest-income category of a few aberrant cases of very well educated, low-income respondents, we shift our focus from the extremes in family income to a more general definition of socioeconomic advantage and disadvantage. We define the advantaged as those with at least some college education and a family income over $50,000 and the disadvantaged as those with no education beyond high school and family incomes below $20,000. These are groups of roughly equal size representing about one-sixth of the sample each.

Table 12-1. *What Respondents Say: Issue-Based Political Activity*[a]

Percent

| Issue | | Proportion of issue-based activity animated by concern about | | |
	All	Advantaged[b]	Disadvantaged[c]	Received means-tested benefit
Basic human needs	10	8	21	32
Taxes	6	6	4	8
Economic issues (except taxes)	5	7	1	1
Abortion	8	11	0	4
Social issues (except abortion)	2	1	5	6
Education	12	15	10	18
Environment	9	8	2	2
Crime or drugs	9	6	10	8
Foreign policy	3	3	0	0
Number of respondents[d]	2,517	425	480	228
Number of issue-based acts[d]	1,556	432	123	73

a. This table records only information-rich acts, those in which an explicit message can be sent to policymakers: contacting officials, protesting, doing campaign work or making contributions accompanied by a communication, informal community activity, or voluntary service on a local board. The numbers in the cells represent the proportion of such acts having identifiable issue content for which there was a reference to the particular issue.

b. The advantaged were those with at least some college and a family income of $50,000 or more.

c. The disadvantaged were those with no education beyond high school and family income below $15,000.

d. Numbers shown are the weighted numbers of cases and issue-based acts.

to basic human needs occupy relatively greater space in the bundle of communications emanating from the disadvantaged.

These findings might suggest that, although the disadvantaged are underrepresented with respect to participatory input, their concerns and needs are nonetheless being expressed by others. When the disadvantaged speak for themselves on issues of basic human needs, however, their communications differ fundamentally from those sent by others. First, when the disadvantaged communicated with public officials about basic human needs, they were much more likely than the advantaged to be concerned about problems that affected them personally. Even affluent citizens may need government assistance with meeting basic human needs: they may have health problems or a handicapped child in school, or, if elderly, receive Medicare and Social Security. Still, a much larger proportion of the messages from the disadvantaged about basic human needs involved particularized communications about problems specific to themselves or their families—a question about eligibility for Social Security, a complaint about the conditions in a housing project, and a request by a disabled respondent for special transportation, to cite some actual examples.

Among respondents who mentioned human needs issues as associated with their issue-based activity, 56 percent of the disadvantaged but only 8 percent of the advantaged were animated by such particularized concerns. Even when the human needs issue was framed as a policy issue rather than a particularized concern, the disadvantaged were much more likely to report that the problem affected themselves or their families as well as others in the community. When discussing basic human needs policy issues, 15 percent of the disadvantaged—as opposed to 21 percent of the advantaged—indicated that the issue affected them as well as others. Taken together, of those who communicated to public officials about issues of basic human needs, 71 percent of the disadvantaged but only 29 percent of the advantaged discussed something with an immediate impact upon themselves or their families. It is axiomatic in the literature on lobbying that public officials listen more carefully to self-interested advocates who are affected by the policies they discuss. Presumably, the analogous principle applies to communications from individuals: stories about basic human needs sound different to policymakers when told by those who are themselves in need.

Furthermore, when they communicate with public officials about policy matters concerning issues of basic human need, the advantaged and disadvantaged convey quite different messages. The appropriate governmental role in addressing problems related to basic human need is an issue about which there is profound disagreement in American society. Close reading of what people actually said about the issues and problems associated with their participation allowed us to differentiate among messages about public efforts on behalf of the needy. On the one hand were expressions of concern about the "homeless plight" and "the Commission for visually handicapped Blind Association. To increase their benefits." On the other were such identifiably conservative statements as "welfare should be done away with" and "[I] dislike big government, [the] welfare state, and big brothers." Not all the policy statements about basic human needs could be so readily categorized. However, to the extent that the disadvantaged—whether liberal or conservative in their overall opinions as expressed in the interview—made identifiable policy statements about basic human needs in association with political activity, none of their statements urged that public attention to issues of basic human need be reduced. In contrast, the views about basic human need expressed by the advantaged through their activity were quite mixed. Because they are so much more active than the disadvantaged, however, public officials actually receive more messages from the advantaged, suggesting a curtailment of government intervention on behalf of the needy, than messages from the disadvantaged urging the opposite.

Overcoming Participatory Inequality through Mobilization

What can be done to diminish the participation gap that separates the advantaged and the disadvantaged? Social scientists have long paid attention to the processes by which citizens are mobilized into politics.[15] In particular, they have focused on the way that social movements—whether composed of assembly-line workers, civil rights activists, environmentalists, advocates of school prayer, or opponents of higher taxes—bring new issues and therefore new publics into politics.[16] Presumably because they

15. On the effects of close interpersonal networks on participation, see Knoke (1990). Among the few studies of networks and electoral mobilization is Huckfeldt and Sprague (1992). Rosenstone and Hansen (1993) stress the important role of mobilization in explaining activity. Their focus, however, is on the role of strategic elites in mobilizing citizens, not on the more proximate interpersonal networks within which citizens live. For a review of contextual studies, see Huckfeldt and Sprague (1993).

16. A few examples in a vast literature include Oberschall (1973); Boyte (1980); McAdam (1982); Freeman (1983); Luker (1984); Morris (1984); McCarthy and Zald (1987); and Tarrow (1994).

can provide a vehicle for the political activation of those who would otherwise be quiescent, social movements among the disadvantaged have received considerable attention.[17] Nonetheless, dating back at least as far as the abolitionists, there is a well-known tradition of middle-class protest in American politics.

Social movements fascinate precisely because they are not simply political business as usual. Less colorful—and less often studied—are the day-to-day processes of citizen recruitment by which neighbors, workmates, fellow organization members, or strangers who call during dinner make requests for political activity. The request might be to attend a meeting to support a local school bond referendum; to give a campaign donation to the incumbent governor; to volunteer in the campaign of his opponent; to write a legislator about the impact of cuts in National Science Foundation funding on research in the social sciences; or to attend a pro-life demonstration. These solicitations may be, but are not ordinarily, associated with a social movement.

Using an innovative battery of questions contained in the Citizen Participation Study, we have been able to investigate patterns of recruitment across the entire citizenry and thus to understand the workings of the recruitment process more generally.[18] What we found is that those who wish to recruit others to politics—from professional fund-raisers in search of large campaign contributions to community residents concerned about the local crime rate—act as "rational prospectors," seeking to expend their time and effort as efficiently as possible.[19] Rational prospectors seek to maximize the probability that the people they ask to get involved will not

17. See, for example, Piven and Cloward (1977).

18. The survey included batteries of questions designed to probe experiences with requests for activity. We asked respondents whether, over the past twelve months, they had received any requests to take part in a campaign (to work in the campaign or to contribute money, or both); to contact a government official; to take part in a protest, march, or demonstration; or to take some active role in a public or political issue at the local level. If they had, we followed up by inquiring whether they had received more than one such request and whether they said yes to the request. If there had been more than one request for a particular kind of activity, we asked the follow-up information about the most recent one. In addition, we probed the characteristics of people making requests and the nature of their connections to respondents. We should make clear that these data provide information about recruitment attempts and that what we know about the characteristics of recruiters is derived from reports of targets. Thus, to the extent that we make inferences about the intentions of recruiters, we do so—in the best traditions of economists—on the basis of revealed preferences.

19. This discussion draws heavily on the analysis and data in Brady, Schlozman, and Verba (1999).

only respond positively to their entreaties but also be effective as participants.

When taken as a whole, these processes of rational prospecting through which citizens are asked by others to take part politically do not, by and large, mobilize excluded constituencies to politics. Rather, the overall thrust is to reinforce the tendencies of a participatory process anchored in the individual characteristics that predict political participation. That is, those who are, by dint of their desire and ability, more likely to be politically active are also more likely to be the targets of appeals for activity. In short, when viewed in its entirety, the process of citizen recruitment does not mobilize the marginal and dispossessed. In fact, by recruiting activists on the basis of the same factors that would lead individuals to participate on their own, rational prospectors bring to politics a set of activists whose participatory characteristics are even more pronounced than the characteristics of those who would have taken part spontaneously.

Who Is Recruited?

By searching for targets who are likely to be willing to take part in politics and who will be effective as activists when they do, those who seek to get others involved in politics use as cues the kinds of characteristics that are associated with participation in politics. The single best predictor of political activity is education: those who are well educated are more likely both to be motivated to take part and to be endowed with the resources that facilitate participation.[20] Across various types of activity, the higher the level of education, the more likely an individual will be targeted by recruiters. Thus, beyond the individual endowments that make them likely to be active, the well educated are also exposed to recruitment efforts. The result is that those citizens who come to their activity through recruitment are not only, as expected, better educated than the population as a whole but also better educated than those who come to their activity spontaneously. The difference is substantial: 45 percent of those who undertook at least one participatory act in response to a request have a college degree; only 31 percent of those who undertook at least one act spontaneously have a

20. See Verba, Schlozman, and Brady (1995, chap. 15) for an extended discussion of the multiple ways in which education fosters political activity. On the role of education in participation, see also Nie, Junn, and Stehlik-Barry (1996).

Table 12-2. *Spontaneous and Recruited Political Activity by Family Income*

	Percent of respondents who engaged in at least one political act that was	
Family income	Spontaneous[a]	Recruited[b]
Less than $15,000	29	9
$15,000–34,999	32	17
$35,000–49,999	36	28
$50,000–74,999	48	33
$75,000–124,999	38	37
$125,000 and over	48	47

a. An act for which there was either no request or a single request that was denied.

b. An act for which there was at least one request that was granted.

college degree.[21] Analogous figures about income tell a similar story. We have already seen in Figure 12-1 that political activity rises with income. Table 12-2, which shows the proportion in each income group who undertook at least one political activity spontaneously and the proportion who undertook at least one act in response to a request, indicates that activity undertook spontaneously is much less highly structured by income than is activity undertaken as the result of recruitment. In the lowest income category, respondents were much more likely to have taken part spontaneously than to have been active after being asked. In the top two categories the proportions active in each way are nearly equal.

The exaggeration of participatory stratification through the process of recruitment is especially pronounced for political contributions. Earlier we noted that political giving is the most stratified of all activities: the well heeled are more likely to contribute, and the more affluent they are, the more they contribute.[22] In making requests, recruiters selectively target those with deep pockets. In our survey, contributors were, as a group, more affluent than noncontributors, whose mean family income was $35,300.

21. We define as spontaneous activists those who either received no requests to become active in that particular way or were asked once and did not say yes. We consider as recruited activists those who were asked to take part at least once and who assented to the most recent solicitation. We omit from the discussion those ambiguous cases in which the respondent reported more than one request for a particular kind of activity but said no to the most recent one. In those cases, we could not ascertain whether there had been assent to a previous request—even though the most recent one was turned down.

22. For elaboration of these themes see Verba, Schlozman, and Brady (1995, chaps. 7 and 12).

However, among contributors, those who gave in response to a request were especially well heeled: their average family income was $56,400, whereas the average income was $48,000 for those who contributed spontaneously. Considering the size of the donation rather than the size of the pocketbook of the donor demonstrates especially clearly that recruiters look where the money is and find it. Contributions given spontaneously averaged $120—only a fraction of those given in response to a request, which averaged $352.

The process by which contributors are recruited thus reinforces the overrepresentation of the well heeled in participation. Figure 12-5 presents data on the proportion of campaign money contributed by various income groups. In Figure 12-3 we saw that the affluent 9 percent of the population (those with incomes over $75,000) were responsible for fully 55 percent of all campaign money given, while the poorest 19 percent (those with incomes under $15,000) were responsible for only 2 percent. However, if we consider separately donations given spontaneously and donations given in response to a request, we see that the process of recruitment further exaggerates this pattern. Of all funds contributed in response to requests, nearly two-thirds, 64 percent, derives from the most affluent 9 percent of the public and only 1 percent from the least affluent 19 percent of the public. The pattern for donations made spontaneously, while still skewed, is much less pronounced.

Those who are brought into politics through these processes of selective recruitment differ not only in their demographic characteristics but also in their need for government assistance. Consider the beneficiaries of government programs discussed earlier. Fifty-two percent of the respondents to the survey said they had been asked at least once to become politically active. Medicare recipients, 49 percent of whom received at least one request for activity, were recruited with about the same frequency as members of the general public. In contrast, only 30 percent of those receiving Medicaid—a means-tested health program for the poor—were recruited at least once. The figures for participants in the principal income-maintenance programs are almost identical: 48 percent of Social Security recipients, but only 30 percent of AFDC recipients, indicated having been asked at least once to take part. With respect to housing, a policy area that often generates political conflict, 58 percent of home owners reported at least one request for participation; only 40 percent of those who do not own their own homes reported receiving at least one such request. Only 28 percent of recipients of government housing subsidies, however, received such requests.

Figure 12-5. *From Which Income Groups Do Political Contributions Come?*

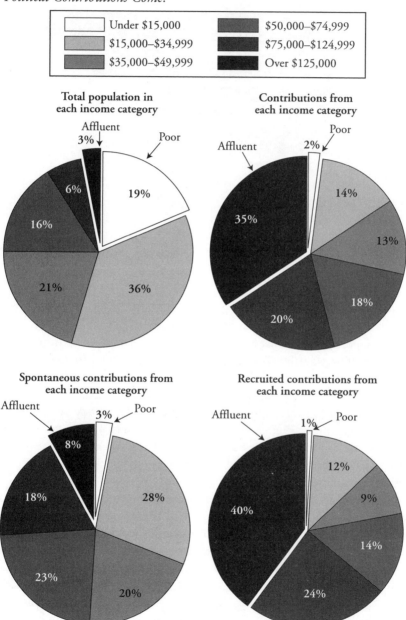

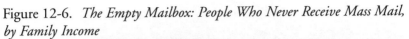

Figure 12-6. *The Empty Mailbox: People Who Never Receive Mass Mail, by Family Income*

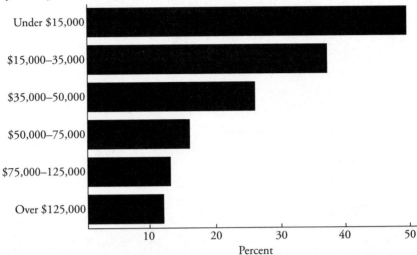

In contrast to the organizational, neighborhood, and workplace networks of personal ties that figure so importantly in the recruitment of political activists are impersonal processes of direct-mail fund-raising. It seems as if everybody's mailbox is crammed with requests for political contributions. However, as shown in Figure 12-6, political direct mail is not sent out indiscriminately. Half of those in the lowest income category indicated that they never receive political mail. Only a small fraction of those in the highest income categories—who presumably are on other mailing lists and are concentrated in promising zip codes—reported never getting any political mail.

In short, while processes of mobilization may bring new issues and points of view to those who govern, our data demonstrate that they do not—when considered in their totality—bring new kinds of people into politics. Because recruiters act as rational prospectors, they seek out people who would be likely not only to participate but to participate effectively—that is, people with the characteristics already overrepresented among participants. In short, the net result of the recruitment process for political activity in general—and for financial contributions in particular—is to exacerbate participatory stratification.

Can Institutions Make the Difference?

Since the ordinary processes by which individuals are asked to take part in politics—for example, to attend a school board meeting, make a campaign donation, or march for or against abortion—do not ameliorate participatory bias, what about voluntary institutions? Voluntary institutions, even ones that are utterly apolitical, operate in many ways other than advocacy to foster political participation. As Tocqueville noted a century and a half ago, associations act as the schools for democracy. Moreover, activity in institutions that has nothing to do with politics or public issues can foster the development of organizational and communications skills that are relevant for politics and thus can facilitate political activity. Organizing the PTA Book Fair, chairing a large charity benefit, or serving on the search committee for a new minister are not overtly political activities. Yet they foster the development of skills that can be transferred to politics. In addition, voluntary institutions can act as the locus of attempts at political recruitment; members make social contacts and, thus, become part of networks through which requests for participation are mediated.[23] And of course association members are exposed to political cues and messages—in communications from officers and staff, on the agendas of meetings, even in informal conversations with fellow members.

It is naive to expect the institutions of civil society to be the magic remedy to overcome the class-based participatory deficit, for the proposed cure contains the seeds of the malady. Just as also those who are well educated and well heeled are more likely to be active in politics, they are more likely to be affiliated with voluntary organizations. Data collected in 1967 indicate that those on the highest rung of the income ladder were three times as likely to be active members of organizations as those at the bottom. In 1990 the

23. For an empirical analysis of the ways in which class-based institutions mobilize individuals to politics, see Verba, Nie, and Kim (1978). Rosenstone and Hansen (1993) demonstrate the importance of efforts by strategic elites in parties and organizations in explaining changes over time in rates of citizen participation. Many studies of parties have illustrated their role in getting out the vote or of organized interests in mobilizing grass-roots constituents. A pioneering study of efforts to bring out the vote is Gosnell (1927). See also Eldersveld (1964); Huckfeldt and Sprague (1992); and Wielhouwer and Lockerbie (1994). On the efforts of organized interests to organize latent constituencies and get members involved in politics, see Schlozman and Tierney (1986) and Walker (1991). Among the many case studies that illustrate these processes, see Browne (1988) and Rothenberg (1992). Cohen and Dawson (1993) show that contacting increased campaign contributions and attendance at community meetings in Detroit.

ratio was exactly the same.[24] Thus, the participatory benefits of organizational activity are being reaped by those who are likely to be politically involved already. However, even though affiliation with voluntary organizations, when taken in toto, has a strong socioeconomic bias, particular institutions of civil society might function to overcome that bias.

What about the citizen groups whose growing importance is documented in Jeffrey Berry's contribution to this volume? Certainly a few of the groups—for example, the American Civil Liberties Union and the National Association for the Advancement of Colored People—that received a great deal of television coverage in 1995 act as advocates for, among others, the economically disadvantaged. Nevertheless, Berry indicates that these groups hold values that are "sometimes at odds with the interests of those further down the economic ladder" and concludes by observing that, at the same time that groups espousing postmaterial values have flourished, unions and other traditional liberal interest groups who have pushed for greater economic equality for workers and the poor have weakened. In short, we cannot expect that citizen groups will carry this representational burden.

Where, then, might we find institutions with counter-stratificational effects? Political parties are an obvious answer. Within a democracy an important function of political parties, especially parties of the left, is the mobilization of ordinary citizens—in particular, those who might not otherwise be active. During the nineteenth century strong political parties played a critical role in organizing and mobilizing voters in America. Nonetheless, American political parties are well known for being weak and fragmented, and there are no working-class or peasant parties.

The Citizen Participation Study is deficient in material about the operation of political parties as institutions, but we can use the information about the characteristics of those who ask others to get involved to shed light on the implications of recruitment through partisan networks. Table 12-3 shows, not surprisingly, that Republican identifiers had higher average incomes—and Democratic identifiers had lower average incomes—than the average for the population. It also shows, again not surprisingly, that those recruited to work in campaigns—and, especially, those recruited to contribute to campaigns—had higher than average incomes, higher even than the average for Republican identifiers. When we focus more narrowly on recruitment among fellow partisans, we find more

---

24. The data for 1967 are reported in Verba and Nie (1972, chap. 11). The 1990 data are from the Citizen Participation Study.

Table 12-3. *Family Income and Recruitment for Campaign Activity: The Partisan Connection*

	Average family income
All respondents	$40,300
All Republican identifiers	45,400
All Democratic identifiers	36,900
All who were asked to work in a campaign	48,800
Republican asked by a Republican	51,700
Democrat asked by a Democrat	49,800
All who were asked to contribute to a campaign	52,900
Republican asked by a Republican	56,700
Democrat asked by a Democrat	54,700

skewing in an upward direction. The intraparty nexus involved recruitment of targets who had, on average, higher-than-average incomes for their respective parties. For contributions, the pattern is especially striking. Those asked by a fellow partisan had, on average, incomes that were quite high. The data make it difficult to argue that the processes of intrapartisan recruitment are in any way expanding participatory representation. When Democrats solicited Democrats and Republicans solicited Republicans, the targets of the requests had family incomes that were substantially higher than the average incomes for their fellow partisans but also higher than the average for all who were asked to contribute. Partisan recruitment to take part in a campaign—and especially to contribute money—seems to increase the stratification of political participation in both parties.

In short, while parties have unambiguously played an important historical role in mobilizing voters who might otherwise not go to the polls and in representing the concerns of broad groups whose views might otherwise not be voiced, with respect to the recruitment of activists, the result is more mixed. When seeking contributions rather than votes or campaign workers, the parties hunt where the ducks are and target the affluent among their supporters.

What about Unions? What about Churches?

Aside from parties of the left, what other institutions might serve as the vehicle for the political activation of the less privileged? A student of comparative politics might immediately suggest that we consider unions; a student of American society might propose that we look at churches.

Among the ways in which American politics is alleged to be exceptional among the world's democracies is the weakness of the institutions that, in other nations, bring disadvantaged groups to full participation in political life. We have already mentioned that the Democratic Party plays only very imperfectly the role adopted elsewhere by social democratic and labor parties in mobilizing those who might otherwise not take part politically. In many other democracies, politically engaged trade unions serve as partners of parties of the left in organizing the less affluent. However, in contrast to their counterparts abroad, American labor unions have traditionally been relatively weak and enroll a relatively small—and diminishing—proportion of the work force.

An aspect of American exceptionalism that receives less attention in discussions of politics is the depth of religious commitment of American citizens and the relative frequency of their religious attendance. As Robert Wuthnow's chapter in this volume demonstrates, participation in religious institutions is the least class-biased form of voluntary activity. In fostering participation, American churches function in a manner similar to voluntary associations: they nurture politically relevant skills, generate requests for political participation, and expose members to explicitly political messages. Thus, religious institutions in America might partially compensate for the weakness of unions and the absence of a labor or social democratic party by bringing into politics those who might not otherwise be involved.

Figure 12-7 presents data for various income groups about these involvements. As anticipated, organizational involvement is structured by income and is almost universal in the higher-income groups. Church membership, in contrast, varies very little among income groups. Among those with the lowest incomes, the same proportion, 63 percent, were organizational and church members. At the top of the income hierarchy, however, fully 96 percent were affiliated with an organization, but only 66 percent were church members. In contrast to organizational affiliation, union affiliation does not seem to rise with income. Instead, the pattern is curvilinear, with those in the highest and lowest income groups having the lowest levels of union affiliation. Thus, it would seem that engagement with unions and religious institutions presents the possibility of, if not overcoming, at least not exacerbating participatory stratification.

Nevertheless, the other obvious lesson provided by the data in Figure 12-7 is the extent to which church membership overshadows union affili-

Figure 12-7. *Civic Involvement, by Family Income*

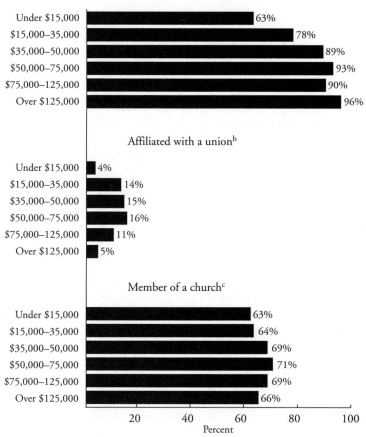

Affiliated with an organization[a]

Income	Percent
Under $15,000	63%
$15,000–35,000	78%
$35,000–50,000	89%
$50,000–75,000	93%
$75,000–125,000	90%
Over $125,000	96%

Affiliated with a union[b]

Income	Percent
Under $15,000	4%
$15,000–35,000	14%
$35,000–50,000	15%
$50,000–75,000	16%
$75,000–125,000	11%
Over $125,000	5%

Member of a church[c]

Income	Percent
Under $15,000	63%
$15,000–35,000	64%
$35,000–50,000	69%
$50,000–75,000	71%
$75,000–125,000	69%
Over $125,000	66%

Percent

a. Member or contributor.
b. Member.
c. Member or regular attender of services at a local church.

ation. At every income level, the proportion who are church members simply dwarfs the proportion in unions. If they were merely nominal, these memberships would mean little in terms of exposure to institutional political stimuli. However, in this respect as well, churches appear to have the advantage. Church members are more likely actually to attend services than are union members to attend union meetings. Of union members, 52 percent indicated having gone to at least one union meeting within the past year; 94 percent of church members reported having attended services within the past year.

Participatory Equality and the Structure of Civil Society in America

The unusual institutional configuration characteristic of American society has important consequences for the outcomes with which we are concerned. Since churches and organizations, including unions, function similarly in fostering political activity, we might argue that the strength of religious institutions would counterbalance the weakness of labor unions. A blue-collar worker is more likely to have politicizing experiences that develop civic skills in church than in a union—not because American unions are particularly deficient in building civic skills and providing exposure to political messages and requests for political activity, but because so few American blue-collar workers are union members and so many are church members. Hence, because churches can pinch hit for unions in encouraging participation, we might conclude that the weakness of American unions has no implications for the representation of the needs and preferences of the less well off in American politics.

Nonetheless, these institutions are not interchangeable when it comes to reducing participatory inequality. Churches and unions are not simply politically neutral sites that encourage political participation as a by-product of other purposes; they are institutions with political concerns of their own. It has long been a part of the union mission to represent the less advantaged in the halls of government. Although religious institutions sometimes take on this function—the Catholic Church, for example, often acts as an advocate for the poor—the economic needs of the less well off rarely top their lists of political priorities. Thus, when a church makes institutionally based attempts to mobilize the flock for political action, or when it gets involved directly in politics, the policy matter at stake is relatively unlikely to be an economic agenda focused on the less advantaged. Over the years, churches in America have embraced many issues ranging from temperance to civil rights. At this juncture religious institutions are active on behalf of a wide range of issues and diverse points of view. However, the center of gravity of the religious agenda in politics is a conservative concern with social issues, with a particular focus on advocacy of pro-life views on abortion. Though the issue priorities of American religious institutions are likely to continue to evolve, there is no reason to expect them to act as a substitute for unions or other organizations representing the less well off in bringing to the attention of public officials the economic needs and preferences of the disadvantaged.

In comparison with other democracies, political conflict in America has traditionally been less deeply imbued with the rhetoric of class. In recent years, however, references to class seem to have become less common in our political vocabulary than at any time since the New Deal, a circumstance that we could, speculatively, attribute to a number of developments over the past decade or two: the success of the Republican Party in defining itself as the party of the common folk; the focus by the Democratic Party on the needs of the middle class rather than the poor as the object of government attention; the erosion of the membership and power of labor unions; the emphasis on multiculturalism; the fall of communism in Russia and Eastern Europe and the declining appeal of Marxist social analysis as an intellectual tool; and changing occupational structures and the concomitant reduction in manufacturing employment. Nevertheless, it is clear that, in spite of the absence of references to class in our political discourse, when it comes to political participation, class matters profoundly for American politics.

At present, the decline of civic engagement is a matter of contention. The inequality of civic engagement is unambiguous. Moreover, analysis of a new and rich data set, the Roper Trends in American Political Participation, suggests that participatory inequality is a consistent attribute of civic life. In spite of minor fluctuations, there is no clear secular trend between 1974 and 1994: participatory inequality rose somewhat in the late 1970s, fell during the early 1980s, and ended the two-decade period almost exactly where it started.[25] Extrapolating from these findings, we can expect that, as long as inequalities in education and income persist—and income inequality in America has become more pronounced of late—as long as jobs continue to distribute opportunities to practice civic skills in a stratified manner, and as long as citizens increasingly donate money rather than time to politics, the voices heard through the medium of citizen participation might be loud and clear, but they will be far from equal.

25. Analysis of the Roper data is contained in Brady, Schlozman, Verba, and Elms (1998).

References

Bachrach, Peter. 1967. *The Theory of Democratic Elitism: A Critique*. Boston: Little, Brown.

Berman, Sheri. 1997. "Civil Society and Political Institutionalization." *American Behavioral Scientist* 40 (March/April): 562–74.

Boyte, Harry C. 1980. *The Backyard Revolution*. Philadelphia: Temple University Press.

Brady, Henry E., Kay Lehman Schlozman, and Sidney Verba. 1999. "Prospecting for Participants: Rational Expectations and the Recruitment of Political Activists." *American Political Science Review* 93: 153–68.

Brady, Henry E., Kay Lehman Schlozman, Sidney Verba, and Laurel Elms. 1998. "Who Bowls?" Paper prepared for the Annual Meeting of the American Political Science Association. Boston.

Browne, William P. 1988. *Private Interests, Public Policy, and American Agriculture*. University of Kansas Press.

Cohen, Cathy J., and Michael C. Dawson. 1993. "Neighborhood Poverty and African-American Politics." *American Political Science Review* 87 (June): 286–302.

Coleman, James S. 1988. "Social Capital in the Creation of Human Capital." *American Journal of Sociology* 94: 95–120.

Edwards, Bob, and Michael W. Foley. "Social Capital and the Political Economy of Our Discontent." *American Behavioral Scientist* 40 (March/April): 669–78.

Eldersveld, Samuel. 1964. *Political Parties: A Behavioral Analysis*. Chicago: Rand McNally.

Foley, Michael W., and Bob Edwards. 1997. "Escape from Politics? Social Theory and the Social Capital Debate." *American Behavioral Scientist* 40 (March/April): 550–61.

Freeman, Jo. 1983. *Social Movements of the Sixties and Seventies*. New York: Longman.

Gosnell, Harold F. 1927. *Getting Out the Vote*. University of Chicago Press.

Huckfeldt, Robert, and John Sprague. 1992. "Political Parties and Electoral Mobilization: Political Structure, Social Structure, and the Party Canvass." *American Political Science Review* 86 (March): 70–86.

———. 1993. "Citizens, Contexts, and Politics." In *Political Science: The State of the Discipline*, edited by Ada W. Finifter. Washington, D.C.: American Political Science Association.

Knoke, David. 1990. "Networks of Political Action: Toward Theory Construction." *Social Forces* 68 (June): 1041–63.

Luker, Kristin. 1983. *Abortion and the Politics of Motherhood*. University of California Press.

Mansbridge, Jane J. 1980. *Beyond Adversary Democracy*. New York: Basic Books.

McAdam, Doug. 1982. *Political Process and the Development of Black Insurgency*. University of Chicago Press.

John D. McCarthy, and Mayer N. Zald. 1987. "The Trends of Social Movements in America: Professionalization and Resource Mobilization." In *Social Movements in an Organizational Society*, edited by Mayer N. Zald and John D. McCarthy. New Brunswick, N.J.: Transaction.

Mincer, Jacob. 1962. "Labor Force Participation of Married Women: A Study of Labor Supply." In *Aspects of Labor Economics*. Princeton, N.J.: National Bureau of Economic Research and Princeton University Press.

Morris, Aldon D. 1984. *The Origins of the Civil Rights Movement: Black Communities Organizing for Change*. Free Press.

Newton, Kenneth. "Social Capital and Democracy." *American Behavioral Scientist* 40 (March/April): 575–86.

Nie, Norman, Jane Junn, and Kenneth Stehlik-Barry. 1996. *Education and Citizenship in America.* University of Chicago Press.

Oberschall, Anthony. 1973. *Social Conflict and Social Movements.* Englewood Cliffs, N.J.: Prentice Hall.

Parry, Geraint. 1972. "The Idea of Political Participation." In *Participation in Politics*, edited by Geraint Parry. Totowa, N.J.: Rowman and Littlefield.

Parry, Geraint, George Moyser, and Neil Day. 1992. *Political Participation and Democracy in Britain.* Cambridge University Press.

Pateman, Carole. 1970. *Participation and Democratic Theory.* Cambridge University Press.

Piven, Frances Fox, and Richard A. Cloward. 1977. *Poor People's Movements.* Random House.

Putnam, Robert D. 1993. *Making Democracy Work.* Princeton University Press.

———. 1996. "Robert Putnam Responds." *American Prospect* 25 (March/April): 26–28.

Rosenstone, Steven J., and John Mark Hansen. 1993. *Mobilization, Participation, and Democracy in America.* Macmillan.

Rothenberg, Lawrence. 1992. *Linking Citizens to Government.* Cambridge University Press.

Schlozman, Kay Lehman, and John T. Tierney. 1986. *Organized Interests and American Democracy.* Harper and Row.

Schlozman, Kay Lehman, Sidney Verba, and Henry E. Brady. 1995. "Participation's Not a Paradox: The View from American Activists." *British Journal of Political Science* 25 (January): 1–36.

Skocpol, Theda. 1996. "Unravelling from Above." *American Prospect* 25 (March/April): 20–25.

Tarrow, Sidney. 1994. *Power in Movement: Social Movements, Collective Action, and Politics.* Cambridge University Press.

Verba, Sidney, and Norman H. Nie. 1972. *Participation in America.* Harper and Row.

Verba, Sidney, Norman H. Nie, and Jae-On Kim. 1978. *Participation and Political Equality.* Cambridge University Press.

Verba, Sidney, Kay Lehman Schlozman, and Henry E. Brady. 1995. *Voice and Equality: Civic Voluntarism in American Politics.* Harvard University Press.

Warren, Mark E. 1998. "Democracy and Associations: An Approach to the Contributions of Associations to Democracy." Paper prepared for the Annual Meeting of the Western Political Science Association. Los Angeles.

Wielhouwer, Peter W., and Brad Lockerbie. "Party Contacting and Political Participation: 1952–1990." *American Journal of Political Science* 38 (February): 211–33.

13 | *Advocates without Members: The Recent Transformation of American Civic Life*

THEDA SKOCPOL

SINCE THE 1960S, Americans have dramatically changed their ways of associating for civic and political purposes. A civic world previously centered in locally rooted and nationally active membership associations—like the American Legion, the Elks, and the PTA—has gone the way of the once-popular television program "Leave It to Beaver." There may still be reruns, but they seem rather quaint. Much of America's civic life has moved into new venues and modalities.[1]

Nowadays, Americans volunteer for causes and projects usually not furthered by associations of which they are members and send checks to a dizzying plethora of public affairs and social service groups run by professionals. Thousands of new advocacy groups have set up national headquarters, and the prime-time airways echo with debates among their spokespersons: The National Abortion Rights Action League debates the National Right to Life Committee; the Concord Coalition takes on the

Many of those acknowledged in Chapter 2 should also be thanked here, especially the researchers and funders of the Civic Engagement Project. Extra thanks go to Ziad Munson, who prepared most of the tables for this chapter; Jocelyn Crowley and Jillian Dickert, each of whom provided important data; and Abby Peck, who retrieved information at the library. As always, my thinking has been stimulated by conversations with Marshall Ganz.

1. Wuthnow (1998) provides a good overview of contemporary patterns of individual civic involvement, especially at the community level.

461

American Association of Retired Persons; and the Environmental Defense Fund counters business groups. Entertained or bemused, people watch as polarized advocates debate.

"In democratic countries," Alexis de Tocqueville once wisely observed, "knowledge of how to combine is the mother of all other forms of knowledge."[2] Understanding the causes and consequences of civic America's recent transition from membership to advocacy is vital if we are to reflect wisely on prospects for our democracy. Shifts in mass attitudes, individual behaviors, and patterns of voter turnout are routinely probed by scholars and pundits. Important as these matters may be, changes in organized civic activities deserve equal or greater attention. Voluntary associations have always rivaled voting as pathways Americans follow into community and public affairs. Organized voluntary groups mediate between government and society, empower participating citizens, and embody relationships between leaders and supporters. Associations are, moreover, sites where citizens learn—and practice—the "knowledge of how to combine" so vital to democracy.

By international standards the United States remains a "nation of joiners."[3] Americans are still, by far, the most churchgoing people of the advanced industrial world; and in comparison with citizens elsewhere they excel at other kinds of associational belonging, apart from union membership.[4] But tallies of group affiliations across nations do not tell the whole story, because the kinds of groups Americans led and joined several decades ago added up to a very different universe of associations than the civic universe we know today.

This chapter examines the forces that have reshaped organized American civic life since the middle of the twentieth century. As my collaborators and I did in Chapter 2, I shine the spotlight on how publicly active voluntary groups relate to government, politics, and community affairs. American civic life has been reoriented by an explosion of advocacy groups. Privileged and well-educated citizens have led the way in reshaping the associational universe, withdrawing from cross-class membership federations and redirecting leadership and support to staff-led organizations. The result is a new civic America largely run by advocates and managers without members and marked by yawning gaps between immediate involvements and larger undertakings.

2. Tocqueville ([1835–40] 1969, p. 517).
3. Schlesinger (1944).
4. Curtis, Grabb, and Baer (1992).

A Changing Group Universe

More than at any time since the civically generative decades just before and after the Civil War, recent times have witnessed extraordinary associational change. Old-line voluntary associations have contracted, and some have virtually faded away. Yet the tale is not only of decline; unprecedented group innovation and proliferation have happened too. From the 1960s, massive social movements bypassed federated membership associations and set the stage for the proliferation of new kinds of civic groups. Contemporary Americans, in short, may be organizing more than ever before, but they have fashioned a very new civic universe.

Old Federations and New Movements

Consider the largest American membership associations of the 1950s. Table 13-1 lists twenty-three associations that enrolled as "members" 1 percent or more of men, women, or both sexes in 1955. This list provides a fascinating window into the framework of American civil society in that time. Included are occupationally based membership federations—the American Federation of Labor and Congress of Industrial Organizations (which merged in 1955) and the American Farm Bureau Federation—as well as a number of recreational associations and two national service institutions (the Red Cross and the March of Dimes).[5] Dominating the list, however, are male-led fraternal and veterans' groups and female-led religious and civic associations.

The largest membership groups of the 1950s were old line and well established, with founding dates ranging from 1733 for the Masons to 1939 for the Woman's Division of Christian Service (a Methodist women's association formed through a cross-denominational merger of multiple "missionary" societies with roots in the nineteenth century). Like most of the large membership associations throughout American history, most of

5. The list of large membership associations presented here comes from the research of the Civic Engagement Project that I described in Chapter 2. Obviously, voluntary associations vary considerably in what they mean by "membership." Our research allows each group to use its own definition, and the Red Cross and the March of Dimes indicate some of the outer limits of what groups may mean. "Members" of the Red Cross include persons who donate even a small amount of money in a given year; and "members" of the March of Dimes include those who volunteer during the annual fund drive. As Sills (1957) explains, the National March of Dimes Foundation also has local chapter-based members, far fewer in number than the participants in the annual drives. On such national health associations in general, see Carter (1992).

Table 13-1. *U.S. Membership Associations Enrolling One Percent or More of American Men, Women, or Both in 1955*

Name	Year founded	Membership	Percent of adults[a]
AFL-CIO	1886	12,622,000	12.05
National Congress of Parents and Teachers	1897	9,409,282	8.99
American Automobile Association	1902	5,009,346	4.78
Ancient and Accepted Free Masons	1733	4,009,925	7.86 (m)
American Legion	1919	2,795,990	5.48 (m)
Order of the Eastern Star	1868	2,365,778	2.26
Young Men's Christian Association	1851	2,222,618	2.12
United Methodist Women	1939	1,811,600	3.37 (w)
American Bowling Congress	1895	1,741,000	3.41 (m)
American Farm Bureau Federation	1919	1,600,000[b]	1.53
Boy Scouts of America	1910	1,350,000[b]	1.29
Woman's Missionary Union	1888	1,245,358	2.32 (w)
Benevolent and Protective Order of Elks	1867	1,149,613	2.25 (m)
Veterans of Foreign Wars	1899	1,086,859	2.13 (m)
Loyal Order of Moose	1888	843,697	1.65 (m)
General Federation of Women's Clubs	1890	826,458	1.54 (w)
Knights of Columbus	1882	800,486	1.57 (m)
Nobles of the Mystic Shrine	1872	761,179	1.49 (m)
Fraternal Order of Eagles	1898	760,007	1.49 (m)
Women's International Bowling Congress	1916	706,193	1.31 (w)
Independent Order of Odd Fellows	1819	543,171	1.07 (m)
American Red Cross	1881	23,196,000	
March of Dimes	1938	3,000,000[b]	

Source: Civic Engagement Project, Harvard University; data as of January 1999. A few of the membership numbers and percents given in this table and table 13-2 may be slightly overestimated because small numbers of Canadian members (always under 5 percent) cannot be removed from association records.

a. (m) means men only; (w) means women only.

b. Estimated.

the 1950s associations listed in Table 13-1 recruited members across class lines. They held regular local meetings and convened periodic assemblies of elected leaders and delegates at the state or regional and national levels. Engaged in multiple rather than narrowly specialized pursuits, many of these associations combined social or ritual activities with community service, mutual aid, and involvement in national affairs. National patriotism was a leitmotif, so perhaps it is not surprising that during and after World War II, a passionate and victorious national endeavor, all of the associations sharply expanded their memberships and renewed the vigor of their local and national activities.[6]

To be sure, very large associations were not the only membership federations that mattered in postwar America. Also prominent were somewhat smaller, elite-dominated civic groups—including male service groups like Rotary, Lions, and Kiwanis, and long-standing female groups like the American Association of University Women and the League of Women Voters.[7] Dozens of ethnically based fraternal and cultural associations flourished, as did African American fraternal groups like the Prince Hall Masons and the Improved Benevolent and Protective Order of Elks of the World.[8] Yet all of the aforementioned operated much like the largest membership federations, and most also experienced membership gains and renewals of energy following World War II. Encompassing very large and somewhat smaller groups, the world of American membership federations was riding high from the late 1940s through the mid-1960s.

For many membership federations, the mid-twentieth century was a golden era of national as well as community impact. Popularly rooted membership federations rivaled professional and business associations for influence in policy debates. The AFL-CIO was in the thick of struggles about economic and social policies; the American Legion and the Veterans of Foreign Wars advanced veterans' programs; the American Farm Bureau Federation (AFBF) joined other farmers' associations to influence national and state agricultural policies; and the National Congress of Parents and Teachers (PTA) and the General Federation of Women's Clubs were influential on educational, health, and family issues. As suggested by the graphic reproduced here from *Your Farm Bureau* (Figure 13-1), a 1958

6. This statement is based on yearly membership totals collected by the Civic Engagement Project.

7. Charles (1993); Young (1989).

8. For ethnic fraternals, see the yearly listings for the late 1950s and early 1960s in Gale Research Company (1959–99). On the twentieth-century expansion of the African American Elks, see Wesley (1955).

Figure 13-1. *The Farm Bureau's Policy Highway*

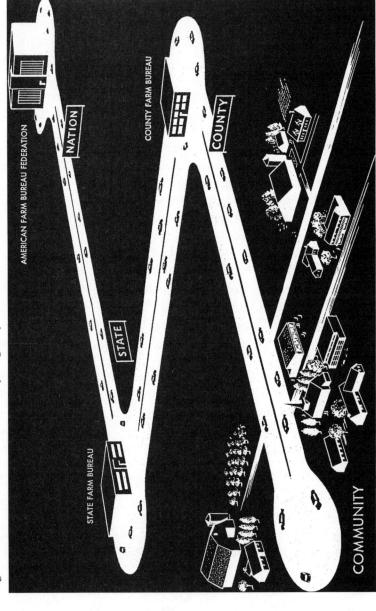

Source: Alice Sturgis, *Your Farm Bureau*, 1958.

civics manual for AFBF members, voluntary membership federations served as two-way "highways" between local communities and government.[9] The results could be decisive, as exemplified by the pivotal role of the American Legion in drafting and lobbying for the GI Bill of 1944.[10]

Then, suddenly, old-line membership federations were no longer where the action was. Upheavals shook America during "the long 1960s," stretching from the mid-1950s through the mid-1970s. The southern Civil Rights Movement challenged white racial domination and spurred national legislation to enforce legal equality and voting rights for African Americans.[11] Inspired by civil rights achievements, additional "rights" movements exploded in the 1960s and 1970s, promoting equality for women, dignity for homosexuals, the unionization of farm workers, and the mobilization of other nonwhite ethnic minorities.[12] Movements arose to oppose U.S. involvement in the war in Vietnam, champion a new environmentalism, and further a variety of other public causes. At the forefront of these groundswells were younger Americans, especially from the growing ranks of college students and university graduates.

"Social movements" are vast and somewhat unstructured endeavors, whose participants express new ways of thinking and agitate for institutional transformations. Never the work of just one organization, movements are pushed forward through shifts in public opinion and the efforts of many contending as well as cooperating groups. As Elisabeth Clemens's chapter in this volume illustrates for an earlier era, actors comfortably situated in previously dominant institutions and associations do not spearhead movements for fundamental social change. New leaders take the initiative, sometimes working through previously existing but somewhat marginalized organizations, yet often launching new associations. Activists in movements for social change are notable for their moral determination, strategic agility, and capacity to help people combine in new ways. Such leaders, and the redirected or newly created associations through which they work, are vital agents of democratic revitalization. Again and again in American history this has been true.

Innovation and fresh leadership certainly marked the great American social movements of the long 1960s. The southern Civil Rights movement

9. Sturgis (1958, pp. 192–93). On the AFBF's involvement in federal policymaking, see Hansen (1991).

10. Skocpol (1997, pp. 106–9); Bennett (1996, chaps. 2–3).

11. McAdam (1982); Morris (1984).

12. Gitlin (1989); Jenkins and Perrow (1977); Minkoff (1995, chap. 2).

of 1955 to 1965 was sparked by direct actions—the "freedom rides," the Montgomery bus boycott, the Greensboro sit-ins, and citywide nonviolent demonstrations—sustained and pushed forward by a remarkable combination of African American churches and leadership cadre groups.[13] Ordinary people were mobilized through social ties within church congregations, while strategic innovation came from the Southern Christian Leadership Conference (SCLC), a coordinating group of African American ministers founded in 1957; and the Student Non-Violent Coordinating Committee (SNCC), a coordinating association of student activists founded in 1960. Previously, the National Association for the Advancement of Colored People (NAACP), an interracial federation founded in 1909, had been the nation's leading civil rights organization. Although the NAACP was decisive in legal advocacy, it never recruited more than 2 percent of African Americans (mostly professionals and ministers) before the civil rights upheavals. When activists shifted to new, direct-action tactics, NAACP chapters and Youth Councils played key roles, but the SCLC and SNCC moved to the fore as coordinators of the mass protests.[14]

The feminist movement of the late 1960s and 1970s was propelled by a combination of loosely interconnected circles, assorted cadre organizations and single-issue groups, and a few newly launched membership associations.[15] Launched during the Civil Rights movement, radical "women's liberation" efforts were grounded in consciousness-raising and direct-action groups. Reform-oriented "women's rights" feminism took shape when participants in government commissions decided in 1966 to launch the National Organization for Women (NOW) as an activist and chapter-based association.[16] The vanguard of feminist reform included the Women's Equity Action League (founded 1968) and the National Abortion Rights Action League (created in 1973 through a reorientation of an earlier group)—both leadership groups that eventually developed mailing-list memberships of modest size. Although a number of them joined in support of feminist projects during the 1970s, old-line membership federations such as the American Association of University Women, the Young Women's Christian Association, the General Federation of Women's Clubs, and the League of Women Voters did not initiate or drive the new

13. See especially Morris (1984).

14. Ibid. (chaps. 1–2).

15. Gelb and Palley (1982, chap. 2). My discussion of organizations involved in the new feminism draws on Gelb and Palley's study.

16. Freeman (1973).

feminism. Describing "feminist mobilization" in 1982, Joyce Gelb and Marian Lief Palley concluded that the "groups . . . [of] the past twenty years have tended to be leadership and not membership based."[17]

The modern environmental movement took shape when long-standing concerns about land conservation and the protection of particular animal species were supplemented by a broader ecological awareness. This transition was spurred by a "new breed of . . . organizations" led by lawyers, scientists, and dissident breakaways from earlier associations. Spark plugs included the Environmental Defense Fund, formed in 1967 amidst "the battle to ban DDT"; the Friends of the Earth, founded in 1969 by a former Sierra Club director fired for independent activism; Environmental Action, founded in 1970 by the student organizers of the first national Earth Day; the Natural Resources Defense Council, founded in 1970 out of "an environmental law firm run by lawyers"; and Greenpeace USA, launched in 1971 by activists who eschewed legislative lobbying for more colorful direct actions.[18] From the 1970s to the 1990s, modern environmental groups proliferated, redefining issues and pursuing fresh tactics. At the same time, such old-line membership federations as the Sierra Club (founded in 1892) and the National Wildlife Federation (founded in 1936) reoriented their efforts and became major players in the new environmentalism.[19]

The great social movements of the long 1960s were, in sum, propelled by combinations of grass-roots protest, activist radicalism, and professionally led efforts to lobby government and educate the public. Some older membership associations ended up participating and expanding their bases of support, yet the groups that sparked movements were more agile and flexibly structured than preexisting membership federations.

The Advocacy Explosion

Still, we can wonder about what happened next. Once protests achieved victories and began to wane, associational innovation might have subsided in the late-twentieth-century United States. The upheavals of the 1960s might have left behind a reconfigured civic world in which some

17. Gelb and Palley (1982, pp. 14–15).
18. Mitchell, Mertig, and Dunlap (1992, pp. 13–14).
19. In addition, these included the National Audubon Society (founded 1905) and the Wilderness Society (founded 1935). All of these were relatively small membership associations before the 1960s.

Figure 13-2. *Women's and Racial-Ethnic Groups, by Constituency,*
1955–85

Number of groups

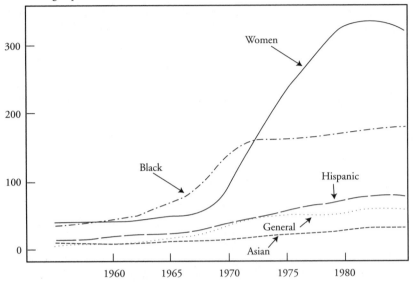

Source: Minkoff (1995, p. 62). Reprinted by permission of Rutgers University Press.

old-line membership associations had declined but others had reoriented
and reenergized themselves to take advantage of new issues and sources of
support. Within each great social movement, memberships might have
consolidated and groups coalesced into new omnibus federations able to
link the grass roots to state, regional, and national leaderships, allowing
long-standing American civic traditions to continue in new ways.

But this is not what happened. Instead, the 1960s, 1970s, and 1980s
brought extraordinary organizational proliferation. At the national level
alone, the *Encyclopedia of Associations* listed approximately 6,500 associations of all sorts in 1958.[20] This total grew to some 10,700 national
associations in 1970, and to 14,726 in 1980. By 1990 the number of
national associations was almost 23,000—a level at which it remained

20. Editions of Gale Research Company (1959–1999) before 1975 do not present total accounts or
enumerate groups in particular categories. I have found that total estimates provided at the front of
these volumes are not accurate. Counting average numbers of entries per page within each of twenty-
some categories of groups, I have estimated national and categorical totals for the 2d edition (published
1959) and the 6th edition (published 1970).

Figure 13-3. *Women's and Racial Ethnic Groups, by Strategy, 1955–85*

Number of groups

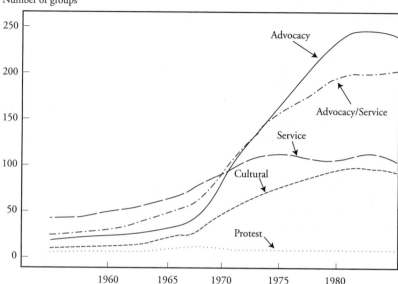

Source: Minkoff (1995, p. 62). Reprinted by permission of Rutgers University Press.

during the 1990s. Between 1958 and 1998, the number of American national associations grew by some 253 percent overall, and almost all of this proliferation came between 1960 and 1990. Within the expanding group universe, moreover, new kinds of associations came to the fore: relatively centralized and professionally led organizations focused on policy lobbying and public education. What political scientist Jeffrey Berry aptly calls the "advocacy explosion" has come in several overlapping waves.[21] "Rights" groups led the way, followed by a proliferation of "citizens' " or "public interest" groups, and by a further expansion of the always substantial ranks of trade and professional associations.

Sociologist Debra Minkoff has studied "organizing for equality" in some depth, and Figures 13-2 and 13-3 display central findings from her analysis of some "975 national minority and women's membership associations that were active at some point between 1955 and 1985."[22] Groups

21. Berry (1997, chap. 2). See also Walker (1991).
22. Minkoff (1995, p. 17). All of the associations were listed in the annual *Encyclopedia of Associations*, 1955 to 1985.

acting on behalf of the rights or welfare of women, African Americans, and Hispanic or Asian Americans multiplied sixfold—from 98 groups in 1955 to 688 groups in 1985.[23] As Figure 13-2 shows, many groups speaking for African Americans were launched immediately after the civil rights victories of the mid-1960s; the ranks of groups advocating equality for women and ethnic minorities expanded a bit later, especially during the 1970s. If anything, Minkoff's study understates the proliferation of rights-oriented groups, because her database includes only associations claiming memberships of some sort, setting aside "government bodies and staff-run not-for-profit organizations such as research centers and operating foundations."[24] All the more telling, then, are the findings displayed in Figure 13-3, which sorts Minkoff's groups by organizational strategy rather than constituency. During the 1970s and 1980s, the mix of rights groups shifted sharply from cultural, protest, and social service associations toward policy advocacy groups and service providers also engaged in policy advocacy (see Figure 13-3).

Minkoff's findings complement those of other scholars. When Kay Lehman Schlozman investigated Washington, D.C.–based associations at the beginning of the 1980s, she found that recently founded women's groups—especially those with a "rights" orientation—already used the same mix of advocacy methods as other Washington pressure groups.[25] The feminist "groups that emerged as a social movement in the late 1960s," concur Gelb and Palley, "evolved in the later years of the 1970s into a stage of political development that emphasized interest-group organization and professionalization."[26] Feminist associations appeal to general public sympathy, while pursuing legal, research, and lobbying activities. "Like their black civil rights counterparts," note Gelb and Palley, "feminist groups are frequently based in Washington or New York."[27]

Another wave of the advocacy explosion involved "public interest" or "citizens'" groups seeking to shape public opinion and influence legislation.[28] Citizens' advocacy groups espouse "causes" ranging from environmental protection (for example, the Sierra Club and the Environmental

---

23. Minkoff (1995, p. 61).
24. Minkoff (1995, p.17).
25. Schlozman (1990).
26. Gelb and Palley (1982, p. 14). See also Costain (1981).
27. Gelb and Palley (1982, p. 25).
28. Berry (1977); McFarland (1984); Walker (1991, pp. 33–35).

Defense Fund), to the well-being of poor children (the Children's Defense Fund), to reforming politics (Common Cause), and cutting public entitlements (the Concord Coalition). As Jeffrey Berry explains in Chapter 10, citizens' associations represent the aspirations of their members and financial supporters along lines not simply reducible to vocation or occupation. They make claims about the public interest, not about the material self-interests of their supporters. Citizens' associations, explains Berry, are "avowedly political" groups that use "substantial financial resources to hire large staffs of lobbyists and researchers."

Many citizens' advocacy groups emerged out of social movements; others were founded amidst policy or partisan struggles—with liberal groups predominating at first, soon followed by conservative contenders. Empirical studies by political scientists confirm that citizens' advocates proliferated from the 1960s through the 1980s. In a survey of eighty-three public interest groups active in Washington in the early 1970s, Jeffrey Berry found that almost half had been launched between 1968 and 1973.[29] Kay Schlozman and John Tierney analyzed groups listed in a 1981 lobbying directory, noting that 40 percent were founded after 1960 and 25 percent after 1970.[30] In the most comprehensive study, Jack Walker and his associates examined 564 groups based in Washington, D.C., in the early 1980s and found that 30 percent were launched between 1960 and 1980, with citizens' groups increasing much more sharply than other kinds of lobbying organizations.[31]

The final wave of the recent U.S. advocacy explosion has been, at least in part, a response to the previous two. During the entire post–World War II period, trade and professional associations were a substantial and gradually growing presence in Washington, D.C. When rights groups and citizens' advocates markedly increased their presence on the national scene, however, previously dominant kinds of interests did not just sit idly by. Segments of business and the professions organized new lobbying groups or moved their offices to Washington, D.C.[32] In the advocacy arms race, action has led to counter-action very rapidly.

Nevertheless, recent decades have brought a marked change in the balance between business and other civically active associations. In 1958,

---

29. Berry (1977, 31–37).
30. Schlozman and Tierney (1986, pp. 75–76).
31. Walker (1991).
32. Walker (1991, chap. 4); Berry (1997, pp. 37–42); Phillips (1994, p. 32). See also Judis (1992).

"trade, business, and commercial" associations accounted for some 34 percent of U.S. national associations. Over the following four decades, trade, business, and commercial groups grew in absolute number—from 2,230 in 1958 to 3,831 in 1998—but declined to only 17 percent of all national associations. Meanwhile, public affairs associations expanded their share from 2 percent to 9 percent; and social welfare associations grew from 4 percent to 8 percent of all U.S. national groups. Not all "public affairs" and "social welfare" groups are what Minkoff or Berry would call "rights" or "citizens'" associations, of course. But by the 1990s these associational sectors had gained proportional parity with the business sector.[33]

The Fortunes of Membership Associations

As the associational explosions of 1960 to 1990 took off, America's once large and confident membership federations were not only bypassed in national politics; they also dwindled as locally rooted participant groups. Most of the largest membership federations of the 1950s starting losing membership shares of the adult population in the 1960s or 1970s—especially after the mid-1970s (see Table 13-2).[34] A few have held their own or gained membership shares, including the Women's International Bowling Congress; the YMCA, which shifted from fostering men's physical and spiritual development toward managing facilities for family recreation; the American Farm Bureau Federation, which has expanded its insurance programs as the farm population has declined; and the Veterans of Foreign Wars, which has proved appealing to many veterans who served in Korea and Vietnam. But fifteen of the twenty associations listed in Table 13-2 have faltered in recent decades.[35]

Trade unions have plummeted—not just the percent of adults enrolled in the AFL-CIO but also the proportion of the employed labor force

33. The numbers and percentages presented in this paragraph were calculated by the author from Gale Research Company (1959, 2d ed.) and (1999, 34th ed.). See note 20 above.

34. Two groups listed in Table 13-1, the Red Cross and the March of Dimes, are not included here. These associations base their "membership" claims on general counts of yearly contributors or volunteers, and claims for recent years are not as clear as earlier counts.

35. In recent years the Fraternal Order of Moose has become a mixed-gender association. But historically men and women were in separate lodges, and the numbers represented here are for men only, tracing changes from 1955 to 1995.

Table 13-2. *Membership Change in Large Associations, 1955–95*[a]
Percent

Associations for men	U.S. men enrolled					Decade shifts				Total shift, 1955–95
	1955	1965	1975	1985	1995	1955–65	1965–75	1975–85	1985–95	1955–95
Fraternal										
Ancient and Accepted Free Masons	7.9	7.1	5.3	3.7	2.4	−10.1	−25.2	−30.1	−35.7	−69.8
Fraternal Order of Eagles	1.5	1.0	1.1	0.9	0.8	−31.2	4.5	−14.6	−11.2	−45.5
Loyal Order of Moose	1.7	1.5	1.7	1.7	1.3	−11.9	18.3	−3.6	−22.0	−21.6
Benevolent and Protective Order of Elks	2.3	2.4	2.4	2.0	1.4	7.0	−1.2	−15.2	−30.0	−37.2
Knights of Columbus	1.6	1.8	1.5	1.4	1.3	14.3	−16.8	−4.8	−8.4	−17.0
Independent Order of Odd Fellows	1.1	0.6	0.3	0.2	0.1	−44.1	−46.3	−48.7	−47.9	−92.0
Nobles of the Mystic Shrine	1.5	1.5	1.4	1.1	0.7	0.3	−6.6	−21.3	−38.9	−55.0
Veterans'										
American Legion	5.5	4.5	4.1	3.3	3.3	−17.7	−10.1	−17.5	−2.7	−40.6
Veterans of Foreign Wars	2.1	2.2	2.7	2.6	2.3	4.2	21.1	−4.7	−8.9	9.5
Recreational										
American Bowling Congress	3.4	8.1	6.5	4.6	2.7	136.2	−19.8	−28.4	−41.5	−20.6

Table 13-2. (continued)

Percent

| Associations for women | U.S. women enrolled | | | | | Decade shifts | | | | Total shift, |
	1955	1965	1975	1985	1995	1955–65	1965–75	1975–85	1985–95	1955–95
Religious										
United Methodist Women	3.4	2.8	1.8	1.4	1.0	−16.7	−34.6	−23.2	−28.4	−70.0
Woman's Missionary Union	2.3	2.4	2.39	1.3	1.1	2.9	35.6	−12.7	−19.5	−53.4
Civic										
General Federation of Women's Clubs	1.5	1.2	0.8	0.5	0.3	−22.5	−33.3	−39.7	−45.8	−83.1
Recreational										
Women's International Bowling Congress	1.3	4.4	5.0	4.3	2.2	237.9	12.8	−14.6	−47.9	69.7

Mixed-gender associations	U.S. adults enrolled					Decade shifts				Total shift, 1955–95
	1955	1965	1975	1985	1995	1955–65	1965–75	1975–85	1985–95	
Occupational										
AFL-CIO	12.1	10.9	10.0	7.9	6.9	–9.2	–8.3	–21.2	–12.9	–42.9
American Farm Bureau Federation	1.5	1.4	1.7	2.0	2.1	–1.6	22.4	14.0	8.8	49.4
Fraternal										
Order of the Eastern Star	2.3	2.0	1.5	1.0	0.6	–11.5	–27.0	–29.9	–38.0	–71.9
Educational										
National Congress of Parents and Teachers	9.0	10.0	5.0	3.4	3.6	11.2	–49.6	–32.8	6.3	–60.0
Boy Scouts of America	1.3	1.6	1.2	1.0	1.1	21.8	–21.9	–23.0	17.7	–13.7
Recreational										
Young Men's Christian Association	2.1	2.8	4.3	3.3	3.5	29.6	57.1	–22.7	3.3	62.5
Other										
American Automobile Association	4.8	8.0	12.4	15.8	20.2	66.2	56.4	27.1	27.7	322.0

Source: Civic Engagement Project, Harvard University; data as of January 1999.

a. Percents are rounded to one decimal point, but decade shift figures are based on underlying unrounded numbers.

involved in any union. More than one-third of the nonagricultural labor force was unionized in the 1950s, but by the 1990s less than one-sixth of workers were enrolled in any union.[36] Fraternal and civic membership associations have also been hard-hit. Once predominant groups like the Masons and the Eastern Star, the American Legion, and the General Federation of Women's Clubs persevere with shrinking memberships, cajoling people to attend less-frequent meetings. Annual reports portray portly, graying men and women because younger Americans simply have not joined such groups in the proportions their elders once did.

Some membership associations have been founded or expanded in recent decades. The appendixes in Chapter 2 show which groups have developed membership of at least 1 percent of adults since the 1950s. By far the largest is the American Association of Retired Persons (AARP), which now boasts more than 33 million adherents, about half of all Americans age fifty or older.[37] Launched in 1958 with backing from a teachers' retirement group and an insurance company, the AARP grew rapidly in the 1970s and 1980s by offering commercial discounts to members and establishing a Washington headquarters from which to monitor and lobby about federal legislation affecting seniors. The AARP has a legislative and policy staff of 165 people, 28 registered lobbyists, and more than 1,200 staff members in the field.[38] After recent efforts to expand its regional and local infrastructure, the AARP involves about 5 to 10 percent of its members in membership chapters—like the one that proudly proclaims its existence (along with traditional service, fraternal, and women's groups) on the civic billboard that graces the entrance to the town of Princeton, Illinois. But for the most part, the AARP national office—which covers an entire city block and has its own zip code—deals with masses of individual adherents through the mail. Individualized contact is also the norm for other recently enlarged membership associations such as the Mothers Against Drunk Driving, which was founded in 1980 and reaches out to most supporters with advertising and direct-mail solicitations. Founded in 1971, Greenpeace USA relies on door-to-door canvassing as well as direct mail.

Four additional recently expanded vast membership associations use modern mass-recruitment methods yet are also rooted in local and state

36. Berry (1997, p. 27, fig. 2.4).
37. Loomis and Cigler (1998, p. 12). My account of the AARP also draws on Morris (1996).
38. Loomis and Cigler (1998, p. 12).

units. Interestingly, these groups are heavily involved in partisan electoral politics. Two of them, the National Right to Life Committee (founded in 1973) and the Christian Coalition (founded in 1989), bridge from church congregations through which they recruit members and activists to the conservative wing of the Republican Party through which they exercise political influence. Two old-line membership federations—the National Education Association (founded in 1857) and the National Rifle Association (founded in 1871)—experienced new explosive growth after reorienting themselves to take part in partisan politics. The NRA took off in the 1970s, when right-wing activists opposed to gun control changed what had traditionally been a network of marksmen's clubs into a conservative, Republican-leaning advocacy group fiercely opposed to gun-control legislation.[39] During the same period, the NEA burgeoned from a relatively elitist association of public educators into a quasi-union for public school teachers and a stalwart in state, local, and national Democratic Party politics.[40]

Although they fall well short of enrolling 1 percent of the adult population, some additional chapter-based membership associations were fueled by the social movements of the 1960s and 1970s. Two previously small conservation groups caught the winds of the new environmentalism. From 1960 to 1990, the Sierra Club (founded in 1892) ballooned from some 15,000 members into a giant with 565,000 members meeting in 378 "local groups." And the National Audubon Society went from 30,000 members and 330 chapters in 1958 to about 600,000 members and more than 500 chapters in the 1990s.[41] Another recently growing group is the National Organization for Women, which signed up 1,122 members and established fourteen chapters within a year of its founding in 1966 and by 1978 had 125,000 members meeting in 700 chapters in all fifty states.[42] But notice that "sixties" movement associations do not match the organizational scope of old-line membership federations. At its post–World War II high point in 1955, for example, the General Federation of Women's Clubs boasted more than 826,000 members meeting in 15,168 local clubs, themselves divided into representative networks within each of the fifty

39. Patterson (1998).
40. West (1980).
41. These numbers are pieced together from Mitchell, Mertig, and Dunlap (1992, p.13) and Gale Research Company (1959–1999).
42. Gelb and Palley (1982, p. 29); Gale Research Company (1959–1999).

U.S. states and the District of Columbia. By contrast, at its high point in 1993, NOW reported some 280,000 members and 800 chapters, with no intermediate tier of representative governance between the national center and local chapters.[43]

Ranging from NOW to the Christian Coalition, these newly large membership associations certainly matter. But we should not imagine that such groups are anything except counter-examples to dominant associational trends. Summary statistics about 2,966 "social welfare" and "public affairs" organizations founded in the 1960s, 1970s, and 1980s show that close to half of these associations indicate no members at all, and another quarter claim fewer than 1,000 "members."[44] In some instances, a number under 1,000 indicates a modest individual membership, but it may also connote an association that has other organizations as its constituents (as many trade and professional associations do). Reconfigured by the advocacy explosion, the new universe of national American associations not only features thousands more groups than the civic universe of the 1950s. New kinds of groups are the trend-setters. Specializing in this or that constituency, cause, or activity, the vast majority are either advocacy organizations without individual members or groups with organizational constituents or modest complements of mass adherents.

Why America's Associational Universe Has Changed

After nearly a century of civic life rooted in nation-spanning membership federations, why did the focus of America's associational universe change so abruptly from membership to advocacy in the late twentieth century? I suggest that a variety of factors, taken together, account for this transformation, including racial and gender change, shifts in the political

---

43. Data for the General Federation come directly from the association's records. Data for NOW come from the 1993 volume of the *Encyclopedia of Associations*; see Gale Research Company (1959–99).

44. Calculated by the author from 1998 CD-ROM data provided by Gale Research Company. There can be a problem using retrospective data on founding dates, but in this case I think it is entirely appropriate because surviving groups from those founded in the 1960s through the 1980s have had a chance to build up their memberships (if any). Some groups say nothing at all about memberships; a few of these may actually have members, but probably not many. The names and statements of purpose of most such groups indicate that they are usually memberless or based on organizational constituencies.

opportunity structure, new techniques and models for building organizations, and recent transformations in U.S. class relations.

Changing Race Relations and Gender Roles

Until recent times, most American membership associations enrolled business and professional people together with white-collar employees, farmers, and craft or industrial workers. There was a degree of fellowship across class lines—yet at the price of other kinds of exclusions. With only a few exceptions, old-line associations enrolled *either* men or women, not both together (although male-only fraternal and veterans' groups often had ties to ladies' auxiliaries). Racial separation was also the rule. As late as the period after World War II, there was nothing subtle about white racism in associational life. Many group constitutions echoed the words of a 1950s orientation pamphlet called *What It Means to Be an Elk*: "Membership in the Order is limited to white male citizens of the United States . . . who believe in the existence of God [and] who subscribe themselves to the objects and purposes of the order."[45] Although African Americans did manage to create and greatly expand fraternal associations of their own, they unquestionably resented exclusion by the parallel white fraternals.[46]

Given the pervasiveness of gender and racial separation in classic civic America, established voluntary associations were bound to be shaken after the 1950s. As Table 13-2 documents, most male-only and female-only groups enrolled smaller and smaller percentages of adults; some began declining in the 1960s and the rest after the mid-1970s. Membership erosion came as new racial and gender ideals took hold in American public life and female labor-force participation climbed. This was the period when hundreds of new advocacy associations came into being, some speaking for the rights of women and African Americans, others pursuing causes that appealed to gender-integrated constituencies.

In Chapter 7, Susan Crawford and Peggy Levitt analyze how a long-standing and important American membership federation, the National Congress of Parents and Teachers (PTA), coped with racial desegregation and changing family and work patterns. The PTA was relatively successful

---

45. Benevolent and Protective Order of Elks (n.d.[1950s]), p. 8). This paperback pamphlet is in the author's personal collection of association ephemera.

46. What is more, the historical record shows that white groups made repeated legal efforts to force counterpart African American groups to disband.

in adapting to new social conditions, yet it lost members and local units in the process and deemphasized many long-standing group activities. Other membership federations also struggled to adapt to new social conditions. Associations dropped explicit racial bars and undertook new public-service projects. Some built new recreational facilities. Such steps kept membership losses minimal for some groups, but many federations could not stave off decline. Socially segregated associations simply lost their appeal to younger Americans coming of age in an era of social toleration and hopes for racial and gender integration. A 1997 survey asked Americans how likely they would be to join groups with various characteristics. Fully 58 percent said they would be "very unlikely" (not just "somewhat unlikely") to join a group that "accepts only men or women," and 90 percent said they would be very unlikely to join a group with "a history of racial discrimination."[47]

Changing gender roles and identities in post-1950s America undercut not just membership appeals but also long-standing routes to associational leadership. Historically, former soldiers and educated women outside the paid labor force were mainstays of voluntary membership federations. On the male side of the associational equation, military veterans were influential not only in obvious cases like the Veterans of Foreign Wars and the American Legion. Veterans—and the ideals embodied in the national service they rendered—mattered just as much to fraternal groups (which made up a large proportion of classic U.S. voluntary associations). Values of patriotism, brotherhood, and sacrifice were celebrated by all fraternal groups—and military service was touted as a sure way to achieve such virtues. During and after each war, the Masons, Knights of Pythias, Elks, Knights of Columbus, Moose, Eagles and scores of other fraternal groups celebrated and memorialized the contributions of their soldier-members. So did women's auxiliaries, not to mention men's service clubs and trade-union "brotherhoods."

But "manly" ideals of military service faded after the early 1960s. Cohorts of U.S. males maturing in the last third of the century are extraordinarily less likely to have served in the military. Two-thirds or more of American men born in the 1920s and early 1930s served; but the proportion plummeted afterward: only one-fifth or fewer of American men born since the mid-1950s have spent stints in the military.[48] Nor is direct participation the

47. Wuthnow (1998, p. 253, n. 51).
48. Based on data from Robert D. Putnam.

only issue. America's bitter experiences during the war in Vietnam disrupted the intergenerational continuity of male identification with martial brotherliness. Across most of U.S. history, even sons who did not serve in the military or participate in wars idolized the martial experiences of their fathers and grandfathers. Punctuated now and again by actual mobilization into victorious wars, intergenerationally shared ideals of martial valor, sacrifice, and comradeship helped to sustain fraternal and veterans' associations as the United States became a class-divided industrial nation. The "Loyal Order of Moose is a militantly patriotic organization," declared the 1944 pamphlet *Moose Facts*, which added that "the desire of fathers—long members—to see the day when they may witness the initiation of their sons . . . has always been a potent . . . factor in stabilizing and building the Order's membership."[49] But from the 1970s increasing numbers of fraternal fathers would not see the initiation of their sons (or mothers the enrollment of their daughters in fraternal partner groups). Standard fraternal histories of the 1960s and 1970s describe mature lodge brothers staging ceremonies to celebrate "Americanism," deplore civil disturbances, and announce support for national military efforts in Vietnam.[50] At the same time, military service lost its élan for many younger people—and a cultural chasm opened between them and the aging World War II generation.

The break was sharpest for privileged, college-educated young people—the ones most likely to avoid being drafted into an unpopular and indecisive war, and those first influenced by new gender ideals. What national data we have on declining fraternal affiliations indicate disproportionate drops among men and women with college degrees or some years of college education. Table 13-3 displays such results using data from General Social Surveys conducted in the mid-1970s, mid-1980s, and mid-1990s. It would be nice to have earlier comparable evidence, but even these limited data indicate a disproportionate decline of fraternal memberships among the college-educated, with an abrupt drop occurring between 1975 and 1985. The aftermath of every previous war in American history brought rising fraternal enrollments, especially among elites, but not the aftermath of the war in Vietnam.

Table 13-4 presents six sets of forty persons—the vast majority of them college- and graduate-educated business and professional men in their

49. Loyal Order of Moose (1944, p. 29). Each page in this little pamphlet has an inspirational heading, and this one is called "FATHER-AND-SON."

50. See, for example, Nicholson, Donaldson, and Dobson (1978, secs. K and L).

Table 13-3. *Educational Attainment and Membership in Fraternal Groups, 1974–94*[a]

Percent

Educational attainment	1974, 1975	*Members of fraternal organizations and change from the previous period*		
		1984, 1986 (change)	1993, 1994 (change)	Change, 1970s to 1990s
16 years or more	20.0	14.3 (−29)	12.7 (−11)	−37
More than 12 years	18.1	9.6 (−47)	6.9 (−28)	−62
12 years	10.4	8.0 (−23)	8.4 (+5)	−19
Less than 12 years	8.1	6.8 (−16)	7.7 (+13)	−5

Source: Author's calculations from General Social Survey.

a. Each cell shows the average of pairs of General Social Surveys. This was done to smooth out variability.

forties and fifties—who served in the Senate of the state of Massachusetts at various points over the past half century. Every year the state of Massachusetts publishes a little leather-bound book showing the picture of each senator and providing his or her self-reported information in a format that has not changed since the 1930s. Very high proportions of Massachusetts senators listed memberships in (one or more) fraternal and veterans' groups from 1950 to 1970. These elite men (and the occasional woman) were proud to claim membership in dozens of fraternal and veterans' groups. At times one-fifth or more of the Senate belonged to some of America's largest membership associations: the Masons and Eastern Star; the Benevolent and Protective Order of Elks; the Knights of Columbus; the American Legion; and the Veterans of Foreign Wars (VFW).

But from the 1970s on, the associational profile of the Massachusetts Senate changed sharply. By the 1990s, one-fifth of senators stopped listing group affiliations of any kind (they simply provided information about their education and stated occupations such as "lawyer" or "legislator"). Among those who listed affiliations, many listed ties to advocacy groups and nonprofit institutions (in the latter case, senators usually said they were trustees or "corporators"). Meanwhile, the proportion involved in veterans' groups plummeted from more than three-fifths in the 1969–70 Senate to less than 10 percent of those serving in the 1997–98 Senate. And the proportion indicating any fraternal tie went from 85 percent or more in the Senates of 1949–50, 1959–60, and 1969–70 to less than

Table 13-4. *Civic Affiliations of Massachusetts State Senators, 1950–98*

Affiliation	1949–50	1959–60	1969–70	1979–80	1989–90	1997–98
Democrats/Republicans	20/20	24/16	27/13	34/6	32/8	33/7
Male/female	39/1	37/3	39/1	36/4	35/5	33/7
Senators reporting any group affiliation	38	38	33	36	32	32
Affiliated senators reporting one or more memberships (percent)						
Fraternal groups	87	95	85	53	47	30
Veterans' groups	39	58	61	36	22	9
Public affairs and advocacy groups (not purely local)	3	5	12	17	25	31
Nonprofit institutions and social service agencies	3	5	18	47	63	72
Membership groups enrolling eight or more senators						
Masons/Eastern Star	X	X				
Elks (B.P.O.E)	X	X	X			
Knights of Columbus	X	X	X	X	X	
Fraternal Order of Eagles	X					
American Legion	X	X	X	X		
Veterans of Foreign Wars		X	X	X		
American Veterans of World War II and Korea (AMVETS)		X				

Source: *Public Officers of the Commonwealth of Massachusetts* (Boston: State of Massachusetts, published annually) for specified years.

one-third in the 1997–98 Senate. This last number, moreover, is thinner than it looks, because most senators still listing fraternal affiliations in the 1990s were Democrats with a single membership—in the Knights of Columbus (the leading Catholic fraternity) or in an ethnic fraternal like the Ancient Order of Hibernians or the Sons of Italy. In earlier eras, most senators listed up to half a dozen affiliations with a variety of fraternal and veterans' groups, including some that crossed partisan or religious lines. But by the end of the twentieth century, Massachusetts senators indicated little involvement in groups like the Masons, the Elks, and American Legion and VFW—affiliations that once were de rigueur for publicly visible leaders.

In the last one-third of the twentieth century, female civic leadership changed as much as or more than male leadership. Historically, U.S. women's associations—ranging from female auxiliaries of male groups to independent groups like the General Federation of Women's Clubs, the PTA, and church-connected associations—benefited from the activism of educated wives and mothers. Although they constituted a tiny fraction of all U.S. females, college-educated women were a surprisingly substantial and widespread presence—because the United States was a pioneer in the schooling of girls and the higher education of women. By 1880 some 40,000 American women constituted one-third of all students in all kinds of U.S. institutions of higher learning; and women's share rose to nearly half at the early-twentieth-century peak in 1920, when some 283,000 women were enrolled in institutions of higher learning.[51] Many college-educated women of the late 1800s and early 1900s married immediately and never entered the paid labor force. Others taught for a time in primary and secondary schools, then usually got married and stopped teaching (either voluntarily or because school systems would not employ married women). Former teachers accumulated in every community. With skills to make connections within and across places—and some time on their hands as children grew older—former teachers and other educated women became mainstays of classic U.S. voluntary life.

Of course, more American women than ever before are now college-educated.[52] By 1990, about 14 percent more women than men earned bachelor's degrees; and large numbers of female college graduates go on to

51. Newcomer (1959, p. 46, table 2). See Skocpol (1992, pp. 340–43) for more discussion and references.
52. See Mare (1995, pp. 164–67).

achieve graduate degrees and pursue professional and managerial careers.[53] But contemporary educated women face new opportunities and constraints. Paid work and family responsibilities are no longer separate spheres, and the occupational structure is less sex-segregated at all levels. Today even married women with children are very likely to be employed, at least part time. In 1960, 28 percent of married women with children were employed, but by 1996 the number had risen to 69 percent.[54]

Despite new time pressures, educated and employed women have certainly not dropped out of civic life. Women employed part time are more likely to be members of groups or volunteers than stay-at-home housewives; and fully employed women are often drawn into associations or civic projects through work.[55] Yet styles of civic involvement have changed—much to the disadvantage of broad-gauged associations trying to hold regular meetings. Employed women, like men, often prefer to send checks to advocacy groups. At the community level, an active woman may get involved intensely and episodically—running a fund-raising drive, for example—rather than attending a traditional-style club that melds sociability with community service. Similarly, a woman employed as a "helping professional" or at a nonprofit agency may take part in a campaign or coalition to address a pressing social issue. As sociologist Robert Wuthnow astutely points out, nonprofit social service agencies, issue-oriented advocacy groups, and volunteers often work together in civic campaigns focused on particular problems or challenges.[56] Both men and women participate, of course, yet educated women are especially likely to join such efforts, either as community volunteers or as social service employees.

The Lure of Washington, D.C.

If recent civic transitions have resonated with changing social identities and relationships, the response of contemporary activists to political challenges and opportunities has been equally decisive. At the national level especially, the advocacy explosion of the 1960s to the 1990s responded to—and in turn helped to fuel—major changes in U.S. government and electoral politics.

53. Ibid. (p. 167); Bianchi (1995, pp. 124–25, tables 3.6 and 3.7).
54. Figure from the U.S. Bureau of the Census, cited by Wuthnow (1998, p. 241, n. 5).
55. Wuthnow (1998, p. 76).
56. Ibid. (pp. 78–79).

A story illustrates the point I have in mind here. Fresh from grass-roots struggles in Mississippi, civil rights lawyer Marian Wright Edelman arrived in Washington, D.C., in the late 1960s to lobby for Mississippi's Head Start program. She soon realized that arguing on behalf of children might be the best way to influence legislation and sway public sympathy in favor of the poor, including African Americans. So between 1968 and 1973 Edelman obtained funding from major foundations and developed a new advocacy and policy-research association, the Children's Defense Fund (CDF).[57] With a skillful staff, a small national network of individual supporters, ties to social service agencies and foundations, and excellent relationships with the national media, CDF has ever since been a determined proponent of federal antipoverty programs. The CDF has worked with Democrats and other liberal advocacy groups to expand such efforts; and during periods of conservative Republican ascendancy, the CDF has been a fierce (if not always successful) defender of federal social programs.

The CDF story suggests the lure of Washington, D.C., for activists, including those who originally got their start far afield in mass-based social movements. "Since about the time Martin Luther King, Jr., led a 'march on Washington' by thousands of citizens in the civil rights movement in 1963," notes political scientist Jack Walker, "there has been a march to Washington by interest groups as well."[58] Activists have gone where the action is, seeking to harness a more active federal government to their purposes. Contrary to what many conservatives believe, the post-1960s U.S. government has not steadily expanded as a taxer and spender. But in recent times the federal government has undertaken a broader range of interventions than ever before.[59] Social movements demanded that the federal government immediately right old wrongs and address pressing issues of broad public concern—and partial responses did come from presidents, courts, and the Congress. Spurred by the upheavals of the long 1960s, the "age of improvement" arrived.[60]

In this same period, congressional subcommittees and their staffs proliferated, and more aides were hired to support individual members of Congress.[61] The number of assistants to House and Senate members went

---

57. This draws on my account of CDF in Skocpol (1995, pp. 299–300).
58. Walker (1991, p. 72).
59. Loomis and Cigler (1998, pp. 11–12).
60. This phrase comes from Heclo (1978, p. 89).
61. Fiorina and Peterson (1998, p. 352 and chap. 12).

from 6,255 in 1960 to 10,739 in the 1970s, then doubled to about 20,000 in 1990.[62] For associations, larger congressional staffs meant more people to contact and additional institutional niches through which to attempt influence. Beyond Congress as well as within it, the Washington scene offered escalating opportunities and challenges. Lawyers could make headway in the courts, researchers and lobbyists could monitor the federal executive, and media people could try to shape the climate of public opinion. For all sides on every issue, there were heightened incentives to be in the national capital with an expert staff at hand. "Washington lobbying is very much a day-to-day activity," explains Jeff Berry, because "influence is achieved through continuous work in the trenches. Simply being in Washington, monitoring what is going on, is important."[63] Responding to the new incentives, staff-heavy research and lobbying associations—the proliferating "public affairs" and "social welfare" groups we have already discussed—took much of the action away from more cumbersome popularly based voluntary federations that had previously served as important conduits between the federal government and citizens in the states and districts.[64]

During the later 1970s and 1980s, moreover, the process of group formation became self-reinforcing—not only because groups arose to counter other groups, but also because groups begot more groups. Civic entrepreneurs in each issue area created more specialized groups to pursue sub-issues or marshal specific expertise. For example, new "legal defense" groups and policy-research "think tanks" were formed as partners to existing associations or added to clusters defined by issue area or ideological outlook.[65] Federal tax laws encourage proliferation by establishing different advantages and penalties for groups more or less directly involved in legislative lobbying.[66] And after a key Supreme Court ruling in 1974 facilitated the flow of electoral contributions through political action committees (PACs), many advocacy sectors set up groups for this specific purpose.[67]

---

62. Phillips (1994, pp. 25, 32). According to Fiorina and Peterson (1998, p. 352), congressional staffs are currently split about 60/40 between aides working in Washington and aides serving in district offices.

63. Berry (1997, p. 220).

64. For one instance of this transition, see Hansen (1991, part II).

65. Phillips (1994, chap. 2); Ricci (1993); Rich and Weaver (1998).

66. Paget (1990).

67. On PACs, see Berry (1997, pp. 55–58 and chap. 7) and Conway and Green (1998).

Indeed, the rise of advocacy groups parallels changes in U.S. parties and elections as well as government. Because businesses and citizens use advocacy groups to influence government outside of parties and between elections, it is not surprising that the contemporary group explosion coincides with waning voter loyalty to the two major political parties. But we should not simply posit a zero-sum trade-off, because advocacy groups and party politicians also maneuver together in transformed routines of electoral politics.[68]

As late as the 1950s, U.S. political parties were networks of local and state organizations through which (in many if not all locales) party officials brokered nominations, cooperated with locally rooted membership associations, and sometimes directly mobilized voters.[69] Then demographic shifts, reapportionment struggles, and the social upheavals of the 1960s disrupted old party organizations; and changes in party rules led to nomination elections that favored activists and candidate-centered efforts over backroom brokering by party insiders. Such "reforms" were meant to enhance grass-roots participation but in practice have furthered oligarchical ways of running elections. No longer the preserve of party organizations, U.S. election campaigns are now managed by coteries of media consultants, pollsters, direct-mail specialists, and—above all—fund-raisers. Because campaigns depend so much on paid television advertising, they are becoming more and more costly, even as voter turnout declines. Candidates compete for winning margins within a shrinking electorate, using expert advisers to help them target mailings or media messages on narrow slices of "swing" voters.[70]

In this revamped electoral arena, advocacy groups have much to offer, hoping to get access to elected officials in return for helping candidates. In low-turnout battles to win party nominations, even groups with modest mail memberships may be able to field enough (paid or unpaid) activists to make a difference. At all stages of the electoral process, advocacy groups with or without members can provide endorsements that may be useful in media or direct-mail efforts. And PACs pushing business interests or public-interest causes can help candidates raise the huge amounts of money they need to compete.

---

68. Berry (1997, chap. 3).

69. This paragraph draws especially on Walker (1991, pp. 23–27). Transformations in party politics inside and outside of government are also analyzed by Aldrich (1995, part 3).

70. Ganz (1994).

A New Model of Association-Building

But, one might observe, attempts to influence the public officials are nothing new for American voluntary associations—and historically as well as in recent times many groups have set up offices in Washington, D.C. Taken alone, a desire to influence the federal government is hardly sufficient to explain the current vogue for staff-led advocacy groups. New techniques and models of association-building are also very pertinent—and the changes affecting voluntary associations parallel those in political parties.

Classic American association-builders took it for granted that the best way to gain national influence, moral or political, was to knit together national, state, and local groups that met regularly and engaged in a degree of representative governance.[71] Leaders who desired to speak on behalf of masses of Americans found it natural to proceed by recruiting self-renewing mass memberships and spreading a network of interactive groups. There were good reasons why this model came to be taken for granted. After the startup phase, associational budgets usually depended heavily on membership dues and on sales of newsletters or supplies to members and local groups. Supporters had to be continuously recruited through social networks and person-to-person contacts. And if leverage over government was desired, an association had to be able to influence legislators, citizens, and newspapers across many districts. For all of these reasons, classic civic entrepreneurs with national ambitions moved quickly to recruit activists and members in every state and in as many towns and cities as possible within each state. Like Frances Willard of the Woman's Christian Temperance Union—who was always on the train and hardly ever "at home" in Evanston, Illinois—leaders traveled around the country, convened face-to-face meetings, and recruited and encouraged intermediate leaders who could carry on the work of member recruitment and retention. "Interact or die" was the watchword for classic American association-builders.

Today nationally ambitious civic entrepreneurs proceed in quite different ways.[72] When Marian Wright Edelman got the inspiration to launch a new advocacy-research group to lobby for the needs of children and the poor, she turned to private foundations for funding and then recruited an expert staff of researchers and lobbyists. In the early 1970s, when John Gardner launched Common Cause as a "national citizens' lobby" demand-

71. My associates and I developed the basis for this generalization in Chapter 2.
72. For a good overview, see Hayes (1986).

ing governmental reforms, he arranged for startup contributions from several wealthy friends, contacted reporters in the national media, and purchased mailing lists to solicit monetary contributions from masses of members.[73] As these examples suggest, new routes to civic influence opened in late-twentieth-century America. Patron grants, direct-mail techniques, and the capacity to convey images and messages through the mass media all changed the realities of organization-building and maintenance.

The very model of civic effectiveness has been upended since the 1960s. No longer do civic entrepreneurs think of constructing vast federations and recruiting interactive citizen-members. When a new cause (or tactic) arises, activists envisage opening a national office and managing association-building as well as national projects from the center. Members, if any, are likely to be seen not as fellow citizens but as consumers with policy preferences.

Money matters for association-building, and new flows have certainly become available of late. In the 1980s, Jack Walker and his associates surveyed hundreds of associations with headquarters in Washington, D.C., ranging from trade associations whose "members" were economic organizations to professional associations, non-profit groups, and citizens' advocacy groups, many of which had individual adherents. What Walker calls "patron grants"—financial aid from wealthy donors, foundations, corporations, government agencies, and previously established associations—figured heavily in the founding of all types of associations. Institutional aid proved to be especially crucial for citizens' groups. Across all eras of group foundings from the nineteenth century onward, 89 percent of the citizens' groups in Walker's study benefited from some sort of financial startup help. Before the 1960s, grants from individuals or other associations were the typical sources of help; from the 1960s on, citizens' associations relied much more heavily on startup grants from foundations, corporations, and government agencies.[74] Tax-exempt private foundations, especially the Ford Foundation, channeled a lot of new money to civil rights and public interest advocacy groups after the 1960s.[75] Foundation

---

73. McFarland (1984, pp. 1–2, 75–76).

74. Walker (1991, chap. 5, especially tables 5-1 and 5-2).

75. See Jenkins (1998); Gelb and Palley (1982, pp. 42–50); and Berry (1977, pp. 71–76). In a 1972–73 study of eighty-three public interest associations, Berry found that nearly half got significant funding from foundations. Unfortunately, he does not report variations within funding categories by founding dates of associations.

grants, moreover, were especially likely to go to associations with expert professional staffs.[76]

Continuing support as well as startup help comes from foundations and other patrons. Again, this is especially true for contemporary citizens' associations focused on "purposive" appeals—that is, promises to represent constituents' views in politics and policymaking. Citizens' associations, according to Jack Walker, are "very likely to rely heavily upon outside patrons rather than their members for financial support. . . . On average, nearly 40 percent of the budgets of the citizens groups is supplied by patrons—a level of support four times higher than the average received by groups in the profit sector whose memberships are most heavily made up of institutional representatives."[77]

Today's advocacy groups can also use patron grants to get started and then turn to computerized direct-mail solicitations as well as media advertising to develop continuing support from individual supporters. Pioneered by "new right" groups, direct-mail solicitation spread during the 1970s and 1980s. To name just a few examples, this technique has been used by Common Cause, big environmental groups, the Concord Coalition, and Mothers Against Drunk Driving. Civic entrepreneurs need generous seed grants to start direct-mail solicitation because appropriate lists must be purchased and hundreds of thousands of letters sent.[78] And staff expertise is equally necessary, because mailings must be honed and deployed again and again.[79] Only a small portion of people who get a cause letter in the mail actually look at it; and an even smaller fraction send back money, with or without a "membership" application.

Ready access to national media outlets is the final circumstance allowing today's associations to forgo recurrent contacts among leaders and members. Today's elite television and news reporters are often recruited directly from universities and operate out of major metropolitan centers.[80] In punditry hubs like Boston, New York, Los Angeles, and Washington, reporters, politicians, and advocacy spokespersons participate in endless talk shows; and print reporters are always on the phone to advocates as well

76. On trends in foundation grants and their impact, see especially Jenkins (1998).

77. Walker (1991, pp. 93–94).

78. In starting up Common Cause, John Gardner sought $300,000 for mailings and newspaper ads alone; see McFarland (1984, p. 76).

79. For a good overview of direct-mail techniques, see Berry (1997, pp. 77–80) and Godwin and Mitchell (1984).

80. This transition is described in Fallows (1996).

as politicians.[81] National media outlets want to stage debates among po-larized spokespersons, and advocacy associations need to keep their causes and accomplishments visible. By dramatizing causes through the national media, advocates can enhance their legitimacy and keep contributions flowing from patrons and direct-mail adherents.

In short, all sorts of new organization-building techniques encourage contemporary citizens' groups—just like trade and professional associa-tions—to concentrate their efforts in efficiently managed headquarters located close to the federal government and the national media. Even a group aiming to speak for large numbers of Americans does not absolutely need members. And if mass adherents are recruited through the mail, why hold meetings? From a managerial point of view, interactions with groups of members may be downright inefficient. In the old-time membership federations, annual elections of leaders and a modicum of representative governance went hand in hand with membership dues and interactive meetings. But for the professional executives of today's advocacy organiza-tions, direct-mail adherents can be more appealing because, as Kenneth Godwin and Robert Cameron Mitchell explain, "they contribute without 'meddling' " and "do not take part in leadership selection or policy discus-sions." Contacted individually, "direct-mail members depend for informa-tion about the organization on the materials the leadership sends them, and therefore may be more easily manipulated."[82] Thus professionals in the central office can keep themselves free to set agendas and maneuver flexibly in the fast-moving worlds of legislation and the media.

Change at the Top

This brings us, finally, to what may be the most civically consequential change in late-twentieth-century America: the rise of a very large, highly educated, upper middle class in which "expert" professionals are prominent along with businesspeople and managers. "Since World War II," notes sociologist Michael Schudson, "higher education has mushroomed. Of people born from 1911 to 1920, 13.5 percent earned college or graduate degrees; of those born during the next decade, 18.8 percent; but of people born from 1931 to 1950"—who became adults from the mid-1950s through the mid-1970s—"the figure grew to between 26 and 27 per-

81. Kurtz (1996).
82. Godwin and Mitchell (1984, p. 836).

cent."[83] Along with expanded higher education has come a proliferation of "professionals"—defined by Steven Brint as "people who earn at least a middling income from the application of a relatively complex body of knowledge." Before World War II, reports Brint, "only one percent of all employed people were college-educated and classified by the Census Bureau as 'professional, technical, and kindred' workers. Today the comparable group is twelve times as large."[84]

Together with business owners and managers and their families, professional families now constitute the top quarter or so of the American class structure. Since the 1970s, such Americans at the top of the educational hierarchy have enjoyed rising incomes, even as less-educated salary and wage employees have suffered declining or stagnant incomes.[85] America's managerial and professional families—often headed by a man and woman married to each other—are not just unprecedentedly numerous. They constitute a comfortable and privileged segment of society.

Professional people today look at themselves and their civic responsibilities in new ways. When U.S. professionals were a tiny, geographically dispersed stratum, they understood themselves as "trustees of community," in the terminology of Steven Brint.[86] Working closely with and for nonprofessional fellow citizens in thousands of towns and cities, lawyers, doctors, ministers, and teachers once found it quite natural to join—and eventually to help lead—locally rooted, cross-class voluntary associations. But today professionals as well as business leaders live less rooted lives. Meritorious high-school students are recruited into leading universities, perhaps located far from their childhood homes to which they may never return.[87] After many years of education and career development, professionals and managers live and work among themselves, frequently crowded in or near metropolitan centers. Understandably, today's professionals see themselves as experts who can best contribute to national well-being by working with other specialists to tackle complex technical and social problems.

Among different kinds of professionals, perhaps the most civically self-aware are some 18 million people, roughly 8 percent of the labor force,

83. Schudson (1996, p. 19). See also Mare (1995, pp. 166–67).
84. Brint (1994, p. 3).
85. Danziger and Gottschalk (1995); Mare (1995, pp. 203–07).
86. Brint (1994).
87. Frank and Cook (1995, p. 12 and chap. 8).

who work as "human service workers, technicians, and staff people who serve their communities in paid positions provided by nonprofit agencies."[88] Nonprofit professionals are likely to see their own work—mostly funded through government—as the very embodiment of community responsibility. "Nonprofit professionals," explains Robert Wuthnow, believe that today's complex social problems "must be addressed by people with special skills who have ample resources at their disposal and who are sufficiently committed to devote themselves to full-time efforts."[89]

A civic world centered in advocacy and service-providing groups complements America's reconfigured class structure. Managers, businesspeople, and all sorts of professionals have their own advocacy associations in Washington, D.C., and many state capitals—and this certainly includes nonprofit professionals, whose livelihoods typically depend on government funding. In addition, the proliferation of staff-led advocacy and service organizations opens new careers for lawyers, researchers, "helping professionals," and assorted other white-collar people and activists. But occupational links and careerism are far from the only synergies at work. In more fundamental ways, privileged Americans and staff-led civic groups need one another.

Cause-oriented advocacy groups offer busy privileged Americans a rich menu of opportunities to, in effect, hire other professionals and managers to represent their values and interests in public life. Why should highly trained and economically well off elites spend years working their way up the local, state, and national leadership ladders of traditional membership federations when they can simply send checks to advocacy groups or contribute to service providers? If so inclined, they can also work personally on projects managed by such groups. The new universe of staff-led civic groups, both associations without members and groups with mailing-list constituencies, is in many ways ideally suited to the aspirations of today's most privileged and confident Americans—busy career men and women who are choosy individualists as well.

From the point of view of staff-led groups, moreover, well educated and relatively well off Americans are ideal supporters. Supporters of Common Cause are an excellent case in point. Heavily tilted toward liberal Democrats, Common Cause also attracts moderate Republicans. Yet privilege rules across the partisan divide. A 1982 survey showed that an as-

---

88. Wuthnow (1998, p. 47).
89. Ibid. (p. 46).

tounding 42.6 percent of Common Cause adherents had completed graduate or professional degrees; 14.5 percent had some graduate or professional education short of degrees; and another 18.7 percent had college degrees. In the same survey, the median Common Cause member had a family income 85 percent above the national median at that time.[90] Common Cause has managed to do quite well, thank you, with several hundred thousand of such relatively privileged and sophisticated supporters and has little need to dig deeper for more "members."

There is a certain irony here. Early in the current era, civic entrepreneurs argued that mass media and mailing lists might reach masses of people left out of traditional associations, thus enlarging the universe of potential recruits to causes and groups and shifting power away from "fat cats." Yet evidence beyond the example of Common Cause questions this hopeful expectation. In a 1984 study, Kenneth Godwin and Robert Cameron Mitchell compared people recruited into the environmental movement through either social networks or direct mail. Overall, the environmental movement disproportionately attracts white, middle-class Americans, but the associations involved include some that are chapter-based and others that are more centralized and reliant on direct mail. Direct-mail recruits, Godwin and Mitchell hypothesized, might include more females, shorter-term residents, and either single or elderly people. These scholars set out to explore possibilities that mailing-list recruitment could enlarge civic participation.

But the results suggest otherwise. The study found no gender differences, and the only significant age-related finding was the opposite of expectations: students were more likely to be drawn into environmental groups through social networks than by direct mail. Direct-mail recruits to environmentalism turned out to be more established types than Godwin and Mitchell had expected: they were longer-term residents of larger communities and reported higher incomes than people recruited to environmental associations through social networks. We should not be surprised at this result. Kay Schlozman, Sidney Verba, and Henry Brady report in this volume that privileged Americans today are not only more numerous than ever before; they also have both the inclination and the means to substitute money for time. Well-educated professionals and managers are more likely than others to attend to public events and develop clear "policy

90. McFarland (1984, pp. 48–49).

preferences"—and they can afford to write checks. For the large numbers of staff-led groups that seek support for their causes, privileged Americans are ideal mailing-list members.

Associational Change and Democracy

If America has experienced a great civic transformation from membership to advocacy—so what? Most traditional associations were racially exclusive and gender-segregated; and their policy efforts were not always broad-minded. More than a few observers suggest that recent civic reorganizations may be for the best.[91]

American public life has been rejuvenated, say the optimists, by social movements and advocacy groups fighting for social rights and enlarged understandings of the public good. For an increasingly well-educated and socially tolerant citizenry, public interest groups may be "a highly efficient use of civic energy. The citizen who joins them," explains Michael Schudson, "may get the same civic payoff for less personal hassle. This is especially so if we conceive of politics as a set of public policies."[92] In Chapter 10 of this book, Jeffrey Berry shows that citizens' advocacy groups have been remarkably successful at broadening public agendas in Congress and the national media.

The personal involvements of contemporary Americans may not be so worrisome either. Just because the local chapters of old-line membership federations are waning, we should not conclude that Americans are uninvolved. Local community organizations, neighborhood groups, and grassroots protest movements nowadays tap popular energies and involve people otherwise left out of organized politics.[93] And social interchanges live on in small support groups and occasional volunteering. According to the research of Robert Wuthnow, about 75 million men and women, a remarkable 40 percent of the adult population, report taking part in "a small group that meets regularly and provides caring and support for those who participate in it."[94] Wuthnow estimates that there may be some 3

---

91. For arguments along these lines in addition to those cited below, see Ladd (1999), Pettinico (1996), and Stengel (1996).

92. Schudson (1996, p. 18).

93. Paget (1990); Freudenberg and Steinsapir (1992).

94. Wuthnow (1994, pp. 4, 45–46).

million such groups, all organized to some degree, including Bible-study groups, twelve-step self-help groups, book discussion clubs, singles groups, hobby groups, and disease-support groups. Individuals find community, spiritual connection, introspection, and personal gratification in small support groups. Meanwhile, people reach out through volunteering. As many as half of all Americans give time to the community in this way, their efforts often coordinated by paid social service professionals. Contemporary volunteering can be intermittent and flexibly structured, an intense one-shot effort or spending "an evening a week on an activity for a few months as time permits, rather than having to make a long-term commitment to an organization."[95]

In the optimistic view, the good civic things Americans once did are still being done—in new ways and in new settings. Social, charitable, and public activities once bundled together in multipurpose membership associations may now simply be separated out into more specific arrangements, allowing people to do things more efficiently and flexibly in a society characterized by what Wuthnow calls "loose connections." The reorientation of national associations toward memberless advocacy may not matter if grass-roots efforts, support groups, and professionally coordinated volunteering are picking up the slack, while citizens' advocates improve the tenor of national politics.

A Top-Down Civic World

Many of these points strike me as valid responses to the notion that sheer social disconnection lies behind America's current civic troubles. In personal lives and local communities, contemporary Americans *are* finding new ways to relate to one another and accomplish shared tasks. But if we look at U.S. democracy in its entirety, and bring issues of power and social leverage to the fore, then optimists are surely overlooking the downside of our recently reorganized civic life. Too many valuable aspects of the old civic America are not being reproduced or reinvented in the new public world run by memberless organizations.

Despite the multiplicity of voices raised within it, America's new civic universe is remarkably oligarchical. Because today's advocacy groups are staff-heavy and focused on lobbying, research, and media projects, they are

95. Wuthnow (1998, pp. 77, 79, 50–52).

managed from the top with few opportunities for member leverage from below. Even when they have hundreds of thousands of adherents, contemporary associations are heavily tilted toward upper-middle-class constituencies. Whether we are talking about memberless advocacy groups, advocacy groups with some chapters, mailing-list associations, or nonprofit institutions, it is hard to escape the conclusion that the wealthiest and best-educated Americans are much more privileged in the new civic world than their (less numerous) counterparts were in the pre-1960s civic world centered in cross-class membership federations.

Of course, better-educated and wealthier people have always been on top in U.S. associations other than labor unions. But pre-1960s membership associations were much more likely to involve less-privileged participants along with the privileged. In huge membership federations, local chapters were widespread, full of leaders and members seeking to recruit others. Hundreds of thousands of local and supralocal leaders had to be elected and appointed every year. Privileged men and women who climbed the ladders of vast membership associations had to interact in the process with citizens of humble or middling means and prospects. Classic membership federations built two-way bridges between classes and places and between local and translocal affairs. Now, in a civic America dominated by centralized, staff-driven advocacy associations, the bridges are eroding.

We cannot safely conclude that either intimate support groups or sporadic volunteer efforts will serve to rebuild the civic bridges that have fallen down. Most small groups are intensely focused on personal concerns and do not draw individuals into larger community projects, let alone into state, regional, or national policymaking.[96] Volunteer efforts, meanwhile, are usually professionally coordinated sporadic or one-shot undertakings. They involve people in "doing for" others—feeding the needy at a church soup kitchen; tutoring children at an after-school clinic; or guiding visitors at a museum exhibit—rather than "doing with" fellow citizens. Important as such volunteering may be, it cannot substitute for the central citizenship functions that membership federations performed. Volunteers do not form as many reciprocal ties; they are normally not elected to responsible leadership posts; and they are unlikely to experience what millions of members once did: a sense of brotherhood or sisterhood

---

96. Wuthnow (1994).

and shared American citizenship. And the staffs or trustees of the social service agencies that run civic campaigns or volunteer efforts do not practice fellowship either.

What about grass-roots groups involved in community projects or protest campaigns—including as many as 7,000–8,000 groups mobilized around community or neighborhood environmental issues?[97] Although such efforts can certainly involve "doing with" rather than just "doing for," they can also be fragmented and parochial—as some "not in my backyard" environmental protests have proved to be. Purely local activists may not learn how problems and solutions are interconnected. And unless they speak for the most privileged neighborhoods, local activists are unlikely to enjoy sufficient leverage to make a real difference: to change the behavior of corporations, to persuade city, state, or local governments to act. Nor are worries about parochialism and lack of leverage the only issues. Touted as spontaneous and locally driven, many "community organizations" and grass-roots undertakings are not quite what they seem. Sparked by well-connected leaders, they frequently have—or soon obtain—outside funding from tax-exempt private foundations. There is nothing wrong with this, but we should not imagine that these arrangements are democratic. Movements and groups that receive outside funding have to apply and reapply for resources while meeting detailed regulatory guidelines. Professionals often become key unelected leaders because groups depend on their expertise and connections to the outside funders.

Who elects—or in any way holds accountable—the large private foundations that channel so much funding to grass-roots and community voluntary associations? In the 1960s and 1970s, liberal foundations were pioneers in stimulating grass-roots action; now conservative foundations are also very much involved. My question holds for both ends of the ideological spectrum. In effect, considerable "local" voluntary civic activity in turn-of-the-twenty-first-century America is actually tightly connected to translocal institutions and resource flows—just as local associational activity always has been. The difference is that today's supralocal institutions are not accountable and the leaders are not elected. As professional experts and managers, foundation people do not arrive at their positions by working up from the grass-roots groups they supervise. The money they dispense comes not from membership dues but from wealthy do-

97. This estimate comes from Freudenberg and Steinsapir (1992, p. 29).

nors—who receive indirect tax subsidies from all Americans without being held democratically accountable.

A top-heavy civic world not only encourages "doing for" rather than "doing with," it also distorts national politics and public policymaking. Imagine for a moment what might have happened if the GI Bill of 1944 had been debated and legislated in a civic world configured more like the one that prevailed during the 1993–94 debates about the proposal for national health insurance put forward by the first administration of President Bill Clinton. This is not an entirely fanciful comparison, because goals supported by the vast majority of Americans were at issue in both periods: in the 1940s, care and opportunity for millions of military veterans returning from World War II; in the 1990s, access for all Americans to a modicum of health insurance coverage.[98] Back in the 1940s, moreover, there were elite actors—university presidents, liberal intellectuals, and conservative congressional representatives—who could have produced outcomes like those in the 1990s health security debacle. University presidents and liberal New Dealers initially favored versions of the GI Bill that would have been bureaucratically complicated, niggardly with public expenditures, and extraordinarily limited in allowing most veterans access to subsidized higher education. Elite ideas about post–World War II veterans' legislation were not so different from elite proposals for health care reforms in the 1990s. A GI Bill fashioned in today's advocacy world would not have opened the doors of colleges and universities to millions of working-class veterans.

But in the actual civic circumstances of the 1940s, elites did not keep control of public debates or legislative initiatives. Instead, a vast voluntary membership federation, the American Legion, stepped in and drafted a bill to guarantee every one of the returning veterans up to four years of post-high-school education, along with family and employment benefits, business loans, and home mortgages. Not only did the Legion draft one of the most generous pieces of social legislation in American history; in addition, thousands of local Legion posts and dozens of state organizations mounted a massive public education and lobbying campaign to ensure that even conservative congressional representatives would vote for the new legislation.

Half a century later, the 1990s health security episode played out in a transformed civic universe dominated by advocacy groups, pollsters, and

98. The following paragraphs draw especially on Bennett (1996); Skocpol (1996); and Skocpol (1997).

big-money media campaigns. Top-heavy advocacy groups did not mobilize mass support for a sensible reform plan. Hundreds of business and professional groups influenced the Clinton administration's complex policy schemes and then used a combination of congressional lobbying and media campaigns to block new legislation. The American people, especially low-income families, ended up without the desired extension of health coverage. American citizens recoiled in disgust at the expense and gridlock of the whole episode.

Even as today's advocacy universe encourages class-biased policy outcomes, it also magnifies polarized voices.[99] In Chapter 11, Morris Fiorina explores advocacy struggles in a community setting and analyzes how skewed incentives for participation can magnify extremes and undercut compromises. We can see analogous phenomena at the national level. Conditions in American politics encourage clashes among advocacy groups because advocates need visibility and media outlets look for opposites. Research shows that even associations with substantial mailing-list memberships have an incentive to go for drama and controversy. In comparison with members recruited through social networks, mailing-list members tend to be at once fickle and motivated by intense policy preferences.[100] Such members will keep sending checks only to advocacy groups that speak out for their strong policy preferences. So advocacy staffs have every incentive to carve out narrow issues and take dramatic, polarized positions. Although the general public might be genuinely ambivalent about many issues, a world of advocacy groups operating in symbiosis with media looking for controversy is not likely to represent the messy middle. Shouting and deadlock can easily result.

Both the artificial polarization and the elitism of today's organized civic universe may help to explain why increasing numbers of Americans are turned off and pulling back from public life. Large majorities say that wealthy "special interests" dominate the federal government, and many Americans express cynicism about the chances for regular people to make a difference.[101] People may be entertained by advocacy clashes on television, but they are also ignoring many public debates and withdrawing into privatism. Voting less and less, American citizens increasingly act—and claim to feel—like mere spectators in a polity where all the significant

---

99. A similar point is made in another context by Skerry (1997).
100. Godwin and Mitchell (1984).
101. King (1997); Orren (1997).

action seems to go on above their heads, with their views ignored by pundits and clashing partisans.

What Could Be Done?

Irreversible changes have propelled civic America's transition from membership to advocacy in both electoral politics and associational life. So it is not easy to imagine ways to recapture in new forms some of the advantages of an earlier civic America. This is not the place for an extended disquisition, but in closing let me offer a couple of observations about how our nation's civic democracy might be revitalized.

Difficult as it may be in a highly commercialized culture that celebrates the market and unfettered individual choices, Americans may need to reknit aspects of social and political life that have become unraveled in recent decades. Many highly educated, individualistic elites find it hard to believe that there could be any advantages in groups or institutions that mix family life with community involvement, recreation and fun with an occasional venture into electoral politics or public affairs. But as America's group life has become more fragmented and disarticulated, regular citizens have lost some of the clout that can be indirectly generated by mixing politics and civic activity with family life and socializing. Multiplex associations draw people in and help to sustain public discussions that resonate with the values and needs of ordinary citizens.

Actually, many of the tens of millions of Americans who still regularly participate in religious congregations experience the advantages of such a mix. It is hardly incidental that family-oriented civic movements continue to be mobilized out of religious networks and values. Christian-right efforts are one example. So are other cross-class and cross-denominational efforts such as the Texas Interfaith Alliance and the Greater Boston Interfaith Organization. When social and political activities intertwine, specific issues and instrumental public policy choices do not have to bear all the weight—as they do in the class-skewed world of advocacy group politics.

Americans need to find ways to extend or build multiplex associations. The biggest challenge, of course, is to recreate associational ties across class lines while progressing toward racial and gender integration. Such ties cannot be fashioned just within residential neighborhoods or workplaces—or just within particular religious worlds. Ways must be found to weave connections among institutions and places, classes and cultural groups. A new national movement focused on family needs and public policymaking for families may be part of the answer—especially if such a movement can connect and energize old membership associations, or even launch a new national membership federation.[102]

Civic revitalization in America is unlikely to happen in a purely partisan fashion—but it cannot happen entirely apart from electoral politics and routines of governance either. Many reformers today recoil from politics in disgust, but politics and associational life have always been closely intertwined in America. Effective associations naturally seek to influence and work with government. How else can market forces be channeled and harnessed to democratic ends? In turn, government and electoral activities not only respond to civil society. They also act back on civil society—by offering opportunities, resources, and incentives for association-builders and leaders. Americans today can hardly expect to revitalize cross-class associational life until we find ways to reduce the role of money, media, and professional consultants in politics, until we find ways to encourage government officials to reengage with broad cross-sections of the citizenry outside the money-and-media-obsessed worlds of Washington, D.C., New York City, and Los Angeles. Yet to draw politicians away from those magnets, broad groups of citizens will themselves have to engage with politics and politicians.

From the nineteenth through the mid-twentieth century, American democracy flourished within a unique matrix of state and society. Not only was America the world's first manhood democracy and the first nation in the world to establish mass public education, it also had a uniquely balanced civic life, in which markets expanded but could not subsume civil society, in which governments at multiple levels deliberately and indirectly encouraged federated voluntary associations. In classic civic America, millions of ordinary men and women could interact with one another, participate in groups side by side with the more privileged, and exercise influence in both community and national affairs. The poorest were left out, but many others were included. National elites had to pay attention to the values and interests of millions of ordinary Americans.

In recent times the old civic America has been bypassed and shoved to the side by a gaggle of professionally dominated advocacy groups and nonprofit institutions rarely attached to memberships worthy of the name. Ideals of shared citizenship and possibilities for democratic leverage have

---

102. Weir and Ganz (1997) offer some ideas along this line.

been compromised in the process. Since the 1960s many good things have happened in America. New voices are heard, and there have been invaluable gains in equality and liberty. Vital links in the nation's associational life have frayed, though, and we may need to find creative ways to repair those links if America is to avoid becoming a country of detached spectators rather than fellow democratic citizens. There cannot be any going back to the civic world we have lost. But Americans can and should look for ways to recreate the best of our civic past in new forms suited to a renewed democratic future.

References

Aldrich, John H. 1995. *Why Parties? The Origin and Transformation of Political Parties in America.* University of Chicago Press.

Almond, Gabriel A., and Sidney Verba. 1963. *The Civic Culture: Political Attitudes and Democracy in Five Nations.* Princeton University Press.

Benevolent and Protective Order of Elks. N.d. [1950s]. *What It Means to Be an Elk: Information Relating to the Order Collected and Published Specially for the Instruction of Initiates.* N.p.

Bennett, Michael J. 1996. *When Dreams Came True: The G.I. Bill and the Making of Modern America.* Washington, D.C.: Brassey's.

Berry, Jeffrey M. 1977. *Lobbying for the People: The Political Behavior of Public Interest Groups.* Princeton University Press.

———. 1997. *The Interest Group Society.* 3d ed. New York: Longman.

Bianchi, Suzanne M. 1995. "Changing Economic Roles of Women and Men." In *State of the Union: America in the 1990s.* Vol. 1: *Economic Trends,* edited by Reynolds Farley. New York: Russell Sage Foundation.

Brint, Steven. 1994. *In an Age of Experts: The Changing Role of Professionals in Politics and Public Life.* Princeton University Press.

Carter, Richard. [1961] 1992. *The Gentle Legions: National Voluntary Health Organizations in America.* Rev. ed. New Brunswick, N.J.: Transaction.

Charles, Jeffrey A. 1993. *Service Clubs in American Society: Rotary, Kiwanis, and Lions.* University of Illinois Press.

Clemens, Elisabeth S. 1997. *The People's Lobby: Organizational Innovation and the Rise of Interest Group Politics in the United States, 1890–1925.* University of Chicago Press.

Conway, M. Margaret, and Joanne Connor Green. 1998. "Political Action Committees and Campaign Finance." In *Interest Group Politics,* edited by Allan J. Cigler and Burdett A. Loomis. 5th ed. Washington, D.C.: CQ Press.

Costain, Ann N. 1981. "Representing Women: The Transition from Social Movement to Interest Group." *Western Political Quarterly* 34 (March): 100–13.

Curtis, James E., Edward G. Grabb, and Douglas E. Baer. 1992. "Voluntary Association Membership in Fifteen Countries." *American Sociological Review* 57(2): 139–52.

Danziger, Sheldon, and Peter Gottschalk. 1995. *America Unequal.* New York: Russell Sage Foundation, and Cambridge, Mass.: Harvard University Press.

Dunlap, Riley E., and Angela G. Mertig, eds. 1992. *American Environmentalism: The U.S. Environmental Movement, 1970–1990.* New York: Taylor and Francis.

Fallows, James M. 1996. *Breaking the News: How the Media Undermine American Democracy.* New York: Pantheon.

Fiorina, Morris P., and Paul E. Peterson. 1998. *The New American Democracy.* Boston: Allyn and Bacon.

Frank, Robert H., and Philip J. Cook. 1995. *The Winner-Take-All Society.* Free Press.

Freeman, Jo. 1973. "The Origins of the Women's Liberation Movement." *American Journal of Sociology* 78: 792–811.

Freudenberg, Nicholas, and Carol Steinsapir. 1992. "Not in Our Backyards: The Grassroots Environmental Movement." In *American Environmentalism,* edited by Riley E. Dunlap and Angela G. Mertig. New York: Taylor and Francis.

Gale Research Company. 1959–1999. *Encyclopedia of Associations.* Vol. 1: *National Associations.* Detroit: Gale Research.

Ganz, Marshall. 1994. "Voters in the Crosshairs: How Technology and the Market Are Destroying Politics." *American Prospect* (Winter 1994): 100–109.

Gelb, Joyce, and Marian Lief Palley. 1982. *Women and Public Policies.* Princeton University Press.

Gitlin, Todd. 1989. *The Sixties: Days of Hope, Days of Rage.* Bantam.

Godwin, R. Kenneth, and Robert Cameron Mitchell. 1984. "The Implications of Direct Mail for Political Organizations." *Social Science Quarterly* 65(3): 829–39.

Hansen, John Mark. 1991. *Gaining Access: Congress and the Farm Lobby, 1919–1981.* University of Chicago Press.

Hayes, Michael T. 1986. "The New Group Universe." In *Interest Group Politics,* edited by Allan J. Cigler and Burdett A. Loomis. 2d ed. Washington, D.C.: CQ Press.

Heclo, Hugh. 1978. "Issue Networks and the Executive Establishment." In *The New American Political System,* edited by Anthony King. Washington, D.C.: American Enterprise Institute.

Jenkins, J. Craig. 1998. "Channeling Social Protest: Foundation Patronage of Contemporary Social Movements." In *Private Action and the Public Good,* edited by Walter W. Powell and Elisabeth S. Clemens. Yale University Press.

Jenkins, J. Craig, and Charles Perrow. 1977. "Insurgency of the Powerless." *American Sociological Review* 42: 249–68.

Judis, John B. 1992. "The Pressure Elite: Inside the Narrow World of Advocacy Group Politics," *American Prospect,* no. 9 (Spring): 15–29.

King, David C. 1997. "The Polarization of American Parties and Mistrust of Government." In *Why People Don't Trust Government,* edited by Joseph S. Nye Jr., Philip D. Zelikow, and David C. King. Harvard University Press.

Kurtz, Howard. 1996. *Hot Air: All Talk, All the Time.* New York: Times Books.

Ladd, Everett Carll. 1999. *The Ladd Report.* New York: Free Press.

Loomis, Burdett A., and Allan J. Cigler. 1998. "Introduction: The Changing Nature of Interest Group Politics." In *Interest Group Politics,* edited by Allan J. Cigler and Burdett A. Loomis. 5th ed. Washington, D.C.: CQ Press.

Loyal Order of Moose. 1944. *Moose Facts.* 4th rev. ed. Mooseheart, Ill.: Supreme Lodge Supply Department.

Mare, Robert D. 1995. "Changes in Educational Attainment and School Enrollment." In *State of the Union: America in the 1990s.* Vol. 1: *Economic Trends,* edited by Reynolds Farley. New York: Russell Sage Foundation.

McAdam, Doug. 1982. *Political Process and the Development of Black Insurgency, 1930–1970.* University of Chicago Press.

McFarland, Andrew S. 1984. *Common Cause: Lobbying in the Public Interest.* Chatham, N.J.: Chatham House Publishers.

Minkoff, Debra C. 1995. *Organizing for Equality: The Evolution of Women's and Racial-Ethnic Organizations in America, 1955–1985.* Temple University Press.

Mitchell, Robert Cameron, Angela C. Mertig, and Riley E. Dunlap. 1992. "Twenty Years of Environmental Mobilization: Trends among National Environmental Organizations." In *American Environmentalism: The U.S. Environmental Movement, 1970–1990,* edited by Riley E. Dunlap and Angela E. Mertig. New York: Taylor and Francis.

Morris, Aldon D. 1984. *The Origins of the Civil Rights Movement: Black Communities Organizing for Change.* Free Press.

Morris, Charles R. 1996. *The AARP: America's Most Powerful Lobby and the Clash of Generations.* New York: Times Books.

Newcomer, Mabel. 1959. *A Century of Higher Education for American Women.* New York: Harper.

Nicholson, James R., Lee A. Donaldson, and Raymond C. Dobson. 1978. *History of the Order of Elks, 1868–1978.* Rev. ed. Chicago: Grand Secretary's Office of the Benevolent and Protective Order of Elks of America.

Orren, Gary. 1997. "Fall from Grace: The Public's Loss of Faith in Government." In *Why People Don't Trust Government,* edited by Joseph S. Nye Jr., Philip D. Zelikow, and David C. King. Harvard University Press.

Paget, Karen. 1990. "Citizen Organizing: Many Movements, No Majority." *American Prospect,* no. 2 (Summer): 115–28.

Patterson, Kelly. 1998. "The Political Firepower of the National Rifle Association." In *Interest Group Politics,* edited by Allan J. Cigler and Burdett A. Loomis. 5th ed. Washington, D.C.: CQ Press.

Pettinico, George. 1996. "Civic Participation Is Alive and Well in Today's Environmental Groups." *Public Perspective* 7(4): 27–30.

Phillips, Kevin. 1994. *Arrogant Capital: Washington, Wall Street, and the Frustration of American Politics.* Boston: Little, Brown.

Ricci, David M. 1993. *The Transformation of American Politics: The New Washington and the Rise of Think Tanks.* Yale University Press.

Rich, Andrew, and R. Kent Weaver. 1998. "Advocates and Analysts: Think Tanks and the Politicization of Expertise." In *Interest Group Politics,* edited by Allan J. Cigler and Burdett A. Loomis. 5th ed. Washington, D.C.: CQ Press.

Schlesinger, Arthur M., Sr. 1944. "Biography of a Nation of Joiners." *American Historical Review* 50(1): 1–25.

Schlozman, Kay Lehman. 1990. "Representing Women in Washington: Sisterhood and Pressure Politics." In *Women, Politics, and Change,* edited by Louise A. Tilly and Patricia Gurin. New York: Russell Sage Foundation.

Schlozman, Kay Lehmann, and John C. Tierney. 1986. *Organized Interests and American Democracy*. Harper and Row.

Schudson, Michael. 1996. "What If Civic Life Didn't Die?" *American Prospect*, no. 25 (March–April): 17–20.

Sills, David L., ed. 1957. *The Volunteers: Means and Ends in a National Organization*. Free Press.

Skerry, Peter. 1997. "The Strange Politics of Affirmative Action." *Wilson Quarterly* (Winter): 39–46.

Skocpol, Theda. 1992. *Protecting Soldiers and Mothers: The Political Origins of Social Policy in the United States*. Belknap Press of Harvard University Press.

———. 1995. *Social Policy in the United States: Future Possibilities in Historical Perspective*. Princeton University Press.

———. 1996. *Boomerang: Clinton's Health Security Effort and the Turn against Government in U.S. Politics*. W. W. Norton.

———. 1997. "The G.I. Bill and U.S. Social Policy, Past and Future." *Social Philosophy and Policy* 14(2): 95–115.

Stengel, Richard. 1996. "Bowling Together: Civic Engagement in America Isn't Disappearing but Reinventing Itself." *Time*, July 22, pp. 35–36.

Sturgis, Alice. 1958. *Your Farm Bureau*. McGraw-Hill.

Tocqueville, Alexis de. [1835–40] 1969. *Democracy in America*, edited by J. P. Mayer and translated by George Lawrence. Garden City, N.Y.: Doubleday, Anchor Books.

Verba, Sidney, Kay Lehman Schlozman, and Henry E. Brady. 1995. *Voice and Equality: Civic Voluntarism in American Politics*. Harvard University Press.

Walker, Jack L., Jr. 1991. *Mobilizing Interest Groups in America: Patrons, Professions, and Social Movements*. University of Michigan Press.

Weir, Margaret, and Marshall Ganz. 1997. "Reconnecting People and Politics." In *The New Majority: Toward a Popular Progressive Politics*, edited by Stanley B. Greenberg and Theda Skocpol. Yale University Press.

Wesley, Charles H. 1955. *History of the Improved Benevolent and Protective Order of Elks of the World, 1898–1954*. Washington, D.C.: Association for the Study of Negro History.

West, Allen M. 1980. *The National Education Association: The Power Base for Education*. Free Press.

Wilcox, Clyde. 1996. *Onward Christian Soldiers? The Religious Right in American Politics*. Boulder, Colo.: Westview.

Wilson, Margaret Gibbons. 1979. *The American Woman in Transition: The Urban Influence, 1870–1920*. Westport, Conn.: Greenwood.

Wuthnow, Robert. 1994. *Sharing the Journey: Support Groups and America's New Quest for Community*. Free Press.

———. 1998. *Loose Connections: Joining Together in America's Fragmented Communities*. Harvard University Press.

Young, Louise M. 1989. *In the Public Interest: The League of Women Voters, 1920–1970*. Westport, Conn.: Greenwood.

About the Contributors

Jeffrey M. Berry is professor of political science at Tufts University. He has written widely and is currently at work on a study of citizen groups and the rise of postmaterialism in American politics.

Henry E. Brady is professor of political science and public policy and director of the Survey Research Center and UC DATA at the University of California, Berkeley. He has contributed to many journals, writing about political methodology, political participation, the dynamics of primaries, referendums, and general elections, rational decisionmaking, and political behavior, and has cowritten books on the Canadian election process and civic voluntarism.

John Brehm is an associate professor of political science at Duke University. He is the author of books and articles on opinion surveys, compliance behavior, and public opinion. He is currently writing a book on conflicting values in American public opinion and is engaged in research on the causes and consequences of social and political trust.

Steven Brint is professor of sociology at the University of California, Riverside. Much of his work concentrates on the institutions, culture, and politics of professionals in advanced industrial societies. His most recent book is *Schools and Societies* (Pine Forge Press, 1998). He is currently at work on a study of American colleges and universities.

Neil Carlson is a doctoral candidate in political science at Duke University. A 1997 recipient of a National Science Foundation graduate research fellowship, Carlson is currently working on the role of nonprofit organizations in the creation of social capital and community development.

Elisabeth S. Clemens is associate professor of sociology at the University of Arizona. Building on both organizational theory and political sociology, her work addresses the role of voluntary organizations and social movements in processes of political change.

Susan Crawford is a doctoral candidate in sociology at Harvard University and also in the Multidisciplinary Program in Inequality and Social Policy at the John F. Kennedy School of Government. She is writing a dissertation about the provision of social services after welfare reform and social action by religious congregations and faith-based nonprofit institutions.

Morris P. Fiorina is professor of political science and senior fellow of the Hoover Institution at Stanford University. He taught at the California Institute of Technology and at Harvard University before joining Stanford. A member of the American Academy of Arts and Sciences and the National Academy of Sciences, Fiorina has written widely on American government and politics, with special emphasis on representation and elections. He has received several National Science Foundation research grants and has served on the editorial boards of a dozen journals in the fields of political science, economics, law, and public policy. From 1986 to 1990 he served as chairman of the Board of Overseers of the American National Election Studies.

Peter Dobkin Hall is senior research scholar at the Yale Divinity School and director of its Program on Non-Profit Organizations (PONPO). He has written widely on American culture and the nonprofit sector, as well as philanthropy and voluntarism. He is coeditor of the chapter on voluntary, nonprofit, and religious entities and activities for the Millennial Edition of Historical Statistics of the United States.

Peggy Levitt is an assistant professor in the Sociology Department at Wellesley College and an associate at the Weatherhead Center for International Affairs at Harvard University. She is currently conducting a comparative historical study of transnationalism among eight immigrant communities in Boston.

Charles S. Levy is a doctoral candidate in the Department of Sociology at the University of California, Riverside. His current work focuses on the measurement of "core values" and their influence on class prejudice in the United States.

Wendy M. Rahn is an associate professor of political science at the University of Minnesota. She is assistant director of the Center for the Study of Political Psychology at Minnesota and coedits *Political Psychology*, the journal of the International Society of Political Psychology. She is also a member of the Board of Overseers of the American National Election Studies. Her current research focuses on American national identity and its intersection with social capital.

Marcella Ridlen Ray is a doctoral candidate in the Institute of Public Policy at George Mason University. Her dissertation is entitled "An Empirical Analysis of Civil Society in the United States in Comparative and Historical Perspective."

Kay Lehman Schlozman is professor of political science at Boston College where she teaches courses in American politics. Her writings include works on unemployment and civic voluntarism, as well as numerous articles in professional journals. Her current research is a collaborative study on the role of gender and families in voluntary participation in political, civic, and religious life in the United States.

Theda Skocpol is Victor S. Thomas Professor of Government and Sociology at Harvard University. A member of the American Academy of Arts and Sciences and past president of the Social Science History Association, Skocpol is the author and coauthor of numerous works dealing with social policy. Her 1992 book, *Protecting Soldiers and Mothers: The Political Origins of Social Policy in the United States*, won five awards, including the Woodrow Wilson Prize from the American Political Science Association and the Ralph Waldo Emerson price from Phi Beta Kappa. Skocpol is currently coordinating the Civic Engagement Project at Harvard University, from which contributions to this book come.

Sidney Verba is Carl H. Pforzheimer University Professor and director of the University Library at Harvard University. He is the author or coauthor of numerous books and articles on American and comparative government. Verba is a member of the National Academy of Sciences and the American Academy of Arts and Sciences. A past president of the American Political Science Association, Verba is also a recipient of the association's highest award, the James Madison Prize.

Robert Wuthnow is the Gerhard R. Andlinger Professor of Sociology and director of the Center for the Study of American Religion at Princeton University. His recent publications deal with the moral dimension of work, business, and money and Christianity and civil society.

Index

AARP. *See* American Association of Retired Persons

ABA. *See* American Bar Association

ABC (network news), 380–81

Abortion, 412, 456–57

ACS. *See* American Chemical Society

Activists, 19, 409–13, 418–23, 467. *See also* Citizen groups; Interest groups

Advocacy organizations. *See* New Haven

AFBF. See American Farm Bureau Federation

AFDC. *See* Aid to Families with Dependent Children

AFL. *See* American Federation of Labor

AFL-CIO. See American Federation of Labor–Congress of Industrial Organizations

African Americans: activism, 472; civic responsibility, 238; in Civil Rights movement, 1; evangelicals, 339–40; fraternal groups, 465; parental participation in education, 266–67, 269, 270–71, 289; political orientation, 237–38; post–Civil War period, 56; voluntary associations, 42. *See also* Civil Rights movement; New Haven, ethnic groups

Agriculture, U.S. Department of, 57

AHA. *See* American Historical Association

AIA. *See* American Institute of Architects

Aid to Families with Dependent Children (AFDC), 438, 440, 448

Allen, Henry, 192

Allentown (Pa.), 356

Almond, Gabriel, 29, 31, 70

AMA. *See* American Medical Association

American Association of Retired Persons (AARP), 440, 478

American Association of University Women, 465, 468–69

American Bar Association (ABA), 167; civic engagement, 179, 180, 181–82, 197; membership and dues, 195, 198; presidential speeches, 172, 174, 175, 177, 178, 200–01

American Boy Scouts, 64

American Chemical Society (ACS), 167; budget, 197; civic engagement, 179, 184, 185–86, 197; growth, 195; presidential speeches, 174–75, 201

American Farm Bureau Federation (AFBF), 62, 69, 378, 463, 465, 474

American Federation of Labor (AFL), 64, 101, 102, 103. *See also* Federation of Organized Trades and Labor Unions

American Federation of Labor–Congress of Industrial Organizations (AFL-CIO), 64, 463

515

American Female Moral Reform Society, 38

American Historical Association (AHA), 167, 178, 187, 201–02

American Institute of Architects (AIA), 167; civic engagement, 179, 184, 186, 197; growth, 195; presidential speeches, 175, 179, 202

American Legion, 59, 63, 64, 465, 467, 502

American Medical Association (AMA), 167; civic engagement, 179, 180, 184, 186–87, 197; membership and dues, 194, 195, 198; presidential speeches, 174, 175, 177, 178, 202–03

American National Election Studies (NES), 7–8, 116, 120, 142–53, 403

American Political Science Association (APSA), 167; civic engagement, 187, 188; presidential speeches, 175, 177, 203

American Protective Association, 62

American Psychological Association (APA), 167; civic engagement, 187, 188, 197, 198; growth, 195; presidential speeches, 174, 178, 203

American Red Cross, 57, 64, 463

American Society of Mechanical Engineers (ASME), 167; civic engagement, 187, 189, 197; presidential speeches, 175, 179, 204

American Temperance Society, 40

American Textile Manufacturers Association, 378

Ancient Order of Hibernians, 41–42

Anderson, Christopher J., 126

APA. See American Psychological Association

APSA. See American Political Science Association

Asians, 267, 472

ASME. See American Society of Mechanical Engineers

Associated Charities of San Francisco, 93

Associations: changes in, 16, 18, 50–51, 463–506; commercial, 212; constitu-
tions and rules, 47, 49, 65; effects of government on, 17–18, 47, 49; ethnic groups, 58–59, 471–72; face-to-face settings, 13; government and, 488–91; industrialization, 50–54, 62; leaders, 8, 41n47, 66–68, 483–86; local and translocal, 36–37, 49, 50–51, 52–54, 55, 56–57, 59, 66; locations, 473, 487–94; listings, 72–75, 464, 475–77; meetings, 49, 491; members, 463, 465, 481–87, 491; membership federations, 60–62, 66, 463–69, 474–81, 482, 500; multiplex, 504–05; newspapers and postal services, 45, 46; political issues, 82, 88, 465, 491; pre– and post–Civil War periods, 46–47, 50, 52, 53, 55–58; professional, business, and trade, 163–207, 473–74; proliferation and decline, 37, 50–52, 54–64, 463, 470–71, 474–80, 481; research, 10–11, 35–36; religion, 44; role and effects, 5, 14, 17–18, 63, 64–66, 68–71, 163, 164–65, 463, 465; service groups, 51; technology, 323–24; urban and rural, 54; in the United States, 20, 32, 33, 36–37, 43, 50–51. See also Civic engagement; Fraternal organizations; New Haven; Social connections; United States; Women's organizations

Ayer/Gale database, 302

Baptist Church, 44

Barber, Benjamin, 368

Bath (Maine), 36

Batzell, E. Digby, 234

Beneficial organizations, 42

Benevolent and Protective Order of Elks, 51, 64, 482

Bennett, William, 3

Bernhardt, Annette, 269

Berry, Jeffrey, 471, 473, 474, 489

Bill of Rights, 44

Birney, Alice McLellan, 255–56, 260

Black, Gordon S., 310

Bonchek, Mark S., 321

Boston, 38–39

Bourne, Randolph, 193
"Bowling Alone" (Putnam), 5–6, 8, 241, 334
Bradley, Bill, 3
Brady, Henry E., 235, 237, 389, 391, 412
Brint, Steven, 495
Britain, 29, 41
Broadhead, James, 174
Brown, Richard, 37, 38, 39, 45
Bureaucratic organizations, 217
Busby, John, 200
Business of Being a Clubwoman, The (Winter), 90
Business sector, 376, 377, 384–85, 387
Busy Parent's Guide to Involvement in Education, The (National PTA), 281
Butler, Selena Sloan, 257

California, 98–99, 321–22. *See also* San Francisco; University of California, Berkeley
California Club, 94
California State Federation of Women's Clubs, 98
"Call to Civil Society, A," 32
Campaigns. *See* Elections
Carnegie Foundation, 188
Carter, James C., 177
CBS (network news), 380–81
CDCs. *See* Community development corporations
CDF. *See* Children's Defense Fund
Charities, 92–93, 95
Charity Organization Societies, 92
Chemical Abstracts, 197
Children's Bureau, 97, 99–100
Children's Defense Fund (CDF), 488
Children's Year of *1918*, 97
Christian Coalition, 338, 354, 359, 389, 479
Churches. *See* Religion and religious congregations
CIS. *See* Congressional Information Service
Citizen groups: budgets, 387, 473; financial support, 493; historical background, 371, 473; location, 473; media access, 493–94; members, 391, 480, 499–500; Olson, Mancur, 370–71; participatory biases, 452; political factors, 388–91, 473, 498; press coverage, 378–79, 381–85, 387–88; proliferation of, 470; representation, 376–77, 379; research stories, 387–88; significance, 368–70, 388–91, 431; testimony at hearings, 375–76. *See also* Interest groups; Lobbies and lobbying
Citizen Participation Study, 430, 438
Citrin, Jack, 126
Civic communities, 165
Civic Culture, The: Political Attitudes and Democracy in Five Nations (Almond and Verba), 29, 31, 70
Civic engagement: advocacy, 496; charitable nonprofits, 239–40; citizen recruitment, 444–50, 451, 452–53, 497; civic skills acquisition, 235, 333, 346–49, 354, 451; decline, 334, 457; definition, 164; democratic processes, 241, 427; knowledge workers, 243; political issues, 133, 136, 505; privatization, 244; problems, 395–423; professional bureaucracies, 199–200, 495–97; protection of interests, 427; religion, 240, 243–44, 341–52; scholarship, 7–12; significance, 428–29; social organizations, 82; social welfare and, 413–17; trust, 138–39, 395–413; voluntary associations, 240; women, 249–50. *See also* Associations; Social connections; United States
Civic Engagement Project, 34, 35
Civic Voluntarism Model, 431
Civil Rights movement, 1, 331–32, 467–68, 472
Civil War: associations before and after, 46–47, 50, 52, 53, 55–58; development of civil society, 39–40
Clemens, Elisabeth, 15, 16, 467
Clinton, Bill, 137, 404, 502–03
Clubs: adoption of "business practices," 94; political factors, 87, 90–91;

women's club movement, 83–84, 97, 102–03, 104
CNN Headline News, 380–81
Coast Seamen's Journal, 102
Coleman, James, 4–5, 113, 114, 122, 130, 137
Common Cause, 389, 491–92, 496–97
Commons, John R., 84
Community Chest, 225
Community development corporations (CDCs), 356–57
Concord (Mass.), 397–403, 415
Congress, 46, 406, 409, 488–89
Congressional Information Service (CIS), 372
Congressional Quarterly Weekly Report, 372, 378
Congress of Industrial Organizations, 64, 463.
Conservatism: citizen groups, 371, 382, 384, 473; religious groups, 339, 340; view of extralocal government, 32; view of social reforms, 4, 62
Constitution, U.S., 44, 86, 89
Consumers' League, 98
Cotton, Sallie, 256
Croly, Jennie June, 87, 89

Dahl, Robert, 390–91, 407
Danielian, Lucig, 381–82, 384–85
Dartmouth College, 167, 174, 178, 187, 189, 204
Daughters of Samaria, 56
"Declaration of the Rights of Man and Citizen" (France), 89
Democracy: activism, 467–69; in America, 1, 3, 5–6, 9–10, 13–14, 19–20, 163, 389, 405–17; associations, 15, 17, 67, 68, 70, 498–506; changes, 407; citizen groups, 389; citizens, 112, 123, 367–68, 416–17;civic culture, 29; conflict and distrust, 14, 16, 112–13, 116–18, 119, 123; education, 129; extremists, 409, 418–23; involvement in public affairs, 14; participatory and representative, 367, 405–17, 430–57; per-

ception of leaders, 126; political parties, 452; social capital perspective, 13, 116; television, 315; "thick" and "thin," 368; Tocqueville, Alexis de, 9, 163, 164; voting, 14–15, 18, 43, 89; women's associations, 15. *See also* Elections
Democracy in America (Tocqueville), 120, 122, 163, 164–65
Democratic party, 409, 452, 454, 457, 479
Direct mail, 493, 497
Directories, 36–37
Division of Labor in Society, The (Durkheim), 129
Dixwell United Church of Christ, 237
Dole, Bob, 137
Domestic Cotton Price Equalization Bill, 378
Donaldson, Paschal, 68–69
Downs, Anthony, 409
Drucker, Peter, 211, 243, 244
Durgin, William W., 27–29, 64–65, 71
Durkheim, Emile, 127, 128, 129, 130, 138, 140
Durkheimians, 13, 14, 50
Dykstra, Joan, 259

Eastern Star, 64
East Harlem (N.Y.), 356
Eastside Ministries (Cleveland, Ohio), 356
Economic issues: *1980s* anxiety, 6; consumer capitalism, 193; cross-class alliances, 100–105; declining trust in government, 404; financial autonomy, 93–94; organization as business, 91–97, 104; political activity, 441–44. *See also* Socioeconomic issues; Women
Edelman, Marian Wright, 488, 491
Edelman, Murray, 126–27, 130
Editor and Publisher International Yearbook, 299
Education, U.S. Department of, 250
Educational Reform Act of 1993, 273
Education: busing, 276; "democratic enlightenment," 128–29; female civic

leadership, 486–87; increase, 494–95; military service, 483; parental participation, 250, 266–67, 268–70, 272, 281–82, 284, 289, 292; political education, 85, 97; political participation, 431, 446–47; post–World War II, 224; religious groups, 339, 340; research, 386–87; teachers, 275–76. *See also* National Congress of Parents and Teachers; New Haven; individual institutions

Educational societies, 38

Edwards, Bob, 113

Ehrenhalt, Alan, 6–7

Elections: *1992* elections, 124; *1996* elections, 116–17, 120–21; *1998* elections, 123; advocacy groups and, 490; campaigns, 123–30, 133, 136–38, 490; candidates, 125–126; comparisons, 121; effects, 122, 131, 132–39, 140–41; importance of cash, 431; as institutions, 126; model and analysis, 130–39, 154–57; negative campaigns, 136; political parties, 123; as rituals, 126–27, 127–28, 138–39; social capital, 112–16, 130, 136, 139–40; social integration, 129–30; social obligations, 114–15, 122, 137; voting, 125–26, 136, 431, 490. *See also* Democracy

Elementary Forms of Religious Life (Durkheim), 127

E-mail. *See* Technology

Employment issues. *See* Women

Encyclopedia of Associations, 11, 312–13, 318, 376, 470

Entman, Robert, 385

Environmental Action, 469

Environmental Defense Fund, 469

Environmental movement, 368, 375–76, 469, 479, 497

Epstein, Joyce, 284

Estabrook Woods. *See* Concord (Mass.)

Ethnic and racial issues, 40–41, 226, 340, 481–82

Evangelical movements. *See* Religion and religious congregations

Exchange clubs, 51

Extremists. *See* Activists

Falwell, Jerry, 338

Family and Medical Leave Act, 285

Federal Communications Commission (FCC), 308, 310

Federal Highway Administration (FHA), 313

Federation of Organized Trades and Labor Unions, 100. *See also* American Federation of Labor

Fellers, James D., 174

Feminist movement. *See* Women's movements

FHA. *See* Federal Highway Administration

Fischer, Claude S., 309

Foley, Michael W., 113

Ford Foundation, 242, 492

Foundations, 491–93, 501–02

Fraternal Order of Eagles, 51, 63, 64, 482

Fraternal organizations: African American, 56; constitutions, 47, 49; decline, 474n35, 478; insurance provision, 58, 63, 225–26; leadership and membership, 41n47, 67; spread of, 40, 41, 51, 52–53, 63; veterans groups, 36. *See also* Associations; New Haven; Social organizations; individual organizations

Frazier, E. Franklin, 244

Friends of the Earth, 469

Funding, 491–93

Galaskiewicz, Joseph, 243

Gamm, Gerald, 11, 35, 51–52, 53, 58, 216–17

GAR. *See* Grand Army of the Republic

Gardner, John, 491–92, 493n78

Gelb, Joyce, 469, 472

Gellner, Ernest, 324, 325

General Federation of Women's Clubs (GFWC): feminism, 468–69; membership, 86–87, 479–80; methods, 97; role, 15, 58, 62–63, 465

General Social Survey (GSS): daily newspaper reading, 299; membership in fraternal organizations, 483; parental involvement in school organizations, 270–72; political participation, 352; religious characteristics, 334, 336, 339, 346–47; social changes among envangelicals, 339; telephone ownership, 307; trust, 117n19; use of, 7–8

General Union for Promoting the Observance of the Christian Sabbath, 46

German-American Alliance, 62

Germany, 29, 60, 226

Gender issues: changing gender roles, 482–87; charities, 95; male political participation, 81; membership restrictions, 34, 100–01;parental participation in education, 269, 270, 283; political organization, 89–100, 104; women's suffrage, 81–82. *See also* Women

GFWC. *See* General Federation of Women's Clubs

G.I. Bill, 63, 467, 502

Gilman, Daniel Coit, 191

Girls' Union, 102

Goals 2000: Educate America Act, 281

Godwin, Kenneth, 494, 497

Goldwater, Barry, 406

Good Housekeeping magazine, 281

Government: activities and, 488; association-building, 47, 49, 70; big government era, 190, 198; benefits and political participation, 438–40, 448; civil society, 31; creation of state agencies, 95–96; opening of, 406; provision of services, 224–26; research, 386; trust, 2, 4, 31, 126, 136, 139, 396, 403–13; view of professionals, 177

Grand Army of the Republic (GAR), 28, 59, 62

Grand United Order of Odd Fellows, 42, 56. *See also* Independent Order of Odd Fellows

Grand United Order of True Reformers, 56

Grangers. *See* Patrons of Husbandry

Granovetter, Mark, 129, 323

Grass-roots organizations, 501

Gray Panthers, 322

Great Depression, 305, 311

Greater Boston Interfaith Organization, 504

Greenpeace USA, 469, 478

GSS. *See* General Social Survey

Guillory, Christine A., 126

Hansen, John Mark, 125

Hatch, Nathan, 43

Health care: reforms, 502–03; sector, 376

Health Insurance Association of America, 377

Henley, Don, 397

Heroines of Jericho, 56

Hibbing, John, 409, 414

Hill-Burton Act of *1946*, 222

Hispanics, 266–67, 269, 472

Hofstadter, Richard, 191

Holbrook, Josiah, 38

Hospital of St. Raphael, 218, 220

Household of Ruth, 56

Humphrey, Dan, 242

Iannacone, Laurence, 234

Improved Benevolent and Protective Order of Elks of the World, 465

Improved Order of Red Men (IORM), 41

Independent Order of Good Samaritans, 56

Independent Order of Good Templars (IOGT), 40, 55, 62, 89

Independent Order of Odd Fellows (IOOF), 28, 30, 41, 55–56, 63. *See also* Grand United Order of Odd Fellows

Industrialization, 32, 50–54, 62

Inside New Haven's Neighborhoods, 236

Institutions. *See* Associations; Social organizations

Interest groups: advocacy groups, 461–62, 472–73, 489–91, 499–500, 503–06; environmental groups, 368; extremists, 19, 409–13, 503; funding, 491–93;

members, 368, 492, 499–500; political factors, 19, 84–85, 369, 380, 388–91, 410, 490; press and media coverage, 377–85; proliferation of, 2, 19, 368, 407, 489; resources, 368; state agencies, 95; testimony at hearings, 374–79. *See also* Citizen groups; Lobbies and lobbying

International Directory of Little Magazines and Small Presses, 302

International Order of Twelve, 56

Internet. *See* Technology

IOGT. *See* Independent Order of Good Templars

IOOF. *See* Independent Order of Odd Fellows

IORM. *See* Improved Order of Red Men

Irish Americans, 41–42

Italy, 5, 122, 138–39

Jews, 59, 225, 234

John, Richard, 46

Jones, Howard Mumford, 196

Joyce, Michael, 6–7, 33

Junior Order of United American Mechanics, 62

Junn, Jane, 129

Kelley, Oliver, 57

Kennedy, John F., 406

Kerbow, David, 266, 269

Kiwanis, 465

KKK. *See* Ku Klux Klan

Knight and Ladies of Tabor, 56

Knights of Columbus, 51, 59–60, 64, 218, 482

Knights of Labor, 62, 100, 101, 103

Knights of Pythias, 29, 31, 41n47, 53, 57, 482

Ku Klux Klan (KKK), 62, 69

Kuttner, Robert, 3, 321

Labor, U.S. Department of, 386

Labor and labor unions: decline, 474, 478; female participation, 100–04; federal government and, 63; membership,

454–56; political participation, 81, 391, 453–54, 456–57; research stories, 387; role of, 69; women's labor reform groups, 95–96, 98; working conditions, 101

Law Day, 181

Leadville (Colo.), 36

League of Women Voters, 465, 468–69

Liberalism: interest groups, 370, 371, 382, 384, 387–88, 391, 473; view of social reforms, 4

Life Magazine, 64

Lincoln, Abraham, 28

Lions clubs, 51, 465

Little, Arthur D., 191

Lobbies and lobbying: associations, 69; business, 384–85; citizen and interest groups, 369, 382, 384; as information sources, 385–88; politicians, 443–44; in public policy, 374–79; registration, 373; women's groups, 16, 91, 97–100, 102. *See also* Citizen groups; Interest groups

Logic of Collective Action, The (Olson), 370

Los Angeles Times, 322

Lost City, The (Ehrenhalt), 6

Loyal Order of Moose, 51, 64, 482, 483

Lunt, Paul S., 234

Lyceums, 38, 40

Lynch, Ann, 259

MacKuen, Michael B., 125–26

Magazine Publishing Association, 303

Maine, 37, 38–39

Maine Register, 51

Making Democracy Work (Putnam), 5, 241

Manent, Pierre, 324

Mann, Hester McKeen, 29, 31

March of Dimes, 463

Marcus, George E., 125–26

Marriage. *See* Sociocultural issues

Marrs, Ida Caddell, 261

Masons: admission of minorities, 41n47, 42; African Americans, 56; during and after Civil War, 55; Massachusetts, 38; military service and, 482; founding,

463; New Haven, 226; spread of, 40, 51, 54n88, 64

Massachusetts, 37–39, 483–86

Massachusetts Special Education Law 776, 273

Matthews, Lillian, 103

McGovern, George, 406

Media: access by associations, 493–94; coverage of business, 384–85; coverage of declining community, 6; coverage of interest groups, 377–85; coverage of politics, 405; coverage of public policy, 380–81; coverage of research, 386–88; "imagined community," 128n48; network news, 380–81; newspapers, 45, 299–301; periodicals, 301–05, 306; social connections, 299, 301–02, 305, 314, 315, 316–19, 323; television, 313–19, 323–25, 385; use of, 300, 324

Medicare, 439, 440, 448

Medicaid, 439, 440, 448

Mendelson, Edward, 322

Methodist Church. See Religion and religious congregations

Michels, Robert, 96

Middlesex School (Concord, Mass.), 397–403

Middletown (Ind.), 311–12, 313, 317, 318

Military service, 482–83

Militias, 384

Mill, John Stuart, 428

Milwaukee Consumer's League, 99

Minkoff, Debra, 471–72, 474

Mitchell, Robert Cameron, 494, 497

Modern Language Association (MLA), 167, 174, 187, 204

Moral Majority, 338, 354, 359

Mothers Against Drunk Driving, 478

Muller, Chandra, 266, 267–68

Mutual benefit organizations. See New Haven

NAACP. See National Association for the Advancement of Colored People

National Abortion Rights League, 468

National American Woman Suffrage Association, 62, 69

National Association for the Advancement of Colored People (NAACP), 468

National Audubon Society, 479

National Congress of Colored Parents and Teachers (NCCPT), 257, 276–77

National Congress of Mothers, 15, 58, 62–63, 255–56, 260. See also National Congress of Parents and Teachers

National Congress of Parents and Teachers (NCPT or PTA), 64; busing, 276; as civic force, 18, 465; dues and fundings, 259, 277, 279; efficacy , 275–76, 282; historical perspective on missions and issues, 260–63; membership, 250–51, 252–54, 257, 263–80, 282–83, 286, 481–82; modern missions and structure, 257–60, 273–74, 275–76, 280–82, 284, 285–86; organizational development, 255–57; racial desegregation, 259–60, 276–77, 278, 481–82; replacement by local parent-teacher organizations, 222, 253, 273–75, 285

National Cotton Council, 378

National Directory of Magazines, 302

National Education Longitudinal Study (NELS:88), 265

National Education Association (NEA), 167; civic engagement, 187, 189–90, 198; membership, 194, 195, 479; presidential speeches, 174, 175, 178, 205; size of, 35

National Network of Partnership Schools, 283

National Organization for Women (NOW), 468, 479, 480

National Parent-Teacher, 262

National Personal Transportation Surveys, 313

National PTA Handbook, 258–59

National Rifle Association (NRA), 35, 382, 384, 479

National Right to Life Committee, 479

National Wildlife Federation, 469, 478

Natural Resources Defense Council, 469

NBC (network news), 380–81
NCCPT. *See* National Congress of Colored Parents and Teachers
NEA. *See* National Education Association
Nelson, Edward, 332, 344
NES. *See* American National Election Studies
New Deal, 63, 178, 193
New England Women's Club, 83
New Haven (Conn.): advocacy groups, 221–22; arts and culture, 219, 221, 222, 223, 228; civic engagement, 244–45; dynamics of change, 222–27; economic trends, 217–18, 227–29; ethnic groups, 230–32, 233, 235, 237–39; fraternal and sororal organizations, 225–26; location of organizations, 229–32, 235–37; mutual benefit organizations, 218, 227; nonprofit organizations, 218, 219, 222, 227–29, 230, 232; nonproprietary organizations, 215, 217, 219–22, 226–27, 229; organizational trends, 214–22; political factors, 241–43; redevelopment, 242–43; religious organizations, 219, 220–21, 225, 232–39, 244; schools, 216, 220, 222, 223–24; secular and quasi-governmental organizations, 235; service organizations, 218, 219, 220, 222, 224–25, 227–29, 230, 232; suburbs, 216
New York City, 275
New York Times, 372, 378, 386
Nie, Norman H., 129, 412
Nonprofit organizations, 211, 213, 243–44. *See also* New Haven
Nonproprietary organizations (NPOs), 213, 217. *See also* New Haven
NOW. *See* National Organization for Women
NRA. *See* National Rifle Association

Odd Fellows. *See* Independent Order of Odd Fellows
Odd-Fellow Text Book, The, 41, 68–69
Ogden, Peter, 42

Oklahoma City, 384
Olson, Mancur, 370
Order of Harugari, 42
Order of the Iron Hall, 58
Order of the Sons of Hermann, 42
Order of the Sons of Temperance, 40
Organizations. *See* Associations; Social organizations; Religion and religious congregations
Organized Interests and American Democracy (Schlozman and Tierney), 373–74

PACs. *See* Political action committees
Page, Benjamin, 381–82, 384–85
Palley, Marian Lief, 469, 472
Parent-Teacher Association. *See* National Congress of Parents and Teachers
Parent-teacher organizations (PTOs), 222, 253, 273–75, 285
Park, Maud Wood, 99
Patrons of Husbandry (Grange), 28; background, 57, 62; badge, 30; female participation, 29, 89, 100–01; role and mission, 66, 69
Patterson, Thomas, 385
Penn. *See* University of Pennsylvania
Periodicals. *See* Media
Perot, Ross, 124, 416
Philadelphia (Pa.), 234, 357
Political action committees (PACs), 489, 490
Political and social movements: Civil Rights, 1, 331–32, 467–68, 472; environmentalist, 368, 375–76, 469, 479, 497; evangelical and fundamentalist, 16, 19, 44, 337–41, 342–44, 345–46, 358; temperance, 40, 45, 57–58; Washington, D.C., 488. *See also* Women's movements
Politics, national: "advocacy explosion," 487–90; associations, 82, 122; campaigns, 125; changes, 2, 82, 85; citizen recruitment, 444–50, 451, 452–53, 497; contributions, 447–49, 450; educational strategies, 97–98; elections, 112; extremists, 409–13, 418–23; fe-

male participation, 87–90, 91, 95–100, 103–04; gender issues, 89; income factors, 441–44; ideology, 410–13; interest groups, 19, 84–85, 369, 380, 388–91, 410; organizational repertoires, 105–07; party contact and politics, 82, 84, 123, 136, 406, 409–10, 413–14, 452, 490; political efficacy, 127, 132–33, 136; political participation, 81–82, 114–15, 120–23, 130–31, 415–17, 428–57; professionals, 177, 191–93, 194, 199, 502–03; public perceptions, 405; religious groups, 338, 339; representation, 369; social trust, 136; use of newspapers, 46; voting, 89. *See also* Lobbies and lobbying; United States

Politics of Progress, The (Wolfinger), 242

Polls, public opinion: American self-orientation, 325; automobiles, 313; Internet, 319–20; magazines, 303; media coverage, 407; newspapers, 300, 314–15; new technology, 298; proliferation, 407; religion, 333, 334; sources, 300–01, 314; telephone services, 308, 309, 310; television, 314–15, 316–18

Pollsters and surveyors: Allen and Dillman, 316–17; Gallup, 300, 301, 303, 308, 316, 334; Gallup Organization for Independent Sector, 333, 349; Hart and Teeter Research, 315; Kane, Parsons and Associates, 315; Leisure Development Center/Gallup, 316; Louis Harris, 301, 316; Luntz Research Company, 308; Minnesota Opinion Research, 315; NBC News/ *Wall Street Journal*/Hart Teeter, 310; Nielsen Media Research, 314, 319–20; Ohio University, 315; Pew Research Center, 300–01, 309; Princeton Survey Research, 303; Roper Organization, 300, 308, 310, 314, 316; Roper-Starch Worldwide, 314, 318; Roper Trends in American Political Participation, 457; *Time*/CNN/Yankelovich, 298; Times Mirror, 308, 315, 320; United Media

Enterprises, 316, 318; *USA Today* (Black), 310; *Washington Post*/Kaiser/Harvard, 310, 313; Wirthlin Group, 308; Yankelovich Partners, 298, 325

Pomona College, 167, 174, 187, 205

Population, 51, 52, 336–37, 372–74

Porteous Club, 94

Portland (Ore.), 36

Postal service, 45–46

Post Office Act of *1792*, 45–46

Preface to Democratic Theory, A (Dahl), 390–91

Prince Hall Masons, 42, 55, 465

Professionals and professional organizations: bureaucratization of civic engagement, 179–98; community and civic activities, 166, 168, 181–90, 197, 198–200; elites as guardians of social values, 166, 193, 194, 195, 199; operating budgets, 197; organizations as a source of change, 194–98; in politics, 177, 191–93, 194, 199, 502–03; presidencies, 197; presidential inaugural speeches, 167–68, 169–79, 190; professional ideals, 175, 177–78, 191–92; professional roles, 462, 469, 470, 490, 494–96; structure and size of organizations, 168–69, 195–96

Progressive Era: nonpolitical associations, 14; National Congress of Parents and Teachers, 257, 261; professional elites, 192–93, 199; social reform, 178; women's groups, 15, 87, 91–92

Protestant movements. *See* Religion and religious congregations

PTA. *See* National Congress of Parents and Teachers

PTOs. *See* Parent-teacher organizations

Public interest groups. *See* Citizen groups; Interest groups

Public policy. *See* Politics, national

Putnam, Robert: associational density, 8, 11, 216–17; church membership, 334, 335; civic capacity, 211; group participation, 138–39, 389; lost community,

6–7; parent-teacher organizations, 253, 268, 274; problems in the United States, 13–14; post–Civil War period, 53–54; Progressive Era, 14, 15; research and methods, 35–36, 58; social capital, 5–6, 15, 122; social trust, 13; spread of associations, 51–52, 54; television, 315

Pythian Sisters, 29, 31

Racial issues. *See* Ethnic and racial issues

Reagan, Ronald, 404

Rebekahs, 63

Recruitment, 444–50, 451, 452–53. *See also* Politics, national

Reeve, Margaretta Willis, 260–61

Religion and religious congregations: African American, 235, 244, 468; attendance and membership, 332, 334–38, 357, 358–59, 360, 454–56; Baptist, 233, 339; Catholic, 59, 225, 233–34, 235, 332, 337, 338, 340–41, 361–62; civic engagement, 19, 234, 240, 243–44, 332–33, 341–46, 354–62, 504; civic skills acquisition, 235, 333, 346–49, 354, 454; churches, 212, 217; demographic issues, 336–37, 358; Durkheim, Emile, 127; effects of income, 437, 454; evangelical and fundamentalist movements, 16, 19, 44, 337–41, 342–44, 345–46, 358; history and background, 331–32; Massachusetts, 38; Methodist, 44, 233; Pentecostal, 233, 339; political participation, 338, 352–54, 359, 454–57; professional mission, 192; Protestant, 16, 19, 59, 225, 233–34, 235, 337, 338, 340, 345–46, 359–61; Quaker, 234; Second Great Awakening, 43–44; social ministry, 18; Internet, 321; volunteering, 334, 343, 349–52. *See also* New Haven; individual religions and organizations

Religious Right, 338

Religious Roundtable, 354

Republican Party, 409–10, 452, 457

Research: Civic Engagement Project, 34; historical approaches, 9–12; by lobbies and lobbyists, 385–88; sources and methods, 33, 166–69, 213, 287–93; studies of civic engagement, 7–12, 17, 33–37; studies of interest groups, 371–72; surveys, 7–9, 10, 31, 113–14. *See also* Polls, public opinion; Scholarship

Research Committee on Social Trends, 301–02, 311

Revolution. *See* United States

Robertson, Pat, 338, 354

Roe v. *Wade*, 338, 412

Rosenstone, Steven J., 125

Rotary clubs, 51, 465

Rush, Gary, 332–33, 338–39, 342

Russell, Ernest, 196

SACs. *See* School Advisory Councils

Sandel, Michael, 3

San Francisco (Calif.), 93, 102, 103, 322. *See also* California

Sanitary Commission, 57

Schambra, William, 6–7, 33

Schlesinger, Arthur, 29

Schlozman, Kay Lehman: acquisition of civic skills, 235, 237; interest groups and lobbies, 373–74, 375, 376, 389, 391, 473; political activism, 412; women's groups, 472

Schoff, Hannah Kent, 260

Scholarship: association membership, 8; civic engagement debate, 3–6; historical-institutional perspective, 16; lines of research, 7–13, 16; neo-Durkheimian scholars, 13, 14; rational-choice scholars, 13, 14. *See also* individual scholars and institutions

School Advisory Councils (SACs), 273–74

Schudson, Michael, 494, 498

SCLC. *See* Southern Christian Leadership Conference

Search for Order, The, 1877–1920 (Wiebe), 50

Secret societies, 40

Selbourne, David, 324

Sheppard Towner Act, 69
Shoulders, H. H., 177
Sierra Club, 469, 479
Sklar, Kathryn Kish, 44–45
Skocpol, Theda, 15, 16, 35–36, 53, 284
SNCC. *See* Student Non-Violent Coordinating Committee
Social capital: church members, 334, 346; as a concept, 5; in democratic governance, 13; elections, 112–16; group membership, 389; obligations, 114; political institutions and mobilization, 111, 122, 133; Putnam, Robert, 5–6, 15, 122; recent scholarship, 17; survey responses, 113–14; trust, 114, 136, 137, 138–39
Social connections: media, 299, 301–02, 305, 314, 315, 316–19, 323; technology, 298, 305, 307–08, 309, 311–13, 320–25; in the United States, 498–99. *See also* Civic engagement
Social movements. *See* Political and social movements
Social organizations: "advocacy explosion," 471–74; business methods, 91–95, 104; changing race relations and gender roles, 481–87; charitable nonprofits, 239–40; civic engagement, 282–86; civic skills acquisition, 235, 333, 346–49, 354, 451; cross-class alliances, 100–05; definitions, 212–13, 239, 349–50; "iron law of oligarchy," 96; location, 472, 487–94; membership, 391, 480; nonproprietary entity, 213; organizational repertoires, 82, 83–86, 87–88, 104–07; political and social movements, 467–69; political participation, 451–57; trends, 217; volunteering, 349–52; women's organizations, 82–83, 85–86, 87, 90–97, 104–05. *See also* Associations; Labor and labor unions; New Haven; Religion and religious congregations
Social reforms, 4, 88
Social Security, 439, 440, 448
Sociocultural issues: family structure,

249–50; inauguration speeches, 172–79; marriage, 270, 271, 287, 289, 292; political involvement, 432–33, 435; professional ideals, 175, 177–78; technology, 298–99; transition from membership to advocacy, 499–506
Socioeconomic issues: associations, 500; individual integration into society, 128; parental participation education, 266–67, 271, 287, 289, 292; political involvement and money, 431–57, 497–98; religious groups, 339–40; rise of professional class, 494–96; social integration, 129–30; spread of voluntary groups, 37–38
Sons of Temperance, 47, 55, 62
Southern Christian Leadership Conference (SCLC), 468
Sprague, Barbara, 275–76
Sprague, Lila F., 92
Standard Periodical Directory, 302, 304
Standard Rate and Data Services (SRDS), 303, 304
Stanfield, John, 238–39
Stehlik-Barry, Kenneth, 129
Strong, Edward, 179
Student Non-Violent Coordinating Committee (SNCC), 468
Suburbia, 311
Suffrage. *See* Women's movements
Suicide (Durkheim), 128
Surveys. *See* Research
Swartz, David, 234
Swidler, Ann, 165

Tarrow, Sydney, 122, 133
Taxation, 223–24
Technology: automobiles, 311–13; computers, 321–22; effects, 19, 297–98, 407; Internet, e-mail, and World Wide Web, 297, 301, 319–22; resistance to, 298; social connections, 298, 305, 307–08, 309, 311–13, 320–25; telephone, 305, 307–10, 324. *See also* Media
Television. *See* Media

Temperance movement, 40, 45, 57–58
Texas Interfaith Alliance, 504
Theiss-Morse, Elizabeth, 409, 414
Thelen, David, 319
Thoreau Country Conservation Alliance, 397
Tierney, John, 373–74, 375, 376, 473
Time Online, 305
Tocqueville, Alexis de: associations in America, 212–13, 362; associations in the political process, 120, 122, 241, 451, 462; group participation, 138; newspapers, 45, 299; organizing, 322; political parties, 133; United States democracy, 9, 163, 164–65; used by Robert Putnam, 5
Townsend movement, 63
Tyack, David, 191

UCB. *See* University of California, Berkeley
Union List of Serials, The, 302
Unions, labor. *See* Labor and labor unions
United Fund, 225
United Order of True Sisters, 226
United Parents Associations (UPA), 275
United States: in the *1980s*, 6; civic culture, 29, 70–71; civic engagement, 3, 5, 6–7, 12–13, 20, 461–62, 498–99, 505–06; civil society, 33, 36, 37–60; Civil War period, 39–40; communications, 45; distribution of wealth, 432; distrust of government, 31, 396, 403–13, 503–04; inequalities, 20; institutions, 126; nation of joiners, 9, 462; participation, 165–66, 413, 431–50, 454; politics, 2–3, 43, 105, 395–413, 454; privacy, 323–24; problems, 13–14, 19–20, 395–418, 454; religion, 43–44, 454, 462; Revolutionary period, 37–39, 43; social capital, 5–6; technology, 298; travel and relocation, 53; volunteering, 461; voter turnout, 431; welfare state, 87, 99, 180, 190, 193; wars, 33. *See also* Democracy; Elections; Government

United States Census of Manufactures, 304
United Way, 225
University of California, Berkeley (UCB), 167; civic engagement, 179, 182–84; presidential and chancellor speeches, 175, 178, 179, 205–06
University of Chicago, 167; civic engagement, 179, 184, 185; presidential speeches, 174, 206
University of Pennsylvania (Penn), 167; civic engagement, 179, 184–85; presidential speeches, 174, 207
UPA. *See* United Parents Associations

Verba, Sidney: acquisition of civic skills, 235, 237, 333, 348; meeting attendance, 389; participant culture, 29, 31, 70; political activism, 412; recruitment, 391
Veterans of Foreign Wars, 64, 465, 474
Vietnam War, 483
Voluntary groups. *See* Associations
Volunteering, 334, 343, 349–52, 499, 500–01
Voting. *See* Democracy; Elections

Waid, D. Everett, 194
Walden Woods (Concord, Mass.), 397
Walker, Jack, 473, 488, 492
Wall Street Journal, 372, 378, 386
War, 33, 54–60, 70. *See also individual wars*
Warner, W. Lloyd, 234
War on Poverty, 4
Washington, D.C., 487–94
Washingtonians, 40
Washington Representatives, 373
Washington State, 99
WCTU. *See* Woman's Christian Temperance Union
Webzine, 305
Weissberg, Robert, 127
White, Lois Jean, 259, 283
Wiebe, Robert, 50, 191
Wiedersheim, William A., 226

Willard, Frances, 58, 491
Will, George, 3, 32
Winter, Alice Ames, 90
Wisconsin, 99
Wolfinger, Raymond, 242
Wood, Donald E., 197
Woman's Christian Temperance Union
    (WCTU), 15, 57–58, 62–63, 69, 86,
    90
Woman's Division of Christian Service,
    463
Women: activism, 29, 389–90, 471–72;
    in churches, 342, 344–45; civic leader-
    ship, 486–87; feminist movement,
    468–69; in labor force, 249–50, 262,
    263, 267–68, 269, 271–72, 487; paren-
    tal participation in education, 267–68,
    269, 271–72, 292, 294; in school
    service groups, 251–52; training, 256
Women's associations: clubs, 84, 90–91,
    94; cross-class alliances, 100–05; Massa-
    chusetts, 38; economic factors, 86,
    91–94; methods of organizing, 101; or-
    ganizational innovation, 82–83, 85–86,
    87, 90–97, 102, 104, 106; political fac-
    tors, 105–08; Progressive Era, 15, 87,
    91–92; religious disestablishment,
    44–45; spread of, 52, 58; trade unions,
    101–04. See also Lobbies and lobbying
Women's Equity Action League, 468
Women's Industrial Exchanges, 92
Women's International Bowling Congress,
    474

Women's movements: disenfranchisement,
    82–83, 86, 95; feminist movement,
    468–69; organizational innovation,
    82–83, 85–86, 87, 90–97; political ac-
    tivity, 87–90, 91, 95–100, 105–07;
    scope and sources, 86–89; state agen-
    cies, 95–97; suffrage, 62, 69, 81–82,
    103–04; women's club movement,
    102–03, 104
Women's Trade Union League (WTUL),
    101–02, 103–04, 105
Working Girls Clubs, 102
World War I, 59, 60, 192
World War II, 63–64, 257, 262–63, 313,
    465, 473
World Wide Web. See Technology
WTUL. See Women's Trade Union
    League
Wuthnow, Robert, 16, 487, 496, 498–99

Yankee City study, 233
Yale–New Haven Hospital, 218
Yale University, 218, 221
Young Men's Christian Association
    (YMCA), 59, 64, 474
Young Women's Christian Association,
    468–69
Young Men's–Young Women's Christian
    Association (YM-YWCA), 216

Zill, Nicholas, 267
'Zine, 305